Financial Market Reform in China

The Political Economy of Global Interdependence
Thomas D. Willett, Series Editor

Financial Market Reform in China: Progress, Problems, and Prospects,
edited by Baizhu Chen, J. Kimball Dietrich, and Yi Feng

Exchange-Rate Policies for Emerging Market Economies, edited by
Richard J. Sweeney, Clas G. Wihlborg, and Thomas D. Willett

Capital Controls in Emerging Economies, edited by
Christine P. Ries and Richard J. Sweeney

Judging Economic Policy: Selected Writings of Gottfried Haberler, edited
by Richard J. Sweeney, Edward Tower, and Thomas D. Willett

Political Capacity and Economic Behavior, edited by
Marina Arbetman and Jacek Kugler

*Interest Groups and Monetary Integration: The Political Economy
of Exchange Regime Choice,* Carsten Hefeker

*Growth, Debt, and Politics: Economic Adjustment and the Political
Performance of Developing Countries,* Lewis W. Snider

*Closure in International Politics: The Impact of
Strategy, Blocs, and Empire,* John A. Kroll

Financial Market Reform in China

Progress, Problems, and Prospects

EDITED BY

Baizhu Chen
J. Kimball Dietrich
Yi Fang

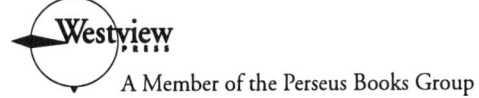

A Member of the Perseus Books Group

The Political Economy of Global Interdependence

All rights reserved. Printed in the United States of America. No part of this publication may be reproduced or transmitted in any form or by any means, electronic or mechanical, including photocopy, recording, or any information storage and retrieval system, without permission in writing from the publisher.

Copyright © 2000 by Westview Press, A Member of the Perseus Books Group

Published in 2000 in the United States of America by Westview Press, 5500 Central Avenue, Boulder, Colorado 80301-2877, and in the United Kingdom by Westview Press, 12 Hid's Copse Road, Cumnor Hill, Oxford OX2 9JJ

Find us on the World Wide Web at www.westviewpress.com

A CIP catalog record for this book is available from the Library of Congress.
ISBN 0-8133-3619-8

The paper used in this publication meets the requirements of the American National Standard for Permanence of Paper for Printed Library Materials Z39.48-1984.

10   9   8   7   6   5   4   3   2   1

Contents

Acknowledgments		*vii*
List of contributors		*viii*
Foreword: Central Bank Credibility, Inflation, and Financial Reform Robert Perry		1
1	An Overview of China's Financial Markets: Progress, Problems and Prospects Baizhu Chen, J. Kimball Dietrich and Yi Feng	5
2	China and the Asian Financial Contagion Nicholas R. Lardy	27
3	Roots of the Financial Crisis in Asia and Implications for China Jianping Zhou	39
4	Why Has China Survived the Asian Crisis So Well: What Risks Remain? John G. Fernald and Oliver D. Babson	55
5	Capital Account Liberalization: Sequencing and Implications Yi Feng	87
6	What Lessons US Financial Markets Can Provide to China J. Kimball Dietrich	109
7	Political Power Transitions and Chinese Economic Policy Brian Buford-Efird	127
8	Financial Development and Macroeconomic Stability in China Barry Naughton	143
9	Money Market in China Hong Chang, Baizhu Chen, and Yang Li	171
10	Credit Quota as a Banking Risk Control in China: A Retrospect Ding Lu and Qiao Yu	195
11	Noise Trading in the Chinese Stock Market Shang-Jin Wei	221

12	Explaining IPO Underpricing in China *Dongwei Su and Belton M. Fleisher*	243
13	China's Experience with Indexed Government Bonds, 1988-1996 *Richard C. K. Burdekin and Xiaojin Hu*	261
14	Trust and Investment Corporations in China *Zhaohui Hong and Ellen Y. Yan*	285
15	Lessons from a Survey of Urban Credit Cooperatives in China *Eric Girardin and Stephen Bazen*	299
16	Improving Access to Credit in Rural China *Wing Thye Woo*	321
17	Restructuring China's State-Owned Enterprises: A Corporate Governance Perspective *Tian Zhu*	347
18	Insider Control, Corporate Governance, and the Soft Budget Constraint: Theory, Evidence, and Policy Implications *David Li*	361
19	Transparency and China's Aspirations *Hilton Root*	383
20	Provincial Distribution of Direct Foreign Investment in China, 1992-1996: A Pooled Time-Series Empirical Study *Yi Feng and Hui Zhang*	401

Acknowledgments

As editors, first of all, we would like to thank the authors of this volume for their conscientious work that makes this volume possible. Many ideas in this book were first explored at an international symposium on financial market reforms in China, which was organized by the Chinese Economists Society. We would like to express our thanks to the sponsors of the conference: Center for International Business Education and Research, China Reform Foundation, MetLife, Hausman & Shrenger LLP, Lincoln National Insurance Company, City National Bank, Marshall School of Business, University of Southern California and The Chinese Economists Society. The Lincoln Foundation also provided generous support to this project through a grant made to Claremont Graduate University where this book was finalized.

Throughout the editorship, we have received invaluable encouragement and sound advice from our colleagues at Claremont Graduate University and the University of Southern California. Our most heartfelt gratitude goes to the Administrations of these two institutions for their understanding and support. In particular, we would like to express our deep appreciation to Thomas D. Willett, who has inspired this book.

We are deeply grateful to Marcus Boggs, Janie McKenzie, Jennifer Thompson, Jane Raese, and their associates at Westview for their guidance and participation in making this book possible.

Special thanks go to Brian Buford-Efird for his excellent work in copy editing and preparing the camera-ready manuscript.

B.C.
J.K.D
Y.F.

Contributors

Oliver D. Babson
Federal Reserve Board, Washington, DC

Brian Buford-Efird
Claremont Graduate University

Hong Chang
University of Southern California

J. Kimball Dietrich
University of Southern California

John G. Fernald
Federal Reserve Board, Washington, DC

Eric Girardin
University of Montesquieu

Xiaojin Hu
Rockwell International Corp

David Li
University of Michigan, Ann Arbor

Ding Lu
National University of Singapore

Robert Perry
Federal Reserve Bank, San Francisco

Dongwei Su
University of Akron

Wing Thye Woo
University of California, Davis

Qiao Yu
National University of Singapore

Tian Zhu
Hong Kong University of Science and Technology

Stephen Bazen
University of Montesquieu

Richard C. K. Burdekin
Claremont McKenna College

Baizhu Chen
University of Southern California

Yi Feng
Claremont Graduate University

Belton M. Fleisher
The Ohio State University

Zhaohui Hong
Savannah State College

Nicholas R. Lardy
The Brookings Institute

Yang Li
Chinese Academy of Social Sciences

Barry Naughton
University of California, San Diego

Hilton Root
Milken Institute

Shang-Jin Wei
Harvard University

Ellen Y. Yan
Key Corp

Hui Zhang
Claremont Graduate University

Jianping Zhou
The International Monetary Fund

Foreword

Central Bank Credibility, Inflation, and Financial Reform

Robert T. Parry
President and Chief Executive Officer,
Federal Reserve Bank of San Francisco

This text is based on a speech delivered to the International Symposium on Chinese Markets Reform on August 1, 1997.

The Federal Reserve Bank of San Francisco has long had a special interest in the Pacific Basin as a whole, and in China in particular. Indeed, the San Francisco Fed's relationship with China, and especially with the People's Bank, began back in 1980, when my predecessor, John Balles, hosted a delegation to the Bank led by Governor Li Baohua; later that year he was part of a delegation to China led by Federal Reserve Chairman Volcker.

My role as President has given me the opportunity to make several visits to China and to be a close witness to the process of financial reform in that country. And each time I visit, I'm impressed once again with the economic progress that China has made in such a relatively short period of time. At the same time, of course, challenges remain—not the least of which is the process of financial market reform, the theme of this conference.

One important element of that reform is the structure and conduct of the central bank, the People's Bank of China—in particular, the conduct of monetary policy in pursuit of low and stable inflation. As China continues to transform itself, it can learn a lesson about monetary policy from the U.S. experience—and indeed, from the experience of much of the rest of the world. The lesson is this: The main thing monetary policy can do is control inflation. This lesson has been learned at a price: High inflation can be costly— very costly, as the U.S. discovered in the late 1970s, when the year-to-year inflation rate reached over 13 percent.

How is it costly? Higher inflation is generally associated with higher uncertainty about inflation. And higher uncertainty about inflation means more difficult planning and contracting by business and labor. It also means higher risk premia in long-term rates of return, which depress capital formation and productivity. In addition, it makes people spend their time hedging against inflation instead of pursuing more useful, more productive activities.

How does a central bank conduct a low-inflation policy? For the U.S. and many other industrialized countries, a good deal of emphasis has been placed on the importance of making such policies "credible." At issue is the difference between the short-run and long-run impacts of policy. *In the short run*, an "easy" monetary policy sometimes can give a boost to employment and economic growth. That makes it tempting for the government to pressure the central bank to "go for the quick fix" — that is, to use monetary policy to boost growth now, and worry about inflation later.

But what happens in the long run? Both empirical and theoretical research indicate that in the long run there *is* no tradeoff between the rate of inflation and growth — in other words, any gains in employment or output are only temporary. A central bank simply doesn't have the power to push an economy beyond its capacity to produce goods and services for very long. The reason, of course, is that the capacity to produce depends on real factors, factors beyond the reach of monetary policy, such as population growth, capital accumulation, and productivity improvements.

In addition, if a central bank *were* pushed to follow an expansionary policy for very long, the inevitable result would be accelerating inflation and financial instability — *without* either more production of goods and services *or* a lower unemployment rate. In fact, there's evidence that prolonged high inflation — especially double-digit inflation — can even *reduce* the growth of GDP.

And that's not all. The private sector also would end up with higher inflation expectations. Why? Because the private sector believes that if politicians and bureaucrats can pressure the central bank into an "easy" policy once, they can do it again. Under these circumstances, a central bank would have a hard time convincing *anybody* it was serious about maintaining low inflation. In other words, the central bank's commitment to a low-inflation policy wouldn't be credible.

How can central banks achieve credibility? One way is to create a formal legal structure that makes the central bank *independent* of short-term political and bureaucratic pressures. The usual model of independence is the German Bundesbank. According to German law, the Bundesbank is "independent of instructions from the federal government," and its assigned task is "preserving monetary stability." Many industrial countries are starting to follow that model. The U.K. gave the Bank of England more independence from the government immediately following the election of Tony Blair as Prime Minister in the spring of 1997. In addition, the European Community's move to a monetary union of 11 of the European economies required establishment of a European Central Bank — and it's expected to be independent of member nation governments and finance ministries. This is known as "structural" or "institutional" independence, and it's a hallmark of the Federal Reserve System.

Another way to create central bank credibility is to establish a clear rule for the central bank to follow, such as making inflation the sole objective. A striking example of such a rule is found in New Zealand. In 1990, after struggling with years of double-digit inflation, a bold program was established. It requires that the government set a policy target—currently it's 0 to 2 percent annual inflation—and then bars the government from telling the central bank how to reach it. It also makes the head of the central bank personally responsible—he signs an agreement to keep to the policy target, and he can be dismissed if he fails to do it!

Another example of a rule that can create monetary discipline for a central bank is establishing an exchange rate peg to a stable foreign currency. Here I might mention Hong Kong's peg to the dollar as a good example. Financial markets can easily *test* its commitment to maintain the peg—and, indeed, they have done so in the aftermath of the Asian financial crises. Therefore, Hong Kong has sought to enhance its credibility by establishing a currency board that limits discretionary actions of the central bank, the Hong Kong Monetary Authority.

There *are* other ways to gain credibility for a low-inflation policy besides structural independence and rules. Japan provides an excellent example. During most of the postwar period, the Bank of Japan has had far fewer *structural* features of independence than the German Bundesbank or the Fed. For example, by law, the Ministry of Finance had the authority to direct the Bank of Japan to take any actions it deemed necessary. And there is no explicit inflation *rule* or exchange rate peg that the Bank of Japan follows. Yet, since 1980, Japan's inflation rate has been even lower than Germany's.

How has the Bank of Japan managed it? First, the Bank of Japan gets consistent *support* in fighting inflation from the Ministry of Finance. Second, and just as important, there's a strong public consensus in Japan in favor of low inflation. Finally, the Bank of Japan has established a strong track record in fighting inflation. In other words, it has *earned* its credibility. I should note that, even with this success, the Bank of Japan has been given greater explicit independence from the Ministry of Finance.

I'm pleased to see China has begun to move in the direction of central bank independence as well. The Central Bank Law passed in March 1995 gives the People's Bank a significant degree of independence from local governments, other ministries and state entities, and individuals that had a heavy influence on its operations in the past. For example, the People's Bank is no longer required to finance Ministry of Finance budget deficits, nor does it now make directed policy loans. Furthermore, the People's Bank is now being restructured somewhat along the lines of the Federal Reserve—that is, with regional branches that would have jurisdiction over a number of provinces. This might prove helpful in centralizing the control over monetary policymaking. In addition, the People's Bank has moved to increase its institutional ability to use indirect policy instruments—for example, they have begun to experiment with open market operations.

These and other financial liberalization measures are important first steps towards the kinds of reforms that will allow markets to work to allocate capital more efficiently in China. But, of course, significant challenges remain in moving forward. Looking ahead, I'd say that one of the main areas of concern, both for the central bank and for further financial reform, is the problem of the state enterprise sector. This sector continues to absorb scarce resources, either through budgeted subsidies or through government-directed loans by the banking system.

This is complicating life for Chinese policymakers in two ways. First, it constrains monetary policy. The People's Bank must ensure that credit continues to grow in order to help support state firms, and that clearly can add fuel to inflationary pressures. Second, it complicates reform of the financial sector, especially banks. A large portion of bank loans in China are to state firms, and they're not likely to be repaid. In that event, banks will have to roll over or even expand these loans, making it that much harder to move banks toward a market orientation.

How policymakers deal with the problems of the state enterprise sector, of course, has significant political and social implications as well. In dealing with them, I believe China's policymakers can benefit from the lessons of other countries' experiences—lessons about the ultimate costs of inflation, and the virtues of central bank credibility, discipline, and independence.

Without question, China has come far; yet there is still much to do, and the path ahead will be difficult. The Asian financial crises of the last two years have placed additional barriers for China to surmount. But I trust that their past successes will provide the stimulus for keeping the process of financial reform—and improving the well-being of the Chinese people—moving in the right direction.

1
An Overview of China's Financial Markets: Progress, Problems and Prospects

Baizhu Chen, J. Kimball Dietrich and Yi Feng[1]

As the economic reform in China initiated in 1978 continues, the reform of China's financial markets has moved to center stage. However, several major problems challenge the deepening of China's financial markets reform. First, even though China has in place the composition of a financial market—such as the central bank, commercial banks and non-banking financial institutions (insurance companies, trusts, brokerages, etc.) as discussed below—it does not possess the essence of a well-functioning market. The central government dominates other economic agents in the markets. Even the central bank, subject to discretion at both central and local governments, has been ineffective in guiding the financial markets. The recent merger of the People's Bank at the provincial level into nine national branches will help the central bank overcome parochialism, contributing to its independence of local governments, though this will have little effect on central government control.

Moral hazard underlies China's financial markets. The commercial banks still have not become economic agents whose behavior is determined by the rate of return on investment. They secure loans from central banks, but lack accountability for investment performance. As of 1997, non-performing loans by the four state commercial banks constituted about 20 percent of their total loans (Di and Ye 1998:53). The transformation of the specialized banks into commercial banks is far from complete. The structure and objectives of these banks are more compatible with making policies rather than profits. Similarly, state-owned enterprise have been able to secure loans from the commercial and policy banks without assuming the adequate risks and consequences of bad performance. They are not institutionalized to compete with other entities in the marketplace and lack the incentive to pursue the highest possible returns on their investment.

Related to the problems above, financial instruments are lacking in the market. Stocks and bonds as a percentage of GDP are significantly lower than those in advanced economies. The intrusive and abrupt intervention by the government in combination with a lack of institutionalized management centered on both market mechanisms and supervision leads to irregularity and disorder in the financial markets and decreases efficiency in the optimal use of financial resources. As mentioned above, these problems have been embedded in China's long-standing central command economy prior to the economic reform and are expected to be resolved as economic reform deepens.

The articles in this volume deal with important issues in China's financial reform, such as the central bank and monetary policies, equity and bond markets, banking and non-banking financial institutions, and corporate governance and capital flow. In addition, the lessons from and implications of other countries' experiences in financial reforms are also discussed in this volume in order to shed light on the rationale and strategies associated with China's financial reform.

The purpose of this book is three-fold. First, it provides a forum for academic research on China's financial reform, still the most important area in its economic reform. The book should add to our understanding of China's financial reform by rigorous state-of-the-art research, while provoking heated academic discussion on what is currently the most fundamental aspect of the economic transformation of China. Second, this book provides policy guidance to China's financial market reform, as well as investment guidance to private investors both in and outside China. Readers in the policy community may utilize this book to enhance policy formulation, and investors may improve their opportunities based on the analysis in this book. Third, this book can be used as a textbook in graduate or training programs at major universities in courses focusing on International Finance, International Economics, International Political Economy, and area studies in China or Pacific Asia. The sections below provide an overview of China's financial markets, followed by a summary of the chapters in this book.

Reform of the Central Bank

The central bank in China, the People's Bank of China, was established soon after the new government was founded in 1949. Before 1979, the People's Bank of China served as the only bank in the country. It performed the tasks typical of a central bank, e.g. credit distribution, currency issuance and foreign exchange reserves management. Additionally, it functioned as a commercial bank by receiving deposits from households and firms, making loans to and providing clearance services for business entities. No separate commercial banks other than the People's Bank existed. In fact, the need for the separate commercial banks did not exist then because the centrally planned economy only needed an accounting system to balance the books of various state-owned enterprises. A mono-banking system in which the central bank also served as the accounting entity was sufficient for this purpose.

Since 1978, economic reform has gradually empowered the non-state sectors as well as increased the incentives for state-owned enterprises to be self-reliant. Consequently, the mono-banking system became increasingly incompatible with the emerging economic system. On September 17, 1983, the Chinese government issued a decree to formally restructure the People's Bank of China into a central bank, effective January 1, 1984. Its commercial businesses were turned over to four state-owned commercial banks that were established during the period of 1979-1984. The People's Bank continued commercial businesses such as making loans to state-owned enterprises until 1994 when comprehensive financial market reforms were initiated. Since then, the People's Bank no longer issued loans to enterprises. It became more like a real central bank whose charges comprise adjustment of money supply and regulation of financial firms. The Central Bank Law passed in March 1995 explicitly banned the People's Bank from financing government budget deficits. It also prohibited the People's Bank from making loans to various levels of central and local government agencies. Thus the direct monetization of budget deficits is out of the question.

The People's Bank has also made adjustments regarding its objectives in conducting monetary policy. For a long time before the Central Bank Law was promulgated, the People's Bank was accustomed to pursuing multiple objectives, e.g. maintaining monetary stability while concurrently promoting economic growth. These two objectives were inconsistent with each other most of the time, as the operation of the People's Bank of China was not independent of the government. When the government felt that economic growth needed to be accelerated, it would instruct the People's Bank to issue more credits to firms. Higher economic growth induced by more credits would be accompanied by higher inflation. As inflation spiraled upward, threatening social stability, credits were then cut and economic growth was reduced. Once the economy slowed down, another monetary expansion would soon be on the horizon. Thus, for a long period of time, the Chinese economy was characterized by a high frequency of boom-bust cycles. The Central Bank Law of 1995 states that the objective of monetary policy is to maintain monetary stability, which facilitates economic growth.[2] This policy outcome reflects consensus among policy makers and economists that stable economic growth can only be achieved within a stable monetary environment. It deviates from the past practice of the People's Bank in that its only goal now is to maintain monetary stability; economic growth is no longer be the principal charge of the central bank.

However, the Central Bank Law of 1995 has not transformed the People's Bank of China into a truly independent central bank capable of carrying out monetary policy without being influenced by government politics. According to the Central Bank Law, the People's Bank formulates and implements monetary policies under the supervision of the State Council (Article 3 and Article 7). The decisions made by the People's Bank regarding the money supply, interest rates, exchange rates, and other important matters must be approved by the State Council (Article 5). Thus the State Council, rather than the People's Bank of China, is the ultimate decision-maker of monetary policy. Inevitably, political considerations become an important factor in the formulation of monetary policies.[3] Though the People's Bank is restructuring itself along the line of the Federal Reserve System of the United States, it is unlikely that the People's Bank will be empowered by the Chinese government with the autonomy in monetary policy that the Federal Reserve System has.

One important task in financial market reform is to transform the traditional direct administrative control of credits by the People's Bank to indirect market-based macroeconomic management, which relies on open market operation, reserve requirement and discount window borrowing. The traditional credit planning system adopted by the central bank in its management of credits and funds is a natural derivative of the centrally planned economy in which credit, interest rate and fund usage are all closely linked to government production programs. Credit planning has become increasingly ineffective as a major way of adjusting fund flows on the financial markets (Yang 1998; Lu and Yu 1998; Chang, Chen, and Li 1998). First of all, banks in China, including the central bank, are not able to independently direct their funds without instruction from the central government. Whenever the government pursues the goal of accelerating economic growth, the central bank has to loosen its total credit quota, exceeding the original level of credit planning. This practice allows commercial banks to inject funds into state-owned as well as non-state owned enterprises to expand production. Some studies have found that each session of the National People's Congress signals a new wave of economic expansion followed by yet another wave of inflation (Xu and Ni 1997).

Second, state-owned banks are generally expected to provide funds to state-owned enterprises. As the government, rather than the market, determines the interest rate, the rate is often set below the market level, which leads to excess borrowing by state-owned enterprises from state-owned banks. Because investment risks and interest rate costs are not among the major factors to be considered when borrowing is made. Additionally, out of concern for the social impact of closing of state-owned enterprises, the government requires that state-owned banks continually provide funds to the non-performing state-owned enterprises. Thus, commercial banks will issue additional credits when economic growth slows down.

Third, China's economic structures have changed significantly since 1978, with rapid growth of the non-state sectors. The percentage of GDP accounted for by the non-state sectors has grown at an annual average of 2 percent since 1980 and has expanded at an annual rate of 4 percent after 1992. The total non-state sector output accounts 51.9 percent of the total industrial output by 1992. By contrast, the amount of credits used by the non-state sectors accounts for only 20.7 percent of the total credits of being utilized by the whole economy in 1992. The funds acquired through regular channels by non-state sectors are far from sufficient, which makes them actively seek unplanned credit. The large amount of off-plan credits remedies the ineffectiveness of credit planning (Yang 1999).

Financial Structures

As the country moved away from a centrally planned economy, the Chinese financial structure was reformed gradually so that the needs of the economy could be satisfied. Between 1978 and 1984, various financial institutions were established. Four state commercial banks – the Bank of China, the Agriculture Bank of China, the Construction Bank, and the Industrial and Commercial Bankwere set up to assume the role of commercial banking business that had been part of the People's Bank. Since 1986, share-holding company-based commercial banks have been established at both national and regional levels. Non-bank financial institutions have also grown very fast. As township and village enterprises (TVEs) expanded dramatically during the 1980s, the number of rural credit cooperatives (RCCs) and urban credit cooperatives (UCCs) experienced a significant increase so as to suit the needs of emerging TVEs. By the end of 1995, 5,217 urban credit coops and 50,219 rural credit coops had been in existence. These rural and urban credit institutions provide liquidity and credit so as to enable many township and village enterprises to develop into major exporters. Investment trust companies, security firms, insurance companies, leasing companies, finance companies, closed-end mutual funds have all been set up. In 1994, state owned commercial banks ceased to be required to carry out policy loans to state-owned enterprises. The newly established policy banksthe State Development Bank, the Export-Import Bank of China and the Agriculture Development Bank – are now responsible for the provision of preferential loans to projects that are deemed to be important according to the government industrial and agricultural policies. By the mid-1990s, the financial structure in China had become more diverse as suggested in Figure 1.1.

The financial institutions in China are dominated by the four state commercial banks. Table 1.1 lists some basic quarterly statistics of deposit-taking financial institutions, calculated as the average of the period from the first quarter of 1993 to the first quarter of 1997. The total assets owned by the state commercial banks are 4,310 billion yuan. The total assets of the other four deposit-taking financial institutions are a little more than 1,200 billion yuan. The assets owned by the state commercial banks are almost 3.6 times as high as those by the other four institutions. Contrary to common belief, the rural credit cooperatives own more assets than the other commercial banks, though the rural and urban credit corporations do not own foreign assets.

FIGURE 1.1 The Structure of China's Financial Markets

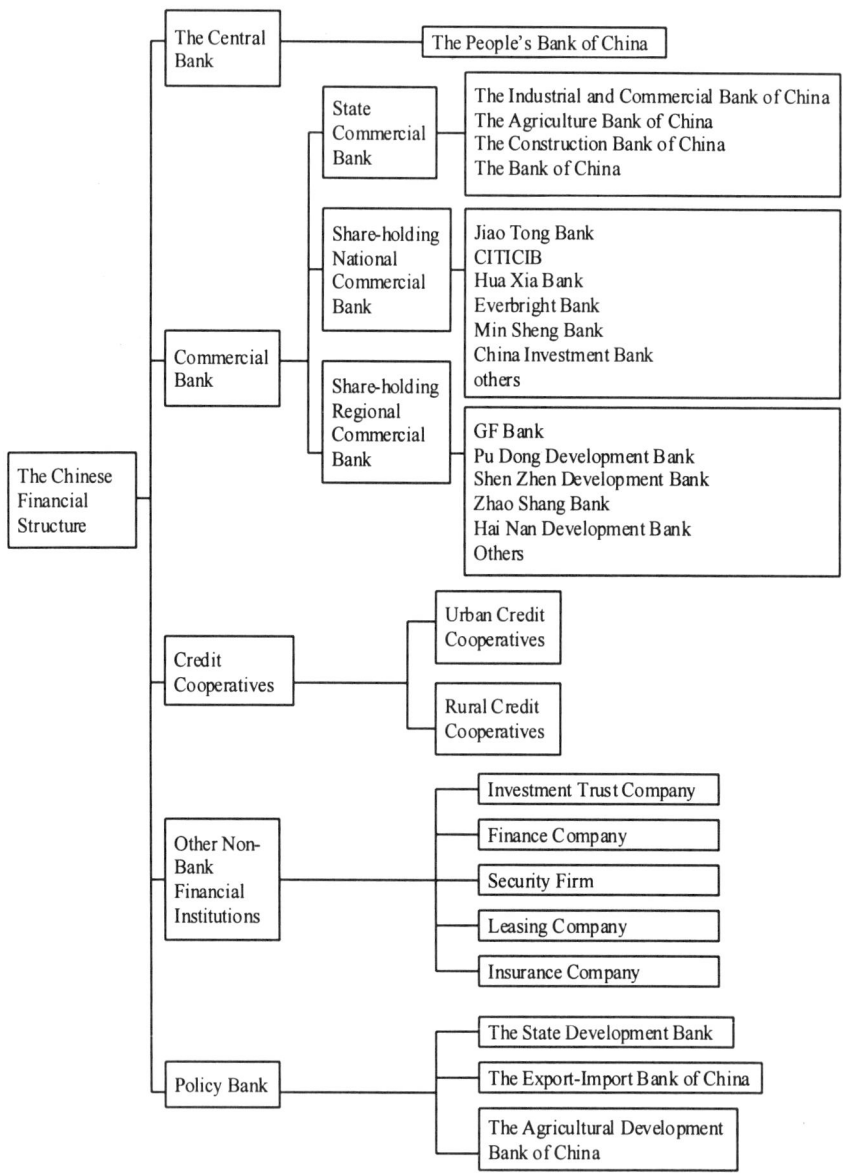

TABLE 1.1 Basic Statistics of the Deposit Taking Financial Institutions in China (in billion yuan)

	State Commercial Banks	Other Commercial Banks	RCC	UCC	Finance Company
Total Assets	4310.51	361.35	571.25	229.16	41.04
Foreign Assets	327.79	46.10	0	0	0.01
Reserve Assets	643.64	75.48	99.24	47.24	3.15
Reserve-Total Asset Ratio	15%	21%	17%	21%	8%
Required Reserve/ Total Asset	9%	9%	13%	11%	5%
Excess Reserve in Central Bank/Asset	5%	10%	3%	8%	2%

Source: The People's Bank of China Quarterly Statistical Bulletin.

The foreign assets owned by the financial companies are negligible, compared with the amount owned by the state-owned banks. The reserve ratios of the deposit-taking financial institutions in China are relatively high (except for the finance companies), ranging from 15 percent for state-owned banks to 21 percent for urban credit corporations and other commercial banks.

The market share of state commercial banks in terms of financial assets declined steadily from more than 85 percent in 1988 to 72.7 percent in 1995. Other commercial banks at the national level also saw their share decline. The market shares of both urban and rural credit cooperatives have increased. The policy banks did not exist in 1988, but its share as a percentage of total institutional financial assets rose to almost 7 percent.

The reserve assets of deposit-taking financial institutions have three components: the required reserves, deposits with the People's Bank and cash in the vault. The required reserves are directly deducted by the People's Bank from the deposits received by the deposit-taking financial firms. The deposits with the People's Bank, which are not required, can be regarded as excess reserves, which constitute a large component of the total reserves. For some financial institutions (e.g. other commercial banks), this component can be even larger than the mandatory component of the required reserves. Since this component is not mandatory, it can be loaned to firms, if necessary, which makes it the most volatile component of the monetary base.

Despite the comprehensive reform programs in China, traditional elements of the planned economy linger. For example, the state owned commercial banks are supposed to make loans in accordance with market principles. However, many state-owned enterprises have accumulated a substantial amount of non-performing debts. Some argue that these firms will go bankrupt if lending is made strictly according to market principles, which will surely lead to serious social problems. Thus, it is expected that state owned commercial banks will continue to issue preferential policy loans to many loss-making and inefficient state-owned enterprises, so that they can be kept floating. Meanwhile, the newly established state-owned policy banks are not capable of assuming all the historical responsibilities of the state-owned commercial banks in issuing policy loans to the state-owned enterprises, due to the fact that their capital is not sufficient to carry out policy loans.

TABLE 1.2 Market Share of Financial Institutions, 1988-1995

	1988	1993	1994	1995
Policy Banks	0.0	0.0	5.6	6.7
State Development Bank	0.0	0.0	1.0	1.8
Agricultural Bank of China	0.0	0.0	4.6	4.9
Export and Import Bank of China	0.0	0.0	0.0	0.1
State Commercial Banks	85.4	84.2	79.8	72.7
Industrial and Commercial Bank of China	27.2	31.1	29.5	28.0
Agricultural Bank of China	14.6	16.8	14.0	11.1
Bank of China	27.1	19.4	20.6	18.1
Construction Bank of China	16.4	16.9	15.7	15.5
Other Commercial Banks at the National Level	6.2	5.8	4.9	4.6
Other Banks	0.2	1.1	1.6	1.8
Credit Cooperatives	8.2	8.9	8.1	13.7
Urban Credit Cooperatives	1.0	3.0	2.4	4.1
Rural Credit Cooperatives	7.2	6.0	5.7	9.6

Note: The numbers are the percentages of the total of financial institutions' assets that exclude foreign banks and non-bank financial institutions. Data for these institutions are not available for years prior to 1995. For 1995, the commercial banks' share in the total financial assets, including foreign banks and non-bank financial institutions, was about two thirds.
Sources: The People's Bank of China Quarterly Statistical Bulletin, various years and Almanac of China's Finance and Banking (1996).

The Government Bond Market

The government issued bonds to finance public expenditures during the early postwar period of the 1950s. The issuance of bonds was stopped because of the increasingly rigid ideological dogma that financial securities were the by-products of capitalism. Since then, for a long period of time, government bonds did not exist as the Chinese government proudly acclaimed to the world that no national debt existed in China. As the imbalance of government budget emerged after 1978, government bonds again became necessary tools for the government to narrow the gap between revenue and expenditure. Table 1.3 indicates that for the eighteen years since economic reform was started, the government has run a budget surplus in only three years. It also shows that the budget deficit has increased over the years. In tandem with the rising budget deficit, the bonds issued in each year have increased. The total value of bonds in each year as a percentage of the total government expenditure in the same year increased from less than 5 percent in 1981 to more than 25 percent in 1996. Notice that government bonds can be quite different from the government budget deficits in each year and most of the time the bonds issued were much larger than the budget deficits.

TABLE 1.3 Budget Deficit and Government Domestic Bond Issued (in billion yuan)

Year	Revenue	Expenditure	Surplus	Bond	Bond/Expenditure Ratio
1978	113.23	112.21	1.02	-	-
1979	114.64	128.18	-13.54	-	-
1980	115.99	122.88	-6.89	-	-
1981	117.58	113.84	3.74	4.87	0.043
1982	121.23	122.99	-1.76	4.38	0.036
1983	136.69	140.95	-4.26	4.16	0.030
1984	164.29	170.1	-5.81	4.25	0.025
1985	200.48	200.43	0.05	6.06	0.030
1986	212.2	220.49	-8.29	6.25	0.028
1987	219.94	226.22	-6.28	11.69	0.052
1988	235.72	249.12	-13.4	18.88	0.076
1989	266.49	282.38	-15.89	22.39	0.079
1990	293.71	308.36	-14.65	19.72	0.065
1991	314.95	338.66	-23.71	28.13	0.083
1992	348.34	374.22	-25.88	46.08	0.123
1993	434.89	464.23	-29.34	38.13	0.082
1994	521.81	579.26	-57.45	113.76	0.196
1995	624.22	682.37	-58.15	151.08	0.221
1996	740.79	793.76	-52.97	212.60	0.268

Sources: China Statistical Yearbook (1997) and The People's Bank of China Quarterly Statistical Bulletin, various years.

Table 1.4 displays the total national debt accumulated as a percentage of GDP. This ratio steadily increased from 2.46 percent in 1984 to 6.10 percent in 1995. As GDP was about 5,826 billion yuan in 1995, the total accumulated national debt was 355 billion yuan in the same year. The government bond issued as a percentage of GDP increased from less than 0.69 percent in 1984 to 2.79 percent 1995. The central government has been highly dependent upon government bonds to finance its expenditures, which has accounted for 22 percent of total government expenditures and more than 52 percent of central government expenditures. As debt is accumulated, the interest payment becomes even larger. The interest payment on government debt in 1995 was 77.95 billion yuan, constituting approximately 11 percent of the government expenditure in that year.

TABLE 1.4 Ratio of National Debt to GDP (1984-1995), %

Year	Total Debt/GDP	Government Bond Issue/GDP	Government Bond Issue/ Central Government Expenditure
1984	2.46	0.59	5.76
1985	2.65	0.68	7.25
1986	2.87	0.61	6.49
1987	3.27	0.53	6.11
1988	3.74	0.89	12.46
1989	4.55	0.82	12.57
1990	4.81	1.06	14.37
1991	4.90	1.30	18.53
1992	4.82	1.73	25.35
1993	4.46	1.10	19.48
1994	5.08	2.29	47.00
1995	6.10	2.79	52.98

Sources: China Statistical Yearbook (1997), The People's Bank of China Quarterly Statistical Bulletin, various years and Almanac of China's Finance and Banking (1996).

When the State Council decided to issue government bonds again in 1981, a total amount of 4.87 billion yuan was issued to the working units only. In the early years, the interest rate of the bond issued to the working units was substantially smaller than the interest rate of the same bond issued to the individuals. The difference in the interest rates is due to the allocation scheme of the government bonds.

The government bonds issued to the working units were placed largely through administrative allocation that enabled the government to offer bonds with lower interest rates. Since 1989, the issuing interest rates of government bonds for the working units have been set the same as those of individuals. Over the years, the variety of the government bonds has increased. The terms of maturity of government bonds now range from a half year to ten years. The short-term maturity bonds have become an increasingly important government financing instrument. In addition, the Ministry of Finance issued the financial bonds through private placement to state commercial banks, other commercial banks, and non-banking financial institutions. Finally, special purchase bonds have been issued, but to the working units only.

The secondary bond market emerged in 1988. Since then, many financial intermediaries have been established. These financial intermediaries underwrote one quarter of the bonds issued in 1991, the year the government decided to experiment with the alternative bond distribution mechanism. Though the interest rates were not determined completely by market supply and demand, the introduction of bond underwriting to the distribution mechanism brought in market mechanisms, as the negotiations between the bond issuers and bond underwriters were also important in setting the interest rates. To accommodate the exchange of bonds in the secondary market, bond-trading centers were set up in various localities. However these bond markets were segmented, as suggested by the regional price spread of the bonds deviating from the price of the same bond traded in Shanghai. In 1990, the average price spread of major trading centers was more than 4 yuan (Fang 1998). Nevertheless, the price spread of bonds declined as soon as the Securities Trading Automated Quotations System (STAQ) – a system connecting securities trading in major trading centers – was put in use in April 1991.

TABLE 1.5 Interest Rates and Types of Government Bonds

Year	Categories	Interest rate % (working units)	Interest rate % (individuals)	Maturity
1981	T-bill	4	-	5-9 years
1985	T-bill	5	9	5 years
1988	T-bill	6	10	3 years
	Financial Bond	7.5-8	-	2 and 5 years
	State Construction Bond	9.5	-	2 years
1989	T-bill	-	14	3 years
	Special Bond	-	15	5 years
	Price Index Bond	14.14	14.14	3 years
1990	T-bill	-	14	3 years
	Financial Bond	10	-	5 years
	Special Bond	15	-	5 years
1991	T-bill	-	10	3 years
	Financial Bond	9	-	5 years
	Special Bond	9	-	5 years
1992	T-bill	-	9.5-10.5	3 and 5 years
	Financial bond	9	-	5 years
1993	T-bill	-	13.96-15.86	3 and 5 years
	Financial Bond	13	-	5 years
1994	T-bill	-	9.80-13.96	6 mo.-3 years
	Special Purchase Bond	15.86	-	5 years
1995	T-bill	-	11.98-14.50	1 and 3 years
	Special Purchase Bond	15.86	-	5 years
1996	T-bill	-	8.5-14.5	6 mo.-10 years
	Special Purchase Bond		8.8	

Sources: same as Table 1.3

The Equity Market

The equity markets in China remain underdeveloped. In 1996, China's Gross Domestic Product reached 6,770 billion yuan. Residents' savings amounted to 3850 billion yuan or about 57 percent of GDP. By contrast, the total value of stocks was only 984 billion yuan, or less than 15 percent of GDP. In 1993, the stock value in Singapore, which has a highly developed financial system, was 5.8 times its GDP. In 1996, China spent 2,360 billion yuan in its fixed capital investment, of which only 263 billion yuan (about 11 percent) was generated from the equity markets.[4]

Shanghai used to boast the largest stock market in the Far East. But stock trading and issuing were discontinued in China for nearly forty years due to ideological misperception that stocks are capitalism incarnate. In the 1980s, some firms started to raise capital by issuing bonds and stocks. The Shanghai Stock Exchange was inaugurated on December 19, 1990, and later the Shenzhen Stock Exchange was established on July 3, 1991. Only eight stocks were listed when the Shanghai Stock Exchange started to operate. The numbers of listed firms, trading volumes and total market capitalization have all increased dramatically since the opening of the exchanges.

China has explicitly segmented its stock market, establishing separate classes of shares for domestic and foreign investors respectively. In each stock exchange, there are two classes of shares traded. Share A, denominated in the Chinese currency, is available to domestic Chinese residents only. Share B, denominated in U.S. dollars in Shanghai and Hong Kong dollars in Shenzhen, is open to foreign investors only. Almost all companies that have issued B shares also have issued A share stocks. The two classes of shares have identical voting rights and stakes for the claim on the firm's cash flow. In order to open an account to purchase a B share, one must satisfy two conditions. The buyer has to show proof of foreign residence and must have a foreign exchange account. Though the B shares are reserved for foreign investors only, the rule is not strictly enforced. Many domestic residents are believed to have purchased large sums of B shares through various channels. Some companies are also listed in Hong Kong (H-shares), the New York Stock Exchanges (N-shares), or both.

Besides these tradable shares, each listed company often issues non-tradable shares. The non-tradable shares include the state shares that represent the state ownership and the legal entity shares that represent the ownership by other registered companies. The ownership of the non-tradable shares can be transferred via negotiation. With permission, a small portion of non-tradable shares can be traded in the nation-wide electronic trading system: STAQ (Security Trading Automatic Quotation) and NETS (National Electronic Trading System).

Tradable shares can be listed in either the Shanghai or Shenzhen Stock Exchange. Dual listing is forbidden. Trading is conducted via an automatic electronic order-matching system. Orders are matched first by the price and then by the time. Since 1993, the Shanghai Securities Central Clearing and Registration Corporation has been responsible for registration, clearing, settlement and depositary management. For A shares, clearing and settlement take one business day (T+1) and for B shares, they take three business days (T+3). The transaction costs are different between A and B shares. There is a stamp fee of 0.3 percent of the market value and a 0.1 percent transfer fee based upon the par value for both classes of shares. However the commission fees for A shares and B shares are not the same. The commission fee for A shares is fixed at 0.6 percent of the market value. The commission for B shares is not fixed; it usually remains below 0.6 percent of the market value for a large trading block.

TABLE 1.6 Basic Statistics of China's Stock Markets

Shanghai Stock Exchange								
	1991	1992	1993	1994	1995	1996	1997	1998*
# A listed	8	38	101	169	184	287	372	413
# B listed	0	9	22	32	36	42	50	52
A-share Mkt Capitalization (billion RMB)	-	52.1	207.6	248.3	243.4	531.6	903.2	1103.3
B-share Mkt Capitalization (billion RMB)	-	3.8	12.9	11.7	9.2	16.2	18.5	11.7
A-share Trade Volume (billion RMB)	-	232.8	238.0	562.7	304.2	902.0	1355.0	966.5
B-share Trade Volume (billion RMB)	-	1.5	9.0	10.6	6.1	9.5	21.3	6.8

Shenzhen Stock Exchange								
	1991	1992	1993	1994	1995	1996	1997	1998*
# A listed	6	24	75	116	122	227	348	388
# B listed	-	6	19	23	34	43	51	54
A-share Mkt Capitalization (billion RMB)	7.9	45.8	125.1	103.2	87.7	413.2	812.1	917.5
B-share Mkt Capitalization (billion RMB)	-	3.2	8.4	5.8	7.2	23.2	18.9	12.7
A-share Trade Volume (billion RMB)	3.5	41.7	126.1	237.6	91.6	1203.2	1674.5	885.5
B-share Trade Volume (billion RMB)	-	1.7	2.6	1.6	1.7	18.5	21.4	3.7

*Sources: GF Security Research Department, *: ending in September 1998.*

The long-term development goal of Chinese stock markets is a unified market with a segmented structure. National markets and local markets complement each other. Without the formation and growth of local markets, it is difficult to develop the national markets. Currently, the pressures on the Shanghai and Shenzhen Exchanges are enormous. A segmented system with national and local exchanges will provide an efficient solution to the demand and supply of stocks so that stocks not meeting the national standards can be downgraded to local markets. In the fifteen years, the level of capitalization in China's stock markets will be among the highest in the world, but the challenge is to also make them among the most efficient ones (Zhao and He 1996).

Non-Banking Institutions

China's non-banking industries consist of investment trust companies, security firms, finance firms, and leasing companies. By the end of 1996, China had 244 trust companies with total assets valued at 510 billion yuan, 96 security firms with total assets at 159 billion yuan, 64 finance companies with total assets at 6.7 billion yuan, and 16 financial leasing companies with total assets at 18.7 billion yuan.

In 1979, China International Trust and the Trust Division of the Bank of China were established. Since then, a large number of trusts emerged across the country. By 1982, there were about 620 trust companies, among which about 520 were run by banks and about 50 by local governments (Di and Ye 1998). In 1982, government branches were ordered to shut down their trusts. In 1984, however, another wave of trusts swept the country, adding to inflationary pressures. The government required that trusts not take any new transactions. From 1984 to 1994, banks and government departments set up numerous investment trusts. The multitude of trust companies resulted in an expansion of investment that competed with existing banks and caused financial instability. Specialized banks transferred funds into investment trusts as a way of avoiding control by the People's Bank. In 1996, the state commercial banks disowned their trust investment divisions; the branches of the People's Bank were also separated from their brokerage divisions. According to the audit of 206 trust companies by the People's Bank, the major problems of the trust companies lay in the inaccurate report of capital, a large number of non-performing assets and unlawful practices such as the use of high interest rates. As a result, a large number of trust companies incurred losses and some of them went bankrupt (*Almanac of China's Finance and Banking* 1997:39).

Finance companies were the product of financial needs within the consortium of enterprises. The first finance company was established in 1987. The People's Bank approved the finance company for the Dongfeng Automobile Group. Since then, various finance companies were set up for such industry groups as chemical engineering, iron and steel, aerospace, textile products, energy, computer, automobiles, metallurgy, and electronics.

These finance companies have the potential of turning into commercial banks. However, as their performance depends upon that of the industrial group, the risk is not diversified. The poor performance of the industry may result in and compound the problems of bad and non-performing loans.

The concept of leasing was introduced in China in the 1980s. Currently, China has two kinds of leasing companies. The joint-venture leasing companies specialize in leasing equipment manufactured abroad. They purchased and leased equipment based on requests from customers. The other type of leasing company specializes in domestic transactions and is run by domestic enterprises, sixteen of which are financial leasing companies. The transactions of financial leasing companies include the lease of assets used in production, science and research, education, health, tourism and transportation. Rules and regulations are generally lacking with respect to financial leasing companies, negatively affecting the development of leasing industries.

Credit Cooperatives

There are two types of credit cooperatives in China – rural credit cooperatives and urban credit cooperatives. While the former existed in China since 1949, the latter started in 1979. Both have played important roles in savings and investments. They have made the loan process accessible to collectively and privately owned enterprises in both cities and the countryside.

Rural Credit Cooperatives

The guiding principles for rural credit cooperatives have been popular involvement, democratic management and flexible operation. Since the 1980s, the role of rural credit cooperatives has been enhanced to support the household responsibility system in the countryside. Though China's Bank of Agriculture supervised the credit planning of rural credit cooperatives, the latter had the power to make decisions on individual loans. In the past, the loans were made to the collectives, but now are made also to individual households to start or expand production. The Bank of Agriculture also reduced reserves for rural credit cooperatives from 30 percent to 25 percent in 1985 and allowed the interest rates at the rural credit unions to be close to the market interest rate. It no longer paid subsidies to those cooperatives that incur losses, making rural credit cooperatives strive for self-reliance. In terms of management, the involvement of peasants has increased substantially, enhancing their incentives to increase deposits with the credit cooperatives. As of 1996, rural credit cooperatives had deposits of 879 billion yuan and made loans of 629 billion yuan. They took the deposits of 396.5 billion yuan from the collectively owned enterprises and 291.5 billion yuan from peasants. Meanwhile they made 561.9 billion yuan in loans to agricultural production and 123.6 billion yuan to township and village enterprises (*Almanac of China's Finance and Banking* 1997).

Urban Credit Cooperatives

The first urban credit cooperative emerged in 1979, as a response to urban economic reforms that led to an increase in collectively owned and privately owned enterprises. Due to the lack of these enterprises' access to funds, the branch offices of the People's Bank and specialized banks helped the set-up of urban credit cooperatives to facilitate loans to them. Two factors contributed to the fast expansion of urban credit cooperatives before 1988. First, the entry cost was low, as the minimum capital for the urban credit cooperative was set at only 100,000 yuan. Second, during that time, the country still experienced tight credit control, particularly to collectively and privately owned enterprises.

The increase in the number of urban credit cooperatives was accompanied by high-risk loans, low quality of assets and blind pursuit of the number and size of loans. In addition, some sponsors of urban credit cooperatives intervened in the operation of cooperatives and even used their funds and assets. In 1988, the People's Bank promulgated the Regulations of Urban Credit Cooperatives to remedy the problems mentioned above, thus reducing the unhealthy expansion of the urban credit cooperative system. In 1996, there were a total of 4,630 urban credit cooperatives with total assets valued at 401.8 billion yuan. Deposits were at 304.4 billion yuan and loans amounted to 196.4 yuan, with a loss of 7.3 billion yuan (*Almanac of China's Finance and Banking* 1997).

Contributions of This Volume

The articles in this volume deal with and analyze many problems we have summarized here. They give insight into a number of policy issues facing China's financial market reform.

Assessing the impact of the Asian financial crisis on China, Nicholas R. Lardy compares China with other countries in the region, with a focus on why China was largely unaffected by the Asian financial crisis of 1997. China shares several characteristics with those nations involved in the crisis, such as bank dominated financial systems, weak central bank regulation and supervision of commercial banks, excessive growth of lending, and a large buildup of non-performing loans. However, it is shielded from crisis because its currency is not convertible for capital account transactions, its capital inflows are primarily in the form of foreign direct investment, it registers trade surpluses, and its foreign exchange reserves are sufficient to finance future imports.

Similarly, Jianping Zhou compares the current Asian financial crisis with the Mexican peso crisis of 1994 and finds many similarities in capital inflows, subsequent policy reactions and vulnerabilities of the linkages between economies. A lack of flexibility in exchange rates can put markets at risk when uncertainty surrounds economic policies and structural weaknesses. Moreover, the current crisis has shown that large capital inflows combined with weak domestic financial systems can be destabilizing. This suggests that China should proceed with its capital account liberalization only when the banking system has in place an effective regulatory and supervisory framework.

John G. Fernald and Oliver D. Babson explore features of China's financial system that helped insulate it from the crisis, and assess whether China has avoided crisis or simply deferred it. They argue that regardless of whether the Asian crisis resulted from weak fundamentals or from "country runs" by investors, it is not surprising that China has survived so far. In a market-oriented system, pressures generally force rapid adjustment when institutions are, or are perceived to be, insolvent; these mechanisms do not operate fully in China. In addition, China's external accounts remain strong. Even in the absence of capital controls, the strength of these external fundamentals would plausibly preclude a self-fulfilling "country run" on China. Nevertheless, capital controls may have played a role in preventing poorly supervised financial institutions from borrowing excessively abroad, and hence may have helped keep China's external fundamentals strong.

In the same vein as the preceding three chapters, Yi Feng analyzes the implications of the sequence of capital account openness in relation to current account openness, domestic financial markets liberalization, and political openness and decentralization. China has gradually liberalized its current account, so as to slowly absorb the political costs of economic liberalization. The sequence of liberalization is unimportant so long as the process is undertaken slowly. Simultaneous liberalization of both capital and current accounts would have produced much higher political costs, perhaps undermining efforts at reform. The fundamental task, he argues, is political reform, without which economic and financial reforms would stagnate.

J. Kimball Dietrich examines the savings and loan and banking crisis in the United States during the 1980s to derive insights for the current Asian financial crisis and the implications for China's financial market reform. He finds that the power to tax is used to protect specific institutions, which distorts financial flows and market incentives. Additionally, market segmentation limits competition and creates barriers between financial markets. Moreover, attempts to control "unhealthy" economic activity have unintended consequences and reduce the efficiency of financial markets. Finally, activity limitations and price controls designed to control financial systems distort market activity and are difficult to remove.

Brian Buford-Efird utilizes power transition theory to explain competition between different actors in the Chinese economy. The political process in Chinese economic decision making is dynamic. Regional and local governments vary in their power over time, so that their ability and incentives to manipulate monetary policy vary as well. When power between competing regions or between the central and local governments is asymmetrically distributed, conflict is unlikely and the more powerful actor's preferences tend to be adopted. However, in order to create a stable economic environment over the long term, the central government in China must increasingly surrender its control over the country and necessarily make its political competitors more powerful.

Barry Naughton traces Chinese financial reform to date. China is at a critical point in its reform due to rapid changes in the economic environment. It is going through both macroeconomic stabilization and acceleration of state enterprise reforms. As state banks dominate the financial markets, financial deepening has been applied primarily to the banking sector. Though the banking sector has improved, it still suffers from a large stock of bad loans, since many lending decisions are not made on a commercially sound basis in an attempt to pursue macroeconomic stabilization. While the stock markets are still extremely volatile and are still limited by government ownership and the strength of large institutional players, they are growing rapidly.

Hong Chang, Baizhu Chen and Yang Li gauge the reform in China's money market, an integral component of any financial structure. While the Chinese money markets have grown in relation to the size of the economy and its financial system, they are still in a preliminary stage as only limited market instruments are available. Both the repo and commercial paper markets are segmented and their interest rates are not market-driven. However, interbank markets are relatively well-developed and relatively efficient with interest rates driven by market mechanisms. Finally, the People's Bank of China has successfully curbed inflation by targeting monetary aggregates.

Ding Lu and Qiao Yu study the performance of the credit quota plan as a banking risk control lever and macroeconomic policy instrument. They find that a number of factors, such as uneven distribution of financial risk, volatility of political preferences, and local leverage over credit quotas eroded its effectiveness prior to its abandonment. They conclude that the failure of the credit quota system demonstrates the necessity for an independent central banking system.

Shang-Jin Wei analyzes the importance of investor sentiment, unrelated to economic fundamentals, in explaining the return variation in China, relative to the stock markets in the US and Hong Kong. He finds that the system of initial public offering is not related to the high volatility in mood swings. While limited disclosure may cause a volatile assessment of fundamentals and hence raise the volatility of the Chinese market index, it does not explain all of the excessive volatility. He concludes that the two most likely explanations for the apparently high Chinese volatility are the absence of an enforced capital gains tax and the dominance of small individual traders relative to institutional traders.

Dongwei Su and Belton M. Fleisher examine the reasons for initial public offering (IPO) underpricing in China. They find that IPO underpricing was at its largest in the earliest developmental stages of the stock market, that goods industries exhibit higher underpricing and that underpricing is not affected by information about firms, the amount of time between announcement of an IPO and trading or various lottery mechanisms. They conclude that IPO underpricing results because only a small aggregate supply of equity instruments is available to investors, that underpricing is better explained by a signaling model relating underpricing to subsequent equity offerings (SEOs) than by one linking ownership to equilibrium underpricing, and that issuers with larger underpricing are more likely to raise capital more quickly.

Richard C. K. Burdekin and Xiaojin Hu compare and analyze the role of government indexed bonds before and after 1992. They find that in the pre-1992 period, the optimal strategy was for the government to lower the inflation rate right before the bond payoff date. If the government failed to lower inflation right before the payoff date, as in 1992 and 1993, then the public would feel that the government could not control inflation. After 1992, the public had undergone a learning process about how to evaluate government behavior, probably reducing its confidence in the government's anti-inflationary policies.

Zhaohui Hong and Ellen Y. Yan study the role played by trust and investment corporations (TICs) on China's financial markets. They maintain that TICs are important to economic development as they can compensate for shortcomings in the banking sector. However, the current TIC liquidity crisis in China is caused by the duplication of bank and securities companies' services. Lessons from other countries indicate that to resolve the crisis, TICs should eliminate their duplicated financial business and instead refocus on their unique trust services.

Eric Girardin and Stephen Bazen conclude that Urban Credit Cooperatives bridge the needs of small and medium-sized businesses that are excluded from bank credit, an important component of economic expansion in a transitional economy such as China's and are a source of faster than planned credit expansion. They find that there are major regional differences in the performance of UCCs, driven by the size of the city they are based in, the region's level of development, the number of directors in the UCC, the extent to which UCCs granted loans to state-owned enterprises, and total assets.

Wing Thye Woo analyzes the problems associated with financing township and village enterprises, particularly those in rural areas. He uses the Indonesian case to suggest further reforms in China. The still heavily regulated financial system directs funds into state-owned enterprises at the expense of Township and Village Enterprises (TVEs). Furthermore, TVEs lack property rights, deterring private investors. Under these circumstances, rural credit cooperatives play an important role in allocating funds to rural TVEs. Woo provides detailed suggestions for the reorganization of Rural

Credit Cooperatives (RCCs) in terms of legal status, accountability, supervision, and accommodation.

Tian Zhu examines the potential problems in China's restructuring of its state-owned enterprises. He finds that enterprise restructuring should be a gradual process that addresses the incentive problems facing managers and owners, as well as the development of market mechanisms in the financial market and its associated legal system. He also suggests that the potential for failure has been overestimated, and that with a corporate governance structure, China can enjoy a successful restructuring of its enterprises.

David Li demonstrates that insider control in China is associated with the lack of government control of enterprises, which results in soft budget constraints. He argues that the maintenance of a proper degree of bureaucratic control of enterprises helps reduce insider control in the short run. In the long run, the solutions to the problem of insider control and the soft budget constraint lie in the creation of large private stakeholders and the establishment of institutions of corporate governance.

Similar to David Li's argument, Hilton Root maintains that competitive financial markets are as essential to China's future as the development of competitive product markets. Inadequate information about the creditworthiness of national financial institutions and unpredictable behavior by government render long-term business planning difficult. When financial intermediaries are able to overcome the problem of asymmetric information, they can reduce transaction costs. So far, the measures taken to provide information to sources outside government have subjected information flow to political considerations. As long as politics, rather than rules, determine access to the information needed to price financial assets, markets will be unstable, because political risks are added to business risks.

Finally, Yi Feng and Hui Zhang study the determinants of foreign direct investment across different regions in China from 1992-1996 and find that expenditures on fixed capital, the degree of openness of the provincial economy, transport systems and communications networks all encourage foreign direct investment. By contrast, higher labor costs and a stronger environmental protection sector hinder foreign direct investment.

Concluding Remarks

China's financial market reform is not confined to the financial markets themselves. It is a part of a comprehensive reform that is increasingly challenged when the reforms are deepened to include the restructuring of state-owned enterprises as well as the political system. China has yet to establish a truly independent Central Bank. The central bank should set its paramount objective as the maintenance of long-run price stability for the country, as called for by Robert Perry in the Foreword of this volume. Any economic decision made by the government is essentially a political one. The Chinese government is faced with the challenge of allowing independence of the central bank, together with an ongoing effort to fight economic corruption and political rent-seeking. In this process, commercial lending and policy lending must also be truly separated.

While allowing markets to function according to price incentives, monitoring and supervisory functions of the financial markets by the central bank should be enhanced by institutionalization of laws and codes to maintain market stability and long-term development. The role played by market intermediary agencies should also be strengthened. They must keep the markets transparent and law-abiding; the firms that violate the equity markets laws should be duly prosecuted.

One of the major sources of the series of financial crises in Pacific Asia is the lack of regulations that safeguard the sound operation of financial markets. During the early 1990s, international funds increasingly flew into emerging equity markets, particularly those in Latin America and Pacific Asia. Because of the lack of transparency on the emerging financial markets and the failure to base investments on the rate of returns, international investment suffered from a rise in non-performing loans. It is essential that the People's Bank be empowered to make and enforce regulations so as to keep the financial markets open, fair and transparent.[5] As several chapters in this volume point out, China should make use of the experiences of Western financial markets by allowing the markets to function in accordance with the efficiency criterion while at the same time institutionalizing and enforcing rules and regulations.

Notes

1. The authors thank Thomas D. Willett for helpful comments. Yi Feng thankfully acknowledges a Fletcher-Jones faculty research grant.
2. Another stated objective is to supervise and regulate financial institutions.
3. Some studies indicate that money supply in China tends to increase after each Party Congress as well (see Xu and Ni 1997).
4. See Weiping Zheng and Qiang Ding, "Retrospectives and Perspectives of China's Capital Markets," *Almanac of China's Economy 1997*, 759-763.
5. Wang (1997) makes some concrete suggestions as to the management of the financial markets in China, including the role played by the People's Bank, the operating standards for banks, risk control, deposit insurance, etc.

References

Chang, H., B. Chen, and Y. Li. 1998. "Central Bank and Monetary Policy in China." Research Paper submitted to The Chinese Eurasia Studies of Taiwan.

China's Finance Society. 1996. *Almanac of China's Finance and Banking, Volume 11.* Beijing: China's Finance Society Press.

———. 1997. *Almanac of China's Finance and Banking, Volume 12,* Beijing: China's Finance Society Press.

China Statistical Bureau. 1997. *China Statistical Yearbook Volume 16.* Beijing: China Statistical Publishing House.

Di, W., and X. Ye. 1998. *The Reform and Opening of China's Financial Industry.* Beijing: Qinghua University Press.

Li, Y. 1998. *The Development of the Chinese Capital Market.* Beijing: Economics and Management Press.

———. 1999. *A Study on the Chinese Financial Market Reform.* Nanjing, China: Jiangsu People's Press.

Li, F. 1998. "The Government Securities Market During the Economic Transformation in China." Working Paper, Monash University.

People's Bank of China. various years. *The People's Bank of China Quarterly Statistical Bulletin.* Research and Statistics Department of the People's Bank of China.

Wang, Z. 1997. *On China's Financial Markets and Globalization.* Beijing: China's Finance Press.

Xie P., et al. 1992. *China's Financial Reform and Deepening.* Tianjin People's Press.

Xu, D., and J. Ni. 1997. "China's Multiple Policy Goals and Business Cycles." Working Paper, 12th Annual Conference of the Chinese Economists Society.

Xue, M., et, al. 1997. *Almanac of China's Economy.* Beijing: Almanac of China's Economy Press.

Zhao, X., and D. He. 1996. *The Structure of Financial Markets in China.* Beijing: Economics and Management Press.

Zheng, W., and D. Qiang. 1997. "Retrospectives and Perspectives of China's Capital Markets." In Muqiao Xue, et al, eds., *Almanac of China's Economy.* Beijing: Almanac of China's Economy Press.

2
China and the Asian Financial Contagion

Nicholas R. Lardy[1]

China appears to be largely unscathed by the Asian financial contagion. In contrast to plummeting currency values in several other countries in the region, the RMB actually has appreciated vis-à-vis the U.S. dollar since the onset of the crisis. In real terms the Chinese economy also has fared quite well. The growth of gross domestic product in 1997, while slower than the blistering pace in the immediate prior years, was almost 9 percent. Price inflation was at a five-year low. Exports grew over 20 percent in 1997, contributing to an unprecedented US$40.3 billion trade surplus. In 1997, foreign direct investment inflows rose for the seventh consecutive year, to reach US$45.3 billion and China raised an additional US$16 billion in debt and equity offerings on international markets. Official holdings of foreign exchange reserves rose sharply, reaching US$139.9 billion by year-end 1997, second in size only to those of Japan.

The official outlook for 1998 is also relatively bright. The government is predicting 8 percent growth of real gross domestic product, which would make China far and away the most rapidly growing economy in the region. It also is forecasting positive growth of imports and expects to maintain the value of the RMB. All of these should be warmly welcomed for their contribution to Asia's financial and economic recovery.

Nonetheless Chinese policy makers are genuinely concerned that they are at risk of being drawn into the Asian financial contagion and have taken a number of bold steps they hope will reduce their vulnerability. Given the weaknesses in their domestic financial structure and the many risks involved in implementation of the reform program, it is too soon to offer a definitive prognosis for its success.

China's Vulnerabilities

China shares many of the characteristics that contributed to the financial crises in Korea, Thailand, and Indonesia. These include, most notably, bank dominated financial systems, weak central bank regulation and supervision of commercial banks, excessive growth of lending, and a large build-up of non-performing loans.

Bank Dominated Financial Systems

Even in a region in which banks dominate financial systems, China stands out. Banks account for fully nine-tenths of all financial intermediation between savers and investors in China, a ratio that exceeds that found in almost all other Asian countries.

Bank dominated financial systems, where markets for equity and debt are very small, tend to share several closely related problems. First, the lack of well-developed capital markets creates a high potential for systematic underpricing of loans. That, in turn, encourages excessive borrowing by firms with preferred access to credit — state-owned firms in China, the chaebol in Korea, those well connected to the government in Indonesia and Thailand — while leaving the rest of the economy starved for funds. More generally, in bank dominated financial systems capital markets do not provide sufficient competition for banks, contributing to lower efficiency of financial intermediation and lower rates of returns for savers who have little alternative but to put their savings in bank deposits. Finally, it is easier for politicians, whether in China or elsewhere in the region, to influence the pattern of bank lending than to determine which borrowers get access to funds raised through capital markets.

Weak Bank Regulation and Supervision

China's financial and banking system, like some others in Asia, suffers from weak central bank supervision and weak prudential regulation of banks. China's largest banks, for example, are not subject to independent audits. Indeed three of China's four largest banks do not even report their financial results on a consolidated basis, meaning that losses can be buried in subsidiary firms whose financial results are not incorporated with those of the parent bank. Classification of nonperforming loans by banks is based on standards that are more lenient than those commonly used internationally, impairing the value of these data as a means of measuring bank performance. China's system of setting aside reserves for nonperforming loans is also flawed, since the magnitude of reserves that banks are required to set aside is not linked directly to the quality of each bank's loan portfolio but rather is set at an arbitrary low percentage of total loans.

More alarmingly, losses caused by fraud, corruption, and other lending irregularities in Chinese banks may be similar to those associated with crony capitalism in Indonesia or with corrupt Korean bank lending practices that were used to channel hundreds of millions of U.S. dollars into the pockets of Korea's highest leaders. The People's Bank of China, China's central bank, in 1996 acknowledged that some banks had lent funds without recording them in their account books, and that some nonbank financial institutions created false assets to cover up the black holes in their balance sheets caused by large financial losses. Ominously, the central bank admitted that the number of serious financial crimes was on the rise and that the manner in which such crimes were committed was making them more and more difficult to detect. Since these astonishing admissions, the situation seems to have worsened. An editorial appearing in November 1997 in *People's Daily*, the Chinese Communist Party newspaper, admitted that some financial institutions operate in violation of laws and regulations; criminal activities in banking and finance are rampant.

Whether in China or elsewhere in the region, the common elements leading to fraud, corruption, and political direction of lending is inadequate regulation and supervision of banks by central banks and the lack of sufficient central bank independence. In Korea, for example, the central bank was formally subordinate to the Ministry of Finance. The latter focused on providing a continuous flow of funds to major industrial groups at low cost and effectively precluded the central bank from exercising effective supervision. A key condition of the IMF bail out was legislation making the Korean central bank an independent entity. In China the weakness of the central bank reflects the extreme reluctance of powerful political leaders, especially at the provincial and local level, to relinquish their power to direct loan funds to specific industries and firms.

Excessive Growth of Lending

China shares with several countries in Asia region an excessive build-up of domestic credit. From the beginning of reform in 1978 through the end of 1997, credit outstanding by all financial institutions grew from RMB 190 billion to RMB 7.5 trillion. Credit outstanding as a percent of gross domestic product almost doubled, from about 53 percent in 1978 to 100 percent in 1997. The build up of credit in China is almost as rapid as that in South Korea and Thailand just prior to the onset of their financial crises in 1997.

The judgement that credit expansion in China has been excessive is based on several criteria. First, the build-up of excessive bank credit is mirrored by an extraordinary deterioration in the balance sheets of state-owned enterprises, which have been the chief recipients of bank credit. At the outset of reform their balance sheets were quite strong, as reflected in a debt to equity ratio of about 10 percent, a level only about one-fourth or a fifth one would expect to find for firms in a market-oriented economy. Because of an extraordinarily rapid increase in their borrowing, by year-end 1995 the debt to equity ratio of all state-owned firms, including commercial and other establishments as well as manufacturing firms, was in excess of 500 percent.

This extraordinary deterioration in the balance sheets of state-owned firms has several important implications. First, a significant portion of

China's state-owned firms are insolvent, i.e. the value of their liabilities exceeds the value of their assets. Second, it suggests that many firms are not able to cover their operating costs with the income they receive from the sale of their output. Their balance sheets have been deteriorating not only because they have been borrowing heavily to finance expansions of their plant and equipment but also to pay for purchased inputs, wages, taxes, and all too frequently growing inventories of unsold and unsaleable goods. This evidence of operating losses is important because even insolvent firms may be able to improve their balance sheets over time if they have operating profits and their lenders are willing to allow them to continue to operate.

Third, enterprises in China are so highly leveraged that an economic slowdown could undermine further the weak financial position of banks. The average state-owned enterprise in China is even more highly leveraged than the Korean chaebol, which are notorious for their high gearing ratios of from 300 to 400 percent. In an economic downturn the earnings of more firms could easily fall below the level necessary simply to pay interest on their heavy debts.

A second indicator of an excessive growth of domestic credit and overinvestment is excess capacity in many industries. This is evident not only in Thailand, Indonesia, and Korea, but also in China where industries with excess capacity include automobiles, beer, home appliances, machine tools, and chemicals and chemical fibers. An industrial census in 1995 showed that the rate of capacity utilization was less than 60 percent for more than 900 major industrial products.

These countries face a shared challenge not only to reform their financial systems but to restructure their productive sectors as well. In Korea increased competition is needed to curb the market power of the chaebol. China's lack of competition is evident not in the domination of the economy by a few large firms, but the birth and survival, through access to bank credit on soft terms, of many small local producers that are grossly inefficient.

One outstanding example of excess investment in China is the automobile industry. In the mid- and late-1980s more than 120 vehicle manufacturers were established in China. This was an astonishingly large number given the initially tiny market for vehicles and the economies of scale that are characteristic of the automotive sector. Although production of vehicles of all types tripled from about a half million in 1990 to 1.6 million in 1997, the vast majority of the 120 manufacturers have production levels that are far too low to take advantage of scale economies.

The Chinese government has sought, since at least 1994 when it promulgated an automotive industrial policy, to engineer a consolidation in the industry. But dozens of provincial and local level governments have resisted fiercely, each determined to maintain a presence in what the central government has identified as a pillar industry. Some of these localities have fostered their own producers by imposing restrictions within their jurisdictions on the sale and licensing of vehicles produced elsewhere. They have been abetted by a highly restrictive national auto import policy. After several cuts, tariff rates on imported sedans are still as high as 100 percent and imports are also subject to quotas and other restrictions. In a more market-oriented economy, with more efficient intermediation of capital and less restrictive trade practices, it is highly unlikely that 120 vehicle producers could have been established over a period of almost a decade. If they somehow had been created, it is even more unlikely that they would have had ongoing access to funds, not only to cover their operating losses and thus sustain their existence, but even to continue to expand their fixed assets.

A third indicator of excess lending has been the creation of asset bubbles, particularly in the property market. In the wake of Deng Xiaoping's famous southern tour in 1992, investment surged. That stimulated property development on a massive scale throughout China, much of it financed by bank lending.

By the mid-1990s it became clear that there had been massive overbuilding. The cities of Beijing, Shanghai, and Shenzhen appear to have the greatest absolute concentrations of unleased luxury villas and townhouses and first-class office space, but there is a significant problem of overbuilding in many smaller cities, ranging from Haikou on Hainan Island to Beihai in Guangxi, and in county-level towns as well. In Pudong, Shanghai's new financial and manufacturing center, the total stock of office space in mid-year 1997 stood at 13.5 million square feet, an astounding five times the 2.7 million square feet at year-end 1994. But more than 70 percent of this space in the latter part of 1997 was vacant. Vacant office space in Shenzhen in late 1997 was the equivalent of three years of take up. The vacancy problem in most large cities is almost certain to grow since the anticipated additions to the stock of space over the next few years exceed by a several-fold multiple the rate of take up of space in the past few years. By mid-1997 office rental rates had already declined substantially—by almost 50 percent in downtown Shanghai, over 40 percent in Pudong, and by 40 percent or more in Beijing—and were forecast to fall by as much as 70 percent before bottoming out. In retrospect, the repeated boast of Shanghai's mayor that one-fifth of the world's construction cranes were at work in Shanghai should have been seen as a premonition of over building and a coming collapse of property prices rather than an auspicious sign reflecting the city's economic resurgence following the creation of the Pudong Development Area in 1991.

Build-Up of Non-Performing Loans

A fourth vulnerability that China shares with other Asian countries undergoing financial crises is a huge build-up of nonperforming loans. Nonperforming loans, in international practice those loans on which either an interest or principal payment is 90 or 180 days past due, are an important indicator of the health of a banking system. Ultimately the borrowers of loans that become nonperforming may default, requiring the lender to absorb the loss, either from loan loss reserves or from its own capital.

According to statements of high officials, including People's Bank of China Governor Dai Xianglong, the share of nonperforming loans in the portfolios of the four largest state-owned banks has increased steadily in recent years—from 20 percent at year-end 1994, to 22 percent at year-end 1995, and then 25 percent at year-end 1997. The ratio of nonperforming loans in China is substantially higher than in South Korea or Thailand prior to the onset of their financial crises.

The Sources of Chinese Insulation

Despite these vulnerabilities, in the short run China is unlikely to experience a crisis like that of several Southeast Asian countries and Korea in 1997-98 for several reasons. First, and most important, the Chinese currency is not convertible for capital account transactions. This means that Chinese savers who are concerned about the viability of the country's financial institutions do not have the option of legally converting their RMB deposits and then purchasing foreign currency-denominated financial assets. Because their ability to convert back into dollars is severely limited, foreigners own only small amounts of RMB-denominated financial assets such as bank deposits or RMB-denominated shares. Indeed, nonresidents legally are precluded from purchasing A shares, the shares bought and sold for local currency on the Shanghai and Shenzhen stock markets. They must buy foreign currency-denominated B shares that are priced independently from the A shares of the same underlying company. If foreign sentiment on the value of B shares turns negative, there are no adverse consequences for the value of the Chinese currency. Would-be sellers, in effect, cannot exit the market unless they find a foreign buyer who will pay dollars for their shares. This contrasts sharply with Southeast Asian markets in the summer and fall of 1997. Foreign portfolio managers all rushed for the exits simultaneously, contributing to a sharp decline in local currency share prices. And, when they then sold the *baht* and other local currencies they had gained from the sale of their shares for dollars, they contributed to the plummet of currency values in these countries. Within a matter of weeks the foreign currency values of shares listed in these markets had fallen 50 percent or more.

The absence of capital account convertibility also means that speculators, either foreign or Chinese, have no way to act on the belief that the RMB is overvalued and likely to depreciate. Only buyers with a demonstrated need related to trade, tourism, or repatriation of profits derived from a prior direct investment are allowed to purchase foreign exchange. Similarly, access to the forward market for foreign exchange in China is limited to those with a documented trade-related need for future foreign exchange, precluding speculators from taking short positions in the Chinese domestic currency. Even domestic firms that have foreign currency-denominated loans are not allowed to purchase foreign exchange to repay their loans until their loan is actually due. That prevents an acceleration of demand for foreign exchange on the part of those that have such loans outstanding.

Second, China's capital inflows predominantly take the form of foreign direct investment. In 1997, for example, China was the recipient of US$ 64 billion in foreign capital. But the largest component, US$ 45.3 billion, was direct investment. Cumulatively, by year-end 1997 foreign direct investment in place stood at US$225 billion, more than half again as large as the level of officially reported foreign borrowing. In contrast, in other countries experiencing financial and banking crises, borrowing exceeds direct investment, sometimes by as much as five or ten times. Direct investors differ fundamentally from financial investors since they invest with a long time horizon and their investments are illiquid. Financial investments, such as lending, bank deposits, stocks, and bonds are frequently of short duration and can be reversed quickly if the investors reevaluate the risk of lending to a particular country. Some financial assets can be sold in the market immediately. Lenders can wind down their exposure over somewhat longer periods by refusing to roll over loans when they come due.

Third, in contrast to Korea, Thailand, and several other countries in Southeast Asia that experienced currency crises in 1997-98, China in the mid-1990s experienced record trade surpluses. Its trade surpluses were US$ 16.69 billion, US$ 12.3 billion, and US$ 40.3 billion in 1995, 1996 and 1997, respectively. Thus China was not dependent on continued foreign capital inflows to finance a trade deficit.

Finally, at the end of 1997 China's foreign exchange reserves were enough to finance almost a full year of imports.

In short, the absence of capital account convertibility, the nature of China's capital inflows, and a strong trade and foreign exchange reserve position mean that a banking crisis is unlikely to be precipitated by a change in the sentiment of foreign lenders, foreign or domestic speculators, or domestic firms that have outstanding foreign currency-denominated liabilities.

This does not mean, however, that China is immune to the adverse consequences of a weak financial system characterized by a continuing rapid build up of non-performing loans to state-owned enterprises financed largely by household deposits. The real consequences are several-fold. First is the inescapable cost of the poor domestic lending decisions that banks have made and are continuing to make. Unless reversed this ultimately can be expected to lead to a slow down in economic growth, which of course means lower rates of job creation and increased potential for social unrest.

Second, poor lending decisions are leading to a huge accumulation of bank liabilities to households, the ultimate source of most of the funds in the banking system. But these liabilities are not matched by real assets. The longer the banks continue to support money losing state-owned enterprises, the greater is the risk that savers will lose confidence in the banking system, triggering a crisis. Even if a crisis can be avoided, the continued accumulation of nonperforming loans means the ultimately required bank recapitalization or the financial losses imposed on depositors grows ever larger.

Third, Chinese banks are unable to offer savers consistently positive rates of real return, creating a disincentive to save, possibly leading to a decline in the savings rate.

Fourth, China faces a higher cost of raising money on international capital markets. The higher costs stem from an increasing perception that China suffers from some of the same underlying economic problems evident elsewhere in the region, including a significant understatement of its external debt. Moody's in early 1998 downgraded the outlook for nine Chinese banks and for China's foreign currency debt from stable to negative. Even prior to the downgrade, the margins on Chinese sovereign debt trading in the secondary market had widened somewhat compared with pre-crisis levels. As a result, the Minister of Finance in March announced that China was postponing a planned sovereign bond offering. They hope that margins will come down, facilitating a placement of the issue in the second half of 1998. Prices of Chinese securities available for purchase by foreigners, including B shares as well as Chinese firms and Chinese majority owned firms listed in Hong Kong, have all fallen sharply. The result is that fewer Chinese companies are being offered on international equity markets and they are priced at a much, much lower multiple of earnings than companies that came to market prior to the crisis.

The Chinese Policy Response

The Chinese government recognizes the risks associated with delaying further fundamental economic reforms. Intense high-level discussion of these risks began on November 17, 1997 when China's State Council convened an National Financial Work Conference in Beijing to discuss the problems of China's financial and banking system. The meeting was held against the backdrop of financial crises in three Asian countries — Thailand, Indonesia, and Korea — that had sought massive international financial assistance coordinated by the International Monetary Fund. Indeed, in an unprecedented move, China contributed US$ 1 billion to the IMF-led bailout of Thailand in 1997.

China is at least temporarily insulated from a currency crisis and is not subject to an IMF-imposed restructuring program. There can be little doubt, however, that Premier Zhu Rongji believes that a restructuring program for banks and their principal borrowers, state-owned enterprises is urgently needed. Commentary in China's leading financial newspaper, published jointly by the central bank and several of China's largest financial institutions, immediately after the financial conference concluded suggested that the problem of an increasing share of non-performing loans is endemic. According to the chapter, a considerable amount of loans extended by banks are disappearing like stones dropped into the sea; principle and interest is difficult to recover; thus the non-performing assets of these banks are increasing.

China's leadership at the Ninth Party Congress in the spring of 1998 confirmed its commitment to take aggressive steps to insure that the Asian financial contagion would not spread to China. Most dramatically Premier Zhu Rongji announced that the long standing twin problems of money losing state-owned enterprises and weak banks would be solved within three years through an accelerated program of privatizations, mergers, and closures and a series of steps that would lead banks to operate on a commercial basis.

Among the most important of these steps was a reorganization of the local branches of the People's Bank along regional lines in order to reduce political interference in lending decisions at the local level. The initial experiment in creating new supraprovincial branches of the People's Bank is underway in south China where previous provincial branches in Guangdong, Jiangxi, Guangxi, and Hainan are being consolidated to form a single regional office in Guangdong's provincial capital, Guangzhou. The goal of the reorganization remains the same as that of several earlier reforms promoted by Mr. Zhu — ending the common practice of provincial governors and party officials influencing the flow of lending in their regions. He has been widely quoted as stating the power of provincial governors and mayors to command local bank presidents is abolished as of 1998.

A second major step is a planned capital injection of RMB 270 billion into the four largest state-owned banks. This injection, which will double the capital of the four largest state-owned banks, is a prerequisite to the commercialization of the banking system. Its relatively large size is perhaps a reflection that the leadership believes that the process of commercialization is well begun.

The central government also has committed substantially more funds to finance the write-off of enterprise bad debts to banks. This program began in 1996 with an allocation of RMB 20 billion to write-off bad debts of enterprises that were being restructured. In 1997 the funds earmarked for this purpose were RMB 30 billion. In 1998 the amount was increased to RMB 40 billion with further increases to follow in 1999 and 2000. These funds are generally allocated to assist in the merger of two or more state-owned firms, thus their use is tied to enterprise restructurings.

In addition to stepped up write-offs of bad debt, the authorities announced several other steps designed to encourage banks to operate on a more commercial basis. Perhaps the most important is that the central bank is to allow banks greater flexibility in setting interest rates on loans. The long-standing practice of the central bank setting uniform lending rates for each type of loan precluded banks from pricing loans according to risk. Under the plan, banks will be given increased authority to set lending rates and will be encouraged to take risk into account when setting rates for specific borrowers. To further encourage commercial banking behavior, report-edly the presidents of banks where non-performing assets increase will be fired. The system of mandatory lending quotas, which has placed a ceiling on total lending and required loans to specific projects is also being phased out. The precise implications of this remain to be seen since a system of guidance quotas for lending is to remain in place.

In the wake of the meeting the Chinese central bank also tightened supervision and regulation of both banks and non-bank financial institutions. The central bank has closed dozens of unauthorized financial institutions, in some cases providing billions of RMB to prevent individual depositors from losing their savings. One element of the enhanced supervision and regulation of banks is a new scheme for classifying non-performing loans, which will come into effect by the end of 1998. This will move China from its lax system of loan classification to a system more closely aligned with international standards. Most importantly classification will be based partly on risk rather than exclusively on payment status.

Finally, the State Administration of Foreign Exchange has been charged with the responsibility of insuring both that all international commercial borrowing by domestic institutions is approved in advance and that borrowed amounts do not exceed certain multiples of the borrowers' net assets and foreign exchange earnings. If followed rigorously, these new regulations would appear to limit the ability of non-financial firms without foreign currency earnings to incur additional foreign exchange risk. They are also designed to limit off-shore borrowing by subsidiaries or affiliates of Chinese firms operating abroad. In some cases the proceeds from such borrowing enter China as the foreign contribution to a joint venture. Thus they are reported in Chinese statistics as foreign direct investment, whereas they are actually foreign currency-denominated debt.

Implications

The leadership has embarked on a daunting transition. If the reform program is successful it would constitute a major breakthrough. It would mean the leadership had found solutions to the problems of money-losing state-owned enterprises and failing banks that have eluded them for two full decades. Domestically success would improve the efficiency of resource allocation, helping to sustain rapid economic growth. Restoring the health of the domestic banking system would reduce the prospects of a systemic failure of banks and help to sustain the high rates of domestic savings that underlie China's rapid growth in the reform era. Success would mean it would be more likely that China would restore its competitive position in Asia through reforms that increased productivity via internally generated efficiencies, rather than through a competitive devaluation of its currency that could set off another round of currency devaluations in the region. It would help to restore China's favorable access to international capital markets and maintain large inflows of foreign direct investment, indirectly contributing importantly to the viability of peg of the Hong Kong dollar to the U.S. dollar. All of these developments would contribute significantly to recovery from the Asian financial crisis.

Finally, the successful implementation of the reform program would provide a striking contrast with Japan, which has seemed unable to contribute significantly to a solution to the Asian financial crisis. Thus China could come to be regarded as central as Japan to the future of the Asian economy, assuring China's ascendancy not only in Asia but also on the world economic stage.

But implementing the reform program is filled with risks. China is already experiencing an unprecedentedly high rate of unemployment and it is not clear that the political system can withstand the strain caused by the even higher rates that will accompany the restructuring of money losing enterprises. Moreover, the transition is being undertaken under unfavorable external conditions. Major currency devaluations in Southeast Asia and Korea in 1997 have already reduced the growth of Chinese exports and slowed inflows of foreign direct investment. The resulting softness in the domestic economy will place further stress on an already fragile domestic banking system.

Another risk would be a premature liberalization of domestic financial markets, most likely in response to external pressure. While the United States has an appropriate interest in assuring that China allows U.S. and other foreign banks the right to take domestic currency deposits and offer domestic currency loans, the insistence of U.S. trade negotiators that China open up its market for banking services on an accelerated basis has the potential to trigger a domestic banking crisis. That would set off a major recession in China, depriving Asia of its most important engine of growth in recent years. The United States has a major interest in seeing countries recover from the Asian financial crisis. This interest will be best served by supporting China's energetic domestic reform program and tempering demands for rapid liberalization of China's banking market.

Notes

1. This chapter is a reprint of an article published in the July/August 1998 edition of Foreign Affairs. Thanks go to the publisher for allowing the article to be included here.

3
Roots of the Financial Crisis in Asia and Implications for China

Jianping Zhou

Introduction[1]

During the past seven years, three major financial crises have hit different continents: the 1992-93 ERM crisis in Europe, the 1994-95 Mexican peso crisis in Latin America, and the recent financial crisis in Asia. These crises have been costly both in terms of lost output and in terms of fiscal costs to shore up fragile financial sectors. Among them, the Asian crisis was most unexpected and has caused financial turmoil in Indonesia, Korea, Malaysia, Thailand, and the Philippines. Its large scale exchange rate devaluations and devastating social and economic concequences have shocked academics as well as the policy-makers. Within less than one year, the currencies of Korea, Malaysia, the Philippines, and Thailand have lost over 40 percent of their value against the U.S. dollar, while the currency of Indonesia has lost over 80 percent (see Figure 3.1). Equity markets in these countries also tumbled, loosing between 60 and 80 percent of their dollar value since the onset of the Asian crisis (see Figure 3.2). In Indonesia, social unrest caused by soaring inflation and rising unemployment forced President Suharto to step down from the post he had held for more than thirty years. At the moment, the Asian crisis seems to continue unabated, as each week still brings new signs that Asia's economic troubles are getting worse. The latest arise from the slide of the Japanese yen, which has caused a new round of speculative attacks against the Hong Kong dollar and new worries on the possible devaluation of the Chinese RMB.

While financial crises are not a recent phenomenon,[2] the frequency in which the crises have occurred over the last couple of years, as well as the contagious nature of these crises have raised concerns about the impact that the financial innovations and the increased integration of global financial markets might have on individual economies. In particular, the fact that the recent Asian crisis has involved countries which seem to have established relatively sound macroeconomic fundamentals, has raised questions concerning the underlying causes of these crises; and most importantly, about whether there are some common symptons which could be detected in advance of a crisis, so that policy makers can adopt pre-emptive measures.

FIGURE 3.1 Developments in the Currencies of Indonesia, Korea, Malaysia, Thailand, and the Philippines (Jan. 1990=100)

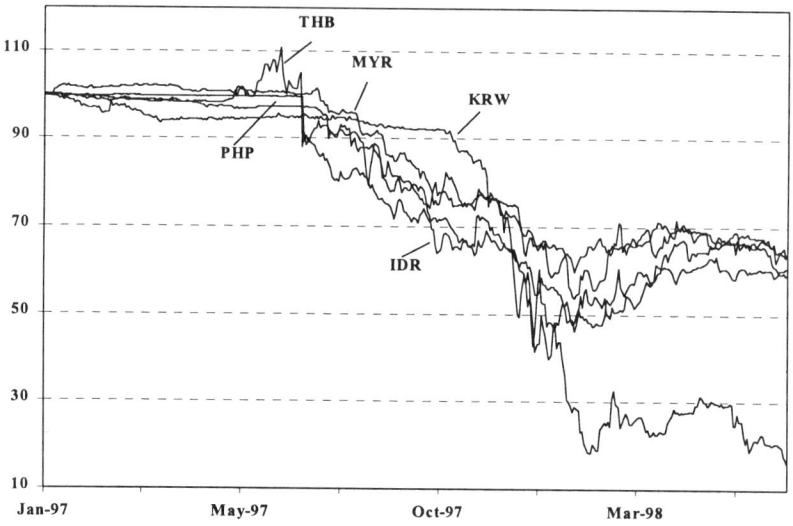

This paper analyzes the main causes of the recent financial crisis in Asia, with a view to drawing some implications for China. After a brief review of the theoretical and empirical literature on currency crises, this paper examines the roots of the Asian crisis, and compares it to the Mexican crisis in 1994 to see whether there are common patterns in the periods leading up to these currency crises. The discussion on implications for China focuses on the issues related to banking and exchange rate policies.

There have been two main approaches in the theoretical literature on currency crises: the classical models stress the role played by weak economic fundamentals in inducing a currency crisis; and the new crisis models show that a crisis may develop without a significant change in fundamentals. Krugman's (1979) seminal paper presents a classical model, where under a fixed exchange rate regime, domestic credit creation in excess of money demand growth leads to a gradual loss of reserves and, ultimately, to a speculative attack against the currency. This attack immediately depletes reserves and forces the abandonment of the fixed exchange rate and the adoption of a flexible rate regime. This model suggests that the period preceding a currency crisis is characterized by a sharp decline in foreign exchange reserves, a rapid growth of domestic credit relative to money demand, and large fiscal imbalances if the excessive money creation is caused by financing needs of the public sector. The decision to abandon a fixed exchange rate may result from the government's concern about other economic objectives, such as growth and interest rates (Obstfeld 1996). In particular, expectations of a currency collapse could lead to higher interest rates, prompting the government to abandon the exchange rate peg out of concern that high interest rates may cause a banking crisis and depress economic activity.

FIGURE 3.2 Developments in Equity Markets in Indonesia, Korea, Malaysia, Thailand, and the Philippines (Jan. 1990=100)

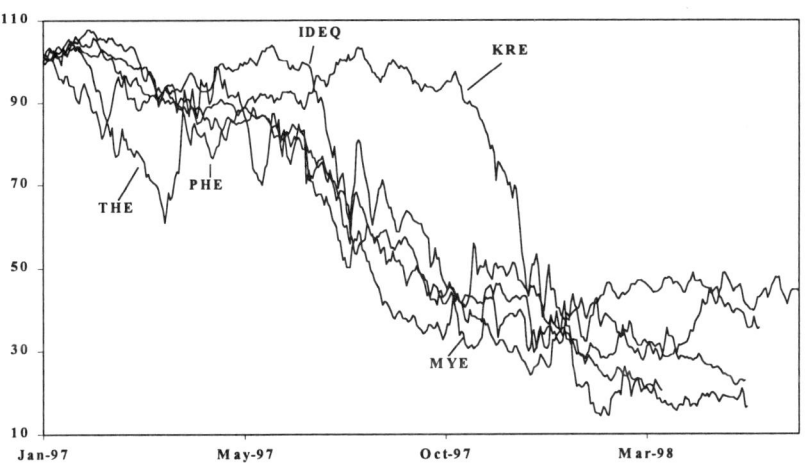

Review of Literature on Currency Crises

In contrast to the classical models, new crisis models suggest that crises may develop without any noticeable changes in macroeconomic fundamentals and that other factors, such as the presence of banking problems and contagion effects, could eventually lead to a currency crisis. For example, problems in the banking sector could trigger a sudden loss of confidence in the currency, prompted by the fear that the central bank has to finance the bail-out of troubled banks. Most recently, the increased integration of the world economy has motivated a group of studies which regard the contagion effects as the main reason for causing a currency crisis. These studies find that a currency crisis in one country can spread to other countries which share similar economic fundamentals, or face common external shocks as the crisis country, or are closely related to it, either as a trading partner or as a competitor. The contagion effects may also be explained by the behavior of investors. For instance, Frankel and Schmulker (1996) argue that the incentive structure of fund managers and traders may encourage them to follow common investment decisions, as the performance of those fund managers is usually measured against the performance of other fund managers (i.e. herding effect). In this case, fund managers follow the common investment strategy, even if such an investment decision is not based on economic fundamentals.

Most recent empirical literature on currency crises has focused on identifying and assessing the usefulness of potential early warning indicators of crises. For example, Dornbusch et al. (1995) examine the currency crises that took place in Argentina, Brazil, Chile, Finland, and Mexico during the period of 1975-95 and discuss the common patterns in the periods leading up to these currency crises. They find that these countries all shared some similar symptoms before crises, including an appreciation of the real exchange rate, high real interest rates, slower GDP growth, relatively high inflation, large fiscal deficits, high credit growth, large trade and current account deficits, declining reserves, and large foreign debt burden. A similar study by Sachs et al. (1996) also finds that for a set of twenty emerging markets, a high ratio of M2 to reserves, an initial real exchange rate misalignment, and a significant increase in bank lending to the private sector can largely explain why some countries were more affected by the Mexican crisis than others. However, Kaminsky et al. (1997) suggest that an effective early warning system should consider a broad range of indicators, since currency crises in the recent years were usually preceded by symptoms that arise in a number of areas.

To a certain extent, Asia's crisis was triggered by the psychology of the Czech crisis when the Czech crown was forced to float on May 29, 1997. After that, the speculative attacks on Thailand's currency intensified. In defending its currency, the foreign exchange reserves of Thailand's central bank fell substantially, by $4 billion in May alone. Later on July 2, Thailand's central bank finally was forced to give up its long fight and abandoned its exchange rate peg to the U.S. dollar. Immediately, the Thai baht fell about 16 percent against the U.S. dollar. Subsequently, Thailand's currency crisis has spilled over to other Asian economies, resulting in large scale devaluations of the Indonesian rupiah, the Philippine peso, the Malaysian ringgit, and the Korean won.

Causes of the Recent Currency Turmoil in Asia

In contrast to previous currency crises, the macroeconomic fundamentals in these Asian economies gave little indication of the crisis before it occurred. In fact, the macroeconomic performance of these countries has been exemplary prior to the crisis, as reflected in their strong economic growth and low inflation over the past decade (see Table 3.1). Most of them ran either balanced or surplus fiscal accounts with little or no government debt, and their exceptional rates of investment were supported by high private sector savings. Current account deficits in these Asian countries were mainly investment rather consumption driven, and were often accompanied by strong export growth.

TABLE 3.1 Main Macroeconomic Indicators Prior The Crises

Indonesia	1994	1995	1996
GDP growth (%)	7.5	8.2	8.0
Inflation (%)	8.5	9.4	7.9
Savings (% of GDP)	29.2	29.0	28.8
Investment (% of GDP)	27.6	28.4	28.1
Fiscal balance (% of GDP)	0.0	0.8	1.4
Current account (% GDP)	-1.7	-3.3	-3.3
Malaysia	**1994**	**1995**	**1996**
GDP growth (%)	9.2	9.5	8.6
Inflation (%)	3.7	3.4	3.5
Savings (% of GDP)	32.7	33.5	36.7
Investment (% of GDP)	40.1	43.0	42.2
Fiscal balance (% of GDP)	1.4	1.3	1.1
Current account (% GDP)	-7.8	-10.0	-4.9
Philippines	**1994**	**1995**	**1996**
GDP growth (%)	4.4	4.8	5.7
Inflation (%)	9.0	8.1	8.4
Savings (% of GDP)	19.4	17.8	19.7
Investment (% of GDP)	23.6	22.2	23.2
Fiscal balance (% of GDP)	-1.6	-1.4	-0.4
Current account (% GDP)	-4.6	-4.4	-4.7
South Korea	**1994**	**1995**	**1996**
GDP growth (%)	8.6	8.9	7.1
Inflation (%)	6.3	4.5	4.9
Savings (% of GDP)	34.6	35.1	33.3
Investment (% of GDP)	35.7	36.6	36.8
Fiscal balance (% of GDP)	1.0	0.0	0.0
Current account (% GDP)	-1.2	-2.0	-4.9
Thailand	**1994**	**1995**	**1996**
GDP growth (%)	8.9	8.7	6.4
Inflation (%)	5.1	5.8	5.9
Savings (% of GDP)	34.9	34.3	33.1
Investment (% of GDP)	39.9	41.8	40.8
Fiscal balance (% of GDP)	2.0	2.6	1.6
Current account (% GDP)	-5.6	-8.0	-7.9

Source: IMF

So what went wrong in these Asian countries? Is it true, as some policymakers in Asia believe, that they were the innocent victims of vicious speculative attacks, irrespective of their underlying economic fundamentals? In the following section, the evidence on the recent currency turmoil in Asia is discussed and compared to the Mexican crisis in 1994, to see whether these crises were driven by the same forces. The following discussion will reveal that despite their economic, geographical, and political differences, there were striking similarities between the recent Asian crisis and the 1994 Mexican crisis, particularly in the way how capital inflows, the subsequent policy response, and the vulnerability of their economies were linked.

Surge in Capital Inflows Preceding Crises

Like Mexico, all the five Asian countries experienced a surge in capital inflows in the years immediately preceding the crises (see Table 3.2). For example, net private capital flows to Thailand surged from $10.8 billion in 1994 to $22 billion in 1995, while that to Indonesia and Korea increased from $7.4 and $1.5 billion to $12.1 and $25.2 billion, respectively. In the case of Mexico, net private flows increased rapidly from $8.4 billion in 1990 to more than $25 billion in 1992, and reached a peak of $34 billion in 1993, the year before the crisis. While capital inflows to Mexico prior to its peso crisis were dominated by short-term portfolio investment, capital inflows to these Asian countries over the past few years were increasingly dominated by bank lending and non-bank credits such as bond issurance and trade credits. By 1996, direct investment into these five Asian countries accounted for only 23 percent of their total capital inflows. In Thailand's case, bank lending accounted for almost 80 percent of capital flows in 1995, and in Korea it accounted for more than half.

A number of factors may have contributed to the surge in capital inflows in these economies. First, the low level of interest rates in the United States, Germany, and particularly Japan since the early 1990s has prompted investors to search for higher yields in emerging markets. Second, improved economic performance, as well as the growing liberalization of domestic financial markets and the removal of capital account restrictions in these countries have encouraged capital inflows. In some cases, capital inflows were also encouraged by tax incentives. For example, both Malaysia and Thailand gave their banks tax incentives to borrow from overseas. Overseas borrowing was also encouraged by the fact that their fixed exchange rate regimes implied a lower cost of foreign as compared to domestic funding. Finally, the globalization of international bond and equity markets and the growing role of institutional investors have also contributed to the surge in capital flows, as they continued to seek the benefits of portfolio diversification across emerging markets.

The surge in capital inflows, although initially beneficial for most recipient countries, has also exposed them to the volatility of global financial markets. In particular, unlike direct investment flows which are typically hard to reverse, much of the bank lending and portfolio investment are of short-term nature and can be easily reversed. Capital inflows, which began to accelerate at the beginning of the 1990s, become a major source of credit in these Asian countries by 1994. When these capital flows did reverse—for example, in Thailand in 1996 and Korea and Indonesia in 1997—the negative impact on their economy in an adverse external environment was devastating.

TABLE 3.2 Capital Inflows Prior the Crisis (in millions of US$)

	1992	1993	1994	1995	1996e
Indonesia					
Private inflows, net	2880	4439	7404	12080	17738
Commercial bank credits,net	663	1573	2030	5648	9509
Portfolio investment,net	1200	1805	1549	2492	2639
Direct investment,net	747	887	1024	1793	2556
Other private creditors,net	269	173	2801	2147	3034
Korea					
Private inflows, net	7820	8566	15093	25199	34050
Commercial bank credits,net	2428	1034	8506	16062	18720
Portfolio investment,net	2288	6077	3123	3954	6100
Direct investment,net	-497	-540	-1318	-1880	-3300
Other private creditors,net	3600	1995	4781	7063	12530
Malaysia					
Private inflows, net	6651	14980	693	6055	9119
Commercial bank credits,net	2046	4479	-3191	3431	5000
Portfolio and direct investment,net	3765	7456	5990	2324	3243
Other private creditors,net	839	3045	-2106	300	876
Philippines					
Private inflows, net	-712	1169	5990	9441	8019
Commercial bank credits,net	-506	-1907	730	1229	2570
Portfolio investment,net	40	-52	269	248	480
Direct investment,net	228	864	1289	1361	1700
Other private creditors,net	299	2530	3702	6603	3269
Thailand					
Private inflows, net	7293	12009	10872	22045	12465
Commercial bank credits,net	4630	3964	11451	17699	9215
Portfolio investment,net	445	2679	-389	2123	-500
Direct investment,net	1534	1220	797	1073	1800
Other private creditors,net	674	4146	-986	1150	1950

Source: Institute of International Finance.

Inappropriate Policy Response to Inflows

The surge in capital inflows had complicated the implementation of monetary polices in these countries. In both Mexico and the five Asian countries, macroeconomic policy in response to the surge in capital inflows mainly relied on central bank intervention to prevent a nominal exchange rate appreciation. Before the crises, their currencies were basically pegged to the U.S. dollar. Using the exchange rate as the nominal anchor initially helped to bring down inflation in several countries. However, maintaining the exchange rate peg over a long period in the presence of large inflation differentials to the US has eventually led to a real appreciation of these currencies. To a certain extent, this eroded their external competitiveness and resulted in large current account deficits. As discussed earlier, an overvalued exchange rate had also encouraged excessive credit expansion, contributed to asset price bubbles (as in the case of Thailand) and to excessive consumption of foreign goods (as in the case of Mexico). Excessive bank lending occurred in all these countries which experienced a surge in capital inflows, which led to the emergence of unsustainable macroeconomic imbalances. Moreover, as these countries all went through substantial external liberalization, the rigid exchange rate arrangements had become increasingly incompatible with the opening of capital accounts, and consequently, had given rise to uncertainty on the part of investors, as well as speculators, as to the sustainability and future course of exchange rate management, and exchange rates eventually became one-way bets for depreciation.

External Shocks and Reversal of Capital Flows

These countries all suffered a sudden reversal of capital flows, due to unfavourable external developments, coupled with a weakening of their domestic economies. While the U.S. interest rate hike in the early 1994 was partly responsible for the reversal of capital flows to Mexico, it was the sharp appreciation of the U.S. dollar against other major currencies since mid-1995 that had a negative impact on the Asian economies. In some countries, the situation was further aggravated by the sharp decline in export prices. The resultant slowdown in their economic activities and weak export growth in 1996 have aggravated their external imbalances, leading to increasing investor concerns about their large current account deficits and exposing them to speculative attacks. For example, in Thailand, a significant slowdown in growth in 1996, largely due to a disappointing export performance, led to a worsening current account deficit, which was almost 8 percent of GDP. Countries that have been affected by the Thailand crisis, such as Indonesia, Malaysia, the Philippines, and Korea all seem to have shared similar symptoms. For instance, the weak export in Korea, mainly due to the sharp decline in the semiconductor prices, led to the widening of Korea's current account deficit, which increased from $9 billion in 1995 to a record high of $23 billion in 1996. Investor concerns about these economies have led to the reversal of capital flows and a further erosion in their balance of payments. The weaknesses in their ecnomy were only exposed after a wave of contagion.

Problems in Banking Systems

Weaknesses in banking systems were one of the main causes of these currency crises, particularly the Asian crisis. These weaknesses stemmed largely from excessive credit expansion under inadequate prudential supervision, resulting in a large share of high risk loans in their banking sector portfolios. Prior to the crisis, credit expansion in these Asian countries far outpaced even their exceptional nominal GDP growth rates (see Table 3.3). Pegged exchange rates have encouraged borrowers to underestimate exchange rate risks. For example, in Thailand's case, problems in its financial sector were also evident before the crisis, as reflected in a massive credit expansion during the period of 1994-96, as Thai borrowers were eager to take advantage of low dollar interest rates on the assumption of a stable baht vis-à-vis the dollar. The result was excessive investment, much of it in the property sector, which led to the real estate and stock market booms, often based on highly leveraged structures. Prior to the crisis, the problem loans carried by Thailand's finance companies and banks amounted to almost 16 percent of GDP, with as much as 50-60 percent believed to have been in default.[3]

TABLE 3.3 Lending Booms Prior The Crises

Domestic credit as % of GDP*						
	1991	1992	1993	1994	1995	1996
Indonesia	50.3	50.1	52.6	55.1	57	59.3
Korea	94.5	101.6	106.4	115.4	117.9	126.8
Malaysia	116.7	121.4	136.9	125.8	141.7	142.2
Philippines	30.2	33.4	41.9	46.5	53.6	65.3
Thailand	96.3	103.7	116.3	132	142.8	147.7

Annual growth rate					
	1992	1993	1994	1995	1996
Indonesia	-0.4	5.0	4.8	3.4	4.0
Korea	7.5	4.7	8.5	2.2	7.5
Malaysia	4.0	12.8	-8.1	12.6	0.4
Philippines	10.6	25.4	11.0	15.3	21.8
Thailand 7.7	12.2	13.5	8.2	3.4	

Note: *Credits by banks and non-bank financial institutions.
Source: IMF: International Financial Statistics.

Banking sector problems in these countries were magnified in the wake of currency turmoil, as the speculative attacks were accompanied by bank runs and by a period of high domestic interest rates, resulting from central bank interventions to defend their currencies. Companies in these Asian countries were typically far more deeply indebted than their western and Latin American counterparts. High domestic interest rates have pushed them much more quickly from illiquidity into insolvency, thus amplifying the banking sector problems. The underlying weaknesses in their banking sectors became more apparent following the reversal of capital flows from abroad, as many companies became increasingly unable to service their debt. As in the case of Thailand, when capital inflows reversed and the Thai baht was forced to devalue, the authorities were left to cope with the collapse of the property sector and the stock market in an adverse external environment.

Speculative Factors

Moreover, speculative factors have also played an important role in triggering these crises. The rapid globalization and institutionalization of international capital markets imply that institutional investors have the capacity to take substantial short positions, within a very short time period, in a weak currency through spot, forward, and currency options markets. The capital of institutional investors such as pension funds, mutual funds, and hedge funds is believed to have exceeded $20 trillion in the mature markets alone. It was suggested that these institutional investors have played an important role in the recent financial crises in Asia. In particular, the hedge funds, whose capital was about $100 billion in the second half of 1997, appear to have contributed to major movements in asset prices in Asia. Countries with perceived inconsistent economic policies and structural weaknesses are likely to be particularly vulnerable to speculative attacks on their exchange rates. For instance, before the crisis in July, speculators had taken substantial short positions in the Thai baht through the forward market, betting on the devaluation of the currency. Investors and domestic corporates, in the fear of devaluation, also sold baht forward to hedge their positions, thus adding more pressure on the baht. In defending the baht, the central bank was believed to have sold some $15 billion in the forward markets — almost half of Thailand's foreign exchange reserves at the end of June.

In sum, both economic and speculative factors might have contributed to the 1997 Asian crisis and the 1994 Mexican crisis. This experience suggests that countries with unsustainable macroeconomic imbalances, inflexible exchange rate management, heavy reliance on volatile short-term external financing, and weak financial sectors are particularly vulnerable to internal or external shocks and thus susceptible to speculative attacks.

Some Implications for China

Despite the currency turmoil in the region, the Chinese RMB has so far remained steady agaisnt the U.S. dollar. On one hand, the restrictions on capital account transactions make it very difficult for speculators to take any short position against the currency. On the other hand, China's large foreign exchange reserves (US$140 billion at the end of 1997), and manageable foreign debt position (US$131 billion at the end of 1997, of which 80 percent is long-term) also enabled China to withstand the turbulence in the region's financial markets. However, Asia's financial problems have profound implications for China, especially at the time when China's economic reform have reached its critical stage, as the reforms of the financial sector and the state-owned enterprises have just begun. In this respect, the regional financial crisis can provide valuable lessons for China, and help it avoid similar policy mistakes during its process of economic liberalization and integration with the global economy.

Urgent Need For Banking Sector Improvement

The Asian financial crisis has shown that problems in the banking sector could eventually give rise to a currency crisis. In particular, when the financial system is liberalized without an adequate regulatory and supervisory framework, the result could be destabilizing. The large credit expansion, often as a result of an import boom, is prevalent in many troubled Asian economies. Moreover, a fragile banking sector is likely to tie the hands of central banks in implementing prudent financial policies.

China has so far avoided the worst of the Asian financial turmoil, protected by its lack of capital account convertibility and large foreign exchange reserves. However, the region's problems have raised serious issues and there is an urgent need to reform its weak banking system. According to a conservative estimate by China's central bank, the Chinese commercial banks currently have problem loans exceeding $180 billion or 20 percent of total assets. The problem could be exacerbated by the economic slowdown. Problems in the banking system can also hinder the banks' role in allocating capital for the restructuring of the state-owned enterprises. In this regard, policy measures are urgently needed to reform China's banking system, which would include cutting back on government-mandated loans, as well as improving the bank supervision and increasing bad-debt provisioning. In addition, the gradual opening up of domestic markets to foreign banks will also help to improve the competitiveness of the Chinese banks.

There is also an urgent need to reform the investment trust companies, which have grown rapidly as fund-raising vehicles for government agencies but often used funds inefficiently. In this case, there have been encourging signs that in the light of Asia's financial crisis the Chinese government is starting to take action against profligate financial institutions. For instance, in June 1998, the central bank ordered the closure of Hainan Development Bank, which collapsed under the bad loans to investments in Hainan's burst property bubble. It is thought to be the first time the government has decided to close a commercial bank. China's Venturetech Investment Corporation, another prominent financial institute and one of the country's earliest and most prominent investment companies, was also shut down for its insolvency.

Is The Current Exchange Rate Arrangement Between China and Hong Kong Sustainable?

Since 1983, the Hong Kong dollar has been pegged to the U.S. dollar in a currency board arrangement. The Chinese RMB, on the other hand, has been kept virtually fixed vis-à-vis the U.S. dollar since the middle of 1995. Amid the Asian currency turmoil, the peg has become the target of the vicious speculative attacks, sending Hong Kong's share prices plunging and causing serious difficulties in the property sector and the banking sector. The Hong Kong Monetary Authority has so far been able to defend the peg, thanks to Hong Kong's sound banking system and stable politial and economic environment. However, this has come at the extremely high price of soaring interest rates and declining economic activity. Tung Chee-hwa, Hong Kong's chief executive, recently admitted that regional crises had pushed Hong Kong into recession.[4] However, he insisted that Hong Kong would stick to its exchange rate peg in spite of its high cost, since there would be unthinkable concequences if the peg was broken — an event which could lead to capital flight and a further bout of regional instability.

The Hong Kong dollar's peg to the U.S. dollar should have been viewed as a transitory arrangement when it was introduced, since it was driven by the need to end the 1983 crisis of confidence in Hong Kong. The peg, which once contributed to the stability of the territory, has led to a serious erosion of Hong Kong's competitiveness. For instance, Hong Kong's real effective exchange rate, an indicator of its international competitiveness, appreciated by more than 50 percent during the period of 1990 to 1996. The recent large devaluation in other Asian currencies has further undermined Hong Kong's competitiveness, and therefore raised the question as to how long the peg can be maintained. It is precisely this uncertainty that has led to speculation against the HK$. The credibility of the peg can only be maintained if the public clearly understands the rationale for the peg. But such a rationale has become increasingly questionable. Not only the political reason for the peg has largely diminished after Hong Kong's smooth unification with China on July 1, 1997, also economically it has become undesirable that Hong Kong, whose economy is closely integrated with the Chinese economy, should still be subject to the monetary policy and associated business cycle of the United States.

The recent Asian crisis has demonstrated that a country is particularly vulnerable to speculative attacks if there are uncertainties regarding the sustainability of its economic policies. The uncertainty surrounding the future exchange arrangements between Hong Kong and China could indeed put China, and particularly Hong Kong, increasingly at risk of being subject to speculative attacks. But when should Hong Kong exit from its current currency board arrangement? As far as the financial turmoil in Asian markets is unsettled, it might not be the right time to abandon the peg just now, as it could lead to a large depreciation of the Hong Kong dollar and cause serious bank runs. However, it is the time now for policy-makers in both Hong Kong and China to work out a credible 'exit strategy,' and make it public as soon as possible, so that there will be no ambiguity left for speculation. For instance, a pre-announced move to a currency union between Hong Kong and China could be a way to minimize the credibility cost of breaking the peg.

Concluding Remarks

This chapter compared the current Asian financial crisis with the Mexican peso crisis in 1994, and found striking similarities among these crises, particularly in the way how capital inflows, subsequent policy reactions, and the vulnerability of their economies were linked. Both economic and speculative factors might have contributed to these crises. Countries with unsustainable macroeconomic imbalances, over reliance on short-term foreign capital, and weak financial systems were particularly vulnerable to internal or external shocks and thus susceptible to speculative attacks Their experience has shown that a lack of flexibility in exchange rate arrangements can put individual emerging markets increasingly at risk of being subject to a speculative attack, whenever there are uncertainties regarding the sustainablity of economic policies and structural weaknesses. This could have important implications for China and Hong Kong both in terms of more flexiability for the Chinese RMB and in terms of a credible 'exit strategy' for the Hong Kong dollar. The current financial crisis in Asia has also demonstrated that the combination of large capital inflows and weak domestic financial systems can be potentially destabilizing. In this regard, China should proceed with its capital account liberalization only when prudential regulation and supervision framework in the banking system are in place.

Appendix: Twin Crises - Banking and Currency Crises

Recent currency crises in Asia have shown that banking and currency crises often appear closely linked. Problems in the banking sector could eventually give rise to a currency crisis. In the case of Thailand, when the central bank had to bail-out the troubled financial institutions, its ability to maintain the prevailing exchange rate commitment eroded. Banking sector problems, on the other hand, can be magnified by a currency crisis if the speculative attacks on the currency is accompanied by bank runs and by a period of high interest rates.

According to a study by Kaminsky and Reinhart (1996), there has been an increasingly strong link between banking and currency crises since the 1980s when financial liberalization took place in many countries. Their study finds no apparent link between these crises during the 1970s, when the financial markets were highly regulated. However, following the liberalization in 1980s and 1990s, more than half of the banking crises were followed by a currency crisis within three years. Most often, the banking crisis erupted one to two years before the currency crisis. In a large number of cases, the bail-out of troubled banks may contribute to the acceleration in credit expansion, often observed prior to the currency crisis. Even in the absence of a large-scale bail-out, a fragile banking sector is likely to tie the hands of central bank in defending its currency, for the higher interest rate further weakens the banking sector. Their study finds only weak evidence of causality from the currency crisis to the banking crisis. However, in 18 of the 25 banking crises in their study, the financial sector had been liberalized during the preceding five years, suggesting that the twin crises may have their common origins in the deregulation of the financial system without an adequate regulatory and supervisory framework. The resultant credit expansion, often as a result of an import boom and followed by the current account deterioration, is prevalent in the periods prior to a currency crisis.

Notes

1. The author is currently on leave from the International Monetary Fund where she is an economist in the Asia and Pacific Department. However, the views represented in this chapter do not reflect those of the IMF.
2. For example, there were the sterling and French franc crises in 1960s; the breakdown of the Bretton Woods system in the early 1970s; and the debt crisis in the 1980s.
3. Oxford Analytica, May 1997.
4. Financial Times, June 23,1998.

References

Calvo, S., and C. Reinhart. 1996. "Capital Flows to Latin America: Is There Evidence of Contagion Effects?" *Policy Research Working Paper*, No. 1619. The World Bank.

Dornbusch, R., I. Goldfajn, and R. Valdes. 1995. "Currency Crises and Collapses." Discussion Paper, Massachusetts Institute of Technology, August.

Eichengreen, B., et al. 1998. "Hedge Funds and Financial Markets Dynamics." *IMF Occasional Paper*, No. 166, International Monetary Fund.

Frankel, J., and S. Schukler. 1996. "Crisis, Contagion, and Country Funds: Effects on East Asia and Latin America." *Pacific Basin Working Paper Series*, No. PB96-04, Federal Reserve Bank of San Francisco.

Goldfajn, I., and R.. Valdes. 1997. "Capital Flows and the Twin Crises: The Role of Liquidity." *IMF Working Paper*, WP/97/87, International Monetary Fund.

Goldstein, M., and P. Turner. 1996. "Banking Crisis in Emerging Economies: Origins and Policy Options." *BIS Economic Paper*, No. 46.

International Monetary Fund. 1997. *World Economic Outlook*. May.

___. 1997. *International Capital Markets: Developments, Prospects and Key Policy Issues*. November.

Kaminsky, G., S. Lizondo, and C. Reinhart. 1997. "Leading Indicators of Currency Crises." *IMF Working Paper*. International Monetary Fund.

Kaminsky, G., and C. Reinhart. 1996. "The Twin Crises: The Causes of Banking and Balance-of-Payments Problems." *International Finance Discussion Papers*, No. 544, Board of Governors of the Federal Reserve.

Krugman, P. 1996. "Are Currency Crises Self-Fulfilling?" in Ben Bernanke and Julio Rotemberg, eds., *NBER Macroeconomic Annual 1996*. Cambridge: The MIT Press.

___. 1979. "A Model of Balance of Payments Crises." *Journal of Money, Credit, and Banking* 11:311-25.

Obstfeld, M. 1996. "Models of Currency Crises with Self-fulfilling Features." *European Economic Review* 40:1037-47.

Sachs, J., A. Tornell and A. Velasco. 1996. "Financial Crises in Emerging Markets: The Lessons from 1995." *Brookings Papers on Economic Activity* 1:147-215.

4
Why Has China Survived the Asian Crisis So Well? What Risks Remain?

John G. Fernald and Oliver D. Babson

Introduction[1]

Given the apparent collapse of many of the "Asian miracle" economies in 1997 and 1998, China's continued strong growth performance is striking. In this chapter, we ask why China has performed so well, focusing on aspects of China's financial system that may have helped insulate it from the crisis so far. As of early 1999, clear risks remain. We discuss some of these risks, trying to assess whether China has avoided crisis or simply deferred it.

In 1998, China's growth rate of 7.8 percent was its lowest rate since the early 1990s. However, most economies in Asia showed negative growth, not robust positive growth. Table 1 gives a sense of China's relatively strong performance. Economies are ranked according to the first column, which shows the change in GDP growth from 1995-96 to 1998-99 (based on Consensus Forecasts for 1998-99). The Table also shows various salient characteristics for these economies. The characteristics are for 1996, and hence are not affected by the crisis. In the first column, China and Taiwan clearly stand out for their strong performance, with growth declining less than 3 percentage points.[2] The median slowdown, in Singapore, was 7-3/4 percent, and the "frontline economies" suffered double-digit declines.

To understand why China has so far avoided crisis, one must first assess why the crisis was so severe elsewhere. Explanations tend to emphasize either weak fundamentals in the affected countries, or else a "run" by financial participants on economies in the region.

In terms of fundamentals, a clear lesson of the crisis is that it is dangerous for a country to have weak, poorly regulated banks making policy loans to inefficient, over-leveraged state enterprises—a reasonable description of China. Some commentators argue that China's financial system looks at least as bad, and perhaps far worse, than those of other regional economies (see for example, Lardy 1998a, b). Weak banking systems are a particularly important problem if the banking system is large relative to the economy.

TABLE 4.1 China versus Other Asian Economies, Selected Indicators 1996 (%)

	Change in Real GDP: 98-99 Avg minus 95-96 avg	Bank Loans/ GDP	Current Account/ GDP	Total Debt/ Resources	Short-Term BIS Bank Claims/ Resources
	(1)	(2)	(3)	(4)	(5)
Indonesia	-17.5	55.4	-3.4	707.0	150.3
Malaysia	-12.2	93.4	-5.2	147.3	38.3
Thailand	-11.5	100.5	-8.0	240.7	50.6
Korea	-11.0	61.5	-4.7	307.6	82.9
Singapore	-7.7	96.0	15.2	-	-
Hong Kong	-7.2	162.4	-1.7	-	-
Philippines	-4.9	49.0	-4.3	410.9	24.3
China	-2.7	92.7	0.9	162.0	25.1
Taiwan	-1.2	143.7	4.0	25.6	21.4

Notes: Column (1) compares growth for the two years after the 1997 crisis to growth two years before the crisis. The remainder of the columns show indicators for 1996, and hence are not affected by the crisis itself. Debt figures for offshore banking centers (Hong Kong and Singapore) in Column (5) are not comparable with data from other countries due to the large size of external claims and liabilities: in 1996 the ratio of gross short-term commercial debt to reserves was 267.8 percent for Hong Kong and 228.0 percent for Singapore.
Sources: Historical GDP figures are taken from IMF International Financial Statistics, 1998 and 1999 GDP figures are taken from the 12/98 Consensus Forecast. Current Account data, column (2), are from FRB INTL databases. Bank loans data, column (3), are from IMF International Financial Statistics, as are data for foreign exchange reserves in columns (4) and (5). Total debt figures for China and Korea are from FRB databases, the remaining figures are from World Bank Global Development Indicators. Short-term BIS bank claims data, column (5), are from the BIS semi-annual survey.

As indicated by the second column of Table 1, the size of China's banking system is similar to that in the rest of Asia. In particular, the median ratio of bank loans relative to GDP was 93 percent in Malaysia, almost identical to the ratio in China. Nevertheless, despite the large banking system, and despite the prevalence of bad loans and other institutional weakness, we argue that these problems need not lead to imminent crisis in China. In a market-oriented system, pressures generally force rapid adjustment when institutions are, or are perceived to be, insolvent; these mechanisms do not operate fully in China. For example, banks can continue to operate regardless of balance-sheet weaknesses, because of the government's support.

In contrast to these weak internal fundamentals, China's external accounts look favorable compared with the rest of Asia, as shown by columns (3) to (5). China runs current account surpluses (about 1 percent of GDP in

1996, but closer to 3 percent in 1997 and 1998), and total debt relative to reserves was lower than in most Asian economies. Measures of short-term debt relative to reserves look particularly favorable for China, as shown by column (5).[3]

Suppose the crisis in Asia reflects runs by creditors. Sachs and Radelet (1998), for example, argue that "financial panic" by investors — essentially, the Diamond-Dybvig (1983) model of rational bank runs applied to countries — played an important role in Asia. For example, financial markets may be subject to multiple equilibria if short-term debt exceeds short-term assets, since it then becomes rational for an individual creditor to "flee" from a borrower if other creditors are fleeing as well.[4] China's capital controls are sometimes cited as a reason for China's strong performance in the crisis, on the grounds that they prevented a destabilizing speculative attack on the Chinese RMB. However, the strength of China's external fundamentals would plausibly preclude a self-fulfilling "country run" on China.

We make a different argument for the potential role of China's capital controls in contributing to stability: Regardless of their other (often adverse) effects, capital controls prevented Chinese financial institutions from borrowing excessively abroad, and hence helped keep the external fundamentals strong.

Clear risks remain for China's economy moving forward. As we discuss, financial market indicators suggest an increased risk premium associated with China. This increased risk premium is likely to lead to reduced capital inflows. To the extent that reduced inflows include foreign direct investment (FDI), reforms also become difficult, since FDI provides an important source of financing for the more dynamic non-state sector.

Given China's strong balance of payments position and substantial foreign reserves, it is unlikely that external pressure on the currency will, in and of itself, provoke a crisis. However, growth could slow sharply, perhaps reflecting continued declines in exports and non-state investment, an overhang of inventories, and widespread consumer unwillingness to spend. Foreign investors could become less willing to invest in and lend to China — because of rising uncertainty about the economy and about the viability of Chinese financial institutions — reducing investment further.

Chinese authorities appear aware of the risks, but the problems are inherently difficult. China is attempting to balance conflicting concerns — a desire for short-run stability and growth (which tends to slow reforms) versus a need for long-run improvements in the allocation of resources (which requires that reforms move forward). This tension was apparent in 1998. Growth slowed in the first half of the year, and as a result, investment by state firms rose sharply in the second half of the year, financed by lending from state banks. Hence, China appeared to have slowed the pace of enterprise and bank reforms, certainly compared with the pace announced at the beginning of the year. Nevertheless, some reforms continued. For example, China announced that the People's Bank of China (PBOC) would be restructured by the end of 1998 with the establishment of nine branches that cut across provincial lines, and also ordered the Communist Party, state ministries, and the army to end their involvement in business.

The first section discusses recent economic developments in some detail. The second discusses why China has avoided crisis so far. The third section assesses the likelihood and implications of slowing capital inflows. The fourth explores risks facing China over the next few years. The final section concludes.

Recent Economic Developments

As shown in the top panel of Figure 1, real GDP growth slowed steadily from 1992 through the first half of 1998. In the second half of 1998, however, official statistics indicate that GDP growth reversed its recent declines. For all of 1998, GDP was 7.8 percent higher than a year earlier, with output in the fourth quarter about 9 percent higher than a year earlier.[5] Industrial production growth also reversed recent declines in the second half. In the context of the collapse of many of the "Asian miracle" economies, China's continued strong growth performance is striking.

Another indicator of China's stability amidst the Asian crisis is the strength of its currency, the RMB. China's nominal exchange rate vis-à-vis the U.S. dollar — the solid line in the lower left panel — has been virtually unchanged since early 1995. The stability of the nominal dollar rate contrasts with the sharp appreciation of China's trade-weighted real exchange rate, shown with the dotted line.

China's large foreign exchange reserves have helped insulate it from the worst effects of the crisis. The solid line in the lower right panel shows the sharp rise in total foreign reserves (less gold) since 1994, as China's central bank accumulated foreign exchange to offset pressure for a nominal appreciation. At the end of 1998, China had about $149 billion in total reserves less gold (including about $145 billion in foreign exchange). The growth in foreign reserves has slowed since late 1997. However, reserves began increasing again at the end of 1998. This increase presumably reflects primarily revaluations stemming from substantial yen appreciation in October.[6] The increase may also reflect the effects of new controls aimed at stemming capital flight. For example, authorities have ordered state enterprises to repatriate offshore holdings of foreign exchange and have tightened inspection of trade documents.

Given China's reserves, its sizeable external debt remains manageable. China reported external debt of $130 billion in mid-1998. In other Asian economies, it turned out after the crisis began that actual external debt was much larger than authorities had thought. (For example, according to a Reuters report from December 30, 1997, the South Korean government estimated in early December 1997 that Korea's end-November total external debt was $116 billion; by the end of December, the government had raised

FIGURE 4.1 External Indicators and Output

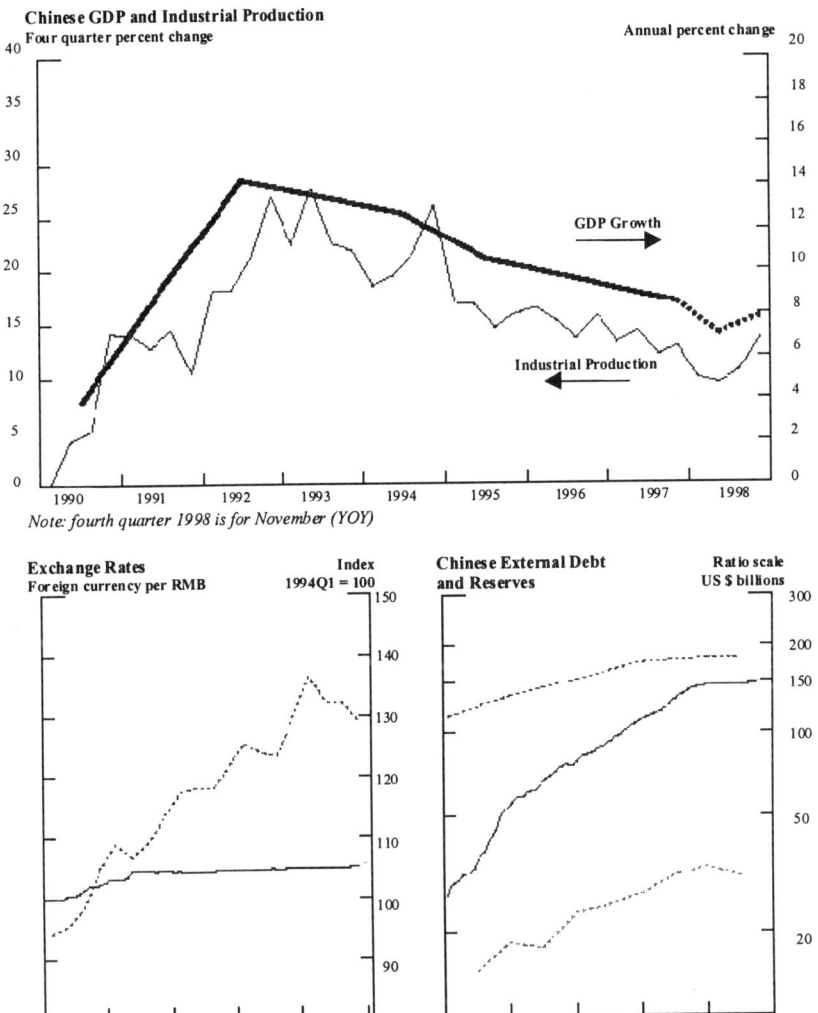

FIGURE 4.2 Trade

Chinese Exports and Imports

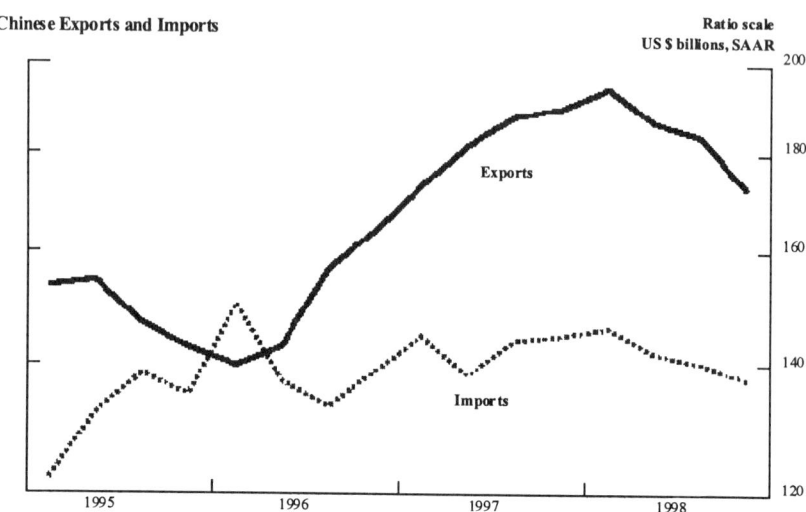

Source: IMF International Financial Statistics and Reuters

Chinese Export Growth by Destination

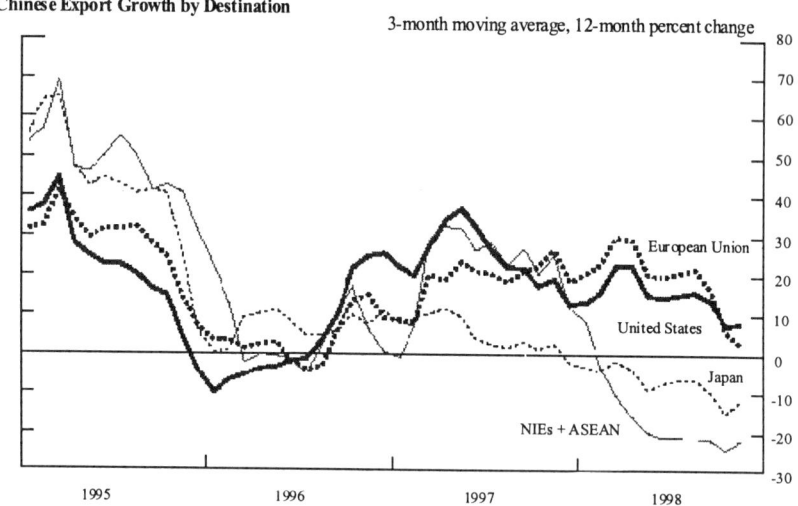

Notes: Newly industrialized Economies (NIEs) are South Korea, Singapore, and Taiwan. ASEAN is Indonesia, Malaysia, Phillipines, and Thailand

that estimate to $157 billion.) Chinese authorities have also become concerned about unreported external debt.[7] One very large discrepancy is in external bank liabilities. At the end of 1997, for example, Chinese statistics indicated external debt to foreign banks of $40.3 billion, compared with bank claims on China from BIS statistics of $89.9 billion.[8]

However, even using the larger BIS number for bank claims, China's debt remains moderate. The dotted line in the top right panel shows estimated gross nominal external debt, which was only about $180 billion in mid-1998. From the BIS statistics, less than $35 billion of this debt was short-term debt to foreign banks as of mid-1998. BIS statistics also show that gross bank lending to China fell in the first half of 1998.

Net exports have remained strong, although this primarily reflects weak import growth. China reported a trade surplus of almost $44 billion in 1998, with the value of exports roughly constant and the value of imports falling several percent. The top panel of Exhibit 2 shows the seasonally adjusted quarterly level of total Chinese exports and imports. Exports have declined steadily since the first quarter of 1998, reflecting weak demand from Asia and the real appreciation of China's currency. Imports remained relatively flat in 1998, with moderate declines over the year. China's current account surplus amounted to more than 3 percent of GDP in 1997, and is likely to be around the same level in 1998.

The bottom panel shows year-over-year growth in China's exports to various regions of the world. Until late 1997, export growth to all regions tended to move together, although export growth to Japan, shown in the dotted line, remained weak throughout 1997. In early 1998, the data show a clear divergence between continuing strong export growth to the United States and Europe—shown by the thick solid and thick dotted lines—and negative growth to Japan and the rest of Asia. Export growth to Asian economies appears to have bottomed out in the third quarter of 1998, but export growth to the United States and Europe also appears to have weakened.

The continued strong output performance is surprising. Sectors other than public investment appear weak: consumer demand (reflecting uncertainty associated with reforms), non-government investment (reflecting lack of financing), and the external sector. The adverse shock to the external sector alone appears likely, in an accounting sense, to have contributed directly almost 3 percentage-points less to growth in 1998 than in 1997.[9] The recovery in growth appears to reflect substantial increases in investment in infrastructure and by state enterprises, including strong inventory investment. Nominal state investment in 1998 was 22 percent higher than a year earlier; most of the increase was in the second half, since investment rose only 11 percent in the first half. (State investment in 1998 accounted for 27 percent of GDP). The increase in investment by state enterprises appears to have been financed by substantially faster third-quarter lending by the four major banks. Hence, the increase in growth appears to be at the expense of previously announced enterprise and bank reform.

Of course, given the strong forces for a continuing slowdown, numerous observers have also questioned the reliability of the output data,[10] particularly given the clear political commitment to an 8-percent growth target. Given long-noted problems with Chinese statistics, most analysts tend to interpret Chinese statistics as indicating trends, even if levels (or even levels of growth) are uncertain. The concern now is that the "biases" in the statistics are not constant, so that the economy might be continuing to weaken despite the recent reported upturn in growth.

Such mismeasurement need not reflect intentional manipulation by authorities in Beijing. First, local authorities may respond to political targets for growth by feeding the center incorrect information. For example, in December 1998, press reports quoted Premier Zhu Rongji's skepticism about local figures—in particular, only one province or region had failed to meet the national 8 percent growth target. The ability of central statisticians to control for this misreporting may be limited. Second, a lot of data is not collected at all, or is inadequately collected. Even in developed economies, statistical agencies find it difficult to keep pace with structural change; China's transformation since 1978 dwarfs the pace almost anywhere else. In particular, data on the non-state sector remains poor, so statistics are likely to miss fluctuations over time in non-state activity. Hence, if state units expand production (as they apparently did in 1998), the aggregate statistics are likely to show an increase in activity, regardless of what happened elsewhere in the economy.

Why Has China Survived So Well?

Understanding China's resilience requires some understanding of why the crisis was so virulent elsewhere. Although the underlying cause or causes remain controversial, explanations tend to fall into one of two broad categories: (1) weak fundamentals in the affected countries, or (2) multiple equilibria. This section argues that neither explanation would lead to an imminent crisis in China. In a market-oriented system, pressures generally force rapid adjustment when institutions are, or are perceived to be, insolvent; these mechanisms do not operate fully in China. Hence, despite serious fundamental weaknesses in Chinese enterprises and financial institutions, a crisis need not develop. In contrast to the weakness of internal fundamentals, China's external accounts remain strong. Even in the absence of capital controls, the strength of these external fundamentals would plausibly preclude a self-fulfilling "country run" on China.

Weak Fundamentals

Perhaps the most common view is that the crisis reflects fundamental macroeconomic and microeconomic weaknesses in the most affected economies. Externally, large short-term external borrowing—especially when used to finance current account deficits — left the economies vulnerable to capital flow reversals. Domestically, inadequately supervised and capitalized banks made excessively risky loans to poorly governed firms.[11]

The story is typically some variant of the following (the emphasis differs across analysts, and not all aspects of the story are relevant for every economy in Asia). Widespread moral hazard existed because financial institutions were poorly regulated and companies had little accountability to shareholders. As a result, corporations borrowed heavily to invest in risky projects, financed by loans from banks who, in turn, borrowed excessively (and unhedged) from abroad. At the same time, foreign creditors were willing to lend large amounts to banks and corporations in these economies: The region had a strong track record for economic performance, and the borrowers were often state-owned banks and corporations who, the lenders thought, had implicit or explicit sovereign guarantees. Hence, risky investments were financed through excessive leverage, and especially through excessive short-term unhedged external borrowing.

These fundamental weaknesses left economies vulnerable to crisis from several directions. First, consider external pressures. The large short-term external borrowing — especially when used to finance current account deficits — left the economies dependent on sustained short-term capital flows. If these flows slowed or reversed for any reason (for example, because of changes in monetary policy in industrial countries, changes in perceptions of the riskiness of these loans, or a "run" on the country of the type discussed in the next subsection), then the economy and the currency were vulnerable. Reversal of inflows contributed to slower growth of the real economy as a result of the need to reduce current account deficits; the reversal also contributed to downward pressure on the exchange rate peg, which might prove to be unsustainable. A substantial depreciation, in turn, weakened banking systems because of the unhedged currency exposure.

Second, consider domestic forces. Poor supervision of banks, particularly those with inadequate capital, led to excessively risky bank lending. If the risks turn out badly, then banks might find themselves without enough capital to make new loans, or even insolvent. In addition, excessive leverage by corporations meant that if risky or speculative projects (office buildings and other real estate investments, say, or a high-tech chip factory) did not pay off, then firms might not have sufficient cash flow to pay workers and suppliers, let alone to repay their creditors. If they could not repay loans, then bad loans in the banking sector again would contribute to a banking crisis.

Are these considerations relevant for China? The external considerations are probably not of great concern to China, since external debt is relatively small in proportion to GDP: As noted earlier, China's short-term external bank debt relative to reserves is among the lowest in Asia. We return to these external considerations in the next subsection when we consider speculative attacks and the role of capital controls in China.

Domestically, however, it is often argued that China looks very similar to some of the frontline crisis economies, with poorly regulated banks making policy loans to inefficient, over-leveraged state enterprises.[12] The PBOC has undertaken a widely publicized campaign to improve financial supervision and the operations of the banking system. In the meantime, however, Chinese banks continue to operate with an enormous overhang of bad loans. In January 1999, for example, People's Bank of China Governor Dai stated that more than 20 percent of bank loans are nonperforming, although he argued that only 5 to 6 percent of loans are unrecoverable; Western observers generally estimate that the proportion of nonperforming and unrecoverable loans may be far higher.[13]

In most Asian economies, policymakers' post-crisis concern with banking-sector health reflects not only long-run concerns about the allocation of capital, but short-run concerns as well. In particular, poor bank health can lead to a "credit crunch," as banks reduce lending even to viable non-financial firms. This credit crunch exacerbates the real effects of the crisis. For example, banks may lose the funding base (deposits) with which to make loans; and even if they have the funding, they may not have adequate capital to make loans. In addition, creditors (depositors and foreign lenders) may lose confidence in financial institutions, leading to fund withdrawals or even bank runs.

These short-term concerns are probably not relevant for China: Banks can and will continue to lend even if loans go bad.[14] That is, it is unlikely that in order to restore their "profitability," Chinese banks will be forced to cut back on other loans. First, it is fairly clear that the Chinese government continues to guarantee bank deposits—which are, after all, primarily held in state banks. Hence, depositors continue to have faith in the banking system, and the deposit base remains sound.

Second, if a severe credit crunch begins to impinge on the real economy, Chinese authorities can in essence order the banks to lend. In the first quarter of 1998, for example, bank loans grew particularly slowly amid reports that banks were concerned about loan quality, and amid reports of a credit crunch; in the second half of the year, loans grew very quickly amid reports of new loans to state enterprises in order to maintain growth. In other words, despite substantial moves in recent years to make the banking system more competitive and commercially oriented, neither the Chinese authorities nor anyone else believes the banking system is fully commercially oriented, or operates independently from the government. Hence, Chinese banks can continue to operate even with substantially negative net worth.

Would Chinese banks operate more soundly if they had adequate capital? The U.S. savings and loan problem highlighted the moral hazard problems of financial institutions with low net worth and access to deposit insurance. In 1998, Chinese authorities announced a 270 billion RMB ($33 billion) program to recapitalize the banks.

Nevertheless, it is advisable to plug the holes in a bucket before trying to fill it with water. Before Chinese banks can operate on a fully commercial basis, China needs to reduce the need make policy loans (through enterprise reform), provide banks with experience and skill in assessing loans on commercial grounds, and ensure that banks are transparent and accountable. These are necessary — but obviously difficult — steps before Chinese policymakers can successfully recapitalize the banks or otherwise try to solve the underlying problems of inherited bad loans of the banking system. Chinese authorities certainly appear to recognize the need for these steps, and have made substantial progress in recent years in training bankers and examiners and in increasing the accountability of banks.

But progress is inherently slow. Suppose, for example, that Chinese banks were successfully recapitalized so that they would meet capital adequacy standards under the best of accounting systems. Key enterprises would still need loans to pay wages and pensions. In principle, the government could move these quasi-fiscal operations onto the official budget. However, financial instruments (including taxes but also bond markets) remain underdeveloped, so such a move is likely to happen later rather than sooner. In addition, inherent incentive problems could remain. In the United States, there were clear incentives for the *owners* of poorly capitalized savings and loans to engage in risky behavior; more capital would have mitigated these incentives. For Chinese banks, however, the issue is the incentives faced by bank *managers* (rather than owners). Individual managers may continue to have incentives to make loans to, say, friends or powerful politicians.[15]

In sum, there are no magic bullets for China's weak financial system. China faces the very difficult task of sequencing, that is, of trying to move from having a non-commercial banking system where market mechanisms do not fully work, to having a viable commercial banking system where incentives are appropriate. The transitional stage — where controls have been lifted but incentives remain inappropriate — holds clear dangers, as was evident in the Asian crisis economies.[16] China's approach is to try applying pressure for reform throughout on the system — for example, pushing ahead with sales of small and medium sized state enterprises, telling banks that they are responsible for any new bad loans, and cleaning up balance sheets. But each step causes dislocations or problems that need to be addressed, as suggested by the apparent backtracking in some areas in 1998. Moreover, in a system with numerous distortions, the theory of the second best tells us that eliminating any single distortion need not improve the functioning of the system. Hence, one should not expect any quick panaceas or progress.

Multiple Equilibria

A second view of the Asian crisis, most clearly associated with Sachs and Radelet (1998), is that the Asian crisis reflects financial panic, akin to self-fulfilling bank runs on the affected economies. China is often cited as an example of a country using capital controls successfully and avoiding a destabilizing currency attack.[17] China's controls take various forms, including restrictions on foreign borrowing by Chinese entities, restrictions on portfolio outflows by Chinese citizens and inflows by foreigners, and a ban on futures trading in the RMB. (Note that a major reversal in capital flows—an apparent panic—need not reflect a situation of multiple equilibria. It may reflect informational revelation: The fundamentals of these economies are in bad shape.)

Did controls spare China from speculative pressure on the RMB? Perhaps. Without a freely accessible onshore futures market,[18] it is difficult to speculate against the future value of the RMB, and controls on outflows make it harder for Chinese investors to convert their RMB if they expect the currency to weaken. Without these controls, it seems likely that many investors would have tried to invest abroad for precautionary reasons.[19]

However, it is worth noting that China's external fundamentals are more favorable than in most Asian economies. As noted earlier, China runs sizeable current account surpluses, its external debt is relatively low, and, in particular, short-term external debt is manageable (less than a quarter of reserves). Multiple-equilibria models of speculative attacks generally allow multiple equilibria only in cases where fundamentals are worse than some threshold. Hence, even if the Asian crisis reflects "runs" on countries, it seems plausible that China would not have been subject to such a run.

Capital controls could well have contributed indirectly to financial stability, however, by keeping China's fundamentals strong. Chinese financial institutions suffer moral hazard problems that are at least as severe as those in other countries: Financial institutions are inadequately regulated and supervised, and they bear little responsibility for losses. Had they been allowed full access to international capital markets, they would have sought to borrow far more from abroad than was optimal from a social perspective. (Until the October 1998 GITIC default, discussed in the fourth section, foreign lenders generally considered Chinese borrowers to have implicit or explicit guarantees from the state and were therefore willing to lend large quantities at favorable rates). Hence, regardless of their other effects, capital controls could have helped keep China's external fundamentals sound, and hence arguably played an important role in sparing China the worst aspects of the crisis.

Prospects for Continued Capital Inflows

China has survived well so far. Nevertheless, Chinese officials as well as foreign financial market participants continue to express concerns about China's vulnerability. China receives enormous gross inflows of foreign capital, primarily in the form of FDI,[20] although bank lending is also substantial (as suggested earlier by Figure 4.1). The first part of this section assesses indicators of foreigners' perceptions of China. The evidence suggests that foreign investors appear to require a greater risk premium than before the crisis. The second part of this section argues that a fall in foreign investment makes reforms more difficult at the margin, since FDI is an important source of financing for the non-state sector.

Actual inflows of FDI were above $45 billion in 1998, virtually unchanged from 1997. The sustained strength of FDI is somewhat surprising, given that about 80 percent of it comes from Asia. At a minimum, it seems likely that gross and net inflows will grow more slowly in the future than they have in the past; given continued economic weakness in Asia, and, given the post-crisis increase in the risk premium associated with almost all Asian economies including China, the level of inflows could even fall sharply.

FDI inflows rose at an average annual rate of 28 percent from 1983 to 1997, with a standard deviation of 27 percent (measured as log-changes). A two-standard deviation fall in the growth rate implies a $10 billion fall in inflows, to about $35 billion in 1999. Such a decline amounts to only about 1 percent of GDP, and is modest relative to the overall favorable balance-of-payments situation. Nevertheless, it would imply lower investment and growth in the non-state sector, in turn making it more difficult to transfer resources out of the state sector.

Evidence of China Risk: Stock Prices

Several measures of "China risk" show an increased China risk premium since the crisis began in mid-1997. The top panel of Figure 4.3 shows stock indices in Shanghai and Hong Kong.[21] China has separate classes of shares for domestic residents (so-called A shares) and foreigners (B or H shares). Foreigners cannot buy the domestic-only shares; domestic residents can neither purchase the foreign-only shares, nor, given China's capital account restrictions, generally invest legally in assets abroad. The Shanghai foreign shares have sometimes tracked the domestic shares, sometimes the Hang Seng, and sometimes neither. From late 1996 until October 1997, the foreign and domestic Shanghai shares (the dashed and solid lines) generally tended to move together. (Although not shown, domestic and foreign share prices in Shenzhen generally move similarly to their counterparts in Shanghai.)

Following sharp declines in the Hong Kong stock market in October 1997, Shanghai foreign share prices followed the Hang Seng down. Indeed, in the second half of 1998, Shanghai foreign shares have underperformed relative to the Hang Seng. Domestic share prices, by contrast, remained largely unaffected by the crisis and as of early 1999, were close to their October 1997 levels. Since the dividend stream is the same for the foreign and domestic classes of shares, the most plausible interpretation for the divergence is an increase in the return required by foreign investors. This increase in returns could reflect an increase in the risk-free real rate, an increase in the risk premium, or both.

FIGURE 4.3 Financial Indicators

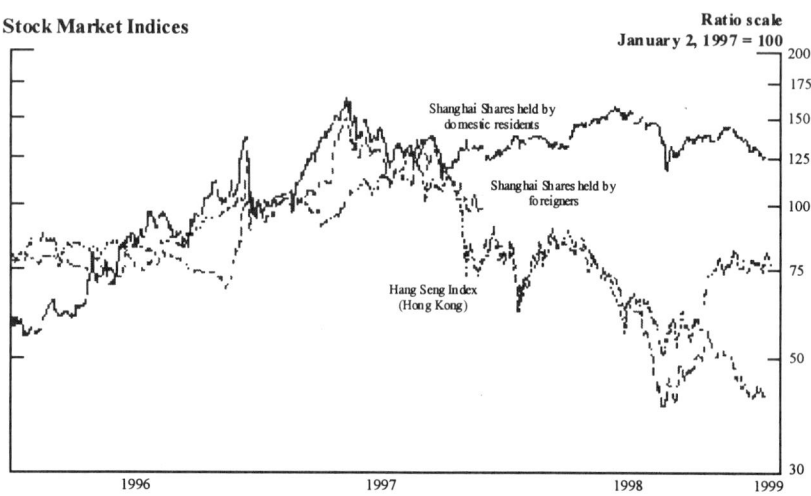

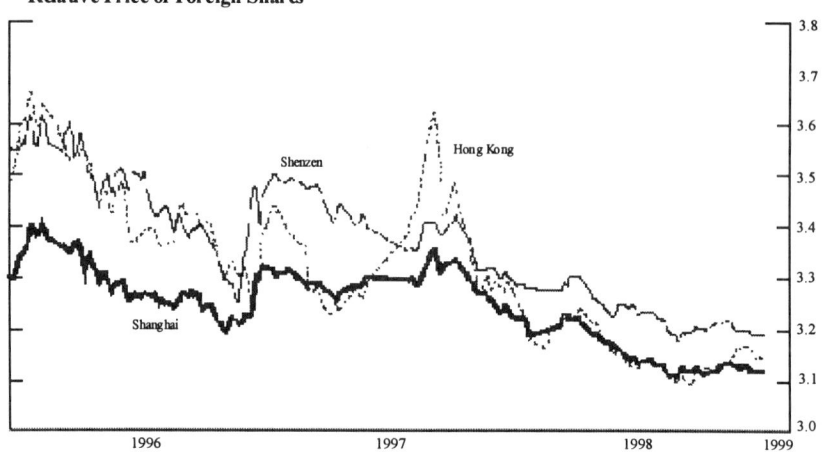

Notes: Chart shows the average price of a foreign share (known as a B- or H-share) relative to its corresponding domestic share (known as an A-share), for companies with both classes of shares. Share prices are converted to a common currency using market exchange rates.
Source: Bloomberg

FIGURE 4.4 Forwards and Yield Spreads

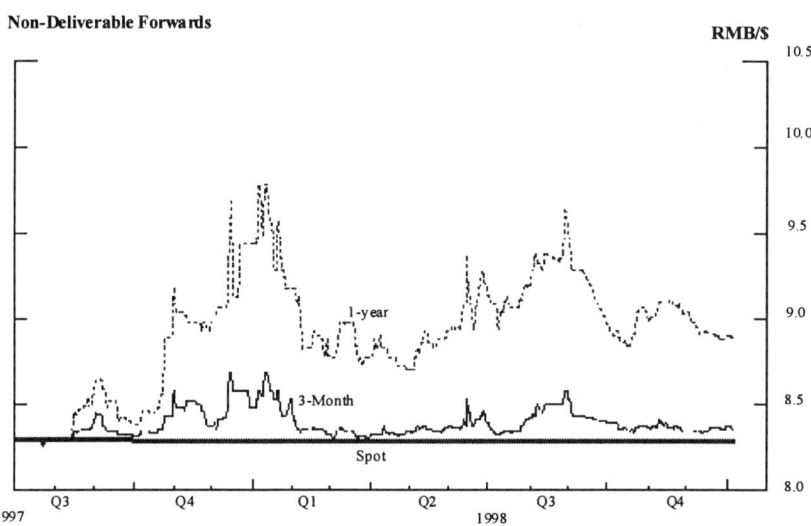

Note: Rates from offshore forward market, where all transactions are settled in US dollars based on the value of the RMB

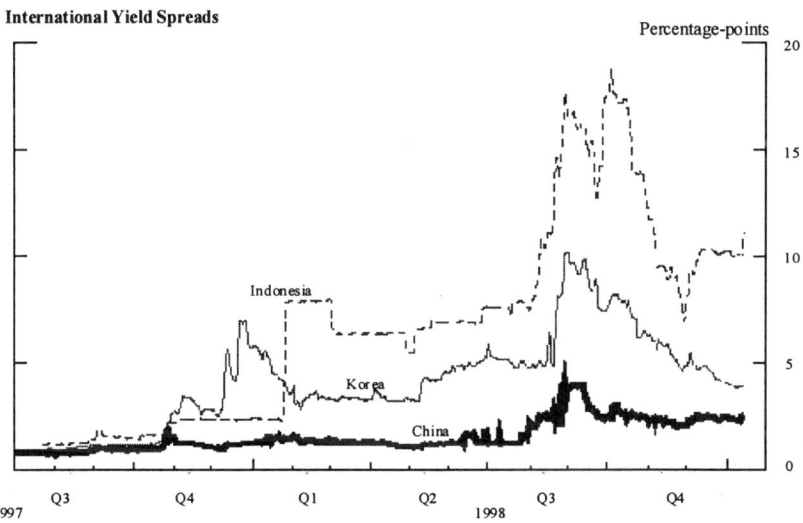

Note: Government bonds relative to US treasuries

An even more striking way to see this divergence is to look at the average relative price paid by foreigners in the three markets, shown in the bottom panel. Although at times there have been wide differences across markets — for example, Hong Kong shares in 1994 and 1995 traded near parity — by mid-1998, foreigners in all three markets typically paid less than one-fifth the price paid by Chinese residents for the corresponding share. China thus contrasts with most markets with investment restrictions, where foreigners pay a premium.

The most plausible reason for the pricing difference is that Chinese investors' have a lower required rates of return, reflecting their lack of access to alternative investments. The main alternative is bank deposits, since financial markets remain poorly developed and Chinese capital controls make it difficult to invest overseas. Bank deposits tend to pay interest rates below world levels. In addition, Chinese investors may have a low equity premium, because stocks offer one of the few opportunities available to diversify their investments at all.

As noted earlier, the Asian financial crisis appeared to raise the risk premium demanded by foreign investors. Fernald and Rogers (1998) estimate how much required returns must have widened, given data on earnings-price ratios and dividend-payout ratios in China. In particular, they calibrate the standard Gordon (1962) pricing formula, which says that $P=D/(r-g)$, where P is the price, D is the current dividend, r is the investor's expected return, and g is the growth rate of dividends. Everything except r is the same for foreign and domestic investors.

Fernald and Rogers rearrange this formula to show that the difference in expected returns is:

$$r_{Foreign} - r_{Domestic} = \left(\frac{D}{E}\right)\left(\left(\frac{E}{P}\right)_{Foreign} - \left(\frac{E}{P}\right)_{Domestic}\right)$$

The dividend-payout rate D/E for listed stocks averaged about ½ from 1993 to 1997. The 1997 peak in relative prices was around one-half (larger in Hong Kong, smaller in Shanghai). With earnings-price ratios of about 0.05 for foreign shares and 0.025 for domestic shares, this equation implies that the difference in expected returns was only about 1-1/4 percent. By mid-1998, the earnings-price ratios had risen to about 0.1 for foreign shares and 0.025 for domestic shares, implying a difference in expected returns of 3-3/4 percent. Hence, the Asian crisis widened the difference in expected returns by about 2-1/2 percentage points.

This equation does not tell us whether domestic required returns fell, or foreign required returns rose. However, domestic share prices changed little while foreign share prices fell sharply. Hence, much of the movement presumably reflected an increase in the foreign required return.

Evidence of China Risk: Other Financial Market Evidence

The top panel of Figure 4 shows RMB prices from the offshore non-deliverable-forward market. This market offers one direct (though somewhat illiquid, and hence imperfect) way to hedge RMB exposure, and prices may reflect either expected currency depreciation, or a currency risk premium. Until Hong Kong's stock market crashed in late October, the forward premium remained relatively small at all horizons. The forward premium then widened sharply, and widened further in December and January. Since then, pledges by Chinese leaders not to devalue contributed to the narrowing of premiums. However, premiums remain quite wide, suggesting continuing perceptions of China risk.

Finally, the lower right panel shows the widening of the yield spread between Chinese sovereign debt and U.S. Treasuries, using a dollar-denominated Chinese government bond due in 2006. The spread widened from under 100 basis points to a high of around 400 basis points in September 1998. In early December, spreads stood at around 230 basis points. If anything, this spread is probably artificially narrow: trading in this issue has tended to be limited, and press reports suggest that Chinese banks and other institutions may often purchase the bonds, and help keep the yield relatively low.[22] Consistent with this interpretation, in mid-December, China successfully launched a $1 billion global issue with a somewhat wider spread of 288 basis points over Treasuries. This spread, though wider than the spread shown in Figure 3, remains low relative to that for other emerging markets. Nevertheless, it is more than 200 basis points wider than the spread before the Asian crisis.

What Role Does Foreign Investment Play in Enterprise Finance?

Given the apparent increase in China's risk premium, reduced capital inflows seem likely. Of course, China does not rely on foreign capital in a macroeconomic sense. That is, China has a current-account surplus and hence is a net exporter of capital (taking the form, especially, of central bank purchases of U.S. Treasuries and other foreign exchange assets). Therefore, if foreign investment such as FDI declines, China can in principle offset the direct effect on domestic investment by reducing its investments abroad (e.g. by converting its investments in U.S. Treasury bonds into investments in, say, factories in China).

Nevertheless, foreign direct investment has played an important role in improving China's economy. One direct benefit of FDI is that foreign firms provide new products, improved technology, and examples of a "reengineered" employer-employee relationship (see Rosen 1999).

A second, indirect benefit of FDI is the support it provides to the dynamic non-state sector. Gross inflows of foreign capital allow the non-state sector to bypass domestic intermediated channels, and hence allow profitable investments that otherwise would not be made. As a result, slowing FDI would tend to make enterprise restructuring more difficult. Downsizing SOEs requires destroying existing jobs and laying off workers, which is socially and hence politically much easier if new jobs are being created.

The top panel of Figure 5 shows an estimate of the enterprise loans going to state-owned enterprises (SOEs) and non-state enterprises (NSEs); the left panel shows these results as a share of total loans, while the right panel shows the actual quantities. Chinese statistics leave a large share of loans unallocated between either sector. We have allocated that share fairly generously to the non-state sector, so that our estimate probably overestimates the share going to the non-state sector.[23] Nevertheless, as of 1997, more than two-thirds of net bank lending went to the state sector, even though this sector accounted for only about one-quarter of industrial output (a share that has steadily shrunk over time).

FIGURE 4.5 Sources of Enterprise Funds

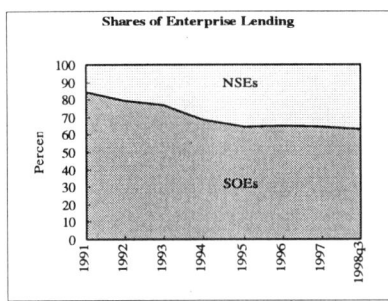
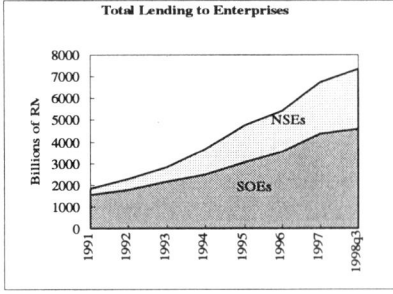
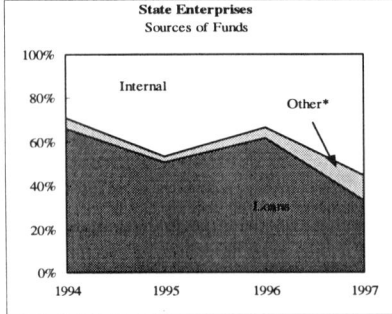
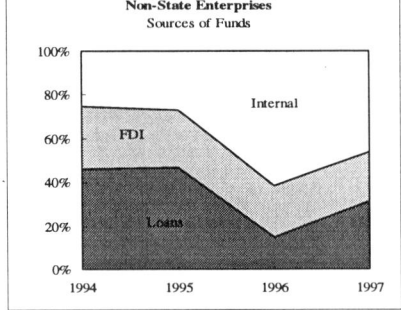

* *Other refers to stocks, bonds, and state appropriations.*

The bottom panels show estimates of the sources of funds for state and non-state firms. As described in the appendix, we have followed standard flow-of-funds conventions to the extent possible. We first estimate the "uses" of funds, which equal gross investment plus accumulation of financial assets (in China, mainly enterprise bank deposits). Sources of funds must equal uses of funds; internal funds, shown in white, are calculated as a residual to ensure that this equality holds.[24]

By 1997, total sources of funds were about equally divided between the state and non-state sectors (about $183 billion for state-owned enterprises and $197 billion for non-state enterprises). The panels show that both sectors rely heavily on internal funding. The state sector, shown in the left panel, relies primarily on loans for non-internal funding; bond and stock issues remain very small.[25] The non-state sector, shown in the right panel, has depended primarily on internal funds and foreign direct investment. (Internal funds include some funds illegally diverted from the state sector; see, for example, Lardy 1998b) Even with the generous estimate of lending to the non-state sector, loans account for only about a third of non-state funds.

Reducing the role of SOEs in the economy requires a massive reallocation of labor and capital, which in turn requires substantial investments in new non-state firms. FDI is a major source of financing for the non-state sector, so any decline in FDI is likely to make this reallocation more difficult. In other words, downsizing SOEs requires destroying existing jobs and laying off workers, a politically difficult step. This downsizing is easier if new jobs are being created, and the pace of job creation is likely to slow because of reductions in the financing available to the non-state sector. But since FDI is a major source of financing for the non-state sector, any decline in FDI is likely to make this reallocation more difficult.

Assessing the Plausibility of Crisis

Conceptually, two broad and potentially interlinked types of "crisis" are possible: (1) an external payments crisis that leads China to devalue, and (2) a sharp slowdown in domestic growth, perhaps reflecting domestic financial weakness. China could certainly choose to devalue even if market forces do not require it; in the near term, though, the most likely reason for such a policy choice would be concerns about the balance of payments or about domestic growth.

As of early 1999, financial markets elsewhere in Asia appeared to have stabilized somewhat. One concern is that a Chinese devaluation could spark a new round of financial turmoil; another concern is that slower growth in China could reduce demand for exports from elsewhere in Asia, thereby slowing their real recoveries.

It is not completely clear, despite widespread concern, that a Chinese devaluation would inevitably lead to a further round of destabilizing depreciations in Asia. It does seem likely that if China had devalued when emerging-market financial turmoil was particularly high (in January or August 1998, for example), then this devaluation probably would have increased financial market uncertainty and led to renewed sharp depreciations elsewhere. Nevertheless, no one thinks the appropriate policy for China is to keep its de facto nominal peg to the U.S. dollar forever. When financial markets have stabilized sufficiently, the effects on the rest of Asia would likely be relatively minor. As shown in Exhibit 1, China's real exchange rate remains about 6 percent stronger than its mid-1997 level, and more than 40 percent stronger than its first-quarter 1994 level. Some of this trend strengthening may reflect rapid productivity increases in tradeables. However, some of the post-1997 appreciation may reverse.

In any case, the timing of any adjustment is largely a political decision by Chinese authorities, and Zhu Rongji has pledged not to devalue in 1999. Given China's current account surplus (around $30 billion for 1998), continued inflows of foreign direct investment (about $45 billion in 1998), and sizeable foreign reserves, it is unlikely that any conceivable shocks will *force* a depreciation. After all, with $149 billion in foreign reserves, a sharp and continued decline in reserves is sustainable for a long time. However, policymakers could decide that any loss in reserves is unacceptable—particularly if it appears to be a symptom of deeper economic weakness. Hence, if exports (and output growth) continue to slow, Chinese exporters could successfully lobby for a devaluation. In addition, there are costs to China if traders and investors expect a depreciation in the future, since they then have an incentive to defer exports from and foreign investment in China, and accelerate imports.

A sharp slowdown in growth does remain a risk. Net exports could continue to slow, and consumption and non-state investment could well remain weak. If state investment cannot fully take up the slack, then growth could slow sharply. On the production side, reduced capital inflows could also work to slow growth. As discussed in the previous section, China's intermediated financial system directs resources largely to state-owned enterprises (SOEs) and former-SOEs. Hence, capital inflows, particularly FDI, have been an important source of financing for the more dynamic non-state sector.

The remainder of this section considers various scenarios and issues that are sometimes mentioned as causes for concern. For the most part, one can dismiss each of these individual stories. Nevertheless, it remains plausible that a crisis could develop that draws on various of the scenarios below, and which is compounded by political turmoil in China. For example, suppose that growth slows sharply in 1999, reflecting a plunge in exports and non-state investment, an overhang of inventories, and widespread consumer unwillingness to spend. Social and political pressures are mounting in response to rising unemployment and stagnating real wages. The perception that China might devalue (in order to spur exports) leads to a widening black market premium and capital flight (evading capital controls). Foreign investors become less willing to invest in and lend to China—because of rising uncertainty about the economy and about the viability of Chinese financial institutions — reducing investment further. In the face of slowing growth, steadily falling foreign exchange reserves, and lobbying by exporters, China devalues. Economic weakness could potentially lead to political infighting in China as well, thereby raising uncertainty and exacerbating all of the problems above. This scenario, though unlikely, remains possible.

Questions and Scenarios

We now discuss some of the more specific questions and concerns that have been raised by observers. Most can be dismissed fairly easily, although as noted in the previous section, they could together form individual pieces of a broader crisis.

1. *If China's capital controls can be easily evaded, could massive capital flight put pressure on the currency and balance of payments?* Errors and omissions are, indeed, large, averaging a $17 billion outflow from 1995-1997. However, this is roughly an order of magnitude smaller than international reserves. With continuing current account surpluses and inflows of foreign direct investment, outflows would have to rise very sharply before foreign exchange reserves began to fall substantially, and before there is irresistible pressure on the currency.

2. *What if foreign lenders refuse to lend to Chinese entities?* In October 1998, if not before, foreign banks began reconsidering their China exposure. At that time, central government authorities closed the Guangdong International Trust and Investment Company (GITIC) because of the institution's inability to repay maturing debt obligations. Many so-called ITICs were formed in the 1980s, generally by local authorities, in order to access international credit markets. GITIC was owned by Guangdong Province and was one of China's largest non-bank financial institutions. Although the four state banks dominate China's financial landscape, accounting for almost 80 percent of financial assets, non-banks grew relatively rapidly in the 1990s and were largely unregulated. The closure of GITIC indicates that authorities may be serious about trying to crack down on financial "irregularities." However, most foreign creditors had assumed that since the ITICs were owned by governmental authorities in China, their liabilities were implicitly guaranteed — a presumption that the central government now disclaims. Hence, as of January 1999, press reports suggest that foreign banks have become much less willing to lend to Chinese entities.

Total external liabilities of ITICs are generally estimated to be about $10 billion (though the Figure could turn out to be larger). Suppose concerns about repayment led foreign creditors to refuse to lend to Chinese non-banks. Even if all of these loans were short-term, the decline in capital inflows would be small compared with foreign reserves. Somewhat more serious would be the case where lenders refuse to roll over loans to other Chinese borrowers—mainly the major state banks and the government itself. Even then, as indicated by Figure 1, China would not suffer a liquidity crisis, because short-term bank liabilities amount to less than one-quarter of reserves. (Government guarantees for the major state banks still appear fairly credible; in December 1998, Moody's downgraded the long-term foreign currency ratings of most major Chinese financial institutions, but they remain investment grade.)

3. *As China defers necessary reforms, will it become more vulnerable to a crisis?* As discussed earlier, China's weak enterprises and financial institutions probably do not pose severe short-term risks. Given the extent to which China relies on quasi-fiscal operations of the banking system to finance enterprises, China could be subject to inflation if savers withdraw funds from the banks. Nevertheless, it is probably possible for China to shift these quasi-fiscal operations onto the budget, given the low level of outstanding public debt (less than 10 percent of GDP). That is, the government's fiscal obligations seem sustainable. Instead, deferring reforms is undesirable because of its implications for the long-term allocation of financial resources, not because it will cause a collapse in the short-term. Indeed, given China's concerns about unemployment and social stability, some deferring of reforms may even be appropriate. (Of course, it is not clear that the best way to address these concerns is renewed investment by state enterprises rather than, say, an expansion of the social safety net.)

4. *What if the yen depreciates sharply?* In 1998, the value of the yen fluctuated widely. Although by early 1999 the yen had strengthened considerably, there were times in 1998 when market commentary suggested widespread concern that the yen might weaken dramatically. Yen depreciation harms China by reducing net exports and Japanese FDI in China. Consider net exports first. In 1997, China exported $32 billion to Japan and imported $29 billion from Japan. Suppose import and export elasticities with respect to the exchange rate are unity. Then a 25 percent depreciation of the yen (e.g. from 120 to 160 yen/dollar) would reduce exports by $8 billion and increase imports by $7 billion, for a net decline of $15 billion. Although substantial, China's current account balance would remain sizeably in surplus. (China and Japan are not major competitors in third markets, so indirect trade-competition effects are likely to be fairly small.)

Now consider FDI. If the yen depreciates sharply, then China becomes more expensive for Japanese investors. In 1997, foreign direct investment in China from Japan was $3.4 billion, less than 10 percent of total FDI and swamped by foreign reserves.

5. *Is there chronic excess supply of goods in China?* Excess supply is often posited as a cause of "deflation," but the two are logically distinct. Conceptually, the overall level of inflation is ordinarily thought of as a monetary phenomenon, whereas chronic excess supply of some goods

(steel and autos, for example) is a relative price issue.

In autumn 1998, China has imposed price floors for major products, in an attempt to minimize price-cutting and hence, it is hoped, deflationary pressures. In a low-inflation environment, however, the main effect of price ceilings is to make relative-price adjustment more difficult. Hence, the problems of deflation—which, as discussed in the previous point, are probably not too severe in China—are compounded by increased micro-economic inefficiency.

More generally, authorities may fear that at market-determined relative prices, some enterprises will not be viable, and their closure would increase unemployment. This problem is, of course, fundamental to the reform effort itself. If China wants to delay reforms, out of concerns for employment, then some sort of subsidies may well be appropriate. It seems unlikely, however, that the appropriate way to do so is to distort relative prices.

6. *Will deflation cause a growth slowdown?* Consumer prices have declined during 1998. In general, deflation has two contractionary effects, but these effects may be relatively weak in China. First, unexpected deflation raises the real value of debts, thereby transferring resources from debtors to creditors. If debtors have a higher marginal propensity to consume than creditors, this transfer reduces spending on goods and services. In China, however, it is unclear that the real value of a borrower's debt has a major effect on his or her activities. SOEs and other politically connected enterprises (regardless of who technically owns them), continue to operate with negative net worth. Second, expected deflation raises real interest rates for any given nominal rate, thereby reducing investment and other interest-sensitive expenditures. Major Chinese borrowers–primarily SOEs–are probably not very interest sensitive, since many of them do not repay their debts anyway.

7. *What if widespread bank runs develop in China?* Despite the fact that banking system weakness is unlikely to result in an immediate credit-crunch, one short-term risk is that a slowdown in output and increases in bankruptcies might cause some banks to become illiquid, if interest income and new deposits cannot cover normal deposit withdrawals. Alternatively, if depositors decide to increase their withdrawals–perhaps because they lose faith in the banking system, or perhaps because they simply decide to reduce their (currently large) holdings of broad money–banks may find themselves illiquid. If the government is then forced to rescue the banks, the most accessible source of funding is the central bank. Then the government may face the undesirable choice of seeing an increase in inflation, or a substantial slowdown in growth (as banks are unable to extend new loans and are forced to call in outstanding ones).

Conclusions

China has so far avoided crisis, but though an economic crisis is not inevitable, clear risks remain. Hence, it remains possible that China has deferred, not avoided, the "Asian flu." Given China's strong balance of payments position and substantial foreign reserves, it is unlikely that external pressure on the currency will, in and of itself, provoke a crisis. However, a risk is that growth could slow sharply. Such a slowdown would raise the likelihood that foreign investors become less willing to invest and lend (as the slowdown compounds lenders' post-GITIC concerns about the creditworthiness of Chinese borrowers); bank runs would also become more likely as Chinese citizens attempt to evade capital controls and invest abroad. With weak growth and downward pressure on the currency, China might choose to devalue in an attempt to increase exports and avoid losing foreign exchange.

In such a combined scenario, how bad might things get? Growth could perhaps slow to 3 to 4 percent—far less severe than the recent output declines elsewhere in Asia, but comparable to China's post-Tiananmen "recession," when growth slowed from more than 11 percent in 1988 to about 4 percent in 1989 and 1990.

The increased downside risks to the economy make rapid enterprise and bank restructuring less likely. In general, radical reforms are costly in the short run. For example, enterprise restructuring was enormously costly in terms of output in Eastern Europe and the former Soviet Union. One can argue about whether China is, or is not, similar to those countries. But even for industrial countries, there is a substantial body of macroeconomic literature that explores the importance of sectoral shifts, suggesting that reallocations are costly in the short-term. The controversy in this literature is not whether reallocations/restructuring are costly in principle, but whether they are important in practice (they might not turn out to be a significant source of shocks to the United States, say). So macroeconomic literature suggests that a slowdown is likely in the short term, should China attempt radical restructuring.

Chinese leaders appear to find the political risks of a short-term contraction greater than the risks from a long-term slowdown in growth. Enterprise reform appears to have slowed, and banks have increased their lending to the state sector. Hence, even if China avoids a near-term slowdown, one cost of the Asian crisis for China is a slower pace of enterprise and banking reforms. Without such reforms, China's long-term prospects become worse.

Appendix: Estimating Sources of Enterprise Funding

Estimates of enterprise funding in China are limited by the availability of Chinese data. Nonetheless, we have pieced together available information to construct a rough picture of enterprise finance in China. Below, we describe the sources of our data and the assumptions we have made in reaching our estimate.

Basic Assumptions

1. *Total uses of enterprise funds in a given year equal the sum of fixed asset investment and acquired liquid assets over the same period.*

    Essentially, enterprises use their money (net of factor payments) in two ways: to invest in fixed assets and to accumulate liquid assets. Uses of funds must equal sources of funds; what goes out of the system must have come in. Hence, fixed asset investment and liquid asset accumulation equals total enterprise expenditure which, in turn, equals total sources of enterprise funding.

2. *We identify five sources of enterprise funding: internal financing (i.e. revenues net of factor payments), foreign direct investment, net issues of stocks and bonds, bank credit, and state appropriations (i.e. government fiscal subsidies).*

The last four sources are considered sources of non-internal financing. We estimate internal funds as the residual of total uses of funds less total non-internal funding.

Balance sheet of Enterprise Flow of Funds

Using our basic assumptions, we construct the following balance sheet of enterprise flow of funds:

(1) Total uses of funds *(2) + (3)*
(2)   Fixed asset investment
(3)   Acquisition of liquid assets

(4) Total sources of funds *(1)*
(5)   Internal funds *(1) - (6)*
(6)   Non-internal funds *(7) + (8) + (9) + (10)*
(7)   Foreign direct investment
(8)   Net equity and bond issues
(9)   Loans
(10)   State appropriations

Data Sources and SOE/NSE Breakdown

We make several assumptions and draw data from several sources in determining the breakdown of funding between SOEs and NSEs. For each element of the basic flow of funds account above, we note both the source of the data and the method used to divide funds between SOEs and NSEs.

1. *Fixed Asset Investment*
   Data on fixed asset investment of SOEs and NSEs were taken from the Chinese State Statistical Bureau, 1998 Statistical Abstract, and China Statistical Yearbooks.

2. *Acquisition of Liquid Assets*
   We assume acquisition of liquid assets is equivalent to the total deposits by enterprises in Chinese financial institutions. Figures for enterprise deposits are found in PBOC "China Financial Outlook." We assign deposits to SOEs and NSEs according to shares in gross output value. Shares in gross output value are taken from China Statistical Yearbooks and data provided by Chinese authorities. We apply 1996 output shares to 1997 and 1998 data, as figures were available only up through 1996.

3. *Internal Funds*
   For both SOEs and NSEs, internal funds are calculated as the residual of total uses of funds (which equal total sources of funds) less external funding.

4. *Foreign Direct Investment*
   Annual utilized FDI data are taken from the CEIC database. We assume that all FDI is directed towards NSEs.

5. *Net Stock and Bond Issues*
   Data on net stock and bond issues for 1994-1997 are drawn from the PBOC flow of funds accounts. The 1997 Figure is from the PRC State Statistical Bureau's 1997 statistical communique. We assume that all stock and bond issues are made by SOEs.

6. *Loans*
   Loans are the most important source of non-internal funding for Chinese enterprises. Lending data are taken from PBOC "China Financial Outlook," which provides tables on the lending activities of Chinese financial institutions in aggregate and, separately, of the state banking system.[26] In 1997 the PBOC changed its methodology for measuring sources and uses of credit funds. In particular, the new methodology expanded data coverage to better reflect the activities of real estate and credit card departments within banks. Despite the change in methodology, there do not appear to be any large breaks with pre-1997 data and we assume the integrity of the time series has not been seriously breached.

   Under its new methodology, the PBOC provides a breakdown of credit by borrower for short-term loans only. Fixed asset loans under the pre-1997 have been reclassified as long- and medium-term loans. These data are adequate for our analysis, as short-term loans (73 percent of all non-agricultural enterprise loans in 1997) and loans for fixed assets (22 percent of all non-agricultural loans in 1997) account for about 95 percent of all lending by Chinese financial institutions.

To determine the flow of bank credit to SOEs and NSEs we make the following assumptions:

a) All loans for "urban and township collective enterprises" and to "joint-venture, foreign, and cooperative enterprises" are made to NSEs.
b) Long- and medium-term loans (fixed asset loans under the pre-1997 methodology) and "other" loans are made to NSEs in proportion to NSE share of gross industrial output value.
c) Loans to SOEs are calculated as the residual of total non-agricultural loans less loans to NSEs.

Our second assumption likely overestimates the NSE share of bank credit. In 1997, fixed asset loans and "other" loans accounted for a little over 1/3 of total non-agricultural lending (22 percent for fixed assets and 12 percent for "other") from Chinese financial institutions. We allocate 72 percent of this to the non-state sector, and 28 percent to the state sector. The NSE share of these loans could be much lower than this method implies, suggesting that NSEs may be even more dependent on FDI and internal funds than we estimate. Nevertheless, we still find that the majority of intermediated lending goes to the state sector.

7. *State Appropriations*

Data on government fiscal support to SOEs are from the China Ministry of Finance. For 1998 we assume the same level of state appropriations as in 1997. State appropriations are directed to SOEs only.

Notes

1. We thank numerous colleagues for helpful comments, particularly Sally Davies, Hali Edison, Peter Hooper, Steve Kamin and John Morton. We also thank Nick Lardy, Prakash Loungani, Hunter Clark, and Bruce Richardson for comments on an earlier draft. The views in this chapter are solely the responsibility of the authors and should not be interpreted as reflecting the views of the Board of Governors of the Federal Reserve System or of any other person associated with the Federal Reserve System.
2. Section I notes some of the concerns about the quality of Chinese statistics. Even if statistics were particularly biased in 1998, China's performance would still likely look relatively strong compared with other Asian economies.
3. To obtain consistent data across countries, we measure short-term debt from creditor data, using short-term bank claims by BIS reporting banks.
4. See the discussion in Sachs and Radelet (1998), page 5.
5. China's annual GDP growth figures were released on December 30, following China's tradition of reporting annual statistics before the end of the year. They are likely subject to revision.
6. The currency composition of China's reserves is not generally announced publically; however, according to a newspaper report in late 1998 (*Ta Kung Pao*

1998b), the proportion was about 62 percent U.S. dollars, 11 percent Deutsche marks, 8 percent yen, and 19 percent other. Suppose that yen have a weight of 8 percent. The yen value of the dollar fell (i.e. the yen appreciated) from 135 at the end of September to 116 at the end of October. This revaluation should have increased the value of China's $141 billion in foreign exchange holdings by about $1.8 billion. This compares with an actual increase of 2.6 billion that month. We thank Hunter Clark for emphasizing this point to us.

7. See, for example, *Ta Kung Pao* 1998a and Reuters (1999a).

8. The BIS has two reports: locational (reported on a quarterly basis), and consolidated (reported on a semi-annual basis). The locational BIS bank claims on China exceed the consolidated BIS claims. The main differences are that the locational numbers are unconsolidated (and hence subject to some double-counting, presumably small for China) but also include activity in offshore banking centers such as Hong Kong (very important for China) and Singapore of banks headquartered outside the 18 countries that report for the consolidated BIS statistics. Given the importance of Hong Kong, we use the locational numbers.

9. Exports were about 20 percent of GDP in 1997, while imports were about 15 percent. In 1997, exports grew 21 percent and imports grew 3 percent; in 1998, exports were roughly unchanged and imports fell about 4 percent. Hence, in 1998, exports contributed about 4 percentage points (0.2× 21 percent slower growth) less to output, while the import slowdown added about 1 percentage point (0.15×7 percent slower growth), for a net accounting subtraction of about 3 percentage points. (The trade figures are nominal dollar values, but no deflators are easily available.)

10. See, for example, "The Chinese Economic Puzzle; Bond Offering Raises Questions About True Growth Rate," *Washington Post*, December 10, 1998, pB01; "China's Dismal Statistics," The *Economist*, January 9-15, 1999; and "China vows to improve accuracy of statistics," Reuters, January 14, 1999.

11. See, for example, IMF Staff (1998), Goldstein (1998), and Krugman (1998).

12. See, for example, Lardy (1998a, b), Business Week (1998), Rennie (1998), and Harding (1998).

13. For coverage of People's Bank Governor Dai Xianglong's comments on the need for improved supervision see, for example, O'Neill (1998) and Reuters (1999c).

14. The paragraphs that follow draw on Fernald, Edison, and Loungani (1998).

15. China has undertaken a high-publicity anti-corruption campaign. One feature of this campaign is its focus on the financial sector, evidenced by the arrest of several high-profile business and bank executives. See, for example, Dow Jones (1999a, b) and Faison (1999).

16. For a discussion of sequencing, see Johnston (1999).

17. See, for example, Lardy (1998a) and Joseph Stiglitz, "Second-Generation Strategies for Reform for China," address given at Beijing University July 20, 1998. Available at: http://www.worldbank.org/html/extdr/extme/jssp072098.htm

18. As discussed below, there is an offshore non-deliverable forwards market in Hong Kong, where all transactions take place in U.S. dollars, based on the underlying value of the RMB. Given the non-convertibility of the underlying currency, the existence of the NDF market does not bring much pressure onto the RMB.

19. Of course, that capital account liberalization improves opportunities for risk diversification is one of its important benefits. Eichengreen et. al. (1998) provide a

comprehensive review of the benefits and potential costs of capital account liberalization, arguing that "...with appropriate safeguards, orderly and properly sequenced capital account liberalization and the broader financial liberalization of which it is part are not only inevitable but clearly beneficial."

20. Anecdotal evidence suggests that some of China's FDI is disguised lending, done to evade capital controls. First, some FDI contracts specify fixed dividends that look a lot like interest payments. Second, Chinese firms sometimes circumvent the severe restrictions on foreign borrowing by establishing subsidiaries in Hong Kong, who borrow from international markets and then undertake FDI in China. Conceptually, both of these examples are closer to being debt than to being FDI.

21. This subsection draws heavily on Fernald and Rogers (1998). See Fernald and Rogers for an expanded discussion of the market, and additional references.

22. "Roadshow Kicks Off for an International Bond Offering," *Asian Wall Street Journal*, December 7, 1998 (Weekly edition), page 3.

23. In the Chinese data on enterprise lending by type of enterprise, the unallocated category accounted for about 35 percent of loans in 1997. As the appendix describes, we allocate these loans to NSEs and SOEs using their shares in output. Since SOEs are much more dependent on intermediated lending, our estimates almost surely *overestimate* the share of loans going to the non-state sector.

24. Chinese statistics report sources of financing for enterprise investments, but these statistics are less useful than the flow of funds approach. For example, suppose that a firm obtains a "working capital" loan from a bank which it uses to pay its workers, and then uses retained earnings to finance investments. The Chinese statistics would show the source of investment funds as being retained earnings. By contrast, the same firm could have chosen to borrow to finance the investment, and then paid its workers out of its earnings. The two cases are economically identical, but in the second case the Chinese statistics would show the source of investment funds as being a bank loan. In both cases, the flow of funds conventions we follow would show that the source of enterprise funds was a bank loan.

25. We have allocated all securities issues to the state sector; a very small share of that, for which we do not have data, should be allocated to the non-state sector. Since bond and stock issues are small relative to other sources of funds, allocating some of them to the non-state sector would not affect any of our conclusions here.

26. The state banking system includes the PBOC, the State Development Bank of China, the Export and Import Bank of China, Agricultural Development Bank of China, Industrial and Commercial Bank of China, Agricultural Bank of China, Bank of China, China Construction Bank, Bank of Communications, CITIC Industrial Bank, and postal savings institutions.

References

Business Week. 1998. "Can China Avert a Crisis?" March 16, 1998.
Diamond, D., and P. Dybvig. 1983. "Bank Runs, Liquidity, and Deposit Insurance." *Journal of Political Economy* 91:401-419.
Dow Jones. 1999a. "China Newspaper Says 1998 Corruption Could Pass $10 billion." January 8.
_____. 1999b. "Chinese Bank Executive Given 10-Year Prison Term for Corruption." January 13.
Eichengreen, B., and M. Mussa, with G. Dell'Ariccia, E. Detragiache, G. Maria Milesi-Ferretti, and A. Tweedie 1998. "Capital Account Liberalization: Theoretical and Practical Aspects." *IMF Occoasional Paper 172.* Washington, D.C.: International Monetary Fund.
Faison, Seth. 1999. "China Points Finger at Culprit of the Week." *New York Times*, January 13, p. A8.
Fernald, J., H. Edison, and P. Loungani. 1999. "Was China the First Domino? Assessing Links Between China and the Rest of Emerging Asia." *Journal of International Money and Finance.* Forthcoming. Working paper version available as *International Finance Discussion Paper* no. 604. Washington, D.C.: Board of Governors of the Federal Reserve System. http://www.federalreserve.gov/pubs/workingpapers.htm.
Fernald, J., and J. Rogers. 1998. "Puzzles in the Chinese Stock Market." *International Finance Discussion Paper* no. 619. Washington, D.C.: Board of Governors of the Federal Reserve System. http://www.federalreserve.gov/pubs/workingpapers.htm.
Goldstein, M. 1998. *The Asian Financial Crisis: Causes, Cures, and Systemic Implications.* Washington: Institute for International Economics.
Gordon, M. *The Investment, Financing, and Valuation of the Corporation.* Homewood, IL: Irwin.
Harding, J. 1998. "China: Survey-Tighter Controls Increase the Pain." *Financial Times.* November 16.
IMF Staff. 1998. "The Asian Crisis: Causes and Cures." *Finance and Development* 35(June):2.
Johnston, R 1998. "Sequencing Capital Account Liberalization." *Finance and Development* December 35:4.
Krugman, P. 1998. "What happened to Asia?" http://web.mit.edu/krugman/www/DISINTER.html.
Lardy, N. 1998a. "China and the Asian Crisis." *Foreign Affairs.*
_____. 1998b. *China's Unfinished Economic Revolution.* Washington, D.C.: Brookings Institution.
O'Neill, M. 1998. "China: No Hurry to Make Yuan Fully Convertible." *South China Morning Post.* December 1.
Reuters. 1999a. "China warns foreign banks - 'no lending without state approval.' January 14.
_____. 1999b. "China vows to improve accuracy of statistics." January 14.

____. 1999c. "Full Text—China Central Bank Governor's Speech." January 27.

Rennie, D. "Street Protests as Chinese are Bled of Their Savings." *Telegraph Group*, November 19, 1998.

Rosen, D. 1999. *Behind the Open Door: Foreign Enterprises in the Chinese Marketplace*. Washington, D.C.: Institute for International Economics.

Sachs, J., and S. Radalet. 1998. "The Onset of the East Asian Financial Crisis." National Bureau of Economic Research Working Paper No. 6680.

Ta Kung Pao. 1998a. "China's Policy on Asian Financial Crisis—Interviewing Dai Xianglong, Governor of the People's Bank of China." November 4, p 8. FBIS document FTS19981109000541.

____. 1998b. "Central Bank to Boost Euro Asset Holdings." December 13, 1998, p A2. FBIS document FTS19990101000613.

5

Capital Account Liberalization: Sequencing and Implications

Yi Feng[1]

Domestic and international financial liberalization can have ambiguous effects on economic development. On the one hand, a free and open financial market may lead to an efficient allocation of investment capital; on the other, such a market may attract speculative capital into the economy, causing financial instability and catastrophe. The recent and ongoing financial crises in East and Southeast Asia have sobered investors with a cruel reality: international financial mobility can spell disaster.

The deepening of economic integration and globalization raises questions about the rationale of complete capital account liberalization. The financial crises in Asia, Russia, and Latin America further sharpen the tantalizing poignancy of the trade-off of financial liberalization in the emerging markets. Globalization is embodied by three fundamental processes: trade, payment for trade flows and services, and capital flows. "During the past half-century, liberalization has proceeded in the first two of these areas, within institutional frameworks offered by the World Trade Organization (for trade) and the IMF (for current account payments). But the equivalent for the capital account began to be considered for emerging countries only recently" (Camdessus 1998).

The Asian financial debacle seems to have confirmed the worst fears of Chinese policy makers about an open financial market. Over the years, despite an overreaching effort to attract foreign direct investment, the Chinese government is far from relinquishing control over its capital account, particular over the regulations and restrictions on portfolio investments by foreign investors and domestic access to foreign capital markets. It is evident that the Chinese economic reformers are aware of the potential problems caused by short-term investment, which, capable of moving in and out of the country instantaneously, can have disastrous consequences on governmental fiscal and monetary policies. By contrast, long-term investment in fixed capital accumulation (e.g. infrastructures, plants or equipment) is less mobile or liquid than portfolio investment and is considered likely to have a positive long-run effect on economic development. This chapter focuses on the sequence of capital account openness relative to current account openness, domestic financial markets liberalization and political openness. A study of the sequence of capital account liberalization vis-à-vis other kinds of liberalization, with implications to China's economic reform, is important in understanding the rationale and logic of financial market reforms in China.

Capital Account and Current Account Liberalization

Capital account liberalization is achieved by allowing economic agents' access to foreign exchange for the international transactions in both financial and real assets through the removal of all foreign exchange controls. Current account liberalization is accomplished by allowing individuals to obtain foreign exchange at the prevailing market rate in order to conduct international trade in pursuance to the IMF's Articles of Agreement. The implication of current account liberalization is that such liberalization reveals comparative advantage by ensuring that prices of key inputs are consistent with world market conditions (Dickinson and Mullineux 1997).

China has not liberalized its capital account yet. By comparison, it has significantly liberalized its current account and started to reform its domestic financial markets. Why not its capital account? This and subsequent sections review the literature on the pros and cons of the sequence of capital account and current account liberalization and the implications of such a sequence to China's transitional economy.[2]

There has been a healthy debate on the sequence of the opening of capital and current accounts. As Woo (1993) argues, most of the sequencing literature is based upon the premise that policymakers can only liberalize one market at a time. Empirically, some countries (e.g. Chile and Taiwan) liberalized the current account first, followed by the opening or gradual opening of the capital account, while others (e.g. Uruguay and Argentina) prioritized the liberalization of the capital account over that of the current account. The success of economic reform is, at times, ascribed to the difference in the sequential opening of the two accounts.[3]

The economic arguments in favor of liberalizing the current account before the capital account "depend generally on distortions in goods and factor markets, adjustment costs, the need for macroeconomic stabilization, and domestic financial market distortions" (Wihlborg and Willett 1997:118). In detail, McKinnon (1973) examines the rationale of sequencing current account liberalization before capital account liberalization. According to him, current account liberalization tends to result in real depreciation of the real exchange rate, while capital account liberalization tends to entail appreciation of the exchange rate. If the net transfer on the capital account (capital inflow minus interest payment) is stable, then the simultaneous liberalization of capital and current accounts will likely lead to an equilibrium real exchange rate. However, the assumption regarding stable net transfers is likely to fail. Initial net transfers following the opening of the capital account must be larger than the final net transfer, since capital inflows must be paid for (Hanson 1996). Large capital inflows could lead to substantial appreciation of the real exchange rate, "either directly under flexible exchange rates, or by inducing monetary expansion and inflation under a pegged exchange rate," causing a reduction in export expansion (Wihlborg and Willett 1997:115).

Between the two accounts, the capital response to capital account liberalization is faster than the responses of the goods and services to current account liberalization, resulting in the appreciation of the real exchange rate (Frankel 1982). The precedence of the liberalization of the capital account over that of the current account will reallocate resources, leading to suboptimal outcomes (Krueger 1986). Moreover, capital account liberalization preceding current liberalization will lead to the allocation of resources in the wrong direction — i.e. into import competing industries (Brecher and Diaz Alejandro 1977, Williamson 1997). Several scholars — e.g. Edward (1984), Frenkel (1982), Khan and Zahler (1983), and McKinnon (1973) — recommend that current account liberalization precede capital account liberalization so as to forestall the inefficiency in resource allocation caused by the differentials in the response to the opening of the two accounts.

The liberalization of the capital account is often considered an instantaneous process (e.g. Frenkel 1982, Edwards 1984), while the consensus is that liberalization of the current account has the option of gradual or radical reform (Krueger 1986, Michaely 1986, and Edwards and van Wijninbergen 1986). A third opinion is that the opening of the capital account may also assume a gradual or rapid approach (Hanson 1986). For instance, taxes on capital inflow and limitations on the use of foreign capital by banks can be varied to phase in the liberalization of the capital account.[4] In Chile, after the economic crisis in 1982, a minimum permanence period of ten years was required for foreign capital. Later, it was reduced to three years in 1991 and to one year in 1993. In 1991, Chile established the encaje (a one-year mandatory noninterest-bearing deposit with the central bank, the financial cost of which is equivalent to a tax on capital inflows). "The purpose here was not to regulate the exit of foreign capital but the entrance. There were two objectives: to relieve some of the pressures of capital inflows that were complicating policy, and to discourage short-term debt" (Massad 1998).

In contrast to scholars who maintain that the current account should be liberalized before the capital account, others argue for the simultaneous liberalization of current and capital accounts. Little, Scitovsky and Scott (1970), Michaely (1986), and Krueger (1981) view capital account openness as a way of alleviating transitional friction associated with current account liberalization. Foreign funds can be utilized to offset the cost of friction in reducing domestic protection. As a matter of fact, the "unnecessary" allocation of resources due to capital inflows may be exaggerated, as once the rate of return in the capital-scarce economy is reduced by the influx of foreign capital, the inflow of foreign capital will decrease. Guitián (1997) argues that in parallel with current account liberalization, freedom of capital movement will enhance economic efficiency, promote growth and increase wealth.

The sequence of current and capital account openness can also be understood in the perspective of the relationship between current account liberalization and domestic investment (Hanson 1996). The liberalization of the current account is accompanied by the depreciation of the real exchange rate to offset the current account deficit. There are two ways to induce real depreciation, through depreciating the nominal exchange rate or through reducing domestic wages or prices. The political cost of the latter is larger than the former.

Therefore, the government tends to go with the former. Doing so, however, will raise the real domestic interest rate. In tandem with the gains from holding financial assets denominated in foreign exchange, the domestic real interest rate needs to rise so as to maintain the attractiveness of financial assets denominated in domestic currency. Meanwhile, the increase in the real interest rate dampens investment, slowing economic growth. The liberalization of the current account therefore tends to have an adverse effect on investment and growth by increasing the real interest rate, most likely in the case of gradual openness. Very slow trade liberalization does not require deep real depreciation, having little effect on the real interest rate. Similarly, rapid trade liberalization implies that a high interest rate will be a temporary phenomenon, thus lowering the expected rate of devaluation and having little effect on the real interest rate (Hanson 1996). Therefore, in the case of very slow or very rapid liberalization of the current account, it does not matter a great deal if capital account liberalization precedes current account liberalization. It is the gradual liberalization of the current account that would make the sequence of capital account liberalization crucial. The simultaneous existence of gradual liberalization of the current account and rapid liberalization of the capital account would likely result in the rise of the real interest rate, depressing investment and slowing growth. As discussed below, China has gradually liberalized its current account and reduced domestic protection over a fairly long period. Capital account liberalization might have derailed China's export promotion strategies.

Capital Account and Domestic Financial Markets Liberalization

Another part of the sequencing literature regarding capital account openness deals with the order of liberalizing the capital account and domestic financial markets. As Wihlborg and Willett (1997) point out, the arguments on the sequence of capital account and current account liberalization does not have to preclude the sequence of capital account and domestic financial liberalization.

First, large capital outflows may drive up the domestic interest rate and slow down domestic investment. Second, capital liberalization before the establishment of sound domestic financial markets will lead to inefficient allocation of resources. Third, such a sequence is likely to serve only to "provide temporary financing for budget deficits that are ultimately unsustainable" (Williamson 1997:14). The high cost of New Zealand's capital account liberalization is a case in support of sequencing domestic liberalization before capital account liberalization.[5]

Historically, people are concerned about the consequences of capital inflows because of the market failures in the movements of factors and goods, as well as policy failures in achieving a consistent and credible domestic macroeconomic policy. Both may be associated with the policies of previous nonmarket-oriented economies (Wihlborg and Dezseri 1997, Dickinson and Mullineux 1997). China has failed almost all these preconditions. The heritage of central planning still exists in China, as manifested by many nonperforming state-owned enterprises. The price information on the stock markets is far from transparent. Adverse selection and moral hazard tend to act as norms, rather than exceptions, in financial transactions. Though the People's Bank has nominally metamorphosized into a central bank, it has not established itself as the ultimate financial authority with effective policy leverage such as discount rates, reserves and open market operations.

Wihlborg and Willett analyze two schools of thought on the sequencing of capital account liberalization and domestic financial markets liberalization. The first school, termed as "exogenous," assumes capital inflows as exogenous destabilizing forces. Higher international capital mobility ensuing from a liberalized capital account, as discussed previously, increases the adjustment costs and causes a misallocation of resources in the domestic market. If the government has chosen a set of economic policies regardless of international financial mobility, then it is plausible that restrictions on capital inflow can decrease the costs of government economic policy. The financial debacle caused by international capital mobility in Asia seems to indicate that a domestic market open to international capital has inherent risks and may disrupt domestic economies.

The other school, termed as "endogenous," treats international financial mobility as endogenous to the underlying economic conditions of the recipient country. As a result, it is no longer useful to think of government policy as fixed. In the context of free capital movement, a government must design a policy that maximizes efficiency so as to increase capital acquisition and to avert "capital flight." To the extreme, Friedman (1953) argues that speculative capital inflow of the inter-war experience stabilized, rather than destabilized, the economy in the sense that they moved the exchange rate toward its equilibrium value.

Scholars ensconced in these two schools would see the recent financial crises in Asia, Latin America and Russia from entirely different perspectives. The scholars in the "exogenous" school of thought will place the blame on the disruptive forces of speculative international capital and those in the endogenous school will attribute capital movement to the existing distortionary government policy and market conditions in the emerging markets. In the light of sequencing capital account liberalization and domestic financial market liberalization, the "exogenous" thinking would support the view that the domestic financial markets should be put into order first, followed by the opening of the capital account, if the latter has to be liberalized.

By contrast, the "endogenous" view would advocate simultaneous liberalization of the domestic financial markets and the capital account, and even would suggest that capital account liberalization precede domestic financial market liberalization. While the view that the liberalization of the capital account should be conditioned upon a stable macroeconomic environment is generally correct, it is difficult to justify waiting on the liberalization of the capital account so that the economic house can be put in order first. This argument is based upon the assumption that stabilization of the economy is only relative and temporary, and international capital mobility will improve the incentives of the government to reduce market distortions and to increase economic efficiency, which will help stabilize the economy and macroeconomic fundamentals in the long run.

Using a mathematical model, Wihlborg and Willett (1997) demonstrate that liberalization of the capital account may induce liberalization of financial markets and enhances the credibility of a domestic liberalization program. The assumption of the model is that the government pursues redistribution and provides insurance against risks in the financial markets. The efficiency losses associated with the two governmental objectives increase with capital account liberalization, inducing the government to liberalize the domestic financial markets to lower the costs.

In addition, they introduce an intertemporal structure into the model and show that the probability of government change leads to a reduction in the openness of the capital account. They also show that liberalization of domestic financial markets induces a higher degree of capital account convertibility. Admittedly, risks to early capital liberalization exist. However, the costs of continuing capital controls may be onerous in the long run. Capital account liberalization will make government's resolve in and commitment to market reform credible, which generates support for government policy.

By contrast, some other scholars warn that liberalization of domestic financial markets can lead to crises. "Attempts to liberalize the financial system in the absence of appropriately staffed and funded regulatory bodies and prudent and well-organized credit bureaus are likely to end in financial crisis" (McKinnon and Pill 1998:352). They show how financial liberalization and the opening of capital accounts can lead to excessive borrowing to finance speculative or risky investment, eventually resulting in the burst of a bubble economy.

Even though we can give full credit to the logic of simultaneously liberalizing capital accounts and domestic markets in the light of improving market efficiency, this scenario may not happen in reality. Policy-makers' incentive structure is not necessarily consistent with the efficiency criteria. Maximization of economic returns may intensify inequity and accelerate political instability. In order to keep political order and to remain in office, political elites may want to slow down economic liberalization and reduce exposure to economic risks that threaten their political tenure.

Financial Liberalization and Political Decentralization

The sequence of political decentralization and economic liberalization has been under a great deal of scrutiny since the end of the Cold War. While some scholars contend that political decentralization is a prerequisite for economic prosperity, others maintain that strong political authorities capable of effectively reallocating resources are required for developing countries to experience rapid economic growth.[6]

The relationship between political decentralization and economic openness is fraught with a fundamental quandary. As Weingast observes, "the fundamental political dilemma of an economic system is this: A government strong enough to protect property rights and enforce contracts is also strong enough to confiscate the wealth of its citizens" (Weingast 1995:1). The protection of property rights, which is the centerpiece of economic freedom, requires a strong and efficient government. Weak governments are often the victims of riots, revolutions, and coups d'état, which often lead to violations of property rights and destruction of property. However, a strong government possesses the potential for expropriating property from its citizens as a result of its capacity to maintain political and economic order.

Feng and Li (1997) find that the strength of the Chinese government's political capacity is related to the national agenda in favor of either political mobilization or economic priorities. When the political campaign intensifies, government political capacity is on the rise; when economic development dominates the national agenda, government political capacity decreases. The centralized politics in China did not square well with economic reforms that pivot upon the incentive structure and revolve around prices. Therefore, in order to ensure the deepening of its economic reform, the Chinese government has decentralized itself to the extent that the local leaderships can have sufficient incentives to facilitate economic growth. The market preserving federalism, as studied by Weingast (1995) and Montinola, Qian and Weingast (1995), presupposes that the central government delegates power to local governments, that local governments are constrained by a hard budget and that a common market exists for all localities. Feng (1997a) finds that the origin and progression of China's economic reform follow the rationale and dynamism of the provinces that vary a great deal in economic endowment.

Despite all the effort to decentralize, the market economy "with Chinese characteristics" is premised upon central control, including the political control by the government and the governing party. Total financial liberalization weakens the central government's autonomy of economic decision-making and therefore forfeits the political and economic benefits associated with such control. Keeping everything else constant, it is easier to have an open financial market where the political process is open and decentralized than where it is closed and centralized.

An autonomous financial market depends on flows of signals, including political and economic information. A closed political system inhibits or hinders the exchange of political and economic information to which the market is sensitive. Furthermore, the political elites under a closed political system are especially wary of the loss of control. Financial openness may introduce elements of financial instability threatening the centralized command. Finally, a perfectly free financial market requires total economic freedom, at the center of which is the protection of property rights. A liberalized financial market presupposes a high degree of privatization, which itself may lead to economic and political instability. Therefore, even if full credit could be given to financial liberalization based upon the efficiency criterion, the Chinese government would likely slow down, if not outright reject, full capital account liberalization.

Cross-Country Empirical Evidence

This section conducts a preliminary statistical test of the impacts on capital account liberalization of current account liberalization, domestic financial markets, and political decentralization. One appropriate method is the Granger test of causality. However, it is infeasible to have such a test in this essay due to the lack of time-series data. At this moment, the data on capital and current liberalization are available for only forty-three emerging markets in 1980, 1987 and 1988 (see the Appendix). Instead, we conduct a cross-country analysis for these emerging markets. The result here therefore should be considered only preliminary.

The statistical model is

$$KA_i = \beta_0 + \beta_1 CA_i + \beta_2 FI_i + \beta_3 PC_i + \beta_4 PI_i + \varepsilon_i$$

Where KA is capital account liberalization, CA is current account liberalization, FI denotes financial institutional strength, PC is political capacity, PI stands for political instability, and ε is the error term. The last independent variable is included to test Wihlborg and Willett's hypothesis that the probability of government replacement has a negative effect on capital account liberalization.

The dependent variable takes its value in 1988. To alleviate reverse causality, the independent variables take values prior to that of the dependent variable. CA takes the 1980 value and where the 1980 value is missing, it takes the 1987 value. The quality of financial institutions, political centralization and political instability all take the three-year average value prior to 1988.

The measures of capital account and current account liberalization utilize the composite indices recently developed by Quinn and Inclán (1997). They determine the degree of liberalization in the capital and current accounts based upon the International Monetary Fund's annual report on exchange restrictions. In the report, the IMF reviews the laws governing current and capital account payments and receipts for those member nations that restrict some international payments, and are therefore of "Article XIV" status. The IMF report distinguishes between restrictions on payments and restrictions on receipts. Under restrictions on payments, the IMF reviews import restrictions, payments for invisibles, and payments on capital income and investment. Under restrictions on receipts, the IMF reviews restrictions on export proceeds, proceeds on invisibles, and receipts of income from capital.

The decision rules for goods and services payments and receipts are as follows. If receipts or payments are necessarily surrendered or blocked, $X=0$. If transfers require approval (unless automatic) $X<1$. If transfers require approval (usually automatic) and are heavily taxed then $X=1$. If transfers are effected through market mechanisms and taxed, then $X>1$. If transfers are free, then $X=2$.

The decision rules for restrictions on capital payment and receipts are as follows. If approval is rare and surrender of receipts required, then $X=0$. If approval is required, and is sometimes granted, $X=0.5$. If approval is required and is frequently granted, $X=1$. If approval is not required and is heavily taxed, $X=1$. If approval is not required and taxed, $X=1.5$. If approval is neither required nor taxed, then $X=2$. We expect that current account liberalization has a positive effect on current account liberalization.

There is no satisfactory direct measure of the extent of financial liberalization. In this section, a variable that measures the quality of banking institutions is used. Clague, Keefer, Knack and Olson (1995) have developed an index for contract-intensive money (CIM). It is defined as $\frac{M2 - Currency}{M2}$. CIM is supposed to be a measure of institutional quality.[7] "In societies where contract and property rights are secure and well defined...currency is normally used only for small transactions. In such environments, it is also profitable to provide extensive banking and financial intermediation services...It is safer and more convenient to hold most money in banks or financial instruments" (Clague, et al. 1995, 8). In the context of developing countries, CIM, however, may have negative implications for capital account liberalization for the following reasons.

First, the presence of strong banking indicates the availability of loans, thus potentially reducing the need to acquire international capital. Second, the money in the bank indicates that the government can tax the population effectively, which reduces the need for international financing. A strong government by itself is also a precondition for imposing effective capital controls. Until recently, Chile has practiced strict entry control of foreign capital; meanwhile Chile has had higher domestic savings than most other Latin American countries. "In the first part of the 1990s," Zahler (1998), past president of the central bank of Chile, commented, "if we had not put some sort of disincentives to the short-term capital inflows, what we would have found in Chile would have been huge amounts of foreign savings that would not have complemented domestic savings, but would have substituted for domestic savings." It should also be noted that during this period of time, Chile has had a strong government. "Chile has a tradition of obedience to the law, especially regarding foreign-currency transactions. So the money flows through the central bank as opposed to going through the black market" (Zahler 1998). Therefore, the effect of CIM on capital account liberalization may be ambiguous, if not decisively negative.

Political capacity is measured through government's extractive capacity in collecting taxes. Taxes embody governmental presence. In this study, I utilize the relative political extraction (RPE) measure developed by Arbetman and Kugler (1995), based on the ratio of the *observed* taxation level in a country to the *expected* taxation level determined by economic factors. A country of high political extraction (with a score larger than one) presupposes a strong and centralized government. I postulate that government capacity has an ambiguous effect on capital account liberalization. A strong government may or may not open its market, dependent upon whether it perceives economic openness as a threat to its regime.

Political instability is measured through the probability function of the limited dependent variable model (Chen and Feng 1996, Feng 1997b). The probability of irregular government change is calculated as a function of recent economic performance, political violence, electoral structure, and continental dummy variables. It has been found that the likelihood of irregular government change, defined as extra-constitutional power transfer, has a very pronounced effect on economic activities (Feng and Chen 1996). It is expected that political instability will be negatively related to capital account liberalization.

Table 5.1 reports the multivariate regression result. Three out of the four independent variables are statistically significant at the 5 percent error level. Current account openness has a positive effect on capital account openness; contract-intensive money has a negative effect on capital account openness; and political instability has a negative effect on capital account openness. Political capacity is not statistically significant.

For this group of emerging markets, past levels of current account liberalization, contract-intensive money and the probability of irregular government change appear to affect the current level of capital account liberalization. A liberalized current account is conducive to opening the capital account, as some of the works summarized above claim. Currency convertibility in the current account will directly involve domestic industries in a competition with an international market based upon comparative advantage, thus increasing the long-term gains from improved technology and management, which is consistent with further decreases in trade tariffs. Current account liberalization will also increase foreign investors' confidence in their direct investment in the recipient country, as their profits will not be subject to currency control, thus increasing their commitment to long-term business ventures. Current account liberalization will compel financial markets to deepen, setting conditions for capital account liberalization.

TABLE 5.1 Regression Results

Dependent variable: Capital Account Openness

Variable	Parameter Estimate	Standard Error	T-Ratio	P-Value
INTERCEPT	3.112	0.994	3.132	0.004
CA	0.310	0.045	6.819	0.0001
CIM	-2.509	1.224	-2.049	0.049
PC	-0.289	0.270	-1.069	0.293
PI	-12.269	4.450	-2.757	0.009

$\overline{R}^2 = 0.584$; $\sigma=0.554$; N=38

The negative impact of contract-intensive money on capital account liberalization seems to confirm the view that the institutionalization of the banking industry may not promote capital account liberalization. Normatively, we have examined the pros and cons of sequencing domestic financial markets and capital account liberalization. In reality, the political elite and interest groups may have preferences that deviate from the apolitical market equilibrium. Domestic capital owners have the incentive to improve the quality of financial institutions and meanwhile to keep the capital account from opening so that they can prevent international competition. This scenario is likely to be true of developing countries where capital is scarce.

Political instability negatively affects the investors' decision to invest. Feng and Chen (1997) demonstrate in a mathematical model and cross-country empirical analysis over forty developing countries that capital tends to exit the domestic market to seek havens where the political system is stable. When political turbulence reigns, capital flight ensues. The government under political uncertainty, naturally, will practice capital controls to avoid capital flight. Similarly, a centralized government levies heavy taxes on domestic and international agents, decreasing the incentives to invest and creating barriers to complete financial openness.

The probability of irregular government change instills great amounts of political uncertainty in the marketplace by introducing unpredicted policy change. Political uncertainty shakes the people's confidence in the economy and their commitment to savings and investment, potentially causing irreversible damages to the course of economic development. The growth trajectories of many Latin American and Sub-Saharan African countries attest to the negative relationship between political uncertainty and investment (Feng 1999).

The China Experience

It has been alluded to throughout this essay that China lacks the conditions for completely opening up its capital account. China's current account liberalization has so far experienced three stages. In the first stage (1949-1979), the state required that enterprises sell foreign currency to the central government, which also determined who should be provided with foreign currency. In the second stage (1979-1994), enterprises still had to return foreign currency to the state, but the state would set aside a percentage of the returned foreign currency, which could be purchased back by the enterprise for future use. In the third stage (1994-present), a unified foreign currency market has been established among banks, based upon the market demand. Under this system, enterprises have access to foreign currency with valid invoices from their current account transactions. On November 27, 1996, Dai Xianglong, Governor of the People's Bank, wrote to the IMF, announcing that as of December 1, 1996 China would assume obligations prescribed in Article VIII of the IMF Agreement and make RMB convertible in the current account.[8]

In tandem with the gradual openness of its current account, China has reduced its mean tariff rate from 47.2% in 1991 to 17.8% in 1997,[9] with an annual average reduction rate of 5%. As mentioned previously, it is the gradual liberalization of the current account that would make sequencing capital account liberalization crucial. The liberalization of the capital account prior to or concomitant with the gradual liberalization of the current account could have several consequences on China's economic reform. First, foreign capital may flow to the still protected, but inefficient state owned enterprises. Second, the influx of foreign capital may work against the real depreciation and make it difficult to offset the external deficits caused by the reduction in protection. Third, an increase in foreign capital intensifies inflationary pressures in China.

China significantly reduced its tariff rates in 1992 and 1996. By the early 1990s, the reform of China's export sectors was far ahead of its reform in its import-competing industries. For instance, export subsidies had been suspended and the extent to which permits were required of exported goods had been reduced. By contrast, imports remained largely controlled by the state. In addition to high tariffs, severe non-tariff barriers existed, such as import quotas, exchange control, and permit authorization. The imports subject to quotas, permits and import control numbered 1,247, or about 20% of total imported items. The losses of the enterprises due to imports were also subsidized by the state (Yang 1997). The inconsistency between the deregulation of the export and the protection of the importing industries ran counter to the establishment of price mechanisms. The reduction of tariffs in 1992 and 1996 marked a turning point in China's trade liberalization.

FIGURE 5.1   Foreign Exchange, Inflation and Tariff Rates in China, 1987-1997

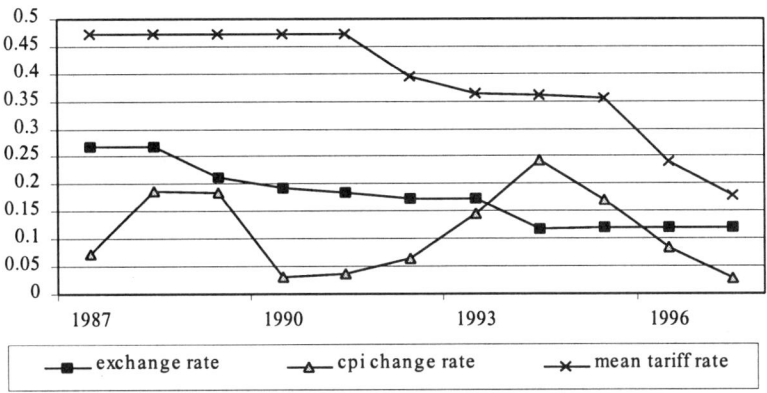

Notes: *The data on exchange rate are from the International Monetary Fund's International Financial Statistics. It is defined as the period average rate in units of the U.S. dollars per RMB. CPI is based on Consumer Prices (line 64) in International Financial Statistics. The 1987-1995 data on tariff rates are obtained from Yang, ed., Reforming China's Tariff System, p. 259 and the 1996-1997 data are from World Development Indicators by the World Bank.*

In general, China's economic liberalization adopts a gradual and phased-in approach. After experimenting with linking RMB to the U.S. dollars through locally managed foreign exchange adjustment centers, China unified its exchange rates on January 1, 1994, adopting a single-rate, market-driven and floating system for the exchange market between banks. Since then, RMB has stabilized and even appreciated slightly. The liberalization of the capital account would lead to a massive injection of additional foreign capital into China's economy, further causing RMB to appreciate, which will discourage exports and may induce inflation. In response to a trade deficit in 1993, devaluation of RMB in 1994 quickly turned the deficit into a surplus of 7.08 billion U.S. dollars in the first quarter of 1995.

Pressure on inflation was also caused by a continuous inflow of foreign direct investment. Because of bright prospects for economic growth in China, direct foreign investment increased to $30 billion in 1994. In addition, some domestic enterprises exchanged foreign currencies for RMB to increase their domestic investment. Finally, since the current account was liberalized in 1994, some international "hot" money, chasing the relatively high interest rate, found its way into China (Pang 1997). All this has led to excess supply of foreign exchange, causing RMB to appreciate. As the Chinese government had to absorb all foreign currencies through China's exchange market, it has built a large foreign currency reserve (currently about 140 billion U.S. dollars) and at the same time increased pressure for inflation. All this indicates that it will not be soon before China significantly opens its capital account and makes its currency fully convertible.

An examination of China's contract-intensive money shows that CIM has been increasing, indicating that the quality of financial institutions may have been strengthened. The increase in savings implies that more domestic resources have been allocated through the banking system, which is the most important player in China's financial market. The amount of money that stays in the financial institutions symbolizes the consumers' and investors' confidence in the stability of the national currency and their rationalization with the interest rate.[10]

FIGURE 5.2   China's Contract-Intensive Money

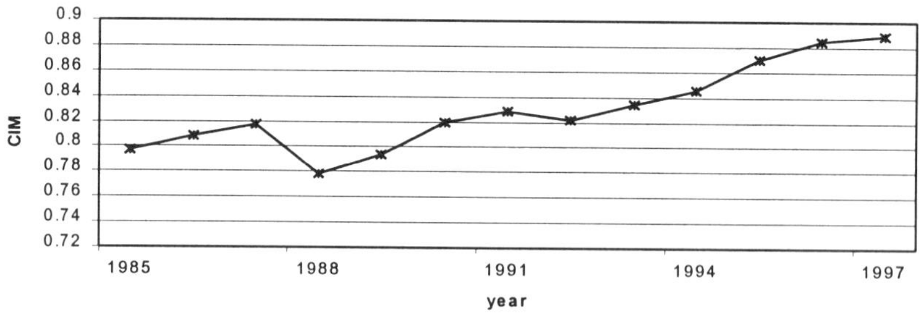

Note: CIM is constructed from International Financial Statistics. The formula is

$$\frac{line\ 34\ +\ line\ 35\ -\ line\ 14a}{line\ 34\ +\ line\ 35} \text{ or } 1 - \frac{line\ 14a}{line\ 34\ +\ line\ 35}$$

Contract-intensive money is positively correlated with political capacity, which is consistent with our previous claim that governments can tax a population more effectively if contract-intensive money is relatively large. A strong and centralized government may rationally forestall full liberalization of the capital account for the sake of political and economic control, which is particularly true when the nation does not have comparative advantage in capital-intensive products.

The endogenous view of simultaneously liberalizing the capital account and domestic financial markets may be normatively correct, as it is based upon the assumption that a nation maximizes its long-run growth through improving economic efficiency. Positively, economic efficiency achieved through opening both areas may not be consistent with political efficiency, the criterion of which is for the political elite to remain in office. The endogenous approach may require massive resource allocations and therefore intensify social conflict. If China opens its capital account, inefficient state-owned enterprises may eventually take the brunt of bankruptcy and income inequality may deteriorate in the society. In this case, speculative capital inflow and outflow would tend to destabilize, rather than stabilize, the transitional economy in the sense that it would create political and social unrest. Though speculative capital has the potential for moving the exchange rate toward its equilibrium value, China's political elite may eschew the risk of opening the financial markets to foreign investors without serious restraints. It should be emphasized that the Chinese government is not averse to foreign capital; on the contrary, it has been coveting direct international investment over the entire course of its economic reform, as the last chapter of this book demonstrates. China has been seeking to upgrade its production structure from labor-intensive goods to high-tech products through acquiring advanced technology and management. It is foreign direct investment—which tends to comprise long-term ventures—that helps China realize dynamic comparative advantage. By contrast, short term portfolio investment, which may take a speculative objective, can cause financial instability, though it may improve market efficiency in the long run.

Wang (1997) summarizes the difficulties that prevent China from opening up its capital account, which are consistent with the implications of the multivariate statistical results. First, the demand and supply of foreign currencies in China have not been fully marketized. The People's Bank remains the largest buyer of foreign exchange and the operation of inter-bank market lacks sophistication, which adds to inflationary pressure. Second, many of China's enterprises remain backward and inefficient, which can be characterized by high indebtedness, low outputs and heavy losses. Financial instability associated with opening the capital account can cause social instability. Third, large fiscal deficits and a lack of effective monetary policy prevent the country from optimizing capital flow in domestic production. All this suggests that an open capital account is likely to result in large-scale volatility of exchange rates, an increase in trade deficits, high inflation, and capital flight, all fomenting social unrest and political instability.

In order to correct for those limitations, the government should improve the micro-foundation of capital account liberalization. It remains a tall order to reform and restructure state-owned enterprises by transforming them into efficient agents in the market economy. The ultimate success of China's 20-year old market reform depends, at this juncture, upon reducing the X-inefficiency and political rent of the state-owned enterprises. When state-owned enterprises can economically rationalize their production decisions and compete effectively with each other and with other entities of enterprises, capital account openness can bring more opportunities without releasing political instabilities.

Two other related tasks are to improve macroeconomic control and to speed up financial market reforms. The government should adopt the principle of "market-preserving federalism," by providing both incentives to compete and excel as well as assuring political and policy stability. More freedom should be allowed in the marketplace while at the same time, a sound supervisory system should be established to monitor and remedy macroeconomic mistakes or high-risk ventures. Particularly, it is essential to perfect the operation of an independent and effective central bank.

China should continue its financial market reform by devising laws, regulations and accounting and auditing systems that are compatible with advanced economies. Transparency should be emphasized and the rate of returns, rather than personal relationships or government-business connections, should become the main criterion of credit and lending. Moral hazard and adverse selection should be institutionally eliminated. For instance, in China, the agencies that assess assets are often designated by state enterprises that are also the owners of the assets being assessed. This kind of market malfunction is a major source of non-performing and bad loans.

Ultimately, economic challenges are political ones. Political reform should not be viewed as a taboo to the society, but rather as a solution to the long-run economic and social wellbeing of the most populous country in the world. Economic justice, fairness and openness cannot be guaranteed without an open political infrastructure that is based upon the full participation by the people who can mandate policies and choose their political leaders to carry them out. "Village democracy" has been tried out in the countryside in recent years. It is not a coincidence that economic reform was first experimented with in the rural areas in China two decades ago. Compared to economic reform, political reform in China faces daunting challenges. However, in the presence of sustained economic development, democratization will take root and grow and blossom in the country.[11]

It will be awhile before China's capital account can be fully liberalized. The pace of capital account liberalization in China is determined by both further liberalization of an economy that is being integrated into the global market and further institutionalization of economic and political participation. Given the particulars of Chinese politics, what we will witness in the process of economic liberalization is likely to be a playoff between economic efficiency versus political stability. Bhagwati (1998) summarizes a sentiment that, increasingly prevalent in the countries still floundering in the recent financial woes, presages the prospects of China's financial reform. "For many developing countries today, including India and China, the question is not whether to impose capital controls but whether to drop them. To them, I say: Cease moving toward free capital flows until you have political stability, sustained prosperity, and substantial macroeconomic expertise.

Concentrate instead on internal reforms such as privatization and external reforms such as a freer trade. Allow 'targeted' convertibility for dividends, profits and invested capital for direct foreign investment. It brings capital and skill and is more stable than short-term capital flows." To his menu of advice, I would like to add the importance of institutionalization of political reform, without which the progress of decades of economic reforms will stagnate, reverse, and even disappear.

Appendix: Countries in the Cross-Country Regression

Egypt, Ethiopia, Ghana, Liberia, Nigeria, South Africa, Tunisia, Costa Rica, Dominican Republic, El Salvador, Guatemala, Haiti, Honduras, Mexico, Nicaragua, Panama, Argentina, Bolivia, Brazil, Chile, Colombia, Ecuador, Paraguay, Peru, Uruguay, Venezuela, Myanmar, Hong Kong, India, Indonesia, Iran, Iraq, Israel, Jordan, Republic of Korea, Malaysia, Pakistan, Phillipines, Singapore, Sri Lanka, Syria, Thailand, and Turkey

Notes

1. This essay was conceived during a series of inspiring conversations with Thomas D. Willett. The author thanks the Fletcher-Jones Foundation for a faculty research grant.
2. Much of the literature review in this section is guided by Hanson (1996).
3. McKinnon (1982) attributes Chile's economic success and Argentina's transitional problems to their difference in sequencing the liberalization of their current account and capital account.
4. Hanson (1996) also discusses the use of dual foreign exchange markets, where the rate applicable to capital account transactions appreciates initially, relative to the current account rate. After the first burst of capital inflow slows, the two rates are then unified.
5. See Margaritis (1996) for a case study of the rationale and experience of financial reform in New Zealand.
6. For various arguments on democracy and economic growth, see Larry Sirowy and Alex Inkeles (1990).
7. It is strongly correlated with another variable – M2 as a percentage of GDP, which is a measure of financial depth. See King and Levine (1993) and Snider (1996).
8. Wang Zili, *Financial Marketization and Globalization in China*. Beijing: China Finance Press, 1997, p. 69.
9. See notes for Figure 5.1.
10. Since 1993, the discount rate in China has been around 10%.
11. See Chen and Feng (1999) and Feng and Zak (1999) for the theoretical discussion and empirical evidence regarding the relationship between economic development and democratic transitions.

References

Arbetman, M., and J. Kugler. 1995. "The Politics of Inflation: An Empirical Assessment of the Emerging Market Economies." In *Establishing Monetary Stability in Emerging Market Economies*, ed. T. Willett, R. Burdekin, R. Sweeney, and C. Wihlborg. Boulder, CO: Westview Press.

Bhagwati, J. 1998. "Yes to Free Trade, Maybe to Capital Controls." *The Wall Street Journal*, November 16, p. A38.

Brecher, R., and C. Alejandro. 1977. "Tariffs, Foreign Capital, and Immiserizing Growth." *Journal of International Economics* 7:317-322.

Camdessus, M. 1998. "Toward an Agenda for International Monetary and Financial Reform." Address to the World Affairs Council, Philadelphia, November 6.

Caprior, G. Jr., I. Atiyas, and J. Hanson, eds. 1996. *Financial Reform: Theory and Experience*. New York: Cambridge University Press.

Chen, B. and Y. Feng. 1999. "Political Regime Change and Economic Development: A Formal Model." *Social Choice and Welfare*. forthcoming.

———. 1996. "Some Political Determinants of Economic Growth." *European Journal of Political Economy* 12:609-627.

Clague, C., P. Keefer, S. Knack, and M. Olson. 1995. "Contract Intensive Money: Contract Enforcement, Property Rights, and Economic Performance." Working Paper.

Diaz-Alejandro, C. 1970. "Direct Foreign Investment in Latin America." In *The International Corporation*, ed. C. Kindleberger. Cambridge, MA: MIT Press.

Dickinson, D., and A. Mullineux. 1997. "Currency Convertibility, Policy Credibility and Capital Flight in Poland and the Czech and Slovak Federal Republic." In *Capital Controls in Emerging Economies*, ed. C. Ries and R. Sweeney. Boulder, CO: Westview.

Edwards, S. 1984. "The Order of Liberalization of the External Sector in Developing Countries." *Princeton Essays in International Finance*, No. 156.

———. 1989. "On the Sequencing of Structural Reform." *NBER Working Paper* 3138, National Bureau of Economic Research, Cambridge, MA.

Edwards, S., and S. van Wijnbergen. 1986. "The Welfare Effects of Trade and Capital Account Liberalization." *International Economic Review* 141-148.

Feng, Y. 1999. "Political Institutions, Economic Growth, and Democratic Evolution: The Pacific Asian Scenario." In *Governing for Prosperity*, ed. Bruce Bueno de Mesquita. Yale University Press.

———. 1997a. "China's Economic Reform: Logic and Dynamism." *International Interactions* 23:315-332.

———. 1997b. "Democracy, Political Stability and Economic Growth." *British Journal of Political Science* 27:391-418.

Feng, Y., and J. Li. 1997. "Internal Constraints and International Competitiveness: A Research Note on China." *Journal of Contemporary China* 6:377-387.

Feng, Y., and B. Chen. 1996. "Political Environment and Economic Growth." *Social and Economic Studies* 45:77-105.

_____. 1997. "Government Capacity and Private Investment: A Study of Developing Countries." In *Political Capacity and Economic Behavior*, ed. Marina Arbetman and Jacek Kugler. Boulder, CO: Westview Press.

Feng, Y., and P. Zak. 1999. "Determinants of Democratic Transitions." *Journal of Conflict Resolution*. forthcoming.

Frankel, J. 1982. "The Order of Economic Liberalization: A Comment." In *Economic Policy in a World of Change*, ed. K. Brunner and A. Meltzer. Carnegie Rochester Conference Series. Amsterdam: North Holland.

Friedman, M. 1961. "Capitalism and Freedom." *New Individualist Review* 1: 3-10.

_____. 1953 "The Case for Flexible Exchange Rates." In *Essays in Positive Economics*. Chicago: University of Chicago Press.

Guitián, M. 1997. "Reality and the Logic of Capital Flow Liberalization." In *Capital Controls in Emerging Economies*, ed. C. Ries and R. Sweeney. Boulder, CO: Westview.

Hanson, J. 1996. "An Open Capital Account: A Brief Survey of the Issues and the Results." In *Financial Reform: Theory and Experience*, ed. G. Caprio Jr., I. Atiyas, and J. Hanson. New York: Cambridge University Press.

Khan, M., and R. Zahler. 1983. "The Macroeconomic Effects of Changes in Barriers to Trade and Capital Flows: A Simulations Analysis." *IMF Staff Papers* 30, no. 2: 223-82.

King, R. and R. Levine. 1994. "Finance and Growth: Schumpeter Might Be Right." *Quarterly Journal of Economics* 108:717-737.

Krueger, A. 1981. "Interactions between Inflation and Trade-Regime Objectives inn Stabilization Programs." In *Economic Stabilization in Developing Countries*, ed. W. Cline and S. Weintraub. Washington, D.C.: Brookings Institution.

_____. 1986. "Problems of Liberalization." In *Economic Liberalization in Developing Countries*, ed. A. Choksi and D. Papageorgiou. London: Basil Blackwell.

Little, I., T. Scitovsky, and M. Scott. 1970. *Industry and Trade in Some Developing Countries: A Comparative Study*. Oxford: Oxford University Press.

Margaritis, D. 1996. "Financial Policy Reform in New Zealand." In *Financial Reform: Theory and Experience*, ed. G. Caprio Jr., I. Atiyas, and J. Hanson. New York: Cambridge University Press.

Massad, C. 1998. "Chile's Massad Discusses Capital Control: An Interview." *The Wall Street Journal*, October 1, p A17.

McKinnon, R. 1991. *The Order of Economic Liberalization: Financial Control in the Transition to a Market Economy*. Baltimore: Johns Hopkins University Press.

———. 1982. "The Order of Economic Liberalization: Lessons from Chile and Argentina." In *Economic Policy in a World of Change*, ed. K. Brunner and A. Meltzer, 159-186. Carnegie Rochester Conference Series. Amsterdam: North Holland.

———. 1973. *Money and Capital in Economic Development*. Washington, DC: Brookings Institution.

McKinnon, R., and H. Pill. 1998. "The Overborrowing Syndrome: Are East Asian Economies Different?" In *Managing Capital Flows and Exchange Rates: Perspectives from Pacific Basin*, ed. Reuven Glick. Cambridge: Cambridge University Press.

Michaely, M. 1986. "The Timing and Sequencing of a Trade Liberalization Policy." In *Economic Liberalization in Developing Countries*, ed. A. Choksi and D. Papageorgiou. London: Basil Blackwell.

Montinola, G., Y. Qian, and B. Weingast. 1995. "Federalism, Chinese Style: The Political Basis for Economic Success in China." *World Politics* 48:50-81.

Pang, J., et al. 1997. *Change and Development in China's Foreign Currency Market*. Beijing: China Finance Press.

Quinn, D.P., and C. Inclán. 1997. "The Origins of Financial Openness: A Study of Current and Capital Account Liberalization." *American Journal of Political Science* 41.

Rodrik, D. 1987. "Trade and Capital Account Liberalization in a Keynesian Economy." *Journal of International Economics* 113-129.

Sirowy, L., and A. Inkeles. 1990. "The Effects of Democracy on Economic Growth and Inequality: A Review." *Studies in Comparative International Development* 25:126-157.

Snider, L. 1996. *Growth, Debt and Politics: Economic Adjustment & the Political Performance of Developing Countries*. Boulder, CO: Westview Press.

Wang, Z. 1997. *Financial Marketization and Globalization in China*. Beijing: China Finance Press.

Weingast, B. 1995. "The Economic Role of Political Institutions: Market-Preserving Federalism and Economic Development." *Journal of Law, Economics, and Organization* 11:1-31.

Wihlborg, C., and K. Dezseri. 1997. "Precondition for Liberalization of Capital Flows: A Review and Interpretation." In *Capital Controls in Emerging Economies*, ed. Christine P. Ries and Richard J. Sweeney. Boulder, CO: Westview.

Wihlborg, C., and T. Willett. 1997. "Capital Account Liberalization and Policy Incentives: An Endogenous Policy View." In *Capital Controls in Emerging Economies*, ed. Christine P. Ries and Richard J. Sweeney. Boulder, CO: Westview.

Williamson, J. 1997. "Orthodoxy is Right: Liberalize the Capital Account Last." In *Capital Controls in Emerging Economies*, ed. C. Ries and R. Sweeney. Boulder, CO: Westview.

Woo, W. 1994. "The Art of Reforming Centrally Planned Economies: Comparing China, Poland and Russia." *Journal of Comparative Economics* 276-308.

World Bank. 1998. *World Development Indicators*. Washington, D.C.: The World Bank.

Yang, S., ed. 1997. *Reforming China's Tariff System*. Beijing: China Social Science Publishers.

Zahler, R. 1997. "Closing the Door: Two Economists Discuss the Wisdom of Exchange Controls for Emerging-Market Countries." *The Wall Street Journal,* September 18, p. R21.

6
What Lessons US Financial Markets Can Provide to China

J. Kimball Dietrich

Introduction: Asian Financial Crisis

The currency and financial market events of the summer and fall of 1997, the Asian Financial Crisis, resulted in enormous economic losses to the affected economies in terms of sharp reductions in economic output and costly restructuring of their economies. The crisis continues to provoke substantial debate about the appropriate policy response by governments and multilateral organizations like the International Monetary Fund. Although China has thus far escaped the direct impact of the crisis, the effects of the crisis have spread to developed country trading partners and investors. The crisis certainly contributed to the market's reaction and official response to financial market crises in Russia and Brazil in 1998. A feeling of gloom and pessimism pervaded the October, 1998, meetings of the World Bank and IMF in Washington, D.C., and the assembled economists and financial market practitioners there.

There is a broad consensus concerning the causes of the currency and financial market crisis in Asia: government policies and economic conditions which resulted in weakness of the financial systems in the countries involved, particularly the banking systems. Unlike previous currency crises, the affected economies had low rates of inflation, substantial international reserves (although not substantial enough in some cases), and controlled levels of government deficit spending. Domestic savings rates in all of the countries were very high. Attention of most observers has focussed on how to improve the financial systems in these countries. The long-run objective is to create sound financial market institutions and markets characterized by the best financial market practices.

In all of the Asian economies involved in the crisis, Indonesia, Malaysia, the Philipines, South Korea, and Thailand, financial institutions had been subject to government influence over credit decisions. In Korea, the relation between the government-favored *chaebols* and banking was well recognized by the market, resulting in market performance well below the non-financial averages (see chart). In the other crisis economies, bank stocks surged from 1993, peaking in all cases except Indonesia well before the onset of the Thai bhat crisis in July, 1997. Except for Korea, where stock prices were depressed relative to the market after 1993, and Indonesia, the crisis economy bank stocks fell before and continued to fall after the baht devaluation. Over the time period, bank stocks exhibited much greater variability than the market in general. This evidence suggests that bank performance was much more sensitive to general economic conditions than non-financial firms, possibly reflecting the importance of politics and government policy to bank profitability and investor returns.

Government actions which promoted bank expansion when the underlying financial system was weak characterized policies toward the savings and loan and banking crisis in the United States in the 1980s. That crisis was similar to the Asian crisis economies in the sense that policy response represented what I call a "hide and grow" strategy of dealing with weakening bank balance sheets. Rather than recognizing the accumulation of poor credits and substandard risk management, policy makers embarked on a strategy of favoring thrift institutions and banks through guarantees on their liabilities, expanding their allowable investments in assets and non-bank businesses, and finally following policies favoring regulatory forbearance in the enforcement of asset quality and capital adequacy regulations. All of failed policies in the United States in the 1980s have been observed in the Asian economies, including China, in the 1990's. In this chapter, I review this history with an eye to deriving lessons for China.

US Financial Markets

Americans in recent times take pride in the performance of their financial institutions and markets. As stock market indices hit historical highs in the late autumn of 1998 and interest rates fell, American policymakers are satisfied with their performance in guiding financial institutions and markets in the recent performance of the American economy. American financial firms are dominant players in many financial markets, for example, US investment banks dominate local German and French competitors in underwriting activity and advising on mergers and acquisitions in Europe (e.g. Salomon advised Thyssen Steel in its hostile takeover attempt and Merrill Lynch is one of the largest underwriters). Citigroup competes for consumer credit effectively against domestic competitors in Japan, Germany, and Korea, and American brokers and fund managers have moved aggressively into Japanese markets in the face of that country's lingering malaise.

FIGURE 6.1 Indonesian Market and Bank Stocks

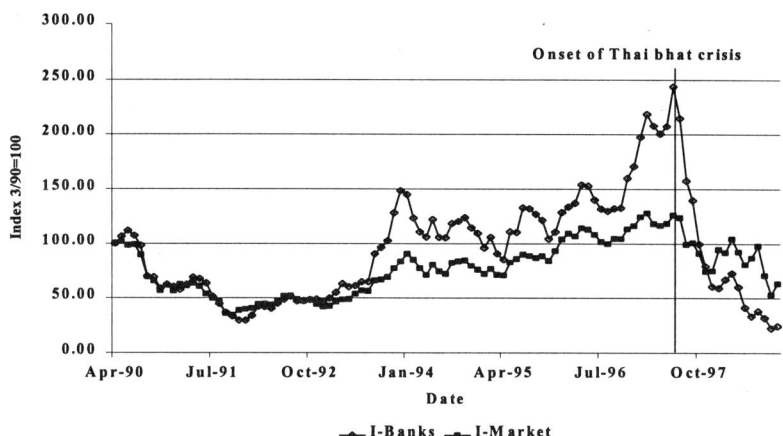

FIGURE 6.2 Korean Market and Bank Stocks

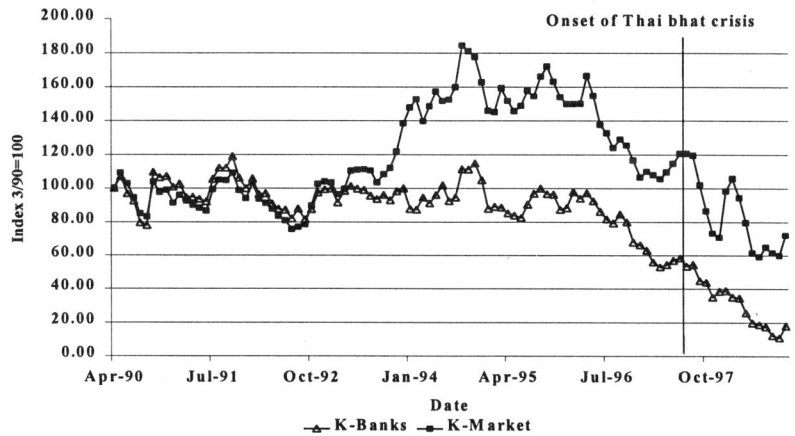

FIGURE 6.3 Phillipine Market and Bank Stocks

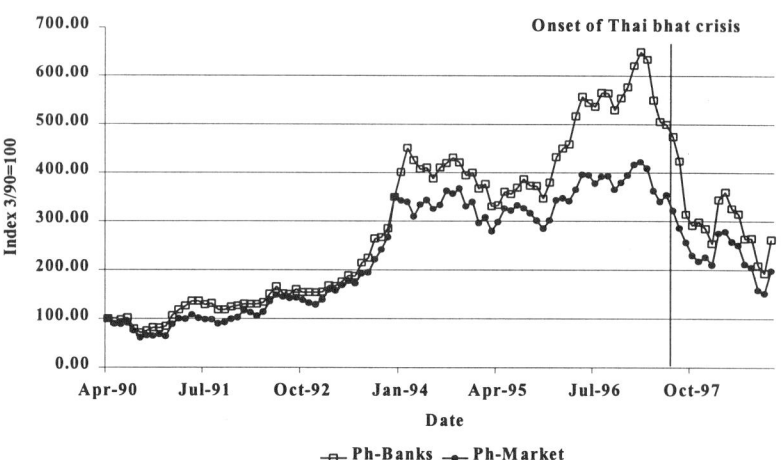

FIGURE 6.4 Thai Market and Bank Stocks

Along another dimension, American financial market observers are smug about the relatively easy financing of innovative small firms though equity and (junk) debt initial offerings and private placements. New products and innovative services offered by creative American firms abound. Other observers of American financial market events are impressed with the impatience of investors who unseat poor management in industrial firms in a very active market for corporate control, where hostile takeovers and many mergers and acquisitions occur. Active institutional investors press boards of directors to improve performance or be removed, pressure by impatient investors which is in marked contrast to more indulgent European and Asian bank investors and owners of enterprises.

Performance of financial institution share prices in the United States reflects their changing fortunes. During the early 1980's, bank stocks under performed the market as investors recognized the extent of deposit-taking institution problems, much as Korean bank stock performance anticipated problems well before the summer of 1997. During the last few years, bank share prices have lagged the US market but tracked it much closer, reflecting banks' improved competitiveness. The improvement in US banks can be seen as the reward for tough adjustments made in the past. One lesson is that market prices of financial institutions reflect valuable guides to anticipating trouble in the future. Moreover, markets reward financial firms that have met their difficulties and restructured, thereby becoming able to profit from business opportunities going forward.

Nonetheless, American financial markets can be used as examples of many mistaken strategies and policies. It is to these I turn for lessons because of the importance of learning from experience. Many of the mistakes were not readily recognized as mistakes by non-technical observers, like politicians and the press. For example, few observers disagree that the regulatory response to the savings and loan crisis represented mistaken policy, but how many observers recognize that regulatory inaction following Stock Market Crash of 1987 represented a success. The performance of financial markets in 1987 provided a demonstration of how strong our securities markets are, not as Congress and many investors believed, a mandate for government intervention to "protect" the financial system. The purpose of this chapter is to stress the important lessons for emerging markets, especially China, to be gained from our mistakes. I should mention that academic observers like myself are often at odds with financial service firm managers and government legislators and regulators who are eager to have regulation and law used to defend market advantages without regard for economic efficiency and growth.

Recent academic work (see Thakor 1997 and Levine 1997 for suggestive surveys) emphasize that financial institutions provide real benefits to the economy. In my book (1996), I lay out a framework which describes the six basic financial services — credit, securities, insurance, transaction processing, asset management, and information and advisement — which create real value to savers and investors. I also stress the real resource commitments, largely labor- and information-technology intensive, which must be made in order to offer financial services to market participants. As discussed in the surveys and studied extensively by researchers, broad availability of basic financial services and effective performance of the required financial activities promote growth and economic efficiency, which in turn have very important long-term social welfare implications. This point is worth stressing since the traditional bias of economists is to focus on monetary policy and the role of money on interest and exchange rates and the demand and supply of savings and investment, largely ignoring the services financial institutions and markets offer, services which are necessary for maximum growth and the most efficient development in any economy.

America's vital and competitive financial firms and active financial markets are the result of a unique historical development, one that no other nation could or should replicate. The economic energies which shaped our current financial markets are common however to all economic systems: demand for the six basic financial services. Our current financial system represents the accumulated historical interactions of investors and savers in financial markets under prevailing economic and technological conditions and the accompanying government policies, rules, and regulations. The lessons to be learned from US financial markets are not to be gained by close scrutiny of our current institutional structure but rather to study the effects of policies on the quantity and quality of financial services provided to the economy.

US Experience

Most major policy mistakes in the United States which have caused dislocations or reduced effectiveness of US financial system can be discussed under four broad headings: government guarantees for financial institution liabilities or financial instruments, efforts to segment financial services markets, policies to control "speculation", and finally, efforts to "design" or control the financial system according to a policy objectives or theory. I provide examples of each of these mistakes drawn from recent US experience. Following this discussion, I discuss the temptation for Chinese policy-makers to make the same types of mistakes in the economic environment facing them.

Financial Guarantees

As mentioned above, a great deal of attention of economic analysis has focused on the role of the financial system in terms of money. Because of the importance of deposit money as a medium of exchange, many governments have focused special attention on the preserving the perception of safeness of bank liabilities, mainly deposits, to avoid the costs of panic-induced deposit withdrawals, forcing liquidations of assets at "fire-sale" prices and inefficiencies associated with a flight from deposit money during bank runs. Possible breakdowns in economic activity due to extreme concern about the security of the payments systems limiting transactions to barter or, worst, an end of commerce, justifies regulators' concern with preserving confidence in bank and thrift deposits. For that reason, the most important use of official financial guarantees backed by the government's ability to tax in the United States has been deposit insurance. But many other financial guarantees not related to money have been granted by policy-makers, for example the "too big to fail" doctrine for large bank liabilities and many types of credit guarantees intended to foster specific credit flows. Financial guarantees have a high cost because they distort relative prices and perceptions of risk and more importantly distort the incentives of managers of financial institutions. Furthermore, guarantees create value for powerful financial market constituencies which become addicted to them – financial guarantees rarely go away once created.

Deposit Insurance

Deposit insurance is credited by most financial market observes to have been the essential factor in the savings and loan crisis, which is estimated to have cost US taxpayers upward of $150 billion (Barth, 1991). Because savings and loan liabilities in the form of deposits were guaranteed by the government, they were riskless to depositors. Savings and loans were granted expansive new powers in the 1980s. Management incentives to maximize returns led the entire industry to obtain the maximum amount of funds through deposits insured by the government and to invest those funds in the highest expected return, hence highest risk, investments allowed by regulation. Risky investments in commercial real estate lending, construction lending, commercial loans, low grade bonds, and newly authorized businesses like casualty insurance and asset management, resulted in enormous losses.

All the evidence suggests that fraud was a minor part of the US savings and loan crisis. The biggest problems came from a rapid increase in total assets of thrifts financed by insured deposits, which after a change in the law in 1980 could be in amounts up to $100,000. Large sums were routinely raised by brokers from wealthy investors unconcerned about the risks of insured deposits. Brokers combined many $100,000 accounts into multimillion dollar investable sums for eager thrift borrowers. The original purpose of deposit insurance in 1933, to protect small ($2,500) depositors, was overwhelmed by the availability of large sums of government guaranteed funds providing incentives to savings and loan managers to maximize growth of the thrift industry, undertaking high-risk investment strategies with cheap funds. Most commentators on the thrift crisis argue that the *moral hazard* problem from investor indifference to risks from investments made with guaranteed deposits and management's understandable urge to maximize returns was the fundamental cause of the financial crisis in the United States in the late 1980's and early 1990's.

Too Big to Fail

During the 1980s, US bank regulators pursued a policy of implicit financial guarantees on the largest banks and financial institutions by assuring non-deposit creditors that important banks, like Continental Bank, would not be allowed to fail, or if they did, all creditors—including uninsured creditors—would be protected. The theory was that a large failure would disrupt the financial system, so-called *systemic risk* destroying confidence and possibly the entire economic system. On the other hand, most observers argue that allowing large failures early in the 1980s would have put the large creditors to banks, mainly corporations and financial institutions, on notice to be wary of risks and could have avoided the large problems later in the decade. The Continental Bank bail-out in the early 1980s had the effect of reducing financial market participants' concern with large bank risks. Since governments cannot eliminate economic risk, the too big too fail doctrine could not be sustained and was officially dropped by Congress in 1991.

Accompanying government guarantees, either explicit guarantees like deposit insurance or implicit assurances like too big to fail doctrines, is the requirement that deposit-taking institutions be monitored by the government insurers to control the risk they have assumed. When regulators wish to postpone recognition of the risks, they have assumed through guarantees, they can relax regulation of asset quality and capital, as happened in the United States. Deposit insurance thus undermines not only the incentive structure of the management of deposit-taking institutions, but can also distort the willingness of regulators to recognize inevitable losses in a timely fashion. This is precisely what happened in the United States, when early problems with thrift losses in the early 1980s resulted in a *reduction* of capital requirements.

Segmentation

US financial markets have been highly segmented, with insurance and investment banking legally separate from commercial banking. In the United States, financial industry officials soon became comfortable with such legal barriers to intermarket competition because they could develop profitable strategies behind government enforced barriers to entry. The losers are consumers of financial services. The costs of financial market segmentation in economic efficiency from reduced competition is augmented with the losses due to difficulty for laws and regulations to adjust to changing market conditions. In the United States, changing laws governing bank holding companies are aggressively fought by energetic and well-financed lobbies.

Glass Steagall

The Glass Steagall Act separating investment banking and commercial banking has prevented banks from realizing synergies available from combining the offering of credit directly with the possibility of arranging funds through public or private placements of debt issues. US investment banking is highly concentrated as a result. The entry of commercial banks into new markets, such as risk management, unrestricted because unknown, and relaxation of regulatory interpretation of restrictions implied in the law, has unleashed commercial bank competition with investment banks which is in part responsible for the creative competition and stimulus for innovation which has made American securities firms among the best in the world. The successes of US financial institutions in securities markets in some ways reflects the breakdown of regulatory segmentation of securities firms' and commercial banks' markets.

Bank Holding Company Act

The Bank Holding Company Act and amendments represented Congress' efforts to prevent commercial bank control of the economy through large size and control of non-financial firms. The unintended effect was to protect insurance companies and their inefficient sales structure relying heavily on independent insurance agents. This strong lobbying force used its large numbers to restrict bank competition in the sale of insurance products, producing one of the most egregious inefficiencies in US financial services markets. Sales and distribution of insurance have until recently been dominated by independent agents who charged extremely high sales commissions. The unintended effect of restrictions on bank holding companies has been the stifling of competition in an important insurance market.

Controlling Speculation

Speculation is considered by many to be an evil. Critics of speculation believe that speculators gain by others' mistakes, that speculators do not create real value, and that speculators can create over inflated or over depressed prices and profit from illusory bubbles or crashes. However, economists know that speculators perform a real economic service in bearing economic risks on behalf of producers and consumers who would rather not worry about future prices or rates. Furthermore, speculation is not just performed by flamboyant individuals with instantaneous access to sensitive financial markets. Every importer who delays payment, or every manufacturer who stores large inventories, is speculating. In the United States, as in China, speculation has a bad reputation and policies have been implemented to control speculation. Nearly all of these efforts have proven to be mistakes.

Margin Requirements

After the Stock Market Crash of 1929, following a presumed speculative bubble, the Federal Reserve was authorized to control the purchase of securities on credit. These restrictions remain, although they are not often important. The reason that these restrictions are not too important today is that it became clear in the past that use of margin requirements to control "speculative" activity was itself a source of enormous market risk. Furthermore, there were present among market participants, principally brokers, exchanges, and their customers, incentives to provide less intrusive controls on excessive use of credit for securities purchases.

One very real problem from efforts to control speculation was caused by policy-makers' confusion about margin requirements on other financial instruments, like futures contracts, in contrast to margin for purchases financed partly by credit. Credible commitments in futures contracts may require a performance bond guaranteeing performance on the contract in the future, but they do not represent an advance of credit when a contract is made. Exchanges and brokers know this, yet some policy-makers were convinced in 1987 that futures contracts margins had to be made uniform with stock market margins, even though they are two entirely different things. Control of margin requirements cannot control speculation, even if controlling speculation were a desirable policy objective. Policy induced changes in margin requirements can disrupt markets and limit their usefulness to the economy.

Prohibited Instruments: Put Options

Concerns about speculation have led to strange policies. For example, when the Securities and Exchange Commission (SEC) authorized trading in call option contracts, it chose not authorize put option trading. But by deciding that put options were "more speculative", the market was made less efficient because risk-takers were less able to tailor their price risk. Furthermore, options are not used exclusively or even predominantly for speculation. They are widely used to reduce risk. The use of options to shift and tailor risk exposure has been one of the most important developments in modern financial markets. These developments occurred, however, in spite of at times serious resistance by regulators and firms specializing in the trading of traditional financial instruments.

Control of Financial Channels and Design of Financial System

Government policy makers often believe that they can plan a financial system. US experience suggests that planning does not work—markets work too fast. For example, the Banking Acts of the 1930s prevented the payment of interest on demand (transaction) accounts and limited payment of interest on savings accounts. The reason given for these regulatory authorities was to prevent cutthroat competition that weakened banks. The result was far different: banks were forced to compete using variables other than interest rates. Many analysts believe that the overinvestment in branches by banks in the United States was the result of competition for deposits in the form of service and convenience rather than in the form of the (more efficient) payment of interest. The real cost of this overinvestment is now being paid by banks as they consolidate though mergers and acquisitions.

One example of US government influence on the structure of the financial system reflects the commitment to provide low-cost financing for home purchases. An entire system of deposit-taking charters, for federal thrift institutions, and regulatory and support structure, the Federal Home Loan Bank System, was founded to funnel savings into home financing. This structure grew to be nearly as large as the banking system over the period of the 1930's to the 1980's, when it collapsed. The result of the was indeed an enormous flow of savings into home ownership, but also underdiversified and fragile financial institutions like thrifts, which were required to invest 82% of their assets in home mortgages. Another result was a large federal bureaucracy which depended on satisfying its constituents in the thrift industry through subsidized services, credit, and forceful representation to lawmakers. Needless to say, revision of the thrift industry became a political issue and took much longer to achieve than if left to unrestricted economic forces.

What is particularly interesting about such efforts to control or design parts of a financial system is that they create their own rigidities, making it hard to remove the distortions. For example, academic policy makers urged the removal of deposit interest-rate ceilings for decades (starting with the Commission on Money and Credit in 1954) before inflation and high unregulated market interest rates forced the issue in the 1980s. Even then, entrenched interests, such as banks and savings and loans benefiting from low-cost deposits relative to market rates, made elimination of the market restrictions designed by policy-makers a difficult process. Only in 1982 did real interest-rate competition break out among deposit-taking institutions in the United States. And then, it was a difficult adjustment for thrifts and added to the earnings difficulties they had with their policy-induced historical commitment to low-return mortgage assets.

Economic forces will strain against barriers to competition or restrictions on fair returns. Interest-rate restrictions were untenable in the 1980s. When rates were finally freed, financial institutions had to make adjustments in a disastrously short time period, rather than gradually developing their abilities to deal with changing market conditions over a longer time period. If interest rates had not been regulated, and portfolios not restricted, deposit-taking institution officials would have learned through relatively painless trial-and-error rather than through catastrophic short-term changes.

Relevance of US Experience to Current Developments in Chinese Financial Markets

Because of vast differences between China and the United States and the development of their financial systems, it would seem that there is little relevance of US experience to policy-making in China. This is not the case. Chinese economic development will depend on the provision of the six financial services, and it is the requirement that these services be supplied to the market which makes US lessons applicable to China. In this discussion, we have maintained the topic outline from above, to stress the problems facing China in the future evolution of its financial system which parallel challenges facing US policy-makers in the 1980's.

Of course, the main difference between China and the United States is in the dominance of state ownership of assets in China. This includes the banks. Furthermore, previous Chinese policy in terms of designing a financial system raised banks to a prominence never seen in the United States. Banks are nearly the exclusive repository of household savings in China. In the United States, insurance and securities investments have always been important alternatives to bank deposits as savings. Furthermore, the US has always had competitive financial markets, with many firms offering of all financial services in protected by nonetheless competitive markets.

The role of state-owned banks in China remains dominant despite recent efforts to redefine the role of some of the banks as commercial banks and others as "policy banks" performing government functions. There has been very little progress in converting Chinese banks, and the vast household deposits they hold, into a free and competitive banking system. For example, recent policy initiatives promoting growth in China in the summer and autumn of 1998 (to achieve the officially adopted target growth rate of 8% for the year 1998) has been accompanied by directives to the banks to increase their lending to money-losing state-owned enterprises (SOEs). This policy demonstrates the key role banks play in China in gathering savings and allocating those savings to state-favored investments.

Financial Guarantees

The importance of deposits as the only significant means of household savings means that allowing banks to fail when their assets, primarily loans to SOEs, go bad, would be accompanied by enormous political costs as households' most important assets were threatened. Allowing banks to fail is felt by most China observers to be a cost too large to be borne by the Chinese government. This leaves policy-makers with only a few alternatives, all of which interfere with efficient investment and economic growth in China. SOEs will probably not be allowed to fail to the extent that economic reality dictates that banks will not be forced to fail. If depositors' confidence in bank deposits erodes because of awareness of bad SOE loans, the state will no doubt be tempted guarantee the liabilities of the bank. Policy-makers will certainly be tempted by a "hide and grow" policy consisting of implicit, or as below, explicit state commitments of support for banks, and policies promoting growth of SOEs with the hope that they can be solvent by becoming larger. Banks may be encouraged to diversify in order to derive profits from new and unfamiliar businesses, such as riskier lending to high potential return projects, in order to grow out of the bad-debt problems.

Government underwritten deposit insurance is a policy which may someday tempt Chinese policy makers. The large portfolios of non-performing state-owned enterprise (SOE) loans in Chinese bank portfolios will make deposits at those institutions less desirable than other forms of savings which would emerge in partially regulated and informal markets, such as deposits or notes from non-banks or newly chartered banks. To prevent the deposit withdrawals which could force recognition of bad loans at existing banks, government officials will be tempted to insure the old bank deposits. Chinese policy makers should resist the temptation to try to paper over the real economic losses of SOEs to delay the reckoning of those losses through policies discouraging deposit withdrawals by implementing deposit insurance. The incentive effects of deposit insurance, in view of US experience, could unleash further risky expansion of insured banks at the cost of more productive investments elsewhere in the economy.

No doubt when the insolvency of one or more large banks becomes too much to paper over with regulatory forbearance on capital and asset quality, officials will be tempted to use extreme measures to postpone closure and liquidation because of the banks' enormous size and importance to household savings. Desperate combinations of large, sick institutions, such as that observed in the United States in the late 1980s, may well be tolerated and encouraged by regulators. Further, as the losses accumulate, the ultimate cost of the required restructuring will mount. Given current estimates of the non-performing loans on the balance sheets of Chinese banks, the ultimate losses could be an enormous cost relative to the size of the Chinese economy. The costs are growing daily.

Segmentation

Chinese financial institutions are not as segmented by regulation as US financial institutions simply because bank deposits are already so important that other means of savings and sources of financial services are minor factors in the markets. However, there may well be a temptation in the future for Chinese policy-makers to limit the products and services offered by non-bank financial intermediaries when the inevitable banking crisis occurs. When deposit-taking institutions appear unsafe to Chinese savers, to prevent deposit runs and disintermediation, tempting stop-gap measures such as those observed in the US financial crisis may be considered to limit non-banks' ability to compete with banks. These measures will likely result in more financial market segmentation to protect against widespread deposit withdrawals. For example, in the United States, banks were allowed to offer insured deposits which competed with money-market mutual funds in terms of rates but had government insurance, limiting the attraction of managed funds to savers.

The attractiveness of many savings instruments depends on how readily they can be converted to cash for payments purposes. Non-banks were denied direct access to the payments system in the United States through Glass-Steagall prohibitions of brokers and investment banks, who offered money market funds as a substitute for deposits to wealthy households, from operating banks which could provide transaction accounts. While fund managers were able to get around these prohibitions by forming alliances with banks, this was possible in the United States because of the large number of financial institutions competing in the financial markets. In China, prohibiting access to the payments system to limit the attractiveness of non-bank savings instruments would be easy to adopt and enforce because of the small number of institutions.

Given the dominance of deposits in household savings, a critical issue in China will be whether policy-makers will allow the development of alternative savings instruments offered by non-banks. The pattern in the Asian Crisis economies was to limit the development of savings instruments that are an alternative to bank deposits, such as debt securities. In the United States, the development of securities markets and mutual funds was advanced by the 1980s, therefore policies to limit the development of savings instruments alternative to bank and thrift deposits could not be too effective. There was little regulators could do to stop funds from moving out of deposit-taking institutions. In China, on the other hand, securities markets and managed funds are fledgling activities. If banks weaken notably such that the willingness of savers to hold deposits erodes, Chinese policy-makers may be tempted to reduce the danger by segmenting markets and limiting competition from non-banks for household savings.

In the end, a policy stunting the development of securities markets could make the ultimate resolution of the banking crisis more costly. In the United States, active securities markets were used to sell pools of bad assets from banks and thrifts in the form of asset-backed securities in the 1980's. These instruments allowed sick or failed institution assets to be sold for higher prices than would be the case in tedious negotiated sales. The use of non-performing loans to crease asset-backed securities created liquidity in the markets. The development of markets in distressed assets reduced the costs of resolving the financial crisis. If, on the other hand, securities markets are not developed enough to absorb distressed assets stemming from deposit-taking institution failures, the liquidation of failed firms will be slower and more costly. More importantly, the restoration of liquidity for the further development of a healthy financial system offering the full range of services will be delayed or made impossible.

Controlling Speculation

In China, futures markets have been closed several times due to excessive "speculative" activity. The fact that some traders may make large profits from a change in expectations should not obscure the value of trading in instruments which can be used not only to speculate but also to hedge risk. The US experience suggests that efforts to control speculative markets either diminishes their value to the economy or forces them to close or move elsewhere. One of the most important roles of financial markets is creating liquidity. Closing any market because of fears of speculative fever is very costly to the effective functioning of the financial system both in terms of the specific market interruption and the impact the policy has on investors' confidence that other markets will remain open and liquid.

The main reason to control speculation is to prevent unexpected losses to naïve investors, especially those presumed to be most subject to speculative fevers. Market participants in emerging market economies must learn, however, that there is no such thing as a sure thing. Risk exists in all economies and cannot be eliminated by government policy. Financial markets serve to distribute and price risk. The bursting of speculative bubbles is a necessary experience to make risk a compelling part of savers' calculation, not only in emerging markets but in established markets. Limitations on speculation also limits the ability of investors to hedge risks stemming from their balance sheets or operating activities. Yet experience in the United States suggests that it is very difficult, if not impossible, to tell the difference between speculators and hedgers. Restrictions on speculation can be very costly to the functioning of financial markets.

Why then do policy-makers try to control speculation? For example, in China, the hysteria and riots experienced in some cities recently when stock market vouchers were rationed was felt to justify limiting the issuance of new securities. The argument was that demand for these high-risk securities was not rational. But is it not rational for investors to invest in highly risky, positive expected return securities, i.e. speculative securities, when real returns on alternatives like bank deposits are low or negative in real terms? In other words, policy makers may be tempted to restrict investor activity in the name of controlling speculation when in fact the purpose is to limit the competition for investment funds to favored instruments, such as bank deposits.

Control of Financial Channels and Design of Financial System

The temptation to design a rational financial system is not limited to economies with a tradition of central planning. In the United States, as discussed above, certain markets and activities were favored by the design of the regulatory system, producing imbalances and rigidities which contributed to the bank and thrift crisis of the late 1980's. The key point about financial systems is that they evolve in response to needs of the economy to the extent they are not restricted. Confining savings flows to certain channels to promote favored investments, like housing in the United States or export industries as in Korea, have the effect of creating imbalances and bottlenecks.

Stiff regulation may control or influence market forces and savings flows for indefinite time periods, but pressures will build up against inefficiencies and price controls which make the ultimate adjustments more costly. For example, thrift institution mortgage portfolios were extremely sensitive to changes in the term structure. Lawmakers created a system of interest-rate controls in the 1960s and 1970s to protect thrifts from market forces. These controls were unsustainable in the high-interest rate 1980s and were short-circuited by market innovations. Thrifts failed as a result of not having developed flexible portfolios and not having learned to deal with term-structure risk. The Korean banks excessive loans to *chaebols* is another example of imbalances coming from designing a financial system to serve specific purposes, in the case major industrial development. At the same time, newer, smaller and more innovative businesses in Korea were starved for capital and the securities markets were stunted.

Chinese policy-makers cannot design an appropriate financial system for their economy. The task is too dynamic and too complex. By delaying the recognition of existing inefficiencies and losses, the costs of restructuring the system only increase. Moreover, the gains from an efficient financial system, providing each of the six financial services needed by the economy in the most efficient way, are lost. This means slower growth and less efficient allocation of savings.

It is true that the financial system which would emerge from uncontrolled Chinese development would be uniquely Chinese, reflecting China's history, culture, and legal environment. It would be responsive to the economic opportunities which only the Chinese understand completely. Institutions providing the six financial services could be very different than those observed in the United States or in other Asian countries. The system should be, to the extent possible considering real political concerns, allowed to evolve naturally. The economic forces which would shape the Chinese financial system should be allowed free play, and not be distorted or twisted by short-term policy objectives which in the long run increase the costs of adjustment and retard development.

Important Lessons from US Experience for China

We can summarize the important lessons to be learned from US experience. First, deposit-insurance and other financial guarantees relying on government's power are tempting for policy-makers facing a lack of confidence in financial institutions, specifically deposit-taking institutions, in order to calm investor concerns and avoid painful adjustments in the financial system. The temptation to use the power to tax to protect specific institutions is pervasive and invariably produces costly distortions in financial flows and management incentives. Second, market segmentation prevents healthy competition and creates barriers between financial markets that are inefficient but can be difficult to remove. Further, stifling the creation of innovative markets and instruments can increase the cost and retard the development of the financial system into its required role in a growing economy. Third, policy-makers' attempts to control presumed unhealthy economic activity such as speculation can have unintended effects reducing the flexibility and usefulness of financial markets. Finally, efforts to design and control financial systems through activity limitations and pricing controls can produce inefficient and wasteful policies on the part of financial institutions and markets and may be harder and more costly to remove after the accumulation of distortions and establishment of privileges over time.

What is the relevance of these lessons for China? First, China's financial system has not really evolved much: many of the implications of the US experience can be translated into a policy committed to few restrictions on financial institutions and their activities and a tolerance for experimentation and failures early in the development of the system. However, the main practical issue facing China's economy is the creation of financial institutions that can increase the provision of the six financial services to promote economic development and efficiency. The large problems resulting from historical evolution, namely large banks with large portfolios of low quality loans, cannot be eliminated by financial system design. These problems will be reduced in significance if they are not allowed to grow bigger and are allowed to decline in relative importance as the rest of the economy grows. Policies built on a strategy of delaying and hiding real economic inefficiencies, either by retaining funds in banks through deposit insurance and guaranteeing credits to SOEs, by designing special purpose institutions intended to solved specific policy problems, or by limiting competition and activities of financial institutions, delay the inevitable marking of bad assets to market values. More importantly, they deny China the important real benefits the full range of financial service required to develop a healthy financial system.

References

Barth, James R. 1991. *The Great Savings and Loan Debacle*. Washington, DC: The AEI Press.

Dietrich, J. Kimball. 1996. *Financial Services and Financial Institutions: Value Creation in Theory and Practice*. Engelwood Cliffs: Prentice-Hall.

Levine, Ross. 1997. "Financial Development and Economic Growth: Views and Agenda." XXXV(2):688-726.

Thakor, Anjan V. 1996. "The Design of Financial Systems: An Overview." *Journal of Banking and Finance* 20:917-948.

White, Lawrence J. 1991. *The S&L Debacle*. New York: Oxford University Press.

7
Political Power Transitions and Chinese Economic Policy

Brian Buford-Efird

Introduction[1]

An extensive theoretical and empirical discussion examines the relationship between the relative power of nations and the initiation of war in the international relations literature. Power transition theory suggests a dynamic relationship between actors in the interstate system, in which a number of factors cause variation in the relative power of nations over time. The opportunities to impose preferences on the world system are a function of a nation's power *vis-à-vis* the remaining set of global powers. When one nation is preponderant (i.e. strong enough to withstand an attack by any potential challenger) the rest of the world is ordered in that nation's best interests. Over time, the strongest nation's preeminence will wane, and the preferences of a new country will be asserted on the world. The dominant country can choose to step down from its perch of preeminence, or seek to prevent the rise of a nation with interests that do not correspond to its ideal vision of interstate relations. Similarly, the challenging nation can choose to alter interstate relations violently, competitively, or cooperatively once it has achieved preponderance. A broad literature has demonstrated strong empirical support for the initiation of war under conditions of parity between nations, and a strong set of formal arguments also serve as a logical foundation for this literature.[2]

The logical basis of this argument need not be restricted to analysis of interstate relations. The fundamental argument of this theory specifies the conditions that probabilistically increase the initiation of conflictual (or competitive) behavior, suggesting that the ability of actors with different preferences to assert themselves varies over time. The most powerful actor in a group will tend to have his or her preferences satisfied by the others, which generates dissatisfaction among the weaker actors and provides the motivation for conflict once a potential challenger is sufficiently powerful to defeat the preponderant opponent. Olson (1965) argues that collective action problems explain the absence of collective objections to the imposition of the leading actor's will — there is no unilateral incentive for any of the lesser actors to oppose their opponent's viewpoints. Over time, however, the power of the preponderant actor will erode relative to one or more of its former lackeys as its scheme to remain most powerful inevitably fails. The power transition literature addresses the obvious question if we can observe such a transition in power: how will each of these actors react to conditions of parity and overtaking?

This chapter applies power transition theory to the domestic decision making environment in China. In particular, the rate at which politicians discount the future and hence the type of policies pursued, varies based on perceived threats to their political survival. A leader is most powerful when she or he is assured of remaining in office indefinitely. Parity in political power (*vis-à-vis* a potential opponent, e.g. a rival politician or rival regional power center) implies the greatest probability of a leader losing control of a country or of resources, whereas asymmetry implies relative comfort in office. As in the power transition literature on war, this chapter suggests that conflict is mostly likely to ensue once the parity condition is fulfilled. Preponderance of a politician, his or her party, or their particular governmental group ensures the relative absence of conflict.

In the domestic political environment, politicians try to maximize their stay in office. At parity they must focus on immediate threats to their power, using whatever tools are at their disposal. The time horizon with which leaders view the implications of policy choices narrows to the immediate future when faced with extreme and rapidly growing threats to power. Under conditions of asymmetry, they can focus on policies that ensure their survival in the long-term, which generally tend to be policy decisions with widely enjoyed benefits such as a healthy economy, a careful fiscal, or an apolitical monetary policy. An unbridled (read irresponsible) fiscal policy might distribute a lot of rents and create popularity in the short-term, but have deleterious consequences in the longer term. Similarly, monetary policy, and specifically in China the ability for the local governments to distribute more and bigger loans to constituent business interests, might be politically-desirable in the short term but have negative consequences for lending in the long term. The perception of a stable status quo can produce policies and options which are hoped to be favorable to the dominance of the leader's party, peers, and heirs. The execution of policies that elicit more stable support over the long term — in this case restricted to growth-enhancing or economically-healthy decisions — ironically allows opponents to gain in strength.

China has traditionally been a planned economy, but has made dramatic moves to open up its financial markets to market forces since 1984. In particular, the government has, at least in spirit, tried to create an independent central bank that is unmotivated by political concerns. However, it appears that instead it has ceded an increasing degree of political control over monetary policy to local and regional governments in China. While an apolitical monetary policy is more likely to reflect economic necessities rather than political concerns, the central government has responded with a more short term focus, suggesting a threat to its power by local and regional governments. Indeed, Bueno de Mesquita, Newman, and Rabushka (1996) predict that competition between central and local powers is likely to involve intense conflicts over the coming years as the power of local governments increases. They suggest that a number of issues between central and local authorities, both political and economic, will remain unresolved and increasingly drive regionally-dispersed tensions. This chapter suggests that the distribution of local-central power has been shifting, at least since 1983, in favor of the local governments.

Power transition theory treats convergence of relative power as a timing game (Alsharabati and Kugler 1997, Powell 1996). The question for such models is *when* conflict will occur, and the *degree* to which it will occur. At the very least, such models suggest when leaders will be most likely to engage in clearly *politicized* policy-making, and when they are most likely to engage in policies that accrue long-term benefits to the population. The intent may be more sustainable policies, but the success of such attempts will vary from actor to actor based on any number of factors. As mentioned above, the important point is that economically *damaging* policies are less likely to be pursued when few political threats are perceived.

The layout of this chapter is as follows. The next section surveys the literature on political business cycles and begins to apply them, in the context of power transition theory, to the Chinese case. The third section applies power transition theory to the apparent competition between local and central actors in the determination of Chinese economic policy, and in particular the allocation of bank credit. The fourth section seeks to understand the reason for such changes in the distribution of power in China. The final section concludes the discussion.

Political Business Cycles in China

The political business cycle provides a framework for the more general model suggested by this chapter. The literature's application is restricted to democratic societies, since the fundamental argument of is that short-term economic fluctuations are tied to electoral cycles. To be precise, the term "political business cycle" should only be applied to a narrow set of the broader literature I am referring to. As suggested by Feng (1997), the primary distinguishing characteristic between the models suggested in this field revolves around assumptions of rationality and partisanship of key actors involved in the process.

In the classic political business cycle formulation, Nordhaus (1975) argues that governments utilize the short-term effects of a Phillips curve to generate preelectoral booms, and will reduce inflation with postelectoral contractionary policy. Over time, little empirical evidence has supported his model (Alesina 1995, Mueller 1990). In the Rational Political Business Cycle formulation, Rogoff (1990) and Persson and Tabellini (1990) suggest that voters are playing a game in which they asses the economic competence of policy makers by evaluating economic performance (voters must distinguish between cyclic/exogenous variations and economic mishandling). In the Partisan formulation, Hibbs (1987) argues that different types of voters select different parties, based on their preferences. In turn, parties identify themselves with a particular set of policies (the left associates itself with and is willing to move more toward policies attempting to obtain full employment, while the right applies the same effort at obtaining zero inflation). In the Rational Partisan formulation (Alesina 1995, Alesina and Sachs 1988), voters forecast an average of the expected policy output of both parties (weighted by the probability of each party winning the election). Victory by the left is associated with a short-term economic boom, as the expectations allow for the government to take advantage of a Phillips curve relationship in while economic expectations adjust to the new policy environment, while victory by the right is associated with a short-term contraction for the opposite reason.

This basic outline of the literature suggests a few conclusions relevant to the present discussion. The primary difference between China and the countries addressed by this literature is an institutional constraint on policy makers that is inherent in democracies, namely elections. The distinguishing characteristic of a stable democracy is that elections are the only time a political actor can be removed from office.[3] In non-democracies, removal can come any time that the power of opponent is sufficient to initiate a coup or irregular government change. The arguments concerning how politicians respond to threats, and how the public views politicians in a system without elections, are largely unchanged. Immediate threats to political power incite immediate solutions. The public's support for politicians is balanced between the short term acquisition of rents and their assessment of the leader's long term ability to continue this supply of rents (the rational political business cycle's notion of competence). A more general conception of the political business cycle argument is provided by power transition theory.

The assumptions of the political business cycle literature are reflected in power transition theory: politicians maximize political support, voters (or in China's case the politically-active public) and politicians are rational and select what they perceive to be an optimal set of policies, and the public updates beliefs based on observed behavior. More importantly, political agents are motivated by temporally competing concerns. On the one hand, they are concerned with their survival and prosperity in the short term. In democracies, this means that they are concerned with winning the next election. In non-democracies there are not clearly identifiable and institutionalized opportunities for a change in power, so that politicians are constantly worried about the potential for a non-institutional change in government control. The question they face is then how to maximize power in the short term? One common argument is that support can be purchased through the strategic use of fiscal policy: transfers, tax breaks, social programs designed to benefit specific constituents, and patronage-based hiring patterns to name a few examples. In a planned economy, such policies are easily embedded in the government's scheme for the economy. Areas where support needs to be shored up are allocated a higher proportion of government resources and attention. In a transitional economy, this becomes more difficult as market forces place some limits on purely-political actions. The case of most Latin American nations demonstrate that the use of economic policy to compensate for losses of political power, which are unavoidable during a transition to a market economy, may often times derail attempts at economic reform by dispersing power toward competitors (Ames 1987).

On the other hand, politicians also have more long-term interests. If one is to be reelected in a democracy, or even kept in power over a long period of time in a non-democracy, the issue of providing a stable political and economic environment becomes important. People are happy if they have a job (full employment) and their wages enable them to purchase the goods they desire (growing wages and stable prices)—this argument in particular is reminiscent of the political business cycle/electoral cycle literature. Particularly in Latin America, there is a widespread public sentiment in favor of a growing economy (Geddes 1994). The problem is that growth-enhancing policies require a direct tradeoff with the types of policies that provide immediate political gains. To reduce inflation, the fiscal deficit needs to be lowered (Arbetman and Kugler 1995). To construct a productive bureaucracy so that policies may be effectively executed and selected based on their economic potential, merit-based hiring approaches need to replace patronage-based hiring practices (Geddes 1994). Geddes' aptly articulated "politician's dilemma" is the tension between the desire to reconcile short-term electoral concerns with the generation of widely shared benefits. When push comes to shove, individuals prefer immediate payouts to a sacrifice in the interest of some future collectively enjoyed benefits (Ramseyer and Rosenbluth 1993, Olson 1965). Politicians recognize this and act accordingly.

The fundamental assumption of this chapter is that political agents are concerned with one thing: maximization of political power. How do they actualize this goal? The common answer is by staying in office. This is accomplished by some combination of the policies alluded to in the previous paragraph. Incentives and opportunities are a function of the change in political power of the key actors over time. What do I mean by political power? In the context of this chapter, a political agent is most powerful in a democracy when she or he can expect to remain in office for the duration of their elected term and receive 100% of the vote in the next election. In a non-democracy, a politician is most powerful when there are few or no viable challengers to power and the public provides near-complete support for her or his policies. To put it simply, political power is directly related to the quantity of public support. In this sense, political power refers to the ability to ignore: (1) satisfying constituent concerns to generate support, (2) the necessity of building extra-governmental coalitions, and (3) garnering of votes for the next election, if a democracy (notice that there are no claims made about the ability of such an agent to push through reforms in the legislature or political system itself). Since politicians compete against each other for a finite quantity of votes, the gains of one politician generally come at the expense of another — in a concrete sense they are zero sum (rather than constantly increasing in scale, as in the parity literature on war). In a democratic polity, support may vary over the course of tenure, but the only institutionalized threat to power emerges during election years. At election time, the more politically powerful candidate will win (assuming that the elections and votes are a perfect indicator of public support).[4] Thus, as suggested by the political business cycle/electoral cycle literature, a strong short-term incentive exists during these years to generate even greater levels of political support through the use of irresponsible policy. Individuals who are politically powerful can ignore the relative gains of their opponents since they are assured of support come the next election. Unfortunately for the popular politician, political power can be a very fleeting asset.

Political agents vary in their level of support over time. When a political agent is assured of being provided with the short-term political support that is required for reelection, and has few threats to their power in the foreseeable future, they are more likely to institute reforms that provide a public good (i.e. growth-enhancing policies, the hiring of technically knowledgeable and capable bureaucrats, etc.). However, when faced with an immediate political threat, whether in the form of a potential military coup or intraparty defection, they resort to the short-term solution: buying support through hiring processes, transfers, subsidizing projects, and economic policy (Ames 1987).

The timing of such events is critical. If we assume that presidential candidates compete against each other, and that political parties compete against each other for a majority in the legislature, then we would expect them to anticipate a change in the distribution of their power. Without formalizing my intuitive assessment of the situation, I can draw only loose conclusions. The anticipation of parity should provide an incentive for the preponderant actor to preempt an overtaking with politically-driven fiscal policy.[5] However, politicians cannot always account for threats to their tenure. Loosening the assumption of certainty, a fast political power transition means that political agents face quick changes in public opinion, which should be more difficult to track than incremental changes in support — unless there are clear signals of emerging public dissatisfaction (e.g. riots, mass protests, etc.).[6] Slower transitions are easier to deal with — policy can be more effectively geared to generate support if given the time. Additionally, a more healthy mix of long-term growth-enhancing policies and myopic fiscal policy is likely. If given more time to produce substantive results, the rate at which the politicians discount the future would probably diminish. In stable democracies, then, more healthy economic policy is likely since the immediacy of political threats are institutionally limited.

The type of groups competing may vary from country to country. Institutional constraints condition the type of political coalitions that are formed. For example, the closed list system in Venezuela helps maintain party competition and the predominance of a single party in electoral politics over time (Geddes 1994). The same is true, for different reasons, with the relative unity and dominance of the LDP in Japan and the PRI in Mexico. The United States and other democratic policies are dominated by two-party competition— alternating control of the government over the course of many years and many elections. China is a particularly interesting case. There should be competing interests at the national level, as different politicians draw on different portions of the population for support and thus reflect the different concerns. In small countries, the central government can keep a close on the affairs of individual cities since it need not concern itself with the broad variations in policy and phenomena that come when a nation spans almost an entire continent. Because China is such a large country, the central government must attempt to create policies that are relatively uniform, but also recognize that different regions of the country will have different demands and variations in their ability to force their demands. The collapse of the Soviet Union demonstrates the dangers of maintaining a large, planned economy. The power of all regions may become such that the central government can no longer retain control. Thus, the central Chinese government must not only contend with national competition for power but also with a variety of subnational opponents.

The variety of implications generated by the myriad possible combination of electoral rules and institutional constraints is a troublesome barrier to the generalization of such a theory. This is particularly the case when the only real consistent empirical observations, across both democratic and non-democratic polities, are discrete events such as a change in regime or governmental control. As Sanders (1981) suggests, political stability and instability are "relative tendencies, not discrete states." However, the logic of this argument highlights some of the potential pitfalls for market economies, and in particular for transitional economies. The creation of a market system does not eliminate the political influences on economic policy, it merely shifts the timing of challenges to power and places some limits on the ability of opponents to alter policy.

Power and Chinese Economic Policy

Forster and Tam (1990) argue that centralism has been the dominant mindset governing the Chinese state since 1949. They suggest that trends toward decentralization or regionalism have historically been the result of short-term responses to economic and political crises. For example, in 1956 Mao Zedong decentralized economic power to local party committees in response to economic crisis as a prelude to the Great Leap Forward. In the early 1970s, investment projects were regionally dispersed to contend with short-term strategic threats to central power. However, the degree of decentralization since Mao's death in 1976 has been more dramatic.

FIGURE 7.1 Relative Political Extraction of China, 1960-1991

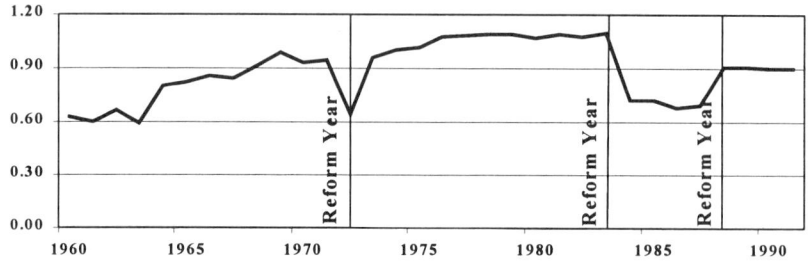

Source: Arbetman and Kugler (1997)

Figure 7.1 traces the China's Relative Political Extraction (RPE) from 1960 to 1991. RPE measures the ability of the central government to extract resources, in this case taxes, from its population, and is based on the notion that a more powerful government can extract a greater proportion of resources than a less powerful government (Arbetman and Kugler 1997). Thus, higher RPE scores suggest a more powerful government. Note that this score suggests a fairly large drop in central government power from 1983 to 1984.[7] Hafer and Kutan (1994) indicate that prior to the 1984, the State Council controlled macroeconomic policy in China and set it according to national concerns, yet reforms in that year are associated with a dispersion of government power to local power centers (more on this in the next section). Moreover, Ma (1996) indicates that before 1983 investment was not driven by bank loans, but rather was driven by central government expenditures. Thus, monetary policy more clearly reflected the interest of the central government primary to the 1984 reform, which marks a dramatic shift in financial and monetary policymaking of China. The theoretical perspective adopted by this chapter suggests that this dispersion of economic decision making power can be explained by a relative gain in power by political opponents. In particular, local power centers seem to have become more powerful at this time than ever before.

Table 7.1 traces the expenditures of the central and local governments from 1953 to 1994. While these data do not necessarily measure the relative power of the central and local governments, it is likely that they reflect the underlying power dynamic to some degree, such that the more powerful set of actors are more likely to spend more government money. In 1982, the local government begins to exceed the central government expenditures and by 1984 the differential in expenditures begins to shift even more dramatically. By 1994 this amount the asymmetry present in 1953-57 has reversed. Now, the critical point to be extracted from these data is that a change in the distribution of power between center and regions appears to be taking place. As this chapter will contend, the regional governments are increasingly provided the ability to manipulate the central bank and monetary policy during this transition in power. The shift from a wholly-planned monetary policy to a pseudo-independent central bank has not created a politically-shielded monetary policy. Indeed, even the Bundesbank, commonly considered to be the most independent central bank in the world, is subject to political manipulation (Alesina, Cohen, and Roubini 1992). The issue is merely *which* political concerns tend to influence its policies. In China, it appears that the local governments play an increasingly important role.

TABLE 7.1 Total Expenditures of Central and Local Governments in China (in 100,000,000 yuan)

Year	Central Expenditures	Local Expenditures
1953-57	997.3	348.4
1958-62	1101.6	1187.1
1963-65	718.9	486.1
1966-70	1538.0	980.5
1971-75	2125.1	1794.3
1976-80	2590.2	2657.2
1981	602.2	512.8
1982	575.1	578.2
1983	642.5	649.9
1984	738.7	807.7
1985	836.5	1008.2
1986	962.3	1368.6
1987	1031.9	1416.2
1988	1060.4	1646.2
1989	1105.2	1935.0
1990	1372.8	2079.4
1991	1517.7	2295.8
1992	1817.9	2571.8
1993	1957.2	3330.2
1994	1754.4	4038.2

Source: *China Statistical Yearbook*, various years

Cardoso and Yusuf (1994) and Naughton (1991) argue that Chinese inflation, especially in the late 1980s, was caused primarily by government budget deficits. Chang and Hou (1997), on the other hand, claim that much of the inflation experienced by China has been structural. Their claim is that prices tend to be distorted in a planned economy, and that in China food tends to be underpriced while other products have tended to be overpriced.[8] Feltenstein and Ha (1991) argue that the government increasingly has responded to "true" inflation with price controls since 1979. The government must coordinate prices and monetary policy in a planned or transitional economy since the market does not equilibrate them, so their finding implies that some decisions are being made with less political motivation. This change suggests that, at least in terms of the central government's fiscal policy, a more long-term view has been accepted.

In 1992, the Party officially noted that a market system was not incompatible with the ideals of socialism. The proposed economic system for China was a socialist market economy, implying central planning over an economy that is largely governed by market forces. The plan that was outlined for this new system included financial reform, intended to create efficient financial markets and strengthen the central bank's abilities to conduct macroeconomic management with monetary policy (Mehran and Quintyn 1996). The intent seems to be a more healthy economic policy for the most part, yet the central government has still made concessions to local powers.

The People's Bank of China (PBC) is the central bank as well as the main commercial bank. Yu (1997) identifies three tools that the PBC uses to control monetary policy. It provides the overall credit plan, provides loans to banks throughout the country, and sets the nation's interest rates. His analysis finds that the PBC generally and successfully used periods of tight monetary control to manage economic overheating and slow growth in industrial output, retail sales, and prices since 1977. However, the effectiveness of its policies declined in the 1990's because of erosion of the bank-credit control system. The overall credit ceiling is jointly determined by the central government's growth target and bargaining between the central and local banks.

Ma (1996) contructs a central-local game that explains why local governments force inflationary monetary policy, suggesting that the central bank does not have central control. He contends that politically-motivated monetary policy has caused macroeconomic instability. Ma also identifies three tools with which the central bank can control monetary policy but analyzes them in a different light. First, it uses reserve rates to control monetary policy. Such a tool can be changed to control the quantity of funds available to local/specialized banks, but is ineffective because they must keep excess reserves. Second, the central bank can control interest rates, which affects demand for credit as intended, but is ultimately ineffective because, due to the credit plans, lending is insensitive to the interest rate for state-run businesses.

Finally, the central bank uses credit plans to designate credit ceilings intended to limit loans to local and regional banks. This tool, more than any other, reflects the degree of newfound local power. The State Council, in cooperation with the State Planning Commission and the central bank, formulates the actual credit plan. Then the money supply for the next year is forecasted by the central bank based on various macroeconomic indicators, providing the basis for a tentative credit plan. Specialized banks are informed of this plan and allocate quotas and deposit targets to provincial, regional, and local banks, who in turn construct their own credit plans. These plans are then transmitted to the specialized banks, aggregated, and then passed back on to the central banks to finalize the overall credit plan — providing the local banks with a lot of flexibility to manipulate the credit quotas. Moreover, Ma (1996) contends that the planned figures are repeatedly revised upwards during the course of the year as local banks exceed the credit targets. The central bank is hamstrung by such action because it is required by the central government to ensure proper funding is allocated to certain essential projects around the country. Since the local banks know that essential projects must be maintained at particular credit levels, they are able to allocate the quantity of loans within the targeted limits to non-essential projects of political importance to the local government, and then rely on the central bank to increase the credit limits so that the essential projects may also be funded.

The changes wrought by the local governments do not end there. Ma (1995a, 1995b) argues that decentralization of the Chinese market system has shifted power to the local governments, which they have in turn used to restrict competition. This suggests the stake that local governments have in local and regional businesses. In most cases, the largest economic powers in a region also control the government, so that the economic interests of the primary corporate players in a particular region control both market relations and the distribution of credit. The shift in decision making power allows local governments to more adequately provide for local businesses, shoring up their political power and support.

Political Power Transitions in China

What has caused this shift of power from the central to local governments? Fleisher and Chen (1997), and Feng and Zhang in this volume, find that the coastal provinces have a higher level of productivity than the noncoastal provinces because they have a higher investment in education and higher foreign direct investment. Some of the more profitable regions in the country were among the first to experience near-free market conditions. The concentration of capital in those regions has created a large and powerful industrial and commercial sector that does not answer to the central government to the degree that traditionally-planned state-owned enterprises have. The interests of economic powers in such regions thus varies from the policies prescribed by the central government. Local governments, to remain in power, must represent the interests of their business constituents. When provided the opportunity by a change in their relative power *vis-à-vis* the central government, local politicians should, and have, push for greater control over policy. To date, the transition in power has produced largely-peaceful transfers of control. The Soviet Union has demonstrated how such a national-local competition may produce more intense conflicts, so that the Chinese government has a continuing incentive to peaceably manage their relationship with all localities.[9] Ironically, the opportunity for challenging central power, however, has come because of the very policies taken by the government to allow long term growth. As the market increasingly governs economic relations, the central government in China should increasingly lose its grasp on power. Opposition groups will have more frequent opportunities to affect policy when they are no longer subject to detailed central planning. How China manages its transition to a market economy will determine to a large degree the continued viability of it as a single nation.

For example, whereas many authors contend that the money supply in China is driven by output growth (Walker 1989; Feltenstein and Ha 1991; Chen, Deavers, and Wang 1992), Ma (1996) contends that price increases are driven by expectations of government announcements of price reforms, which creates an expectation of high prices by the public and results in a short-term in the purchase of goods, in turn causing the government to increase the money supply. As inflation becomes managed more effectively, this particular tool of central government support-generation becomes eroded. The PBC literature suggests that a Phillips curve can be used to generate short term support. This ability is present even in a democratic, market economy such as the US, so the power to sway public opinion will not be eliminated. However, the degree to which the central government can control such policies will be limited. More importantly, potential opponents, such as local governments, can a firmer grasp on manipulating such policies for their own purposes. Thus, one consequence of reform to a market economy is less control over the economy by the central government so that local governments necessarily become more powerful. The exercise of the preponderant power's attempts to ensure long term economic health thus undermine its hold on power. The question is then merely how it will contend with the increase in competition (Bueno de Mesquita, Newman, and Rabushka 1996).

Conclusions

This chapter utilizes power transition theory to explain competition between different actors in the Chinese economy. The political process in Chinese economic decision making is dynamic in that regional and local governments vary in their power over time, so that their ability and incentives to manipulate monetary policy vary as well. When power between competing regions or between the central and local governments is asymmetrically distributed, conflict is unlikely and the more powerful actor's preferences are likely to be adopted. In China, this has generally meant that the central government controls most aspect of economic policy. When power parity between actors is achieved, conflict is likely to emerge and the challenging actor is likely to use whatever tools available to affect monetary, or more broadly economic, policy in its favor. Since 1983, the local governments in China have gained an increasing degree of control over economic policy, and in particular the allocation of credit to local businesses. This chapter contends that such a process is an inevitable consequence of maximizing the long term interests of a healthy economy. Even in nations with an "independent" central bank, policy is subject to political concern. When a preponderant actor, such as the central government in China, seeks to promote long term interests, rents must be distributed much more broadly and in a much more sustainable manner. Competitors for power then have the opportunity to offer much more concentrated benefits to unhappy parties, and can increasingly vie for power as their foothold in the policy making arena is solidified. Many authors contend that China must transform itself to a market economy indeed much of this volume describes the advantages of such a transition. Such decisions come with a price, however. To create a stable economic environment over the long term, the central government in China must increasingly surrender its control over the country and necessarily make its political competitors more powerful.

Notes

1. The author would like to thank Yi Feng, Rebecca Buford-Efird, Gaspare Genna, and Siddharth Swaminathan for helpful comments and discussions on this chapter.
2. For the most recent review see Tammen, et al 2000.
3. This is not entirely true. The Clinton impeachment hearing in the US states suggests another potential method of removal from office. However, this a fairly rare occurrence and can be generally ignored by politicians as long as they place *some* restriction on the degree to which they politicize their decision making.
4. Clearly this may not always be the case. Elections can be rigged. Supporters may not actually come out to vote for their preferred candidate. Any number of factors may create a noisy correlation between voting outcomes and public support. That said, this chapter will assume that votes are a direct measure of public support.
5. Note that I am borrowing some terminology from the Parity approach to interstate war. Overtaking suggests that the weaker party is approaching (and will surpass) the majority party in strength. Parity suggests two parties that have equivalent political power. A transition refers to the period of time in which the change in relative political power drives the two (or more) parties toward parity.
6. This is consistent with the findings of the timing game presented in Alsharabati (1997) and Alsharabati and Kugler (1997).
7. Indeed, RPE is at its lowest point in ten years in 1984.
8. This reflects a common political motivation. The public tends to be happy when

it is fed, so that distorting food prices downward tends to be an important way to prevent or at least limit unrest and to maximize political power. If the costs of such policy can be absorbed over the long term, such a strategy may even be stable for many years, which appears to have been the case in China.

9. Of course, there are *many* differences between the Chinese and Soviet cases. The important point to extract is merely that the Soviet Union fell prey to a conflictual transition in power, which ultimately resulted in the dissolution of that country.

References

Alesina, A. 1995. "Elections, Party Structure, and the Economy." in J. Banks and E. Hanushek, eds., *Modern Political Economy*. Cambridge: Cambridge University Press.

Alesina, A., G. Cohen, and N. Roubini. 1992. "Macroeconomic Policy and Elections in OECD Democracies." in A. Cukierman, et al, eds., *Political Economy, Growth, and Business Cycles*. Cambridge: The MIT Press

Alesina, A., and J. Sachs. 1988. "Political Parties and the Business Cycle." *Journal of Money, Credit, and Banking* 20:63-82.

Alsharabati, C., and J. Kugler. 1997. "Dynamics of War Initiation." School of Politics and Economics, Claremont Graduate University. Paper Presented at the Annual Meeting of the American Political Science Association, Washington, D.C.

———. 1995. "The Politics of Inflation," in T. Willett, et al, eds. *Establishing Monetary Stability in Emerging Market Economies*. Boulder: Westview Press.

Ames, B. 1987. *Political Survival: Politicians and Public Policy in Latin America*. Berkeley: University of California Press.

Arbetman, M., and J. Kugler. 1997. *Political Capacity and Economic Behavior*. Denver: Westview Press.

Bueno de Mesquita, B., D. Newman, and A. Rabushka. 1996. *Red Flag Over Hong Kong*. Chatham: Chatham House.

Cardoso, E., and S. Yusuf. 1994. "Red Capital Growth and Inflation in China." *Challenge* May-June:49-56.

Chang, G., and J. Hou. 1997. "Structural Inflation and the 1994 Monetary Crisis in China." *Contemporary Economic Policy* 15(3):73-81.

Chen, M., R. Deaves, and C. Wang. 1992. "An Analysis of Money and Output in the Industrial Sector in China." *Journal of Asian Economy* 3(2):271-80.

Feltenstein, A., and J. Ha. 1993. "The Sectoral Implications of Macroeconomic Policy: The Case of Postreform China." *Journal of Policy Modeling* 15(3):277-96.

———. 1991. "Measurement of Repressed Inflation in China: The Lack of Coordination between Monetary Policy and Price Controls." *Journal of Development Economics* 36:279-94.

Feng, Y. 1997. "Political Stability, Democracy, and Economic Growth." *British Journal of Political Science* 27:391-418.

Fleisher, B., and J. Chen. 1997. "The Coast-Noncoast Income Gap, Productivity, and Regional Economic Policy in China." *Journal of Comparative Economics* 25:220-36.

Forster, K., and O. Tam. 1990. "Introduction." *Chinese Economic Studies* 24(1):5-14.

Geddes, B. 1994. *Politician's Dilemma*. Berkeley: University of California Press.

Hafer, R., and A. Kutan. 1994. "Economic Reforms and Long-Run Money Demand in China: Implications for Monetary Policy." *Southern Economic Journal* 60(4):936-45.

———. 1993. "Further Evidence on Money, Output, and Prices in China." *Journal of Comparative Economics* 17:701-9.

Hibbs, D. 1987. *The American Political Economy: Electoral Policy and Macroeconomics in Contemporary America.* Cambridge: Harvard University Press.

Ma, J. 1997. "Intergovernmental Fiscal Transfers in Nine Countries: Lessons for Developing Countries." *World Bank Policy Research Working Paper #1822.* September.

———. 1996. "Monetary Management and Intergovernmental Relations in China." *World Development* 24(1):145-53.

———. 1995a. "Defining the Limits of Local Government Power in China: The Relevance of International Experience." *Journal of Contemporary China* 10:3-22.

———. 1995b. "Macroeconomic Management and Intergovernmental Relations in China." *World Bank Policy Research Working Paper #1048.* January.

Mehran, H., and M. Quintyn. 1996. "Financial Sector Reforms in China." *World Bank World Development Report #040396.* March.

Mueller, D. 1990. *Public Choice II.* Cambridge: Cambridge University Press.

Naughton, B. 1991. "Why Has Economic Reform Led to Inflation?" *American Economic Review* 81(2):207-211.

Nordhaus, W. 1975. "The Political Business Cycle." *Review of Economic Studies* 42:169-90.

Oi, J. 1992. "Fiscal Reform and the Economic Foundations of Local State Corporatism." *World Politics* 45(1):99-126.

Olson, M. 1965. *The Logic of Collective Action.* Cambridge: Harvard University Press.

Persson, T., and G. Tabellini. 1991. *Macroeconomic Policy, Credibility, and Politics.* New York: Harwood Academic Publishers.

Powell, R. 1996. "Uncertainty, Shifting Power, and Appeasement," *American Political Science Review.* 90(4):749-64.

Rogoff, K. 1990. "Equilibrium Political Budget Cycles," *American Economic Review* 80:21-36.

Ramseyer, J., and F. Rosenbluth. 1993. *Japan's Political Marketplace.* Cambridge: Harvard University Press.

Sanders, D. 1981. *Patterns of Political Instability.* New York: St. Martin's Press.

Tammen, R., J. Kugler, D. Lemke, A. Stam, M. Abdollahian, C Alsharabati, A. Organski, and B. Buford-Efird. 2000. *Power Transitions: Strategic Policies for the 21st Century.* Chatham: Chatham House.

Walker, D. 1989. "Effects of Economic Reforms on the Banking System in China." *Economica International* 42(August/November):244-57.

Yu, Q. 1997. "Economic Fluctuation, Macro Control, and Monetary Policy in the Transitional Chinese Economy." *Journal of Comparative Economics* 25:180-95.

8
Financial Development and Macroeconomic Stability in China

Barry Naughton

The global financial crisis that began in Thailand in the summer of 1997 has led to an increased awareness of the fragility of financial systems in developing countries, and inevitably to heightened scrutiny of China's financial system and reform. The economy of China and the economies of southeast Asia most effected by crisis share some important common features, which are especially evident in the character of their financial systems. In the past, sustained high growth of these East Asian countries had led to a sense of complacency. Despite the fact the deficiencies in their financial systems were widely recognized, many economists neglected the potential for instability. Similarly in China, sustained high saving and rapid growth have long diverted attention from deficiencies in the financial system, despite the fact that these deficiencies have been widely acknowledged.

China shares with most of her Asian neighbors a general pattern of bank-dominated finance. Bank lending is large in relation in GDP, while capital markets are relatively less developed. Corporate bonds, in particular, are a relatively unimportant source of financing. Equity markets are more substantial, but remain relatively thin and extremely volatile. Problems in the banking system, ultimately traceable to poorly specified agency relations, potentially may threaten China's financial stability. In comparison with the Southeast Asian economies, it is natural to ask whether China, with similar growth achievements and equally substantial financial shortcomings, is likely to suffer similar disturbances, originating in the financial system, in the future.

At the same time, the *differences* between recent Chinese and southeast Asian experience can also be interpreted as confirming the caution of China's reform process. Numerous observers have commented lately on China's emergence as a "bastion of stability" in the Pacific region. China's foreign exchange reserves, $140 billion at year-end 1997 appear ample, and the

Chinese currency has remained stable through over a year of financial turbulence. Most fundamentally, China differs from ASEAN in the relationship between domestic and foreign financial markets. The Chinese currency is not convertible on the capital account, and most of the massive capital inflow China has enjoyed in recent years has come in the form of foreign direct investment. As a result, China has relatively little exposure to private debt denominated in foreign currency, and the interactions between volatility in domestic financial markets and foreign currency markets are quite limited. There is thus little danger of a downward spiral caused by mutually reinforcing volatility in the markets for foreign exchange and domestic financial assets, and little immediate danger for China of contagion by the "Asian flu."

However, China faces formidable problems of its own. These problems may prove especially difficult to manage in the next year or two. Successful macroeconomic stabilization is now being followed by a renewed burst of enterprise restructuring. On balance, this creates new opportunities to reform the financial sector, but also complicates the environment in which reform must proceed. It is inevitable that significant efforts will be made in the next few years to clean up bank balance sheets and restructure the financial system. The magnitude of the problems and the uncertainty of the overall economic environment could easily lead to short-term financial problems. These in turn might reduce growth rates and derail essential financial sector reforms.

The first section of this chapter examines the basic trends and main achievements of financial reform to date. The second and third sections look at the banking system and stock market respectively. The fourth and final section examines the current situation, with stress on the impact of current restructuring initiatives in concert with current macroeconomic conditions. The basic message is that while substantial progress has been made, there is a significant danger that financial problems may disrupt further progress.

Overall Trends and Achievements

China is a developing country as well as a transitional market economy. Financial development in China proceeds in a context that reflects both these long-term processes. Economic development is typically accompanied by a gradual process of financial deepening: The ratio of various financial assets to GDP increases steadily as GDP per capita climbs. In general, we should also expect transition from a socialist to a market economy to lead eventually to financial deepening, but the actual experience of transitional economies has been much more complex. In many European transitional economies, conversion to a market economy was preceded or accompanied by substantial inflation that wiped out accumulated financial balances. Many households lost their life savings. In those countries, transition took place in the context of a major disintermediation process: in Russia, broad money declined from 80% to only 20% of GDP between 1990 and 1993, and bank credit to enterprises and households declined from 40% to about 16% (Dittus and Prowse 1996). At the same time, economic disruption caused a decline in current saving. Saving by government and enterprises collapsed, and households were unable or unwilling to increase saving rapidly. Financial systems had to be rebuilt from the ground up.

In China, national saving was high before, during and after reform. However, the composition of saving changed dramatically, and the institutions that channel saving to investment changed as well. Government saving, as in most transitional economies, has dropped sharply, in response to the deteriorating financial position of state-owned enterprises. However, household saving has increased very rapidly in response to the new opportunities created by transition. Total household saving—including both in-kind and financial saving—jumped rapidly from 7% of household income in 1978 to 17% in 1982, and have continued to increase steadily since. Moreover, the increase in household saving rates cannot be explained simply by more rapid growth of houshold income during those years. Instead, saving behavior shifted upward in response to the changed environment (Naughton 1987). Even more crucially, financial saving tripled, increasing from 2.3% of household income in 1978, to an average of 6.8% in the years 1980-83. (Cheng 1991, Macroeconomic Research Office 1987). As of 1995, households were generating 70% of domestic saving, a sum greater than 25% of GDP (Xu 1997).

In response to these changes in saving behavior, China's financial system began to diverge from the standard command economy model, and resemble that of most market economies. Saving surpluses in the household sector were transferred primarily through the banking system to fund investment in the enterprise and government sectors. The banking system has been fundamentally transformed. M2 increased from 32% of GDP in 1978 to 122% in 1997 (Figure 8.1). By this measure, China has had a "deeper" financial system than any other major transition economy since 1992 (Caprio and Levine: 16). Changes in household balances were the largest part of financial deepening, as household saving deposits increased from 6% to 62% of GDP between 1978 and 1997.

During this period, China has put in place the basic institutional structures that govern a modern financial system. The People's Bank of China (PBC) was made into a central bank, with the potential to control lending and monetary aggregates through reserve requirements and central bank lending. The beginnings of competition were introduced into the banking system. Stock markets were established in Shanghai and Shenzhen in 1990, and enterprises were given authority to issue various kinds of stocks and bonds. Government bonds of various types and maturities have been issued since 1981, with Treasury bonds making up the largest share.

FIGURE 8.1 Financial Deepening: M2 and Household Deposits

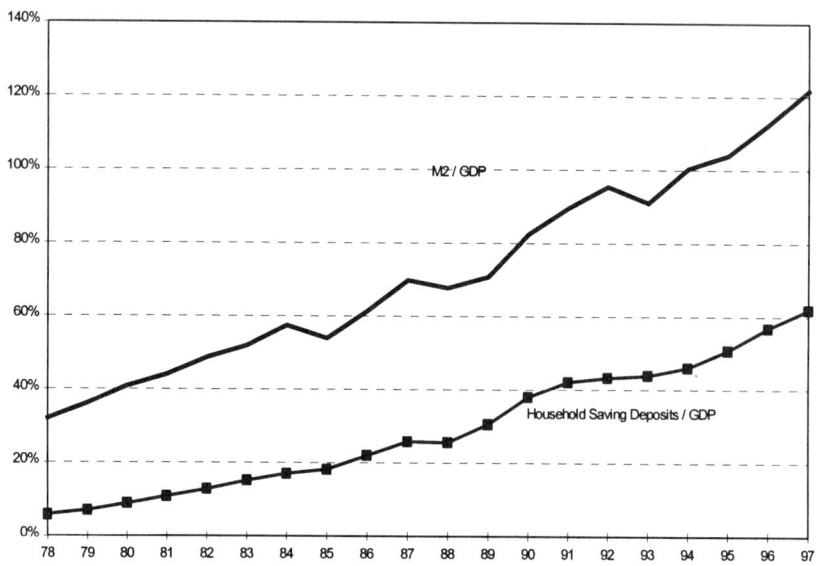

Sources: PBC Research and Statistics Department (1992); Almanac of China's Finance and Banking, various years. China Finance 1997:3, pp. 27-31; Ma Hong, ed., Zhongguo Shichang Fazhan Baogao [China Market Development Report] 1998. Beijing: Zhongguo Fazhan, 1998, pp. 89-99.

Despite these achievements, the development of capital markets in China has not been impressive to date. This is somewhat ironic, given the attention that has been paid to China's nascent stock markets as symbols of capitalism. However, it is indisputable that, at least if we limit our attention to formally recognized and regulated institutions, the development of capital markets has been much less steady, and much less impressive than the growth of the banking system. There was very little capital market development during the 1980s. The stock exchanges in Shanghai and Shenzhen were established in 1990, and a burst of rapid capital market development ensued through 1993. Subsequently, however, development slowed markedly, and the atmosphere shifted from one of financial permissiveness to a renewed stress on control and regulation. As we shall see, that slow-down was intimately related to speculative excesses and regulatory shortcomings in the initial phase of capital market development. Figure 8.2 shows the development of the Chinese stock exchanges, relative to GDP, as well as several comparison economies.

FIGURE 8.2 Stock Market Capitalization

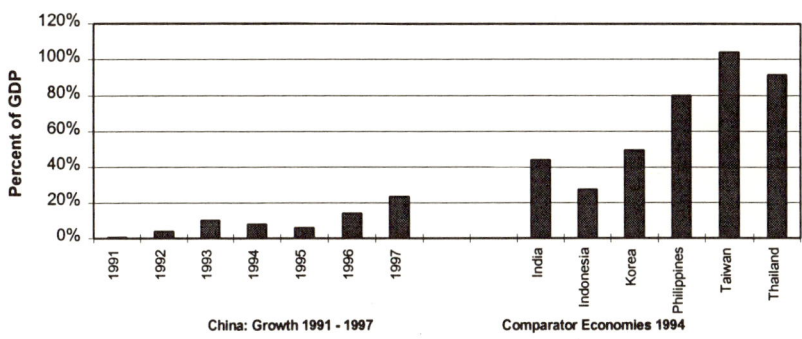

Sources: IFC 1996; China Economic News, August 4, 1997, p. 9. Ma Hong, op. cit., pp. 74-88.

The market for fixed income securities has shown a similar trajectory. Securities of all kinds were issued in significant quantities during the early 1990s, and the value outstanding grew sharply until 1992. At the end of that year, government bonds outstanding equaled 6.1% of GDP, and financial bonds added another 0.6% of GDP. Enterprise fixed income securities outstanding had grown at a rapid pace — in a parallel development to the initial growth of the stock markets — to reach 3.1% of GDP. But this development was not sustained (Table 8.1). Between 1992 and 1996, the stock of government bonds in circulation grew slightly faster than GDP, reaching 6.8% of GDP by year-end 1996. Total government debt grew more rapidly, because most of the increase in bank bonds in this time was to finance government policy lending by the new policy banks (especially the State Development Bank and the Import-Export Bank). But enterprise bonds — even generously estimated by the broadest possible definition — had declined to less than one percent of GDP. By this simple measure, then, the total value of fixed income securities in circulation increased fairly quickly to 9.8% of GDP in 1992, but growth than slowed dramatically, with total value reaching only 11.4% of GDP in 1996. Moreover, between 1992 and 1996, government debt actually increased its already dominant share of fixed income securities, as strict limitations on issuance of new enterprise debt led to a sharp decline in the relative importance of corporate bonds.

TABLE 8.1 Securities Outstanding as a Share of GDP

	1992	1996
Government Bonds & Notes	6.1%	6.8%
Bank Bonds	0.6%	3.7%
Enterprise Bonds & Notes	3.1%	0.9%

Sources: 1994 Zhongguo Jinrong Nianjian [Almanac of China's Finance & Banking], pp. 455-56. 1998 Zhongguo Tongji Nianjian [China Statistical Yearbook], p. 672. Note that both these sources use broad definitions of enterprise bonds, including varying maturities, and firms that may include local government investment firms. Smaller numbers for 1996, based on narrower definitions, are available in the 1997 Finance Almanac, p. 472, and the 1997 Securities Market Annual, pp. 527-30.

Between 1992 and 1996, then, the incipient growth of China's capital markets was drastically slowed, while the real economy—and the banking system—continued to grow. As a result, despite important institutional evolution in virtually every area, the financial system in the late 1990s still displays the same fundamental characteristics that have marked its development since the beginning of reform: it is a system that has undergone very substantial financial deepening, but in which virtually all of the deepening has been channeled into the banking system. Despite renewed growth of the stock market beginning in 1996 (discussed below), it remains a bank dominated system. Moreover, it is also a system in which state-owned banks dominate the banking system: while the growth of competition to the state banks has been real, it has been limited and much too slow.

There is one important caveat, however, to the generalization that China's financial system is dominated by state banks. Informal financial markets in China are large and important, and little studied. Three tiers of informal financial markets can be distinguished. At the "bottom," informal rural credit mechanisms—including credit clubs, money lenders and unregistered private banks—are very significant, particularly in the countryside. In a recent court case, it was decided that private money-lenders were not usurious so long as interest rates were not more than four times officially regulated lending rates. According to estimates based on household surveys, rural informal financial markets surpassed formal rural institutional lending in size in 1986 (Xu 1994:218-220). At the "middle level," many state and collective firms have issued various kinds of promissory notes, "stocks," and other IOUs that are not formally recognized by the government (or included in the statistics in Table 8.1). These IOUs exist in a legal gray area, with the ability of lenders to collect essentially dependent on local government willingness to enforce specific contracts. Finally, at the "top," many local governments dispose of significant funds that are not included in the formal budget, but are available for investment purposes. For example, government statistics on fixed investment reveal that "other" financial sources of investment (outside of bank lending, government funds, or private or enterprise retained funds) equal about 4% of GDP annually, about half as much as formal bank lending. Most of these funds are controlled by local government officials or by entities set up under their patronage (such as local investment corporations or investment funds). Thus, there is a large amount of financial intermediation occurring in China which is captured very imperfectly — or not at all — by officially reported statistics. In the aggregate, it is conceivable that the funds flowing through these channels may be large enough to lead us to modify the assertion that the overall financial system is dominated by state banks.

The Banking System

Banking sector reform is best approached by considering the "stock" problem and the "flow" problem, where the stock problem refers to the stock of bad loans, and the flow problem refers to the fact that current lending decisions are still not made on a commercially sound basis.

The Stock of Nonperforming Loans

The stock problem in China is large, ironically because of some of the successes of China's transition strategy. In both Russia and Poland, bank assets were reduced essentially to zero by hyperinflation on the eve of, or in the early stages of, economic transition. This freed the banks of the burden of the stock of bad loans, but at the enormous cost of wiping out the value of the accumulated saving deposits of households. In China, there was no reduction in the relative value of bank deposits or loans on the eve of transition, and they have in fact grown rapidly throughout the transition process.

Instead, the banking system benefited throughout the transition from the massive inflow of household funds. In this sense, the current Chinese situation is in some respects more like that in a country that has successfully undergone stabilization, rather than a socialist country undergoing transition. That is because after successful stabilization, there tends to be an inflow of funds into the banking system. Particularly if the country were previously undergoing high inflation, stabilization is typically accompanied by high real interest rates and a return of funds into the banking system. As a result, the money multiplier increases, and there is a credit boom. The result is frequently "overlending" and a subsequent financial crisis. This framework is generally applicable to China. China has generally kept real deposit interest rates positive, although on some occasions only after short-run panics or runs on the bank. As a result, the bulk of increased household saving has flowed into the banking system, creating a fairly abundant source of credit funds. Banks have responded by increasing credit rapidly, extending credit generously to state-owned enterprises, among others.

An important related development has been the steady increase in the share of bank debt in enterprise worth since the beginning of the reform process. The aggregate debt of industrial state-owned enterprises (SOEs) is 73% of aggregate book value (depreciated fixed capital plus all inventories). Indeed, SOEs finance 99.8% of their inventories through bank credit. Moreover, the debt load has grown inexorably since the beginning of the reform era. In 1978, the debt burden was only 11% of book value, and by 1988 it had grown to 45%. This ratio is now much higher than in most other transitional economies. For example, in Hungary in 1992 the ratio was 34% and in Poland 41%. Comparable figures for OECD countries are in the range of 42% to 69% (Baer and Gray 1996). In addition, leverage is high for most sectors, and for virtually all ownership forms. Indeed, leverage in the non-state sector (at 70%) is only three percentage points lower than in the state sector.

Because the outstanding volume of bank lending is large, bad loans, default risk, and costs of recapitalization of the banking system, are all large, relative to GDP (Lardy 1998:92-127). There is no firm Figure of problem loans in the banking system, because there is no adequate audit process to accurately determine which loans are really in risk of default. However, the central bank governor, Dai Xianglong, recently put the proportion of nonperforming loans at state banks at 20%, with 8% of total outstanding loans more than 3 years overdue, and another 12 percent overdue less than 3 years (quoted in Faison 1996). A recently released Figure roughly consistent with Dai's comments puts the total of nonperforming loans at 1.06 trillion RMB in 1995 (*China Economic News* 1997). This would actually amount to 21% of all loans in the banking system, and 18% of GDP. It is a huge number.

The proportion of bad loans in China seems to be roughly comparable to those in other transitional economies: for instance, in 1992, Hungary, Poland, and the Czech Republic all had nonperforming loans estimated at between 19 and 26% of total lending, roughly the range within which estimates of Chinese nonperforming loans fall. However, because for each of these economies, the volume of loans relative to GDP is considerably smaller, the potential default burden is considerably smaller (Dittus 1994). The total problem of bad loans in China may be even larger than these overall estimates indicate. In the first place, the classification of bad loans in the Chinese system is quite lax, with loans classified as fully nonperforming (*daizhang*) only when firms are bankrupt or have virtually no possibility of payment; and overdue loans classified as overdue more than three years (*daizhi*) or six months (*yuqi*). Loans repeatedly rolled over are not classified as nonperforming, so long as some interest payments are made. Moreover, non-bank financial institutions also have significant nonperforming loans.

A People's Bang of China study found that 21.6% of a large sample of urban credit cooperative loans were nonperforming, with the proportion expected to be higher for rural credit cooperatives, and probably even higher for Trust and Investment Companies, since they have invested heavily in real estate (Jing and Bingxi 1997:47-48).

Moreover, because of China's gradualist transition strategy, there is no possible "firewall" between the bad old government-controlled lending and current, relatively better, market-responsive lending. As a result, it is almost inconceivable that a principle could be found to segregate past non-performing loans into a separate institution, such as that proposed by Begg and Portes (1993) or carried out by the Japanese government after World War II (Hoshi 1995). The rapid build-up in lending, documented in the previous section, implies that many of these problem loans are of relatively recent provenance. They cannot be simply blamed on the pre-reform economy, but rather represent poor lending decisions made during the transitional process.

Finally, a subsidiary implication is that a relatively large proportion of lending is for long-term fixed assets. In the former government-controlled system, with only a few minor exceptions, banks did not lend for fixed investment. Bank credit for long-term, fixed investment is thus an innovation of the transition process. Long-term lending inevitably carries more risk for the banks than short-term lending. Chinese bank balance sheets show 25% of state bank lending (1,336 billion yuan) as of mid-1997 as being medium to long term (i.e. over one year). In addition, there is universal agreement that this understates total long-term lending, since a significant portion of short-term lending is diverted to fixed investment. Thus, the accumulated financial risk of the banking system, and by implication the entire economy, is large.

The "Flow" Problem: Ensuring Good Lending Decisions

It is insufficient to deal with the "stock" problem of non-performing loans. In addition, it is necessary to create the proper incentives so that the "flow" of new lending is shaped by market return and a prudent attitude toward risk. In principle, a gradual transition should make it easier to gradually improve the incentive environment that works within the banking system. In that vein, it would be nice to be able to report that the accumulation of a stock of problem loans had been the price paid to purchase substantial improvement of the flow problem. But that does not seem to be substantially true. In short, the banks still operate at relatively low levels of efficiency, meaning that poor lending decisions continue to be made, and the stock of non-performing loans continues to increase.

The broader context is the generally low level of efficiency of the banking system as a whole. This inefficiency affects all parts of the banking system's activities. Broadly speaking, the banking system has two jobs: financial intermediation and provision of liquidity services. The above discussion, like most discussions of financial development, stresses financial intermediation, but provision of liquidity services is, if anything, even more important. Other institutions can provide financial intermediation, but only the banking system can effectively provide liquidity services. Provision of liquidity is particularly difficult in a large, diverse, agricultural economy. The fact that the economy is large and diverse means that liquidity needs fluctuate in different areas according to different factors; the fact that it is agricultural means that the seasonal component to the demand for liquidity is large. In the current Chinese banking system, the primary mechanism used to adjust regional and seasonal fluctuations in liquidity demand is to adjust the net position of each regional bank with the central bank. That is, additional central bank lending is used to provide liquidity when necessary, especially at the peak demand season, i.e. the harvest. If possible, the central bank will attempt to draw down liquidity in other regions (and seasons) by having local banks maintain "excess" reserves at the bank. Local bank branches are not in a position to manage their own liquidity needs. Their position is fairly passive, and they approach the central bank for additional funds when needs arise. This system works, but not very well, as is shown by repeated cases in which local banks are unable to provide adequate funds to finance procurement of the harvest, and are reduced to giving farmers promissory notes (*bai tiaozi*) for later payment.

The inefficient banking system reflects the inadequate incentive environment for bank workers. The most important problems include:

1. *ownership*. Since the main banks remain state-owned, they remain subject to serious problems of incentives, risk management and soft budget constraints. Loan officers have been given employment contracts that reward them for increasing revenues and maintaining low default rates. But these contracts do not reward loan officers for accurately assessing future risks or making provisions for future defaults (it is extremely difficult to design contracts that provide adequate risk sharing, and this has certainly not been done in the Chinese case). Given the ease with which individual loan officers may roll over loans, postponing problems indefinitely, no individual has the incentive to carry out the overhaul of administration and procedures necessary to improve operations.
2. *oversight*. Oversight appears to be seriously deficient. Loan officers have a great deal of decision-making power with respect to individual loans, and the identification and monitoring of credit risk is delegated to the loan officer. Once a loan is granted, oversight weakens further. Credit departments classify loans according to repayment status, but there are no procedures for assessing changes in creditworthiness or projected cash flows. There are no specialized problem loan work-out units
3. *skills and reporting*. Credit personnel are seriously lacking in train-

ing relating to analyzing cash flow, assessing repayment ability and risk. Reporting of problem loans follows subjective and inconsistent criteria. Overdue interest payments do not automatically trigger classification. Information is frequently missing, and loan classifications are often inaccurate (much short-term lending is diverted to long-term uses and repeatedly rolled over.)

These characteristics mean that the ability of the banks to discriminate between good and bad loans on commercial principles are quite limited. Moreover, with so much decision-making authority at the loan officer level, and so little specialized oversight, there are also significant opportunities for diversion of funds and corruption. Indeed, a recent public opinion poll ranked workers in financial institutions third in a list of social groups that have benefited from recent reforms, following only private businessmen and artists and musicians (Xu 1998).

Bank Resources

The banking system does not possess sufficient capital to deal with problem loans on its own. Table 8.2 shows that the state-owned specialized banks started off, in 1985, with sufficient capital to meet the 8% ratio required according to the Basle standards. However, capital adequacy has eroded steadily in three of the four specialized banks, with only the Bank of China displaying some increases in capital adequacy, at least up through 1992. After 1992, there is substantial evidence of further worsening in capital adequacy ratios, and comprehensive statistics become increasingly scarce. There was undoubtedly further erosion of bank capital through 1995. Conceivably there has been some improvement since 1995, as inflation has come down and real lending rates and the spread over deposit rates both turned positive. Nevertheless, unadjusted capital adequacy ratios are said to be below 7% currently (Jing and Shen 1997:48).

TABLE 8.2 Capital Adequacy Ratios of Main Chinese Banks

Year	Industrial-Commercial Bank	Agricultural Bank	Bank of Construction	Bank of China
1985	10.0%	12.6%	n.a.	4.4%
1986	8.9%	11.8%	n.a.	5.4%
1987	9.1%	10.7%	n.a.	4.3%
1988	7.2%	9.9%	9.2%	5.6%
1989	7.4%	8.8%	8.2%	7.0%
1990	6.8%	7.4%	7.5%	6.7%
1991	6.7%	6.5%	6.5%	6.6%
1992	6.6%	6.3%	6.5%	7.9%

Sources: Zhao (1996:151), Du (1996:58).

If 20% of bank loans are non-performing, and the banks are ultimately able to collect half of those loans (a generous assumption), then the ultimate reduction in the banks' value will equal 10% of total lending. This is substantially greater than the total owned capital and loss reserves (limited to 1% of outstanding loans) possessed by the banks. Thus, Chinese banks are in a state of chronic insolvency, and the unresolved burden of bad loans contributes to the difficulty in restructuring the incentive environment to improve the quality of new lending. The banking system clearly needs financial strengthening.

FIGURE 8.3 Inflation and Deposit/Lending Rates

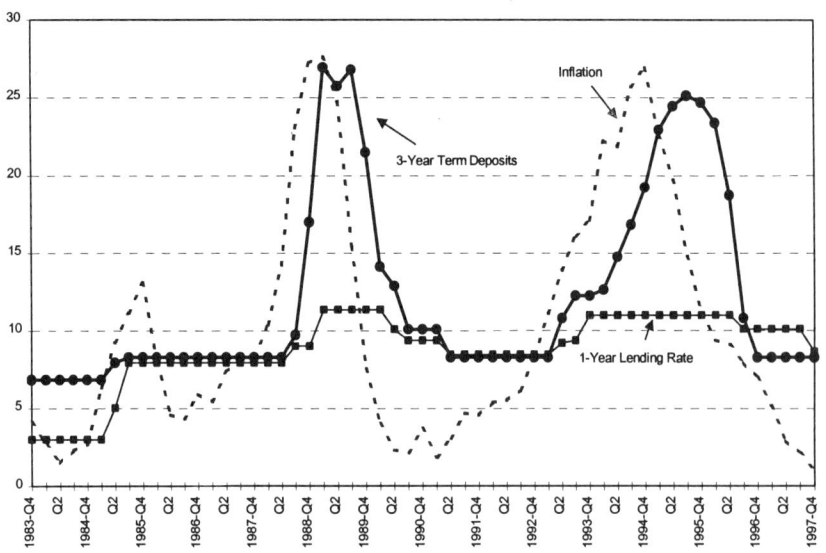

Sources: *Inflation, China Monthly Statistics*, various issues. Interest rates: *Almanac of China's Finance and Banking*, 1987: pp. II-47, 48; 1988: pp. 117-19; 1991 [English], pp. 119-21; *Statistical Yearbook*, 1996: 618-19; Inflation Supplement: *China Price Yearbook* 1996: 391-92.

The erosion of bank capital is easily traced to a single fact: Under the current system, the state banking system is subject to heavy explicit and implicit taxation by the government. As Lardy (1998:170-72) has shown, direct taxes on the banks are very large. Moreover, the government uses the banking system to indirectly achieve objectives that its limited fiscal resources prevent it from achieving directly. The government exacts large implicit taxes on the banking system through a number of channels. Most important, of course, are the mandates given to the banking system to fund government investment projects. Clearly, these lead to extensive resource misallocation and heavy burdens on the banking system. Even in addition to these basic costs, government implicit taxation is large because of three factors. First, interest rates are controlled and interest rate spreads are narrow during the best of times. During inflationary episodes, the government protects households (and the liquidity of the banking system) by indexing long-term savings deposits. Figure 8.3 shows the pattern. When an inflationary episode begins—as in 1988 and 1993—real interest rates turn negative. Soon, the government is compelled to protect the value of household deposits (and the liquidity of the banking system) by providing indexation to term deposits (three years or above), bringing the ex post real interest rate back up to zero. However, the government is unwilling to impose the full costs of positive real interest rates on enterprises, and real lending rates remain negative until inflation is tamed. The result is that the modest spreads in normal periods become large negative spreads of up to fifteen percentage points. The Figure shows 3-year term deposits and working capital loans: spreads are larger for sight deposits and short term loans. Notice that at the end of 1996, spreads turned positive for these two interest rates, reflecting an across the board shift in interest rate policy.

Second, reserve ratios are relatively high. The required reserve ratio has been at the moderate level of 13% since 1988, but commercial banks are never allowed to dip into their reserve funds for clearance purposes. As a result, they maintain substantial additional reserves at the central bank, conventionally termed "excess reserves" in order to meet their normal inter-bank transactions demands. This differs from regulations in, for example, the US, where banks are allowed to use their required reserves with the Federal Reserve for transactions purposes, so long as they have adequate reserves at day end (Meek 1991). Given the relatively inefficient clearance mechanisms that still characterize the Chinese banking system, additional reserves on the order of 5-7% of deposits are required for the normal functioning of the system. Thus, de facto reserve requirements amount to 18-20% of deposits. In turn, the PBC recycles these funds to the specialized banks in the form of central bank lending, which is large. PBC lending to specialized banks averaged 32 and 37 percent of total specialized bank lending between 1988 and 1993 (though it declined thereafter). The specialized banks receive 9.18% interest for reserves deposited at the PBC, but pay over 10 percent on loans from the PBC.[1] As a result, high reserve ratios and central bank lending further erode specialized bank profitability.

Third, banks often have their assets wiped out when enterprises run into financial difficulty. Bankruptcy procedures, whatever the law says, typically involve writing off bank debts first. In a large sample of bankrupt enterprises in 1996, the banks recovered only 15% of their loan values. Moreover, local governments often negotiate forgiveness of bank debt as a part of enterprise bailouts.

How does the banking system continue to attract such high levels of deposits of it is so heavily taxed? The answer appears to be twofold. First, households only partially bear the cost of taxation. In normal times, households receive a lower rate of return to their assets than they would if a more diversified set of financial assets were available. However, in return, they receive implicit insurance of the value of their assets: if inflation accelerates, real interest rates will be prevented from turning negative. This insurance seems to be enough to make saving deposits attractive to households. Second, the supply of alternative assets is rigorously controlled. Although households can always lend funds on the informal market, in such markets risks as well as returns are high. In general, household access to alternative assets with moderate risks and returns is strictly rationed.

The Chinese government bears particular responsibility for the plight of the banking system, and this is recognized in numerous implicit and explicit commitments. Of course, the banks are state-owned to begin with. The government bears additional responsibility because of years of directing bank credit to government-favored projects, many of which are low-return; and also because government policies have drained the banks of capital over the last decade. Governments in most countries provide a level of insurance to the banking system, and China is no different. But in China the government is essentially in the position of providing extensive and ongoing insurance for the banking system. However, this ongoing protection further erodes incentives within the banking system, contributes to a "soft budget constraint" within the banks, and inevitably leads to further accumulation of bad loans.

The high level of central bank lending does provide a mechanism through which government-sponsored write-offs of bad bank debts will occur. Because liabilities to the central bank are a large item on specialized bank balance sheets, commercial loan write-offs can be fairly easily accommodated by writing down liabilities to the central bank. In turn, the central bank can receive new government debt. In this sense, the already high level of government interference in the banking system may make it somewhat easier to restructure assets and liabilities to more adequately reflect government responsibility. As is always the case with bad lending decisions, the misallocation of resources has already occurred, and the highest priority is to reallocate the current burden of non-performing assets in order to slow the future accumulation of bad loans. The relatively low level of outstanding public debt makes this feasible, but it will require the reversal of a long-standing habit of relying on the banking system to compensate for fiscal weakness.

Failed Liberalization

The preceding section described the combination of government controls on the banking system and extensive implicit taxation that leads to a financially weakened banking system. A further implication of the situation is that attempts at incremental liberalization often fail. When the overall financial system is liberalized, there is a large outflow of funds from the state banking system. This creates liquidity shortages and generally leads the government to recontrol the financial system. Depositors looking for higher rates — that is, looking to escape the increasing implicit taxation which is rapidly becoming confiscatory — move funds out of the banking system and into less formal, riskier assets. These episodes are particularly likely to occur when liberalization intersects with accelerating inflation. For example, this combination occurred in 1985, 1988, and 1992-93, and the resultant decline in the ratio of M2 to GDP in those years is clearly visible in Figure 8.1. Disintermediation creates a liquidity crisis in the banking system, to which the government responds in three ways. The central bank injects reserves into the commercial banks; administrative restrictions on non-bank financial institutions (formal and informal, legal and illegal) are tightened; and ultimately the deposit rate is increased, at least to the rate of inflation for term deposits. At this point, the implicit tax on the banking system is at its maximum. Deposit rates are high; lending rates are low; and the implicit subsidies received through increased central bank lending are insufficient to offset the implicit taxation in the interest rate differential.

It is not only households with savings deposits that have an incentive to move funds out of the banking system during periods of liberalization and inflationary growth. Government agencies hold substantial "extra-budgetary" funds, which they manage in ways such that they won't have to pay the punitive taxes levied on funds that go through the banking system. (Note that bank deposits owned by enterprises and organizations never enjoy the inflation protection that household deposits receive). Even more important, personnel of the banking system itself have very strong incentives to move funds out of government controlled channels, and into less regulated institutional forms. For example, the growth of various Trust and Investment Companies (TICs) in China can be understood in part as the attempt by bank officers to avoid punitive taxation on the banking system. Many of the TICs have been established by state banks: 181 of 394 authorized TICs in September 1995 were associated with the specialized (commercial) banks. Many of the others are subordinate to local governments. The TICs provide convenient outlets for bank money to avoid regulatory strictures and seek out higher returns than are available through regulated lending. Moreover, as we will see in the next section, such funds are frequently channeled into the stock markets.

We are now in a position to understand why the development of capital markets faltered after 1992. Concerned about the rapid drain of funds from the banking system, and an acute funds shortage in 1992-93, Vice-Premier Zhu Rongji, in charge of economic policy, adopted a series of measures to restrict the operation of bank subsidiaries. These policies caused the relative shrinkage of the stock market shown in Figure 8.2. However, while these policies retarded capital market development, they were quite effective in restraining the excessive growth of aggregate demand that was building up during 1993. Adoption of restrictive credit policies turned out to be essential and effective. Inflation accelerated to a peak annual rate of 28% during 1994, but thereafter declined steadily. By the end of 1997, inflation had been essentially eliminated. Macroeconomic stabilization—a "soft landing"—was achieved, but at the cost of aborting the financial liberalization of 1992-93, in particular the development of capital markets. If sustained, though, macroeconomic stability will prepare the ground for further financial reform, under more favorable conditions.

Stock Markets: On the Verge of the "Big Leagues"?

It was noted above that China's formal stock markets have remained small, in contrast to the very large changes in the volumes transacted in the banking system. Since early 1996, though, China's stock markets have grown rapidly, and growth continues through the present. Nevertheless, up until now, China's formal stock markets have developed in an artificially controlled environment. Indeed, some observers have dismissed China's two stock markets in Shanghai and Shenzhen as Potemkin villages. It is perhaps more accurate to refer to them as the tip of the iceberg, that is, as the shiny visible pyramid atop a huge murky mass of informal credit relations. In any case, by international comparisons the formal stock exchanges are of modest size. Even after rapid appreciation and expanded listings during 1996 and 1997, the total market value of listed stocks (both A and B-shares) on the Shenzhen and Shanghai stock exchanges came to 1.75 trillion RMB at the end of 1997, equal to 23.4% of GDP (Figure 8.2). In sheer volume terms, then, China's stock markets appear to be just now approaching medium development status.

Nevertheless, there are important characteristics of these markets that limit their ability to play their full economic function. Table 8.3 shows the breakdown of ownership by owner type on the Shanghai exchange. Government agencies own a large proportion of total stock, 46% in mid-1995, down from 65% in 1990. The category of "legal entities" (literally "legal persons" in Chinese) refers to legally constituted autonomous organizations. It is crucial that in the Chinese case these legal entities are generally not mutual funds, pension funds, or insurance companies, but are generally holding companies established by government agencies as a management tool for government-owned stocks. Thus, most Chinese observers consider them "secondary government ownership" (e.g. Du 1996:160). Shares classified as government or legal-entity owned are not allowed to circulate on the exchange. Thus, two-thirds of total share value on the Shanghai exchange did not circulate.[2] The Shenzhen exchange shares this characteristic, but in a less extreme form: the Shenzhen exchange has many more companies listed that are in joint ventures with Hong Kong companies, and have fewer direct government connections.

TABLE 8.3 Ownership of Shares on the Shanghai Stock Exchange

	Total Share Value (at face value) Billion Yuan	of which, percentage held by			
		Government	"Legal Entities"	Individuals	Overseas Funds and Individuals
1990	0.273	65.1%	9.9%	25.0%	-
1991	0.295	61.9%	10.7%	27.4%	-
1992	5.234	51.3%	18.0%	9.8%	20.9%
1993	25.055	56.7%	14.9%	14.0%	14.5%
1994	45.879	49.2%	17.5%	17.6%	15.8%
6/95	52.659	45.7%	20.8%	17.0%	16.5%

Source: Du Xuncheng, *Jingji Zhuanxingzhong de Jinrong Chuangxin* [Financial Innovation during Economic Transformation]. Shanghai: Lixin Kuaiji Chubanshe, 1996, p. 158.

The restricted circulation of shares makes another characteristic of the stock markets even more remarkable. This is the very rapid turnover of stocks: turnover is slightly above total market value in both Shanghai and Shenzhen. However, taking into account the restrictions on circulation, turnover is actually more than 300% of market value of tradable shares, at least in Shanghai.[3] In turn, extremely rapid turnover should be interpreted in light of the extreme volatility of the market. Interesting studies show that the market is highly volatile, even in the developing country context. Moreover, even more interesting studies show that volatility is explained by reactions to government policy changes, particularly those that affect liquidity on the markets. Reactions to changes in underlying fundamentals of individual companies are insignificant in comparison (Su 1996).

Thus, the Chinese markets display extreme volatility and high turnover in a relatively narrow market. It is a casino as much as a market. Who plays at this casino? Although there are a large number of individuals who enjoy gambling on the market (33 million individual accounts in 1997!), anecdotal evidence suggests that the large players are institutional. This relates to the earlier discussion of "flight" from the banking system. Important players on the stock market have been TICs, and other quasi-governmental companies. Managers of these companies enjoy profitable opportunities from weak oversight over public funds. The odds on gambling are greatly improved by the asymmetry of the bargain: individuals can divert a part of large profits, while posting losses to the public account. In essence, there is a large volume of "hot money" that flows in and out of the market. There are persistent reports of market manipulation, and clear examples of large movements of money in advance of shifts in government policy that affect market liquidity.

Clearly, the Chinese stock exchanges have not served until now as a market for corporate control. Since majority control of most listed companies remains firmly in government hands, outside investors can do little beyond speculate on the market's fluctuations. It is also unclear whether the stock exchanges have increased the net availability of investment funds. The individual firms that list on the exchange undoubtedly receive an infusion of cash from their initial public offerings. But given substantial evidence that much of the funds are subtracted from the banking system through various mechanisms, it is unclear that these represent a net increase in available funds. Conceivably the market could provide such a net increment. It is true that in most developed countries, stock markets do not channel large volumes of investment funds to the corporate sector, instead serving primarily as devices for the allocation of existing capital.[4] However, this does not necessarily mean that stock markets cannot serve to raise additional investment capital in developing countries. Singh (1995) studies 9 developing countries and finds that in 5, over 40% of the growth of net assets in the 1980s was financed by new share issues, and in two more countries this ratio was over 25%. Singh suggests that this is because financial deregulation has raised bank interest rates at the same time that stock market booms have lowered costs of raising money there. Chinese stock markets thus may have the potential to generate substantial new funds for the corporate sector, but they are far from playing such a role currently.

Ironically, the limitations imposed on the market by the Chinese authorities probably make it that much easier for large institutional players to manipulate the market, and may discourage individual investor interest. Until recently, the stock markets have been primarily experimental institutions, not playing a significant role either in the flow of funds, or in corporate governance. However, important changes are occurring in the Chinese financial scene. Market values went up significantly during 1997, and large numbers of new joint stock corporations were created. It is conceivable that a new stage of financial reform is beginning. In mid-1997, the government sharply increased the pace at which new companies would be listed on the two exchanges during the course of the year. What is particularly striking is that this accelerated broadening of the stock market came in response to a run-up in stock prices that the government thought was excessive. In order to dampen the speculative fever, the government announced its intentions to release more new initial public offerings to the market, thus signaling its intention to soak up liquidity flowing into the market. This market-broadening measure was combined with increased regulatory measures that had the effect of restricting the flow of liquidity into the market, but at some cost to the pace of liberalization of capital markets overall.

In May and June 1997, immediately following the announcement of expanded initial public offerings, a series of regulations were rolled out that increased the stamp tax on stock transactions from 0.3% to 0.5%; that strictly forbade banks to deal in equity in any form whatsoever; and disciplined several state organizations (including branches of state banks) that were in violation of existing rules (Hong 1998:79). These measures followed a series of earlier regulatory efforts. First, TICs and other agencies controlling public money had been prohibited from participating directly in the stock markets. Subsequently, a number of large securities companies were closed down in the wake of speculative excesses and large losses of public money (Shanghai Wanguo Securities 1995, China Bank Trust and Investment Company 1996). In early 1997, the banks had been ordered to withdraw from the secondary government bond market, in which government bonds were serving as collateral in bank fund-raising, used to generate funds for market speculation. All these measures represented, to varying degrees, the recontrol of financial markets that had already developed. The combined measures had the desired effect: both the Shanghai and Shenzhen exchange indexes declined significantly after June 1997, and the speculative bubble was deflated. In the judgment of government officials, further financial development could take place only after speculation was curbed.

The Contemporary Environment

Since 1997, rapid changes in the economic environment have provided the potential to escape from the limitations of financial reform described in the previous sections. However, the sheer magnitude of change has also introduced new elements of uncertainty and risk into the financial system. Two broad changes are most important: successful macroeconomic stabilization and a dramatic acceleration in the pace of state enterprise reform. Both are fundamentally positive, but each brings with it the possibility of instability.

Macroeconomic stabilization has occurred remarkably smoothly, apparently achieving the much vaunted "soft landing." The inflation rate (consumer price index) has been brought down from a maximum of 28% during 1994, to zero inflation by the first quarter of 1998, and slightly falling prices subsequently (see Figure 8.4). Thus far, the effects of disinflation on the real economy have been modest: GDP grew 8.8% during 1997, and slightly above 7% during the first half of 1998. Growth has been drifting downwards since 1992's 14.2% growth rate, but hardly qualifies as a recession. Stabilization has a number of important effects. With much lower inflation and only modest changes in nominal interest rates, real interest rates are significantly positive to a degree rarely true during the transition period (Figure 8.3). With positive real interest rates, the implicit tax on the banking system has been reduced, and banks have had an opportunity to replenish their capital. Moreover, the tendency toward disintermediation has been strongly reduced, and policy-makers will find it less necessary to impose restrictions on financial innovation in order to maintain the health of the banking system. Overall, stabilization creates favorable conditions for further reform.

FIGURE 8.4 Consumer Price Inflation (YPP)

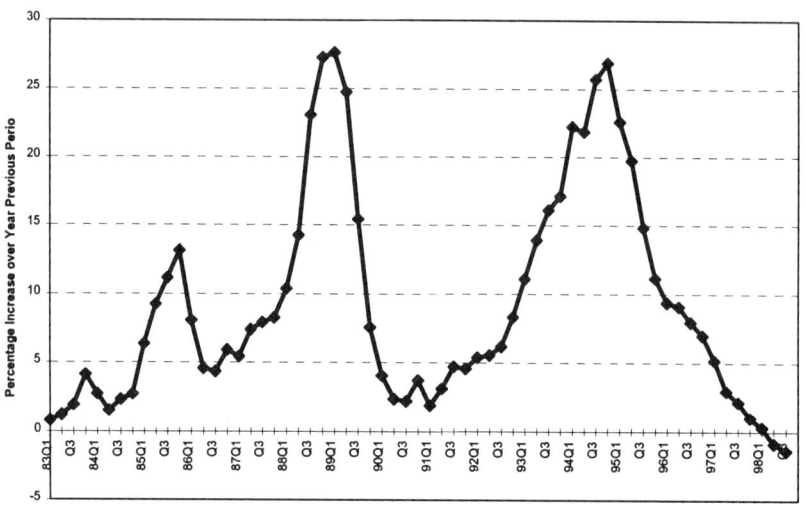

Sources: *China Monthly Statistics*, various issues.

But stabilization also brings substantial new stresses to the system. The current stabilization has reinforced the trend towards an intensely competitive domestic market that has been building throughout the transition period. Entry by rural firms, private companies and foreign invested enterprises has created brutal competition for existing SOEs, making it impossible for many of them to survive. Prices for many manufactured goods have been falling during 1997 (with the CPI propped up by increases in previously price-controlled services). In a sense, the current stabilization is the culmination of the entire market-creating transition process. Firms that were protected for nearly twenty years by the initially underdeveloped market and lack of competition are now fully exposed to tough competition from a variety of competitors. State firms, in particular, have lost the protective market conditions that gave them high profits under the planned economy and during the first decade of reform. Start-up firms and foreign investors that initially enjoyed high profitability in niche markets now find their niches have been invaded by other firms, who may be leaner and more innovative. The burden of interest payments is keenly felt by these highly-leverage and less competitive firms. Under such conditions, all the mistakes of past loans outstanding are increasingly evident. More firms are under intense competitive pressure, and the dangers of a chain of defaults is clearly increased.

There are some markets in which asset bubbles are poised to burst. China's major cities are now seriously overbuilt. Office space in Beijing will jump from 1.5 million meters at the end of 1996 to 2.5 million at the end of 1997; Shanghai luxury rents are already down about 20%, with another 10% fall in the cards (*China News Digest* 10/08/97). Real estate development has been a favorite target of "hot money" speculation in recent years: funds have been diverted in substantial amounts, and some of those funds might not now be recovered. The "TICs" described above will be particularly vulnerable. Another key area where financial disorder might arise is in the management of China's embryonic pension funds. Most regions now collect a percentage of wages for investment in pension funds, but oversight over these funds has been abysmal. Some pension fund managers rushed to invest in real estate when that seemed to promise the highest returns. According to preliminary reports trickling out of China, many of these funds have lost substantial sums of money, and it may well be that significant public scandals are brewing. Without proper management these problems could interact with other weaknesses in the financial system to cause major disruption. Thus, the biggest current danger is that defaults by property companies and defaults by production and trade enterprises might combine to rapidly threaten the solvency of key financial institutions. One can expect the Chinese government to respond promptly to such problems, and move to rectify whatever situation emerges. But such crises can be complex, and not always easy to manage, even by governments with the best of intentions.

The second major factor affecting financial development since 1997 is the stepped up pace of state enterprise reform. During the Fifteenth Communist Party Congress in September, major new impetus was given to the ongoing program of "enterprise restructuring." A central thrust of the restructuring initiative is the conversion of the forms of ownership of public firms. Conversion of form means defining modern corporate entities with explicit ownership stakes, and rights and liabilities. In many cases, this process also involves the distribution or sale of significant ownership stakes to private parties. Thus, the process involves substantial privatization of formerly public firms, as well as significant reorganization, merger and takeover, and bankruptcy. While the regime chooses to under-emphasize the extent of privatization by avoiding the word itself and referring to enterprise "restructuring," there is no doubt that significant conversion of public firms to private ownership is taking place. Moreover, the much greater use of joint stock corporations is a fundamental part of enterprise restructuring, for both privatized firms and those that remain under public management. Thus, for the first time on a significant scale, effective control of joint stock corporations can be contested openly. This is a fundamental factor facilitating further financial reforms, because for the first time we can expect equity markets to begin to function as real markets for corporate control. Government limitations requiring that the state maintain majority or controlling interests are being repealed. Clearly, a flood of new firms is being launched onto the formal and informal markets.

Despite this fundamentally positive development, a number of questions are unresolved. These questions create new uncertainties that may retard the pace of financial reform. First, the role of enterprise restructuring in resolving bank debt problems is not yet clear. The banks have substantial stakes in firms that are being restructured. The recently adopted Banking Law has decreed a separation between the commercial and investment roles of financial institutions, and prohibits bank ownership of equity. Government interpretation of the law has tended to interpret this separation relatively strictly, as part of the attempt to prevent bank-related institutions from using bank funds to speculate in the market. This is unfortunate, since flexibility in this respect could greatly facilitate both enterprise restructuring and the attempt to reduce the bad loan problem. Banks might well package loans and sell them as equity stakes; or swap them to subsidiaries; or sell convertible bonds. Unquestionably, the conversion of bank debt into equity and convertible bonds could be a non-trivial part of the ongoing restructuring of enterprises (Li and Li 1996; Xu 1997). Regardless of the specific forms adopted, it is likely that the overall trend of financial development will shift. Capital market development is likely to accelerate, while bank expansion is likely to slow.

Already, the Chinese government shows signs of being willing to facilitate a large-scale shift of financial structure away from the banking system and towards capital markets. The government has recently given its blessing to creation of mutual funds, and these are likely soon to be joined in the market by other institutional players, including pension funds and insurance companies. At the same time, the banking system faces an unprecedented opportunity to deal with its stock of bad debts. A combined program of enterprise balance sheet restructuring and fiscally supported write-offs of bad debt could make a serious dent in the bad debt problem. As bank customers are converted to joint stock companies and sold off to private investors, there will be more options for dealing with bad debts. But the resulting process will likely be messy and non-transparent. Many banks will be compelled to simply write down old debt in order to facilitate the privatization ambitions of local government officials.

Moreover, China's banks have yet to resolve the flow problem. Ownership of the state banks continues to be expressed in vague and inconsistent ways that do not provide bank managers with adequate incentives for making appropriate loan decisions. The ongoing agency problems within the banks undermine what would otherwise be an obvious avenue of approach to enterprise restructuring, which is to have the banks play a greatly enhanced role as monitors of newly restructured enterprise management groups. Clearly, the banks are important stakeholders in China's corporations. Most SOEs rely on the banks for virtually the totality of their external financing. Moreover, banks provide substantial amounts of long-term capital, which strengthens the argument for long-term links between banks and enterprises, including the formation of financial groups. Obviously this gives the banks a potentially strong role in disciplining enterprise behavior, since enterprises have limited alternative sources of finance. In recognition of the large stake banks hold currently in SOEs, banks should be encouraged to put representatives on Boards of Directors, and the current prohibition of banks holding equity should be relaxed (though not eliminated). Banks should be allowed to hold small equity stakes, perhaps for limited periods (up to two years) as part of restructuring efforts. This would help banks gain experience, provide better incentives, and prepare banks for a more active monitoring role in the future.[5] But such measures can only provide a small incremental benefit under current conditions. In addition, it is essential that the government move quickly and decisively to restructure the banks themselves. Enterprise restructuring without bank restructuring is unlikely, in the long run, to be successful. Control over financial enterprises ought also to be restructured, and the role of government ownership reduced.

In broader terms, the government now seems willing — for the first time — to countenance a withdrawal of household funds from the banking system. If this is accompanied by an orderly write-down of bad debts, and recapitalization of the banking system, we can expect to see the beginnings of a shift away from the bank-dominated financial system. Here the maintenance of a low inflation environment presents a precious opportunity to relax controls over the banking system. With significantly positive real interest rates, returns to bank assets are sufficiently attractive that the threat of large scale withdrawal of deposits should be modest (provided implicit government guarantees remain in place). Thus, the government need not erect barriers to prevent the outflow of bank deposits, and need not restrict household choice of alternative financial assets unduly. At the same time, the potential flood of new listings should soak up substantial liquidity on the stock market, and prevent the launch of an unsustainable speculative bubble. In a word, with macroeconomic stability and significantly positive real interest rates in the banking system, the overall financial system is close enough to equilibrium to permit rapid liberalization.

It should be clear that the current period is one of great opportunity. But it is also one of substantial risk. The complexity of the problems facing China's policy-makers has increased sharply. Chinese leaders have displayed an extremely cautious approach to financial reform over the past decade. Repeatedly, they have retreated from liberalization measures after what they saw as speculative excesses erupted. Premier Zhu Rongji, in particular, seems to have an almost allergic reaction to speculation, and a determination to maintain financial development within a fairly strictly controlled environment. Given the weakness of standard regulatory institutions in China, that preference for control has often meant a slow pace, and even periods of retreat, in the financial liberalization process. Some of these individual decisions certainly seem to have been questionable. Overall, however, the cautious pace and preference for control looks rather good in the light of the widespread financial problems in the rest of Asia. As we have seen, it is not that the Chinese financial system is in fundamentally better shape than elsewhere in Asia: quite the contrary. But the determination of the Chinese government to maintain control and stamp out speculative excesses have thus far prevented financial problems from mushrooming.

One aspect of that caution that has emerged as particularly important in the 1997-98 period is the separation between domestic and international financial markets. China clearly differs from the Southeast Asian economies in the absence of strong links between domestic financial markets and foreign currency markets, which is directly due to the caution exercised by Chinese leaders in not pushing to achieve capital account convertibility more rapidly. In the absence of linkage, the Chinese government has been able to move on at least two occasions to deflate domestic asset bubbles. In 1993-94, and again in mid-1997, that in their judgment threatened to upset financial equilibrium. These measures have been at least partially successful, though they were unable to prevent the emergence of a massive property bubble in major cities during the same time period. Given still fairly rudimentary tools to manage financial markets, it is reasonable to think that relative success in these areas is at least partially due to the cautious pace of liberalization.

However, a cautious approach to financial development and liberalization implies deferring problems for the future, and in some respects may allow problems to build up so that they eventually become unmanageable. China's financial system still suffers from important weaknesses, and these weaknesses are likely to intensify over the next year or two. Default risks are substantial. Economically, there is no intrinsic reason why China cannot deal with the problem of bad debts. However, in practice, China's leaders, managers, and technocrats face daunting problems of actually putting together a workable and politically feasible program to deal with bad debts (Lardy 1998:128-82). At the same time, the favorable configuration of low inflation and rapid progress on public enterprise restructuring, which prevailed during 1997-98, cannot be expected to last forever. Already, during 1998, the Chinese government began to show concerns about excess slowing of the economy. In this respect, both lagged effects from the earlier austerity program, and the external effects of the Asian crisis were implicated. The initial government response was to increase infrastructure investment in order to offset declining external demand and stagnant domestic consumption demand. While this policy was sensible, it required relaxing the attitude toward banks, and encouraging them to expand lending, including lending to state-owned enterprises. Clearly, this policy involves some retreat from the policy package that was driving enterprise restructuring in 1997-98, and will inevitably create future costs making the next stages of financial development more difficult. It will require extreme vigilance and skillful management on the part of China's policy-makers to manage these costs, and to encourage continued and accelerated financial development, without stumbling into a major financial crisis.

Notes

1. Interest rates after July 11, 1993. Specialized banks pay 10.62% for annual loans from the PBC, 10.26-10.44 for seasonal loans, and 10.08 for "overnight" loans of less than 20 days. PBC, *China Financial Outlook '95*, p. 96.
2. This regulation actually conflicts with the July 1, 1994 company law, which states that all shareholders have the right to transfer their shares. Nonetheless, at least until recently, it was the earlier regulation restricting the transferability of government shares that held sway.
3. The Taiwan stock market is also characterized by extremely high turnover. Singh (1997) reports that in 1989, the Taipei market traded nearly $3 billion daily, compared to $2 billion in London, and less than $6 billion in New York.
4. Corbett and Jenkinson (1995) find that between 1970 and 1989, the stock market in the UK made a net negative contribution to corporate investment finance, while that in the US was positive, but quite small. Fry (1997) reports that the Taiwan stock market produces a larger flow of dividends to the household sector than the flow of new stock issues.
5. In Japan, banks hold 19% of corporate equity, and in Germany the Figure is 10%. In the US, of course, banks are prohibited by the Glass-Steagal act from holding equity directly. See Dittus and Prowse, p. 23.

References

Almanac of China's Finance and Banking. *Zhongguo Jinrong Nianjian*. Beijing: Zhongguo Jinrong, Annual.

Baer, H., and C. Gray. 1996. "Debt as a Control Device in Transitional Economies: The Experiences of Hungary and Poland." in R. Frydman, C. Gray, and A. Rapaczynski, eds., *Corporate Governance in Central Europe and Russia: Volume 1: Banks, Funds, and Foreign Investors*. Budapest: Central European University Press [Distributed by Oxford University Press].

Begg, D., and R. Portes. 1993. "Enterprise Debt and Financial Restructuring in Central and Eastern Europe." *European Economic Review* 37:396-407.

Caprio, G., and R. Levine. 1994. "Reforming Finance in Transitional Socialist Economies." *World Bank Research Observer* 9(1):1-24.

Caprio, G., and D. Klingebiel. 1996. "Bank Insolvency: Bad Luck, Bad Policy, or Bad Banking?" in M. Bruno and B. Pleskovic, eds., *Annual World Bank Conference on Development Economics*.

Cheng, X. 1991. "Distribution of National Income during Economic Reform," processed. San Francisco: 1990 Institute.

China Economic News. 1997. "Tizhi fengxian youshei chengdan?" (Who will bear the systemic risk?). *Zhongguo Jingji Xinwen [China Economic News]*, August 18:15.

China Finance. various months. *Zhongguo Jinrong*. Beijing.

China Monthly Statistics. Hong Kong: Economic Information and Agency.

China Price Yearbook. various years. *Zhongguo Wujia Nianjian*. Beijing: Zhongguo Wujia.

Corbett, J. and T. Jenkinson. 1994. "The Financing of Industry, 1970-89: an International Comparison." *Discussion Paper No. 948*. London: Centre for Economic Policy Research.

Dittus, P. 1994. "Bank Reform and Behavior in Central Europe," *Journal of Comparative Economics* 19(3):335-96.

Dittus, P., and S. Prowse. 1996. "Corporate Control in Central Europe and Russia: Should Banks Own Shares?" in R. Frydman, C. Gray, and A. Rapaczynski, eds., *Corporate Governance in Central Europe and Russia: Volume 1: Banks, Funds, and Foreign Investors*. Budapest: Central European University Press [Distributed by Oxford University Press].

Du, X. 1996. *Jingji Zhuanxingzhong de Jinrong Chuangxin [Financial Innovation during Economic Transformation]*. Shanghai: Lixin Kuaiji Chubanshe.

Faison, S. 1996. "Inflation Curbed, But Not Growth, China Asserts." *New York Times* July 16:C1, C7

Fry, M. 1997. "In Favour of Financial Liberalisation," *The Economic Journal* 107(442):754-770.

Hoshi, T. 1995. "Cleaning Up the Balance Sheets: Japanese Experience in the Post-War Reconstruction Period," in M. Aoki and H. Kim, eds., *Corporate Governance in Transitional Economies: Insider Control and the Role of Banks*. Washington, DC; The World Bank.

International Finance Corporation. various years. *Emerging Stock Markets Factbook*. Washington, DC: IFC.

Jing, X., and S. Bingxi. 1997. "Bank Risk: Current Situation, Trends, and Defenses" *Gaige* 1:45-54.

Lardy, N. 1998. *China's Unfinished Economic Revolution*. Washington, D.C.: The Brookings Institution.

Li, D., and L. Shan. 1996. "Guoyou Qiye Zhaiwu Chongzu de Yige Xin Silu" *Gaige* 2:39-47.

Liu, J. 1996. "Doubts and Speculation about 'Legal Person' Stocks" *Gaige* 2:63-68.

Macroeconomic Research Office. 1987. "The Macroeconomic in the Process of Reform: Distribution of National Income." *Jingji Yanjiu* 8:16-28.

Meek, P. 1991. "Central Bank Liquidity Management and the Money Market," in G. Caprio, Jr. and P. Honohan, eds., *Monetary Policy Instruments for Developing Countries*. Washington, DC: World Bank.

Naughton, B. 1987. "Macroeconomic Policy and Response in the Chinese Economy: The Impact of the Reform Process." *Journal of Comparative Economics* XI:3.

_____. 1996. "China's Emergence and Future as a Trading Nation." *Brookings Papers on Economic Activity* 2:273-344.

People's Bank of China Research and Statistics Department. 1992. *China Financial Statistics (1952-1991)*. Beijing: Zhongguo Jinrong.

Rostowski, J. 1995. *Banking Reform in Central Europe and the Former Soviet Union*. Budapest: Central European University Press [distributed by Oxford University Press].

Singh, A. *Corporate Financial Patterns in Industrialising Economies: a Comparative international Study*. IFC Technical Paper No. 2. Washington, D.C.: World Bank.

_____. 1997. "Financial Liberalisation, Stockmarkets and Economic Development." *The Economic Journal* 107(442):771-82..

Statistical Yearbook. various years. *Zhongguo Tongji Nianjian*. Beijing: Zhongguo Tongji.

Su, D. 1997. "A Study of the Behavior of Chinese Stock Markets." Paper presented at the Annual Meeting of the American Economics Association Annual. January 5.

Xu, M. 1997. "How to Deal with the Bad Assets of Specialized Banks" *Gaige* 3:76-84.

Xu, X., et al. 1994. *Zhongguo Nongcun Jinrong de Biange yu Fazhan 1978-1990 [Chinese Rural Finance Change and Development, 1978-1990]*. Beijing: Dangdai Zhongguo: 1994.

_____. 1998. "Views of urban residents on the Social Situation in 1997-1998." In R. Xin, ed., *1998 Nian: Zhongguo Shehui Xingshi Fenxi yu YuCe [Analysis and Projection of Social Situation: China 1998]*. Beijing: Shehui Kexue Wenxian.

Zhao, W. 1996. *Zhongguo Huobi Zhengce Chuandao Jizhi*, Chengdu: Xinan Caijingdaxue.

9
Money Market in China

Hong Chang, Baizhu Chen and Yang Li

Introduction[1]

The economic reform started in 1978 has brought impressively high economic growth to China. But the economic growth in China has not been stable. To achieve stable and persistent economic growth, financial market reforms now become increasingly important. In particular, transforming the People's Bank of China into a relatively independent central bank that relies on market mechanisms to influence the money supply is a critical first step to achieve that goal. However, monetary policy tools relying on market mechanisms cannot be effective only if there is an efficient and sophisticated money market, an integral part of the Chinese financial system.

The money market is generally defined to include all financial instruments, easily converted to means of payment (M1), that are used by government, financial institutions, and non-financial enterprises for short-term funding or placements. They include government or central bank obligations, negotiable notes (including negotiable certificates of deposit, trade bills, and bankers acceptances), commercial paper, foreign exchange swaps or forward contracts, interbank loans, and repurchase contracts ("repos"). Since the short term government obligations and foreign exchange swaps or forward contracts in China are very insignificant, our main focus will be on the interbank market, repurchase agreements, and commercial papers.

The money market is an integral component of a sophisticated financial structure. It first provides short-term liquidity to the market participants and tools of monetary policy to a central bank. The money market interest rates serve as the reference rates for pricing all debt instruments. However, the contributions to the financial development in developing nations have largely been ignored. The pioneering work on financial development in low-income countries by Shaw (1973) focused primarily on the banking system. In McKinnon's classic work (1973) on financial markets in developing countries, the role of money markets was also ignored. Only Fry (1988) and the World Bank Report (World Bank 1989) suggested the importance of money markets in the financial development of a developing country. Even less work has been done on the Chinese money markets. Li's work (Li 1996a, 1996c) documented a very preliminarily description of the money markets in China. Xie (1996) discussed policy issues of liberalizing interest rates in China. He argued for sequential liberalization of interest rates. Zhong (1996) outlined steps to establish a nationwide, unified interbank market. To our knowledge, this chapter is the first comprehensive analysis of the Chinese money market.

We examine each individual instrument of the Chinese money market. We find that the interbank market becomes relatively more sophisticated and more efficient since the establishment of a unified interbank market in 1996. The interbank interest rates are cointegrated and any one of the interbank interest rates can be used as a reference rate in pricing other interbank instruments of different terms of maturity. However, as other interest rates such as the central bank loan rate are not market determined, the overall interest rate structure distorts resource allocation among different segments of the Chinese financial system, such as among the interbank market and other short-term financial loan market. To allow efficient allocation of resources among different markets, all interest rates need to be determined by the market mechanism. Even though the People's Bank of China requires that the interbank interest rates be taken as the reference for pricing the repurchase agreement, the opposite is found as our result indicates that the interest rates in the two markets are not cointegrated. We also find that the repo market seems to be segmented, possibly because different trading centers and stock exchanges set different rules, and information of demand and supply in one place is not quickly transmitted to another due to the nonexistence of a nationwide computer network. Based on the limited data available on the commercial paper market, we suggest that credibility of enforcing the "commercial paper law" and accurate risk assessment are two important factors for further developing the commercial paper market.

The second section of this chapter provides an overview of the financial market in China. The third section is an overview on the Chinese money market. The fourth examines the interbank market. Discussions on repo market and commercial paper market are carried out in the fifth and sixth sections. The seventh section is a brief discussion on the monetary targeting. The final section concludes.

Overview of the Financial Market in China[2]

One measure of financial development is an economy's monetization, or the extent to which transactions are made in domestic currency rather than through barter or the use of foreign exchange. The ratio of M0 or M1 to GDP, thought not a perfect measure, tends to reflect the degree of an economy's monetization. Table 9.1 lists the ratios of currency (M0), narrow money (M1), and broad money (M2) to gross domestic product (GDP). Narrow money consists of currency in circulation plus banks' demand deposits, whereas broad money is M1 plus banks' time and saving deposits. A relatively underdeveloped economy usually has a higher level of home production and self-sufficiency and thus a lower M0/GDP or M1/GDP ratio because of limited market transaction.[3] Usually as economies develop, the M0/GDP or M1/GDP ratio tends to increase. But when income reaches a certain level, these ratios will level off. Japan, Hong Kong, and Singapore, high-income economies that are also international financial centers, all have relatively high M0/GDP or M1/GDP ratios compared with other Asian countries. These are fully monetized economies. By 1996, China's income per person was still far less than these high-income Asian economies, but its M0/GDP or M1/GDP ratio exceeded all of them. It suggests that after twenty years of economic reform, the Chinese economy is quite monetized.

TABLE 9.1 Per Capital GDP and Money Ratios, 1980, 1988 and 1996

	M0/GDP			M1/GDP			M2/GDP		
	1980	1988	1996	1980	1988	1996	1980	1988	1996
China	0.08	0.14	0.13	0.20	0.35	0.42	0.32	0.62	1.11
Japan	0.07	0.09	0.10	0.29	0.31	0.37	0.86	1.12	1.12
Hong Kong	-	-	0.08	0.18	0.21	0.18	0.69	1.89	1.34
Singapore	0.13	0.12	0.08	0.24	0.25	0.20	0.64	0.88	0.84
Korea	0.05	0.04	0.04	0.10	0.10	0.10	0.33	0.38	0.46
Malaysia	0.09	0.10	0.08	0.18	0.20	0.29	0.53	0.72	0.97
Philippines	0.04	0.05	0.06	0.09	0.07	0.11	0.21	0.23	0.54
Indonesia	0.05	0.04	0.04	0.10	0.14	0.10	0.19	0.41	0.53

Data Sources: Cole, Scott and Wellons (1995), International Monetary Fund (various issues), and Research and Statistics Department of the People's Bank of China (various issues).

Because there is an increased propensity to hold financial savings in the form of bank savings and time deposits, the ratio of broad money to gross domestic product (M2/GDP) generally keeps rising with per capita income (Gurley 1967). In 1980, M2/GDP in China was substantially smaller than in Hong Kong, Japan, Malaysia, and Singapore. It was about the same as in Korea. By 1996, China's M2/GDP ratio was ranked third among these economies reaching 1.11 which was almost at the same level as Japan's. It had exceeded Singapore's. From 1980 to 1996, M2/GDP in China had grown almost by 250%. In comparison, the percentage change in M2/GDP was 30.2% for Japan, 94.2% for Hong Kong, 31.3% for Singapore, 39.4% for Korea, 83.0% for Malaysia, 157.1% for Philippines, and 178.9% for Indonesia.

TABLE 9.2 Assets of Deposit Taking Financial Institutions, 100 million yuan

Year	State Bank	Comm Bank	RCC	UCC	Finance Co.	SDI	Total Asset	GDP
1993	33194.5	1965.7	3749.6	1182.4	162.9	2328.1	42583.2	34634.4
1994	41781.4	3182.1	5526.1	2168.7	277	2802	55737.3	46759.4
1995	49945.7	4685.2	7229.4	3081.3	489.6	3261.6	68692.8	58478.1
1996	59470.5	6673.3	9234.1	3870	820.2	5866.1	85934.2	68593.8
Avg	46098.0	4126.6	6434.8	2575.6	437.4	3564.4	63236.8	52116.4
Ratio to Total Asset	0.737	0.085	0.100	0.039	0.006	0.055	1	0.825
Ratio to GDP	0.893	0.075	0.121	0.047	0.0068	0.067	1.212	1

Note: State Bank is the four state commercial banks. Comm Bank is the other commercial banks. RCC is the rural credit cooperatives. UCC is the urban credit cooperatives. SDI is the special depository institutions.

An alternative to look at financial development is to compare the relative importance of various deposit-taking financial institutions. Table 9.2 compares assets of the four state-owned commercial banks, other commercial banks, the rural credit cooperatives, the urban credit cooperate, the financial companies and the special depository institutions. The four state banks are the Bank of China, Industrial and Commercial Bank of China, Agricultural Bank of China, and Construction Bank of China. The assets of UCC cover urban credit cooperatives and urban cooperative banks. The special deposit institutions are financial trust and investment companies, including leasing companies as well as policy banks such as the State Development Bank. From 1993 to 1996, assets of the four state commercial banks accounted on average about 74% of the total assets of all deposit taking financial institutions and about almost 90% of GDP. Assets of other commercial banks and rural credit cooperatives each accounted about 10% while other three deposit taking financial institutions, urban credit cooperatives, financial company and special depository institutions, together took the other 10% of the total assets. The ratio of total assets of depository taking financial institutions to GDP between 1993 and 1996 on average was 1.212. By comparison, the ratio of total assets of depository taking financial institutions to GDP was 8.63 in 1989 in Hong Kong, a financial center in Asia, which was more than seven times of the ratio in China. Deposit-taking financial institutions in China were less developed and were dominated by the four state commercial banks. However, even though other deposit-taking financial institutions together accounted only about a quarter of the total assets, all of them had seen their shares increased during this period while the share of the state commercial bank had declined. The fastest growing deposit-taking financial institution was the financial companies (30% per year) and followed by other commercial banks (21% per year).

Overview of the Money Market in China

Before discussions can be carried out, the definition of a money market has to be clearly specified. There is no universally agreed upon definition of money market. Like in most of other studies, we define a money market to include all financial instruments such as debt instruments with maturity of one year or less which can be easily converted to means of payment (M1). Equity or ownership shares are excluded. This definition covers interbank loan, repurchase agreement, commercial bills, and treasury bills or short-term government bond with maturity less than a year. Though treasury bills have been issued since 1981, most of them have maturity over one year. Short term treasury bills with maturity of one year or less were issued first in 1994, however the quantities were extremely small (table 9.3). The treasury bills issued with maturity one year or less were valued at 13.24 billion yuans, 11.79 billion yuans and 64.98 billion yuans respectively in 1994, 1995, and 1996. They accounted 0.65%, 0.5% and 2.34% of M1 in each year. Though there had been a substantial increase in 1996, the government had decided to stop issuing short-term treasury bills from 1997 on. Thus in this chapter, the money market instruments discussed only include interbank loan, repurchase agreement, and commercial bills.

TABLE 9.3 Treasury bills with maturity of one year or less, 100 million yuans.

	1994	1995	1996	1997
Short term T bills	132.35	117.89	649.81	-
% of M1	0.65	0.50	2.34	-
% of GDP	0.28	0.20	0.96	-

Source: The People's Bank of China Quarterly Statistical Bulletin.

A well-functioning money market is integral as the basis of a well-developed financial system. One of the most important basic functions of a money market is to provide liquidity to those who need and to offer returns to those who have short-term cash surplus. A good example is the interbank market in which financial institutions with a cash surplus position provide liquidity to those with a short-term cash deficit position. Depending on how well developed a money market is, it can help avoid a liquidity crisis by serving as a buffer to absorb unexpected financial shocks or disturbances. In a market where interest rates reflect free and uncontrolled demand and supply conditions for short-term funds, the money market interest rates can serve as the reference guides for pricing all other debt instruments, such as bank loan rates or the central bank's discount rate. To serve as the reference rates, the money market interest rates must be market determined. Often longer-term, more risky forms of debt instruments are priced as increments over a basic reference rate. For example, in many countries, one money market interest rate frequently used as a reference rate is LIBOR (London Interbank Offering Rate). In addition, since most developing countries still have very undeveloped capital markets, a well-developed money market in which short-term debt instruments are properly priced can serve as groundwork for subsequent issues of medium- and long-term debt instruments. Moreover, a well functioning money market can help the central bank achieve its monetary policy objects. The central bank can conduct open market operations to influence the amount of liquidity in the financial system. It can use the fluctuations in money market interest rates as a barometer of the degree of tightness or ease in the money market.

TABLE 9.4 Ratio of Money Market Trading Transaction to GDP

	1993	1994	1995	1996
MM/GDP	0.180	0.188	0.263	0.789

Sources: *The People's Bank of China Quarterly Statistical Bulletin* various issues, *China interbank Market Annual Report*, *China Security Daily*.

The Chinese money market is very primitive. It did not exist in the first few years of the economic reform. It only became a relatively important market in terms of quantity in recent years. To measure the relative importance of the Chinese money market, we calculate the ratio of money market transaction volume to GDP in China. The money market transaction volume is calculated by adding the transaction volumes of the interbank loan, repurchase agreement, and commercial paper. Table 9.4 lists this ratio from 1993 to 1996. The ratio of money market transaction volume to GDP in China in 1993 was 18%, It increased to 26% in 1995 and further increased 79% in 1996. It indicates that the Chinese money market as a percentage of GDP has more than quadrupled from 1993 to 1996. Even though the money market in China has grown at an impressive rate particularly in recent years, it is still a relatively small market compared with other Asian economies. Even in 1988, the ratio of money market transaction volume to GDP in Hong Kong was 314%, in Singapore was 895%, and in Malaysia was 108%, which were all substantially larger than China in 1996.

Interbank Market in China

The interbank market in China began to exist after the January of 1981. Before the economic reform, there was effectively only one bank, the People's

Bank of China. In this kind of monobank system, no interbank borrowing or lending was necessary because liquidity needed by a bank could be provided by the government, while extra cash was channeled to the government. No interest payments on the loan were required. The financial reform in 1984 re-established various financial institutions, such as the Agricultural Bank of China and People's Insurance Company of China. At the same time, subdivisions of the People's Bank of China became relatively independent banking identities more or less responsible for their own financial activities. Further, reserve requirement were mandated for commercial banks. All these changes made necessary the interbank borrowing and lending which were to cover short-term cash positions. Unauthorized small-scale interbank borrowing and lending existed sporadically since 1981 particularly in relatively developed provinces. Only after 1986 when the State Council legitimized the interbank borrowing and lending, did interbank market reached a significant scale.

Figure 9.1 shows the development of the interbank market during the ten-year period since 1986. The interbank market in China experienced a dramatic increase in 1987, when the transaction volume increased to 230 billion yuan, almost eight times the transaction volume in 1986. It further increased to 262 billion yuan in 1988. However, at the time when the interbank market experienced phenomenon growth, very few market regulations were put into place. Market irregularities were common. Many non-bank financial institutions, particularly finance companies, actively participated in the interbank market and a large portion of interbank funds was used to finance fixed asset investments that were generally long-term in nature in stead of covering short-term liquidity position. The excessive flow of funds through the interbank market to fixed asset investments might have exacerbated high inflation in 1988. A series of decrees were issued by the People's Bank of China between late 1988 and early 1990. These decrees were aimed at limiting the market irregularities, limited the participation of non-bank financial institutions in the interbank market, regulated the usage of interbank funds, and imposed an upper limit on terms and rates of interbank loans. The transaction volume of the interbank market hovered around the 1988 level from 1989 to 1991. As economic growth sped up in 1992, the interbank market also steadily expanded, and peaked in 1995 with the transaction volume reaching more than 10,000 million yuan. Large excess demands for interbank funds in the early 1990s existed, as suggested by the fact that the monthly interest rate for the interbank market loan reached 20% in some cities, more than three times of the upper limit, 6%, imposed by the People's Bank of China. A large portion of the interbank funds went to the real estate market and stock market for speculative purposes. More decrees from the People's Bank of China followed in 1993 to regulate the interbank market in terms of the usage of fund and interest rate charged. These decrees suppressed the market irregularities for a period of time. However, with segmented financial market, loose regulations, non-market determined interest rates, and limited transparency, the so-called market "irregularities" would soon emerge again once the government administrative controls were loosened.

FIGURE 9.1 Trading Volume of Interbank Market, 100 million yuan

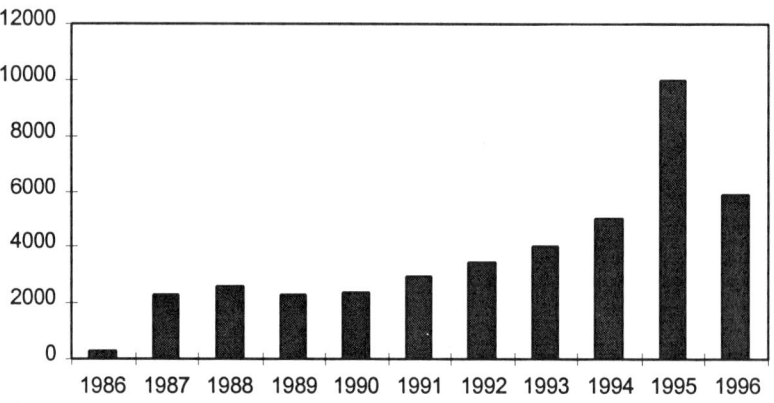

Source: Li (1996a) and China Interbank Market Annual report (1996).

On January 3, 1996, to unify the segmented interbank market, a nationwide interbank market was launched. It consisted of two trading levels: a primary network and a secondary network. The participants of the primary network included the 15 headquarters of the commercial banks that are so authorized by the People's Bank of China, 35 financing centers that are associated with the provincial People's Bank branches, 4 urban credit cooperatives and several national trust and investment companies. The interbank transaction is conducted using the computerized central trading system, the China Foreign Exchange Trade System.[4] The net position of the main office of each commercial bank can be loaned to or borrowed from the main offices of other commercial banks that are authorized to participate in the interbank market. The trading center in a province can also participate in the primary network to balance the demand of and supply for the fund within the province. The secondary network consists of 35 finance centers that are located in 35 provinces, municipal cities, and autonomous regions. The participants of the secondary network include commercial bank branches and sub-branches at the prefecture and municipal level which are authorized by their head offices, local trust and investment companies, urban and rural credit cooperatives, insurance companies, financial leasing companies, and financing companies. The primary and secondary networks are inter-connected. Transaction information of one network enters into the other and thus the interest rates of the two networks closely mirror each other. For example, if there is an excess demand for loans in a finance center in the secondary network, the finance center can access loans from other finance centers, commercial banks, and national investment and trust companies through the primary network.

FIGURE 9.2 Net Position in Interbank Market of four state banks and others, 100 million RMB yuan

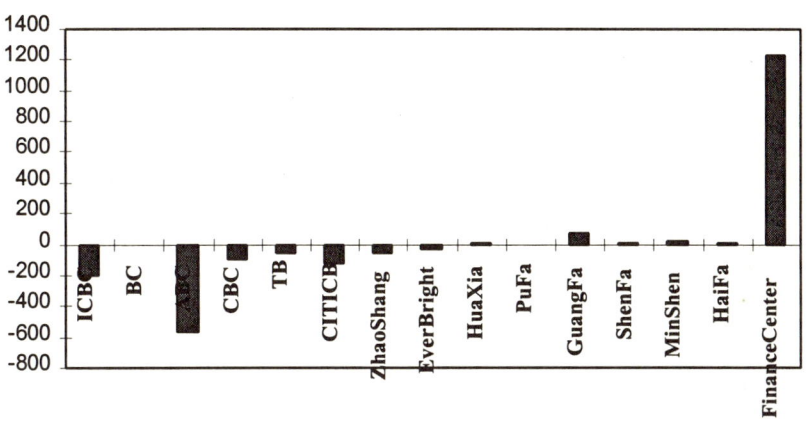

Source: China Interbank Market Annual Report (1996)

As indicated in Figure 9.2, the 35 finance centers were the major borrowers in 1996. While other commercial banks, such as GuangFa and ShenFa, were net borrowers in the interbank market, the state-owned commercial banks tended to be net lenders. This suggested that the state-owned commercial banks might have incentives to channel excess funds to the interbank market instead of lending to state-owned enterprises, as they were often required to. In fact, the four state-owned commercial banks were all net lenders in almost every month of 1996.

The interest rate in the unified national interbank market is determined by the market demand and market supply. The People's Bank of China does not directly intervene in the market through administrative measure. However, interbank interest rates are influenced by the monetary policies of the central bank. The terms of interbank loans cover 1-day, 7-days, 20-days, 1-month, 2-months, 3-months and 4-months. No instruments with maturity longer than 6 month exist. Loans with 7-day maturity accounts 26% of total daily transaction followed by 2-month (25%) and 1-month (15%). Figure 9.3 compares the daily interest rates in the unified national interbank market on

7-day, 1-month, and 3-month loans from the beginning of 1996 to the end of that year. The interbank interest rates fluctuated around 13% in the beginning of the year, which were generally higher than the central bank loan rate—the interest rate on the loan made by the People's Bank of China to financial institutions, 10%-11%. Even during the year as the interbank interest rates moved downward, they were still most of the time higher than the central bank loan rate. This created an arbitrage opportunity for commercial banks that could get loans from the People's Bank of China with a relatively low rate of interest and then channel the proceeds of these loans to the interbank market for a higher rate. It was quite possible that the large increase in the capitalization of the interbank market was partly due to the arbitrage opportunity created by this interest rate structure. This could send a false signal to the central bank that there was excess money demand and wrongly spark calls for the central bank to increase the money supply. In order for the People's Bank of China to conduct monetary policies based on correct market information, an urgent reform is to adjust this interest rate structure.

FIGURE 9.3 Comparison of Interbank Rates

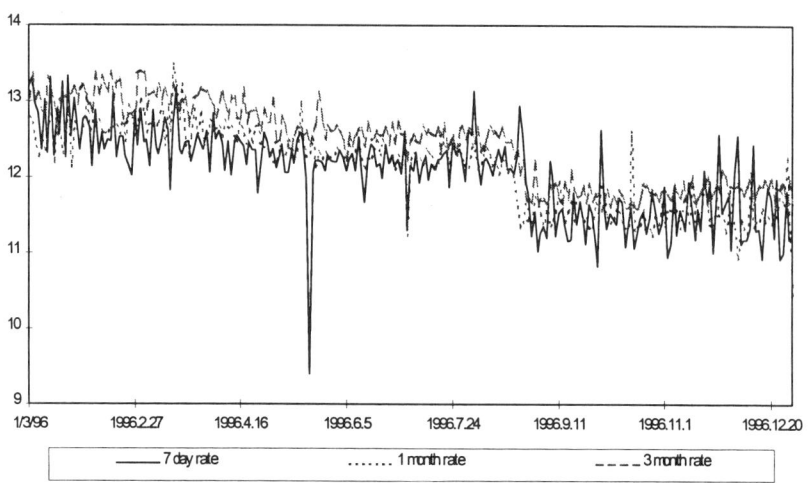

One important question is the time-series properties of interbank interest rates for different terms of maturity. In particular, we first test whether each interest rate can be modeled as a unit root process driven by weakly-dependent innovation sequences, i.e., $y_t = y_{t-1} + e_t$, where e_t is drawn from the ARMA(p, q) class. The alternative hypothesis is that the interest rates are stationary processes drawn from the ARMA(p, q) class. Notice that when the random error, e_t, is drawn from an independent and identical process, the unit root model is in fact a random walk model, which is commonly associated with the efficient market hypothesis literature in the theory of finance.[5]

Also, the unit root hypothesis implies that shocks affecting the time series will not be dissipated for a very long time and therefore the time series will not display mean-reverting properties. Assuming that the data are consistent with the unit root hypothesis, we then test whether the interbank interest rates of various terms of maturity are cointegrated. If they are, this will suggest that the interest rates of different terms of maturity are moving together over time and thus one interest rate can be used as a reference rate that dictates the long-run movement of other interest rates of different terms of maturity.

TABLE 9.5 ADF unit root test and KPSS stationarity test

	ρ_v	η_v
one day	-2.851	1.282
seven day	-2.280	2.150
twenty day	-1.288	1.253
one month	-1.047	0.899
two month	-0.708	0.637
three month	-0.927	0.537
four month	-2.046	1.269

Note: In the Dickey-Fuller test, the lags included in the regressions are chosen according to the Schwarz's Information Criterion. The 5% critical values for ρ_v test is -2.873. The 5% critical value for the KPSS η_v test is 0.463.

Unit root test results on interbank interest rates are given in Table 9.5. We use the Augmented Dickey-Fuller procedure to test the null hypothesis that the interest rate data are drawn from a unit root process. Since the Dickey-Fuller test takes the unit root as the null hypothesis, it is often argued that the test result may biased against the alternative hypothesis. To ensure the accuracy of our result, we apply the KPSS procedure (Kwiatkowski, Phillips, Schmidt, and Shin 1992) which tests the null hypothesis that the time series are stationary against the alternative that the time series contain a unit root. Table 9.5 clearly indicates that the null hypothesis of a unit root cannot be rejected according to the Augmented Dickey-Fuller test. Further, the null hypothesis of stationarity can be rejected according the KPSS test for all the interbank interest rates. Thus we can confidently conclude that all interbank interest rates can be modeled as a unit root process. This implies that the interest rates do not display mean-reverting behavior or the impact of a shock on the interest rates is likely to remain for a very long period.

Given that all the interest rates in the interbank market are consistent with the unit root hypothesis, we can test the cointegration of the interest rates to see if they move together in the long run. In another words, we examine whether there are common factors driving the interest rate movement. Toward that end, we apply the Johansen cointegration procedure. In testing cointegration, we include a trend variable as well as no trend variable in the cointegration equations. Since the data of 1-day interest rate begin on July 1, we exclude the 1-day interest rate first in the whole sample and test the cointegration of 7 day, 20 day, 1 month, 2 month, 3 month, and 4 month interest rates. The result is exhibited in Table 9.6. We have found that the null hypothesis of no cointegration can be rejected for these six interbank interest rates. We also conclude from Table 9.6 that there are five cointegration relations or common factors existing for these interest rates. These results seem to suggest that there is a common factor driving the interbank interest rates. Any one of the interbank interest rates can be used to price other interbank rates.

TABLE 9.6 Johansen cointegration of interbank interest rates with various terms of maturity

No trend in the cointegration equation			
Hypothesized No. of CE(s)	Likelihood Ratio	5% Crit Value	1% Crit Value
None **	204.385	94.15	103.18
At most 1 **	141.563	68.52	76.07
At most 2 **	87.742	47.21	54.46
At most 3 **	54.097	29.68	35.65
At most 4 **	24.232	15.41	20.04
At most 5	0.230	3.76	6.65
Trend in the cointegration equation			
	Likelihood Ratio	5% Crit Value	1% Crit Value
None **	216.329	114.90	124.75
At most 1 **	152.945	87.31	96.58
At most 2 **	98.485	62.99	70.05
At most 3 **	61.463	42.44	48.45
At most 4 **	31.120	25.32	30.45
At most 5	7.109	12.25	16.26

Note: ** indicates significant at 5% level. The number of lags in the cointegration equation is determined by the Schwarz Information Criterion (SIC).

Repurchase Agreements

A significant financial development in recent years in China has been the rapid growth in repurchase agreements, or repos as they are frequently called.[6] A repurchase agreement is an acquisition of funds through the sale of securities, with a simultaneous agreement by the seller to repurchase them at a pre-negotiated price at a later date. The repos are effectively equivalent to a loan that the buyer of the securities lends to the seller. They are in fact secured means of borrowing and lending of short-term funds in which underlying securities serve as the collateral. The same transaction of repurchase agreement viewed from the perspective of the lender is frequently used by participants in the repo market as the reverse repurchase or resell agreement. The reverse repurchase agreement is a purchase of securities, with a simultaneous agreement by the buyer to resell them at a pre-negotiated price at a later date. In the following discussion, we use repo to refer both the repurchase as well as the resell agreements.

An illustration of a typical repurchase agreement transaction is helpful in understanding this financial instrument. Suppose that a firm determines that it has funds that are not needed immediately, but will likely be used to meet expected business expenses in a day or so. The firm wishing to earn interest on these excess funds for a day can arrange to purchase a government security from a commercial bank with an accompanying agreement that the bank will repurchase the security on the following day. If the firm decides that the excess funds will be available for a longer period, a longer-term repurchase agreement can be arranged.

There are many advantages of repo transactions. First of all, through repurchase agreement, firms with large cash balances can earn a secured market rate of return on these balances until they actually are used for payments. Second, repurchase agreements provide banks with a useful source of short-term funds. Third, there is no basic reserve requirement against funds obtained from repurchase agreement so long as the underlying securities are obligations of the government. In short, the repo market provides liquidity, profitability, and security to the parties involved. It enhances the efficiency of the financial market. Besides, the repo market is also a vehicle through which the central bank can conduct its monetary policy.

FIGURE 9.4 Volume of Repurchase Agreements, 100 million RMB yuan (one-sided transaction)

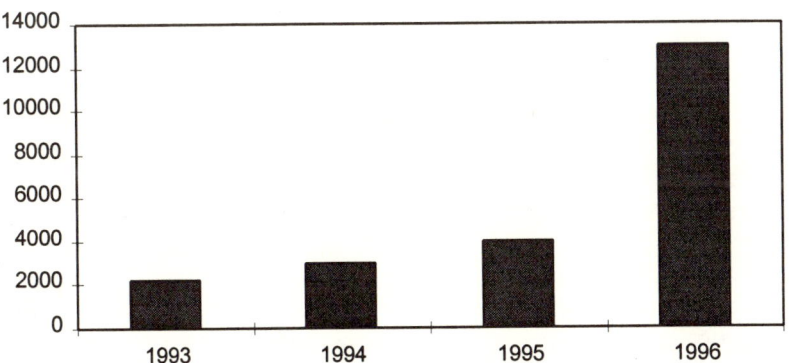

The repo market in China began in 1991 when the Shanghai Stock Exchange and the Security Trading Automatic Quotation (STAQ) system were just established. Many exchanges and trading centers in China participated in the repurchase transactions. Since then the repo market experienced rapid growth (Figure 9.4). The one side transaction volume of repurchase agreement was 225 billion yuan in 1993. It increased to more than 400 billion yuan in 1995 and further more than doubled from 1995 to 1996. The maturity of the underlying securities of the repurchase agreement covered 7 days, 14 days, 28 days, 91 days and 180 days.

TABLE 9.7 Composition of Participants and Trades in the Repo Market, 1995

Participants	On-site Repurchase	Resell
Banking institutions	1%	2%
Non-bank financial institutions	95%	97%
Non-financial institutions	4%	1%

Trades	Off-site Repurchase	Resell
Among financial institutions	43%	91%
Financial institutions and residents	54%	5%
Financial institutions and non-financial firms	2%	3%

There are two kinds of transaction in the repo market: "on-site" trading and "off-site" trading. The "on-site" trading takes place in the Shanghai or Shenzhen Stock Exchanges, the trading centers located in different cities, as well as within the STAQ network. The payment and clearance of the "on-site" trading have to be carried out in the stock exchanges or STAQ system. The "off-site" trading refers to those transactions that do not take place in the stock exchanges and STAQ system, but rather in the security trading centers in cities such as in Wuhan and Chendu. Unlike the "on-site" trading, the payment and clearance of "off-site" trading only occur within the trading centers and do not go through the STAQ system or the stock exchanges. Table 9.7 shows the composition of participants and transactions in the repo market. We find that the main participants in the on-site repo market are the non-bank financial institutions. In the off-site market, about 43% of repurchases occur among financial institutions, 54% between financial institutions and residents, and only 2% between financial institutions and non-financial firms. This implies that repurchase agreements to a large degree are used by the financial institutions to absorb savings from residents. It can also be seen from Table 9.8 that residents and non-financial institutions provide 27% of total fund in the resell agreements while they take 21% of total fund in the repurchase agreements. This suggests that residents and non-financial institutions are the net lenders in the repo market. The major borrowers in the repo market seem to be the non-bank financial institutions.

TABLE 9.8 Fund Source, 1995

	Repurchase	Resell
Residents	13%	20%
Banking institutions	6%	7%
Non-bank financial institutions	73%	66%
Non-financial institutions	8%	7%

No unified repo market exists in China currently. The repo transaction only matches demand and supply of a particular geographic location. The segmentation of the repo market is evident from Figure 9.5, which compares the daily seven-day repo interest rates in the Shanghai Stock Exchange and the Shenzhen Stock Exchange.

FIGURE 9.5   Comparison of Repo Rates in Shanghai and Shenzhen Stock Exchanges

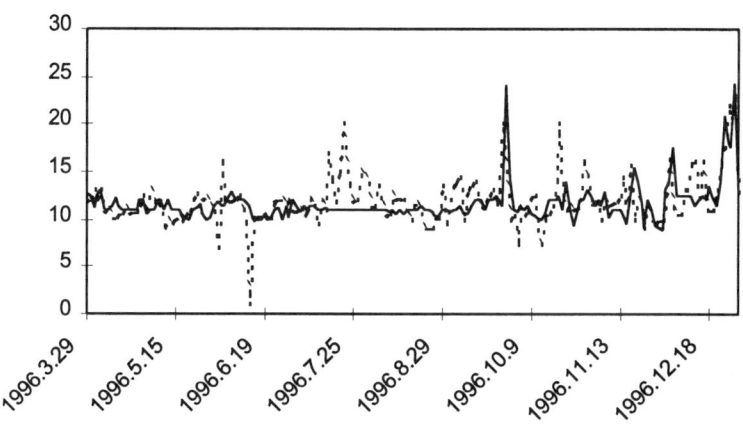

The repo interest rate data available to us starts from March 29, 1996 and ends on December 31, 1996. If the repo market were not segmented, the interest rates in the two stock exchanges would have been equal. Figure 9.5 clearly indicates the opposite. The fact that the difference of repo interest rates between the two stock exchanges does not disappear sometimes even for as long as several months suggests that the repo market is effectively segmented. This market segmentation could both be possibly attributed to government regulation or information segmentation. In fact, most of the transactions of repurchase agreement occur between borrowers and lenders located in the vicinity of a trading center or a stock exchange (Li 1996a, 1996b). There is no computer network to transmit transaction information in a trading center or a stock exchange to another. The market segmentation in the repo market allows the existence of arbitrage opportunity for a relatively long period of time.

FIGURE 9.6 Comparison of Interbank Rate and Repo Rate in Shanghai Stock Exchange

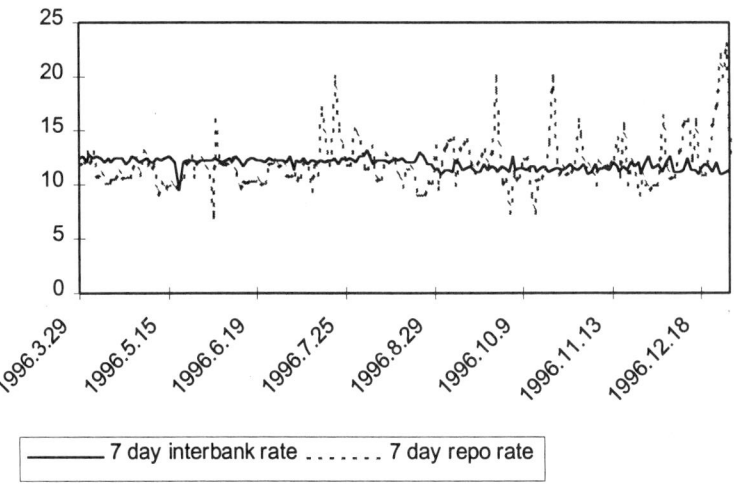

Figure 9.6 compares the daily interest rates of seven-day maturity in the interbank and repo markets.[7] We find that the interest rate in the repo market is more volatile than the interbank rate. The difference between the repo rate and interbank rate sometimes is very large. For example, the repo rate reached 23% but the interbank rate was a little more than 11% on December 30 of 1996; the difference was almost 12%. We also test cointegration between the interbank rate and the repo rate of seven day maturity.[8] The cointegration test result is shown in Table 9.9. We find that the interbank rate and the repo rate of the same maturity were not cointegrated. This casts doubt upon the

idea that the interbank interest rate was taken as a reference for pricing the repo agreement as required by the People's Bank of China. It follows that the interbank rate in China cannot be used as a reference rate in pricing the repurchase or resell agreements.

TABLE 9.9 Johansen Test for Cointegration between Interbank Rate and Repo Rate

Hypothesized No. of CE(s)	Likelihood Ratio	5% Crit Value	1% Crit Value
None	9.924	15.41	20.04
At most 1	2.929	3.76	6.65

A main problem of the repo market is the market segmentation that prohibits efficiently allocating capital in the nationwide economy. The market segmentation also makes government regulation on the repo market difficult. For example, even though the People's Bank of China, the Ministry of Finance, and the China Security Regulatory Commission all required the repurchase agreement to have 100% of the underlying government bonds as the collateral, different trading centers or stock exchanges all had allowed partial collateral in repo transactions. Participants in the repo market could execute a repurchase agreement with a face value substantially higher than the value of the underlying government bonds. For example, one survey (Li 1996b) shows that among the 25 repo market participants surveyed, the ratio of government bond value relative to the repurchase agreement exceeded 40% for only 4 firms and 30% for 6 firms. For the other 15 firms, the ratios (the value of the underlying security to the value of repo agreement) were below 30%. Some firms entered repurchase agreement even without any government bonds as the underlying collateral. In fact, the repo market provided an easy source of capital for firms. Besides, monitoring the usage of capital was difficult. Firms thus had incentives to acquire capital through repo market and then to invest the proceeds in long-term projects or in stocks and real estates properties for speculative purposes. The repurchase agreement, which was to provide short-term liquidity, thus became a source of long-term or speculative financing, which resulted in many cases non-performing loans from the repo market. A nationwide unified repo market with a centralized clearance system would help the government regulatory bodies to monitor the usage of capital as well as any irregularities in the repo market.

Commercial Papers

Commercial paper is a short-term unsecured promissory note that is generally sold by large corporations on a discount basis to finance short-term working capital quickly and for short periods of time. It provides liquidity to issuers and serves as an investment vehicle for purchasers of commercial paper. Large corporations with the highest credit ratings generally dominate the commercial paper market as the commercial paper is unsecured and bears only the name of the issuer. The major issuers of commercial paper in an industrial country often include finance companies, non-financial companies, and bank holding companies.

The commercial paper market in China began approximately in 1982. The growth of commercial paper market was retarded in the first ten-year period due to the fact that no laws or regulations governing the market existed. Even after the passage of the "Commercial Paper Law" by the National People's Delegation Congress, commercial paper still played a very limited role in the Chinese money market. The total transaction volume of commercial paper in 1995 was 140 billion RMB yuan, which was substantially smaller than the interbank market volume 1000 billion RMB yuan as well as the repo market volume 400 billion RMB yuan. Commercial banks in China held 14.9 billion RMB yuan of commercial paper which accounted only about 0.3% of the total loans issued by them. One important reason that might have retarded the growth of commercial paper market was the lack of accurate risk assessment. There was no rating agency that provided coherent risk assessment of issuers of commercial paper. Even if there had been a rating agency, non-transparent accounting rules and business practices in China would prohibit accurate risk assessment. Besides, the lack of enforcement of the "Commercial Paper Law" to punish those issuers who could not honor their commercial papers also contributed to the meager size of the market. Thus to further develop the commercial paper market, enforcement of the law and correctly assessing risks of issuers are the necessarily preconditions.

Monetary Target

An important function of the money market is that it provide the means for monetary authorities to adjust primary liquidity in the domestic economy in order to target the inflation rate. In most industrialized countries, a key instrument of adjusting primary liquidity is the purchase and sale of government bonds by monetary authorities through open market operations. In the absence of government debt markets, countries sometimes adjust liquidity by discounting commercial papers issued by the private sector, but the limited supply of such notes restricts the usefulness of this instrument. Another tool to adjust liquidity is to directly control the credits extended by the central bank to commercial banks. An alternative way is to impose quantitative restrictions, particularly on interbank borrowing or on bank credit issued to corporations. Such quantitative restrictions were effective means of adjusting liquidity but often resulted in shocks and severe disruptions to the money market.

The central bank of China has long been using direct administrative methods such as quantitative restrictions to adjust liquidity. But it has started moving more toward a market-based mechanism in adjusting liquidity, such as open market operations. To maintain a correct level of liquidity in the economy in order to target a certain level of inflation rate, the central bank needs to choose an intermediate target. Often the intermediate target is either an interest rate or the growth rate of a monetary aggregate. The Federal Reserve System of the United States targeted the federal funds rate, an interbank interest rate before it switched to target the M2 growth rate in 1979. But it was found that the M2 demand function in the US was not stable, resulting in inaccuracy of M2 targeting, thus it switched back to interest rate targeting in 1992. The People's Bank of China has started monetary targeting in recent years. It set the growth rate of M1 below 18% and M2 below 25% in order to control inflation rate within 10% in 1996. The actual growth rates of M1 and M2 were 18.9% and 25.3% respectively in 1996, and combined with other administrative measures, resulted in a 6.1% growth rate of the retail price index and 8.3% growth rate of the consumer price index. The 1997 growth rates of M1 and M2 were targeted at 18% and 24% (Ma 1997).

TABLE 9.10 Research on Monetary Targeting in China

	Monetary Aggregate	Income Elasticity	Price Elasticity	Target*
Chow (1987)	real M0	1.16-1.35	-	21.6-23.5%
Feltenstein & Farhadian (1987)	real M2	1.37	-	23.7%
Blejer et al (1991)	real M2	1.53	-	25.3%
Hafer & Kutan (1994)	nominal M2	1.33	1.52	28.5%
Huang (1994)	nominal M2	2.12	1.56	36.8%
Chen (1997)	real M0	1.43-1.50	-	24.3-25%
	real M2	1.79-1.93	-	27.9-29.3%

*assuming 10% income growth and 10% inflation

As macroeconomic data have become more available, there have appeared more studies on monetary targeting in China. Table 9.10 lists several studies on the Chinese monetary targeting in recent years. Chow (1987) was probably the first study applying the quantity theory of money on the Chinese data from 1951 to 1986. He found that the real M0 income elasticity was about 1.16-1.35. If M0 is chosen as the targeted monetary aggregate, his result implies that the targeted M0 growth rate should be 21.6%-23.5% assuming the growth rate and inflation rate both are 10%. Feltenstein and Farhadian (1987) and Blejer, et al (1991) found that the real M2 income elasticity coefficients were 1.37 and 1.53. If the economy grows at 10%, the upper level of M2 growth rate should be 23.7% or 25.3% to control inflation within 10%. Hafer and Kutan (1994) estimated that the income elasticity and price elasticity for nominal M2 in China were about 1.33 and 1.52, while Huang's estimates

(1994) were 2.12 and 1.56. Assuming the income growth rate to be 10%, the upper level of M2 growth rate is 28.5% according to Hafer and Kutan's estimates (1994) in order to have 10% or lower inflation rate. But using Huang's (1994) result, it can be as high as 37%. Chen (1997) found that the money demand for M0 and M2 were both stable between 1951 and 1991, and thus both could be used for monetary targeting. According to Chen's (1997) result, to maintain 10% inflation, M0 and M2 growth rates should not exceed 24.3%-25% and 27.9%-29.3%, assuming 10% income growth rate. His result on M0 is similar to Chow's (1987) and his result on M2 is very close to Hafer and Kutan's (1994).

As indicated above, the M2 growth rate in 1996 in China was 25.3%. If we use Chen's (1997) estimate and the actual growth rate of GDP in that year 9.7%, then the inflation rate can be estimated to be 6.58%-7.9%, which is very close to the actual inflation rate 6.1%-8.3%. According to the *1997 Economic Situation and Prospect of China* (Ma 1997), the GDP growth rate is estimated to be about 10.5% and the retail price inflation rate should be around 6%. This report calls for targeting M2 growth rate at 24%. According to Chen's (1997) result, the upper level of M2 growth rate should be between 24.79%-26.26%.[9]

Conclusion

Several conclusions can be drawn from the chapter:
1. The Chinese money market is still in a very primitive stage. Only very limited money market instruments are available. Short-term government obligations with maturity less than one year only existed for three years before they were prohibited by the government. These short-term government securities are important not only because they form the basis for the pricing longer term government securities, but also they are an integral part of the money market which carry important information for monetary policy of the central bank.
2. Interbank markets are relatively well developed and more efficient compared with other segments of the money market, possibly because of the establishment of a unified national interbank market. The interbank interest rates are cointegrated and any one of the interbank interest rates can be used as a reference rate in pricing other interbank instruments of different terms of maturity. However, as other interest rates such as the central bank loan rate are not market determined, the overall interest rate structure in the Chinese financial system distorts resource allocation among different segments of the financial system, such as among the interbank market and other short-term financial loan markets. To allow efficient resource allocation among different markets, all interest rates need to be determined by the market mechanism. Liberalizing some interest rates but not others will not necessarily improve the efficiency of resource allocation.

3. The repo market seems to be segmented, possibly because different trading centers/stock exchanges set different rules and information of demand and supply, and do not quickly transmit to other centers or exchanges due to the non-existence of a nationwide computer network. We find no cointegration between the repo rate and the interbank interest rate with the same maturity, implying that the interbank interest rate is not taken as the reference for pricing repurchase agreement, as is required by the government. A unified national repo market will improve its efficiency.
4. Even though the commercial paper was among those money market instruments that first experimented in China, its market is still very much underdeveloped. Compared with other segments of the money market, the commercial paper market plays a very limited role. The development of the commercial paper market is largely retarded by the lack of rating agencies for accurate risk assessments, as well as the lack of credibility for enforcing the "Commercial Paper Law."
5. The People's Bank has begun targeting some monetary aggregates, e.g. M1 or M2, to control inflation. We find that properly choosing a monetary aggregate for targeting is able to control inflation. For example, if the GDP growth rate is 9.7% and the targeted inflation rate is 7%, then our result indicates that if M2 is chosen as the targeted aggregate, its growth rate should be less than 24.4%, which is very close to the actual M2 growth rate in 1996, 25.3%.[10]

Notes

1. We are grateful to Mr. Dexu He, Dr. Gang Yi, Dr. Qiren Zhou, and many colleagues in the People Bank of China, Financial Research Institute, China Center for Economic Research for their helpful comments and suggestions. Financial support from the Washington Center for China Studies is acknowledged. We are particularly thankful to Mr. John Hao Jia of the WCCS for his help. All errors are our responsibility.
2. Dipchand, Zhang, and Ma (1994) discuss Chinese financial market before the economic reform.
3. The M0/GDP or M1/GDP ratio also depends on other factors such as the rate of inflation as well as the substitutability of foreign for domestic currency.
4. This is the same system that provides for the settlement of foreign exchange transactions.
5 Recent studies on the efficiency of foreign exchange market or bond market often directly test whether the foreign exchange rate or interest rate contains a unit root.
6. Li (1996b) has an excellent description on the development of Chinese repo market.
7. Since our repo rate started on March 29, we truncate the interbank bank rate so that it has the same sample size as the repo rate.
8. Before the cointegration test can be carried out, the unit root test for the repo rate is done first. We find that the null hypothesis of a unit root cannot be rejected

for the repo rate, but to save space, the result is not listed here.
9. The 1997 growth rate in China is 8.9%. The actual inflation rate is only 3%, substantially lower than estimated by Ma (1997). The main reason is that besides of monetary targeting, the central bank of China still resorts many administrative tools (*Wall Street Journal*, December 31, 1997).
10. The inflation rate in 1996 was 6.1-8.3%.

References

Blejer, M., D. Burton, S. Dunaway, and G. Szapary. 1991. "China: Economic Reform and Macroeconomic Management." *IMF Occasional Paper*, No 76.

Ma, H. 1997. *The Economic Status and Outlook of China*. China Development Publisher.

Chen, B. 1997. "Monetary Policy and Inflation in China." *Journal of Macroeconomics*.

Chow, G. 1987. "Money and Price Level Determination in China." *Journal of Comparative Economics* 11.

David C., H. Scott, P. Wellons. 1995. *Asian Money Markets*.

Dickey, D., and W. Fuller. 1981. "Likelihood Ratio Statistics for Autoregressive Time Series with a Unit Root." *Econometrica* 49.

Dipchand, C., Y. Zhang, and M. Ma. 1994. *The Chinese Financial System*. Greenwood Press.

Feltenstein, A., and Z. Farhadian. 1987. "Fiscal Policy, Monetary Targets, and the Price Level in a Centrally Planned Economy: An Application to the Case of China." *Journal of Money, Credit, and Banking* 19.

Fry, M. 1988. *Money, Interest, and Banking in Economic Development*. Baltimore, Johns Hopkins University Press.

Gurley, J. 1967. "Financial Structure in Developing Countries." In *Fiscal and Monetary Problems in Developing States*, ed. D. Krivine. New York: Praeger.

Hafer, R., and A. Kutan. 1994. "Economic Reforms and Long-run Money Demand in China: Implication for Monetary Policy." *Southern Economic Journal* 60.

Huang, G. 1994. "Money Demand in China in the Reform Period: An Error Correction Model." *Applied Economics* 26.

International Monetary Fund. various issues. *International Financial Statistics*.

Johansen, S. "Estimation and Hypothesis testing of Cointegrating Vectors in Gaussian Vector Autoregressive Models." *Econometrica* 59.

Kwiatkowski, D., P. Phillips, P. Schmidt, and Y. Shin. 1992. "Testing the Null Hypothesis of Stationary Against the Alternative of a Unit Root: how Sure Are We That Economic Time Series Have a Unit Root?" *Journal of Econometrics* 54.

Li, Y. 1996a. "Financial Reform in China: History and Future," Working Paper, Finance Research Center, Chinese Academy of Social Sciences.

———. 1996b. "The Analyses of Government Bond Repo Market in China," *Economic Research* August.

———. 1996c. "Money Market Development: Precondition for Reforming the Macroeconomic Adjustment Mechanism." *Financial Research* January.

Shaw, E. 1973. *Financial Deepening in Economic Development*. New York: Oxford University Press.

McKinnon, R. 1973. *Money and Capital in Economic Development.* Washington DC: Brookings Institution.
People's Bank of China. 1996. *China Interbank Market Annual Report.*
Research and Statistics Department of the People's Bank of China. various issues. *The People's Banks of China Quarterly Statistical Bulletin.*
World Bank. 1989. *World Development Report.* Washington, DC: World Bank.
Xie, P. 1996. "Toward a Market-oriented Interest Rates Policy in the Transformation of China's Economy." In *Interest Rate Liberalization and Money Market Development,* ed. H. Mehran, B. Laurens, and M. Quintun. IMF.
Zhong, Q. 1996. "Basic Outline for the National Interbank Market in Renminbi," In *Interest Rate Liberalization and Money Market Development,* ed. H. Mehran, B. Laurens, and M. Quintun. IMF.

10
Credit Quota as a Banking Risk Control in China: A Retrospect

Ding Lu and Qiao Yu

Introduction

A major lesson to be learned from Asia's recent financial turmoil is the importance of managing the banking sector's exposure to financial risks. A central banking system compatible to the financial needs and risk management of a market economy should emerge from financial market reforms in China. This chapter provides a retrospective of the credit quota plan as the major risk management lever in China's banking sector and discusses the implications of its recent abolition.

The official demise of the credit quota plan by the end of 1997 marked an important milestone in China's central banking reform. The credit quota plan was a crucial feature of China's banking sector, which has been a two-track control system. On the one hand, the sector has the structure of a central banking system and its conventional control levers, which include the central bank's lending to state banks, fractional reserves, discount rates and, more recently, open market operations. One the other hand, China's central bank—the People's Bank of China (PBC)—has been using the monetary-control levers (such as the credit quota plan) typical of a centrally planned economy to achieve ad hoc objectives.

For years, the effectiveness of the credit quota as a shield against financial risk and macroeconomic instability has been a controversial issue among academics and policy makers. In the most recent macroeconomic cycle, China watchers were impressed by the effective role of Beijing's credit squeeze in "soft-landing" the apparently overheated economy while taming double-digit inflation after 1993 (Prystay 1996). Yi (1994) observed that in the beginning of the 1990s, the money supply mechanism was still by and large controlled by the central government through ad hoc administrative orders, rather than through economic leverages. Since its inception, the central bank had shown its ability to control the macroeconomic condition of the economy by credit quota planning. Other economists, however, have cast doubt on the effectiveness of the credit quota plan. The World Bank (1995) reported that the PBC's credit plan had been less binding and vulnerable to leakage and to the diversion of funds in the 1990s. Naughton (1993) argues that only one of the two systems (the credit quota system and the central bank's fractional reserve system) can be binding for any given bank. He points out that in the period of 1992-93, the credit quota control was not effective in containing the loan growth. Ma (1995) also pointed out that the local banks and governments often strategically manipulated the use of investment funds to induce higher credit ceilings from the central bank. The interplay between the central and local authorities made it difficult for the central bank to keep its commitment to the pre-announced credit ceilings and thus created inflation.

Evaluation of the effectiveness of the credit quota plan has great implication upon perspectives for China's financial market. With the credit quota plans removed, will the PBC be able to maintain its control over domestic money supply? Will China's banking sector be exposed to greater financial risks from now on? Some economists, such as Yi (1994), recognized that the absence of real privately owned commercial banks determines the ineffectiveness of a pure central banking system. Administrative controls, including credit quota plans, should continue to be the dominant and effective instrument. The World Bank (1990, 1995) urged China to pursue institutional reforms of the PBC and make the central bank less vulnerable to pressure from local governments. It also recommended accelerating the development of indirect instruments of monetary policy that should reduce Beijing's reliance on ad hoc administrative measures to restore effectiveness of the credit plan. The World Bank, however, stopped short of suggesting an early removal of the credit quota controls. Yet, Mehran and Quintyn (1996) saw that a gradual approach to liberalization (in the financial and banking sector) had perhaps been postponed for too long and might have led to distortions elsewhere in the economy. Naughton (1993) stressed that since banks in China had already made the transition toward a fractional reserve system, it was harmful and unnecessary – even when an austerity policy was needed – to return to a system in which credit was determined primarily by credit quotas.

By reviewing the central bank's performance records in controlling the uses of the banking fund, this chapter evaluates the effectiveness of the credit-quota plan as a banking risk control lever and macroeconomic policy instrument. In retrospect, a number of factors had already seriously eroded the effectiveness of credit controls before its abandonment. Credit-plan-induced rent seeking at the local level had also resulted in undesirable consequences to economic efficiency. We conclude that since the mid-1990s, the time has been ripe for China to facilitate its transition toward a full-fledged central banking system by removing the credit plan.

Performance Record of Credit Quota Plan[2]

During the period 1953-78, China adopted a Soviet-style centrally planned economy (CPE), which had the following main features:

1. Enterprises in manufactures and services were mostly nationalized and all farmers were collectivized.
2. The state set a physical production plan for all production agents and directly allocated material resources.
3. Enterprises were required to turn in profits to the state, while their capital investment and working capital were financed through the government's budget.
4. Apart from use as the exchange medium for retail sales, wage payments, and the procurement of agricultural goods, the role of money was very limited in the economy. Commodity prices, interest rates, and exchange rates were all under the tight control of the state. With no linkage to relative resource scarcity, prices merely served as accounting units in central planing process.

Under the CPE system, the People's Bank of China (PBC) was in essence an accounting subsidiary of the Ministry of Finance. There was no division of roles between a central bank and commercial banks in the system. The PBC simply functioned as a "monobank" to provide financial assistance for the fulfilment of the state physical production plan. It centralized deposits, allotted credits to production agents for their partial working capital needs (mainly wage payments), and issued currency to fill in the mismatch between deposits and loans.[1]

Due to coordinating deficiencies in resource allocation and the lack of working incentives for production agents, the pre-reform Chinese economy was severely plagued by economic inefficiency. Since 1978, however, economic reforms initiated in rural areas have significantly revitalized the economic performance in nearly all respects. For almost two decades, China has proudly displayed a spectacular average annual GDP growth rate of over nine percent.

Although the changes in China's economy have many facets, the most important include the transition toward a market system and the decentralization of economic decision-making power to lower authorities in regional governments and production agents. The first one liberalizes price determination and alters the means of resource allocation. The second grants autonomy to enterprises and localities and motivates the latter to seek profits or local interests, hence allowing the growth of the non-state sectors. Propelled by these two developments, the Chinese economy has been quickly monetized as money has become the medium for all kinds of economic activities. The ratio of M2 to GDP rose from 42 percent in 1978 to 104 percent in 1995.

Banking reform began in 1980 when the so-called *cha-e kongzhi* (credit-gap control) system was introduced between the PBC headquarters and its local branches. The system features a national credit plan to control the range of credit gaps between fund availability and fund usage for all local banks (Zhao 1989). Compared to the previous centrally planned mono-banking system, the reform gave more incentives to local banks to mobilize savings and deposits.

The People's Bank of China was restructured into a central bank in 1984. Meanwhile four big state "specialized banks" were reorganised or established to take over regular banking businesses in the period of 1979-84. These banks include the Bank of China (BOC 1979), the Agricultural Bank of China (ABC 1979), the People's Construction Bank (PCB 1981),[3] and the Industrial & Commercial Bank of China (ICBC 1984). Since the restructure of the Bank of Communications (BOCOM) into a quasi-commercial bank in 1986, there have emerged a few more smaller-sized commercial banks and many non-bank financial institutions that are organized on a share-holding basis. The long-term goal was to develop all the specialized banks into full-fledged commercial banks (SCSR 1993:283).

After its inception, the operation of China's central banking system has followed four principles (SCSR 1993:285):

1. *Unified planning*: The PBC plans all credits available in the banking sector.
2. *Account division:* The specialized banks are financially independent from the PBC, which holds required reserves and excess reserves of the specialized banks.
3. *Fund availability:* Fund availability (the assets of banks in the form of cash and deposits) constrains fund usage (loans).
4. *Inter-bank lending:* Inter-bank lending has been allowed with mandatory restrictions on the range of discount rates and terms of lending. Inter-bank lending was first restricted in provinces and regions, and a nation-wide inter-bank market did not exist until January 1996.

In this less centralized post-reform banking system, the PBC's main control leverage was an overall credit ceiling on financial institutions, which was consistent with the government's annual money supply target. Accordingly, the national credit planning and credit-quota allocation worked together with the control of interest rates to ensure the fulfilment of the credit-ceiling goal.[4] The national credit plan matched annual fund usage with fund sources and decided the volume of new currency issued to balance the gap between fund uses and sources. The PBC combined all of the fund sources and uses for all banks, which were aggregated from the banks' regional branches. The national credit plan controlled credit uses both quantitatively and qualitatively through the specification of mandatory annual credit targets. These targets included the overall bank credit ceiling, the capital investment ceiling, and the "policy loan" assignments to finance agricultural procurement, poverty-alleviation, and other centrally planned uses. In addition, the plan provided non-binding guided targets for lending, such as working capital loans for state-owned enterprises.

Besides using direct plan-based instruments to target the overall credit ceiling, the PBC has gradually developed other alternatives of credit control. One is the central bank's lending. When a bank's deposits and other fund resources are inadequate to meet the loan needs, the bank may seek extra liquidity by borrowing from the PBC. There exist four types of PBC lending. The first is annual lending to banks, which is set by the credit plan and mainly relates to policy-oriented bank loans. The second type is seasonal lending to solve the liquidity shortages of banks caused by production seasons. The third is overnight lending to meet the temporary needs of banks. The last is discount lending for securities, which is trivial in size. The PBC controls the amount of these loans as well as their interest rates (discount rates). Since the PBC's lending accounts for approximately one-quarter to one-third of the fund sources for banks, it has a strong leverage effect on their credit condition.

Other leverages include occasional adjustments by the PBC to interest rates and the reserve requirement for banks. In 1993, for instance, the required reserve ratio was 13 percent, with an additional required special deposit (extra-reserve requirement) of five to seven percent (Yi 1994:66). In addition, credit control is often reinforced by the government's direct administrative interventions. This includes the issuance of ad hoc administrative decrees to direct financial activities, and the dispatch of inspection teams to check upon the enforcement of government orders.

Ironically, the introduction of the present credit quota scheme caused immediate chaos in the money supply. By 1984, the credit-gap control policy had restricted the gap between fund availability and the fund usage, but not the overall credit quantity. A bank that could mobilize more deposits and fund sources was accordingly able to issue more credits. In 1984 (the inception year for the central banking system), the PBC announced that the credit-gap control would be replaced by the credit quota plan and the future credit quota allotment would be based on the banks' credit base for that year. Eager to start at a higher quota base, almost all the specialized banks and their branches rushed to expand their credits before the end of the year. Bank loans rose sharply (Figure 10.1); a consequence of the credit rush was a net increase in the currency circulation of nearly 50 percent for the year (Zhao 1989).

The credit plan had not been effective in binding domestic credit creation, as shown by a comparison between the planned credit use with the real credit use since 1981 (Table 10.1). After the introduction of the central banking structure in 1984, the effectiveness did not improve much in the second half of the 1980s. Entering the 1990s, the credit plan became even more poorly implemented. On a quarterly basis, the Word Bank (1995:52-53) also showed that during the period 1988 to 1993, the credit plan ceased to be binding on domestic credit and loan expansion whenever the economy experienced an upswing.

FIGURE 10.1 Annual Growth Rates of Loans, Nominal GDP, Real GDP and Annual Inflation Rate.

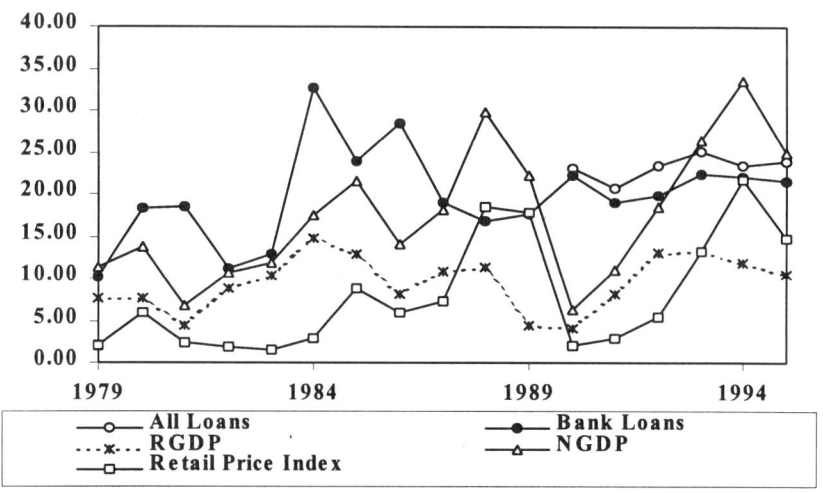

Note: "All Loans" refers to loans from all financial institutions; "Bank Loans" refers to loans from state banks only.
Source: Statistical Yearbook of China, and Almanac of China's Finance and Banking, various issues

Nor did the credit plan successfully anchor the volatility of loan expansion during the 1980s, as shown in Figure 10.1. In years when austerity programmes were fully implemented (1979, 1985, 1988-89), the monetary authorities were able to suppress the bank loan growth rate five to fifteen percentage points lower than that of the preceding year. These efforts had generally created a counter-cyclical movement of loan growth against nominal GDP growth, except for the years 1983-84. However, when the economy felt the pain and slowed down, the loan growth rate would immediately bounce back (1980-81, 1986, 1990). Behind these ups and downs of the loan growth rate were the central bank's repeated upward adjustments of its credit ceilings to accommodate demand, especially in the periods 1984-85, 1987-88, and 1992-93 (Ma 1995).

There were signs that the PBC's credit control had become increasingly less effective in the first half of the 1990s, especially after the austerity programme (1993-94). In the first half of the 1990s, the loan growth rate

201
fluctuated within a much smaller range around the 20 to 25 percent level, despite the austerity programme. The overall loan growth rate was one to five percentage points higher than the loan growth of the state banks. The World Bank (1995:49-51) concluded that bank fund leakage was on a rise due to the rapid growth of inter-bank lending operations and illicit lending activities.

TABLE 10.1 Credit Use: Planned vs. Actualised (RMB billions)

Period	Planned Credit Use	Actual Credit Use	Excess Gap
Sixth 5-Year Plan (1981-85)	Annual credit use increases by 217.0	Increased by 276 on average	27.2%
		Increased by 410 by the end year	88.9%
Seventh 5-Year Plan (1986-90)	Annual credit use increases by 574.5	Increased by 721 on average	25.5%
		Increased by 1046 by the end year	82.1%
Eighth 5-Year Plan (1991-95)	Annual credit increases by 12%	Increased by 2019 on average (equivalent to an annual rate of 21%)	123.1%
		Increased by 3385 by the end year (equivalent to an annual rate of 25%)	168.4%

Notes:
1. "Credit use" is the sum of total credit, bond purchase, gold and foreign reserves, asset at international monetary institutions and fiscal loans. The Eighth Five-Year only specifies annual increase rate for total credit.
2. The amount increased "on average" means the amount increased on five-year average.
3. The amount increased "by the end year" means the amount increase between the end years of the two periods.
4. "RMB", or yuan, Chinese currency unit, US$ 1.00 = RMB 8.35 in 1995.
Source: Almanac of China's Finance and Banking, various issues; China's Sixth, Seventh and the Eighth Five-Year Plans.

The scale of illicit lending in China's banking sector can be estimated by looking at the balancing item "other sources of funds" in the banking sector's balance sheet (Table 10.2). The item refers to the gap between major fund sources (deposits, currency in circulation, long-term debts and bank capital) and the total fund uses (all loans, budgetary borrowing and other assets): Major fund sources + "other sources of funds" = total fund sources = total fund uses.

We may interpret this balancing item as an "errors and omissions" item, which is equivalent to the sum: Errors & Omissions = valuation defects – bad loan write-offs + unaccounted sources of funds + over-accounted (or double-accounted) lending – unaccounted lending.

Of these components, the first term's impact on the errors and omissions should be relatively stable if the accounting rules remain unchanged. Whether the term has a positive sign or a negative sign is also uncertain, depending on the nature of valuation defects. In China's banking sector, the introduction of asset-liability management method in recent years did not lead to drastic changes in the basic accounting principle of recording fund sources and fund uses. Improvement in financial accounting, if any, should have the effect of reducing valuation defects.

TABLE 10.2 "Other Sources of Funds" and Their Weights in Total Fund Uses (RMB Million)

Year	State Banks		Other Financial Institutions	
1986	54,124	6.60%		
1987	72,710	7.37%		
1988	62,730	5.46%		
1989	79,860	5.89%	-5,350	-2.72%
1990	95,520	5.67%	-13,640	-5.37%
1991	77,150	3.74%	-23,910	-7.12%
1992	-117,830	-4.86%	-25,980	-5.37%
1993	-235,060	-8.03%	25,000	3.21%
1994	75,190	1.85%	-406,760	-48.28%
1995	25,060	0.49%	-497,420	-44.23%
	All Financial Institutions			
1986				
1987				
1988				
1989	74,510	4.80%		
1990	81,880	4.23%		
1991	53,240	2.22%		
1992	-143,810	-4.94%		
1993	-210,060	-5.67%		
1994	-331,570	-6.75%		
1995	-472,360	-7.56%		

Note: Statistics of the non-state-bank institutions before 1989 are not available mainly because the weight of these institutions in the financial sector was negligible.
Source: Almanac of China's Finance and Banking, various issues.

The second item, bad loan write-offs, may inflate when banks decide to stop doing business with firms in deep financial trouble, or when banks themselves go bankrupt. As shown in the next section, China's state banks had been obliged to support state-owned enterprises until very recently. As yet, there has been no case of any bank going bankrupt in China. Nor has there been any evidence of large-scale bad loan write-offs occurring in the 1980s and the first half of the 1990s.[5]

The third term, unaccounted sources of funds, may include the liabilities of banks unreported to the PBC. For banks that had hit the credit quota ceilings, the fourth term, over-accounted lending, was unlikely to be significant since they did not want to be reprimanded for over-lending above the quota. The likely case for a bank to over-report its lending was when the bank failed to mobilize enough funds to lend up to its credit quota. In such a case the bank did not want the unused quota to become an excuse for the PBC to cut its quota for the next year.

The last term should increase when banks engage in illicit lending practices unaccounted for in the side of "fund uses." The increase of illicit lending thus negatively affects the item "other sources of funds."

As shown in the last column of Table 10.2, before 1992, the balancing item ("other sources of funds") for the whole financial sector was positive but its share in total fund uses had been declining. The item dropped below zero in 1992 and continued to negatively increase both in value and in its share of total fund uses. In 1995, a total of RMB 472 billion (about 7.6 percent of all financial intermediaries' assets) was categorized as missing value in the financial sector's balance sheet, which was virtually out of the PBC's credit control.

Based on the above analysis of the balancing item — when credit quota control was more effective and illicit lending activities were less prevalent — the over-reporting by banks with unused quota would dominate the value of the item. Therefore, the positive figures in the earlier years reflect the then more effective controls of the PBC's credit plan in the banking sector. The growing negative figures after 1992 imply extensive fund leakage through illicit lending.

TABLE 10.3 Criminal Cases Prosecuted and Amount of Funds Being Investigated for Illicit Transaction in the Banking Sector

Year	Number of criminal cases involving RMB 1 million or above	Amount of funds being investigated for illicit transaction (RMB billion)
1990	-	51.90
1991	56	142.25
1992	26	145.76
1993	74	106.82
1994	116	207.60
1995	150	600.00

Source: *Almanac of China's Finance and Banking*, various issues.

The trend shown in Table 10.2 is consistent with the rise of illegal activities in the banking sector, as displayed in Table 10.3. The PBC's mandatory credit squeeze on fund uses forced an increasing share of lending activities to go underground. China's banking sector has thus been the hotbed of bureaucratic corruption. For instance, the state banking sector was blamed on the illegal collection of funds amounting to RMB 100 billion, and illicit lending of RMB 105.5 billion outside of the state sector through the interbank markets during the first half of 1993. Most of the money went into speculative trading in real estate, stocks, and securities.[6] State banks also engaged in illicit lending beyond the credit quota, by such methods as keeping secret accounts, devising fake financial reports, repurchasing bonds at discounts from firms, and extending repayment deadlines for existing loans.[7] Interestingly, the balancing item for state banks followed a pattern of change as seen similar to that of the whole banking sector up to the year 1993, when the net value of their unaccounted lending peaked at more than RMB 235 billion, accounting for 8.7 percent of their assets. The trend was held and reversed in 1994 and 1995, after China's "economic czar" (whose formal post was Vice Premier), Zhu Rongji, took over as the PBC Governor and strengthened the control over state banks' lending with uncompromising austerity.[8] This successful deed was unfortunately tarred by the sudden jump of unaccounted lending by other financial institutions for the same years. The PBC has a weaker control over these financial institutions, which are organized on share-holding basis and owned by local governments and/or various state departments. For all years except 1993, the "other financial institutions" category recorded negative figures of the balancing item. (The reason behind the positive figure in 1993 could be that the huge amount of illicit lending by state banks in the year overwhelmingly increased the unaccounted sources of funds in the balance sheet of the other financial institutions.) Remarkably, the negative value of fund source-use gap for other financial institutions in 1994 and 1995 exceeded 40 percent of their assets. This suggests that when Zhu Rongji plugged the leak in the state banking sector, illicit lending through the other financial institutions soared, leaving the fund leakage in the whole banking sector even more serious.

Risky Loans, Lucrative Borrowing, and Secured Lending

The ineffectiveness of the PBC's credit quota control mainly stemmed from a highly uneven distribution of financial risks. Under the credit quota plan, bank loans became a lucrative rent seeking target as banking risks were centralized in the central bank which controlled the credit ceilings.

Accommodation to Political Moods

First of all, all state banks, including the central bank, lack a basic political independence from China's Party-state. The PBC and specialized banks are more or less governmental or semi-governmental subdivisions. Recent reforms have yet to place the PBC in full charge of an independent policy goal to pursue in its decisions over money and credit supply. The asset usage of the state banks has been under the strong influence of the central government. Through the 1980s to the 1990s, when the government pursued a higher growth goal, the PBC had to ease credit ceilings and provide additional liquidity for banks to financially accommodate the government-initiated economic expansion. If the government switched to an austerity policy, the central bank had to tighten credit conditions and call in its loans to banks.

The post-reform business cycles in China have demonstrated some unique features. All four Party Congresses (held in 1977, 1982, 1987 and 1992) during the Deng Xiaoping era were immediately followed by periods of economic expansion and boom.[9] Generally, the economy would gain its growth momentum and rapidly expand as soon as a new Party Congress proposed growth targets and relaxed controls over the local levels. Economic overheating would then loom large in the backdrop of galloping inflation, and mounting pressures on the infrastructure would cause bottlenecks in energy and electricity supplies, transportation networks, and communication services. Economic slowdown, however, would not set in until the elite decision-makers reached a consensus and started implementing macro controls. Following the economic booms led by the four Party Congresses, four austerity programmes were respectively introduced in April 1979, April 1985, September 1988 and July 1993.

China's political history demonstrates that the economic decisions of the government have been highly volatile, especially when there was a replacement of the Party leaders. This reality inevitably resulted in a volatile credit expansion. Moreover, the central authorities — being constrained by a deteriorating fiscal status in the post-reform years — must rely heavily on the PBC's direct credit allotment to implement industrial and regional development policies. This practice, again, adds an extra incentive for the government to directly intervene in banking operations. From time to time, the PBC adjusts its mandatory and guided credit targets to accommodate changes in state development policies.

Dancing to the Local Tune

The procedure to determine quota-assignments in the banking system consisted of bargaining between the central authorities and local officials. National credit plans and local credit plans occurred as the result of a complicated political-economic process. Factors that decided annual quotas include: (a) national plan targets; (b) deposits of the previous year by regional banks; (c) regional policies (e.g. policies to promote development of certain regions). Based on the national credit plan approved by the central government, the PBC disaggregated the overall credit ceiling and other credit ceilings. These credit quotas were then allocated to the head-offices of all banks that, in turn, re-allocated them to their regional branches and subsidiaries, respectively. Technically, the PBC pre-announced the next annual credit quotas for banks in advance, allocated quotas quarterly, and monitored their usage monthly. The overall credit ceiling and the investment credit ceiling were mandatory targets by which banks must abide. A bank was not allowed to issue loans beyond the allotted quota even if it had sufficient fund resources, such as savings deposits.

In the post-reform decentralized decision-making structure, however, it has been in the interests of local governments to compete for larger share of bank credits, since most local investment projects are no longer funded by the state's budgetary grants. In this race for bank credits, local governments tried to outperform each other so as to be capable of promoting regional development and enlarging their local revenue bases. To local bureaucrats, pressing banks for more loans for their own development projects and state-owned enterprises involves little risk to their careers, as these bureaucrats are not directly responsible for returning the loans. They can, however, boast of their administrative success in generating higher local revenues or building mammoth projects.

On the other hand, local branch banks had until recently usually been willing to cooperate with the local governmental authorities, reflecting a symbiotic relationship between the local governments and the local bank branches. The hierarchical administration of China's state banks parallels that of the government. Although local bank governors are officially appointed by the central bank, local governments have often been consulted in such appointments and the remuneration. Local governments have thus played a determinant role in the personnel management of regional bank executives. Under the close supervision of local governments, a chronic macroeconomic problem in China has been local banks dancing to the tune of local authorities and acting in the "local interest." With decentralized fiscal resources, the local governments "do not like to see their banks remit excess reserves to the next level in the banking hierarchy, or to see their banks lend excess reserves to those in other localities." (Wong and Chen 1995:124)

Before the PBC worked out the national credit plan and credit quota allocation, a locality might exaggerate its funding needs, since the uses of bank funds were aggregated from regional branches. Working with the regional bank branches, there were many ways for local authorities to push for more credits from the banking system, particularly in the bottom-up process of the formulation of the credit plan. After the credit quotas were allocated, local bank branches were often pressed to extend credit to the favourite revenue-generating projects of the localities. Since bank loans were "free," or nearly free, goods in disguise (see below), local authorities would employ all kinds of administrative measures to restrict the outflow of bank funds and zealously seek more cheap credits. Thanks to the symbiotic relationship between the branch banks and the local government authorities, these banks could hardly decline the aggressive credit requests of the latter. In the past, regional bank branches have behaved like semi-independent local government banks, conducting regular banking business more or less beyond the direct supervision of headquarters. A bank might also divert bank credits from where it had been originally earmarked for use by the PBC to projects that could generate quick revenue for the local government. Funding for the purchase of agricultural products, poverty alleviation, and educational development was often circumvented in the process.[10]

Obliged to Lend

The prevailing relationship between the banking system and state-owned enterprises has been an important cause of autonomous credit growth. During the post-reform years, the government had shifted the budgetary burden of supporting state enterprises to the banking system. Two major reform schemes were introduced for the state-owned enterprises in 1983 and 1984 parallel to the 1984 banking reform. One was the so-called "*li gai shui*" (taxes-for-profits), which was to allow greater financial autonomy for state-owned enterprises. This reform sought to dismantle the centrally planned system whereby all profits, after subtracting a small portion retained for the enterprise, were simply returned to the state. A corporate tax system was to replace the profit-remittance system. By 1986 almost all of the profits from enterprises were taxed, instead of being completely remitted to the government. Another was the so-called "*bo gai dai*" (loans-for-grants), which sought to move away from the practice of providing investment funds on a grant basis from the government budget instead toward allocating working capital and investment funds through the banking system (Hua et al. 1988; Shi and Liu 1989). This jumping-off point for banking reform determined that the state banks would bear an inherent obligation to support the state-owned enterprises.

As shown in Figure 10.2, the deposit rate and the loan rate were almost equal to each other over the years. In some years, the loan rate was even lower than the deposit rate. Meanwhile, during the several years when inflation accelerated, the real interest rate could even become negative. From this, one can conclude that the role of interest rates was supplementary to direct credit controls, and bank credits were nearly-free funds or subsidies in disguise to the borrowing firms. Accordingly, many uses for credit quotas were centrally planned. The state specialized banks were obliged to provide so-called "policy loans" to meet the priorities set by the government which, by 1994, accounted for 40 percent of the loans lent by the four specialized banks (Gan 1995). For example, the Industrial & Commercial Bank of China was responsible to support the circular fund requirements and technology-upgrading needs of some large state-owned firms. The Agricultural Bank of China must provide loans to meet the needs for procurement and warehousing of certain important agricultural products. Loans by the People's Construction Bank went first to national priority-projects and firms. The Bank of China should support the fulfilment of centrally planned export and import items. On top of all that, some policy loans, such as those for capital investment in agriculture and infrastructure development and those for circular-fund needs in grain procurement, must be provided at preferential interest rates even lower than the standard rates. The PBC only subsidises a portion of the losses which arise from these services. The remaining losses must be absorbed by the local banks themselves (Zhu 1993).

FIGURE 10.2 Bank Rates vs. Inflation

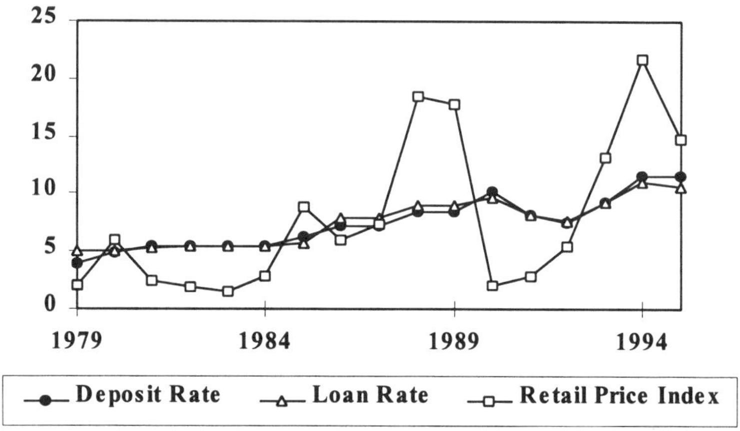

[Chart showing Deposit Rate, Loan Rate, and Retail Price Index from 1979 to 1994, with values ranging from 0 to 25]

Note: Deposit rate refers to average one-year deposit rate. Loan rate refers to the average loan rate for industrial and commercial firms' circular-fund needs.
Source: Almanac of China's Finance and Banking, 1995.

In the past, the risk of these lending activities had been low to banks managers- after all, they were doing their job, following state instructions. Furthermore, classification for non-performing loans had until recently been rather rough and irregular. Loans were recorded as "bad" only when the principal failed to get repaid, even if the borrower had long defaulted on interest payments. Large amounts of non-performing loans thus continued to remain on the banks' books as "valuable assets."

Free to Borrow

Privileged access to easy and low-cost credit has encouraged state-owned enterprises to aggressively expand borrowing from banks, with little concern for interest costs and investment risks. Though their contribution to total industrial output declined from 78 percent in 1978 to 43 percent in 1993, borrowing by state-enterprise still accounts for over 80 percent of total bank credits. According to an official survey, the average debt-asset ratio of the state-owned enterprises increased from 18.7 percent in 1980 to 54.8 percent in 1989, and 83.33 percent in 1994. As a majority of state enterprises have become nil-profit earners and loss-makers in recent years, a large number of bank loans are bad loans or problematic loans in risk of default. In 1995, for instance, the nominal average capital rate of return in the state-owned enterprises was about 6 to 7 percent, well below the 12-percent average interest rate for business loans. By the end of 1995, bad loans accounted for nearly 40 percent of the four specialized state banks' outstanding loans. Nevertheless, fear of touching off social chaos by allowing a widespread shutdown of state enterprises and consequent massive lay-offs led the government authorities to insist on pumping bank loans into the state-owned sector. As a consequence, the volume of loans was expanded by the increasing losses of the ailing state-owned sector during economic slowdowns in 1981, 1986, 1990, and 1994.[11]

The above factors work together to create a vicious cycle in the banking industry. As the Party's top leadership called for faster economic growth and reforms, expansionary policies led to an ease of bank credit control, which would very soon result in economic booms and inflation. Once the concerns over economic and social stability overwhelmed the zeal for rapid growth, the central government would carry out austerity policy to reduce credit quotas and encourage savings by hiking interest rates. As a consequence, bank loan growth slowed and bank deposits accumulated, leaving the banks with increasingly heavier interest payment burdens. As deposit savings increased faster than the credit loans, the woes of declining profits reflected in their balance sheets would press the banks to bargain for higher quotas and more PBC loans, or to find ways to circumvent credit constraints. For instance, according to an official report, in the last austerity period, the four specialized state banks saw their profits decline from RMB 34.3 billion in 1992 to 12 billion in 1994. By 1995, three of the four were in red.[12] In such a context, local initiatives would soon cause the actual loan growth to bounce back. Banks would also lobby for a cut in deposit rates and a hike in loan rates (Liu and Zhang 1996). Pressure for a looser monetary policy would thus arise from the local levels of the banking system. Eventually such pressure would lead to a new round of economic resurgence, once the top policy makers had given in or changed their priorities. Otherwise, illicit lending would have to sharply rise as a substitute.

Risk of Credit Quota Control

In retrospect, the credit quota plan had not only become increasingly ineffective but also perhaps done more harm than good to the financial security of the banking sector in its late years. The distortion induced by credit-quota has left behind a legacy of accumulated bad loans in the banking sector.

During the years when the central government carries out austerity programmes, the credit control may be reinforced by ad hoc administrative measures, as happened in 1989-90 and 1993-94. The increased control was nevertheless costly. As pointed out by Yi (1994), when the PBC squeezed credit with an austerity programme, it did not have the flexibility to achieve its objectives without hurting the overall credit condition more than necessary. When the administrative pressures were applied in 1993 on state banks to call back outside-plan loans, the relatively efficient firms were the first to be hurt since they were able to return the loans and were more care about their credibility for future loans. The lousy state-owned enterprises in the chronicle red, however, did not have the ability or the willingness to return the loans. This whipping-the-winner effect has aggravated the loss-making problem of the state-owned sector. For state-owned enterprises, the debt-asset ratio (excluding inter-firm arrears) rose from 55 percent in 1985 to 66 percent in 1997. While the (nominal) interest rate of bank loans was 12 to 14 percent in 1995, the average (nominal) rate of return in the state-owned enterprises was only 7 percent. It was estimated that the rate of return would decline further down to 5.7 percent in 1996 while the interest rate was around 12 percent (Zhou 1996). Bank loans continue to be the subsidies in disguise to the state-owned enterprises. At the end of the day, the banks must end up with large amount of bad loans. By spring 1997, China's 370,000 state-owned enterprises had already owed RMB 4 trillion debt to state owned banks. More than one in four companies had debts exceeding their assets.[13]

The credit quota and the mandatory interest rate have not only led to inefficient use of funds but also created rent that invites rampant rent-seeking activity in the form of bureaucratic corruption. Our earlier discussion of illicit lending activities shows that the PBC's mandatory credit squeeze forced a growing share of lending activities to go underground. Corruptive practice continues to be a serious problem in the banking sector. In the second half of 1996, banks and financial institutions started pumping huge amount of funds into the domestic securities market and even into the Hong Kong stock market. Alarmed by the surge of fund leakage to stock market speculation, the PBC ordered in early June 1997 all state banks to close their securities trading accounts within 10 days and stop lending to securities brokerages.[14] One example was that the Shenzhen Development Bank (SDB) used more than RMB 320 million of bank funds to speculate in its own companies' stocks between March 1996 and April 1997. In the crackdown starting in May 1997, Beijing sacked a number of officials in banking and securities business, including the head of the China Securities Regulatory Commission and the president of the SDB.[15] These rent-seeking activities waste productive resources and erode the base of the emerging legal framework conducive for doing business.

All this has exposed China's banking sector to very high operation risks. By April 1998, it was estimated that unrecoverable loans, of which the principal were not to be repaid, accounted for about 6-7 percent of the banking assets. Total non-performing loans amounted to around 25 percent of banking assets, or RMB 1.5 trillion.[16]

Demise of credit quota plan became inevitable with three major developments in banking reform after 1996. The first is the landmark promulgation of the PBC Law and the Commercial Bank Law in 1995. These laws laid the basis of a modern financial intermediary sector. This legal framework of banking industry and the emergence of commercial banks and non-bank financial institutions with plural ownership structures have prepared ready institutions for a major change in macroeconomic management of money supply. To prepare the four specialised banks for becoming full-fledged commercial banks, three policy-loan banks, namely, the National Development Bank, the Agriculture Development Bank of China, and the Export & Import Bank of China, were set up in 1994 to shoulder the burdens of providing "policy loans". The move could be a key step towards a more market-oriented banking system if it would eventually and effectively relieve the specialised banks of those burdens.

The second major development is the trial operation of a nation-wide interbank market since January 3, 1996. The largest PBC sponsored interbank market started in Shanghai as early as in 1985 to serve banks' short-term liquidity needs. Shanghai's interbank market alone grew 30 to 70 percent annually from 1985 to 1992. Before 1994, the maximum allowable maturity was 7 days, interest rates were mandated by the PBC, and transactions were mainly restricted to regions.[17] These restrictions were later gradually relaxed. In 1994, the PBC set up 43 regional interbank markets and allowed limited inter-regional transactions. Meanwhile the legal maturity was extended to allow two categories of lending activities, namely the 7-day lending and the 7-day-to-4-month lending, with respectively two ranges of interest restrictions. With these changes, the annual amount of lending in 1994 shot up to RMB 1,000 billion, 1.5 times of the amount in 1993.[18] From January 1995, the PBC increased legal maturity further to allow three lending periods, namely, the 20-day lending, the 20-to-90-day lending, and the 90-to-120-day lending.[19] In June 1996, the PBC removed the daily limits on how much lending rates could move up or down in the interbank market. These developments opened a channel for free movement of banking funds and allowed interbank interest rates to be market-driven for the first time. Funds borrowed can be used exclusively for working capital and not for investment in fixed assets, real estate speculation or purchase of company shares.[20] The nowadays interbank market is a two-tiered system. The first tier comprises the head offices of 20 major domestic banks and 35 short-term financial centres. Other domestic banks, major state bank branches and money brokerages run by the PBC are second-tier members, trading through the centres. A recent step toward opening up the market was to allow eight foreign banks to conduct RMB business in the national interbank market.[21]

The third major development is the PBC's commencement of open market operations in the foreign exchange market and bond market since 1994. With increasing current account surplus and inflow of foreign direct investment, the banks must redeem foreign currencies with the local currency. To offset the inflationary pressure on local currency, the PBC had issued financial bonds for foreign exchanges worth RMB 238 billion by the end of 1996. On April 9, 1996, the PBC started repurchasing government bonds denominated by the local currency to meet the short-term (14-day) liquidity needs of commercial banks. The open market interest rate (or the bond discount rate) is determined through a bidding process participated by the state banks. Although the operation only involved the short-term fund of RMB 2 billion in 1996, it has prepared the PBC for the management of market-driven interest rates (Qian 1997). In March 1997, the PBC boosted its re-discount business significantly by buying discount papers from the four major state banks.[22] By trading these discount papers, which are commercial papers or bonds bought from state firms at a discount rate by the four state banks, the central bank can use floating re-discount rates to influence the quantity of loans supplied by the major state banks as well as market interest rates.

FIGURE 10.3 Loan-Deposit Ratios for All State-Owned Banks and Rural Credit Co-ops

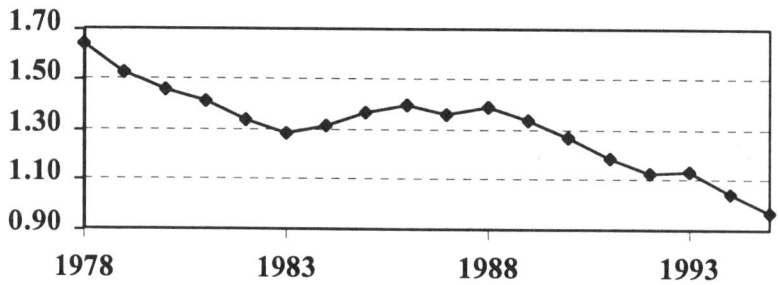

Source: Almanac of China's Finance and Banking, various issues.

Evidently, the PBC in the recent years has developed institutions and techniques to substitute instruments of a fractional reserves system for the direct credit allotment. These are the moves in the right direction toward a full fledged central banking system.

Apart from institutional reforms, the rapid commercialisation and monetisation of the economy called for a banking system to function as an efficient financial intermediary. During the period of 1978-1995, while the GDP rose by about 3.8 times, total deposits in the state banks and RCCs increased by 38 times, forming the major source of bank credits. Meanwhile, deposits by households increased by 132 times (Figure 10.3). This has raised the share of household savings in total deposits from 18.23 percent to 61.23 percent. Consequently the share of household deposits in GDP increased from 6 percent to 48.3 percent during the same period. This fact is mainly a result of the robust economic growth and income distribution in favour of households and enterprises. It is also attributed to the public's high saving propensity and the lack of sophisticated alternative financial instruments.[23] On the other hand, as displayed in Figure 10.4, the banking industry's loan-deposit ratio has been declining continuously in the past two decades from 1.63 to 0.96, indicating that banking finance has become better-founded on deposits. These changes have provided the solid ground for developing a full-fledged commercial banking system in China.

FIGURE 10.4 Changing Shares in Financial Market

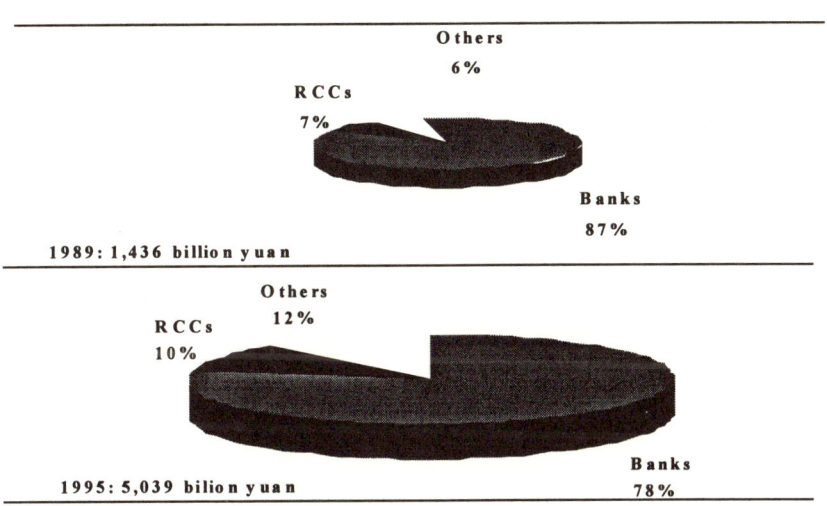

Source: *Almanac of China's Finance and Banking, 1995.*

Concluding Remarks

The retrospect of China's experience of credit quota plan implies that banking reform is irreversible. Centrally planned credit quota allotment had provided little shield against financial risks but proved to have left behind costly consequences.

The luck of future banking reforms hinges on a successful transformation of the state sector. It was estimated that, by 1997, 35 percent of state owned enterprises had debts greater than assets.[24] Since a comprehensive tax reform was introduced in 1994, Beijing has started a wholesale transformation of its ailing state-owned sector. New measures have been taken to restructure the large state-owned enterprises into modern corporations. As for the smaller state-owned enterprises, the policy consensus is to allow them to be leased or purchased by the non-state sectors. In the Fifteenth National Congress of the Chinese Communist Party (September 1997), Jiang Zemin, the General Secretary, called for the reform of the state-owned enterprises to be expedited through developing a share-holding economy. Zhu Rongji, after being made prime minister in March 1998, vowed to turn the state sector around in three years. In addition to the restructure of the state-owned sector, the privatisation of residential housing and the opening of the housing mortgage business for banks are also crucial to a conducive environment for further banking reforms.[25]

As for internal reforms, the PBC has recently beefed up its surveillance over the commercial banks in a bid to reduce their exposure to financial risks. A new accounting standard will be introduced to commercial banks by the end of 1998. All banking loans are to be classified into five categories, namely, "passed," "special mention," "substandard," "doubtful," and "loss." Accordingly, banks' bad loan provisions must be increased.[26] These measures will certainly impose more cautions on banks' lending decision.

FIGURE 10.5 Households' Deposits in Total Deposits
(in State Banks and Rural Credit Co-ops)

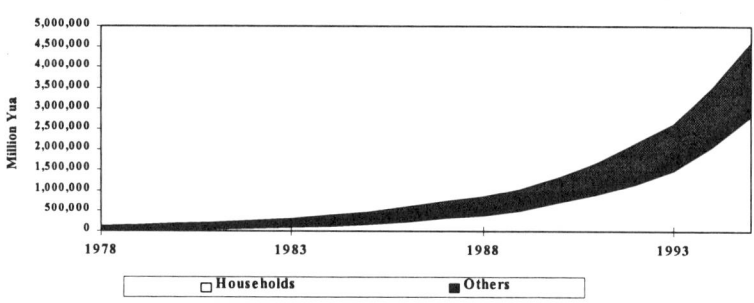

Source: *Almanac of China's Finance and Banking*, various issues.

A new problem emerged after 1996, however, has been the state banks' rising reluctance in making productive loans in the backdrop of newly introduced asset-liability auditing procedure. Stricter surveillance by the PBC has made local bank management unwilling to take business risk in lending. Compared to the banks' over-lending behaviour in earlier years, the source of current inertia did not change much. When the PBC's surveillance was lax and business risks were highly centralised, the local bank managers did not care about business risk because they need not bear the consequence. Now as the local bank management has been taken to be responsible for bad lending, risk aversion becomes a norm. Neither extreme is compatible to commercial banking. The source of the problem lies in the bureaucratic nature of banking officials. The bank's unique ownership by the state determines that the general manager is part of the state bureaucracy. It is hard to design an incentive structure within the bureaucracy to make the banking official behave like an entrepreneur. To tackle the problem, further commercialisation of banking business is crucial.

In 1986, the Bank of Communications (BOCOM) became the first quasi-commercial bank. Since then there have emerged a few more smaller-sized commercial banks and many non-bank financial institutions, many of which are organised on share-holding basis and owned by local governments and/or various state departments. Among the non-bank financial institutions, the most important ones are rural credit cooperatives (RCCs), which have functioned like small commercial banks in the rural area since the 1950s. RCCs used to be placed under the supervision of the PBC in the pre-reform monobank system. In recent years, RCCs operate under the guidance of the Agricultural Bank of China. Since the late 1980s, there have emerged many other non-bank financial institutions as well, such as trust and investment corporations (TICs), financial companies (FCs), financial leasing companies (FLCs), urban credit cooperatives (UCCs),[27] etc (Xie 1995). The share-holding asset structures of the ten commercial banks newly emerged since 1994 have opened the door to a banking sector with plural ownership. Based upon the 5,000 urban credit co-operatives, the PBC has allowed experimental launch of 24 urban co-operative banks in a few cities. In July 1995, China opened the first Sino-foreign joint-venture investment bank, China International Capital Corporation (CICC), with an initial capital of US$ 100 million. The joint venture between the PCBC, Morgan Stanley and other three investment groups provides project financing for Chinese companies.[28] The phenomenal rise of non-bank financial institutions since the late 1980s has remarkably diversified China's financial structure (Figure 10.5). Between 1993 and 1995, in the overall financial credits, the share of the loans issued by the four major state specialised banks has declined from 75 percent to 62 percent.[29]

These developments point to the hope of commercialisation, which must consist of two elements. One is divestiture. China's four major state owned specialised banks have between them 150,000 branches, employing nearly 1.7 million staff. Their returns have become increasingly bleak relatively to the size of their assets.[30] To adapt themselves better to their business environment, these banks must transformed themselves into smaller and slimmer ones to be efficient and nimble, just like the whole banking sector did (as the first step) in 1984. The other element is ownership pluralisation. Only with pluralised ownership can a board representative for shareholders' interests be in charge of the bank's business. Surveillance by the board should be more effective than that by the central bank in making sure that management takes financial risks properly for the bank's sake.

Notes

1. For a more detailed discussion of the pre-reform monetary system in China's centrally-planned economy, see Peebles (1991).
2. Discussion in this section is based on Lu and Yu (1998).
3. It was renamed as Construction Bank of China in 1996.
4. The following exposure of the institutional features of China's financial system is based on Gan (1995), Peebles (1991), the PBC (1994), Xie at el (1992), Xie (1995), Yi (1994), Yu and Xie (1996), Wang (1991), World Bank (1990, 1995), and Zhu (1993).
5. Contrarily, a major retrenchment effort made by the government in the austerity programme of the early 1990s was to clear inter-firm arrears by injecting new bank loans.
6. *Almanac of China's Finance and Banking 1994*, p. 41, p.47.
7. *Almanac of China's Finance and Banking 1995*, p. 46, *1996*, p. 18.
8. Zhu Rongji's measures included: Strengthening the financial disciplines; separating the state banks from their affiliated trust and investment firms; pressing all specialized banks to call back all outside-credit-plan loans immediately; restricting the inter-regional lending; etc. [*People's Daily* (Beijing), 22 July 1993].
9. As usual, the newly selected Party chief presides the next Party Congress and raises new economic development goals. For example, Hua Guofeng, Hu Yaobang, Zhao Ziyang and Jiang Zemin chaired the 11th, 12th, 13th and 14th Party Congress, respectively.
10. Ma (1995) shows that, when the central government's priority projects are under-invested by the local banks, the central bank will have the ex post incentive to revise the credit ceiling upwards.
11. Figures in this paragraph come from Gan (1995) and a news release of a Chinese official report on state enterprises appeared in *Lianhe Zaobao (United Morning Post*, Singapore), 23 December 1995.
12. Xinhua News Agency, *Lianhe Zaobao (United Morning Post*, Singapore), 30 August 1996.
13. Bloomberg News, *Straits Times* (Singapore), 22 April 1997.
14. *Ming Bao* (Hong Kong), 6 June 1997.
15. Bloomberg News, *Straits Times* (Singapore), 13 July 1997.
16. *Economist* (UK), 2 May 1998, pp. 69-70.
17. World Bank (1995), p.49.
18. *Almanac of China's Finance and Banking 1995*, pp. 35-36.
19. *Almanac of China's Finance and Banking 1996*, p. 38.
20. Reuter, *Straits Times* (Singapore), 29 December 1996, p. 38.
21. *People's Daily* (Beijing), 5 May 1998.
22. Reuter, *Straits Times* (Singapore), 14 March 1997, p. 65.
23. China's household saving rate has been above 35 percent in recent years, well above most other countries in the world.
24. *China Daily* (Beijing), 4 October 1998.
25. In April 1997, the PBC promulgated the first bylaw on residential housing mortgage business [*Jingrong Shibao* (Financial Times, Beijing)], 30 April 1997.
26. *Lianhe Zaobao* (Singapore), 27 February 1998, p. 32.

27. In 1995, the UCCs were restructured into 24 Urban Cooperative Banks.
28. Reuters, *Straits Times* (Singapore), 23 May 1995.
29. Xinhua News Agency, *Lianhe Zaobao (United Morning Post,* Singapore), 8 August 1996.
30. *Economist* (UK), 2 May 1998, p. 69.

References

Gan, Y. 1995. "The Significance of China's Commercial Bank Reform" (in Chinese), *Xin Shiji* [New Century Newsweek (China)] 80(December):3-8.
Hua, S., et al. 1988. "A Decade of China's Reform: Looking Back, Reflection, and Prospect" (in Chinese), *Jingji Yanjiu* [Economic Research Journal (Beijing)] 9(September):13-37.
Liu, K., and F. Zhang. 1996. "Will Banks' Interest Rates Go Lower?" (in Chinese), *Xin Shiji* [New Century Newsweek (China)] 85(May):12-14.
Lu, D., and Q. Yu. 1998. "Banking Credit-Quota Plan as a Macroeconomic Policy Instrument in China: Effectiveness and Costs." *Economic Systems* 22(2):147-74.
Ma, J. 1996. "China: Central Government Credibility and Economic Overheating," *Economic Systems* 19(3):237-261.
Mehran, H. and M. Quintyn. 1996. "Financial Sector Reform in China," *Finance & Development* 33(1):18-21.
Naughton, B. 1993. "Monetary Control and China's Most Recent Macroeconomic Cycle," *China Economic Review* 4(2):231-234.
Peebles, G. 1991. *Money in the People's Republic of China: A Comparative Perspective*. Sydney: Allen & Unwin.
People's Bank of China. 1994. *China's Monetary Policy in the 1990s* (in Chinese). Beijing: The Chinese Economic Press.
Prystay, C. 1996. "Easing off the Breaks," *Asian Business* 32(8):24-26.
Qian, X. 1997. "Thoughts on the Gradual Improvement of Open Market Operation in China" (in Chinese), *Jingrong Shibao* [Financial Times (Beijing)] 27(May):3.
Shi, X. and J. Liu. 1989. "Review on 'A Decade of China's Reform,'" *Jingji Yanjiu* [Economic Research Journal (Beijing)] 2(February):11-33.
State Commission of Structural Reform. 1996. *Chronicles of China's Reform and Opening Up*. Guangdong: Guangdong People's Press.
Wang, X., ed. 1991. *An Outline of the PRC Financial System* (in Chinese). Beijing: China Finance Press.
Wong, J., and K. Chen. 1995. "The Evolving Role of Government in China's Transitional Economy," *Journal of Far Eastern Business* 1(3):113-131.
Wong, Y. 1995. "China's Economic Reform: The Next Step," *Contemporary Economic Policy* 13(1):18-27.
World Bank. 1990. *China: Financial Sector Policies and Institutional Development*. Oxford: Oxford University Press,
____. 1995. *China: Macroeconomic Stability in a Decentralised Economy*. Oxford: Oxford University Press.
Xie, P., et al. 1992. *China's Financial Deepening and Financial Reforms* (in Chinese). Tianjing: Tianjing People's Press.
Xie, P. 1995. "*Financial Services in China,*" Discussion Paper, the UN Conference on Trade and Development, No. 94.

Yi, G. 1994. *Money, Banking and Financial Markets in China*. Boulder: Westview Press.

Yu, Q. 1997. "Economic Fluctuation, Macro Control and Monetary Policy in China's Transition Economy," *Journal of Comparative Economics* 25(October):180-195.

Yu, Q. and P. Xie. 1996. "Control Over Money Aggregates: Problems and Prospects in China's Transitional Economy," *Washington Centre for China Studies Papers* 6(6).

Zhao, D., ed. 1989. *Economic History of the PRC* (in Chinese). Henan: Henan People's Press.

Zhou, T. 1996. "An Analysis and Forecast on the Stability of the Money and Banking System" (in Chinese), in L. Guoguang, et al, eds., *China in 1997: Analyses and Forecasts on Economic Situation*. Beijing: Social Sciences Documentation Press.

Zhu, Y. 1993. "China's Credit Fund Management: Problems, Features, and Solutions" (in Chinese). *China Finance* 7.

11
Noise Trading in the Chinese Stock Market

Shang-Jin Wei

Introduction[1]

Noise trading, or trading based on investor sentiment, peudo-signals, or non-information, has been recognized as an important feature of financial markets: it not only exists, but can have imprints on asset prices, causing systematic deviations from the efficient market hypothesis (see the excellent survey by Shleifer and Summers 1990, and the papers cited therein). The emerging equity markets in Asia, Latin America and elsewhere tend to exhibit higher volatility than those in developed countries (World Bank 1995). Is this higher volatility a reflection of greater incidence of noise trading in the emerging markets? If it is, the gains from diversification into these markets by investors in the developed countries may be smaller than otherwise. More noise trading can be thought of as an increase in the spread of the returns in the emerging markets without necessarily increasing the returns or affecting the correlations with the equity markets in developed countries.

This chapter seeks to psychoanalyze a particular emerging market, that of China: how important is the investor sentiment, unrelated to economic fundamentals, in explaining the return variation in China, relative to the stock markets in the U.S. and Hong Kong?[2]

The Chinese stock market has a higher volatility than the U.S. and Hong Kong, as reflected in their respective market indices. For example, between February 2, 1994 and April 26, 1996, the standard deviation of the daily returns in Shanghai (A-share) market, the larger of the two Chinese stock exchanges, is 4.0%, about 250% as high as Hong Kong (with a standard deviation of 1.5% for Hangsheng index) and 650% as high as the U.S. (with a standard deviation of 0.6% for S&P500). Similarly higher volatility is also apparent in the weekly and monthly returns in the Chinese market.[3]

The higher volatility in China suggests possibly a greater presence of investor mood swings that are not based on economic fundamentals, or "noise trading," in the language of Kyle (1985); Black (1986); and De long, Shleifer, Summers and Waldman (1990). But a comparison of unconditional volatility across markets per se does not prove the relative importance of noise or mood swings. A market with more volatile economic fundamentals can be expected to have more volatile stock returns even if the relevant investor pool is no more mood-based than in other markets.

Indeed, there are plenty of reasons why the economic fundamentals in China may be more volatile than the U.S. and Hong Kong. First, there may be greater uncertainty about the Chinese macroeconomic policies. The economy seems in a perpetual cycle of overheat, emergency brake, sluggish growth and overheat. Whenever the government wants to redirect the economy, which it frequently does, it often resorts to drastic, non-market based measures, such as a decree to halt bank lending overnight. On top of that, the timing of decision-making is often unpredictable in contrast to the regularity of the American central bank's FOMC meetings or releases of important statistics in both the U.S. and Hong Kong.

Second, there may be greater uncertainty about the fundamentals specific to individual firms. The disclosure requirement is less detailed and less well enforced relative to the U.S. and Hong Kong. Less publicly available information in China may translate into more volatile assessment of corporate fundamentals.

It is generally hard to distinguish between fundamental or noise (mood swing) explanations of volatility, because neither is directly observable. In this chapter, we seek to control for the contribution of the fundamentals by examining Chinese stocks that are cross-listed inside and outside China. Shares that are listed in different markets represent the same voting rights and claims on the dividend stream. So the economic fundamentals on them are common. Aside from looking at relative volatility of cross-listed shares of the same companies, we make an attempt to quantify the importance of market-wide mood swings in explaining return variations in China.

Hardouvolus, LaPorter and Whizman (1995) and Frankel and Schmukler (1996) make use of data on closed-end country funds that share an important feature with the data examined in this chapter: the same asset is traded both at home and abroad. The prices of the funds and their net asset values are often different from each other. So it is a natural laboratory to study the existence of noise trading in the country where the country funds are traded. These studies do not examine differential degrees of noise trading across countries, which is the central focus of this chapter.

There are two advantages of the Chinese data set in this chapter than the country funds data. First, the Chinese stocks chosen here are highly liquid in both home and foreign markets, whereas the underlying assets for country funds are often illiquid. Second, there are legal restrictions that prevent non-Chinese nationals to trade domestic shares, and Chinese to trade foreign shares. In contrast, many country funds do not have legal restrictions against investors to trade both the funds and the underlying assets, or if they did in the past, the data is not as readily available. The legal restriction is useful for us to trace the sentiment to nationality of the investor pool.

The chapter is organized in the following way. The second section describes basic the data and institutional background. The third section investigates the importance of mood swings in return variations. The final section provides a concluding discussion.

Data and Institutional Background

Chinese stocks that are listed in one of the two Chinese stock exchanges (Shanghai and Shenzhen) and are traded only among Chinese nationals are called A-shares. A subset of the firms that issue A-shares also issue B-shares that are only to be traded by non-Chinese nationals. The B-share market has so far very thin trading, despite of the fact that firms that issue B shares tend to be large. Another non-overlapping subset of firms also issue shares in Hong Kong (H-shares) or New York (N-shares) or both.

To disentangle the importance of mood swings from economic fundamentals, we apply the following criteria in our sample selection: (1) Companies that are cross-listed in several exchanges (to control for fundamentals), (2) Markets that are liquid (which excludes the B-share market), and (3) Markets that are legally segmented (otherwise arbitrage would force prices to be more or less identical). We focus on two cross-listed firms: Shanghai Petrochemicals, which is listed in Shanghai, Hong Kong and New York;[4] and Tsingtao Brewery, which is listed in Shanghai and Hong Kong.[5]

Both stocks are highly liquid. Shanghai Petrochemicals processes a thick and dark liquid,[6] and Tsingtao Brewery produces a trasparent and brownish variety.[7] This is one measure of liquidity (just kidding). Both firms also have large capitalizations and are actively traded in all the exchanges on which they are listed. We choose not to examine any B share stocks precisely because of its infrequent trading or lack of liquidity which could distort its measured statistical properties.

The sample period is February 4, 1994 to April 26, 1996. We deliberately restrict the sample to after 1993. Before January 1, 1994, the Chinese currency was non-convertible. There was a huge black market premium on the U.S. dollar over the official exchange rate, often reaching 50%. Since January 1, 1994, limited convertibility of currency has been instituted. The official exchange, after a sharp depreciation on that day, is now virtually the same as the free market rate. We allow for the possibility that the exchange rate needed time to adjust to its equilibrium in the first month after the exchange rate reform. Since the beginning of February, 1994, the black market has all but disappeared. Anecdotal evidence suggests that it is just as likely to observe a tiny black market discount (on the order of 1-2%) on the U.S. dollar as a tiny premium. Although we do not have data on market exchange rate, we believe that for our sample, the official exchange rate is reasonably reliable to convert Chinese currency denominated stock returns to other currencies. We also look at the broad indices in Shanghai, Hong Kong and New York. Since we later wish to examine the co-movement between individual stocks and the markets on which they are traded, we do not want to use the off-the-shelf Shanghai A-share index, which gives heavy weights to Shanghai Petro and Tsingtao Brewery by virtue of their sizes. Instead, we create our own Shanghai A-share index based on four equally-weighted large stocks: Erfangji (maker of textile machines), Dazhong Taxi Company,[8] Shanghai Diesel Engines, and Shanghai Refrigerator Manufacturer.

For Hong Kong, we use the Hangseng Index, which, according to the Bloomberg screen, "is a capitalization-weighted index of 33 companies that represent approximately 70 percent of the total market capitalization of the Stock Exchange of Hong Kong." To our knowledge, neither Shanghai Petro nor Tsingtao Brewery is part of the index. For New York, we adopt the Standard & Poor 500 instead of the NYSE index, because the former is more widely available.

Table 11.1 reports summary statistics for one-day returns of the two stocks, the four indices and the three exchange rates. In the sample, the two stocks happen to have negative mean returns. It is interesting to observe that Shanghai Petrochemicals' A-share has a standard deviation (3.9%) that is at least 150% as high as its overseas personalities (2.6% for H and 2.4% for N shares). Similarly, for Tsingtao Brewery, its A share's standard deviation (4.1%) is 117% as high as its Hong Kong H share identity (3.5%).

As we remarked at the beginning of the chapter, Shanghai market is 250% as volatile as Hong Kong, and 650% as volatile as New York. There are two pieces of evidence that suggests that more volatile fundamentals in China are part of the explanations for a more volatile Chinese market. First, the returns on the Chinese shares listed in Hong Kong are more volatile than the Hong Kong index itself. Second, the difference between the volatility of the Shanghai market index and those of Hong Kong and New York is much larger than those for the two cross-listed stocks. On the hand, for cross-listed companies, their within-China returns are still more volatile than overseas twins. This suggests that something other than economic fundamentals is also responsible for some of the higher volatility in China.

One possibility is exchange rate volatility. To properly compare return volatility of the shares on different markets, we need to convert all returns into a common currency (say, the Chinese currency, RMB). If the RMB/HK$ rate is volatile, then the H-share return volatility, when denominated in RMB, could be very volatile as well.

The last three variables in the upper panel are pertinent to changes in the exchange rates: RMB/US dollar, Hong Kong dollar/US dollar, and RMB/Hong Kong dollar. The most salient feature here is the relative fixity between the Hong Kong and the U.S. dollars (with an average daily standard deviation of 0.04%). During the sample, the Chinese currency, RMB, had a slight appreciation against both the U.S. and Hong Kong dollars, but its value against the U.S. or Hong Kong dollars is also fairly stable (with a daily standard deviation of 0.24%).

TABLE 11.1 Summary Statistics of 1-day Returns

		Mean (x10^{-4})	Std Dev	Min	Max
Shanghai	A	-3.41	0.039	-0.20	0.31
Petrochemical	H	-2.85	0.026	-0.11	0.10
	N	-2.72	0.024	-0.10	0.08
Tsingtao	A	-7.77	0.041	-0.24	0.32
Brewery	H	-22.70	0.035	-0.23	0.20
Market	Shanghai	0.25	0.040	-0.20	0.28
Index	Hong Kong	-1.32	0.015	-0.08	0.05
	New York	5.20	0.006	-0.03	0.02
Exchange	RMB/US$	-0.74	0.0024	-0.03	0.03
Rate	HK$/US$	0.03	0.0004	-0.00	0.00
	RMB/HK$	-0.77	0.0024	-0.03	0.03

Correlation Matrix
1994:2:4 - 1996:4:26, N=580

	Petro A	Petro H	Petro N	Brew A	Brew H	Shanghai	Hong Kong	New York	RMB/ US$	HK$/ US$	RMB/ HK$
Petro-A	1.00	-	-	-	-	-	-	-	-	-	-
Petro-H	0.07	1.00	-	-	-	-	-	-	-	-	-
Petro-N	0.06	0.59	1.00	-	-	-	-	-	-	-	-
Brew-A	0.80	0.00	0.01	1.00	-	-	-	-	-	-	-
Brew-H	0.03	0.32	0.15	0.01	1.00	-	-	-	-	-	-
Shanghai	0.75	0.03	0.04	0.80	0.03	1.00	-	-	-	-	-
Hong Kong	0.02	0.53	0.33	0.02	0.28	0.04	1.00	-	-	-	-
New York	-0.01	0.06	0.33	0.03	0.05	-0.03	0.05	1.00	-	-	-
RMB/US$	0.00	-0.07	-0.04	0.03	-0.04	0.04	-0.07	-0.01	1.00	-	-
HK$/US$	-0.00	-0.07	-0.09	0.00	-0.04	0.04	-0.14	-0.02	0.07	1.00	-
RMB/HK$	0.00	-0.05	-0.03	0.03	-0.03	0.03	-0.05	-0.01	0.99	-0.09	1.00

Relative to the movements in the (local-currency) stock prices, the volatility of the exchange rates are smaller by at least two orders of magnitude. Moreover, the correlation between the RMB/HK$ volatility and the H-share is negative for both stocks. The H-share (or N-share) volatility, when converted into RMB, will still be much smaller than A-share volatility. For example, for Shanghai Petro, the H-share volatility in RMB is 2.8%

226

(=0.026+0.0024-2*0.05*0.026*0.0024),[9] 28% smaller than its A-share identity. Similar calculations apply to Tsingtao Brewery. Hence, the exchange rate factor will not change any of the earlier inferences made based on local-currency returns.

TABLE 11.2 Summary Statistics of 5-day Returns (Wednesday to Wednesday)

		Mean (x10-4)	Std Dev	Min	Max
Shanghai	A	-34.80	0.083	-0.25	0.51
Petrochemical	H	-26.72	0.062	-0.13	0.16
	N	-24.21	0.058	-0.14	0.14
Tsingtao	A	-48.73	0.082	-0.26	0.39
Brewery	H	-119.42	0.071	-0.18	0.19
Market	Shanghai	-27.99	0.085	-0.28	0.33
Index	Hong Kong	-0.31	0.035	-0.11	0.08
	New York	27.50	0.013	-0.05	0.03
Exchange	RMB/US$	-3.84	0.0011	-0.01	0.00
Rate	HK$/US$	-0.01	0.0005	-0.00	0.00
	RMB/HK$	-3.83	0.0012	-0.01	0.00

Correlation Matrix
N=114

Petro	Petro A	Petro H	Brew N	Brew A	Brew H	Shang-hai	Hong Kong	New York	RMB/ US$	HK$/ US$	RMB/ HK$
Petro-A	1.00	-	-	-	-	-	-	-	-	-	-
Petro-H	0.19	1.00	-	-	-	-	-	-	-	-	-
Petro-N	0.19	0.91	1.00	-	-	-	-	-	-	-	-
Brew-A	0.84	0.11	0.10	1.00	-	-	-	-	-	-	-
Brew-H	0.18	0.47	0.44	0.18	1.00	-	-	-	-	-	-
Shanghai	0.72	0.20	0.22	0.78	0.15	1.00	-	-	-	-	-
Hong Kong	0.11	0.69	0.68	0.06	0.45	0.12	1.00	-	-	-	-
New York	0.15	0.33	0.40	0.13	0.17	0.03	0.45	1.00	-	-	-
RMB/US$	-0.00	-0.13	-0.10	-0.06	-0.06	-0.10	-0.18	-0.04	1.00	-	-
HK$/US$	-0.03	-0.27	-0.18	-0.01	-0.12	0.07	-0.23	-0.07	0.02	1.00	-
RMB/HK$	0.01	0.01	-0.01	-0.06	-0.00	-0.12	-0.05	-0.01	0.89	-0.43	1.00

The lower panel of Table 11.1 presents the correlation matrix among the various identities of Shanghai Petrochemicals, Tsingtao Brewery, the three indices, and the three exchange rates. There are several noteworthy features. First, the Shanghai Petro's returns in Shanghai are not much correlated with the corresponding H-share in Hong Kong or N-share in New York (the correlations are less than 10%). Rather, it is more highly correlated with Tsingtao

Brewery's return in Shanghai (80%) or with the Shanghai A-share index (75%). Similarly, the H shares of Shanghai Petro and Tsingtao Brewery are more highly correlated with each other and with the Hong Kong's Hengsheng index than with their own identities in Shanghai. Note that Shanghai Petro's H-share return is highly correlated with that of its N-share in New York (0.59). This simply reflects that the force of arbitrage is strong between Hong Kong and New York.[10]

In other words, unrelated stocks in Shanghai (or Hong Kong) are more correlated with each other than the shares of same companies inside and outside China. This is quite striking as A, H and N shares are supposed to represent the same claim on the assets and dividend streams. The fundamentals of the stocks (projected future streams of dividends or earnings) are by construction identical. This feature suggests some noise trading that is marketwise within each trading locale. But the influence of the noise is limited at the Chinese border.

It is interesting to note that the extraordinarily high correlation between a stock with its local market appears to be specific to the Chinese market. For the stock (Shanghai Petrochemicals) that we do have data on N-shares, we observe that the H and N shares of the same company are indeed highly correlated (59%). Since there are no formal barriers to arbitrage between the two markets, this high correlation is all to be expected.

It is instructive to see if the correlation pattern varies with the return horizon. Tables 11.2 and 11.3 report summary statistics and correlation matrices for the five-day (Wednesday to Wednesday) and twenty-day (every fourth Wednesday) returns. As the return horizon increases from daily to weekly, the correlation of the multiple personalities of same stocks does increase. For example, Shanghai Petrochemicals' weekly A-share return has a correlation coefficient of 19% with its H and N share counterparts, higher than the 0.07 and 0.06 daily correlation. On the other hand, Shanghai Petro's A-share remains to be more correlated with Tsingtao Brewery's A-share (with a coefficient of 84%) and with the A-share index (72%).

Similarly, the correlation of Tsingtao Brewery's weekly H-share return with its A-share identity (18%) is higher than its daily counterpart (1%), but still lower than with Shanghai Petro's H-share (47%) or with Hong Kong market's Hengsheng index (45%).

Again, between Hong Kong and New York where formal segmentation is absent, the market is very integrated. The correlation between Shanghai Petro's H and N-shares is 91%, higher than each's correlation with the relevant local market (69% between H and Hong Kong, and 40% between N and New York). This indicates that on a weekly basis, the co-movement of the stocks in the Chinese market is also unusually high relative to Hong Kong and New York.

Once we increase the return horizon to twenty days, the correlation between A and H or N shares for Shanghai Petro actually declines a bit, although that between A and H shares for Tsingtao Brewery increases a bit (to 27%). For both stocks, their A-shares continue to be more correlated with the A-share index (70% for Shanghai Petro and 80% for Tsingtao Brewery) than with their H- share identities (13% for Shanghai Petro and 27%).

TABLE 11.3 Summary Statistics of 20-day Returns (Every fourth Wednesday)

		Mean (x10-4)	Std Dev	Min	Max
Shanghai	A	-68.90	0.196	-0.37	0.74
Petrochemical	H	3.72	0.131	-0.30	0.26
	N	4.35	0.110	-0.28	0.20
Tsingtao	A	-196.17	0.176	-0.43	0.63
Brewery	H	-447.29	0.123	-0.33	0.15
Market	Shanghai	-97.37	0.226	-0.47	0.62
Index	Hong Kong	25.81	0.077	-0.18	0.13
	New York	136.64	0.027	-0.04	0.08
Exchange	RMB/US$	-15.99	0.0026	-0.009	0.002
Rate	HK$/US$	-0.12	0.0012	-0.005	0.003
	RMB/HK$	-15.87	0.0031	-0.009	0.004

Correlation Matrix
N=27

	Petro A	Petro H	Petro N	Brew A	Brew H	Shanghai	Hong Kong	New York	RMB/ US$	HK$/ US$	RMB/ HK$
Petro-A	1.00	-	-	-	-	-	-	-	-	-	-
Petro-H	0.13	1.00	-	-	-	-	-	-	-	-	-
Petro-N	0.15	0.98	1.00	-	-	-	-	-	-	-	-
Brew-A	0.95	0.16	0.17	1.00	-	-	-	-	-	-	-
Brew-H	0.24	0.64	0.64	0.27	1.00	-	-	-	-	-	-
Shanghai	0.70	0.31	0.32	0.80	0.20	1.00	-	-	-	-	-
Hong Kong	0.11	0.85	0.84	0.10	0.69	0.18	1.00	-	-	-	-
New York	0.22	0.24	0.25	0.14	0.25	-0.02	0.46	1.00	-	-	-
RMB/US$	-0.24	-0.14	-0.16	-0.25	0.01	-0.40	-0.07	-0.06	1.00	-	-
HK$/US$	0.11	-0.28	-0.28	0.06	-0.30	0.24	-0.38	-0.32	-0.22	1.00	-
RMB/HK$	-0.25	-0.01	-0.02	-0.24	0.13	-0.43	0.09	0.08	0.93	-0.57	1.00

Mood Swings and Returns

In this section, we first look at how the measured return differentials across markets are linked to the broad indices of the markets where the shares are traded. The basic specification is

$$R_{A,i,t} - R_{H,i,t} = a + b_1 HongKong_t + b_2 Shanghai_t + b_3 S_t + b_4 R_{A,i,t-1} + b_5 R_{H,i,t-1} + u_{i,t}$$

where i=Shanghai Petro, S_t=change in log of RMB/HK$ at time t. HongKong$_t$ and Shanghai$_t$ are Hangsheng and Shanghai A-share indicies respectively.

Table 11.4 presents the regression results on the return differentials between the A and H shares for Shanghai Petro. The twelve columns are organized into three return horizons: daily, weekly (Wednesday to Wednesday) and "monthly" (every fourth Wednesday). Within each horizon, the first column relates the return differentials to the indices in Shanghai and Hong Kong, the second one adds the changes in the RMB/HK$ exchange rate, the third adds lagged values of A and H share returns, and last column imposes the constraint on the coefficient for the lagged returns (β_5 = - β_4).Several features stand out. First, the A-share return in excess of that of H-share is positively related to A-share index and negatively related to H-share index. A one percent increase in the A-share index is associated with a 0.7% increase in the gap between A and H returns for Shanghai Petro. Second, this finding is robust across specifications and return horizons, although the magnitudes of the response change gradually with the return horizon. Third, a one percent appreciation of the exchange rate over a daily horizon narrows the A and H return gap by about one percent, but is statistically uncorrelated with the return differentials at the five-day and twenty-day horizons. Finally, past returns do not appear to be correlated with the current return differential. There is no evidence that the return differential between A and H shares reverts toward zero over time.

Table 11.5 examines the return differential between A and H shares for Tsingtao Brewery. All the four important features of Table 11.4 continue to ring true.

To see if the prominent features of Tables 11.4 and 11.5 are specific to the Shanghai market, it is useful to examine return differentials on other markets. Since Shanghai Petro is also listed in the New York Stock Exchange (the N-share, or ADR), we can perform such examination easily. However, the closing prices in Hong Kong and New York are quoted with a few hours of time difference, this non-synchronization of timing could lead to spurious correlation between the stock returns and the index of the market on which it is traded. To deal with this problem, we adopt the Sholes-Williams (1987) procedure. Specifically, for the Hong Kong's Hangsheng and New York's S&P500 indices, as well as the HK$/US$ exchange rate, we add one lead and one lag to the regression in addition to the contemporaneous values. We then test whether the sum of the three coefficients for a given variable is different from zero.

The results are reported in Table 11.6. There are two striking results that contrast sharply with the earlier tables. Most importantly, the return differential between N and H shares is by and large not correlated with the market indices of Hong Kong or New York. This result is unaffected by the inclusion of changes in the exchange rate, and is robust across the return horizons. This suggests that the co-movement of the A shares in the Chinese market is especially strong relative to Hong Kong and New York. Second, there is stronger evidence of a correction mechanism between the Hong Kong and New York market: the return differential is negatively related to the past differential. Over a day, 35% of the differential is eliminated. Over five days, 50% percent of the differential is eliminated. This seems sensible, as arbitrage possibility between the two markets are not impeded by any legal barrier, unlike between the A and H markets.

It is useful to make sure that the differences between Table 11.6 and earlier tables are not artificially created by the adoption of the Sholes-Williams procedure of adding leads and lags of the regressors. In Tables 11.7 and 11.8, we reproduce Tables 11.4 and 11.5, except that we also add one lead and one lag to the market indices and the change in the exchange rate. As one can see, the most important features of Tables 11.4 and 11.5 are basically unchanged. In particular, for both the daily and weekly horizons, the return differentials between the A and H shares are positively related to the A-share market index for both stocks, and negatively related to the Hong Kong index for Shanghai Petro. This is the same as the earlier tables with the leads and lags. The result is weakened for the 20-day horizon. Overall, the different characteristics between the A/H and N/H comparisons are not likely driven by the employment of the Sholes-Williams procedure.

We turn to an alternative way of looking at the data that may provide a clue to the quantitative importance of the market-wide mood swings relative to the fundamentals in explaining return variations. Specifically, for each stock, we run the following regression.

$$R_{A,i,t} = a + b_1 R_{H,i,t} + b_2 S_t + b_3 (R_{H,t,t} \times S_t) + b_4 R_{A,i,t-1} + g\, Shanghai_t + u_{i,t}$$

where I=Shanghai Petro or Tsingtao Brewery. We estimate the regression both with and without the Shanghai index as a regressor. Since our interest is an accounting exercise (to see how much variations in the Shanghai index contribute to the variations in the individual A-share return), we pay special attention to the (unadjusted) R-squared measures. We perform the regression for daily, weekly and monthly horizons. The results are reported in Table 11.9.

For daily horizon for each stock, the returns on the H-share and the changes in the Chinese currency/Hong Kong dollar exchange rate explain a tiny fraction of the A-share returns, less than 1% for Shanghai Petro and less than 2% for Tsingtao Brewery. In contrast, the marginal contribution of the Shanghai index is enormous, over 56% (0.567-0.006) for Shanghai Petro and over 62% (0.643-0.015) for Tsingtao Brewery. Since the contribution of the economic fundamentals should be common to both A- and H- shares of the same company, this suggests that market-wide mood swings account for over 56-62% of the total returns.

TABLE 11.4 Return Differentials between A and H Shares
Shanghai Petrochemical (in RMB, 1994:2:4 - 1996:4:26)

	1-Day Return		5-Day Return	
Constant	-.000	-.000	-.000	-.000
	(.001)	(.001)	(.001)	(.001)
Shanghai	.717*	.720*	.727*	.721*
Index	(.069)	(.069)	(.067)	(.067)
Hong Kong	-.969*	-.977*	-.973*	-.988*
Index	(.085)	(.086)	(.086)	(.085)
RMB/HK$	-	-1.025*	-1.000*	-1.006*
		(.380)	(.397)	(.375)
$R_A(-1)$	-	-	-.102	-
			(.064)	
$R_H(-1)$	-	-	-.074	-
			(.054)	
$R_A(-1)-R_H(-1)$	-	-	-.050	-
			(.051)	
N/ser	580	580	579	579
ser	.03	.03	.03	.03
R^2	.48	.49	.49	.49
DW	2.05	2.04	1.98	1.94
Log Likelihood	1162.30	1163.9	1167.1	1163.0

	20-Day Return							
Constant	.001	.002	.004	.003	.003	.009	.010	.012
	(.007)	(.007)	(.007)	(.007)	(.039)	(.041)	(.042)	(.041)
Shanghai	.622*	.627*	.607*	.626*	.521	.544##	.590*	.605*
Index	(.161)	(.159)	(.145)	(.153)	(.365)	(.369)	(.288)	(.282)
Hong Kong	-1.136*	-1.131*	-1.132*	-1.152*	-1.453*	-1.478*	-1.318*	-1.338*
Index	(.158)	(.161)	(.168)	(.166)	(.348)	(.393)	(.377)	(.397)
RMB/HK$	-	3.082	3.619	2.606	-	3.674	5.102	5.926
		(5.626)	(5.503)	(5.903)		(10.460)	(11.701)	(10.568)
$R_A(-1)$	-	-	.171	-	-	-	-.306	-
			(.139)				(.428)	
$R_H(-1)$	-	-	.037	-	-	-	.396##	-
			(.135)				(.270)	
$R_A(-1)-R_H(-1)$	-	-	.104	-	-	-	-.330	-
			(.100)				(.300)	
N	114	114	113	113	27	27	26	26
ser	.07	.07	.07	.07	.17	.18	.17	.17
R^2	.43	.43	.44	.43	.39	.37	.44	.47
DW	0	0	0	0	0	0	0	0
Log Likelihood	141.67	141.83	142.70	141.26	10.694	10.744	12.747	12.687

Notes: Five day returns are computed using closing prices from Wednesday to Wednesday. Twenty day returns are computed using closing prices every fourth Wednesday. Heterogeneity-robust standard errors are in parentheses. *, # and ## denote significantly different from zero at the five, ten and fifteen percent levels, respectively

Table 11.5 Return Differentials between A and H Shares Tsingtao Brewery (in RMB, 1994:2:4 - 1996:4:26)

	1-Day Return		5-Day Return	
Constant	.001	.001	.002	.002
	(.002)	(.002)	(.002)	(.002)
Shanghai Index	.801*	.803*	.794*	.790*
	(.073)	(.073)	(.068)	(.070)
Hong Kong Index	-.649*	-.655*	-.689*	-.681*
	(.133)	(.132)	(.132)	(.131)
RMB/HK$	-	-.808*	-.939*	-.819*
		(.370)	(.411)	(.386)
RA(-1)	-	-	-.084	-
			(.074)	
RH(-1)	-	-	.256	-
			(.216)	
RA(-1)-RH(-1)	-	-	-.180	-
			(.129)	
N	580	580	579	579
ser	.05	.05	.05	.05
R^2	.30	.30	.33	.33
DW	2.46	2.46	2.08	2.08
Log Likelihood	907.0	907.4	922.3	919.2

	20-Day Return							
Constant	.009	.009	.010	.009	.035	.038	.038	.039
	(.007)	(.007)	(.008)	(.007)	(.022)	(.025)	(.026)	(.026)
Shanghai Index	.685*	.684*	.673*	.683*	.586*	.596*	.648*	.607*
	(.105)	(.104)	(.095)	(.101)	(.172)	(.179)	(.145)	(.143)
Hong Kong Index	-.952*	-.952*	-.987*	-.998*	-1.190*	-1.201*	-1.193*	-1.090*
	(.218)	(.219)	(.230)	(.228)	(.187)	(.165)	(.193)	(.181)
RMB/HK$	-	-.438	-.400	-.401	-	1.611	4.19	.719
		(5.439)	(5.375)	(5.404)		(7.009)	(10.68)	(7.42)
RA(-1)	-	-	.091	-	-	-	-.206	-
			(.097)				(.168)	
RH(-1)	-	-	.010	-	-	-	.008	-
			(.118)				(.211)	
RA(-1)-RH(-1)	-	-	.050	-	-	-	-.162	-
			(.079)				(.154)	
N	114	114	113	113	27	27	26	26
ser	.08	.08	.08	.08	.12	.12	.13	.12
R^2	.40	.40	.40	.40	.59	.57	.57	.57
DW	0	0	0	0	0	0	0	0
Log Likelihood	133.05	133.04	132.30	131.93	20.46	20.48	20.47	20.10

See notes to Table 11.4

TABLE 11.6 Return Differentials between N and H Shares Shanghai Petrochemical (in US$, 1994:2:4 - 1996:4:26)

	1-Day Return		5-Day Return	
Constant	-.000	-.000	-.000	-.000
	(.001)	(.001)	(.001)	(.001)
New York	.035	.061	.441#	.420
Index	(.262)	(.263)	(.266)	(.265)
Hong Kong	-.123	-.103	-.129	-.175#
Index	(.117)	(.116)	(.116)	(.107)
RMB/HK$	-	8.507	8.881#	9.476#
		(5.659)	(5.356)	(5.371)
RN(-1)	-	-	-.377*	-
			(.055)	
RH(-1)	-	-	.332*	-
			(.048)	
RN(-1)-RH(-1)	-	-	-.351*	-
			(.045)	
N	579	579	579	579
ser	.21	.21	.019	.019
R²	.199	.202	.301	.30
DW	2.71	2.72	2.17	2.17
Log Likelihood	1430.3	1432.7	1472.1	1471.51

	20-Day Return							
Constant	-.001	-.001	-.001	-.001	.006	.003	.004	.004
	(.003)	(.003)	(.002)	(.002)	(.005)	(.005)	(.009)	(.008)
New York	.356	.355	.315	.327	.507*	-.291	-.563	-.592
Index	(.447)	(.425)	(.379)	(.381)	(.252)	(.220)	(.504)	(.423)
Hong Kong	-.294	-.317*	-.269#	-.329*	-.038	-.012	.148	.218##
Index	(.158)	(.151)	(.155)	(.134)	(.073)	(.071)	(.204)	(.139)
RMB/HK$	-	-2.733	-4.377	-2.944	-	.715	4.138	6.064
		(10.648)	(9.614)	(8.678)		(4.433)	(9.172)	(9.144)
RN(-1)	-	-	-.535*	-	-	-	-.265	-
			(.091)				(.316)	
RH(-1)	-	-	.468*	-	-	-	.314	-
			(.080)				(.250)	
RN(-1)-RH(-1)	-	-	-.496*	-	-	-	-.387#	-
			(.081)				(.220)	
N	113	113	113	113	26	26	26	26
ser	.08	.02	.02	.02	.022	.021	.02	.02
R²	.03	.09	.29	.29	.45	.48	.49	.52
DW	0	0	0	0	0	0	0	0
Log Likelihood	257.01	262.29	278.00	277.06	63.268	66.185	68.306	68.124

See notes to Table 11.4

TABLE 11.7 Return Differentials between A and H Shares with leads and lags Shanghai Petrochemical
(in RMB, 1994:2:4 - 1996:4:26)

	1-Day Return		5-Day Return	
Constant	-.000	-.000	-.000	-.000
	(.001)	(.001)	(.001)	(.001)
Shanghai	.647*	.646*	.708*	.655*
Index	(.119)	(.119)	(.118)	(.116)
Hong Kong	-1.209*	-1.207*	-1.150*	-1.236*
Index	(.147)	(.147)	(.164)	(.156)
RMB/HK$	-	.024	.061	.003
		(1.376)	(1.382)	(1.374)
RA(-1)	-	-	-.078	-
			(.085)	
RH(-1)	-	-	-.051	-
			(.066)	
RA(-1)-RH(-1)	-	-	-.024	-
			(.057)	
N	576	576	576	576
ser	.03	.03	.03	.03
R²	.48	.48	.48	.48
DW	2.06	2.05	2.00	2.00
Log Likelihood	1158.20	1160.4	1161.9	1160.5

	20-Day Return							
Constant	.001	.004	.004	.004	-.004	.016	.013	.015
	(.007)	(.008)	(.007)	(.007)	(.042)	(.055)	(.052)	(.054)
Shanghai	.634*	.662*	.417##	.586*	.527	.628	.303	.623
Index	(.282)	(.282)	(.265)	(.281)	(.618)	(.618)	(.720)	(.618)
Hong Kong	-1.302*	-1.296*	-1.445*	-1.174*	-.670	-.954	-1.868	-.942
Index	(.334)	(.331)	(.376)	(.355)	(.979)	(1.158)	(1.479)	(1.207)
RMB/HK$	-	7.125	6.298	6.301	-	11.621	7.393	11.403
		(6.112)	(6.102)	(6.447)		(20.123)	(19.464)	(20.159)
RA(-1)	-	-	.304#	-	-	-	.264	-
			(.179)				(.421)	
RH(-1)	-	-	.197	-	-	-	.477	-
			(.164)				(.594)	
RA(-1)-RH(-1)	-	-	.139	-	-	-	.011	-
			(.128)				(.317)	
N	110	110	110	110	24	24	24	24
ser	.07	.07	.07	.07	.17	.18	.19	.18
R²	.40	.39	.42	.39	.47	.42	.37	.37
DW	0	0	0	0	0	0	0	0
Log Likelihood	135.62	136.32	140.69	137.36	12.613	13.874	14.688	13.875

See notes to Table 11.4

TABLE 11.8 Return Differentials between A and H Shares with leads and lags Tsingtao Brewery(in RMB, 1994:2:4 - 1996:4:26)

	1-Day Return		5-Day Return	
Constant	.002	.002	.002	.002
	(.002)	(.002)	(.002)	(.002)
Shanghai	.662*	.660*	.715*	.842*
Index	(.137)	(.136)	(.176)	(.159)
Hong Kong	-.936*	-.939*	-1.116*	-1.099*
Index	(.287)	(.289)	(.340)	(.336)
RMB/HK$	-	-.495	-.300	-
		(1.693)	(1.712)	
RA(-1)	-	-	-.072	-
			(.111)	
RH(-1)	-	-	-.276	-
			(.221)	
RA(-1)-RH(-1)	-	-	-.228	-
			(.167)	
N	576	576	576	576
ser	.05	.05	.05	.05
R^2	.30	.30	.34	.33
DW	2.47	2.46	2.07	2.06
Log Likelihood	903.0	903.9	921.6	919.3

	20-Day Return							
Constant	.008	.009	.010	.009	.035*	.042	.030	.033
	(.007)	(.007)	(.008)	(.008)	(.016)	(.032)	(.028)	(.026)
Shanghai	.800*	.818*	.744*	.858*	.531*	.564*	.354#	.001
Index	(.149)	(.151)	(.163)	(.162)	(.143)	(.185)	(.185)	(.185)
Hong Kong	-1.369*	-1.363*	-1.472*	-1.389*	-.828#	-.919	-.814	-1.037*
Index	(.380)	(.379)	(.368)	(.369)	(.447)	(.542)	(.517)	(.459)
RMB/HK$	-	3.762	2.307	3.605	-	3.209	1.815	-7.698
		(7.108)	(6.988)	(6.954)		(12.095)	(11.787)	(10.811)
RA(-1)	-	-	.078	-	-	-	.650*	-
			(.140)				(.178)	
RH(-1)	-	-	.161	-	-	-	-.055	-
			(.139)				(.168)	
RA(-1)-RH(-1)	-	-	-.068	-	-	-	.296*	-
			(.104)				(.134)	
N	110	110	110	110	24	24	24	24
ser	.07	.07	.07	.07	.11	.12	.11	.11
R^2	.43	.41	.42	.42	.71	.65	.70	.67
DW	0	0	0	0	0	0	0	0
Log Likelihood	134.6	134.8	136.2	135.1	23.57	23.90	27.63	25.26

See notes to Table 11.4

TABLE 11.9 Mood Swings and A share Returns

	Shanghai Petro 1-Day	5-Day	20-Day	Tsingtao Brewery 1-Day	5-Day
Constant	-.000	-.000	.000	.002	-.040
	(.002)	(.001)	(.008)	(.005)	(.030)
RH	.102#	.068#	.208#	.052	.320
	(.056)	(.037)	(.123)	(.073)	(.270)
RMB/HK$	.125	-.298	3.85	7.66	-18.40
	(.367)	(.446)	(6.39)	(4.25)	(13.9)
RH*(RMB/HK$)	6.875	-1.387	-90.10	-25.71	48.34
	(19.023)	(18.127)	(64.15)	(52.42)	(77.03)
RA(-1)	-.045	-.063	.253	.196	-
	(.081)	(.060)	(.232)	(.134)	
Shanghai Index	-	.724* (.064)	-	.690* (.130)	-
N	580	580	114	114	26
R^2	.006	.567	.109	.570	.093
adj R^2	-.001	.563	.076	.550	-.073
DW	1.98	1.93	0	0	0
Log Likelihood	1063.2	1301.4	128.9	168.5	6.715

	Tsingtao Brewery 20-Day						
Constant	.008	-.001	-.001	-.003	-.001	-.041	-.007
	(.030)	(.002)	(.001)	(.008)	(.005)	(.027)	(.019)
RH	.075	.015	.003	.191#	.066	.116	.022
	(.188)	(.029)	(.031)	(.116)	(.056)	(.194)	(.142)
RMB/HK$	5.96	.442*	-.000	-3.41	2.555	-19.41	10.05*
	(7.17)	(.194)	(.232)	(5.51)	(2.835)	(13.19)	(4.85)
RH*(RMB/HK$)	119.99	6.541	4.077	-41.9	-15.63	-96.71	-7.91
	(52.61)	(7.231)	(12.63)	(63.2)	(23.01)	(62.14)	(25.15)
RA(-1)	-.196	-.119	-.076	.122	.032	-.065	-.332#
	(.207)	(.090)	(.055)	(.207)	(.096)	(.114)	(.179)
Shanghai Index	.793* (.190)	-	.806* (.052)	-	.753* (.101)	-	.747 (.135)
N	26	580	580	114	114	27	26
ser	.59	.015	.643	.052	.616	.205	.765
R^2	.49	.008	.640	.017	(.598)	.060	.707
DW	0	1.98	2.11	0	0	0	0
Log Likelihood	17.61	1036.4	1327.9	126.3	175.7	11.86	27.19

See notes to Table 11.4

237

Table 11.10 Mood Swings and H share Returns

	Shanghai Petro 1-Day	5-Day	20-Day	Tsingtao Brewery 1-Day	5-Day
Constant	-.000	-.000	-.001	-.001	.008
	(.001)	(.001)	(.006)	(.004)	(.022)
RA	.045*	.037*	.111#	.062	.160
	(.023)	(.018)	(.067)	(.053)	(.132)
RMB/HK$	-.591*	-.337#	.264	2.59	3.25
	(.261)	(.183)	(6.48)	(4.69)	(9.40)
RA*(RMB/HK$)	5.966	-1.323	-38.0	-31.70	2.58
	(24.568)	(32.783)	(47.1)	(34.63)	(32.89)
RH(-1)	.085#	.043	-.039	-.005	-.246
	(.049)	(.043)	(.098)	(.073)	(.173)
Hong Kong Index	-	.941* (.068)	-	1.197* (.121)	-
N	580	580	114	114	27
R^2	.014	.286	.041	.481	.082
adj R^2	.008	.279	.006	.456	-.085
DW	2.00	2.11	0	0	0
Log Likelihood	1292.9	1386.2	158.9	193.9	18.42

	Tsingtao Brewery 20-Day						
Constant	-.008	-.003	.003	-.013#	-.012#	-.041#	-.048#
	(.014)	(.002)	(.002)	(.007)	(.006)	(.024)	(.018)
RA	.004	.025	.022	.103	.082	.005	-.116
	(.075)	(.039)	(.037)	(.077)	(.075)	(.114)	(.108)
RMB/HK$	-2.29	-.189	.059	-.084	1.407	12.77	7.018
	(6.09)	(.464)	(.541)	(7.031)	(5.502)	(7.19)	(6.375)
RA*(RMB/HK$)	-8.59	10.904	18.961	-75.6	-71.87	-68.62*	-76.29*
	(17.07)	(19.403)	(21.73)	(61.8)	(57.29)	(29.51)	(24.62)
RH(-1)	-.110	-.231	-.241	-.055	-.022	-.278	-.079
	(.079)	(.217)	(.214)	(.096)	(.095)	(.183)	(.137)
Hong Kong Index	1.435* (.201)	-	.638* (.131)	-	.919* (.158)	-	.999* (.177)
N	27	580	580	114	114	27	27
R^2	.730	.054	.096	.042	.240	.277	.604
adj R^2	.665	.048	.088	.006	.205	.145	.509
DW	0	2.03	2.08	0	0	0	0
Log Likelihood	34.92	987.3	1000.5	143.3	156.5	23.18	31.30

See notes to Table 11.4

As the horizon lengthens, the correlation between the A- and H share returns strengthens, and the marginal contribution of the market index, and hence mood swings declines slightly. However, even at the twenty-day horizon, market-wide mood swings still account for 50% of the variations in the A-share returns.

Investment sentiment plays a role even in major stock markets, as suggested by the work of Lee, Shleifer and Thaler (1991) who studied the closed-end fund discounts in the U.S. It is useful to establish a benchmark with which we can compare the relative importance of investor mood swings in the Chinese stock market. In Table 11.10, we look at the contribution of the Hong Kong Hengsheng index to the returns of the H-shares of Shanghai Petro and Tsingtao Brewery, using a specification similar to Table 11.9. The returns on the corresponding A shares are used to control for public information on the economic fundamentals. The coefficients on the Hong Kong index is statistically significant for both stocks over all three horizons.

Comparing the regressions with the Hong Kong market index with those without it, we observe that the marginal contribution to the H-share return variation (as reflected by changes in R-squared) is not trivial but much smaller than in the A-share market. For example, at the one-day horizon, the marginal contribution of the Hong Kong market index is 27% (0.286-0.014) for Shanghai Petro (compared to 56% in Shanghai), and 5% (0.096-0.054) for Tsingtao Brewery (compared to 62% in Shanghai). This suggests that market-wide mood swings are far more important in the Chinese stock market than in Hong Kong.

Unlike the A-share market, the market-wide movement in Hong Kong becomes more important in determining the individual stock returns as the horizon increases. Consequently, the difference between Shanghai and Hong Kong diminishes quickly with the length of the horizon. For example, at the twenty-day horizon, the contribution of market-wide mood swings in Hong Kong rises to 65% (0.730-0.082) for Shanghai Petro and 32% (0.604-0.277) for Tsingtao Brewery. These average out to be only slightly below that for Shanghai (49% for the H-shares compared with about 53% for the A-shares).

Concluding Discussions

In the previous sections, we documented higher volatility for Chinese stocks relative to their twins or triplets outside China. This suggests possibility of more mood swings or noises in the Chinese market. Moreover, the mood swings appear to be market- wide: Chinese market index contributes more than 50% in explanatory power of a company's A-share return even after one takes into accout the H-share return of the same company.

In this final section, we summarize various factors that may give rise to the findings.

It is easy to find fault with the Chinse stock market, from its regulatory structure to its trading mechanism. However, we would argue that many of the popular criticisms of the Chinese market are not likely responsible for the apparently excessive mood swings reported here. First, the system of initial public offering has been criticized for engaging in excessive pre-trading discounts. While the problem is there, it is not likely related to the high volatility documented here since our analysis are based solely on post-offer traded prices.

Second, limited disclosure is often found fault for various deficiencies of the Chinese market. While it may indeed causes a volatile assessment of fundamentals and hence raises the volatilty of the Chinese market index, it does not explain all the excessive volatility, since any informational problem associated with limited disclosure is common to both the H- and A-shares of the same companies.

Third, imperfect legal protection of investors' rights is sometimes held responsible for the observed large discounts on the foreigner-only B shares over the Chinese-only A shares. Some stretch of reasoning is required to argue that it also causes H- and N-shares to be less volatile than the A-shares, or that stocks in Shanghai should co-move to a larger degree than in Hong Kong and New York.

Four, low liquidity in overseas trading can in principle cause a lower measured volatilty for H- and N-shares relative to the A-shares. However, it is unlikely as the explanation for the findings in this chapter since the two stocks studied are reasonably actively traded in their overseas markets.

Finally, if the discount rate of the Chinese investors is more volatile than those in Hong Kong and New York, then the A-share returns can be rationally more volatile than its overseas twins. This explanation is possible in principle and cannot be ruled out easily. On the other hand, it seems surprising that the distribution of the betas in the Chinese market would be so much more narrow than Hong Kong and the United States, which is what is needed to generate the astonishing degree of co-movement of the Chinese A-share prices.

In our judgement, the two most likely explanations for the apparently high Chinese volatility are: (1) absence of an enforced capital gain tax, and (2) dominance of small individual traders relative to stable institutional traders. The effect for each of these is obvious. If this diagnosis is correct, the stock market volatility will stay high until the government makes progress on the reforms of the tax system (particularly its enforcement) and social safety net (e.g., establishment of pension, insurance and mutual funds).

Notes

1. I thank Christian Bordes, Eric Girardin for very helpful comments, Tianlun Jian for collaboration on a related project, and Greg Dorchak for efficient editorial assistance. I blame myself for any shortcoming of the chapter.
2. If we think of a hierarchy of three types of markets in the world according to their maturity (and degree of international participation), we may have devel-

oped markets (of which the U.S. is an example), matured markets in developing countries (or recently emerged market, of which Hong Kong may be an example), and emerging markets (of which China is an example). The hypothesis of interest for this chapter is that the extent of noise trading is inversely related to the maturity of the market.

3. Detailed statistics are reported in Tables 10.1-10.3.

4. Shanghai Petrochemical is the only Chinese firm that has N-share (ADR) listed in New York Stock Exchange and also has an A-share inside China. One N-share is equal to 100 H or A shares. Two other firms, Shandong Power and Huaneng Power, have N-shares in NYSE but no corresponding A-shares in China or H-shares in Hong Kong. Some other firms have both A- and N-shares but the N-shares are only traded over-the-counter which do not have publically available price data.

5. Tsingtao Brewery, Shanghai Petro and Maanshan Steel have H-shares listed from early 1994. Some additional 22 firms have listed H-shares later. The data on these firms are much shorter and hence not used in this chapter.

6. According to the Bloomberg screen, Shanghai Petro "processes crude oil into synthetic fibers, resins and plastics, intermediate petrochemicals and petroleum products."

7. According to the Bloomberg screen, Tsingtao Brewery Co. "owns and operates beer breweries in China." It "produces the internationally recognized 'Tsingtao Beer', new products include brown beer, Gold label, stout, Dragon and Phoenix canned beer, 'Blue Girl' and gift set beer. The Company markets its products throughout China and around the world."

8. Because the line (or lines) of business the company is in may not be adequately reflected in its name, we provide the following description from the Bloomberg screen: "Shanghai Dazhong Taxi Company provides taxi services to the city of Shanghai with its fleet of approximately 1,400 taxis. Through its eleven wholly-owned subsidiaries, seven associated companies and three joint ventures, the Comapny is also active in real estate, tour services, commercial trading, spare parts retailing, import and export, car rental and bus line operations."

9. In this calculation, we make use of the information on correlation between Shanghai Petro's H-share and the RMB/HK dollar exchange rate, reported in the lower panel of Table 11.1.

10. The non-synchronization of the return data in Hong Kong and New York, and the (small) transaction costs in arbitrage are the likely reasons for the lack of perfect correlation between the closing prices of the two locations.

References

Avery, C., and J. Chevalier. 1996. "Identifying Investor Sentiment from Price Paths: The Case of Football Betting," unpublished. Harvard University and University of Chicago.

Black, F. 1986. "Noise," *Journal of Finance* 41(July):529-543.

Chen, N., R. Kan, and M. Miller. 1993. "Are the Discounts on Closed-End Funds a Sentiment Index?" *Journal of Finance* 48(2):795-800.

De Long, J., A. Shleifer, L. Summers, and R. Waldmann. 1990. "Noise Trader Risk in Financial Markets," *Journal of Political Economy* 98(4):703-738.

Errunza, V., and E. Losq. 1985. "International Asset Pricing Under Mild Segmentation: Theory and Tests," *Journal of Finance* 40:105-124.

Fernald, J., C. Harris, and J. Rogers. 1995. "Puzzles in the Chinese Stock Market," working paper, Board of Governors of the Federal Reserve System.

Frankel, J., and S. Schmukler. 1996. "Country Fund Discounts and the Mexican Crisis of December 1994: Did Local Residents Turn Pessimistic Before International Investors?" Federal Reserve Board International Finance Discussion Papers 563.

Froot, K., and E. Dabora. 1996. "How Are Stock Prices Affected by the Location of Trade?" Mimeo, Harvard Business School.

Kyle, A. 1985. "Continuous Auctions and Insider Trading," *Econometrica* November:1315-1336.

Lee, C., A. Shleifer, and R. Thaler. 1991. "Investor Sentiment and the Closed-End Fund Puzzle," *Journal of Finance* 46:75-109.

World Bank. 1995. *China: The Emerging Capital Market.* 1 and 2 (November 3):Report Number 14501-CHA.

12
Explaining IPO Underpricing in China

Dongwei Su and Belton M. Fleisher

Introduction

Initial public offering (IPO) underpricing, or high IPO initial return, is a phenomenon common to most stock markets — both in developed and emerging economies (Loughran, Ritter, and Rydqvist 1994). This chapter studies the underpricing of Chinese IPOs. The Chinese case is of interest primarily because of the extreme magnitudes that have been observed since market trading of stocks began in late 1990. A noteworthy measure is that in our sample, the mean IPO initial returns, defined as the difference between the first-day market closing price minus the IPO price divided by the IPO price, is 948.59%! In other words, the first-day market closing price is on average almost eleven times as high as the initial price offered to the domestic investors. In this chapter, we offer explanations of the high IPO underpricing exhibited in Chinese A-share stock markets. Our data are for 308 firm-commitment A-share IPOs between December 1986 and January 1996.

We first formulate and estimate a baseline empirical model that relates IPO initial returns to variables widely used in studies of IPO underpricing. Then we test three hypotheses that may help explain the high A-share IPO underpricing in China. We find that IPO underpricing is the largest at the earliest stage of development of stock markets in China. The extraordinarily large IPO underpricing is at least partially due to a relatively small aggregate supply of shares. We also find that A-share IPO underpricing is better explained by a signaling model that relates IPO underpricing to subsequent equity offerings (SEOs) than by one linking government or employee ownership to equilibrium IPO underpricing. Issuers with larger IPO underpricing are more likely to raise larger amounts of capital through SEOs more quickly. Moreover, we do not find any evidence that lottery mechanisms have contributed to the high IPO underpricing.

The reminder of the chapter proceeds as follows: In Section 2, we explore empirical regularities in Chinese stock markets, examining the relationship between IPO returns and conditioning variables suggested by various hypotheses that can potentially explain the variation in the degree of underpricing across issuing firms. We also test hypotheses that IPO underpricing is due to a small aggregate supply of shares, can be explained under asymmetric information where issuers possess superior knowledge about the value of the firms, and has been caused by offering mechanisms peculiar to the Chinese situation. In Section 3, we summarize the findings and propose future research in this area.

Institutional Background

There are several noteworthy features of the new-issue and offering process in China.First, the aggregate amount of new shares to be issued each year is determined by a quota set by the State Planning Committee, the central bank and the China Securities Regulatory Committee (CSRC). The quota is then distributed to individual provinces. The stated criteria used for allocation of new issues among provinces reflect the central security regulatory authorities' perceived regional development needs and provincial differences in production structure and industrial base. Within each regional quota, the local security regulatory authorities invite enterprises to request a listing and make a selection based on criteria which combine good performance as well as sector development objectives. Infrastructure enterprises, especially those specializing in electricity and water supply, are given priority for approval.

Second, the Chinese government has introduced a variety of share categories to allow ownership of state-owned enterprises to be dispersed among the government itself, other state-owned enterprises, firms' own employees, domestic public and foreign investors. There are currently five types of shares: (1) government shares, which are retained in the state institutions and government departments and are non-tradable; (2) legal entity shares, or C shares, which can only be held by other state-owned enterprises. C shares can not be listed in the two official exchanges (Shanghai and Shenzhen Security Exchange), but a very small number are traded on the Security Trading and Automatic Quote System (STAQS) and National Electronic Trading System (NETS); (3) employee shares, which are non-tradable until the firm allows their convertibility; (4) ordinary domestic individual shares, or A shares, which can only be purchased and traded by private Chinese citizens in the two official exchanges in China; (5) foreign individual shares, which can only be purchased and traded by the foreign investors in security exchanges in China (B shares), in Hong Kong (H shares) or in NYSE (N shares).

An issuer of B shares must, besides satisfying requirements stated in the securities regulations, meet the following conditions: (1) It must have obtained approval from the relevant authorities for its use of foreign investment or for its conversion into a foreign-funded enterprise. (2) It must have a stable source of adequate foreign exchange income and the total amount of its annual foreign exchange income must be sufficient to pay the annual dividend. (3) The proportion of B shares to the total number of shares must not exceed the ceiling determined by the relevant authority. The aggregate amount of shares is fixed in each year and the total number of firms allowed to issue foreign shares is also limited. An issuer of H or N shares is not subject to the quota restriction, but is subject to case-by-case approval.

Third, most stock sales are partial sales. The government still maintains control in varying degree over many firms. The size of government ownership ranges from 10% to 88%. Only 89 out of 308 issuers going public between December 1986 and January 1996 do not report government ownership of shares. However, none of these 89 issuers has reported IPO size that is above 50% of its total market capitalization, which indicates that a larger portion of its shares are still controlled by other state-owned enterprises.

Fourth, the average time elapsed between the announcement of IPO and the first day market trading is 260 days for A shares and 72 days for B shares, which is considerably higher than other countries. There are a number of steps a firm must take after it is selected for initial public offering and before the market trading begins. Some typical steps include: (1) publication of a prospectus in newspapers and selection of underwriters; (2) purchase of application forms by prospective investors; (3) a lottery to determine which individual and institutional investors will be allowed to purchase new issues at the IPO price; (4) delivery of shares to the lottery winners after payments are made.

Fifth, the lottery mechanism, which remains the primary method of share allocation, has undergone several substantial changes. Before October 1992, the security regulatory authorities designed a lottery system based on a pre-announced fixed number of application forms. Each retail investor was allowed to purchase a limited number of lottery forms from the central bank and its subsidiaries. Lottery winners were entitled to a certain number of shares per winning form. With the number of lottery forms pre-determined, the odds of winning the lottery were known to investors. In October 1992 and January 1993, the security regulatory authorities introduced two new lottery mechanisms to replace the old one: One mechanism was based on unlimited number of application forms. The central bank sold as many lottery forms as investors were willing to buy. Therefore, the odds of winning the lottery was unknown to investors at the time of lottery. The other lottery mechanism was based on savings deposit certificates. Investors were required to deposit a certain quantity of funds into a special saving account when submitting application for shares, which could not be withdrawn until the lottery was completed. These special saving accounts were given relatively low interest.

Under the lottery mechanisms, the IPO prices were fixed for all investors. In the early stage of development in Chinese stock markets, some initial issues were even offered at the shares' face values. Companies that went public before January 1991, such as Shanghai Vacuum Electronics, Jinbei Automotive, Phoenix Chemical, China Textile Machinery, Shenzhen Vanke Co., Gintian Industry, Shenzhen Zhenye Co., and Shenyang Materials Development, all offered shares at RMB 1 yuan.

In April 1994, two kinds of auction mechanisms were introduced. Under the first auction mechanism, an issuer set an initial price and investors were required to bid for the price and quantity. The final offer price was set at the level where the accumulative quantities demanded by investors equaled the total number of new shares available. Under the second auction mechanism, the IPO price was fixed and investors were invited to bid for the quantity of shares. In case of oversubscription, all investors were guaranteed a certain amount of shares and the remaining shares were distributed in proportion to investors' bids.

Empirical Regularities in IPO Returns for Chinese Stocks

First, we estimate a baseline cross-sectional regression using OLS for the full sample of firm-commitment IPOs of A-share common stocks occurring between December 1986 and January 1996 and a subsample of firms issuing IPOs up to June 1994.[1] The dependent variable is *IPORETN*, such that

$$IPORETN = \frac{P_1 - P_0}{P_0} \cong \ln P_1 - \ln P_0$$

The IPO price is P_0, and the first-day market price is P_1.[2] The right-hand variables in our empirical analysis include:

RCIPIPO = the reciprocal of IPO price
LNIPOSZ = logarithm of IPO size measured in Chinese yuan
PROFSHA = ratio of the profit a year before the IPO date divided by the outstanding shares at the time of the IPO
LNTOSIZE = logarithm of the sum of IPO size and SEO size
LNAGE = logarithm of the age of the firm
SIC(k) = six industry dummies: durable goods (SIC1), non-durable goods (SIC2), transportation and public utilities (SIC3), finance, insurance, and real estate (SIC4), services including restaurants (SIC5) and domestic and foreign trade (SIC6).
TIMEIPO = number of days elapsed between the announcement of an IPO and the first-day market trading
YEAR(t) = IPO year dummies, t = 1 if a firm went public before January 1, 1991; t = 2 ... 5 for going public in the years 1992 through 1995.

Descriptive statistics for the above variables are presented in table 12.1.

TABLE 12.1a Definitions for Variables to Explain
IPO Initial Returns

Variable	Description
IPORETN	IPO initial return
RCPIPO	reciprocal of IPO price
LNIPOSZ	logarithm of IPO size
PROFSHA	profit per share
LNAGE	logarithm of firm's age
LNTOSIZE	logarithm of the sum of IPO and SEO sizes
TIMEIPO	time elapsed between offer and trade dates
LNGOVNT	logarithm of the size of government ownership
LNEMPLOY	logarithm of the size of employee shares
LNMKTCAP	logarithm of firm's stock-market capitalization
IPORETN	IPO initial return
RCPIPO	reciprocal of IPO price
LNIPOSZ	logarithm of IPO size
PROFSHA	profit per share
LNAGE	logarithm of firm's age
LNTOSIZE	logarithm of the sum of IPO and SEO sizes
TIMEIPO	time elapsed between offer and trade dates
LNGOVNT	logarithm of the size of government ownership
LNEMPLOY	logarithm of the size of employee shares
LNMKTCAP	logarithm of firm's stock-market capitalization

The OLS regression estimates for A-share IPOs presented in table 12.2 show that: (1) The smaller the IPO price, the larger is the IPO initial return; (2) The smaller the size of initial offering, the higher is the IPO initial return; the larger the size of total offerings, which is the sum of IPO and all SEOs, the higher is the IPO initial return. These findings imply that firms with small IPOs relative to their total offerings have a relatively high degree of IPO underpricing; (3) Time elapsed between the announcement of an IPO and the first-day market trading does not affect the IPO underpricing;[3] (4) The age of the firm and the profit per share variables do not seem to be related to the IPO initial return, indicating that available information about a firm at the time of the IPO is not related to IPO underpricing;[4] (5) Durable and non-durable goods industries have larger IPO underpricing than other industries, suggesting that the proportion of high-value firms going public is larger in durable and non-durable goods industries than in other industries; (6) IPO initial returns were significantly higher at the early stage of development of Chinese stock markets. In table 12.2, the dependent variable is the IPO initial return. The independent variables are the reciprocal of IPO price (*RCPIPO*), logarithm of IPO size measured in dollars (*LNIPOSZ*), profit per share (*PROFSHA*), logarithm of the age of the firm (*LNAGE*), logarithm of the size of total offerings (*LNTOSIZE*), time elapsed between the offer date and the first trading date (*TIMEIPO*), industry dummies (*SIC(k)*) and IPO year dummies

($YEAR(t)$). The six industry dummies are: durable goods ($SIC1$), non-durable goods ($SIC2$), transportation and public utilities ($SIC3$), finance, insurance and real estate ($SIC4$), services including restaurants, department stores and hotels ($SIC5$) and domestic and foreign trade ($SIC6$). IPO year dummies are set to one for the year of issue and zero otherwise.

TABLE 12.1b Descriptive Statistics for Variables to Explain IPO Initial Returns

Variable	Mean	Median	Std. dev.	Minimum	Maximum
A-share full sample, between December 1986 and January 1996 (n=308)					
IPORETN	9.4859	2.3125	29.677	-0.1858	383
RCPIPO	0.3781	0.2632	0.2844	0.0747	1
LNIPOSZ	9.0781	9.2053	0.9955	5.4806	12.241
PROFSHA	0.254	0.1737	0.5002	0.0153	0.9885
LNAGE	2.4849	2.7701	0.8929	0.6931	4.4773
LNTOSIZE	10.681	10.628	1.0975	7.1701	15.772
TIMEIPO	260.12	135	341.24	3	1868
LNGOVNT	6.0294	8.0194	4.0055	0	12.9078
LNEMPLOY	5.6087	5.7038	1.5882	0	9.8522
LNMKTCAP	10.4359	10.4996	1.221	5.4806	14.6162
A-share sub-sample, between December 1986 and June 1994 (n=268)					
IPORETN	10.431	2.7124	31.663	-0.1	383
RCPIPO	0.3811	0.2685	0.2811	0.0978	1
LNIPOSZ	9.0635	9.177	1.0099	5.4806	12.2405
PROFSHA	0.2486	0.1634	0.5258	0.0153	0.9885
LNAGE	2.7743	2.6391	0.9016	0.6931	4.4773
LNTOSIZE	10.77	10.678	1.0583	8.2295	15.772
TIMEIPO	251.04	142	305.98	3	1831
LNGOVNT	6.0898	8.0283	4.0101	0	12.9078
LNEMPLOY	5.6935	5.7038	1.3461	0	9.8522
LNMKTCAP	10.4072	10.4727	1.2207	5.4806	14.6162

In short, we find that issuers with better performance and lower-priced new issues have higher-priced shares after market trading begins. The result is consistent with the signaling hypothesis with separating equilibrium as proposed by Allen and Faulhaber (1989), Grinblatt and Huang (1989), Welch (1989) and Chemmanur (1993)

Hypotheses and Empirical Results

Hypothesis 1: *Underpricing of A-share IPOs is partially due to relatively small aggregate supply of A shares.*

Before the emergence of stock markets, Chinese households had access to a very limited number of investment instruments, mainly savings deposits at relatively low interest rates. At the same time, China's household savings rate was one of the world's highest, about 40% of total disposable income. Potential demand for new shares was extremely high when the stock markets emerged.

TABLE 12.2 OLS Regression Estimates for the Baseline Empirical Model

Variable	Full Sample	Sub-sample
Constant	-69.6048*	-93.6159*
	(-3.0612)	(-3.7446)
RCPIPO	22.9758*	25.1627*
	(3.4019)	(3.4513)
LNIPOSZ	-5.0583*	-4.1532**
	(-2.4754)	(-1.8391)
PROFSHA	-4.1638	-4.4099
	(-1.4312)	(-1.4059)
LNAGE	2.3892	2.5793
	(1.4162)	(1.3741)
LNTOSIZE	10.0695*	11.1672*
	(6.1995)	(5.9527)
TIMEIPO	-0.0172	-0.0141
	(-1.0161)	(-1.2724)
SIC1	7.8147**	9.9033**
	(1.7232)	(1.9049)
SIC2	10.7099*	14.0239*
	(2.1654)	(2.4707)
SIC3	1.6218	3.2262
	(0.2802)	(0.4773)
SIC4	2.8004	3.8525
	(0.4782)	(0.5565)
SIC5	5.0636	8.193
	(0.9657)	(1.384)
YEAR1	43.5243*	44.4975*
	(3.3936)	(3.3733)
YEAR2	-7.6043	-8.5893
	(-0.8122)	(-1.0246)
YEAR3	0.6983	-0.9173
	(0.0868)	(-0.1385)
YEAR4	-3.9135	-3.6153
	(-0.5362)	(-0.6443)
YEAR5	0.7963	-
	(0.1014)	
Adjusted R^2	0.3581	0.3757

Figures in parentheses are t-statistics. *, ** denote 5% and 10% level of significance, respectively.

On the other hand, the aggregate value of new shares to be issued each year is set by the State Planning Committee and China Securities Regulatory Committee and is part of the national investment and credit plan. The aggregate supply of shares in China probably falls far short of the quantity demanded at any price-earning ratio that would be considered "normal" in more mature stock markets. In this sense, there has been a persistent excess demand for new shares in China. For example, the ratio of stock market capitalization to GDP was 4.8% in 1991, which is very small compared to other countries where IPO underpricing is far less than in China.

The regression coefficient (t-statistic) for *YEAR1* in the baseline empirical model is 43.5243 (3.3936) for the full sample, which indicates that IPO initial return was highest when stock markets emerged in China. To test the hypothesis that IPO underpricing has been partially dependent on the relatively small aggregate supply of new shares, we replace the year dummies with the following two variables:

TIME = variable representing time trend, which takes value 1 for a firm going public before January 1, 1991, takes value 2 for a firm going public after January 1, 1991 but before January 1, 1992, and so on.

MKTCAP = the ratio of the total stock-market capitalization to GDP, which is a proxy for the aggregate supply for shares relative to aggregate demand for shares.

The econometric results for the augmented baseline empirical model are shown in Table 12.3. The coefficient estimates for *MKTGDP* (t-statistic) are -4.1977 (-5.2823) for the full sample and -5.1576 (-5.0602) for the subsample, which are consistent with the hypothesis that the smaller the stock market capitalization-to-GDP ratio, or the smaller the excess demand for shares at a "normal" price-earning ratio, the higher is IPO underpricing. The coefficient estimates for the *TIME* variable are statistically insignificant, suggesting that the *MKTGDP* variable has removed the time effect in the cross-sectional regression.

In table 12.3, the dependent variable is the IPO initial return. The independent variables are the reciprocal of IPO price (*RCPIPO*), logarithm of IPO size (*LNIPOSZ*), profit per share (*PROFSHA*), logarithm of the age of the firm (*LNAGE*), logarithm of the size of total offerings (*LNTOSIZE*), time elapsed between the offer date and the first trading date (*TIMEIPO*), industry dummies (*SIC(k)*), IPO time trend (*TIME*) and a proxy variable for investors' relative demand for shares as measured by the stock market capitalization to GDP ratio (*MKTGDP*).

Table 12.4 shows the relationship between the average degree of IPO underpricing and the stock market capitalization-to-GDP ratio for a sample of countries. Countries that have larger stock-market capitalization-to-GDP ratios, such as the U.S., U.K. and Japan, exhibit smaller degree of IPO underpricing. The stock-market capitalization-to-GDP ratio was only 4.8% in China when stock market emerged. At the same time, the average degree of IPO underpricing was enormous.

Therefore, we conclude that one of the causes of high IPO underpricing in China has been the relatively small aggregate supply of shares.

TABLE 12.3 OLS Regression Estimates for the Augmented Baseline Empirical Model

Variable	Full sample	Sub-sample
Constant	-6.2012	-27.562
	(-0.2235)	(-0.8691)
RCPIPO	21.0434*	24.1561*
	(3.1182)	(3.3228)
LNIPOSZ	-4.8632*	-3.8549**
	(-2.3674)	(-1.7061)
PROFSHA	-3.6443	-4.5946
	(-1.2633)	(-1.4769)
LNAGE	2.2085	2.459
	(1.3018)	(1.3081)
LNTOSIZE	9.5395*	10.7874*
	(5.8661)	(5.7598)
TIMEIPO	-0.0118	-0.0096
	(-1.4227)	(-0.883)
SIC1	7.1854**	9.6356**
	(1.6808)	(1.8506)
SIC2	10.1581*	13.9356*
	(2.0432)	(2.4475)
SIC3	2.0087	3.9815
	(0.3449)	(0.5883)
SIC4	2.7036	4.3636
	(0.4594)	(0.6284)
SIC5	5.5267	9.0541
	(1.0522)	(1.5294)
TIME	-0.7321	1.3305
	(-0.3737)	(0.507)
MKTGDP	-4.1977*	-5.1576*
	(-5.2823)	(-5.0602)
Adjusted R^2	0.3484	0.3719

Figures in parentheses are t-statistics. *, ** denote 5% and 10% level of significance, respectively.

TABLE 12.4 IPO Underpricing and Stock-Market Capitalization-to-GDP Ratio

Country	IPO Underpricing	Market Capitalization-to-GDP
China	948.59%	4.8%
Brazil	78%	31%
Korea	60%	37%
Taiwan	45%	74%
U.S.	16%	74%
U.K.	15%	99%
Japan	12%	93%

Hypothesis 2: *Underpricing of A-share IPOs is an equilibrium outcome under asymmetric information among issuers and investors.*

There are two classes of signaling models of IPO underpricing that assume asymmetric information among issuers and investors:

1. IPO underpricing is an equilibrium outcome for an issuer to signal its quality to investors. Allen and Faulhaber (1989), Grinblatt and Huang (1989), Welch (1989) and Chemmanur (1993) have proposed a class of signaling models of IPO underpricing in which issuers have superior information than investors. In their models, an issuer maximizes the value of the firm through initial sale and subsequent equity offerings. In the absence of complete information, investors do not know whether an issuer is of "high value" or "low value." Underpricing is an equilibrium outcome for an issuer to signal its quality to the investors. A "high value" issuer can afford to underprice its IPO because it can capture larger revenues through subsequent equity offerings (SEOs). A "low value" issuer can not afford to underprice its IPO because it can not raise more capital through after-market SEOs. Their models work as follows: An issuer gives out "free samples" to the public by underpricing and induces the public to learn more about the issuer. The learning process leads to a higher price on the first day of market trading than would otherwise occur—but for "high value" issuer only. This effect on the market price allows "high value" issuer to quickly return to the market with SEOs and thereby reap the return from underpricing its IPO. Testable implications from the signaling models include: (1) Issuers with larger IPO underpricing are more likely to issue subsequent equities than issuers with lower IPO underpricing; (2) Issuers with larger IPO underpricing are more likely to issue larger amounts of SEOs; (3) Issuers with larger IPO underpricing will issue SEOs more quickly after the initial sales.[5]

2. Underpricing of state-owned enterprises' IPOs is an equilibrium outcome for a government issuer to signal its commitment to pro-market privatization policies. Perotti (1995) presents a model of IPO underpricing and privatization for state-owned enterprises under government policy uncertainty. In Perotti's model, a government maximizes the sum of expected revenues from IPOs and SEOs plus the dividends on the retained shares during the privatization process. Under policy uncertainty, a government may choose to retain a large stake of the state enterprises and underprice a partial sale to signal its intent to credibly commit to future pro-market privatization policies. The model implies that IPO underpricing is positively related to the uncertainty of government policies, negatively related to the size of IPOs, and positively related to the size of government ownership and the length of time the government is expected to retain significant ownership. Dewenter and Malatesta (1996) argue that government may also pursue political objectives other

than maximizing firm's value in the privatization process. For example, government may allocate underpriced shares to the employees who may otherwise have misgivings about privatization. Therefore, underpricing may be related to the size of the employee shares in an offering.

TABLE 12.5 OLS Regression Estimates for the Signaling Models of IPO Underpricing

Variable	Full sample	Sub-sample
Constant	-2.5967	-25.8576
	(-0.0915)	(-0.7831)
RCPIPO	19.8627*	24.3932*
	(2.8121)	(3.0056)
LNIPOSZ	-8.1461*	-7.1106*
	(-2.5569)	(-1.9984)
PROFSHA	-3.4473	-4.3911
	(-1.1862)	(-1.3951)
LNAGE	1.8791	2.2909
	(1.0675)	(1.1605)
LNTOSIZE	9.6519*	10.7496*
	(5.8777)	(5.6876)
TIMEIPO	-0.0126	-0.0104
	(-1.5071)	(-0.9466)
LNGOVNT	0.4579	0.3293
	(1.1735)	(0.72)
LNEMPLOY	0.3978	-0.0633
	(0.4081)	(-0.0448)
SIC1	5.8185	8.2169
	(1.251)	(1.5269)
SIC2	8.6381**	12.2601*
	(1.701)	(2.0918)
SIC3	0.9076	2.5651
	(0.1521)	(0.3689)
SIC4	0.5589	2.0589
	(0.0925)	(0.2854)
SIC5	5.0107	8.6202
	(0.9494)	(1.444)
TIME	-0.707	1.1064
	(-0.3582)	(0.4179)
MKTGDP	-4.2688*	-5.1365*
	(-5.2362)	(-4.9778)
LNMKTCAP	2.2492	2.7621
	(0.9274)	(0.978)
ADJ. R^2	0.3475	0.3686

Figures in parentheses are t-statistics. *, ** denote 5% and 10% level of significance, respectively.

To test the signaling models of IPO underpricing, we add the following three variables to the augmented baseline empirical regression.[6]

$LNGOVNT$ = logarithm of the size of government ownership
$LNEMPLOY$ = logarithm of the size of employee shares
$LNMKTCAP$ = logarithm of the sum of IPO size, government shares, legal entity shares and employee shares at the time of IPO

The econometric estimates of the signaling hypotheses are contained in table 12.5. The coefficient estimates (t-statistic) for $LNIPOSZ$ and $LNTOSIZE$ are -8.1461 (-2.5569) and 9.6519 (5.8777) for the full sample and -7.1106 (-1.9984) and 10.7496 (5.6876) for the sub-sample, which indicate that the smaller the IPO size relative to the size of the total offerings, or the larger the size of SEOs, the higher the IPO underpricing. Therefore, there is a positive relationship between the degree of IPO underpricing and the size of SEOs. The coefficient estimates for $LNGOVNT$, $LNEMPLOY$ and $LNMKTCAP$ are of the expected signs in the full sample, but not statistically significant. Therefore, of the two classes of signaling models, the one linking SEOs to a process of equilibrium IPO underpricing appears to have greater explanatory power than the one linking government or employee ownership to equilibrium IPO underpricing.

In table 12.5, the dependent variable is the IPO initial return. The independent variables are the reciprocal of IPO price ($RCPIPO$), logarithm of IPO size ($LNIPOSZ$), profit per share ($PROFSHA$), logarithm of the age of the firm ($LNAGE$), logarithm of the size of total offerings ($LNTOSIZE$), time elapsed between the offer date and the first trading date ($TIMEIPO$), logarithm of the size of government ownership ($LNGOVNT$), logarithm of the size of employee shares ($LNEMPLOY$), logarithm of the size of market capitalization ($LNMKTCAP$), industry dummies ($SIC(k)$), IPO time trend ($TIME$) and stock market capitalization to GDP ratio ($MKTGDP$).

Hypothesis 3: *Lottery mechanisms in share allocation contribute to high IPO underpricing.*

Five different offering mechanisms have been used in allocating A shares in China.[7] A team of World Bank specialists argued that offering mechanism affects the degree of underpricing ("China: The Emerging Capital Markets" Vol. II, p. 96).

> ...the allocation mechanism adopted for the new share issue affects the degree of underpricing. Non-discretionary allocation of shares, by mechanisms such as a lottery, exacerbate the tendency to underprice.

TABLE 12.6 OLS Regression Estimates for the Relationship Between IPO Underpricing and Offering Mechanisms

Variable	Full sample		Sub-sample	
RCPIPO	22.972*	22.5151*	25.1338*	24.8412*
	(3.3954)	(3.2211)	(3.4378)	(3.2832)
LNIPOSZ	-5.0359*	-4.9117*	-4.1113**	-4.0008**
	(-2.4233)	(-2.3179)	(-1.7861)	(-1.7066)
PROFSHA	-4.1577	-4.0039	-4.3952	-4.1984
	(-1.4259)	(-1.3432)	(-1.3969)	(-1.2912)
LNAGE	2.3723	2.4539	2.5445	2.6041
	(1.3862)	(1.4143)	(1.3299)	(1.3412)
LNTOSIZE	10.0659*	10.044*	11.1622*	11.1502*
	(6.1827)	(6.1203)	(5.9363)	(5.8862)
TIMEIPO	-0.0172	-0.0175	-0.0141	-0.0144
	(-1.0136)	(-1.0268)	(-1.2722)	(-1.2822)
SIC1	7.8267**	7.8219**	9.9417**	9.9522**
	(1.7214)	(1.7114)	(1.9032)	(1.8937)
SIC2	10.7449*	10.6334*	14.1095*	13.9905*
	(2.155)	(2.1113)	(2.4526)	(2.4068)
SIC3-SIC5	estimation results not reported			
YEAR1	43.4031*	42.4265*	44.2613*	43.6987*
	(3.3404)	(3.185)	(3.2955)	(3.1926)
YEAR2-YEAR5	estimation results not reported			
LD	0.2502	-	0.4713	-
	(0.0624)		(0.099)	
OD1	-	2.579	-	2.9664
		(0.3157)		(0.3088)
OD2	-	0.8813	-	1.7952
		(0.1312)		(0.2161)
OD3	-	2.5108	-	2.5531
		(0.3348)		(0.7778)
OD4	-	0.157	-	1.2298
		(0.0212)		(0.1319)
Adjusted R^2	0.3559	0.3498	0.3733	0.366

Figures in parentheses are t-statistics and *, ** denote 5% and 10% level of significance, respectively.

However, we disagree with their assertion. According to the classical capital asset pricing model (CAPM), available information about a firm and the expected future payoffs affect an investor's demand for shares. The number of investors bidding for an IPO affects the overall demand for shares and therefore affects the degree of IPO underpricing, given the fixed IPO price and the amount of initial sale. Offering mechanisms designed to allocate oversubscribed shares do not affect the demand or the supply for new shares and therefore will not affect the IPO initial return.

Fortunately we are able to identify the offering mechanisms adopted by each individual firms at the time of A-share IPOs, so we test the hypothesis that that the mean A-share IPO initial returns for firms using lottery mechanism is higher than the mean A-share IPO initial returns for firms using other offering mechanisms, after controlling for variables such as the IPO size, the year of an IPO and the industry a firm belongs to.

To estimate the influence of lottery mechanisms on underpricing, we include in the regression equation a dummy variable (LD) that takes value 1 if a firm uses a lottery mechanism in allocating A shares and 0 otherwise and estimate the model. We also examine the effects of five different kinds of offering mechanisms on A-share IPO initial returns by adding a set of offering mechanism dummies (OD) and estimate the regression coefficients again. The estimation results in table 12.6 show that none of the coefficients for LD and OD variables is statistically significant. Therefore, there is no evidence that offering mechanisms affect the degree of IPO underpricing, after controlling for other variables that affect IPO initial returns.

In table 12.6, the dependent variable is the IPO initial return. In addition to the independent variables included in regression 1, the following dummy variables are added to test the hypothesis that offering mechanisms affect IPO underpricing: (i) LD, which takes value one if a firm uses lottery mechanism in allocating new shares and 0 otherwise; (ii) OD, set of five dummy variables representing the lottery mechanism with fixed number of application forms, the lottery mechanism with unlimited number of application forms, the lottery mechanism based on CD receipts, the auction mechanism with quantity and price bids and the auction mechanism with only quantity bids.

Policy Implications

We have investigated several potential causes of the high IPO underpricing in China. We find that a framework in which IPO underpricing is an equilibrium outcome in a world of uncertainty and information asymmetry is a useful paradigm for understanding the Chinese equity offering process. Underpricing arises under a strategy in which insiders who have better information about their firms' intrinsic value signal their information to private investors (outsiders) in order to attract investors' interest. To maximize the value of the firm going public, managers underprice a small fraction of the firm at the time of the IPO and come back to the capital market and issue larger amount of equities (SEOs) when investors learn about the value of the firm and are willing to pay a price closer to shares' "true value." This type of strategic behavior is designed to reduce the indirect cost associated with raising equity in a capital market characterized by an extraordinary degree of information asymmetry.

Although underpricing can be understood in terms of an optimal strategy given current constraints, it is nevertheless costly in terms of firm value, probably hinders the privatization process in China, and may well diminish the power of stock markets to mobilize funds for capital formation. Reducing the indirect cost of equity offerings embodied in IPO underpricing can be achieved only by increasing the informational efficiency of the offering process. This, we believe requires reduction of information asymmetry to achieve a more streamlined transfer of state enterprises to private investors and improved secondary market performance of newly issued equity shares. We suggest the following steps to help achieve these goals: (1) broaden employee share ownership through encouragement of employee stock ownership plans (ESOPs); (2) better preparation of balance sheets, accounting practices, and prospectuses priori to IPOs; and (3) improved procedures for pricing of shares.

Wider Employee Ownership

If the host won't eat the food, what are the guests to do? Surely, share ownership by an enterprises' employees (particularly the management) through ESOPs should send investors favorable signals regarding the intrinsic value of the firm. Wider employee share ownership may be encouraged through incentives to make shares more appealing to employees, by providing information within the firm on the advantages of stock ownership, by providing information on how to purchase shares and participate in securities markets in general; by creating priorities for employees in the allocation of shares, and by permitting employees to pay for shares in installments.

Better Preparation of Firms Going Public

The scope and depth of information provision to investors are critical in reducing information asymmetry between issuers and investors. A basic step in this direction is to assure that standard accounting documents are accurate and complete. In China's ongoing financial reform, accounting and auditing practices are being upgraded, but the speed at which they approach the standards of the world's major financial centers should be accelerated.[8] For example, assets and liabilities must be clearly identified and evaluated by an agency with a national reputation using a consistent set of standards instead of by local audit firms using diverse practices. Balance sheet items should be calculated using current market prices instead of historical prices. Previous debt write-offs, if any, should be recorded. Market research and formal assessments by lead underwriters should be included in prospectuses available to the public. It would also useful to establish share information offices before flotation to disseminate business, managerial and financial information about the firm not included in the formal prospectus.

More Efficient Pricing of Shares

The pricing of shares before going public takes into account, among other things, the quality of the firm, the degree of information asymmetry, and the demand for shares in the primary market. Under current practice, government, underwriters and managers estimate a range of prices usually based on either the dividend yield or the price-earning ratios of "comparable" companies. For all issues, a fraction of equity is firmly placed with the government State Asset Control Bureau and other state-owned enterprises. The reminder is usually sold to retail investors who are successful in their applications for shares through a lottery. The Government's goal seems to have been mainly to retain a minimum level of control over firms being "privatized," not to minimize indirect costs of issuing equity nor to maximize firm value. Managers, for their part, want to maximize their control over assets, and probably view underpricing as a means to increase the amount of funds raised through SEOs. Underwriters want to ensure the success of the issue (especially in firm-commitment underwritten offers), and IPO underpricing reduces their risk. A more efficient mechanism of share pricing may be achieved through open and competitive bidding subject to clawback in the event of oversubscription. In fact, 18 companies including Xiamen Xiahua Electronics and Tianjin Bohai Group adopted auction mechanisms when it was first introduced in October 1994. These companies achieved an average underpricing of merely 3.82%.

Conclusion

In this chapter, we have empirically identified some causes of the cross-sectional differences in underpricing of Chinese IPOs using data compiled for 308 firm-commitment A-share IPOs. We first formulate and estimate a basic empirical model that relates IPO initial returns to variables widely used in studies of IPO underpricing. We find that:

1. IPO underpricing was largest at the earliest stage of development of stock markets in China.
2. Available information about a firm at the time of IPO is not related to IPO underpricing.
3. Time elapsed between the announcement of an IPO and the first-day market trading is not related to IPO underpricing.
4. Durable and non-durable manufacture goods industries exhibit higher IPO underpricing than other industries.

Testing three hypotheses on the high A-share IPO underpricing in China, we find that:

1. Underpricing of A-share IPOs has been at least partially due to a relatively small aggregate supply of equity instruments available to Chinese investors. This hypothesis is consistent with an international (negative) correlation between stock-market capitalization-to-GDP ratios and the average degree of IPO underpricing.

2. Of the two classes of signaling models, the one linking SEOs to a process of equilibrium IPO underpricing appears to have greater explanatory power than that linking government or employee ownership to equilibrium IPO underpricing.
3. Issuers with larger IPO underpricing are more likely to raise larger amounts of capital through SEOs and to do so more quickly. This is consistent with the hypothesis that the primary purpose for Chinese firms going public is to raise capital, not to transfer ownership.
4. There is no evidence that various lottery mechanisms have contributed to the high A-share IPO underpricing in China.

We have offered explanations of the extraordinarily high IPO underpricing that characterizes the Chinese stock markets in this chapter. However, we have not considered possible rent-seeking behavior by the government or individuals who have access to the limited quota during the new-issue and offering process. These fascinating problems await further research.

Notes

1. The subsample will later be used to test hypotheses involving the issue of SEOs. The time period covered by the subsample allows time for firms to issue SEOs.
2. The IPORETN variable defined here is the raw IPO initial return. We do not use the market-adjusted IPO initial return in this investigation because a number of firms have gone public before the emergence of secondary markets in China.
3. This contradicts Chowdhry and Sherman (1996), who show that IPO underpricing is positively related to the time period between IPO date and first trading date.
4. This is in contrast to that of Ritter (1991), who found significant negative relationship between IPO underpricing and past information for the U.S. firms.
5. Jegadeesh, Weinstein and Welch (1993) test this class of signaling models using U.S. data and find weak evidence that firms that underprice their IPOs are more likely to issue subsequent equity and on average have larger subsequent offerings.
6. Obviously, the second implication in the first class of signaling models — that IPO underpricing and the size of SEOs are positively related — is tested and not rejected in the initial empirical model.
7. These offering mechanisms are: lottery mechanism based on fixed amount of application forms, lottery mechanism based on unlimited amount of application forms, lottery mechanism based on certificate of deposit receipts, auction mechanism with quantity and price bids and auction mechanism with only quantity bids.
8. Those interested in this critical link in China's economic reform may wish to consult Tam (1995).

References

Allen, F., and G. Faulhaber. 1989. "Signaling by Underpricing in the IPO Market." *Journal of Financial Economics* 23:303-323.

Chemmanur, T. 1993. "The Pricing of Initial Public Offerings: A Dynamic Model with Information Production." *Journal of Finance* 48:285-304.

Chowdhry, B., and A. Sherman. 1996. "International Differences in Oversubscription and Underpricing of IPOs." *Journal of Corporate Finance* 2:359-381.

Dewenter, K., and P. Malatesta. 1996. "Public Offerings of State-Owned and Privately-Owned Enterprises: An International Comparison." *University of Washington working paper.*

Grinblatt, M., and C. Hwang. 1989. "Signaling and the Pricing of Unseasoned New Issue." *Journal of Finance* 44:393-420.

Jegadeesh, N., M. Weinstein, and I. Welch. 1993. "An Empirical Investigation of IPO Returns and Subsequent Equity Offerings." *Journal of Financial Economics* 34:153-175.

Loughran, T., J. Ritter, and K. Rydquist. 1994. "Initial public offerings: International Insights." *Pacific-Basin Finance Journal* 2:165-199.

Perotti, E. 1995. "Credible Privatization." *American Economic Review* 85:847-859.

Ritter, J. 1984. "The 'Hot Issue' Market of 1980." *Journal of Business* 57:215-240.

_____. 1991. "The Long-run Performance of Initial Public Offerings." *Journal of Finance* 43:789-822.

Su, D. 1998. "The Behavior of Chinese Stock Markets." in *Emerging Markets Finance and Investment*, ed J. Choi and J. Doukas. Greenwood Publishing Groups.

Su, D., and B. Fleisher. 1998. "Risk, Return and Regulation in Chinese Stock Markets." *Journal of Economics and Business* 50:239-256.

_____. 1998. "An Empirical Investigation of Underpricing in Chinese IPOs." *Pacific-Basin Finance Journal.* forthcoming.

Tam, O. 1995. *Financial Reform in China.* New York and London: Routledge.

Welch, I. 1989. "Seasoned Offerings, Imitation Costs and the Underpricing of Initial Public Offerings." *Journal of Finance* 44:421-449.

World Bank. 1995. *China: The Emerging Capital Market.* Washington, D.C.: World Bank. Volumes I and II.

13

China's Experience with Indexed Government Bonds, 1988-1996

Richard C. K. Burdekin and Xiaojin Hu

Introduction[1]

Although there is a quite extensive literature on the experience with indexed bonds in industrialized economies such as the United Kingdom (Arak and Kreicher 1985, Woodward 1990, de Kock 1991, Levin and Copeland 1993), their potential value for developing nations remains largely unknown. The People's Republic of China's indexed bond issues of 1988-1996 provide a novel opportunity for us to examine whether comparison with non-indexed securities of similar maturity provides a useful gauge of inflation expectations in a developing economy.[2] We also address the question of whether the issuance of indexed bonds may have added to the Chinese government's credibility as an inflation fighter and examine the different public reactions to the pre-1992 and post-1992 issues.

Indexed bonds become more expensive with inflation, and their issuance should reduce, if not eliminate, the government's incentive to inflate the debt away (Bach and Musgrave 1941, Friedman 1971). According to the People's Bank of China (*Security Market Weekly* 1994), the objective of issuing indexed bonds in the People's Republic of China was simply to protect the interests of the public and control inflation. The adoption of indexed bonds followed the upsurges of inflation in the late 1980s and early 1990s.

In 1988 and 1989, the public pulled their savings out from banks in the face of inflation rates in excess of 18 percent, the highest since economic reforms began in 1978. Hoarding became a very serious problem. As part of the anti-inflation polices, three-year savings deposits and government bonds were indexed. Inflation slowed temporarily, but quickly rose again, reaching 22 percent in 1993. Once again, the government announced plans to adopt indexed bonds and indexed saving deposits. However, inflation stayed above 20 percent for the rest of 1993, 1994, and the first half of 1995 — before finally falling below 10 percent in the first quarter of 1996.

The impact of indexation in the 1990s was very different from the experience of the late 1980s. This chapter will compare and analyze the role of government indexed bonds in the two periods. Inflation expectations are derived by comparing the trading prices of indexed bonds and nominal bonds for the 1989-1992 and 1993-1996 periods. The expectations series are then used to analyze the public's opinion of government policy and the overall effects of indexed bonds on the economy. The response of market expectations of inflation to government subsidy interest rate announcements over the second indexation period is analyzed through an event study.

China's Bond Market and the Role of Indexation

The first bonds issued by the People's Republic of China in 1950 were indexed, but coercive methods were used to convince individuals and businesses to subscribe (see Burdekin and Wang forthcoming). However, after two series of bond issues in the 1950s, no more government bonds were issued prior to the market reforms that began in 1978. These reforms were accompanied by a dramatic increase in the budget deficit.

Stated on a Western basis, the deficit accounted for 5.2 percent of GNP in 1979. While official figures suggest that the deficit subsequently declined below 4 percent of GNP by 1994, a consolidated deficit measure that takes account of central bank lending to loss-making state enterprises has been much larger — with estimated values typically being near 10 percent of GNP in the 1990s (see Burdekin 1999).

Bond financing was re-introduced to help finance these continuing budget deficits and to soak up excess liquidity in the economy. As in the 1950s, the bond issues that began in 1981 did not rely upon voluntary subscriptions. The mandatory purchases "represented a form of taxation and a continuation of traditional 'directive' state controls" (Bowles and White 1992:369). In an attempt to make treasury bonds more attractive and to secure voluntary purchases, the coupon rates on the bonds were gradually raised and the maturities shortened over the 1980s (see Bei, Koontz and Lu 1992; Hu 1997). By 1988, bond maturities had been reduced from ten years to just two and three year terms.

Despite the rapidly growing volume of treasury bonds over the post-1978 reform period (see Table 13.1), government bonds could be traded only with black marketeers who were apparently able to obtain them "for much lower than par value, sometimes for as little as fifty percent of par" (Bei, Koontz and Lu 1992:158). But on August 5, 1986 the Shenyang Trust and Investment Company started over the counter trading of securities. In June 1988 trading was extended to sixty-three cities. The trading volume in that year was 2.63 billion yuan. Thirty-four security companies were established to specialize in the security business. The development of a secondary market enabled individuals to cash in their holdings of bonds before maturity and made bonds an attractive investment for those individuals with liquid savings.

TABLE 13.1 China's Treasury Bonds, 1981-1995 (in billion Yuan)

Year	1981	1982	1983	1984	1985	1986	1987	1988
Volume of Issuance	4.9	4.4	4.2	4.2	6.1	6.3	11.8	18.9
Coupon Rate (%)	4 or 4	4 or 8	4 or 8	5 or 9	5 or 9	6 or 10	6 or 10	6 or 10
Outstanding Balance	4.9	9.3	13.5	17.8	23.9	30.1	39.9	56.7
Maturity (years)	10	10	9	9	5	5	5	3&2

	1989	1990	1991	1992	1993	1994	1995
Volume of Issuance	18.7	23.4	28	38	38.4	102	154
Coupon Rate (%)	14	14	10	9.5 or 10.5	13.96 or 15.96	11.98 or 13	14 or 14.5
Outstanding Balance	73.8	87.9	97.6	89.6	107	228	n/a
Maturity (years)	3&2	3&2	3&2	3&5	3&5	Up to 5*	

Source: Almanac of China's Finance and Banking, 1994

The first issuance of indexed bonds in 1988 came in response to the first drop in the savings rate and the first rise in the income velocity of circulation since economic reforms began in 1978 (Burdekin 1999). 12.5 billion yuan's worth of indexed bonds — with a three year maturity — were issued in 1988 followed by 12.2 billion yuan's worth in 1989. In 1989 only 5.6 billion yuan of same maturity non-indexed bonds were issued. The interest rate for the non-indexed bonds was 14 percent.

Under the form of indexation adopted in China, the yield is indexed with the payment depending upon: (1) a base interest rate component equal to the same maturity saving deposit rate plus one and (2) a "Subsidy Interest Rate" (SIR) for the month of the maturity date. The SIR is published quarterly by the People's Bank of China. It has a three-month lag. In short, the price index used to calculate the SIR is the one three months prior to the maturity date. The formula provided by the People's Bank of China to calculate the SIR is as follows:

$$\text{SIR} = \{[p_1/p_0 - 1 - r^*n]/n\}*12*100\% \qquad (1)$$

where

p_1 = Price index three months prior to the month of deposit maturity
p_0 = Price index three months prior to the month of original deposit
r = Monthly interest rate of saving deposits
n = Number of months during the period of deposit

The SIR is thus equal to inflation less the fixed interest rate on the deposit over the period and is calculated based on three year savings deposits. The price index used to calculate the value of the SIR is the "Total Commodity Retail Price Index." This index includes retail commodities, service products, and producer goods. It is not published and is different from all the other indexes published by the State Statistical Bureau.

If the inflation rate is less than the savings deposit rate at the time the bond matures, the savings deposit rate plus one percent would be the yield for the indexed bonds. If the inflation rate is higher than the saving deposit rate at the maturity date, the interest rate would be equal to the base interest rate plus one plus the SIR. This interest rate is called the "value protected interest rate." It provides an *ex post* real interest rate of one percent at maturity.

TABLE 13.2   Statistics of China's Security Markets: Trading Volume and Percentage (in million Yuan)

Year	1988	1989	1990	1991	1992	1993
Government Bonds	2421	2126	11593	37017	108257	83057
Share	92.57%	94.44%	73.54%	83.58%	39.43%	10.54%
Investment Bonds			25.67	216	8319	2021
Share			0.17%	0.49%	3.03%	0.26%
Bank & Corporate Bonds	185	102	1917	2541	16323	25675
Share	7.07%	4.53%	12.49%	5.74%	5.94%	3.26%
Stock	9.22	23.15	1812	4515	141684	677041
Share	0.35%	1.03%	11.81%	10.19%	51.60%	85.94%
Total	2615.22	2251.15	15347.67	44289	274583	787794

Source: *Almanac of China's Finance and Banking*, 1994

In 1988-1989 demand for the new indexed bonds outran supply. Bonds were one of the scarcest "commodities" partly for the reason that bonds provided at least some protection against inflation. The percentage of forced purchases declined gradually. In 1991, the first syndicate of financial institutions was formed to underwrite the security issues in place of the old forced allocation method (Bei, Koontz and Lu 1992, 161). In 1993, all the government bonds issued were underwritten by thirty-five financial institutions.

Another milestone was the establishment of a nationwide information and exchange network in October 1990 that brought about more uniform pricing across the different cities and regions of China. The trading volume of government bonds accounted for 75.54 percent of all security trading in China in 1990. When the Shanghai Securities Exchange opened in December 1990, it was dominated by the trading of government securities. Although volume subsequently declined over the 1991-1993 period in the face of growing competition from other financial instruments (see Table 13.2), interest in treasury bonds was rekindled in July 1993 when indexed bonds — along with indexed savings deposits — were adopted again as inflation began an upward climb, peaking at over 24 percent in 1994. However, the indexation method was a little different from the 1989 procedure.

Regular government bonds with both three-year and five-year maturities were outstanding at the time. So the government simply announced that all 1992 and 1993 treasury bonds with maturities over three years would be indexed starting on July 11, 1993. 1992 three-year bonds would be indexed for two years and 1993 three-year bonds would be indexed for two years and nine months. The yield for the period of indexation was set equal to the three-year savings deposit rate plus the SIR of the month at the maturity date. The SIR would be published by the government every month.

To make government bonds more attractive, treasury bond futures were introduced on major exchanges in October 1993. At the same time, a treasury bond repurchase market was established. The 1994 bond issuance amounted to 102.9 billion yuan, which was equal to one third of the total volume of issuance over the previous ten years combined. The People's Bank of China also established open market operations in Shanghai. In 1995, the trading volume for government bonds (including futures trading) on the Shanghai market was 5157.5 billion yuan, 16 times higher than the stock market trading volume in that year. Bond issuance continued to increase, reaching 195.2 billion yuan in 1996.

Extracting Inflation Expectations from Indexed Bond Prices

The nominal interest rate on a non-indexed bond is the sum of the real interest rate, expected future inflation, and the inflation risk premium. If the inflation risk premium is assumed to be constant over time, the difference between the rates on nominal and indexed bonds would reflect changes in expected inflation.[3] The advantage of this method is that the public's opinions and expectations can be measured directly without relying on survey data that are available only for specific points in time.

Using the methodology first applied to UK indexed bonds by Arak and Kreicher (1985), the expected inflation rate can be derived for the two issues of Chinese indexed bonds. Our empirical work spans the 1989-1992 and 1993-1996 periods.[4] The rationale is that prices of the index-linked securities together with yields on conventional bonds can be used to produce estimates of expected inflation because the yield on conventional bonds would incorporate an inflation premium. For example, the price (P) of the indexed bonds is the present discounted value of the expected future cash flow. The formula is

$$P_t^n = C^n \sum_{k=0}^{K} (1 + i/12)^{-(6k+j)} + (1 + i/12)^{-(T-t)} F^n \qquad (2)$$

where F is the face value and C is the coupon payment in six-month intervals. The first payment after period t occurs in period t + j (j ≤ 6), and the last payment coincides with redemption in period T. The discounted stream of coupon payments occurs at six month intervals denoted by k, ending in period (T - t - j)/6 — with this endpoint represented by K.

By assuming that the rate of inflation is expected to be constant, the resulting Fisher equation specifies that the nominal rate of return, i, equals the sum of the real return, r, and the average expected rate of inflation, π^e. Equation (2) can be re-expressed as:

$$P_t^n = \sum_{k=0}^{K} [(1 + r_t/12)(1 + \pi_t^e/12)]^{-(j+6k)} C_{t+j+6k}^1 + [(1 + r_t/12)(1 + \pi_t^e/12)]^{-(T-t)} F$$

(3)

If we have values for the two instruments, with each value dependent upon the real rate of interest and inflationary expectations, the two unknowns can be solved.

Interest payments on the Chinese government's indexed bonds are simple interest rates paid at the maturity date with no allowance for compounding. Moreover, the form of index-linking is unique. Under the conventional indexation method, the expected inflation rate calculated for a particular date is the average annual rate from that date up to the bond maturity date. According to China's indexation method, the expected inflation rate calculated on each particular date is the public's perception on that date of the expected inflation rate for a date three months before the maturity date. This clearly influences our interpretation of the observations, especially as we get close to the maturity date. However, the information obtained will still indicate the public's reactions to government policy and changes in the public's perceptions of future inflation.

Based on China's indexation method, the indexation formula can be described as follows: the price of an indexed bond, B^i, at time t is assumed to be equal to the present discounted value of the expected final redemption interest payment and the principal payment. Thus, at period t the price for a three-year term indexed bond with 100 RMB face value will be:

$$B_t^i = \frac{100(3i^* + 1)}{(1 + r/12)^{36-t}} \qquad 0 \leq t \leq 36 \qquad (4)$$

where r is the period t annual yield to maturity on the bonds, and i^* is the expected "value protected interest rate" (defined below) at maturity date t=36. Similarly, the price of a nominal bond, B, after j periods is:

$$B_t = \frac{100(3i + 1)}{(1 + r/12)^{36-j}} \qquad 0 \leq j \leq 36 \qquad (5)$$

where i is the coupon rate on the conventional bond. The "value protected interest rate" (i^*) consists of two parts. It comprises (1) a base rate component defined as the same maturity savings deposit rate (s) plus one percent for the 1989 indexed bonds and (2) the SIR for the month of the maturity date.

The SIR applies only if the inflation rate defined by the "total commodity retail price index" is higher than the saving deposit rate. If the inflation rate is lower than the savings deposit rate, the SIR is equal to zero. In total, we have:

$$\begin{aligned} i^* &= s + 1\% + \pi_t - s = \pi_t + 1\% && \text{when } \pi_t > s \\ &= s + 1\% && \text{when } \pi_t \leq s \end{aligned} \qquad (6)$$

where π_t represents the inflation rate three months before the maturity date; ($\pi_t - s$) represents the SIR, and (s + 1%) represents the base interest rate. The *ex ante* interest rate will depend on the expected inflation rate, π^e, at time t. The cash flow of these indexed bonds depends on the level of expected inflation. The SIR only comes into play when $\pi^e > s$. Therefore, the pricing of this security would be different from those with fixed cash flow and is influenced by the probability distribution of the public's expectations of inflation.

It would be very complicated and unrealistic to model the subjective probability distribution in this case. We assume that the public did expect $\pi > s$. With this assumption in hand, the equations can be solved for expected inflation (denoted below as Series 1: Calculated based on the prices of both indexed bonds and nominal bonds):

$$\pi_t^e = \frac{1}{3} \left\{ \frac{B_t^i}{100} \left[\frac{100(3i+1)}{B_t} \right]^{\frac{36-t}{36-j}} - 1 \right\} \qquad (7)$$

Due to the unique method of indexation of China's government bonds, the yield on indexed bonds should be the rate of inflation if the inflation rate is higher than the three-year savings deposit rate. Because the interest rates on the bonds are simple interest rates paid in full at redemption, an alternative measure of the public's perception of future inflation can be obtained by using the trading price of indexed bonds to calculate the implied yield when the bond matures. This is denoted below as Series 2: Calculated based on indexed bond prices.

On each particular date, this yield-to-date information will reflect the public's perception at that time. Under the same assumption as before, the implied yield will reflect the expected inflation rate if everyone thinks that the inflation rate will be higher than the three-year savings deposit rate. Otherwise, the rate will be discounted by those people who think that the inflation rate will be lower than the saving deposit rate. This method also assumes that no risk premium exists. Therefore, the calculated inflation rate inferred from the indexed bond price may not correspond exactly to the "true" expected inflation rate. But the overall pattern of the implicit expected inflation series should still provide useful information about changes in the public's perception of inflation.

The formula for this alternative method is described as follows, with the price of an indexed bond, B^i, at time t given by:

$$B_t^i = \frac{100\left(3i^{*e} + 1\right)}{\left(1 + r/12\right)^{36-t}} \qquad 0 \leq t \leq 36 \qquad (8)$$

where $i^{*e} = s + 1\% + \pi^e - s = \pi^e + 1\%$ when $\pi^e > s$ (9)

Therefore, at any time t, the yield to date calculated from the price should reflect the public's perception of expected inflation at maturity. The yield to date (y) is calculated as

$$y = \frac{12\left(B_t^i - 100\right)}{t} \qquad (10)$$

The expected inflation-Series 2 is yield to date minus one for the period of May 1990 to May 1992.

Essentially, the Series 1 expected inflation rate is derived from the relative price of the nominal bonds and indexed bonds whereas the Series 2 is derived from the trading price (and implied yield to date) on the indexed bond alone. In theory, both absolute and relative returns on the indexed bonds depend on the same thing — the inflation remaining in the system at the bond's maturity date.

Figure 13.1 plots the implied expected inflation rate-Series 1 along with the expected inflation-Series 2 and the actual inflation rate for the period of May 1990 to May 1992. In late 1989, monetary policy was sharply tightened and inflation fell below 5 percent by early 1990. The SIR published in June

1990 was zero and stayed zero until 1993. In April 1991, the three-year savings deposit rate was reduced to 8.28 percent from 10.08 percent. The interest rate on three year savings deposits is the benchmark of the indexed bonds based on the government's announced policy. Nevertheless, the expected inflation rate-Series 1 remains quite high and is consistently above the actual inflation rate.

Figure 13.1 Expected Inflation Rates vs. Retail Price Index Inflation: May 1990 to April 1992

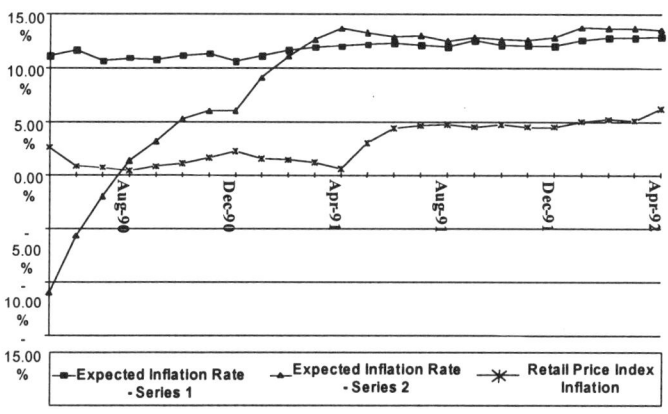

In 1990, the Series 2 measure shows a very different trend. This difference can be explained by the fact that the 1989 indexed bonds were first allowed to be traded only in May 1990. Initially, there was almost no demand, and they traded below par value. From late 1990 to early 1991, prices increased dramatically, reflecting the increasing demand for 1989 indexed bonds.

From April 1991, the expected inflation rates calculated based on indexed bond prices converge to the expected inflation rates calculated by comparing regular bonds and indexed bonds. The expected inflation rates from both methods stay around 12 percent to 13 percent despite the low inflation and the 8.28 percent interest rate that actually prevailed on three-year savings deposits. This seems to confirm that the public did not really trust the government's anti-inflation policy.

For the indexation re-introduced in July 1993, the same methodologies applied to the 1989 bonds are used to calculate the expected inflation rates from December 1993 to February 1996. The data series are for 1992 three-year bonds maturing on July 1, 1995 and 1993 three-year bonds maturing on March 1, 1996 (the last day of trading being February 16, 1996). The initial coupon rate for the 1992 three-year bond was 9.5 percent, which would be indexed for two years after July 1993. The coupon rate for the 1993 three-year indexed bond was 13.96 percent, which would be indexed for the remaining two years and nine months from July 1993.

This time, however, the Chinese government did not issue nominal bonds with the same maturity as the indexed bonds. The closest nominal bond counterparts were the 1994 two-year bonds and the 1994 one-year bonds. The 1994 one-year bonds were issued in February and allowed to be traded on the secondary market in April 1994. The 1994 two-year bonds were issued in April and were traded in August. So the 1994 one-year bond data series is used for the April-August 1994 period, and the 1994 two-year bond data for the rest. Although the yield-to-maturity for different maturity bonds is influenced by term structure issues, these are all short term bonds with only a one year difference in duration. It still seems reasonable to use these nominal bonds in the calculations.

Figure 13.2 Expected Inflation Rates Based on 1992 Indexed Bonds vs. Retail Price Index Inflation: December 1993 to June 1995

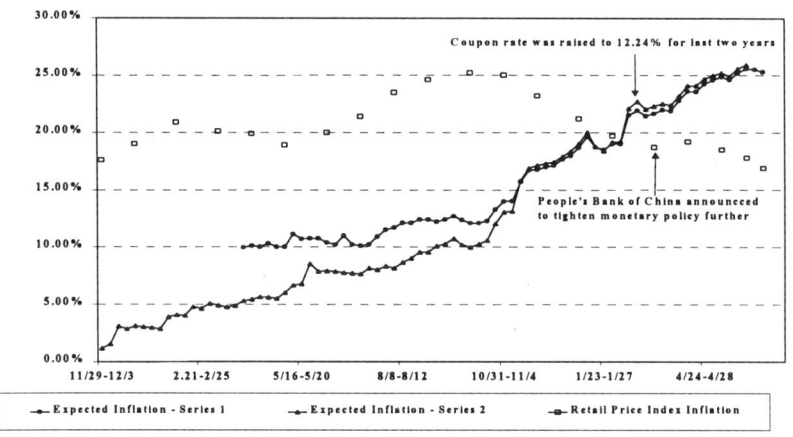

In Figure 13.2, the expected inflation (Series 1) calculated by comparing the indexed bonds with nominal bonds is plotted against the expected inflation (Series 2) derived from the 1992 three-year indexed bonds plus the actual inflation rate. The expected inflation rate derived from prices of 1992 indexed bonds appears relatively low compared to the expected inflation-Series 1 until November 1994. This finding may partially be explained by the fact that, in 1993, China's booming stock markets were much more attractive to investors than government bonds. Consequently, part of the 1993 bonds issued had to be allocated by the government again and several bonds traded below their par value in that year.

However, as the Shanghai Index fell from 1558 in 1993 to 558 in April

1994, investors now transferred funds from the stock market to other investments such as government bonds. Between May 1994 and November 1994, the expected inflation rates-Series 2 gradually converge to expected inflation rates-Series 1. They remain very close from November 1994 until June 1995, when the 1992 indexed bonds were taken off from the market

Figure 13.3 Expected Inflation Rates Based on 1993 Indexed Bonds vs. Retail Price Index Inflation: December 1993 to February 1996

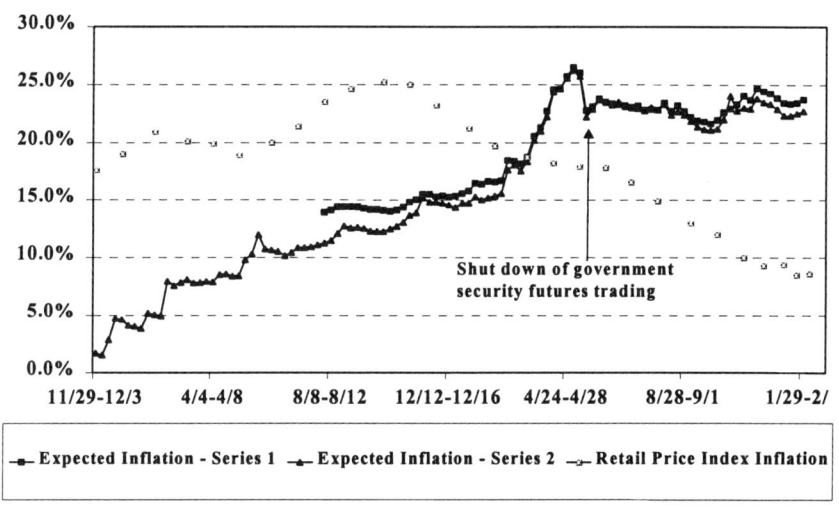

The expectations measured on each particular date are the public's perception of inflation three months before the maturity dates of the bonds. When the observation date approaches the maturity date, the public already has obtained relatively accurate information about the relevant inflation rate. Figure 13.2 shows that the public's forecasts of inflation in July 1995 stayed relatively low at around 10 percent from March 1994 to October 1994, but climbed quickly afterward. Meanwhile, actual inflation rates generally remained above 20 percent and climbed to 25 percent in October and November 1994. The lower expected inflation rates may well have been influenced by the previous indexation experience: even if inflation was high today, it could still be reduced by the government in time to assure that no SIR would exist when the bonds actually matured.[5] After October 1994, the expected inflation measures climbed quickly, and then jumped at the end of February 1995. One important reason for this sudden jump was the announcement by the government that the coupon rate for the 1992 three-year indexed bonds was to be raised to 12.24 percent for the last two years with the first year coupon rate staying at 9.5 percent. By this time it was becoming clear that the government's anti-inflation policies were not working.

In Figure 13.3, the expected inflation-Series 1 from the 1993 indexed bonds and 1994 two-year nominal bonds is plotted along with expected inflation-Series 2 as well as the actual inflation rate. The expectations measured are the public's perception of what inflation would be in March 1996. The data series calculated from the two different methods show quite consistent movements. From August 1994 though March 1995, expectations of future inflation were around 12 to 15 percent. The actual inflation rate was above 20 percent for much of this period, but fell back from its peak level of 25 percent in October and November 1994.

Strikingly, even as actual inflation fell below 20 percent, expected inflation rose sharply from March to May 1995 and exceeded 20 percent. This is consistent with the jump in inflation expectations seen for the 1992 bonds.

Simultaneously, China's government bond market experienced a very special period in the first half of 1995. Funds poured into the bond market in March 1995. Treasury futures were traded heavily on margin. Initially only 2 percent of the contract face value was needed for trading. (Later, China's government increased the margin requirement to 10 percent.) Speculation in the futures markets inflated prices.

Quite aside from any actual increases in the expected future inflation rate, indexed bond prices were driven higher by overshooting due to the speculative demand. On May 17, 1995, China's Security and Exchange Committee shut down all futures market trading. This event knocked the wind out of the market and pushed indexed bond prices back down, thereby accounting for the apparent sharp drop in the inflation expectations series at that time. Expectations of future inflation then remain in a 21-25 percent range until the end of the sample in February 1996. Apparently, the public realized that inflation had begun to fall and that the subsidy interest rate probably would not climb further.

In analyzing the response of expectations of future inflation to subsidy interest rate announcements, we undertake an event study that focuses on the post-1992 indexed bonds (during the earlier period the SIR was always zero and so there are no such announcements to examine). Given that the SIR plus the base interest rate determines the payoff rate of the bonds, the subsidy interest rate should have an impact on bond prices and the implied expected inflation rates. The People's Bank of China announces the subsidy interest rate every month.

By studying the reactions of the public around the announcement date, we hope to gain more specific insight into the relationship between the subsidy interest rate and expected inflation rates. Our event study utilizes the expected inflation rate calculated based on bond prices (the Series 2 method) because the trading prices of the nominal bonds used for the Series 1 method were not available on many announcement days. The percentage changes in rates were calculated for each event date (cf, Smirlock and Yawitz 1985; Johnson and Jensen 1994). Table 13.3 documents the subsidy interest rate changes through December 1995, the dates of the changes, and their magnitudes.

TABLE 13.3 Announcements of Subsidy Interest Rate Changes

Announcement Date	Rate	Change
6/7/94	4.58%	1.20%
7/9/94	4.27%	-0.31%
8/9/94	4.96%	0.69%
9/12/94	5.62%	0.66%
10/12/94	6.57%	0.95%
11/9/94	8.79%	2.22%
12/13/94	9.74%	0.95%
1/10/95	10.38%	0.64%
2/10/95	11.87%	1.49%
3/12/95	11.47%	-0.40%
4/12/95	12.27%	0.80%
5/12/95	12.92%	0.65%
6/13/95	13.01%	0.09%
7/11/95	12.99%	-0.02%
8/10/95	12.64%	-0.35%
9/12/95	12.07%	-0.57%
10/12/95	12.07%	0.00%
11/9/95	13.24%	1.17%
12/12/95	11.31%	-1.93%

Source: Shanghai Security Daily

Expected Inflation and Subsidy Interest Rate Announcements

For every subsidy interest rate change, eight daily closing quotations of bond trading prices were collected from the *Shanghai Security Daily* – one for each of the three days preceding the announcement, one for the day of the announcement, and one for each of the four days following the announcement. The purpose in selecting only an eight-day event window is to avoid contamination from reactions to other separate events.

Expected inflation rate changes associated with subsidy interest rate increases and decreases are separated. For expected inflation calculated from the 1992 series, twelve increases and two decreases occur. Because the two decreases were relatively small they are put aside. For expected inflation calculated from the 1993 series, ten increase and six decrease. Among the six declines, only one is as high as 1.9 percent in absolute value. All the others were trivial in magnitude, and under the assumption that the market will not react to small changes, they were again disregarded. Average announcement period expected inflation rate changes are computed for each event day in Table 13.4.

Test statistics are calculated by taking the mean of the changes in the expected inflation rate across the announcement dates and dividing them by their respective standard errors to test whether they are significantly different from zero. For expected inflation calculated from the 1992 series, Table 13.4 shows that the expected inflation rate had seemingly substantial movements several days prior to the announced change in the subsidy interest rate.

However, none of these t statistics is significant. The announcement date (Day 0) shows a mean of 1.435 percent. This t-statistic *is* significant at the 10 percent level under a one-tail test. This implies that the subsidy interest rate announcement does have a weakly significant effect on the expected inflation rate. It also indicates that the public did not fully anticipate the increase.

TABLE 13.4 Changes in the Expected Inflation Rate Around Subsidy Interest Rate Announcements

Event Day	Expected Inflation Change – 92 (%)	t test	Expected Inflation Change – 93 (%)	t test
-3	0.411	0.55	0.286	0.32
-2	0.622	0.67	0.292	0.18
-1	0.916	1.20	0.112	0.19
0	1.435	1.58	0.105	0.94
1	1.034	1.08	0.094	0.05
2	0.056	1.31	0.108	0.1
3	0.076	0.66	0.425	0.24
4	0.039	1.03	-1.486	-0.31
-3 & -2 & -1	1.957	0.98	0.177	0.21
0 & 1	2.334	1.48	0.791	0.25
2 & 3 & 4	1.435	1.05	-0.954	-0.17

In China, bond transactions are not as easy to conduct as they are in developed countries. Whereas institutional investors can conduct transactions on the same day that an announcement occurs, private investors usually will find it difficult to have the transaction done the same day. Accordingly, the cumulative rate changes for day 0 and day 1 also are calculated in Table 13.4 (along with the cumulative pre-announcement and post-announcement totals for periods -3 through -1 and periods 2 through 4, respectively). The announcement period cumulative percentage change has a mean of 2.33 percent and is significant at the 10 percent level under a one tail test.

For the post-announcement period, no significant reaction on any of the days after day 1 occurs. The post-announcement response of the 1992 indexed bonds seems to imply that the information provided by subsidy interest rate changes is immediately reflected in the bond market. It should be acknowledged that, since this inference is supported only at the 90 percent confidence level, our findings are more suggestive than definitive on this point.

Meanwhile, for expected inflation calculated from the 1993 bond series, there is absolutely no evidence of any changes around the announcement date of the subsidy interest rate. The t-statistics for the 1993 series in Table 13.4 are uniformly insignificant. This may reflect, in part, the fact that the largest fluctuations in the subsidy interest rate occurred in late 1994 at a time when the 1992 bonds were close to maturity but the maturity date for the 1993 bonds was relatively far off. While these developments significantly affected the expected inflation rates applied to the 1992 bonds, investors could not be sure the current changes in the subsidy interest rate would still have any effect more than a year in the future. Only the 1992 indexed bonds rallied at this time. Second, when the 1993 bond was approaching its maturity date, the subsidy interest rate started to decrease a small amount each time. These observations were dropped from the sample.

Finally in early 1995, there seemed to be a shift in sentiment. By March and April 1995, it was becoming clear that, if the government did not change the way the subsidy interest rate was calculated, the subsidy interest rate would probably be high for the rest of the year based on the comparison of inflation in 1995 to 1992. By May 1995, the bond market was in a bull market and trading volume reached an historic high.

Then the government suddenly stopped the trading of bond futures in that month. This shock again had an impact on the 1993 indexed bonds. Therefore, the 1993 indexed bond data seem to have been subject to more distortions than was true of the 1992 indexed bonds. (Although we do see that, in December 1995, when the subsidy rate showed a sharp drop of 1.93 percent, the expected inflation for the 1993 bond series drops by 1.6 percent.)

Lessons from the Chinese Experience with Indexed Bonds

China's indexation scheme is quite different from other countries. Indexed bonds were introduced only when the inflation rate was high and were removed when inflation fell. Moreover, the payoff rate is solely decided by comparison of the inflation rate at maturity and inflation at the issue date. An interesting question is why the government chose this unique indexation method instead of the one that is commonly used by other nations' governments? If the Chinese government pursues revenue maximization, can this unique indexation scheme fit its purpose? The answer depends on the trend of inflation and how the government perceives this trend.

When indexed bonds were first introduced in 1988, inflation was 18.2 percent. If inflation had still been at this high level when the bonds matured, the public stood to receive a higher return on the indexed bonds than on their non-indexed counterparts. At the time the 1989 indexed bonds were issued, retail price index inflation was 21.5 percent. The SIR was 12.59 percent and reached 13.64 percent in the next quarter. The potential nominal interest returns stood to be 25.73 percent and 26.58 percent if this situation persisted until maturity, much higher than the 14 percent payable on regular bonds.

The public's response to the indexed bonds was very positive. Even when the SIR approached zero in mid 1990, the expected inflation derived from the 1989 indexed bonds and nominal bonds showed that the public seemed not to trust the government's efforts and kept inflation expectations high despite the low actual inflation. In reality, the SIR continued to be zero until the maturity date of the 1989 three-year government bonds. The government effectively cut inflation before the maturity date.

The indexation of bonds and saving accounts may well have been instrumental in stopping the inflation panic that prompted widespread hoarding of durable goods in 1988. Shortly after the introduction of indexed bonds, the public seemed to calm down because they felt safe holding bonds as liquid assets, making it less necessary for them to exchange their liquid assets for merchandise in order to keep the asset value from depreciating.[6] Hoarding disappeared. Inflation was quickly brought down to only 2 percent in 1990. Yi (1994:70) documents the public's responses to the indexation program:

> The time deposit increased rapidly in 1989 and 1990. By the end of 1989, the total deposit reached 514.69 billion yuan, which was 134.54 billion yuan higher than the year before... This trend continued in the early 1990s. At the end of 1991, the total residential deposits was 911 billion yuan, which was 46% of the GNP in that year (1985.5 billion).

It was a surprise outcome for everyone. Even the government, while perhaps anticipating that inflation would be brought down by the date when the indexed bonds matured, did not expect that inflation could be lowered so quickly.

If the Chinese government wants to maximize its revenue and minimize its payoff on debt, and if it is able to affect the inflation outcome by manipulating monetary policy, it should keep inflation high over the full holding period prior to cutting inflation just before the maturity date to make the real return on indexed bonds negative. From this standpoint, the government might have cut inflation too soon.

In 1989, when the Ministry of Finance issued indexed bonds, the SIR was 12.59 percent. The indexed bonds would have carried an interest rate of 25.73 percent if the 1989 inflation rate still applied when the debt matured. At maturity in 1992, the inflation rate was held below the same maturity savings deposit rate of 8.28 percent (as shown in Figure 13.4). The government was probably not sure how long it would take to control inflation. Therefore it implemented an overdose of anti-inflation policies. In fact, the government adopted extremely tight monetary policy and fiscal policy from

1989 to 1990 which had some very negative effects on output, putting China's economy in a serious recession.

Figure 13.4 Retail Price Index Inflation, 1988:1 - 1996:2

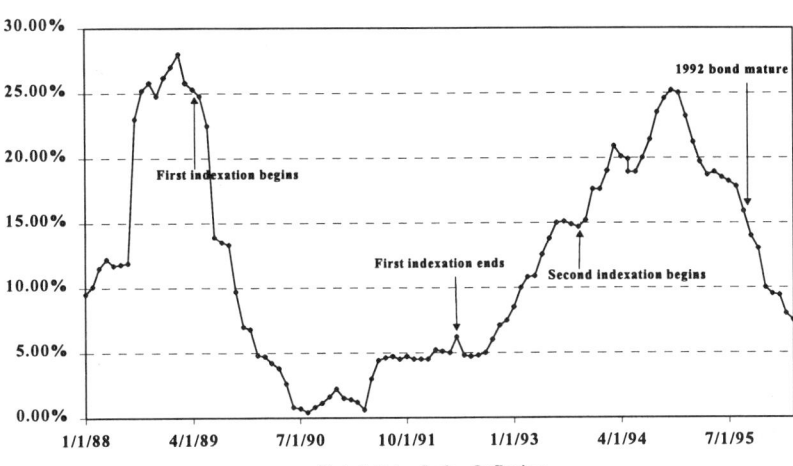

As the SIR was zero at the maturity date of the 1989 indexed bonds, the interest rate payable on indexed bonds was to be the same maturity three-year savings deposit rate (8.28 percent) plus one, i.e., 9.28 percent. This means that the government stood to save 4.29 billion yuan in interest payments with a return of 9.28 percent instead of 25.73 percent. But for those who bought the indexed bonds, this would be a punishment for their overly-high inflation expectations. The Chinese government definitely realized that if the return on the 1989 indexed bonds was actually held down to 9.28 percent, much lower than the 14 percent return on the non-indexed bonds, it would be very difficult to sell government bonds in the future. So, after the fact, the interest rate of the indexed bonds was hiked to 14.14 percent at maturity. The saving for the government was still 3.03 billion yuan relative to the consequences of letting inflation remain at its prior high levels.

In late 1992, inflation took off again, averaging 14 percent for the second half of 1992. The retail price index inflation rose sharply in 1993 and stayed over 20 percent in 1994. The government failed to control inflation. Figure 13.4 shows that inflation continued to be high with no sign of slowing down in 1995. Although indexed bonds were adopted again in 1993, the public's reaction was quite different.

For most of 1993, the indexed bonds traded below their par value. The expected inflation rate calculated from the bond market shows that the public had low inflation expectations in the first half of 1994. They presumably believed that the government would again ensure that there would be no SIR when the indexed bonds matured. But, in late 1994, when there was still no sign that the inflation rate would come down, the SIR rose quickly. The expected inflation calculated from the bond markets started to climb. The public finally realized that the government was unlikely to deliver on its promise.

The SIR for July 1995 reached 13.01 percent. The government ended up paying 25.25 percent for the post-July 1993 indexation period on both the 1992 and the 1993 three-year indexed bonds. For the 1992 bonds, this is derived from a July 1995 SIR of 13.01 percent plus a base interest rate of 12.2 percent. For the 1993 bonds, the 25.25 percent payout reflects a March 1996 SIR of 11.29 percent coupled with a higher base interest rate of 13.96 percent.

While the government seemingly planned to lower the inflation rate in 1994, the initial anti-inflation packages used this time were less restrictive than the 1988 to 1989 anti-inflation policies. The major reason for this policy choice was that the government did not want to repeat the recession experience of 1989 to 1991. In 1994, when the government realized that the inflation rate was still rising, the central bank started to strictly tighten credit. But this policy was hindered by fundamental structural changes in China's financial system. M-2 kept growing because of rising foreign reserves and accommodation of salary growth in the state sector (Dai 1995, Yi 1995). So this time the government ended up paying 21.41 billion yuan more than it would have paid for the 1992 and 1993 bonds if the inflation had been totally eliminated.

Toward a More General Perspective

Chinese bondholders certainly were proven to be overly pessimistic about inflation the first time around, pushing the prices of the 1989 indexed bonds well above levels consistent with the inflation actually in the system. But they then went too far the other way and apparently bid down the 1992 and 1993 indexed bonds because of a misplaced belief that the government would control inflation as quickly as it had in 1988-1989. Such errors may, to some degree, be due to the bond market being in its infancy over the period covered in this study and most participants beginning with little or no experience of trading financial instruments.

But, given that traders in much more established markets often have similarly misinterpreted the course of inflation, we should be careful not to automatically assume the state of development to be the only factor, or even the major factor, at play in this case. Consider, for example, the striking expectational errors made in the face of the great deflation at the beginning of the 1930s and the successive upward and downward swings in the US inflation rate during the late 1970s and early 1980s.

In the former case, commodity futures traders seemed to have repeatedly, and severely, underestimated the rate of price decline during 1929-1932. A blunder, to be sure, but perhaps a justifiable one given that "people could not know at the time that these three years were going to be different from anything seen before or since" (Hamilton 1992:160). More recently, the hypothesized Fisher effect, whereby interest rates rise one-for-one with inflation expectations, has not insulated real interest rates from fluctuations in inflation. Real rates became negative for a time in the 1970s before soaring in the early 1980s. This suggests that US market participants first underestimated inflation and then went to the other extreme and overestimated it — thereby seemingly making the same kind of mistakes as the Chinese, but in the opposite order!

Regardless of the particular inflation expectations that lay behind trading of the Chinese indexed bond issues, these bonds remained an important part of the movement towards a proper market for Chinese government debt, supplanting the past reliance on advances from the central bank and forced subscription from the public. The popularity of the first issue of indexed bonds in 1988-1989 helped make feasible a near doubling in debt issuance from 1987 levels and established government bonds as a viable alternative asset class.

Without the growing importance and acceptance of Chinese government debt, we surely could not have had the 1994 Budget Law that prohibits government borrowing from the People's Bank of China. This law promises to weaken the link between deficits and inflation. As US experience has shown, even sustained deficits need not be inflationary — so long as the market is willing to absorb the bonds without demanding ruinous discounts (as in, say, the financing crisis early in the US Civil War that prompted the issue of the "greenback" PAPER currency to fund deficit spending). The key here is, first, having in place the market for the debt, and second, having sufficient credibility that the public actually wants to hold your bonds (see, for example, Burdekin and Langdana 1995).

We will have to see if the conditions are sufficiently in place for China to avoid the near-automatic link between deficits and inflation evident in so many developing economies.[7] As far as government credibility is concerned, the particular indexation scheme adopted in China, and the use of relatively short maturity periods for the indexed bonds, seemed to give the government every incentive to get inflation out of the system quickly.

More precisely, the optimal strategy for the government seemingly was to lower the inflation rate right before the pay off date. The government could not only help stabilize the economy by encouraging saving when inflation was high, but it also could save significantly in interest payments at maturity and gain credibility in controlling inflation. This is basically what happened with the 1989 indexation.

But if the government failed to lower the inflation before the payoff date — as was the case with the 1992 and 1993 indexed bonds — they would have to pay much more interest on indexed bonds and this could leave the public with the feeling that the government was not able to control inflation. From a short-run perspective, however, the government's initial credibility stemming from the earlier indexation period does seem to have effectively kept inflationary expectations low until 1995, thereby helping to maintain the stability of the economy.

What would happen the next time? It seems that the public went through a learning process to evaluate the government's behavior over the indexation period. In 1989, they learned that the government could control inflation, and this lesson established trust in the government's anti-inflation policy. But in 1994, people obviously learned a different lesson about the government's anti-inflation measures. They probably would be less likely to trust the government's claim that inflation could be so quickly controlled in the future.

If the government still adopted the same old indexation method, it could face a worst case scenario and be a big loser. Perhaps the Chinese government realized the inconsistency in its indexation policy, or maybe the burden of the interest rate payments in 1995 and 1996 was too huge for the government to handle. In any event, the Chinese government announced on April 1, 1996, that the indexation policy was to be stopped permanently.

Notes

1. This chapter is based on Burdekin and Hu (1999) and is reprinted here by kind permission of the publisher. An earlier version was presented at the 1997 meetings of the Western Economic Association in Seattle, Washington, July 9-13. We wish to thank Bill Brown, Charles Hu, Leroy Laney, Tom Willett, Pierre Siklos, Tom Mayer, Tom Goodwin, José Blanco, and two anonymous referees of the *Review of Development Economics* for many helpful comments.
2. While Shen (1995), for example, points to this potential benefit from issuing indexed bonds, the value of the derived expectations may be adversely affected by heterogeneity among economic agents—as well as by shocks that change the variance of inflation expectations (Mayer 1998).
3. While variations in the risk premium could pollute calculations of expected inflation, Woodward (1990:377) argues that this premium is more likely to vary with maturity than with the expected inflation rate. In this case, using same maturity indexed and non-indexed bonds mitigates the problem. The actual behavior of the risk premium in the UK case has been analyzed by Levin and Copeland (1993) using an alternative methodology that compares the yield on indexed bonds of different duration. While this approach relies upon an institutional quirk in the UK market—and cannot be applied to China—it reveals relative constancy of the risk premium in the face of much larger variations in UK nominal rates and inflation expectations.
4. While a small volume of indexed bonds was issued in 1988, no trading took place until 1989 and so we begin with the 1989 series (see Hu 1997 for further details on the calculations).
5. Also, in the first half of 1994, government spokesmen issued repeated assurances that inflation would be cut below 10 percent by the end of the year.

6. Whereas in countries like the United States most Treasury bonds are marketed to institutional purchasers, the vast majority of the Chinese indexed bonds really were put directly into the hands of the public. All 1989 indexed bonds and all 1992 bonds were issued to households, while, of the 1993 bonds, 31 billion yuan's worth were issued to households and only 7 billion yuan's worth went to financial institutions (see World Bank 1996:84). Institutions undoubtedly played a larger role in secondary trading, especially so in bond futures trading, but we do not have access to any data on the breakdown of the trading volume itself. However, it may be added that Chinese regulations forbid any foreign involvement in the bond market—and so contrary to, say, Mexico's experience, domestic agents were the only (legal) participants.

7. Indexed bonds could help other developing countries in this regard. For example, while the Indian government has committed to ending its reliance on automatic monetization of deficits by the Reserve Bank of India, pressures on nominal interest rates due to high inflation expectations coupled with low savings rates threatened to make this a costly strategy. Chitre et al. (1996:5) argue that, in addition to serving as a measure of inflationary expectations, the introduction of indexed government bonds as an inflation hedge could be a "solution to the problems of rising interest rates and the stagnating saving rate."

References

Almanac of China's Finance and Banking 1994. Beijing, China.
Arak, M., and L. Kreicher. 1985. "The Real Rate of Interest: Inferences from the New UK Indexed Gilts." *International Economic Review* 26:399-408.
Bach, G. L., and R. A. Musgrave. 1941. "A Stable Purchasing Power Bond." *American Economic Review* 31:823-25.
Bei, D., A. Koontz, and L. X. Lu. 1992. "The Emerging Securities Market in the PRC." *China Economic Review* 3:149-72.
Bowles, P., and G. White. 1992. "The Dilemmas of Market Socialism: Capital Market Reform in China - Part I: Bonds." *Journal of Development Studies* 28:363-85.
Burdekin, R. C. K. 1999. "Ending Inflation in the People's Republic of China: Some Lessons from Chairman Mao?" Mimeo, Claremont McKenna College, Claremont, Calif.
Burdekin, R. C. K., and X. Hu. 1999. "China's Experience with Indexed Government Bonds, 1988-1996: How Credible Was the People's Republic's Anti-Inflationary Policy?" *Review of Development Economics* 3:66-85.
Burdekin, R. C. K., and F. K. Langdana. 1995. *Confidence, Credibility and Macroeconomic Policy: Past, Present, Future.* London: Routledge.
Burdekin, R. C. K., and F. Wang. forthcoming. "A Novel End to the Big Inflation in China in 1950." *Economics of Planning*.
Chitre, V., et al. 1996. *Inflation, Interest Rates and Index-Linked Bonds.* Mumbai, India: Reserve Bank of India (Development Research Group Study No. 12).
Dai, G. 1995. "1994 nian huobi zhengce xiaoyi chubu fenxi." *Jinji Yanjiu*, April:9-13.
de Kock, G. 1991. "Expected Inflation and Real Interest Rates Based on Index-linked Bond Prices: The UK Experience." *Federal Reserve Bank of New York Quarterly Review*, Autumn:47-60.
Friedman, M. 1971. "Government Revenue from Inflation." *Journal of Political Economy* 79:846-56.
Hamilton, J. D. 1992. "Was the Deflation During the Great Depression Anticipated? Evidence from the Commodity Futures Market." *American Economic Review* 82:157-78.
Hu, X. 1997. *A Study of the Role of Government Indexed Bonds in the People's Republic of China.* Unpublished Ph.D. Dissertation, Claremont Graduate School, Claremont, Calif.
Johnson, R., and G. Jensen. 1994. "Prime Rate Changes and Returns to Industries: Announcement Period Evidence." *Quarterly Review of Economics and Finance* 34:75-93.
Levin, E. J., and L. S. Copeland. 1993. "Reading the Message from the UK Indexed Bond Market: Real Interest Rates, Expected Inflation and the Risk Premium." *Manchester School of Economic and Social Studies* 61(Supplement):13-34.

Mayer, T. 1998. "Indexed Bonds and Heterogeneous Agents." *Contemporary Economic Policy* 16:77-84.

Security Market Weekly (Zhengjuan shichang zhoukan), various issues, Beijing, China.

Shanghai Security Daily (Shanghai zhengjuan bao), various issues,Shanghai, China.

Shen, P. 1995. "Benefits and Limitations of Inflation Indexed Treasury Bonds." Federal Reserve Bank of Kansas City *Economic Review* Third Quarter:41-56.

Smirlock, M., and J. Yawitz. 1985. "Asset Returns, Discount Rate Changes, and Market Efficiency." *Journal of Finance* 40:1141-58.

Woodward, G. T. 1990. "The Real Thing: A Dynamic Profile of the Term Structure of Real Interest Rates and Inflation Expectations in the United Kingdom, 1982-89." *Journal of Business* 63:373-98.

World Bank. 1995. *The Chinese Economy: Fighting Inflation, Deepening Reforms*. Washington, DC: The World Bank.

Yi, G. 1994. *Money, Banking, and Financial Markets in China*. Boulder: Westview Press.

_____. 1995. "Zhongguo de huobi gongqiu yu tonghuo pengzhang." *Jinji Yanjiu*, May:51-57.

14

Trust and Investment Corporations in China

Zhaohui Hong and Ellen Y. Yan

Introduction

On January 13, 1997, one of China's biggest trust and investment corporations, China Agribusiness Development Trust and Investment Corporation (CADTIC), was taken over by China Construction Bank. This highly visible event attracted a lot of international attention and was reported by *The Wall Street Journal*, *Reuters*, and other major newspapers worldwide. This is a remarkable symbol, as China's government is trying to stabilize its trust and investment industry by takeovers or leveraged buyouts. As central bank governor Dai Xianglong announced the same day: "As for some trust and investment companies that incurred serious financial risk, the central bank has taken them over, commercial banks have bought them out or new assets have been injected to shore up their finances" (*Reuters*).

The takeover of CADTIC serves as a milestone as trust and investment corporations (TICs) in China enter a reform stage. In what ways the reform should be carried out, however, needs more serious debate on both the academic and the practical level. We feel that the special conditions of financial and economic transition need to be considered seriously, along with the international trust and investment business standards. How reform can properly combine both features is one of the important issues of this chapter.

Formation and Expansion of TICs in China

Before TICs were formed, most of the firms in China had only one resource for all their financial needs—the state-owned banks. A lot of valuable projects were forgone due to the very restricted lending rules of state-owned banks. Firms had no alternative resources for their valuable projects if they could not obtain funding from state-owned banks.

As the economic reform in China went further in the direction of market principles, the first Chinese TIC, China International Trust and Investment Corporation (CITIC), was formed under the direct supervision of the State Council in October 1979. The first president of CITIC, Mr. Rong Yiren, former vice president of China (1993-1998), successfully attracted a lot of uninvested cash. CITIC's total asset grew very fast. Then, more new TICs were established. They prospered because the interest rates offered by state-owned banks were simply too low to attract civil deposits.

Since TICs can offer higher interest rates to depositors, their assets expand at an astonishing speed. Furthermore, without much regulation or restriction, TICs offer almost all the services that state-owned banks can offer at a much lower cost. They play an important role in facilitating valuable private investment for firms that cannot obtain funding from state-owned banks. They can also carry on foreign-exchange business, while state-owned banks cannot. In fact, CADTIC was initially formed to create a legal entity that could accept agricultural loans from the World Bank because the China Agricultural Bank, the only official bank for agribusiness in China, could not conduct foreign-exchange business in 1980s. Because TICs met the immediate financial needs of an economy that was shifting away from central planning towards a market scheme, they soon developed into an important industry in China.

However, the similar financial services provided by TICs pose an immediate danger to state-owned banks, which are still under tight central-bank control and unable to compete with TICs. In order to ease the problem, the State Council gave state-owned banks permission to conduct trust business on July 10, 1980. Observing the lucrative opportunities in this area, many banks began to operate their own trust business as a subdivision. By 1995, out of only 391 TICs in existence, 186 (almost half) were TICs operated by banks (*People's Daily* 1/4/97).

After more than a decade of reorganization and adjustment, TICs in China can be categorized into five different types. The first type is under direct central government control (e.g., CITIC, CADTIC) and benefits substantially from strong ties with the central government. Their branch offices and subsidiaries are numerous, some in foreign countries. CITIC, the largest TIC in China, has 37 subsidiary companies domestically and internationally with total assets of 166.7 billion yuan. CITIC also has its own commercial bank, which has 17 branch offices and is ranked sixth among Chinese commercial banks in total assets. Profits from its bank subsidiaries are CITIC's main income source and compose 73% of CITIC's total profit (*People's Daily* 4/8/96). CADTIC, however, had more than 50 branch offices in Zhejiang Province alone by 1994. Its total assets reached 26.9 billion yuan, with 260 million yuan net profit in 1994. Its international business brought in more than $64 million profits in U.S. dollars. (*People's Daily* 2/27/95). TICs in the second category are sponsored by local government (e.g., Shanghai International TIC and Beijing Real Estate TIC). Those in the third category are supported by firms in other industries, such as insurance or real estate. TICs in the fourth category are founded by foreign banks or joint ventures. The fifth category consist of TICs that are subsidiary to commercial banks (e.g., the TIC of the China Industrial and Business Bank). However, due to the mandatory legal separation of banks and the trust business, many of the major commercial banks (e.g., China Industrial and Business Bank, China Agricultural Bank, China Bank, and China Construction Bank) had completed the separation process by November 1995. Thus, the number of TICs in the fifth category dropped from 186 to 38 by the end of 1995 (*People's Daily* 1/4/97).

Major Differences Between China's TICs and Those of Other Countries

The trust business is very popular in western countries. Its primary purpose is to facilitate the transfer and management of properties. Settlors (or grantors), the original owners of the trust assets, have a fiduciary relationship with the trustee, that is, a relationship of faith or trust. Any person with the power of control, management, or disposition over the funds of the trust is a fiduciary. Fiduciary duties and powers, as well as the rights of the beneficiaries, are specified primarily by the provisions of the will or trust agreement. This agreement, often referred to as "the governing instrument," controls the administration of the trust account unless its terms violate applicable law or are inconsistent with public policy. The fiduciary duties specified in trust agreements vary widely, but their most common features are as follows (for a more detailed account of these duties, see BAI 1976):

1. *The duty of undivided loyalty.* The trustee must administer the property exclusively in the best interests of the beneficiaries. The trust institution must not allow itself to be placed in a position in which its own interests conflict with those of the beneficiaries. The fiduciary may not profit in any way from his advantageous position. Only the beneficiaries, who sometimes include the settlor himself, should enjoy the benefits derived from the trust property. If a fiduciary is involved in activities against "parties-in-interest," it will be considered a breach of a trust by law.

2. *The duty to take possession and maintain control of assets.* The terms of a trust instrument almost always specify that the trustee is to have exclusive management of the trust property. Occasionally, the trust agreement even serves as a receipt for the original assets transferred to the trustee. Having obtained possession of trust property, the trustee's duty is to protect and manage it. If the trust property is subject to tax liability, a mortgage, or other encumbrance, the required payments should be made to prevent the loss of the property through a tax or foreclosure sale. One of advantage of a trust is the

successive management of trust property, independent of a trustee's situation. If something happens to the trustee (e.g., resignation, bankruptcy, or even death), the court has the right to appoint a new trustee to continue the management of trust property (Zhou 1996).

3. *The duty to separate and earmark trust and estate property.* A fiduciary has a duty to keep trust and estate property segregated from property owned by the fiduciary in his own right. If trust or estate funds are mingled with the trustee's own funds contrary to the terms of the governing instrument, the trustee is guilty of a breach of trust.

4. *The duty to make the trust property produce income.* The usual objectives of a personal trust are to confer immediate and continuous financial benefits on beneficiaries in the form of income, while simultaneously conserving the capital. A trustee, therefore, is generally under a duty to put the trust property into a form that regularly produces economic benefits such as interest, rents, or dividends that can be paid over to the current beneficiaries. For some trusts, such as an employee benefit trust or a charitable trust, the most important function is to produce a satisfactory "total return," rather than current income. Total return includes changes in capital value as well as dividend and interest income.

5. *The duty to remit income to the beneficiary.* The trustee has a duty to distribute the "net income" to the beneficiaries at reasonable intervals (on a quarterly basis, if the governing instrument does not specify the frequency). Net income is defined as gross income less proper deductions, allowances, and reserves.

6. *The duty to exercise care and skill.* A fiduciary is required only to meet the standard of "the prudent man rule." This means that the duty of the trustee is to exercise such care and skill as a man of prudence, discretion, and intelligence would use in dealing with his own property. If an individual fiduciary actually has greater skill or more facilities than the ordinary man of prudence, he may be held to a higher standard (for example, a corporate fiduciary often represents himself to the public as an expert). However, the trustee has only limited liability for the trust property, as long as there is no proof of negligence. None of the trustee's personal assets can be seized as compensation for the lost trust property. This limited liability rule protects the trustee's interest and helps him to provide optimal service for investors and beneficiaries (Meagher and Gummou 1986). If negligence is found, the trustee is subject to a surcharge by the court.

7. *The duty to provide information to beneficiaries.* A fiduciary is obliged

to give complete and accurate information to beneficiaries concerning the administration of the account. A trust remainderman is likewise entitled to receive this information.

8. *The compensation for trustee.* The fee charged by that trustee usually composes a percentage of the market value of the principal assets, or a percentage of gross income, or a combination of both. Using only a percentage of market value of the principal assets as the fee standard allows compensation to fluctuate as investment performance relates to the market. Using only a percentage of income as the fee keeps compensation rather stable, but does not reward or penalize the trustee's investment decisions. A fee structure encompassing both income and corpus fees can provide stability in falling markets and some measure of reward as the market rises. Furthermore, the fiduciary relationship includes not only that of trustee and beneficiary, but also that of principal and agent. The distinction between the responsibilities of an agent and a trustee is explained as follows:

"An agent acts for and on behalf of his principal and is subject to his control; a trustee as such is not subject to the control of his beneficiary, although he is under duty to deal with the trust property for the latter's benefit in accordance with the terms of the trust. The agent owes a duty of obedience to his principal; a trustee is under duty to conform to the terms of the trust" (BAI 1976).

Agency is a special kind of trust service most frequently observed in investment management accounts. The agent's management of assets for a principal may be on a discretionary or an advisory basis. In a discretionary account, the agent can execute transactions without consulting the principal. In an advisory account, the agent must obtain the principal's approval before executing any transaction. Agency services are very popular in western countries.

In China, however, the trust originated as a financial resource to supplement banks when the country's economy shifted away from central planning. Thus, China's TICs have none of the features described above. On the contrary, the settlors in China enjoy debtholders' rights, which are identical to those of commercial bank depositors. Their features are as follows:

1. The trustee pays settlors a fixed rate of interest, which usually is much higher than the rate paid by state-owned banks.
2. The trustee is the residual claimant of the trust property. This means that he enjoys all the benefit derived from the trust property after paying the promised interest rate to settlor.
3. When there is a serious loss in the trust property due to mismanagement or economic recession, the central bank or commercial banks come in to take over the trust business and pay off the settlor.

Therefore, we can see that TICs in China basically perform the role of commercial banks but with much less regulation and restriction. This will inevitably create financial chaos.

Furthermore, the trust industry is unregulated in most western countries. This means that entry to or exit from the industry is determined by market forces without much government intervention. Therefore, TICs place no charter value on their business identities. Counterexamples are regulated industries such as banks, utility companies, etc. To open in the U.S., for example, a new bank must be approved by banking regulatory authorities. It therefore has a charter value on its identity. Whether or not TICs in China carry charter value has not yet been determined.

The regulations of governing TICs in China also need to be clarified. There seems to be some kind of regulation since some authorities must approve the opening of a new TIC. However, it is unclear who has the authority. The Central bank, local government, and some bureaus all seem to have authority to approve TICs' operating licenses. This, of course, creates a chaotic situation for trust businesses and substantially reduces the charter value of existing TICs.

The Origins of China's TIC Crisis

According to the Temporary Regulation on the Management of Trust and Investment Corporations, issued by the China Central Bank in 1986, TICs are allowed to do business in the following categories:

1. trust business specified by settlors or testators
2. general trust business requested by settlors or testators without any special specifications
3. leasing business associated with financing
4. agency services related to trust asset management, including collection, conservation, and issuing securities
5. securing and issuing currency debt
6. other services approved by the China Central Bank

Notice that only the first two categories specified above are considered part of traditional trust business internationally; the other four categories are not (Zhou 1996). The typical loan services that TICs provide should include fixed-asset loans, inventory loans, short-term loans, loans on collateral, etc. However, many Chinese TICs engage in high-risk activities they are forbidden to do, including investing heavily in real estate and/or stock speculations. When the stock market or real estate market goes down, huge losses appear on their TIC balance sheets. This creates a lot of financial instability.

In addition to providing services that banks and securities companies provide, TICs also invest in various other industries. For example, CADTIC used to own businesses in international shipping and handling, traveling, electricity generation, manufacture of automobile parts, and food production. Such TICs, therefore, are "financial giants." In essence, they are not TICs any more.

The composition of TIC clients in China is also quite different from that of other countries. Elsewhere, personal trusts, such as living trusts, investment trusts, property trusts, retirement trusts, heritage trusts, annuity trusts, will trusts, testamentary trusts, net gift trusts, etc., compose most of the trust business. In China, however, the major trust business is the corporate trust. This is because Chinese TICs have put their business emphasis on industry sectors but ignored providing traditional personal trust services for individuals. This phenomenon is also related to some aspect of Chinese ideology, such as devaluing individualism or believing that a curse attaches to dealing with death or will. As a result, the personal trust businesses is almost entirely ignored.

The capital structure of TICs in China, however, resembles that of a bank rather than a trust company. Their asset includes both trust property and the trustee's equity. In particular, both the profit and the risk belong to the trustee instead of the settlors. Settlors receive a fixed rate of return as depositors (Zhou 1997). Further, TICs cannot get loans from banks, according to China's central banking law and commercial banking law. Either they are not allowed to take personal funding as liabilities. This create a very peculiar situation: As a result, many TICs borrow inappropriately, incurring triangle debt, lending out borrowed money, and performing fictitious transitions, etc. (Huang 1995). In order to compete with banks to raise money, TICs offer settlors interest rate as high as 20%, while the loan interest rate they charge for their funding projects is up to 40%. This causes a lot of financial chaos, since TICs' high interest charges directly increase the bankruptcy probability of their debtors.

Finally, changing economic and financial environments also have serious effects. TICs were formed to supplement the inefficient and inflexible state-owned banking system in the 1980s. However, as economic reform has progressed, the commercial banks have undergone substantial reforms. TICs are gradually losing their traditional advantages of high interest rates and flexible services. Now banks can provide better service and engage in businesses that were closed to them before. For example, commercial banks can now conduct business in foreign exchange, which was previously the exclusive domain of TICs. The banking system reform definitely enhances the competition in TICs. In addition, China's securities industry has grown very fast, providing competing services that have caused TIC industry to decline. Numerous TICs now are in financial crisis. Their funding is deficient. Their equity capital ratios are lower than 8%, which is the minimum level required to avoid financial warnings. Many TICs use their short-term deposits to fund long-term debt, which inevitably creates liquidity problems. TICs have now reached the stage where substantial reform is unavoidable to maintain their financial stability. As banking and the securities industry have come to play their own roles in the economy, it is now time for TICs to conduct their own trust business instead of seizing business from banks and securities companies.

The Importance of Reestablishing a Traditional TIC Business in China

The trust industry has unique features that banking and the securities industry cannot provide. One of these functions is managing and protecting trust properties, generation after generation without interruption. The trustee has full authority to manage trust property but does no share the benefits derived or bear the risk. The trustee secures the trust property to the beneficiaries and provides professional services for them. No other industry could perform these functions. The features of the traditional trust business guarantee the fundamental demand for this industry. What TICs in China need to do is to clarify the mixed financial services they provide and concentrate on standard trust business. Doing so will enable them to regain financial stability by attracting clients and distinguishing themselves from banks and securities companies.

In addition, TICs should provide not only private but also public trust services, such as charitable, and employee benefit trusts. When property owners want to donate assets to a beneficiary who is either too young or who lacks the skills to manage the assets properly, TICs are the natural agents to turn to. More commonly, people would like to increase the value of their assets or property but they lack the ability to manage it successfully. TICs are designed to provide them with this expertise without sharing their risks and profits. Thus, traditional trust services are very attractive and have a very good market.

In fact, the potential demand for traditional trust business in China is huge, especially for its unique protective feature. Due to the legal independence of trust property, neither the debtors of the settlor nor the debtors of the beneficiary can claim trust assets that are under a trustee's management. This means that even in the event of the bankruptcy of the settlor or his beneficiary, the trust asset is unseizable. Trust law states that the beneficiary of the trust rather than the settlor's debtors has priority in recovering ownership of the trust assets (Zhou 1996). This protective feature is especially attractive to Chinese, because of the political upheavals and dramatic policy changes they have gone through. Now the economy is growing so fast that many people become millionaires within a few years. They all search desperately for a legal way to protect their private assets or property, worrying that they might be confiscated overnight due to some dramatic change in the political environment. This is especially true for those who gained their fortune through illegal or improper activities. TICs' protective trust services could not only satisfy their personal need but also channel their money back efficiently for reinvestment to stimulate the economy.

China's high rate of economic growth surely provides a large market for trust business. Statistics show that the amount of deposits reached 3,000 billion yuan at the end of 1996 (Nan 1997). Now more and more people are interested in better investment opportunities than just earning the low interest rate available from their banks. The average financial assets per person increased from 40 yuan in 1978 to 2,400 yuan in 1995, while total financial assets owned increased from 39.8 billion yuan in 1978 to 3,000 billion yuan in 1995. In other words, within 20 years, financial assets per person have increased 60 fold (*Financial Times* 6/5/95). This growth lays a very solid foundation for a thriving trust business.

Furthermore, the ongoing reorganization of state-owned firms also provides many chances for trust business growth. Because of changes in governmental function, local and central governments do not have the right to manage money left beyond the initial planning. Therefore, the amount of state-owned assets increased from 20 billion yuan in 1950 to 3,500 billion yuan in 1995. Of these assets, about 1,000 billion yuan are used inefficiently and should be transferred. Assets that are not in use at all amount to 300 billion yuan (*Financial Times* 6/17/95). Therefore, state-owned firms need an external agent to manage those assets. This is the best time to develop corporate trust business. In addition, with an improved shareholder system for state-owned enterprises, state-owned shares also need an agent to represent their interests. This offers a good opportunity for developing an intangible trust business.

In 1993, the State Council issued a new law mandating the separation of financial business among insurance companies, securities, trusts, and banks (Zhou 1997). Although this regulation reduces some service categories that TICs used to provide, it also help TICs resume their traditional trust services. By early 1997, the separation of commercial banks from their sponsored TICs was almost complete. As a result, more than 100 billion yuan of assets have been successfully transferred from banks to TICs. This substantially increases TICs' business opportunities and market share (*People's Daily* 1/4/97). This law provided a good preparation for TICs to totally recover their traditional trust business with their independent identity and assets.

From our current perspective, we can clearly see that TICs in China have great futures, in spite of the current problems. However, we need to ensure that TICs transformation will be as smooth as possible. Some new trust services should be introduced to satisfy Chinese customers' special needs. In addition, an intermediate scheme is necessary for the transition period.

Proposed Measures for China's TICs in the Transition Period

First, TIC regulations need to be clarified and unified. A trust, by its legal nature, is characterized as a fully independent agent. Thus, it requires an independent authority and examiner (Zhou 1996). We suggest setting up a unified authority to impose some transitory regulations on the trust business in order to guarantee its successful transformation. However, the trust business should ultimately be allowed to operate according to market forces, without much regulatory intervention.

Privatizing TICs' ownership will improve their operating efficiency. Publicly-owned TICs are controlled by market forces. If they are not efficient, they can not survive the competition. However, most TICs in China are still state owned. CADTIC, for instance, used to be owned by the Ministry of Agriculture. Since its dissolution in 1996, CADTIC's numerous branches, which are located in different areas, have been owned by local governments. Those state-owned TICs do no have a balanced decision-making process; thus, they cannot prevent the controlling party from being inefficient or abusive (Zhou 1997).

Many Chinese TICs are too small to diversify their financial risks adequately. Their asset quality is low and their services are not professional. Their financial vulnerability seriously affects the trust industry's reputation. If the industry were competitive, those TICs would already be out of business. However, in the transition period, we need to set up a minimum asset requirement to induce mergers and acquisitions to solve this problem.

In the case of big TICs that are financially insolvent, if mergers and acquisitions are necessary, a conservatorship is needed to smooth the transfer of assets. For example, in 1995, when the TIC of the China Bank became insolvent due to excess debt and mismanagement, it was put into conservatorship by Guangdong Development Bank, which officially purchased all its shares one year later and sustains all its debt. This merger enables Guangdong Development Bank to expand its trust business from the local level to the international level. Meanwhile, this transaction pays off the immense debts of China Bank. Thus, it protects the interests of both the debtholders and shareholders in China Bank. In addition, all the former employees of China Bank, following the principle that workers should move with assets, are employed by the Guangdong Development Bank (*People's Daily* 11/7/96).

With regard to trust services, TICs should make more effort to do business in personal trusts, including deposit, investment, estate, retirement, heritage, annuity, will, testamentary, net gift, and donation trusts. In China, which has one-third of the world's population, the market for trusts is huge. However, because most Chinese do not have much knowledge about trusts, a lot of marketing, advertising, and education efforts are needed to stimulate the enormous potential demand. Before long, we should be able to observe thriving business in personal trusts. That is where consumer demand is huge.

For corporate trusts, more emphasis should be put on intangible trusts, in addition to tangible trusts. Three new kinds of intangible trust services should be introduced to Chinese firms. The first one, the "voting right trust," focuses on representing shareholders interests by voting on various occasions. In a well-developed country, most firms have boards of directors involved in major managerial decisions. There is a certain percentage of board members who represent shareholders' interests. However, this is not the case in China, especially for some TICs. Since many companies have numerous shareholders, widely scattered across the country, it is impossible to have a general shareholder meeting when it is imperative to make a decision. In addition, many shareholders have little knowledge about the management and operation of their firms anyway. Therefore, shareholders' interests are inadequately represented in the managerial decision process. Thus, it is necessary for shareholders to turn over their voting rights to TICs, which can represent their interests in case of a vote and also provide a professional monitoring function for the management and operation.

The second kind of service is the "guaranteed debenture trust," which can offer additional security for company debentures. This kind of trust is designed to improve investors' confidence in firms that want to issue bonds and debentures but need a reliable institution to guarantee their debt value. TICs, by nature, could provide this kind of service effectively and reliably.

The third kind of service is the "financial distress turnover trust," in which the trustee specializes in managing a firm under financial distress. A lot of special knowledge is needed when a manager must operate a firm that is close to financial insolvency. Most managers know only how to manage a healthy firm and lack the knowledge to deal with a troubled one. The financial distress turnover trust could provide the specialized knowledge needed to assist the incumbent manager in turning around a bad financial situation. This service should be very valuable, especially for the large number of state-owned firms that are currently in financial trouble.

Public trust services, like charitable trusts and social security trusts, also need to be developed in China, which is undergoing substantial reform of social security and health insurance. The new system incorporates both government assistance and individual payment for the funding. The administrators who control the money are not usually professionals in managing financial assets, but TICs should be suitable for managing those funds. This will not only improve the funds efficiency of usage but also maintain their independent status to avoid mismanagement. For the charitable trust service, many nonprofit organizations have been formed to accept public donations, especially those from overseas (e.g., the fund for the victims of June 4, etc.) The assets of the Hoping Project, the charitable fund for improving educational opportunities for needy Chinese teenagers in rural areas, already exceed 100 million yuan. Those funds definitely need to be managed professionally before they are to be used properly. By ensuring that those funds are well managed and correctly used, TICs will be able to collect more donations, since people will feel secure that the money they contribute will be handled properly.

As to services that TICs provide but which overlap with other sectors: Some of them should continue into the transition period in order to smooth out the transformation process. China should allow TICs to keep their securities business temporarily and with appropriate restrictions. Although incorporating the securities business into trusts will increase the risk of the trust business, the common services they provide, like investment banking or financial consulting, will help stabilized their organizations before new service demands are successfully identified in the general public. We suggest that TICs should be temporarily allowed to operate as investment banks, whose primary role is that of middleman between investors and fund raisers through a securities market (Wang and Tang 1995). The general services that an investment bank provides are listed in the appendix.

Regarding the role of settlor, the change from debtholder to shareholder is very dramatic for most Chinese who are usually very risk-averse. A new middle position is proposed here to resolve the problem of stabilizing the trust business during the transformation. We propose that, during the transition period, settlors' principal should be guaranteed, although standard shareholders could loss all their money in economic downturns. However, trust investors should profit from a trustee's good investment, instead of earning a fixed interest rate. On the other hand, the trustee's incentives need to be aligned with settlor although he is not the residual claimant of the trust assets. One way to achieve this is to give the trustee a certain percentage of the profit he makes as a bonus, so that he has an incentive to work harder and do a good job for settlor. Government assistance might still be needed in this scheme when the trust business turns insolvent. However, the only debt that needs to be cleared up, in the event of default, is the principals. This scheme should be able to serve as an intermediate stage between current TICs and future, well-developed TICs.

We have a lot of confidence in the future of TICs, in spite of their current problems. The process of transformation is always difficult and it takes time and effort. We are sure that before long the Chinese people will realize how important trust services are to their daily life.

Summary and Conclusion

TICs play such an important role in China's economy that their current crisis cannot be ignored. We identify the source of the crisis as TICs' duplication of services already provided by banks and securities companies. This is related to another problem: that settlor in China now play the role of debtholders instead of shareholders. We point out all the major differences between China's TICs and those in other countries.

We recommend that, in order to clear up the chaotic situation and sustain their financial stability, TICs should recover all their normal trust services and give up the financial business they have seized from the banking and securities industry. We also propose various measures for transforming the current TICs, including introducing new trust services and an intermediate scheme to smooth out the transition process. We hope our chapter will serve to encourage more research in this area.

Appendix

General Services of an Investment Bank:

1. Provide the securities investment trust in which investors' asset value could be increased reliably through good securities investment.
2. Supply financing for firms that need long-term investment.
3. Issue, secure, and underwrite new bonds and stocks.
4. Provide consulting services for individuals.
5. Provide consulting services for companies, including mergers, acquisition, capital adjustment, and policies.
6. Provide brokerage services by buying and selling state treasury bonds, government bonds, certificates of deposit, stocks, etc.

References

Baker, P., and P. Langan. 1982. *Snell's Principles of Equity*. London: Sweet and Maxwell.

Bank Administration Institute. 1975. *Trust Operation Manual*. Park Ridge.

———. 1976. *Trust Account Administration*. Park Ridge.

Fang, J. 1994. *The Theory and Practice of Trust Law* (xintuofa zhi lilun yu shiwu). Taipei: yuedan chubanshe gufen youxiangongsi.

Federal Financial Institutions Examination Council. 1995. *Trust Assets of Financial Institutions*. Washington, D. C.

Huang, L. 1995. "The Separated Management of Finance and Outlet of Trust and Investment Corporations (Jinrong fengye jingying yu xintuo gongsi de chulu)." Paper presented at the Symposium of Guangzhou Finance and Enterprise Reform, Guangzhou, China.

Meagher, R., and W. Gummow. 1986. *Jacobs' Law of Trusts*. Sydney: Butterworths.

Miller, M. 1996. "Alternative Strategies for Corporate Governance," in X. Dianqing and W. Guanzhong, eds. *Reform of State Owned Enterprises in China*. Beijing: Zhongguo jingjichubanshe.

Nan, Y. 1997. "Analysis of Personal Financial Assets in China (Geren jinrong zichan fenxi)," Dadi Monthly 64:31-32.

Parker, D., and A. Mellows. 1975. *The Modern Law of Trusts*. London: Sweet and Maxwell.

Wan, F. 1994. *The Practice of Banking Credit and Trust Investment* (Yinhang xindai yu xintuo touzi shiwu), Beijing: zhongguo shangye chubanshe.

Wang, C. and D. Tang. 1995. *Management and Operation of the Investment Banks in the World* (Geguo touzi yinhang guanli yu yunzuo). Guiyang: Guizhou renming chubanshe.

Zhou, X. 1996. *Where to Go – the Identification and Future Direction of China's Trust under a Policy of Separation between Different Financial Businesses* (Zhongguo xintuoye: hequ hecong). Jingji daokan (Journal of Economics), February, 13-20.

———. 1997. *Studies on the Comparative Law of Trust System* (Xintuo zhidu bijiaofa yanjiu), Beijing: faluu chubanshe.

15
Lessons from a Survey of Urban Credit Cooperatives in China

Eric Girardin and Stephen Bazen

Introduction

There is a widespread view that China has achieved record rates of growth, despite the lack of apparent fundamental reforms in key sectors, such as the financial sector, especially banking.[1] Such a lag in reforming the financial sector compared to reforms in other sectors of the economy is indeed generally considered to be a characteristic feature of transitional economies.[2]

However, the experience of other high growth Asian economies[3] shows that despite the shortcomings of the formal banking system, 'the financial system as a whole must have contained enough resilience and elasticity to meet the most urgent needs of a rapidly growing economy in a great transformation process.'[4] In the literature on Asian economies, but curiously not in the case of China, this resilience is usually attributed to non-banking credit arrangements, which bridge the needs of small or medium size business excluded from bank credit. There is thus a need to examine further the structure and dynamics of the Chinese financial institutions to see whether agents other than state owned banks have played an increasing role.

Among non bank financial intermediaries in China, Urban credit cooperatives (UCCs) were both the most dynamic over the last ten years, and one of the least studied. In their otherwise exhaustive study of the 'Chinese Financial System,' Dipchand et al (1994) devote only two pages to UCCs with meagre details compared to extensive developments on Rural Credit Cooperatives (RCCs) or Trust and Investment Companies (TICs). A very short case study of 'UCCs in Shanghai' is provided by a recent World Bank (1995) country study. Furthermore, UCCs are hardly mentioned by Yi (1994) or Yang (1996). This chapter aims at filling such a gap by presenting results from an original survey study on UCCs in cities with different sizes located in regions with varying levels of economic development.

We will provide in the first section a general background on Urban Credit Cooperatives. We first consider recent theoretical advances which have highlighted their comparative advantages in using local information, monitoring and enforcing sanctions. We then go on to consider the Chinese macroeconomic context of UCCs. This will involve examining their history and main characteristics. We also look at their financial specificities, as well as the regulations to which they are subject.

The second section will present the results of the survey study. We firstly examine in a descriptive way the major features of our sample of UCCs and then go on to consider the relationships between their main characteristics by using in turn principal component analysis, and econometric analysis.

Theoretical and Macroeconomic Background

An assessment of the situation and dynamics of Urban Credit Cooperatives in China involves looking both at the comparative advantages as well as the downside of the non-banking credit arrangements, and examining the aggregate dimension of such credit cooperatives in China.

The Advantages and Downside of Credit Cooperatives

In China the non-state financial sector developed in response to controls over, and deficiencies in, the formal banking sector (it was has been reactive rather than autonomous, using the approach suggested by Chandavarkar 1985). Indeed, the state-owned banks are typically poor at solving the problems of asymmetry of information and at monitoring the performance of their borrowers, mostly state-owned enterprises. Non-bank financial intermediaries such as credit cooperatives by contrast have a comparative advantage in these respects, but these institutions present some drawbacks.

Credit cooperatives typically borrow funds from inside sources, mostly their members, and outside sources, mainly banks. They work in some respect like formal sector banks, collecting deposits from and granting loans to their members.

Recent theoretical advances have been made in the study of the motivation for and design of risk sharing institutions in general and credit arrangements in particular.[5]

Two major approaches to analysing credit cooperatives have been put forward. The first has focused on the long term interaction that they ensure. According to this view, cooperatives should be designed to ensure that members have durable long-term relations among themselves or else identify sufficiently with the collective (Banerjee et al 1994).

Another approach considers that credit cooperatives are an organizational form that tries to use local information and enforcement, and aims at providing a closer monitoring of borrowers than do conventional banks

(Besley 1993). They have a comparative advantage in using local information, monitoring and enforcing sanctions on borrowers. This is the so-called peer monitoring view[6] (Stiglitz 1990, Arnott and Stiglitz 1990). Individuals who interact in a variety of non market contexts tend to know each other well. Thus they may have greater ability to monitor each other than do formal financial institutions, such as banks. This can explain why many non-market institutions function effectively where formal institutions fail. For example, the frequent failure of formal banking arrangements in low-income situations is commonly attributed to informational problems such as adverse selection and moral hazard (Braverman and Guash 1986, Binswanger 1986). In such contexts non-market institutions may still be able to work.

While in a large scale bank, an individual may wish to monitor those who have been granted loans and on whose performance the return to his savings depends, it is usually extremely costly for him to do so. By contrast, in a credit cooperative, such monitoring may be easier, given the individual's local knowledge of borrowers and the relatively small size of membership. This may reduce the two kinds of agency problems experienced in banking: the borrower's and the monitor's. Borrowing members of the cooperative undertake projects about which they have some private information. If there is a moral hazard problem, the other members of the credit cooperative have to be induced to monitor.

The comparative advantage of informal non-market institutions in terms of enforcement has two features. The first concerns the scope of sanctions. In most social structures, mechanisms of social control already exist to limit antisocial behaviour. The second feature concerns the depth of sanctions. In low-income countries, many formal institutions, such as banks, are new, but there is a long history of cooperation in informal settings.

The lessons of the experience of Asian countries — excluding China — with informal finance, gathered in an exhaustive study by Ghate et al (1992), are that as a result of its comparative advantages, informal credit is better distributed than formal and is used more productively. However, there are three main concerns, often put forward — that are undoubtedly shared by Chinese monetary authorities. First, informal credit violates the planning objectives that the government sets itself. Second, with respect to stabilization policy, informal credit frustrates, or least dampens, the efficiency of monetary policy. Third, there are prudential concerns. The informal sector cannot offer the same degree of protection to depositors that can be enforced in banks, for example benefiting from the backing of the state or other prudential safety nets.

The Aggregate Dimension of Chinese UCCs

Banking sector reform in China favoured a phased approach. After initially protecting existing state banks both from outside, and from mutual, competition, the Chinese authorities allowed in the eighties successive waves of entry of new types of non-state and non-bank financial institutions. Moreover, even though they should not compete directly with state banks, since they are supposed to exclusively finance the growth of the non-state sector, they tend to gain an increasing share of financial assets. The impressive growth of UCCs, in the late eighties, early nineties was particularly helpful in satisfying the growing demand for investment loans by enterprises. However, this implied an uncontrolled development which led to successive attempts by the authorities to regulate them.

Since the national economic adjustment and economic system reform initiated in 1979, Township and Village Enterprises (TVEs) and private enterprises have developed quickly but encountered difficulties in opening accounts at banks, getting loans from banks, and settling business through banks. As a result, Urban Credit Cooperatives emerged and developed rapidly. They are collectively owned urban financial institutions, which are under the supervision of the People's Bank of China.

Since UCCs emerged with the primary purpose of facilitating the financing of non-state-owned small and medium sized enterprises, the fluctuations in the development of UCCs and that of non-state-owned enterprises were closely related.

TABLE 15.1 Rate of Growth of the Assets of the Different Financial Institutions (in %)

	1988	1989	1990	1991	1992	1993	1994
PBC	20.6	24.2	25.8	24.8	12.7	31.7	33.2
Specialized banks	18.0	21.2	25.9	22.3	20.4	26.2	10.2
RCCs	8.8	18.2	24.6	24.7	29.8	27.8	12.0
UCCs	105	28.6	32.1	51.3	96.4	70.0	15.0
TICs	45.6	6.0	34.0	41.5	37.7	11.3	N.A.
CPI inflation rate	18.8	18.0	3.1	3.4	6.4	14.7	24.1

Source: PBC

The first UCC was set up in Luhoe county, Henan Province in 1979. In 1984, the Industrial and Commercial Bank of China opened Individual Business Departments specializing in granting credit to individual businessmen and private enterprises at urban and township level. Subsequently, UCCs grew fast in terms of their number, their employees, and the volume of the deposits collected and loans granted. By the end of 1993, there were about 4,892 UCCs, with 120 thousand employees and 187.8 billion yuan total assets in the whole country. UCCs appear as the most dynamic element among Chinese financial institutions over the most recent period. As a rule the rate of nominal growth of the assets of financial institutions was higher than the CPI inflation rate from 1988 to 1993 (table 15.1). On average nominal assets grew at the same rate for the PBC, state banks and Rural Credit Cooperatives (*i.e.* 22%), corresponding to more than twice the average official inflation rate, and a little more for the growth of assets of Trust and Investment Companies but with more variance. UCCs represent the main exception to the rule. The average rate of growth of their assets was indeed nearly three times higher than for specialized banks. Some years, like 1988 and 1992 even saw a doubling of the assets of UCCs. Despite their rapid developement, UCCs still account for only a small share of both total loans (3.2 percent in 1994) and total deposits (5.81 percent).

Operational and Fund Management

Among total assets of UCCs, loans saw their share fall from nearly two-thirds until the early 1990s to two-fifths in 1993 (table 15.2). The share of deposits with banks witnessed a much less dramatic fall from around a fifth to a-sixth. Interbank lending was the major beneficiary of these movements, reaching nearly 15 percent of assets in 1993. On the liabilities side, movements were less sharp. However within a share of total deposits with no clear trend, the strong rise in the share of deposits from households (especially time deposits) is quite noticeable. Indeed households savings represent 20 percent of total liabilities of UCCs in 1993. By contrast loans from banks have followed a downward trend.

The balance sheet of UCCs in 1994 has five main characteristics. Firstly, total deposits exceed aggregate credit. Secondly, in the inter-bank market, UCCs are net lenders. Thirdly, the majority of UCCs' liabilities are deposits by collectively-owned enterprises. Fourthly, the major borrowers of UCCs are urban collectively-owned enterprises Fifth, the assets of UCCs are diversified.

The rules governing the management of UCCs are contained in the "Regulation on Management of UCCs" issued by PBC in 1989. "The Regulation" defined UCCs' establishment, their scope of business, and operational management.

The scope of business of UCCs, defined in Chapter 3 of "The Regulation" is: to collect deposits from and grant loans to urban collectively owned enterprises, private enterprises, small-size state owned enterprises which are under the leasing contract; and do the settlement for them; to absorb deposits from urban individuals; to deal with the security business on behalf of security companies; to collect the premium and other commissions and make payments on behalf of the insurance companies and other financial institutions; and to do other business approved by PBC.

In its Chapter 4, "The Regulation" defined the operational management of UCCs as follows:
1. The total amount of its own capital plus the accumulated profit of the UCC shall not be less than 5% of its total assets.

2. The total loans granted by the UCC shall not exceed 80% of its total deposits plus its own capital.
3. The total amount of fixed asset loans granted by the UCC should not exceed 30% of its total credits.
4. The maximum amount of a single loan to collectively owned enterprises and contracted small-size state owned enterprises granted by the UCC shall not exceed 50% of its own capital; the maximum amount of a single loan to individual businessmen granted by the UCC shall not exceed 10% of its own capital.
5. The total amount of the fixed assets of the UCC shall not exceed 20% of its own capital plus its accumulated profit.

TABLE 15.2 Decomposition of Urban Credit Cooperatives' Assets and Liabilities (in % and Yuan)

	1987	1990	1993
Assets			
Loans	64.5	66.9	41.4
Collectives	42.3	43.4	31.8
Individual enterprises	6.9	6.6	3.6
Other	15.3	16.9	5.9
Required reserves	4.7	8.4	7.1
Deposits with banks	22.1	20.8	16.1
Bonds			4.8
Cash in vault			1.1
Interbank lending			14.6
Other	8.6	3.8	14.8
Total Assets	**100**	**100**	**100**
	(9.2 bil)	(37.2 bil.)	(187.9 bil)
Liabilities			
Deposits	76.9	83.2	71.3
Collectives	35.0	26.9	33.2
Individual enterprises	6.3	4.5	3.6
Household savings	8.2	23.0	20.0
Demand	3.1	6.9	7.3
Time	5.0	16.1	12.7
Other	27.4	28.7	14.5
Loans from banks	7.0	3.8	1.5
Own capital			4.5
Interbank borrowing			7.7
Other Liabilities	15.9	12.9	14.9
Total Liabilities	**100**	**100**	**100**

Source: PBC

UCCs shall abide by the principle named "planning the credit issued to customers according to the deposit they have taken." The interest rate paid by UCCs shall be subject to the level set by PBC; the lending rate charged by UCCs may float on the basis of the authorized lending rate, but the floating margin shall be set by PBC. The interest rate for inter-bank lending or borrowing shall be decided by mutual negotiation.

UCCs shall open an account and deposit reserves in the PBC's local branch. The required reserve ratio shall be stipulated by the PBC. If they have difficulties in opening an account with PBC, they may open an account in the specialized banks. UCCs may participate in the intra-city settlement of negotiable instruments. The inter-city settlements among UCCs may be done by mutual agreement between each other. The specialized banks will support them in opening accounts, settlements and the supply of cash.

A Survey of UCCs

In order to remedy the lack of first hand data on Chinese urban credit cooperatives, we conducted a survey among eight cities in three regions with different levels of development, selecting some 57 UCCs. We first present a descriptive overview in order to highlight the structure of their balance sheet, their management structure and financial performance or solvency. In order to examine the relationships between these different characteristics of the sample UCCs, we use principal component analysis. Finally, with an econometric analysis we examine the determinants of UCCs' efficiency in granting loans that are repaid and their profitability.

Descriptive analysis

A survey of Urban Credit Cooperative in China, was conducted by selecting them randomly in representative regions, chosen because of their diverse level of development, and representative cities, chosen because of their differing sizes. We thus selected 57 UCCs from 8 cities accross China (see table 15.1). A questionnaire was sent to the relevant local branches of PBC, with answers established on the basis of annual reports that UCCs are required to submit. In the following, all data are collected (for 1994) from these sample UCCs unless otherwise specified.

Since the start of the reforms and the opening to the outside world, while China's economy as a whole developed rapidly, differences of economic development among regions widened. Three types of development zones have been formed: one is the developed zone which is composed mainly of coastal provinces in the south-east of China. In this region, the economy is outward-oriented, developed and with deep commercialization and monetization. The various economic indices of this zone including population, land area, aggregate agricultural output, aggregate industrial output, retail sales and foreign investment as a share of the total in the whole country are given in table 15.3. Another is the developing zone which mainly contains inland provinces in the middle of China. Economic development in this region is just average, falling behind the coastal areas in the south-east of China and it still keeps parts of planned economy. The third is the under-developed zone which mostly includes north-western parts of China. This region is relatively isolated and under-developed. The market-oriented economy has just started.

TABLE 15.3 Major Characteristics of Selected Regions as a Share of the Whole Country's (in %)

	Southern-Eastern	Middle	Western
Population	48	34.1	17.2
Land area	30.7	41.4	28
Agricultural output	57.2	31.7	12.3
Industrial output	71.1	20.7	9.4
Retail sales	62.7	25.2	12.1
Foreign investment	88.6	8.0	3.4

Source: *Statistical Yearbook of China, 1995*

We selected large, medium and small-size cities in the above three regions (table 15.4). We did not choose small-size cities in the western zone because the number of UCCs in these cities is rather small. We took 9 UCCs in the large-size cities, 6 UCCs in the medium and small-size cities respectively as random samples. Altogether, the 57 UCCs included in our sample investigation, register 1% of all UCCs across China.

TABLE 15.4 Distribution of Sample

	Eastern China	Middle China	Western China
Large cities	9 from Guangzhou (F)	9 from Wuhan (G)	9 from Chengdu (H)
Medium-sized cities	6 from Jinan (C)	6 from Changsha (D)	6 from Xining (E)
Small cities	6 from Changzhou (A)	6 from Kaifeng (B)	

Number of UCCs in the sample: 57. The letters will be used below.

China's four specialized commercial banks are solely owned by the state.[7]. UCCs' share-holding structure is absolutely different form that of the comRMB 16.2 billion, without any equity investment from any level of government budgets.

The equity structure of sample UCCs (table 15.5 and 15.6) shows that they share the following characteristics which distinguish them from commercial banks and are of great significance to their management structure. First, diversification of shareholders. Second, diversification of shareholding structure. Third, UCCs are generally controlled by legal entities.

TABLE 15.5 Equity Structure of Sample UCCs
(Average, in RMB thousand; except * natural numbers)

	EQUITY SHARES			
Paid-up Capital	Legal entity holders' equity	Number of shareholders*	Maximum amount	Minimum amount
301	161	50	30	1.3
Registered Capital	Individual shareholders' equity	Number of shareholders*	Maximum amount	Minimum amount
202	91.3	270	2.1	0.08

It is apparent that UCCs do not follow the structure stipulated by the People's Bank of China which provides that neither individual shares nor collectively-owned shares should exceed 30% of total equity, since they represent respectively 48.5 and 38.9%, thus giving a predominance to individuals.

The borrowers of UCCs are generally non state-owned enterprises. The credit structure of the sample UCCs shows that 31 UCCs lend to state-owned enterprises, accounting for an average of 21.2% of their respective aggregate credit; 57 lend to collectively-owned enterprises, averaging 61.7% of their lending; 14 lend to private enterprises, registering an average of 2.9% of their aggregate loans; 44 lend to self-employed persons, or an average of 5% of their aggregate lending; 47 lend to other borrowers, accounting for an average of 30% of the aggregate lending. No credit is offered to individual residents. Among the 31 UCCs for which data are available, credit to state-owned enterprises exceeds 50% of the total credit in 5 UCCs (with the highest proportion of 87%); in 3 UCCs, credit to state-owned enterprises account for 30-50%; the figure runs from 10% to 30% in 9 UCCs and in 14 UCCs the proportions are below 10%.

Not less than 30% of the total loans, which is listed under "other loans," possibly include many loans to state-owned enterprises. Among the 16 UCCs for which the ratio of other loans over total loans exceed 30%, 11 of them did not report their loans to state-owned enterprises. UCCs are prohibited from providing loans to state-owned enterprises. However, since state-owned enterprises tend to be less risky, it is understandable that UCCs are willing to provide credit to these enterprises. Accordingly, we can presume that UCCs actually provide credit to them but they would rather list such credit under "other loans" than report them explicitly. Based on the above presumption, loans provided to non-state-owned sector by UCCs are believed to be more than 70%, but lower than 78.8% in our sample of UCCs.

TABLE 15.6 Shareholders' Structure of Sample UCCs
(unit: RMB thousand and %)

	Collective entities	Private entities	Individual-run enterprises	Individual residents
avg	502	17.9	100	369
%	29.7	10.6	5.9	21.8
	Staff	Community	Others	Total
avg	172	156	214	-
%	10.2	9.2	12.6	100

Since all UCCs in China are single-office entities, and branching is not allowed, their business scale is limited. In the sample UCCs, the largest asset is RMB 490.56 million and the smallest RMB 9.84 million. Their asset scale distribution shows that more than a third have assets over 100 million, while two-fifths have assets under 70 million.

The quality of risk of the assets of UCCs is generally better than that of state-owned commercial banks. According to the data collected from the sample, the total assets of the 57 UCCs are RMB 6,130.50 million, registering an average of RMB 107.55 million per UCC. The three asset quality indices are: the average asset security ratio reaching 92%; the average credit quality index, 11.2%; and the average capital risk ratio, 81.9%. These three indices are defined as follows:

Asset security ratio = $\{[A - (B + C + D + E)]/A\} \times 100$
Loan quality = $(B + C) / Outstanding\ loans$
Capital risk ratio = $(B + C)/Capital$

with
A = Total assets,
B = Outstanding bad loans,
C = Outstanding over-due loans,
D = Interest receivables, and
E = Other receivables.

Non-performing loans account for 4.7% of the credit that the sample UCCs grant, well below the 20% (official figure) of the state-owned commercial banks. The assets of UCCs are liquid with an average liquidity ratio of 64.5%. UCCs have adequate reserves, with a free reserve ratio of 28.7%. Furthermore, the capital adequacy ratio (ratio of capital over risk-adjusted assets) averages 11.7%.

The asset quality of UCCs seems at first inspection closely related to the economic development of the cities where UCCs operate while the inherent factors come only second. Among the cities where samples are selected, cities with non-performing loan ratios below 3% are Chengdu (1.3%), Wuhan (2.1%), Changzhou (2.4%) and Guangzhou (2.8%), which are three large cities and a small city with a developed economy. Cities with non-performing loan ratios of 3 to 10% are Jinan (4.6%) and Changsha (7.1%) which are two medium-size cities whose economy is not well developed. Two small cities with an underdeveloped economy have non-performing loan ratios exceeding 10%: Kaifeng (17.6%) and Xining (19.1%).

As we mentioned earlier in this chapter, we selected samples from the eastern, middle and western regions of China. Nevertheless, taking as a criterion the credit quality of UCCs, it seems at first sight that the size of different cities tends to have more influence on the operation of UCCs than the location of the city. The large-size cities (e.g. Guangzhou, Wuhan and Chengdu) in the eastern, middle and western regions have a developed economy and UCCs in these cities operate well on this criterion. With comparison, though Jinan locates in the eastern region and Changsha is not far from Guangdong, UCCs in these cities do not have a good performance in terms of loan quality since the level of economic development in these cities is only average.

The earnings of the sample UCCs show that most UCCs are profitable. The 57 sample UCCs have an average earning asset ratio of 2.6%. One (or 1.8%) of the sample has a negative earning ratio; 33 UCCs, or 57.9% of the sample, have earning asset ratios ranging from 0% to 2%; 19 UCCs or 33.3% of the sample have an earning asset ratio of the order of 2-5% and 4 of the sample, i.e. 7%, have an earning asset ratio in excess of 5%.

The average ratio of earnings on capital of 56 sample UCCs is 32.4%. More precisely, 18, or 32.1%, of the sample have a earning-capital ratio below 10% (among which, one has a negative ratio); 23.2% of the sample, or 13 UCCs, have earning-capital ratios running from 10% to 30%; 16, or 28.6%, of the sample have earning-capital ratios of 30 to 60% and 9, or 16.1%, have a earning-capital ratio in excess of 60%.

By contrast, specialized banks are characterized, at a national level, by low and declining earnings. Their earnings in 1994 were RMB 16.6 billion. With total assets of RMB 580 million, this implies an earning asset ratio of 0.29%. In 1994, the outstanding credit of the four state-owned commercial banks increased by 28.4% compared with that of 1992 while earnings declined by 51.8% over the same period.

Principal Component Analysis

In order to isolate the relationships between the different characteristics of UCCs, we use a principal component analysis to classify them on the basis of a number of criteria: i.e. the extent they lend to and borrow from collectively-owned or state-owned-enterprises (SOEs), their profitability and the quality of their loan portfolio.

The usefulness of the method lies in the fact that a large part of the total variance can be explained by a small number of components, thereby reducing the dimension of the problem. Of particular interest in the case of UCCs is that they are based in eight different cities and, given the above observations, it will be interesting to see whether UCCs in a particular region are relatively homogeneous with respect to the variables used.

In previous work (Girardin and Bazen 1998) we examined the deposit and loan structure of UCCs according to where deposits emanate from and to whom loans are granted. We also weighted each observation according to the size of total assets in order to avoid outliers having too much influence on the estimated coefficients. The principal component analysis provided a clear opposition both between UCCs that deal with collectively-owned enterprises and those that loan to SOEs, wich have positive values, and between UCCs that collect deposits mainly from collectively-owned enterprises and make loans to state-owned enterprises. In other words, this analysis pointed to a clear separation of cities in terms of whether they deal more with state-owned or collectively-owned enterprises and the extent to and direction in which they tend to fulfill a function of financial intermediation between the two. UCCs in different cities were found to be relatively homogeneous in the main.

We used the following four variables:

depcol: the percentage of total deposits emanating from collectively-owned enterprises
loancol: the percentage of total loans granted to collectively-owned enterprises
depstate: the percentage of total deposits collected from state-owned enterprises
loanstate: the percentage of total loans granted to state-owned enterprises

Our previous analysis was undertaken mainly in terms of institutional features of the UCCs – their specialization and the predominant form of their intermediation. In order to extend this, we include here two further variables reflecting the financial situation of UCCs. The first is an indicator of the quality of the loans that the UCC makes (*loanqual*) and is measured as the percentage of bad loans to total loans. The higher the value of this ratio, the lower the quality of loans. The second additional variable is an indicator of the profitability of the UCC (*rateprof*) which is measured as the rate of profit on capital.

In order to interpret what the principal components represent, we note that the sign and absolute size of the coefficients or 'loadings' are critical. These attribute positive and negative values to the principal components for different observations, depending on the values of the variables. The latter are standardised to have mean zero and unit variance. In this way, observations are separated along axes and often form fairly distinct groups. The components are determined in a particular order such that the first component 'explains' the largest part of the variance.

The first principal component attributes high positive values to UCCs dealing mainly with state-owned enterprises (in terms of both deposits and loans) and that have a preponderance of bad loans and a low rate of profit (table 15.7). The opposite is true for UCCs dealing mainly with collectively-owned enterprises. This first principal component explains only 37% of the total variance. The coefficients on the first principal component provide a clear opposition of UCCs that deal with collectively-owned enterprises, which have negative values, and those that loan to SOEs, which have positive values. This is in line with our earlier, more limited analysis. Thus cities A, B, C and, to a lesser extent, H tend mainly to lend to and collect deposits from collectively-owned enterprises while D, E and G (i.e. one city with an average level and one with a higher level of development) deal mainly with state-owned enterprises. City F shows no clear separation (figures 15.1 and 15.2).

TABLE 15.7 Principal Component Analysis: Relationship Between Asset Structure and Financial Indicators

	Principal Components		
	First (F1)	Second (F2)	Third (F3)
Deposits from collectives	-0.35	0.32	0.46
Loans to collectives	-0.53	-0.24	-0.26
Deposits from SOEs	0.45	0.14	-0.52
Loans to SOEs	0.52	0.37	0.24
Loan quality	0.26	-0.52	0.61
Profit rate	-0.20	0.64	0.14
Cumulative variance	0.36	0.59	0.74

In the second principal component, the financial variables dominate the others, attributing high positive values to UCCs with a high quality of loans (a low value for the variable *loanqual*) and a high rate of profit. While of much less importance, higher values are also attributed to UCCs with a high proportion of loans to state-owned enterprises and a high proportion of deposits its from collectively-owned enterprises. Thus, UCCs with high values for this principal component are profitable, well-managed, institutions intermediating mainly from collective to state-owned enterprises, and tend to be found in cities A, D, F and G (located in highly or midly developed areas). Those with very low values for the second principal component are B, E and H, (from underdeveloped regions) and the latter form more homogeneous groups than the former along the second axis. This principal component shows the extent to which UCCs are profitable by keeping bad loans to a minimum, which appears to be associated with allocating deposits from collectively-owned enterprises as loans to state-owned enterprises. Together, the first two principal components 'explain' nearly 60% of the total variance. The combination of the classification given by the first two principal components (figure 15.1) generates a rather clear division between four types of cities. The first have UCCs with good financial performance associated with intermediation from collectively owned to state owned enterprises. They are then subdivided between the cities where UCCs mostly intermediate among collective enterprises (cities A, C and F from Eastern China) which enjoy a better financial performance than those which intermediate amongSOEs (cities D, G, from middle China, and F). The second, opposite category, includes cities where UCCs have a poor financial performance and intermediate from SOEs to collectively owned enterprises. The subdivision is then the same as for the first category with now cities B and H (from middle and West of China) with UCCs intermediating between collective enterprises having a better financial performance than UCCs located in cities E (Western China) and G which intermediate between SOEs. This implies that the level of development of the region in which they are located matters more for the financial performance of UCCs than the size of the city in which they operate. Indeed, the better performing ones are located in the most developed regions (eastern and middle of China) while moving westwards tends to imply a deterioration in financial performance.

The addition of the third principal component increases the proportion explained to 74%. The most prominent variable in terms of the size of its coefficient is *loanqual*, the proportion of bad loans. That is high values of this principal component are attributed to UCCs which have high proportions of deposits from collectively-owned enterprises and low proportions from state-owned enterprises, and where the loans made are of poor quality. A high proportion of loans to state-owned enterprises also leads to a positive value for this principal component but it is not one of the prominent variables. Low values for this principal component are found for UCCs in the cities C and G, and high values for cities A, D and H. However, in each city there are exceptions and there is more heterogeneity among cities than for the first two principal components (figure 15.2).

In previous work we undertook an econometric analysis of the determinants of UCCs' efficiency in granting loans that are repaid and their profitability. We used variables that represent the kind of influences highlighted

in the theoretical approaches mentioned above such as monitoring and peer group rating of loans. The explanatory variables used were:
1. the number and quality of the personnel — E is the number of staff emplyed, Q is the proportion of staff with a university degree or higher, and D is the number of directors;
2. the size of the UCC in terms of its assets (Tassets);
3. the proportion of loans made to state-owned enterprises (Lstate).

FIGURE 15.1 Principal Component Analysis:
First and Second Principal Components (F1 and F2)

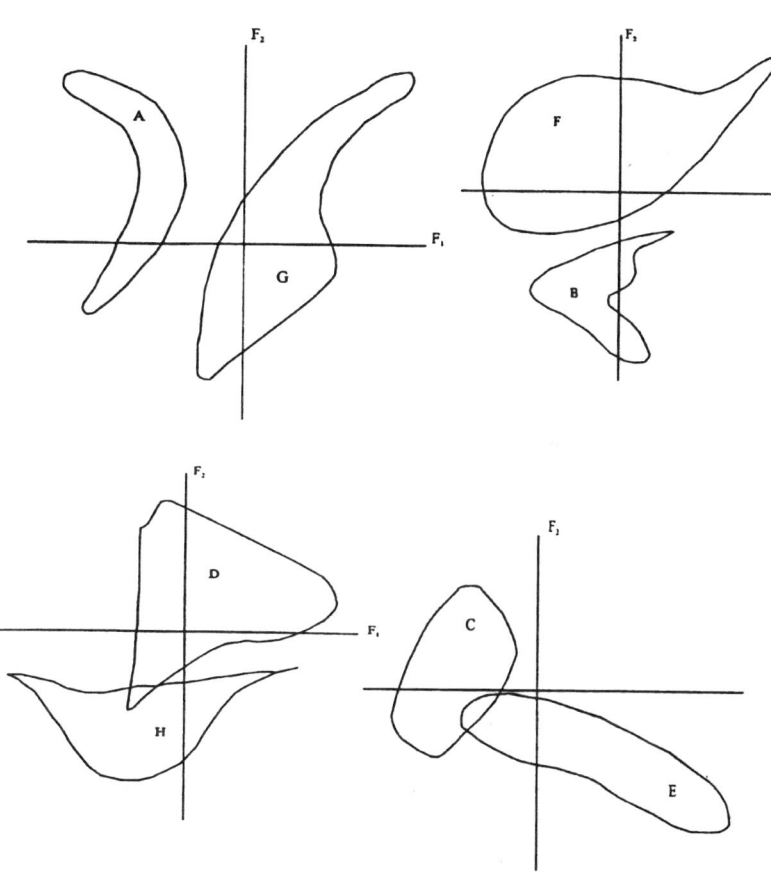

FIGURE 15.2 Principal Component Analysis: First and Third Principal Components (F1 and F3)

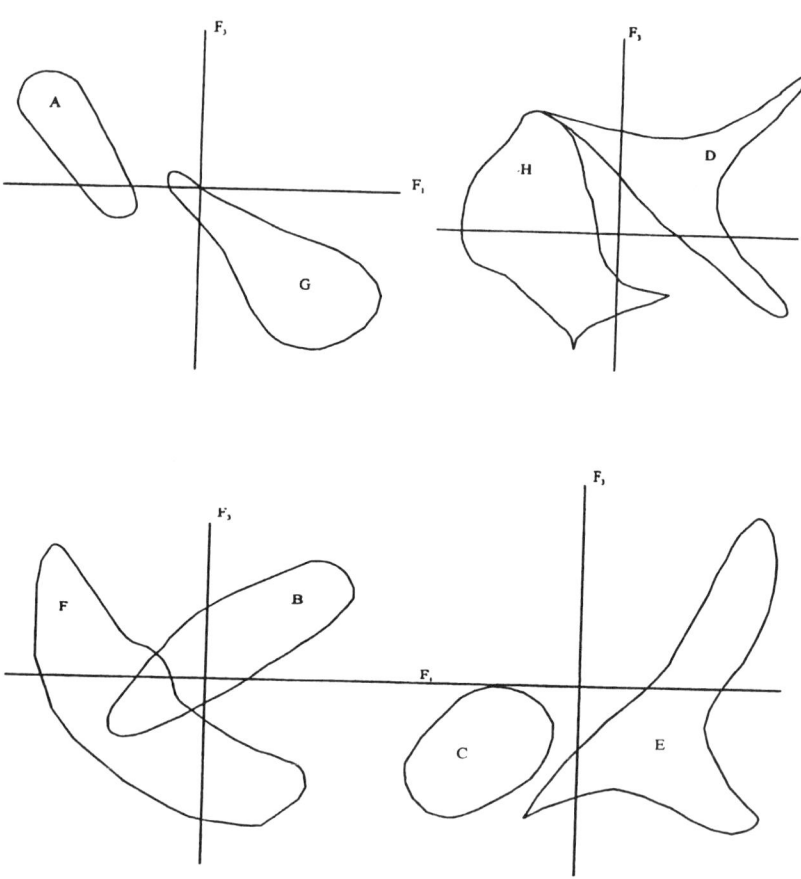

An econometric analysis of the performance of UCCs

As the UCCs come from different regions and cities of different sizes, we also included shift dummies to take account of these spatial influences. Dummy variables are defined for the Eastern and Western regions (with variable names EAST and WEST, respectively) and for small and medium size towns (with names SMALL and MEDIUM, respectively). The constant in the model therefore defines the base towns which are large and in the central region.

TABLE 15.8 Estimates of the determinants of loan quality and profitability in Urban Credit Cooperatives

Dependent variable:	Loan Quality (LQ)	Profitability (π)	
Variable	Estimated coefficient	Estimated coefficient	Estimated coefficient
Number of directors (D)	-0.321* (0.073)	-	-
Number of staff (E)	-0.012 (0.020)	-	-
Proportion with university educ (Q)	-0.024 (0.020)	-	-
Proportion of loans made to state-owned enterprises (Lstate)	-0.042* (0.017)	-	-
Total assets of (UCC/1000)	0.041 (0.035)	-	0.0023* (0.0011)
Total assets of (UCC/1000 squared)	-	-	-0.000005* (0.0000023)
Proportion of bad loans (L*)	-	-0.361 (0.200)	-0.237 (0.150)
EAST	-2.034* (0.680)	22.016* (10.487)	20.054* (10.341)
WEST	-1.696 (0.995)	-11.307 (9.116)	-
SMALL	1.306* (0.593)	-14.148 (8.797)	-12.129 (7.365)
MEDIUM	1.817* (0.626)	9.360 (11.805)	-
Constant	0.206 (1.274)	30.525 (7.628)	15.164* (6.226)
R^2	0.399	0.294	0.313
Test of Heteroskedasticity	1.24 F(14,32)	0.622 F(6,44)	0.302 F(7,43)
Test of Linearity	1.34 F(1,46)	1.026 F(1,50)	0.094 F(1,50)
Number of observations	57	57	57

Notes: * indicates that the relevant null hypothesis is rejected at a 5% significance level. Standard errors in parentheses. For the coefficients the null is that the coeffcient is equal to zero and a standard t test is used. The null of homoscedasticity is tested using the squares of the regressors in an artificial regression. The null hypothesis of linearity is tested using Ramsey's RESET test. All calculations were made with PCGIVE Version 8 (Doornik and Hendry 1995).

According to the estimated coefficients (see Table 15.8, column 1) the key determinants of loan quality are the number of directors in the UCC, the proportion of loans made to state enterprises and the size and location of the UCC. The larger the number of directors, the better the quality of loans madeby the UCC. A higher proportion of loans made to state-owned enterprises also improves the overal quality of loans made. The coefficients of the spatial dummies reveal substantial differences between UCCs in the three regions and according to the size of the town. UCCs in the eastern region, and to a lesser extent in the western region, have substantially fewer bad loans than those in the central region. On the other hand, UCCs small- and medium-sized towns have higher proportions of bad loans than UCCs in large towns.

Overall, the estimated model is an acceptable representation of the determinants of loan quality, however, as is often the case with cross section data, only a minority of the total variation in the sample is 'explained' by the model.

By contrast, in our earlier study, we could not find a satifactory explanation of differences in profitability. The quality of loans granted appears to be a very limited influence in itself (Table 15.8, column 2). Only two coefficients (those of the EAST dummy and the constant) are significant at the conventional 5% level, the loan quality variable is significant at 10%. The addition of a quadratic function of the total assets of the UCCs improves the fit (Table 15.8, column 3), suggesting that larger UCCs are more profitable. However, the quality of loans remains a fairly weak influence

The conclusion that emerges is that there are major regional differences in the performance of UCCs in terms of the quality of loans made and this in turn is influenced by the number of directors in the UCC and the extent to which the UCC grants loans to state-owned enterprises. The profitability of UCCs is only weakly related to the quality of loans made and appears to be more highly correlated with the size of the UCC as measured by its assets..

Conclusion

Credit expansion by credit cooperatives may be viewed as a source of difficulty for monetary control. While such credit expansion is subject to ceilings set by the comprehensive credit plan,[8] compliance with the plan may have proved much more difficult to monitor. Thus UCCs would represent an important source of faster than planned credit expansion. However, this assertion should be qualified since the loans of UCCs have represented only a fraction of the deposits they collect. Of course this does not imply that UCCs have not participated during certain periods in "excessive" credit expansion. These excesses have led the authorities to try to enforce existing regulations and to reinforce them. Furthermore it designed recently asset liability ratios as an alternative form of management to the credit ceilings. The current strategy for reforming the urban cooperative financial system has consisted both in standardizing UCCs and in merging some of them into new urban cooperative banks.

In the survey we carried out, it seems that sample UCCs do not as a rule comply with many existing regulations. Thus their equity structure gives a predominance to individuals, and to collective enterprises, in excess of what is stipulated by existing regulations. Besides, even though UCCs are prohibited from granting loans to state-owned enterprises, such loans represent 20 to 30 percent of credits granted by UCCs. However, this is understandable in as much as state-owned enterprises tend to be less risky. Besides, the financial performance of our sample UCCs is much better than the national performance of state-owned banks. Their share of non performing loans is four times smaller and their ratio of earnings over assets ten times bigger than the latters.'

We selected samples from the eastern, middle and western regions of China. Taking as a criterion the share of non-performing loans granted, a descriptive analysis would imply that the size of different cities tends to have more influence on the operation of UCCs than the region in which they are located. However, a principal component analysis shows that there tends to be a separation of UCCs according to the level of development of the region in which they operate, rather than to the size of the city in which they are located. In highly and mildy developed regions, i.e. the eastern and middle parts of China, UCCs are profitable and have a low proportion of non-performing loans while they to some extent collect deposits from collectives and lend to SOEs. In the western part of China, composed of less developed regions, to some extent UCCs do the opposite type of intermediation and have a poor financial performance. The fact that UCCs do the rest of their intermediation between collective enterprises rather than between SOEs improves their financial performance in both cases. Actually the more developed the region (i.e. the more to the east) the lower the share of intermediation between SOEs. This analysis implies that it is only in these regions that it seems rational for UCCs to side-step regulations in order to grant loans to SOEs. The SOEs which borrow from them may be keen at servicing their debts in order to keep their reputation and may divert funds to put UCCs first on the list among creditors.

The econometric analysis carried out on the cross section of UCCs provided by our survey data implies that there are major regional differences in the performance of UCCs in terms of the quality of loans made. The latter is also influenced by the number of directors in the UCC and the extent to which the UCC grants loans to state-owned enterprises. Profitability however is mainly a function of size (total assets) although there appears to be a weak relationship with loan quality.

Notes

1. Lin (1995)
2. See, for example, the survey by Caprio (1995).
3. Ghate (1992).
4. Lundberg (1979) quoted by Besley and Levenson (1996)
5. In most of this literature, risk sharing and credit are closely tied for three reasons (Besley 1995). First, credit serves as an insurance substitute when market opportunities for risk sharing are limited; an individual may borrow in lieu of

receiving an insurance payment, thus smoothing out transitory shocks. Second, the distinction between credit and insurance becomes blurred when lenders are willing to relend on some part of the repayment in the event of an unforseen negative shock to the borrower. Third, the optimal form of contracts when information is incomplete and/or enforcement is a problem seems to look like a combination of credit and insurance. A pure credit arrangement, rather than a contract with contigencies is unlikely to be optimal in many risky environments.

6. Banerjee, Besley and Guinnane (1994) have studied the optimally designed credit cooperative as a peer monitoring problem. This approach emphasises that the constitution of the credit cooperative can affect the amount of monitoring that is undertaken. They examine how the amount of monitoring will be influenced by any guarantee provided by non-monitoring members, the amount that such members lend to the cooperative, and the interest rate paid on deposits.

7. The Bank of Communications is also controlled by the state. "Controlled" here refers to equity investment of central and local governments, or direct holding by the state in the true sense. This kind of equity is different from the equity investment of the state-owned enterprises (i.e. legal entities).

8. See for instance Girardin (1996) or Montes-Negret (1995).

References

Arnott, R., and J. Stiglitz. 1990. "Moral Hazard and Nonmarket Institutions: Dysfunctionnal Crowding Out or Peer Monitoring." *American Economic Review* 81(1):179-90.

Banerjee A., T. Besley, and T. Guinnane. 1994. "Thy Neighbor's Keeper: The Design of a Credit Cooperative with Theory and a Test." *Quarterly Journal of Economics* 109:491-515.

Besley, T. 1995. "Savings, Credit and Insurance," in Jere Behrman, and T. Thrinivasan eds., *Handbook of Development Economics, Vol. 3*. Pp. 2125-50. Amsterdam: Elsevier.

———. 1995. "Nonmarket Institutions for Credit and Risk Sharing in Low-Income Countries." *Journal of Economic Perspectives* 9(3):115-27.

Besley, T., and A. Levenson. 1996. "The Role of Informal Finance in Household Capital Accumulation: Evidence from Taiwan." *Economic Journal* 106:39-59.

Binswanger, H. 1986. "Risk Aversion, Collateral Requirements, and the Markets for Credit and Insurance in Rural Areas," in P. Hazell, C. Pomerada, and A. Valdes, eds., *Crop Insurance for Agricultural Development*. Pp. 67-86. Baltimore: John Hopkins University Press.

Braverman, A., and J. Guash. 1996. "Rural Credit Markets and Institutions in Developing Countries: Lessons for Policy Analysis from Practice and Modern Theory." *World Development* 14(10-11):1253-67.

Caprio, G. 1995. "The Role of Financial Intermediaries in Transitional Economies." *Carnegie Rochester Conference Series on Public Policy* 42:257-302.

Chandavarkar, A. 1985. "The Informal Financial Sector in Developing Countries: Analysis, Evidence and Implications." *Seminar of South East Asian Central Banks*. Yogyakarta, Indonesia. November.

Dipchand, C., Z. Yichun, and M. Mingjia. 1994. *The Chinese Financial System*. Greenwood Press.

Doornick, J., and D. Hendry. 1994. *PC-Give 8: An Interactive Econometric Modelling System*. Oxford: Institute of Economics and Statistics, University of Oxford.

Ghate, P., A. Das-Gupta, M. Lamberte, N. Paopongsakorn, D. Prabowo, A. Rahman, and T. Srinivasan. 1992. *Informal Finance: Some Findings from Asia*. Oxford: Oxford University Press.

Girardin, E. 1996. *The Dilemmas of Banking Sector Reform and Credit Control in China*. OECD Development Centre Studies.

Girardin, E., and S. Bazen. 1998. "An Empirical Study of Urban Credit Cooperatives in China." *International Review of Applied Economics* 12(1):141-155.

Lin, C. 1995. "The Assessment: Chinese Economic Reform in retrospect and Prospect." *Oxford Review of Economic Policy* 11(4):1-24.

Montes-Negret, F. 1995. "China's Credit Plan: An Overview." *Oxford Review of Economic Policy* 11(4):25-42.

People's Bank of China. 1994a. *Annual Report 1993*. China Financial Publishing House.
___. 1994b. *Almanac of China's Finance and Banking: 1993*. China Financial Publishing House.
___. 1995a. *Annual Report 1994*. China Financial Publishing House.
___. 1995b. *China: Financial Outlook '95*. China Financial Publishing House.
___. 1995c. *Almanac of China's Finance and Banking: 1994*. China Financial Publishing House.
Stiglitz, J. 1990. "Peer Monitoring and Credit Markets." *World Bank Economic Review* 4(3):351-66.
Tam, O. 1995a., ed. *Financial Reform in China*. Routledge.
Wiu, X. 1995. *China's Financial Institutions*, in On Kit Tam, ed., *Financial Reform in China*. Routledge.
World Bank 1990. *China: Financial Sector Policies and Institutional Development*. Washington, D.C.: A World Bank Country Study.
___. 1995. *China, Country Economic Memorandom: Macroeconomic Stability in a Decentralized Economy*. Washington, D.C.: A World Bank Country Study.
___. 1996. *The Chinese Economy: Fighting Inflation, Deepening Reforms*. Washington, D.C.: A World Bank Country Study.
World Development Report. 1996. *From Plan to Market*. New York: Oxford University Press.
Yang, H. 1996. *Banking and Financial Control in Reforming Planned Economies*. MacMillan.
Yi, G. 1994. *Money, Banking and Financial Markets in China*. Boulder: Westview Press.

16
Improving Access to Credit in Rural China

Wing Thye Woo

Recently, in March 1999, the National People's Congress passed the landmark amendment to the constitution of the People's Republic of China to elevate private ownership to be a primary ownership form just like state ownership. Private ownership will no longer be just a supplementary ownership form to state ownership. This deepening of economic reform comes from the recognition that the non-state industrial sector was the most important engine of growth in the reform era, and that significant improvements in the future standard of living requires that the non-state sector maintains its past growth momentum. The latter outcome would certainly be easier to realise with the reduction in legal discrimination against private ownership.

Woo (1998) calculated the sectoral contribution to the high annual GDP growth rate of 9.7 percent in the 1985-93 period to be 12 percent from primary industries, 57 percent from the industrial component of secondary industries, 6 percent from the construction component of secondary industries, and 25 percent from tertiary industries. Within the 57 percent contribution from the industrial component of secondary industries, state-owned enterprises (SOEs) accounted for 12 percentage points, collectively-owned enterprises (COEs) for 29 percentage points, individually-owned enterprises (IOEs) for 8 percentage points, and enterprises of other ownership forms for 9 percent points. Since the bulk of COEs and IOEs are in the rural areas, the important implication is that continued high growth of the Chinese economy depends importantly on the continued high growth of rural enterprises.

However, recent indications of the economic health of rural enterprises give course for concern. Both employment growth and output growth in rural enterprises have slowed down in the 1990s, and this general slowdown cannot be easily dismissed by pointing out that the levels of employment and output in 1994 are several times higher than in 1984. The growth slowdown of the TVEs shows the symptoms of being unnaturally starved of investment funds. This hypothesis comes from the following facts:

	Share of total investment, %		Share of industrial output, %	
	1985	1997	1985	1997
SOEs	66.1	33.8	64.9	25.5
Rural Enterprises	26.7	23.0	33.9	56.0

While the 32 percentage point fall in the SOE share of total investment seemed in line with its 39 percent point fall in industrial output, the 4 percent fall in the rural enterprise share of total investment is at odds with the 22 percentage rise in its share of total industrial output. The data show a grave inability on the part of the rural enterprise sector to raise investment funds: (1) it did not get any of the share of investment funds released by the decline of the SOE sector, and (2) its share of investment funds actually declined!

The opposite movement in the investment share and the output share of rural enterprises could be explained by, one, the extreme labor intensive nature of the goods produced by rural enterprises, and, two, the extreme substitution of labor for capital in the production process of the rural enterprises. However, with the saturation of the markets for labor-intensive goods in the near future (if it has not already occurred), the continued development of the rural enterprise sector would hinge on its ability to obtain investment funds to move into the production of more capital-intensive goods. The fact that its share of investment funds has fallen over time does not bode well for the ability of the rural enterprise sector to continue to grow rapidly.

Even worse yet, as we shall show later in the chapter, the investment of the rural enterprise sector has fallen secularly, from an annual average of 8.5 percent of GDP in the 1985-88 period to 7.7 percent in the 1992-96. There can be little doubt that the proportionally lower, and increasingly even lower, investment by rural enterprises threatens the continued high growth of China's economy. A multi-facetted policy response is required to address the financing difficulties of the rural enterprises. The recent amendment of the constitution to give higher legal status to private enterprises was an important step toward better legal protection of their property rights, and hence will make them more attractive to outside investors. Other important steps that are needed include the improvement of financial intermediation in rural areas, and the permitting of rural enterprises to assume ownership forms that are market-determined.

This chapter confines itself primarily to studying the financing of investments by rural enterprises, and recommending appropriate investment-financing mechanisms in order to accelerate the growth of rural enterprises. In particular, this chapter draws attention to the successful case in Indonesia of setting up rural banks under the leadership of Bank Rakyat Indonesia, a state-owned bank. This successful Indonesian experience provides a natural model to reform China's rural financial system which is dominated by the Rural Credit Cooperatives (RCCs) operating under the guidance of the Agricultural Bank of China (ABC).

Finally, a word on terminology. When rural enterprises were first permitted, they were constrained to be collectively-owned at the township and village level. Hence, the first rural enterprises were commonly referred to as township and village enterprises, TVEs. Over time, the ownership restrictions were relaxed, such that many official statistics on TVEs nowadays encompass all rural enterprises regardless of whether they are collectively-owned or not.[1] This chapter will use the term "rural enterprises" and "TVEs" interchangeably.

An Overview of the Financial System

The state banks[2] dominate the banking system, which, in turn, dominates the financial system. At the end of 1995, state banks accounted for 78 percent of all the loans made by all financial institutions, Y3, 925 billion out of Y5,039 billion — see Table 16.1. The issued value of all stocks[3] at the end of 1995 was only Y30 billion, and the issued value of all (legally registered) bonds outstanding was Y563 trillion. The premier position of the state banks is clearly shown by their 72 percent share of the total deposits in all financial institutions, and 78 percent share of the total loans in 1995 — which is after seventeen years of economic reform.

TABLE 16.1 Distribution of Loans and Deposits Across Financial Institutions, 1995

	Total Deposits (in 100 million yuan)	Total Loans	Loans as proportion of deposits, %	% of total deposits	% of total loans
Total	53862.3	50394.2	93.6	100.0	100.0
State banks	38782.6	39249.6	101.2	72.0	77.9
Other banks	1599.8	1205.1	75.3	3.0	2.4
Urban credit cooperatives	3357.4	1929.0	57.5	6.2	3.8
Rural credit cooperatives	7172.8	5234.2	73.0	13.3	10.4
Financial trust institutions	2498.5	2409.8	96.4	4.6	4.8
Finance companies	451.2	366.5	81.2	0.8	0.7

Source: *1996 Almanac of China's Finance and Banks*

The state bank sector is in turn dominated by the four state commercial banks: the Bank of China (BOC), the People's Construction of China (PCBC), the Agricultural Bank of China (ABC), and the Industrial and Commercial Bank of China (ICBC). BOC was originally the international exchange and remittance bank of the Kuomintang government, and it was designated the state foreign exchange bank in 1953. PCBC was founded in 1954 to finance, and handle the budgetary allocations for, large infrastructure projects. ABC was established in 1955 to provide financial services to the rural sector, channel funds for the grain procurement purchases, and to supervise the rural credit co-operatives. ICBC was founded in 1984 to serve residents and enterprises situated in urban areas.

Rural Credit Cooperatives (Nongcun Xindai Hezuoshe)

Small-scale collectively-owned rural credit cooperatives (RCCs) were started in the early 1950s to be the primary financial institutions serving the rural areas. In line with the 1978 economic reforms, the management of RCCs was reorganised in 1980. Although RCCs are independent accounting units owned by townships, or towns, or villages, or several villages jointly, they are, in practice, grassroot units of the Agricultural Bank of China (ABC), "operating under the leadership of the county sub-branches of the ABC."[4] In 1995, RCCs accounted for 13 percent of deposits in all financial institutions, and 10 percent of all the loans made – see Table 16.1.

Up until the mid-1980s, the RCCs deposited the bulk of their deposits in ABC. In 1978, RCCs lent only 27 percent of the deposits they collected in the rural area to finance rural economic activities, see Table 16.2. With the reduction in legal barriers beginning in 1984 against, (a) non-agricultural economic activities undertaken by farm households, and (b) the establishment of rural enterprises, RCCs were allowed to make more loans in the rural areas. RCCs' loans to rural areas jumped from 34 percent of RCC deposits in 1983 to 57 percent in 1984. The proportion of RCC deposits going to rural loans increased incrementally every year in the 1984-1991 period, and then made a small jump to 71 percent in 1992 when economic deregulation accelerated after Deng Xiaoping's *nanxun* in early 1992.[5] It would be right to say that until the mid-1980s, the RCCs serve primarily as tributaries by which rural savings were channeled to finance economic activities in the urban areas. RCCs still divert a significant proportion of their deposits to finance activities outside of the rural area, 27 percent of their deposits in 1995.

RCCs operate an extensive network of branches, savings deposit offices, and credit stations in market towns and remote areas. The number of RCC units rose from 389,726 in 1981 to 421,582 in 1984, and then fell steadily to 365,492 in 1995.[6] We want to highlight this decline in the number of RCC units after 1984 because this decline means a decrease in the effort to mobilise rural saving, and a decrease in the access of the rural community to investment financing.

Table 16.2 Sources and Uses of Funds in Rural Credit Cooperatives

Part A: Uses of Deposits in Rural Credit Cooperatives, 1978-1995

Year	Total Deposits	Total Loans	loans to agric collective	loans to township enterprises	loans to farmer househlds	Loans as proportion of deposits, %	Distribution of loans across borrowers, %		
	(a)	(b)	(c)	(d)	(e)	(b/a)	(c/b)	(d/b)	(e/b)
1978	166.0	45.1	21.8	12.1	11.2	27.2	48.3	26.8	24.8
1979	215.9	47.5	22.4	14.2	10.9	22.0	47.2	29.9	22.9
1980	272.3	81.6	34.5	31.1	16.0	30.0	42.3	38.1	19.6
1981	319.6	96.4	35.7	35.5	25.2	30.2	37.0	36.8	26.1
1982	389.9	121.2	34.8	42.3	44.1	31.1	28.7	34.9	36.4
1983	487.4	163.7	28.2	60.1	75.4	33.6	17.2	36.7	46.1
1984	624.9	354.5	38.4	135.0	181.1	56.7	10.8	38.1	51.1
1985	724.9	400.0	41.4	164.4	194.2	55.2	10.4	41.1	48.6
1986	962.3	568.5	44.6	265.9	258.0	59.1	7.8	46.8	45.4
1987	1225.2	771.4	64.5	359.3	347.6	63.0	8.4	46.6	45.1
1988	1399.8	908.6	80.1	456.1	372.4	64.9	8.8	50.2	41.0
1989	1669.5	1094.9	107.3	571.9	415.7	65.6	9.8	52.2	38.0
1990	2144.9	1413.0	134.1	760.7	518.2	65.9	9.5	53.8	36.7
1991	2709.5	1808.6	169.9	1007.3	631.4	66.8	9.4	55.7	34.9
1992	3477.7	2453.9	222.6	1471.8	759.5	70.6	9.1	60.0	31.0
1993	4297.3	3143.9	262.1	2001.2	880.6	73.2	8.3	63.7	28.0
1994	5681.1	4168.6	808.4	2279.4	1080.8	73.4	19.4	54.7	25.9
1995	7172.8	5234.2	1094.9	2779.1	1360.2	73.0	20.9	53.1	26.0

Part B: Sources and Uses of Credit Funds of Rural Credit Cooperatives, 1995

	(in 100 million yuan)	% of total
Sources of Funds in total	7550.6	100.0
Deposits	7172.9	95.0
peasant household saving deposits	6195.6	82.1
demand deposits in rural areas	892.0	11.8
time deposits in rural areas	85.3	1.1
Bank's own fund (paid-in capital)	377.7	5.0
Uses of Funds in Total	7550.6	100.0
Loans	5234.3	69.3
loans to township enterprises	2779.1	36.8
loans to agricultural collective units	1094.9	14.5
loans to farmer households	1360.3	18.0
Reserve Assets	1218.3	16.1
required reserves	875.4	11.6
deposits with PBC	187.8	2.5
cash in treasury	155.1	2.1
Claims on central government	338.5	4.5
Other Uses	759.5	10.1

Part A is constructed from the 1993 and 1995 issues of *China Statistical Yearbook*
Part B is constructed from Table 8, 16, 18 and 19 in 1996 *Almanac of China's Finance and Banking*.

Other Methods of Raising Outside Funds by Non-SOEs

The general fact is that non-SOEs face great difficulties in raising funds. The financial system is dominated by the state banks, and the state banks lent primarily to the SOEs. Private and small collective enterprises have always paid the higher interest rates in the informal credit markets. A 1992 field investigation reported that a fast-growing private electronic company[7] paid an interest rate of 2.5 percent each month on its working capital; and its original start-up capital came from the savings of the partners and informal loans from friends. These informal credit markets, popularly referred to as "folk finance" (*minjian rongzhi*), appeared to have increased greatly in scope in recent years.[8]

Given the heavy reliance by rural collectives and individually-owned enterprises on non-formal investment financing, a new informal financial instrument called employee bond (*jizi*) has emerged as a significant source of funds. An employee bond is purchased by the new employee when she joins the enterprise, and it carries an interest rate at least equal to that of a time deposit with the same maturity. Many non-SOEs also issue a hybrid equity-bond instrument which, in addition to paying a fixed base rate, also pays a bonus rate — the size of which is contingent on the profitability of the enterprise. In many cases, especially with collectives, tax exemption turned out to be an important source of investment financing. Since many counties, towns and villages are on tax-contracts with their upper administrative levels that specify a fixed amount of tax to be turned in, they typically start exempting taxes once their tax quotas were reached provided that the extra retained funds would be invested.

Investment According to Ownership

Table 16.3 looks at investment behavior from two angles. Part A of Table 16.3 compares the absolute size of investment from each ownership type by expressing investment spending as a percent of GDP. Part B of Table 16.3 shows the relative size of investment by expressing investment spending of each ownership type as a percent of total investment. There are three phases in investment outlay during the 1985-96 period that correspond to three policy regimes of the period.

The first phase of 1985-88 coincided with the first significant dose of operational autonomy devolved to SOEs, and the relaxation of curbs on the establishment of non-agricultural enterprises in the rural areas. Average annual fixed investment was 29.9 percent of GDP, and SOEs accounted for 63.9 percent of the fixed investment.

The second phase of 1989-91 was a period of tight credit, re-introduction of some administrative curbs on the investment activities of SOEs and some uncertainty as to future state policies on economic reform and opening. The results were that average annual fixed investments in the second phase fell to 25.1 percent of GDP, and the SOE share of fixed investment increased slightly to 64.3 percent.

TABLE 16.3 Investment According to Ownership

Part A: Fixed Asset Investment by Ownership as Percent of GDP

Year	National total	State-owned	Rural collectives	Rural individuals	Solely Hong Kong, Taiwan andd Macao	Foreign-financed firms	Other forms	Rural enterprises*
1985	28.93	19.11	2.27	5.44	0.00	0.00	2.10	7.71
1986	29.80	19.53	2.42	5.67	0.00	0.00	2.18	8.09
1987	30.89	19.50	3.10	5.90	0.00	0.00	2.39	9.00
1988	30.24	18.45	3.11	5.88	0.00	0.00	2.80	8.99
1989	25.13	15.40	2.33	5.42	0.00	0.00	1.98	7.75
1990	24.29	15.93	2.00	4.78	0.00	0.00	1.57	6.78
1991	25.89	17.05	2.32	4.90	0.00	0.00	1.62	7.22
1992	30.37	20.39	3.85	3.89	0.00	0.00	2.25	7.73
1993	36.11	22.20	4.73	3.30	0.13	2.14	3.62	8.03
1994	35.12	19.88	4.22	3.22	0.99	2.81	3.99	7.45
1995	34.55	18.55	3.99	3.38	1.26	2.83	4.54	7.37
1996	34.19	17.65	4.09	3.71	1.38	2.91	4.44	7.81
Averages:								
85-96	30.46	18.64	3.20	4.63	0.31	0.89	2.79	7.83
85-88	29.97	19.15	2.72	5.72	0.00	0.00	2.37	8.45
89-91	25.10	16.13	2.22	5.03	0.00	0.00	1.72	7.25
92-96	34.07	19.74	4.17	3.50	0.75	2.14	3.77	7.68

Part B: Share of Total Investment According to Ownership Form, in percent (each row, excluding memo item, sums to 100)

Year	State-owned enterprises	Rural collectives	Rural individuals	Solely Hong Kong, Taiwan and Macao	Foreign-financed firms	Other forms	Memo item: Rural enterprises
1985	66.08	7.83	18.81	0.00	0.00	7.28	26.65
1986	65.52	8.13	19.04	0.00	0.00	7.32	27.16
1987	63.12	10.04	19.10	0.00	0.00	7.74	29.14
1988	61.01	10.27	19.46	0.00	0.00	9.26	29.73
1989	61.28	9.29	21.56	0.00	0.00	7.88	30.85
1990	65.60	8.23	19.70	0.00	0.00	6.47	27.93
1991	65.86	8.97	18.93	0.00	0.00	6.25	27.89
1992	67.14	12.67	12.80	0.00	0.00	7.40	25.47
1993	61.47	13.09	9.13	0.37	5.92	10.01	22.23
1994	56.61	12.02	9.18	2.82	8.00	11.37	21.20
1995	53.70	11.54	9.78	3.65	8.18	13.15	21.32
1996	51.64	11.97	10.86	4.04	8.52	12.97	22.83
Averages:							
85-96	61.58	10.34	15.70	0.91	2.55	8.92	26.03
85-88	63.93	9.07	19.10	0.00	0.00	7.90	28.17
89-91	64.25	8.83	20.06	0.00	0.00	6.87	28.89
92-96	58.11	12.26	10.35	2.17	6.12	10.98	22.61

*: rural enterprises include collectives plus individuals

TABLE 16.4 Funding for Investment by Type of Enterprise According to Source, in % (for each year, elements within each column sum to 100)

	National total	State-owned enterprises	Rural collective	Rural individuals	Solely Hong Kong, Taiwan and Macao	Foreign-financed firms	Other forms	Rural enterprises
1985								
a) State Budget	17.65	26.42	0.00	0.00	-	-	2.59	0.00
b) Domestic Loans	20.06	23.04	32.12	0.00	-	-	31.96	9.44
c) Foreign Investment	1.98	2.83	0.00	0.00	-	-	1.58	0.00
d) Self-raised funds	53.62	40.43	51.49	100.00	-	-	55.85	85.74
e) Others	6.68	7.29	16.39	0.00	-	-	8.01	4.82
1986								
a) State Budget	15.59	23.68	0.00	0.00	-	-	0.97	0.00
b) Domestic Loans	21.14	22.74	34.01	6.87	-	-	29.61	14.99
c) Foreign Investment	3.38	4.97	0.00	0.00	-	-	1.75	0.00
d) Self-raised funds	49.29	38.43	48.98	81.47	-	-	63.23	71.75
e) Others	10.60	10.18	17.01	11.65	-	-	4.44	13.26
1987								
a) State Budget	13.06	20.55	0.00	0.00	-	-	1.20	0.00
b) Domestic Loans	22.96	24.56	38.03	7.26	-	-	29.10	17.87
c) Foreign Investment	4.82	7.33	0.00	0.00	-	-	2.49	0.00
d) Self-raised funds	47.93	38.20	37.31	79.49	-	-	63.21	64.95
e) Others	11.23	9.37	24.66	13.25	-	-	4.00	17.18
1988								
a) State Budget	9.06	14.67	0.00	0.00	-	-	1.17	0.00
b) Domestic Loans	20.57	24.20	32.09	0.00	-	-	27.10	11.09
c) Foreign Investment	5.72	8.96	0.00	0.00	-	-	2.75	0.00
d) Self-raised funds	54.35	40.49	41.07	100.00	-	-	64.50	79.64
e) Others	10.30	11.68	26.84	0.00	-	-	4.48	9.27

TABLE 16.4 (continued)

	National total	State-owned enterprises	Rural collective	Rural individuals	Solely Hong Kong, Taiwan and Macao	Foreign-financed firms	Other forms	Rural enterprises
1989								
a) State Budget	8.26	13.36	0.00	0.00	-	-	0.89	0.00
b) Domestic Loans	17.31	20.85	23.79	3.97	-	-	18.66	9.94
c) Foreign Investment	6.63	10.15	0.00	0.00	-	-	5.14	0.00
d) Self-raised funds	56.93	42.80	48.48	96.03	-	-	69.75	81.71
e) Others	10.88	12.84	27.72	0.00	-	-	5.55	8.35
1990								
a) State Budget	8.71	13.21	0.00	0.00	-	-	0.77	0.00
b) Domestic Loans	19.57	23.62	24.09	4.08	-	-	19.93	9.98
c) Foreign Investment	6.25	9.11	0.00	0.00	-	-	4.26	0.00
d) Self-raised funds	52.36	42.15	47.37	82.41	-	-	70.69	72.09
e) Others	13.10	11.91	28.54	13.50	-	-	4.35	17.93
1991								
a) State Budget	6.77	10.23	0.00	0.00	-	-	0.57	0.00
b) Domestic Loans	23.46	28.06	27.90	5.10	-	-	24.16	12.43
c) Foreign Investment	5.74	8.34	0.00	0.00	-	-	3.97	0.00
d) Self-raised funds	52.25	43.11	46.23	81.94	-	-	67.35	70.46
e) Others	11.78	10.26	25.87	12.97	-	-	3.94	17.11
1992								
a) State Budget	4.25	6.30	0.00	0.00	-	-	0.30	0.00
b) Domestic Loans	27.40	30.37	34.22	5.11	-	-	27.32	19.59
c) Foreign Investment	5.82	7.99	0.00	0.00	-	-	6.19	0.00
d) Self-raised funds	51.24	46.60	38.93	80.68	-	-	63.42	59.92
e) Others	11.29	8.74	26.85	14.21	-	-	2.75	20.49

TABLE 16.4 (continued)

	National total	State-owned enterprises	Rural collective	Rural individuals	Solely Hong Kong, Taiwan and Macao	Foreign-financed firms	Other forms	Rural enterprises
1993								
a) State Budget	3.72	5.96	0.00	0.00	0.37	0.31	0.41	0.00
b) Domestic Loans	23.49	25.44	30.81	4.73	14.24	20.17	21.30	20.10
c) Foreign Investment	7.28	6.08	6.84	0.00	63.79	37.03	2.25	4.03
d) Self-raised funds	49.92	48.01	39.56	80.68	14.06	28.91	60.86	56.46
e) Others	15.59	14.51	22.79	14.58	7.53	13.58	15.19	19.42
1994								
a) State Budget	3.20	4.95	2.38	0.00	0.13	0.36	0.70	1.35
b) Domestic Loans	22.38	25.58	28.24	4.34	14.88	17.99	19.79	17.89
c) Foreign Investment	10.69	7.14	9.64	0.00	46.66	46.98	3.67	5.46
d) Self-raised funds	48.36	50.77	8.51	93.43	23.77	26.95	63.24	45.29
e) Others	15.37	11.57	51.24	2.23	14.56	7.72	12.59	30.01
1995								
a) State Budget	3.03	4.94	2.20	0.00	0.05	0.36	0.65	1.19
b) Domestic Loans	20.46	23.39	25.60	4.02	15.51	16.11	20.25	15.70
c) Foreign Investment	11.19	7.80	7.68	0.00	45.90	48.62	3.51	4.16
d) Self-raised funds	51.88	48.15	58.59	94.55	18.79	23.19	56.48	75.09
e) Others	13.45	15.71	5.93	1.43	19.76	11.72	19.10	3.86
1996								
a) State Budget	2.69	4.61	1.77	0.00	0.14	0.30	0.53	0.93
b) Domestic Loans	19.54	23.58	19.68	4.67	15.21	14.92	20.18	12.54
c) Foreign Investment	11.73	6.71	9.67	0.00	50.42	53.08	4.25	5.07
d) Self-raised funds	53.22	50.79	58.49	93.35	17.33	21.32	56.55	75.07
e) Others	12.82	14.32	10.39	1.98	16.90	10.37	18.49	6.39

TABLE 16.4 (continued)

	National total	State-owned enterprises	Rural collective	Rural individuals	Solely Hong Kong, Taiwan and Macao	Foreign-financed firms	Other forms	Rural enterprises
Average 1985-96								
a) State Budget	8.00	12.41	0.53	0.00	0.17	0.33	0.90	0.29
b) Domestic Loans	21.53	24.62	29.22	4.18	14.96	17.30	24.11	14.30
c) Foreign Investment	6.77	7.28	2.82	0.00	51.69	46.43	3.48	1.56
d) Self-raised funds	51.78	44.16	43.75	88.67	18.49	25.09	62.93	69.85
e) Others	11.92	11.53	23.69	7.15	14.69	10.85	8.58	14.01
Average 1985-88								
a) State Budget	13.84	21.33	0.00	0.00	-	-	1.48	0.00
b) Domestic Loans	21.18	23.63	34.06	3.53	-	-	29.44	13.35
c) Foreign Investment	3.98	6.02	0.00	0.00	-	-	2.14	0.00
d) Self-raised funds	51.30	39.39	44.71	90.24	-	-	61.70	75.52
e) Others	9.70	9.63	21.22	6.23	-	-	5.23	11.13
Average 1989-91								
a) State Budget	7.91	12.26	0.00	0.00	-	-	0.75	0.00
b) Domestic Loans	20.11	24.18	25.26	4.39	-	-	20.92	10.78
c) Foreign Investment	6.21	9.20	0.00	0.00	-	-	4.45	0.00
d) Self-raised funds	53.85	42.69	47.36	86.79	-	-	69.26	74.75
e) Others	11.92	11.67	27.38	8.82	-	-	4.62	14.47
Average 1992-96								
a) State Budget	3.38	5.35	1.27	0.00	0.17	0.33	0.52	0.69
b) Domestic Loans	22.65	25.67	27.71	4.58	14.96	17.30	21.77	17.16
c) Foreign Investment	9.34	7.14	6.76	0.00	51.69	46.43	3.97	3.74
d) Self-raised funds	50.92	48.86	40.81	88.54	18.49	25.09	60.11	62.37
e) Others	13.71	12.97	23.44	6.89	14.69	10.85	13.63	16.04

TABLE 16.5 Destination of Funds from Each Source, percent going to each ownership type.
(each row, excluding Memo item, sums to 100)

	State-owned enterprises	Rural collective	Rural individual	Solely Hong Kong, Taiwan and Macao	Foreign-firms firms	Other Sector	Rural enterprises
1985							
a) State Budget	98.93	0.00	0.00	0.00	0.00	1.07	0.00
b) Domestic Loans	75.87	12.54	0.00	0.00	0.00	11.59	12.54
c) Foreign Investment	94.21	0.00	0.00	0.00	0.00	5.79	0.00
d) Self-raised funds	49.82	7.52	35.08	0.00	0.00	7.58	42.61
e) Others	72.07	19.21	0.00	0.00	0.00	8.72	19.21
1986							
a) State Budget	99.55	0.00	0.00	0.00	0.00	0.45	0.00
b) Domestic Loans	70.49	13.07	6.19	0.00	0.00	10.25	19.26
c) Foreign Investment	96.21	0.00	0.00	0.00	0.00	3.79	0.00
d) Self-raised funds	51.08	8.07	31.46	0.00	0.00	9.39	39.54
e) Others	62.96	13.04	20.93	0.00	0.00	3.07	33.98
1987							
a) State Budget	99.29	0.00	0.00	0.00	0.00	0.71	0.00
b) Domestic Loans	67.51	16.64	6.04	0.00	0.00	9.81	22.68
c) Foreign Investment	96.00	0.00	0.00	0.00	0.00	4.00	0.00
d) Self-raised funds	50.30	7.82	31.67	0.00	0.00	10.21	39.49
e) Others	52.66	22.06	22.53	0.00	0.00	2.75	44.59
1988							
a) State Budget	98.81	0.00	0.00	0.00	0.00	1.19	0.00
b) Domestic Loans	71.77	16.03	0.00	0.00	0.00	12.20	16.03
c) Foreign Investment	95.55	0.00	0.00	0.00	0.00	4.45	0.00
d) Self-raised funds	45.45	7.76	35.80	0.00	0.00	10.99	43.56
e) Others	69.19	26.77	0.00	0.00	0.00	4.03	26.77
1989							
a) State Budget	99.15	0.00	0.00	0.00	0.00	0.85	0.00
b) Domestic Loans	73.80	12.77	4.95	0.00	0.00	8.49	17.71
c) Foreign Investment	93.89	0.00	0.00	0.00	0.00	6.11	0.00
d) Self-raised funds	46.07	7.91	36.37	0.00	0.00	9.65	44.28
e) Others	72.30	23.68	0.00	0.00	0.00	4.02	23.68
1990							
a) State Budget	99.42	0.00	0.00	0.00	0.00	0.58	0.00
b) Domestic Loans	79.17	10.13	4.11	0.00	0.00	6.59	14.24
c) Foreign Investment	95.59	0.00	0.00	0.00	0.00	4.41	0.00
d) Self-raised funds	52.81	7.44	31.01	0.00	0.00	8.74	38.45
e) Others	59.63	17.92	20.30	0.00	0.00	2.15	38.22

333

TABLE 16.5 (continued)

	State-owned enterprises	Rural collective	Rural individual	Solely Hong Kong, Taiwan and Macao	Foreign-firms firms	Other Sector	Rural enter-prises
1991							
a)State Budget	99.47	0.00	0.00	0.00	0.00	0.53	0.00
b)Domestic Loans	78.79	10.66	4.11	0.00	0.00	6.43	14.78
c)Foreign Investment	95.68	0.00	0.00	0.00	0.00	4.32	0.00
d)Self-raised funds	54.34	7.93	29.68	0.00	0.00	8.05	37.61
e)Others	57.38	19.70	20.83	0.00	0.00	2.09	40.53
1992							
a)State Budget	99.47	0.00	0.00	0.00	0.00	0.53	0.00
b)Domestic Loans	74.41	15.82	2.39	0.00	0.00	7.38	18.21
c)Foreign Investment	92.13	0.00	0.00	0.00	0.00	7.87	0.00
d)Self-raised funds	61.06	9.62	20.16	0.00	0.00	9.16	29.78
e)Others	51.98	30.11	16.11	0.00	0.00	1.80	46.22
1993							
a)State Budget	98.38	0.00	0.00	0.04	0.49	1.10	0.00
b)Domestic Loans	66.59	17.18	1.84	0.22	5.09	9.08	19.02
c)Foreign Investment	51.28	12.29	0.00	3.23	30.12	3.09	12.29
d)Self-raised funds	59.12	10.38	14.76	0.10	3.43	12.21	25.14
e)Others	57.22	19.14	8.54	0.18	5.16	9.75	27.69
1994							
a)State Budget	87.54	8.94	0.00	0.12	0.91	2.49	8.94
b)Domestic Loans	64.69	15.16	1.78	1.87	6.43	10.06	16.94
c)Foreign Investment	37.81	10.83	0.00	12.29	35.16	3.90	10.83
d)Self-raised funds	59.43	2.11	17.74	1.38	4.46	14.87	19.85
e)Others	42.60	40.06	1.33	2.67	4.02	9.32	41.40
1995							
a)State Budget	87.75	8.38	0.00	0.05	0.98	2.83	8.38
b)Domestic Loans	61.41	14.44	1.92	2.76	6.44	13.02	16.36
c)Foreign Investment	37.43	7.92	0.00	14.96	35.56	4.13	7.92
d)Self-raised funds	49.84	13.03	17.83	1.32	3.66	14.32	30.86
e)Others	62.72	5.08	1.04	5.36	7.13	18.68	6.12
1996							
a)State Budget	88.44	7.86	0.00	0.21	0.94	2.54	7.86
b)Domestic Loans	62.30	12.05	2.60	3.15	6.50	13.40	14.65
c)Foreign Investment	29.52	9.86	0.00	17.38	38.53	4.70	9.86
d)Self-raised funds	49.28	13.15	19.05	1.32	3.41	13.78	32.20
e)Others	57.68	9.70	1.68	5.33	6.89	18.72	11.38

TABLE 16.5 (continued)

	State-owned enterprises	Rural collective	Rural individual	Solely Hong Kong, Taiwan and Macao	Foreign-firms firms	Other Sector	Rural enter-prises
Average 1985-96							
a)State Budget	96.35	2.10	0.00	0.03	0.28	1.24	2.10
b)Domestic Loans	70.57	13.87	2.99	0.67	2.04	9.86	16.87
c)Foreign Investment	76.28	3.41	0.00	3.99	11.61	4.71	3.41
d)Self-raised funds	52.38	8.56	26.72	0.34	1.25	10.75	35.28
e)Others	59.86	20.54	9.44	1.13	1.93	7.09	29.98
Average 1985-88							
a)State Budget	99.14	0.00	0.00	0.00	0.00	0.86	0.00
b)Domestic Loans	71.41	14.57	3.06	0.00	0.00	10.96	17.63
c)Foreign Investment	95.49	0.00	0.00	0.00	0.00	4.51	0.00
d)Self-raised funds	49.16	7.79	33.50	0.00	0.00	9.54	41.30
e)Others	64.22	20.27	10.87	0.00	0.00	4.64	31.14
Average 1989-91							
a)State Budget	99.35	0.00	0.00	0.00	0.00	0.65	0.00
b)Domestic Loans	77.25	11.19	4.39	0.00	0.00	7.17	15.58
c)Foreign Investment	95.06	0.00	0.00	0.00	0.00	4.94	0.00
d)Self-raised funds	51.07	7.76	32.35	0.00	0.00	8.81	40.11
e)Others	63.10	20.43	13.71	0.00	0.00	2.75	34.14
Average 1992-96							
a)State Budget	92.32	5.04	0.00	0.08	0.66	1.90	.04
b)Domestic Loans	65.88	14.93	2.11	1.60	4.89	10.59	17.04
c)Foreign Investment	49.63	8.18	0.00	9.57	27.88	4.74	8.18
d)Self-raised funds	55.75	9.66	17.91	0.82	2.99	12.87	27.57
e)Others	54.44	20.82	5.74	2.71	4.64	11.65	26.56

The third phase of 1992-96 saw higher investment outlay; the result of temporarily easier credit, and of renewed confidence that economic reform and opening would actually be accelerated. The first sign of this new policy regime was seen in February 1992 when Deng Xiaoping inspected the southern provinces ("*nanxun*"). In October 1992, the accelerated reform and opening agenda was formally endorsed at the 14th Party Congress when it dropped mention of the "central plan" and made the construction of "a socialist market economy with Chinese characteristics" as its policy goal. The results marked a big shift from the central plan to a market economy: fixed investment increased to 34.1 percent of GDP, and the SOE share of fixed investment fell to 58.1 percent.

While it is desirable that total investment has risen from 30 percent in 1985-88 to 34 percent in 1992-96 — a confirmation of the well-known international experience that economic deregulation increases economic efficiency and capital accumulation — it is extremely troubling that investment by rural enterprises (rural collectives and rural individuals) has actually shrunk over time, from 8.5 percent of GDP in 1985-88 to 7.7 percent in 1992-96. SOE investment, on the other hand, rose slightly from 19 percent of GDP in 1985-88 to 20 percent of GDP in 1992-96. This anomalous situation is a bad sign for future economic growth, and for the reduction of rural poverty.

The biggest absolute increase in investment was from foreign-owned firms (including those owned by oversea Chinese). Their investment rose from negligible levels in 1985-92 to 4.1 percent of GDP in 1995. This big increase in investment in such a short time indicates the tremendous investment potential of foreign firms because of their access to international capital markets. Naturally, the obvious question is how to increase the access of TVEs in the central provinces to foreign capital.

Tables 16.4 and 16.5 track in detail the financing of investments undertaken by enterprises of different ownership type. Table 16.4 focuses on where enterprises of each type of ownership get their investment funds by calculating the percent of investment that is funded by each financing source. Table 16.5 emphasizes the destination of the funds from each financing source by calculating the share of funds from each source received by enterprises of each ownership type. The definitions of the funding sources identified in Table 16.4[9] are as follows:

(a) State Budget: This source finances primarily projects specified in the state investment plan. The funds come from (1) direct budget appropriations, and (2) policy loans from state banks (that are, many times, backed by government deposits). The Chinese economic reforms have drastically reduced the scope of the state investment plan, and hence reduced "state budget" as a source of investment funding.

(b) Domestic Loans: Until the early 1990s, domestic loans were largely loans from the state banks that were backed by the banks' own funds and non-government deposits. Domestic loans also include investment loans from local governments, and from finance companies. As emphasized in Table 16.1, the bulk of all formal credit (78 percent in 1995) is supplied by the state banks.

(c) Foreign Investment: Funds from (1) bonds and shares sold to foreigners (including Chinese from Taiwan, Hong Kong, and Macao) - who may hold the controlling shares – and (2) loans from international organisations that are managed or guaranteed by the government.

(d) Self-Raised Funds: These funds come mostly from (1) retained earnings, (2) bonds/shares sold to workers within the enterprises, and (3) the supervising agencies of the SOEs.

(e) Other Funds: This is more than a residual category. It also encompasses funds that are raised in the formal and informal bond and stock markets. In our usage, there are only two formal bond and equity markets in China because only those in Shenzhen and Shanghai have legal recognition. So we call all the other bond and equity markets (quite numerous but less developed in the poorer regions) "informal financial markets."

Tables 16.4 and 16.5 suggest five immediate policy issues for promoting the growth of the more dynamic TVE sector. The first policy issue is that *even though the SOE share of domestic loans has declined, SOEs continue to have disproportionate access to domestic loans and hence are retarding the growth of TVEs.* The reasoning follows from that:

(loans to SOEs/output of SOEs) = (loans to SOEs/GDP) / (output of SOEs/GDP)

The (loans to SOEs/output of SOEs) ratio has increased very significantly in the 1985-96 period because (a) the annual average (loans to SOEs/GDP) ratio has gone up from 4.1 percent in the 1985-91 period to 5.1 percent in the 1992-96 period, and (b) the (output of SOEs/GDP) ratio has gone down greatly as evidenced by the drop in the SOE share of total industrial output from 65 percent in 1985 to 28 percent in 1996.

The second policy issue is that *despite the drop in SOE share of total domestic loans, the rural sector's share did not go up.* The rural sector's share averaged 18 percent in both the 1985-88 and 1992-95 periods. The loan share "released" by the SOEs went entirely to help finance the investments of the foreign-owned firms. The absolute amount of resources transferred by domestic loans to rural enterprises showed little change over time, 1.1 percent of GDP in 1985-88 and 1.3 percent in 1992-95, a paltry increase of 0.2 percentage point.

The third policy issue is that *while rural enterprises have recently gained access to "foreign investment," their share of this fund is disproportionately small.* TVEs received only 8.2 percent of the total foreign capital inflow into China in the 1992-96 period; and foreign funds financed only 3.4 percent of TVE investment in this period. In the same period, the SOEs absorbed 49.6 percent of the foreign investment.

The fourth policy issue is that *the access of the rural enterprises to funds from the fast growing "other funds" has declined precipitously recently.* "Other funds" which we take to be a proxy for informal credit has grown from 2.9 percent of GDP in 1985-88 to 4.7 percent in 1992-96, but the TVEs' share of it has fallen from 31 percent in 1985-88 to 27 percent in 1992-96, with the share being 6.1 percent in 1995 and 11.4 percent in 1996.

The fifth policy issue from Tables 4 and 5 is that *in light of the limited access that TVEs have to foreign funds and domestic loans, it is troublesome that the chief source for financing TVE investments – self-raised funds – has declined in size over time,* from 6.4 percent of GDP in 1985-88 to 4.8 percent of GDP in 1992-96. The drop in self-raised funds deserves serious study to determine whether it is the result of increased competition from the entry of new TVEs or the result of increased compensation to managers and workers. If the drop in retained earning is due to over-compensation of personnel in rural collectives, then the *corporate governance structure* and *ownership form* of rural collectives has become a barrier to the dynamic growth of the TVE sector.

However, before we discuss solutions to the above five problems, we turn to look at one successful foreign experience in improving financial intermediation in the rural areas in order to make our subsequent policy recommendations more useful.

Improving Investment Financing in Rural Areas: The Unit Desa System in Indonesia[10]

We choose to use an Indonesian example in our discussion on rural finance because Indonesia is very similar to China in key economic and institutional features. Like China, Indonesia is a geographically vast, and heavily populated economy, and its rural financial system is dominated by branches of a state bank (Bank Rakyat Indonesia, BRI) which has been designated to serve the rural areas.

When the Soeharto government took power in Indonesia in 1965, it made rural development a high priority. The Indonesian government used BRI to provide several rural credit programs at subsidised interest rates because BRI had branches in nearly everyone of Indonesia's 241 districts. In 1969, one of the BRI district branches established village offices in order to increase the access of the rural poor to the credit programs, and the village office was called "Unit Desa."[11] When oil revenue started pouring into Indonesia in 1973 in the wake of the first OPEC price increase, the government greatly expanded the subsidised credit programs to the rural areas. In 1974, President Soeharto instructed BRI to make the Unit Desa a nation-wide program.

The government definitely saw cheap credit as the way to jumpstart the rural economy. Low interest loans were given to rural residents upon application, regardless of whether the borrower had defaulted on earlier loans or not. In fact, one key criterion for BRI to judge the performance of a branch was the amount of loans that the branch had extended. The BRI Unit Desa were effectively disbursement agents of the government, if not loan-pushers with no concern for loan repayment in the future.

Transforming Unit Desa from a Subsidised Institution to a Commercially Viable Institution

When the price of oil started falling in 1982, the government could no longer afford to keep the generous subsidy system going. In 1984, BRI faced the choices of abandoning its Unit Desa or restructuring them in the hope of making them self-supporting. With technical assistance from the Ministry of Finance, BRI converted each Unit Desa into a full-service rural bank:
- each Unit Desa was a separate accounting unit that was evaluated in terms of its profitability;
- it started off with an equity investment by its supervising BRI branch;
- it accepted saving and time deposits, and made loans;
- deposits at the Unit Desa were guaranteed by BRI;

- BRI set the loan rates high enough above the deposit rates so that the expenses of the Unit Desa could be covered. The deposit rates were set to produce positive real rates to maintain savers' confidence in the Unit Desa. The expenses of the Unit Desa included the payment of a service fee to the supervising BRI branch, beside the normal payroll and operational costs of the Unit Desa itself.
- the spread between the loan and deposit rates also included an allowance for expected default;
- savings deposits in excess of loans were deposited in the district branch of BRI, and received an interest rate above that the Unit Desa deposit rate paid to the villagers;
- the Unit Desa could borrow from the district branch to meet liquidity crunches or to extend more loans;
- over time, BRI raised the liquidity rate above the Unit Desa loan rate in order to encourage the Unit Desa to mobilise savings, and to accumulate precautionary/loss reserves;
- collateral for loans was not necessary. The first loan could be partly based on the recommendation of the village head because there were no other screening mechanisms. Subsequent loans were based primarily on the borrower's credit record. The amount of loan extended to a particular person would be increased following the on-time repayment of several successive loans; and
- mobile Unit Desa teams serviced isolated villages with low levels of economic activity once or twice a week.

Following three years of losses (which were covered by subsidies from the government), the Unit Desa became profitable in 1987, and has remained so. The Unit Desa system has grown considerably in its operations, the average loan size was US$162 in 1985, US$296 in 1990, and US$512 in 1995; and the profits in these years were: –US$0.8 million (a loss), US$34.3 million, and US$170 million respectively. The profitability of rural banking has led Unit Desa to increase its presence in the countryside, the number of service units has risen from 2,469 in 1985 to 3,957 in 1994.

One might wonder whether the profitability of the Unit Desa was primarily due to BRI setting the loan rate very high above the deposit rate. The fact is that interest rates in Indonesia had been decontrolled in June 1983, before the reorganisation of the Unit Desa system. The deposit and loan rates of the Unit Desa are circumscribed by the informal financial markets in the rural areas, and by the private banks in the urban areas. The Unit Desa, in short, never enjoyed an unchallenged monopoly position. The sweeping financial deregulation in 1988-89 caused the number of banks (deposit money banks, DMBs) to increase from 115 in 1982 to 141 in 1989, and the number of non-DMB credit institutions to explode from 6,073 to 7,757 in the same period.

The loan-deposit rate spread of 20 percentage points in 1990 and 1995 may raise questions on our statements in the preceding paragraph. The fact

is that the Unit Desa loan rates were still below those charged by the rural money-lenders and pawn shops. The primary reason why rural lending rates are high all over the world is because:
- the transaction costs are high because of the processing of a great number of small loans. Transaction cost would have been lower if there was just one big loan equal to the sum of all the small loans.
- there is no easy collateral to possess to make up for unpaid loans. It is almost impossible in many countries (including Indonesia) to confiscate a farmer's land or his livestock or his grain inventory when he could not make payments because of weather conditions or physical disability. It is at least a time-consuming process to do so in most cases.

Comparing the Unit Desa-Bank Rakyat Indonesia (UD-BRI) System and the Rural Credit Cooperative-Agricultural Bank of China (RCC-ABC) System

There are three key differences between the (UD-BRI) System and the (RCC-ABC) System. The first big difference is that *UD-BRI and RCC-ABC have different objectives*. RCC-ABC has several primary objectives, and one of them is to collect rural saving to re-deposit in ABC in order to *finance state projects*. The over-riding objective of Unit Desa is to *intermediate funds locally* on a commercially viable basis.

The second big difference is that *Unit Desa has become more accessible to rural dwellers over time, while RCC has become less accessible*. The number of Unit Desa increased by 60 percent in the 1985-95 period, while the number of RCC decreased by 13 percent in the 1984-95 period. One of the reasons for the decline in the number of RCC units is that the tremendous growth of the urban economy after 1984 and the large amount of foreign capital inflow after 1992 has made urban and state investment financing much less dependent on rural saving.

The third big difference is that *UD-BRI operates in a competitive environment, while RCC-BRI has a near-monopoly position in the countryside*. Because the Unit Desa faces a deregulated financial system where interest rates are market-determined and barriers to entry into any market are low, it has every incentive to be efficient and innovative. An RCC has very little flexibility, both deposit and lending rates are set by the central bank, and the range of its activities are tightly circumscribed. An RCC has neither the incentive nor the autonomy to be innovative.

Increasing Rural China's Access to Investment Financing

As pointed out earlier, the general prospects for future TVE growth is actually not very promising. TVE investment dropped by 1.8 percentage points of GDP during the 1985-96 period, even though total domestic investment increased by over 4 percentage points of GDP; and the TVE share of total domestic investment has dropped from 28 percent in 1985-88 to 22 percent in 1992-96. In our opinion, the primary reason for this drop in TVE investment (as a share of GDP and as a share of total domestic investments) is that TVEs suffer from two big disadvantages in investment financing.

The first disadvantage suffered by TVEs is that the still heavily-regulated financial system is directing too much of the investment funds to the SOE sector, thus starving the TVEs sector of investment funds. SOE investment has actually risen as a share of GDP despite the facts that the share SOE output in GDP has fallen, and that the SOE sector is less profitable and less efficient than the TVE sector.

The second major disadvantage of the TVEs in raising capital is that TVEs generally do not have forms of property rights that attract market-driven investment funds. We see this clearly in the failure of the TVE sector to significantly increase their shares of funds from the banking sector, foreign capital flows, and funds raised in the formal and informal financial markets. As the banking sector began to commercialise its lending activities in the 1990s, a smaller proportion of bank loans flowed to the SOE sector, but the "released share" went entirely to firms of other ownership structure e.g. shareholding companies and foreign-owned companies.

The three most important issues that must be addressed in order to overcome the above two crippling disadvantages faced by TVEs in getting investment financing are:
- that the financial system is over-regulated;
- that the RCC-ABC system lacks the organisational flexibility and incentive to focus on efficient local financial intermediation; and
- that some ownership forms of TVEs discourage outside investment into TVEs.

Deregulating the Financial Sector

This is a much discussed issue in the Chinese press,[12] but unfortunately many of the financial reform proposals are actually proposals for administrative reorganisation of the existing financial institutions rather proposals for using market forces to allocate funds. Marketization of the financial system involves at the minimum:
- allowing the establishment of privately-owned financial institutions;
- freeing deposit and loan rates;
- permitting foreign financial institutions to increase the scale and range of their operations over time;
- imposing identical supervisory oversight and prudential standards on state-owned, and private-owned banks; and
- instructing the state banks to stop giving preferential credit to SOEs, and to process loan applications equally without regard to ownership forms of the enterprises.[13]

The above financial reforms will stop the disproportionate flow of credit to the SOE sector,[14] and free up the funds for the more productive projects in the non-state sector; and allow the appearance of new small-scale local financial institutions that will mobilise local savings to finance local TVE investments. Since the adoption of the policies of economic reform and opening in 1978, folk finance (*minjian rongzhi*) has grown impressively despite the absence of legal recognition and legal protection. Folk finance was definitely the source of the development of TVEs in Wenzhou city in Zhejiang Province. Liu (1992) reported that:

> "Ninety-five per cent of the total capital needed by the local private sector has been supplied by "underground" private financial organizations, such as money clubs, specialized financial households and money shops ..."[15]

It is important to keep in mind that financial deregulation has to be accompanied by the introduction of adequate banking supervision and of prudential standards that comply with international norms. The rash of banking crises in Eastern Europe in the early 1990s and in East and Southeast Asia recently should serve as warnings of financial deregulation without adequate improvement in the government's ability to monitor the activities of the financial institutions.

Reorganising the RCC-ABC system

We are confident that it is well within China's reach to establish a comprehensive rural credit program quite quickly by drawing upon the Indonesian experience with the *Unit Desa* system, and making appropriate adjustments to suit China's specific circumstances. The reorganization of the RCC-ABC system should be guided by five principles.

The first key guiding principle is that *a large-scale subsidised credit program for the rural areas cannot be sustained* because it is both too expensive and too inefficient. A developing country like China should avoid wasting its scarce capital by using the interest rate mechanism to allocate funds to the projects with the highest rates of return.

The second key principle is that *the role of government subsidies is to provide seed money* to (1) provide technical training, (2) start the credit unit's lending activities, and (3) cover the losses for the first few years. Over time, the rural credit unit must (1) mobilise local savings to expand its lending activities, (2) improve its loan assessment activities in order to increase profits, and (3) build a reserve fund to cover losses.

The third key principle is that the rural credit unit must be given the *incentive to maximise profits in a prudent manner*. This third principle necessitates that each credit unit be given a large degree of operational autonomy in return for being financially accountable to the supervising branch of ABC. Bailouts should be used only in exceptional cases where losses are clearly not due to incompetence or recklessness, and bonuses and promotion should be clearly based on contribution to the bank's profitability. Only in an environment with clearly defined individualised rewards and general hard budget constraint, would a credit unit apply itself to mobilize savings diligently, and to assess loan applications carefully.

The fourth key principle is that *rural loan rates are generally higher than in the urban areas.* This situation does not generally indicate exploitation, it reflects instead the higher costs of making many small loans, and the absence of collateral to cover losses.

The fifth principle is that *no rural bank should be given privileges that allow it to monopolise the local market.* This is because providing credit to the rural poor is a hard job. The rural poor are many times unaware of their eligibility for loans, and can be physically hard to reach. Only a bank that is facing competition will attempt to reach these groups with advertisement campaigns, and with mobile teams. Without competition, a bank may even actually reduce its presence in the rural areas like the 13 percent reduction in the number of RCC units in the 1984-95 period — echoing the textbook monopolist who maximises profit by restricting supply.

The following four steps should be simultaneously implemented in order to strengthen the working of the reorganised RCC-ABC system:

1. The existing rural cooperative funds (*nongcun hezuo jijin*), rural credit cooperative (*nongcun xindai hezuoshe*), and other folk finance institutions (*minjian rongzhi*) should be given legal status as independent financial institutions. This will ensure that the RCC-ABC system will no longer enjoy its present near-monopoly status.
2. Various departments of rural development within the different ministries may establish and operate rural financial institutions, but none of them should have regulatory power over institutions that they do not own.
3. The supervision of these independent rural financial institutions should be the sole responsibility of the People's Bank of China in order to ensure consistent regulation of all financial institutions, and to avoid over-regulation of the rural financial institutions.
4. The People's Bank of China should adjust the different mandatory asset-liability ratios to recognise that rural financial institutions face higher transaction costs (due to numerous small loans) and higher risk premia (due to absence of collateral), and that they serve the poorest portion of the population.

It is of fundamental importance to emphasize the point that the proposed ABC credit unit system could work satisfactorily only with competition from other rural financial institutions. Wenzhou's experience with investment financing in the 1980s leaves no doubt about the beneficial effects of vigorous competition from folk finance on state-owned financial institutions:

"In order to compete with [the new folk finance institutions]..., as early as 1980 a local collective credit union, without informing the superior authority, abandoned for the first time the fixed interest rate and adopted a floating interest rate which fluctuated in accordance with market demand but remained within the upper limit set by the state. Despite the dubious legality of the floating interest rate, the local state bank branches and all the credit unions in Wenzhou had already adopted it before the central state officially ratified it in 1984" Liu (1992).

Allowing Rural Enterprises to Assume Market-Determined Ownership Forms

The fact is that *profit-maximising investors do not feel that their interests would be protected in TVEs* where their property rights are less clearly defined, less protected legally, and not freely tradable like the property rights of shareholding firms and foreign-owned companies. The present trend of restructuring TVEs into shareholding cooperatives by dividing their assets among the workers (sometimes, among the original inhabitants of the community) is hence an important step in addressing the difficulties faced by TVEs in raising investment funds.

The transformation of TVE into shareholding cooperatives is akin to the present process of transforming most SOEs into shareholding companies. The transformation of TVES and SOEs into shareholding companies is a natural convergence to an enterprise form which, international experiences have shown, assures investors that managers would have the incentives to maximise profits in a prudent manner. If the property rights of TVEs fail to become freely tradable in formal stock markets, their share of total investment funds will be reduced further because the former SOEs (now transformed into normal corporations) will be the more attractive investment vehicle. The failure to turn TVEs into normal corporations will almost certainly mean that foreign institutional investors, who represent the biggest pool of investment fund in the world and who also have less inside information about the operations of TVEs than Chinese investors, will not become significant investors in TVEs.

Final Remarks

The recent constitutional amendment to accord greater legal protection to private ownership and the ongoing privatisation of collectively-owned TVEs to shareholding cooperatives are giant steps in making rural enterprises more attractive to outside investors. In our opinion, the biggest policy barrier, at the present, to improved financial intermediation in rural China is the government's reluctance to license private financial institutions, especially private banks, more liberally. A restructured ABC-RCC system will not work to its full efficiency potential unless it faces competition from legal, private financial institutions.

Notes

1. See Woo (1999) for a review of the competing interpretations of the TVE phenomenon.
2. The term "state banks" refers the Bank of China, Agricultural Bank of China, People's Construction Bank of China, Industrial and Commercial Bank of China, the three policy banks, Bank of Communications and CITIC Industrial Bank; this usage is from People's Bank of China, *China Financial Outlook '95*.
3. This includes the value of Chinese shares issued in foreign stock markets, primarily the value H-shares, which are shares issued in Hong Kong.
4. 1990 Almanac of China's Finance and Banking.
5. *Nanxun* refers to the February 1992 inspection trip of southern China.
6. The number of RCC units is the number of RCCs plus the number of branches, saving deposit offices and credit stations. The number of RCCs (i.e. institutions with independent accounting systems) went up from 55,044 in 1981 to 60,897 in 1988, and then down to 50,219 in 1995.
7. Bao An county factory, September 28, 1992, Case A27.
8. The term "folk finance" is from China Foreign Trade and Economic Trust and Investment Company (1997).
9. Data are from various issues of the *China Statistical Yearbook*.
10. The discussion in this section draws upon Patton and Rosengard (1990), Woo, Glassburner and Nasution (1994), Woo (1996), and Yaron, Benjamin and Piprek (1997).
11. Desa means village in the Indonesian language.
12. For example, two recent articles in the *China Daily* are "Financial system to undergo five major changes," (February 28, 1998); and "Reforms to target SOEs and State banks," (February 17, 1998).
13. The Export and Import Bank of China has recently decided "to gradually expand its financial services to collectively-owned firms and joint-stock companies" and to continue making "the large- and medium-sized State-owned firms .. as its major clients" (China Daily, "Bank loans to non-State enterprise," January 22, 1998). This decision is a step in the right direction, but it is a very inadequate one because of the continued discrimination against private enterprises – which makes a mockery of the heading of the article.
14. The SOE sector has gotten even more capital-intensive in the post-1978 period of economic deregulation. The subsidised investment funds to the SOE sector are hence offsetting one important thrust of China's economic reforms which is to make enterprises to choose production techniques that are in line with China's vast endowment of labor.
15. The power of market forces (when tolerated by the local authorities) to induce financial institutional innovations is an old story. Taiwan's small and medium private enterprises exhibited dynamic growth in the 1960-1985 period even though they were heavily discriminated against by the (wholly state-owned) banking system because informal financial markets (curb markets) appeared to cater to their needs, Shea and Yang (1994).

References

China Foreign Trade and Economic Trust and Investment Company (CFTETIC). 1997. "Pre-Formulation Study Report on Small Enterprise Guarantee Fund."

Liu, Y. 1992. "Reform From Below: The Private Economy and Local Politics in the Rural Industrialization of Wenzhou." *China Quarterly* 130(June):293-316.

Patten, R., and J. Rosengard. 1990. "Progress with Profits: The Development of Rural Banking in Indonesia." *Harvard Institute for International Development Working Paper.*

Shea, J., and Y. Yang. 1994. "Taiwan's Financial System and the Allocation of Investment Funds." In *The Role of State in Taiwan's Development*, ed. J. Aberbach, D. Dollar, and K. Sokoloff. Armonk: M.E. Sharpe.

Woo, W. 1995. "Indonesia." In *Financial Systems and Economic Policy in Developing Countries*, ed. S. Haggard and C. Lee. Ithaca: Cornell University Press.

———. 1998. "Zhongguo Quan Yaosu Shengchan Lu: Laizi Nongye Bumen Laodongli Zai Pei Zhi de Shouyao Zuoyong (Total Factor Productivity Growth in China: The Primacy of Reallocation of Labor from Agriculture)" in *Jingji Yanjiu* 3:31-9.

———. 1999. "The Real Reasons for China's High Economic Growth." *The China Journal* 41(January):115-37.

Woo, W., B. Glassburner, and A. Nasution. 1994. *Macroeconomic Policies, Crises, and Long-Term Growth in Indonesia, 1965-90.* World Bank.

Yaron, J., M. Benjamin, and G. Piprek. 1997. "Rural Finance: Issues, Design, and Best Practices." *Environmentally and Socially Sustainable Development Studies and Monograph Series.* World Bank. No. 14.

17

Restructuring China's State-Owned Enterprises: A Corporate Governance Perspective

Tian Zhu

Introduction[1]

At the same time that academics outside China are trying to find out how and why China's gradual reform has generated rapid economic growth since 1978 (see Walder 1995, and the references therein), policy-makers and economists inside China find themselves with the unenviable task of reforming the ailing state sector. The 15th Communist Party Congress and the 9th National People's Congress have placed the state enterprise reform at the top of the government's agenda for the coming years. This is a clear signal that the Chinese government is finally aware of and getting serious about the need for a thorough restructuring of its state sector after more than a decade of relatively unsuccessful and piecemeal reforms. While the current emphasis on the reform of state enterprises is long overdue, it is nevertheless a great leap of faith for the Chinese government to take as it faces the daunting fact that almost half of China's state enterprises are losing money.

The new reform plan aims separate the government from enterprises through a corporatization scheme that will convert traditional state-owned enterprises into shareholding companies. In other words, China wants to build a new enterprise system that more or less resembles Western-style modern corporations characterized by the separation of ownership and control.

The move towards corporatization is certainly an important step. Despite years of delegating control to enterprise managers, China's government at all levels still exerts excessive influence on the business decisions of state enterprises. Consequently, the government often has to bear the burden of bailing out money-losing enterprises.

Policy discussions have been focused on how to separate the government from the enterprises and how to restructure and manage state assets. What has been overlooked, however, is a clear understanding of how the modern corporate system actually operates and what institutional environment is required to make the system work in the West. It is particularly striking in these discussions that the critical issue of corporate governance has been basically ignored (but see Qian 1995, 1996 and Wu 1994 for exception), as if once the separation between the government and enterprises is achieved one way or another, the new system will work automatically.

The separation of government and enterprises will not work without certain institutional underpinnings. Western economists and investors are acutely aware of the so-called agency problem resulting from the separation of ownership and control (Berle and Means 1932, Jensen and Meckling 1976, and Jensen 1986). When managers have little ownership stake in their companies, they tend to act in their own self-interest rather than the owners' interests. Managerial misbehavior ranges from shirking duties and the misuse of company funds to flat-out expropriation.

One does not need to look hard to find abundant examples of managerial misbehavior in China. Among the most common offenses are dining and wining on the company, buying luxury cars, traveling for pleasure at company's expense, the promotion of staff based on personal relationships rather than on merit, investing carelessly in infrastructure and plant expansion, diverting state assets to set up subsidiary companies that are financially easier to manipulate, and using company funds to speculate in the property and stock markets.

Corruption by government officials takes similar forms because they are essentially the bosses of enterprise managers. They effectively have the ultimate control rights over the state enterprises but are not legally entitled to the income rights that owners of private enterprises would normally have. It is, therefore, not surprising that the Chinese government finds the socially destabilizing problem of rampant corruption by managers and cadres most difficult to crack. The separation of government and enterprises would certainly help to solve corruption by government officials at the root of the problem. However, managerial corruption could get even worse if a new governance structure is not created to replace the old one. It is also not difficult to imagine that some cadres will try to use their power to convert their government units into enterprises, to set up new companies under their control, or to grab managerial positions in post-separation enterprises.

It is important for China's policy-makers to have a clear understanding that, in the West, the separation of ownership and control is a result of an endogenous, evolutionary process that is based on voluntary exchange of private property rights in pursuit of gains from specialization (Fama and Jensen 1983). In the process, various governance mechanisms have been developed to safeguard owners' interests from managerial infringement. They are legal and economic institutions for owner-investors to have effective control over managers and to assure themselves of a return from their investment. Managers have fiduciary duty to act in the shareholders' interest. Laws have been enacted to prevent self-dealing activities. In addition to legal protection of investors' control and income rights, economic mechanisms have been developed to provide incentives and discipline, including managerial stock options, independent auditing, large shareholders, the market for corporate control, and other specific contractual mechanisms (Hart 1995, Shleifer and Vishny 1997).

In China, there is not enough time for such an evolution. The separation of ownership and management will be largely exogenous at least at the initial stage. Conscious effort needs to be made to develop corporate governance mechanisms in order to minimize the transition costs.

The fundamental question, therefore, is not whether the government and enterprises should be separated. Rather, the questions are how the managers will be governed in the post-separation corporations and how the government can make sure that those who effectively have the ownership rights of the state assets would act in the state's interest.

To address the two questions, this chapter attempts to incorporate the recent development in the theory of the firm and financial structure (Jensen and Meckling 1976, Hart 1995) into the study of China's enterprise reform. The rest of the chapter is organized as follows. In next section, we attempt to assess Chinese state sector's current problems and their causes. We will argue that the poor performance of the state-owned enterprises has often been overestimated and misinterpreted. The actual performance of the state sector does not warrant an urgent solution. We then argue in Section 3 that the creation of a new corporate governance structure is the key to China's enterprise, and that, in turn, requires the development of a well-functioning financial market and a sound legal system. In Section 4, we will draw the lesson from other transitional economies to demonstrate that there is no quick solution to the state enterprise reform and any big-bang style reform plan will end in failure if it does not address the critical issue of corporate governance. We conclude the chapter in Section 5.

Problems and Causes

Since the economic reform in the late seventies, the role of China's state sector in the national economy has been declining. In 1996, the state-owned industrial enterprises accounted for only 28.5% of the gross industrial output. While the share of the total assets by the state-owned industrial enterprises was 58.6%, its share of the total profits was only 27.7% (see *China Statistical Yearbook 1997*) It is widely reported that one-third of China's state-owned enterprises are losing money, one-third barely break even and only one-third are making profits; and it is also said that one in two employees of the state sector is working for a loss-making enterprise. Table 17.1 shows the increasing trend of loss-making by the state-owned industrial enterprises.

The total losses reached 79 billion yuan in 1996 while the losses for 1978 were only 4.2 billion yuan. The annualized growth rate in losses is 17.7%. These losses are absorbed by government subsidies, inter-firm debts, and, more importantly, the state banks. It is estimated that more than 20% of the total bank loans are non-performing.

However, these statistics may not be an accurate indicator of allocative efficiency of the state sector. In addition to the agency problem that is typically associated with state ownership, we identify two other causes that have contributed to the difficulties of the state enterprises.

TABLE 17.1 Financial Indicators of State-Owned Enterprises (100 million yuan)

Year	Total Fixed Assets	Total Profits	Total Loss	Total Tax	Ratio of Pre-tax Profits to Total Fixed Assets
1978	3193.40	508.80	42.06	281.90	0.248
1979	3466.70	562.80	36.38	301.60	0.249
1980	3730.10	585.40	34.30	321.70	0.243
1981	4032.30	579.70	45.96	343.60	0.229
1982	4375.00	597.70	47.57	374.50	0.222
1983	4767.80	640.90	32.11	391.90	0.217
1984	5170.00	706.20	26.61	451.60	0.224
1985	5956.20	738.20	32.44	595.90	0.224
1986	6744.80	689.90	54.49	651.50	0.199
1987	7677.90	787.00	61.04	727.10	0.197
1988	8795.20	891.90	81.92	883.00	0.202
1989	10160.84	743.01	180.19	1030.13	0.175
1990	11610.27	388.11	348.76	1115.03	0.129
1991	13556.75	402.17	367.00	1258.98	0.123
1992	15669.78	535.10	369.27	1409.02	0.124
1993	19066.39	817.26	452.64	1637.44	0.129
1994	23101.98	829.01	482.59	2047.24	0.125
1995	30935.70	665.60	639.57	2208.60	0.093
1996	34764.96	412.64	790.68	2324.49	0.079

Data Source: China Statistical Yearbook, 1997.

First, increasing competition has driven down the profit margin across the whole spectrum of enterprises including non-state enterprises. While competition may be bad news for individual firms, it is good news for the whole economy. Table 17.2 shows that while the state enterprises have performed worse than non-state enterprises, the performance as measured by the ratio of pre-tax profits to total fixed assets has declined over time for both the state sector and non-state sectors. The average profit margin is not an indicator of an economy's health but rather the competitiveness of the market. As the Chinese economy becomes increasingly market-oriented, it is natural to expect that the superficial profits for state enterprises as guaranteed by the planning system in the past would decline over the course of economic reform. Moreover, loss-making is not a unique problem within the state sector. A high percentage of non-state enterprises is also losing money. According to China's Third National Industrial Census in 1995, 33.8% of the state-owned industrial enterprises were making losses, while the percentage of loss-making enterprises for the whole industrial sector was 25%.

TABLE 17.2 State-Owned versus Non-State Industrial Enterprises (Measured by the Ratio of Pre-Tax Profits to Total Fixed Assets)

Year	All Industrial Enterprises	State-Owned Industrial Enterprises	Non-State Industrial Enterprises
1985	23.92	22.40	33.30
1990	13.52	12.90	22.26
1995	11.23	9.29	15.48
1996	9.89	7.87	13.96

Source: Calculated from China Statistical Yearbook, 1997.

Second, relative to non-state sectors, the state-owned enterprises have to shoulder much heavier social responsibilities. They are required to create employment for urban residents even if they already have redundant workers. In addition, the SOEs have a much higher percentage of retired workers on their payrolls. They are also expected to and do indeed provide employees with various fringe benefits such as low-cost housing and free medical care. Moreover, the state enterprises have been paying more taxes than other enterprises.

According to the 1995 census, the average ratio of total tax to pre-tax profits was 0.77 for state-owned industrial enterprises, while the figure for township enterprises and wholly foreign-owned enterprises was respectively 0.54 and 0.35 (see Table 17.3). When we take the state sector's contribution to tax revenue and employment into account, the difference in performance levels between state enterprises and other enterprises becomes narrower. According to the same census, in 1995, the average ratio of net profits to equity was 0.041 for all enterprises and 0.022 for SOEs while the ratio of pre-tax profits to equity was 0.184 for all enterprises and 0.177 for SOEs. In other words, when we take the tax contribution into account, the difference in performance between the state sector and non-state sectors would narrow down dramatically. When we look at the ratio of the sum of total wages, pension and pre-tax profits to equity, the difference would basically disappear.

One may have reservations about the accuracy of Chinese statistics. It is certainly reasonable to question the above statistics. But we are not trying to show that SOEs are just as efficient as other types of enterprises. We simply want to point out that SOEs may not be as inefficient as one might think based on simple statistics widely reported in the press.

TABLE 17.3 The Performance of the State versus Non-State Industrial Enterprises at or above the Township Level

Enterprise Type	Ratio of Total Tax to Pre-Tax Profits	Ratio of Net Profits to Equity	Ratio of Pretax Profits to Equity	Ratio of the Sum of Total Wages, Pension and Pretax Profits to Equity
TOTAL	0.68	0.041	0.184	0.370
State-owned	0.77	0.022	0.177	0.367
Collective Owned	0.64	0.063	0.255	0.570
Private	0.34	0.216	0.372	0.526
Joint Owned	0.67	0.041	0.178	0.371
Shareholding	0.45	0.082	0.186	0.289
Sino-Foreign Joint Venture	0.48	0.074	0.170	0.248
Wholly Foreign Owned	0.35	0.062	0.102	0.223
Mainland-HK-Macau-Taiwan Joint-Venture	0.51	0.061	0.140	0.255
HK-Macau-Taiwan Wholly Owned	0.49	0.030	0.065	0.198
Others	0.43	0.062	0.135	0.242

Source: The Data of the Third National Industrial Census of the People's Republic of China in 1995

Corporate Governance: Key to Enterprise Reform

In this section, we will argue that enterprise reform is not equivalent to the separation of government and enterprises. It is not a simple problem of ownership reform or converting state enterprises to shareholding companies.

The objective of the state enterprise reform should be to address the incentive problem of both the managers and their monitors. Even the most dramatic approach to the separation of government and enterprises, namely, privatization, will not necessarily solve the problem.

To address the problem of managerial incentive, the most obvious approach is to tie managerial compensation to the managers' performances. In China, enterprise managers are provided with little contractual, personal incentive. It is more efficient to change managerial incentives from implicit or illegal benefits to explicit, legal compensations. If a manager personally receives, say, 10 per cent of his company's profit, then, on the one hand, he would have good incentive to take measures to improve his company's performance; and, on the other hand, it would make corruption much more expensive both to himself and to the bribers. The amount of benefits from corruption would have to be large enough for the manager to be willing to take the risk in favor of costly illegal benefits over explicit, legal compensation. Moreover, a large sum of bribes also makes it more visible and easier to detect.

The problem with China's current managerial incentive system is that it either provides too little personal incentive to managers and or it tends to give incentives biased toward short-term accounting profits. Managerial incentive contracts in the form of equity participation or stock options would provide managers with adequate incentives to improve the firms' long-term profitability. Stock options, however, can be an effective incentive device only when stocks are tradable and stock prices reflect the firms' long-term performances. This, of course, depends on the development of a well-functioning stock market.

But incentive pay, by itself, may not be enough to deter excessive on-the-job consumption, misuse of company funds, or outright embezzlement. Monitoring is often necessary to prevent the misuse of company funds and overt or disguised managerial theft. In China, government agencies are supposed to be the monitors of enterprise managers. But the question now becomes: who monitors the monitors? After all, government officials themselves are not the owners of the state enterprises although they exercise control rights that are similar to those of owners. The absence of an effective monitoring system is at the root of China's serious corruption problem. In a typical market economy, a company either has a virtually unified structure of ownership and management, or, when the two are separated, shareholders have the rights to vote for the board of directors which, in turn, has the rights and obligations to monitor the management in the shareholders' interest. More importantly, in even the largest corporations, there are normally shareholders that hold significant ownership stakes. Large shareholders can and have incentives to exercise effective control rights and monitor the management.

Some economists in China propose that the Bureaus of State Asset Management or state-owned banks (after converting loans to equity shares) should assume the role of large shareholders. But unless the new monitors are given adequate incentives, the outcome would not be very different. In addition, the control rights would become too concentrated. When one government agency controls a large number of enterprises, the effectiveness of monitoring is doubtful. Moreover, this may create incentives for the new agencies to adopt anti-competition measures. One alternative is, as we see it, private financial intermediaries. Chinese households already have enough bank deposits to buy a significant portion of the state equity. By encouraging the formation of large private financial intermediaries such as mutual funds,

China can channel a large bulk of household savings to equity investments. But financial intermediaries may have their own governance problems especially in a country that does not possess an adequate financial market and legal system.

The threat of bankruptcy due to a poor performance is another disciplinary mechanism (Grossman and Hart 1982). China, however, has been reluctant to use this mechanism out of the fear for massive unemployment and social instability. But in recent years, many companies have been rushing to declare bankruptcy as it is the cheapest way to get rid of their debt obligations. As a consequence, the Chinese government has recently encouraged mergers and acquisitions of hopeless money losers by profit-making companies. Such administrative maneuvering may only transfer the burden from the state to those well-performing enterprises but not solve the fundamental problem. Some Western economists believe that corporate takeovers through mergers and acquisitions are a powerful force in corporate governance because poorly performing managers are generally replaced after the takeover (Jensen 1986). This imposes a tremendous pressure on those managers who are incompetent but refuse to step down and those who are too busy promoting their own self-interests. In China, takeovers administered by the government are not motivated by the logic of corporate governance. The absence of a well-functioning capital market in transitional economies will also limit the effectiveness of corporate takeovers as a viable mechanism for China in the near term.

There are two factors other than unemployment that limit the use of bankruptcy as a governance mechanism in China. First, the Chinese legal system is weak and debtholders' interests are not fully protected. As a result, bankruptcy is often used by some companies as a way to avoid paying back their debts. Moreover, most debt obligations are in the form of loans from state banks. Under the current system, state banks do not have enough incentives to make loans very carefully and, after default, do not make enough efforts to recover the debt. Therefore, debt payment becomes a soft budget constraint rather than a hard budget constraint as in a typical market economy (Williamson 1988).

Second, state enterprises have an unusually high debt to equity ratio. It is a legacy of the past bank-loans-for-budget-allocation reform. A high leverage ratio makes it difficult for firms to borrow money even if there are good investment projects. And if they can borrow, too much debt may encourage them to pursue highly risky projects (Jensen and Meckling 1976). A more serious problem is that, when debt is virtually the only source of finance, firms become extremely vulnerable to default. In other words, default tends to be more of a result of economic fluctuation rather than of poor performances by enterprise managers. In such situations, bankruptcy would be very inefficient. This, we believe, is the root cause of the debt crisis in China. Unless China reforms its current one-dimensional corporate finance system, all other measures such as clearance of triangular debt by the administration, bankruptcy and mergers will not prevent the problem from recurring.

Corporate governance structure is the key to resolve the agency problem when ownership and control are separated. But all the governance mechanisms need to be supported by an effective legal system and a well-functioning financial market. Managerial stock options require stock prices to reflect firms' true performance. An excessively speculative market will not serve this purpose. Moreover, managers' legal compensations from their hard work should be protected while managerial corruption must be punished. Measures need to be taken to encourage the formation of large private shareholders. In particular, the state monopoly in banking and other financial sectors must be abolished, and non-state financial intermediaries should play an important role in blockholding. This requires the government to devote sufficient financial and human resources to expand and deepen China's financial market. In the mean time, an effective legal and regulatory system needs to develop hand-in-hand with the financial market. In particular, the self-dealing activities by large shareholders to infringe upon small shareholders' interests or manipulate the market should be prohibited and violations should be effectively prosecuted.

The governance function of bankruptcy requires that, on the one hand, debt payment and the transfer of control rights upon bankruptcy be strictly enforced by law (Aghion and Bolton 1992), and, on the other hand, firms need to have more choices in their ways of financing. If non-bank financial intermediaries are allowed to develop and take large equity stakes in the firms, then a large portion of corporate finance will be transferred from bank loans to equity holdings. Consequently, the current high debt-to-capital ratio will be reduced to a more appropriate level.

Lastly, we want to point out that there are no governance mechanisms that are universally applicable. It is difficult either to prescribe or to predict what type of governance structure will emerge in China in the long run. But in all countries that have relatively effective corporate governance structure, there have developed functioning financial and product markets and relatively sound and effective legal systems. For China, therefore, the most important problem is not to find a fixed set of governance models from which to copy, but to establish and start to enforce some basic rules of the market game.

No Quick Solution: Lessons from Other Transitional Economies

It is easy to separate government and enterprise, and it is not a lot more difficult to privatize all the state enterprises, at least not on paper. But an efficient and effective corporate governance structure is much harder to come by. Effective governance structure hinges on the development of market institutions, in particular, on the development of the financial market and the legal system. Institution-building takes time. This is the hard lesson that Russia and some of the other transitional economies have taught us.

The transition to the market economy in Russia and most of Eastern and Central European Countries (CEEC) was carried out in a big-bang fashion. Following recommendations by Western economists (Lipton and Sachs 1990), these countries attempted to implement a shock therapy strategy to liberalization and privatization. Before privatization, there was a wave of corporatization characterized also by the separation of government and enterprises. This was done through incorporation of state owned enterprises and reclamation of the state's property rights. Traditional state enterprises were transformed into joint stock companies. Corporatization was perceived as a preliminary step towards privatization. Although there were variations in the specific ways of privatizing state enterprises, a common feature of various programs for privatization was the direct or indirect distribution of assets of state-owned enterprises at no or low cost to citizens. In particular, enterprise managers and employees often received special treatment.

In both pre-privatization and post-privatization, the problem of corporate governance has been either neglected or underestimated in these countries.

After corporatization in CEEC, several problems emerged that are similar to what we have seen in China's state sector (see Dobrinsky 1996). First, soft-budget constraints were not eliminated but took a different form. Firms treated payments to suppliers and banks as a soft budget constraint. Most CEECs pursued a prolonged macroeconomic austerity such as what was implemented in China after 1993. This caused a snowballing of bad enterprise debt and the resulting crisis in the banking sector that propelled financial restructuring. The restructuring was basically implemented by various forms of government bail-outs. Bankruptcy was not widely used. The negligence of proper governance resulted from the perception that corporatization is only an interim process and subsequent privatization will solve the problems. But actual privatization has been much slower than expected. Consequently, state enterprises were simply left on their own with very little supervision from the state. The governing bodies of state properties have often engaged in corruption and rent-seeking behavior.

The governance problem persists after privatization. The most serious problem is that the ownership of post-privatization enterprises becomes too dispersed. This gives rise to the free-rider problem in monitoring and consequently to managerial misbehavior. Managers are more concerned with promoting their own self-interest rather than carrying out restructuring plans and thus find ways to divert company assets.

In recognition of the potential governance problem, the schemes for privatization have included measures that attempt to create large stakeholders. In an effort to promote blockholding, both Czech and Russian programs have encouraged the creation of private mutual funds that accept citizens' vouchers in exchange for the funds' shares. In the two countries, managers are given the options to acquire large ownership stakes at discounted prices. Poland adopted a top-down program that was to create a few large mutual funds managed by foreigners and then allocate to these funds shares in state enterprises. Each enterprise has a lead fund with a 33% block of shares. Each citizen then receives a share in each of the mutual funds (see Boyco et al 1994).

Having large stakeholders, however, is only one of the governance mechanisms used in modern corporations. Large shareholders may themselves engage in self-dealing activities that sacrifice the interest of small shareholders. Numerous reports on managerial theft in Russia confirm this point (Bim 1996). Moreover, a mutual fund may have its own governance problem. In fact, many investment funds in these countries have played little role in corporate governance. Their activities are not centered on long-term investment but on speculative trading of vouchers or stocks. This, in combination with the fact that a mutual fund often holds stakes in a large number of firms for the sake of diversification, casts doubts on the effectiveness of large shareholdership by mutual funds as a governance mechanism at the initial stage of reform. Moreover, it may take a very long time for large private stakeholders to emerge spontaneously. It is not surprising that in the Czech Republic, most investment funds are eventually controlled by commercial banks. These banks control funds to trade stocks in the secondary market and try to use their stakes in firms to attract banking business (Dobrinsky 1996).

When managers acquire a large stake in the company, they often resist the purchase of shares by hostile outsiders. They do not necessarily take a constructive approach to transition. It is often easier for the managers to extract income and capital for personal benefits than to carry out restructuring. In Russia, both before and after privatization, the ways of capital extraction or other rent-seeking behavior should look familiar to Chinese observers: lease-out of enterprise premises and creation of semi-state or semi-private small businesses around the core ones (Bim 1996). Employees also tended to support managers more than interested outsiders for fear of losing their jobs after restructuring.

All the problems that CEECs have been facing were not unexpected by careful observers. They are the result of their failure to solve the governance problem for lack of a well-functioning financial market and a sound legal system. Lessons from these countries support our assertion that if China does not pay close attention to market and legal institution building, any reform, whether it is corporatization or privatization, is deemed to fail.

We hasten to add that we are not arguing that the Chinese government does not need to do anything with the state sector before a well-functioning financial market and an effective legal institution are in place. The development of market institutions needs participation of market players. The point we are trying to establish is that institution building should go hand-in-hand with corporatization. The pace of reform should be gradual and in accordance with the development of the financial market and legal systems. Although institutions take time to grow, investment in institutions will hasten the process. Therefore, the most important task for the Chinese government is to commit sufficient financial and human resources (i.e., not just words) to developing the country's financial market and legal systems. Any enterprise reform plan should be congruent with the central task of institution building.

Conclusion

In this chapter, we have attempted to argue the following points. First, enterprise reform must address the problem of corporate governance or, in other words, it has to address the incentive problem of both the managers and the owners. Second, an effective corporate governance structure depends on the development of market institutions, especially the financial market and its supporting legal system. Third, the development of market institutions cannot be completed in a big-bang fashion.

We have not been able to offer a quick solution to the reform of China's state sector. We believe, on the one hand, that there is no such solution, and, on the other hand, the performance of the state sector may not be bad enough to warrant an urgent solution. We have argued that the poor performance of state enterprises may be overestimated. There are many factors other than poor management that have contributed to the mounting loss of the state sector.

All in all, we believe that if China is to succeed in its bid to modernize its corporate system, it must accord the first priority to the development of corporate governance structure. The most urgent and essential task is to develop the country's financial market and the supporting legal and regulatory systems. This is, of course, not an easy task and the reward may not be seen in the short term. But, it will be the most rewarding task for China to sustain its long-term growth. Any reform plan that excludes these key elements may end in failure.

Notes

1. Division of Social Science, Hong Kong University of Science and Technology, Clear Water Bay, Kowloon, Hong Kong. The author wishes to thank Shan Li for helpful discussions. This is a revised and retitled version of a paper presented at the 1997 Annual Conference of the Chinese Economists Society, Los Angeles.

References

Aghion, P., and P. Bolton. 1992. "An Incomplete Contracts Approach to Financial Contracting." *Review of Economic Studies* 59:473-494.

Berle, A., and G. Means. 1932. *The Modern Corporation and Private Property*. Macmillan.

Bim, A. 1996. "Ownership and Control of Russian Enterprises and Strategies of Shareholders." *Communist Economies and Economic Transformation* 8:471-500.

Boycko, M., A. Schleifer, and R. Vishny. 1994. "Voucher Privatization." *Journal of Financial Economics* 35:249-266.

Dobrinsky, R. 1996. "Enterprise Restructuring and Adjustment in the Transition to Market Economy: Lessons from the Experience of Central and Eastern Europe." *Economics of Transition* 4:389-410.

Frydman, R., and A. Rapaczynski. 1993. "Insiders and the State: Overview of Responses to Agency Problems in East European Privatization." *Economics of Transition* 1:39-60.

Fama, E., and M. Jensen. 1983. Separation of Ownership and Control, *Journal of Law and Economics* 26:301-25.

Grossman, S., and O. Hart. 1982. "Corporate Financial Structure and Managerial Incentives," in J. McCall, ed., *The Economics of Information and Uncertainty*. Chicago: University of Chicago Press.

Hart, O. 1995a. "Corporate Governance: Some Theory and Implications," *The Economic Journal* 105:678-89.

―――. 1995b. *Firms, Contracts and Financial Structure*. Oxford: Oxford University Press.

Jensen, M. 1986. "Agency Costs of Free Cash Flow, Corporate Finance and Takeovers," *American Economic Review* 76:323-39.

Jensen, M., and W. Meckling. 1976. "Theory of the Firm: Managerial Behavior, Agent Costs, and Capital Structure," *Journal of Financial Economics* 3:305-60.

Lipton, D., and J. Sachs. 1990. "Privatization in Eastern Europe: The Case of Poland," *Brookings Papers on Economic Activity* 2:293-333.

Qian, Y. 1995. "Reforming Corporate Governance and Financial Structure," *Jingji Yanjiu [Economic Studies in Chinese]*, 20-9.

―――. 1996. "Enterprise Reform in China: Agency Problems and Political Control," *Economics of Transition* 4:422-47.

Shleifer, A., and R. Vishny. 1997. "A Survey of Corporate Governance," *Journal of Finance* 52:737-83.

Walder, A. 1995. "China's Transitional Economy: Interpreting its Significance," *The China Quarterly* 144:963-79.

Williamson, O. 1988. "Corporate Finance and Corporate Governance," *Journal of Finance* 43:567-91.

Wu, J. 1994. *Xiandai Gongsi Yu Qiye Gaige (Modern Corporations and Enterprise Reform)*. Tianjin: People's Press of Tianjin.

Zhongguo Tongji Nianjian (China Statistical Yearbook). 1997.
Zhonghua Renmin Gongheguo 1995 Nian Disanci Quanguo Gongye Pucha Ziliao Huibian (The Data of the Third National Industrial Census of the People's Republic of China of 1995). Beijing: China Statistical Press.

18

Insider Control, Corporate Governance, and the Soft Budget Constraint: Theory, Evidence, and Policy Implications

David D. Li

Introduction[1]

The purpose of this chapter is to examine the relationship between insider control of enterprises and the Soft Budget Constraint (SBC) and to explore policy implications for the next stage of China's state enterprise reform. The SBC, which was first introduced by Kornai (1980), refers to a phenomenon where the firm is not concerned with financial losses and always expects to be bailed out. The SBC is widely recognized as a root of many economic problems of the formerly socialist economies and it remains a major obstacle of economic reforms in these economies.[2] Therefore, research on the causes of the SBC carries important policy implications for economic reforms in the post-socialist economies.

Existing literature has focused on two independent causes of the SBC. The first cause is the creditors' lack of information and commitment to terminate bad investment projects. Dewatripont and Maskin (1995) explain the SBC by the lack of information and commitment of a centralized financial system, which is too big to credibly cut off those projects that become profitable (i.e. *ex post* profitable) after the initial investment is sunk. This implies that decentralizing and down-sizing financial institutions are necessary in hardening budget constraints. Following Dewatripont and Maskin, Bai and Wang (1998) theorize that because the principal (the state) knows less about the future return of investment than the agent (the planner), the principal may rationally require the agent to refinance some of the *ex post* inefficient projects. This way, the principal makes the agent suffer a greater financial loss by letting bad project get started. The agent is thus induced to work harder to screen projects. The second cause is explained in Shleifer and Vishny (1994). They argue that the SBC is caused by politicians' desire to influence firms' decisions. Politicians use subsidies as a condition to induce firms to take non-profit maximizing activities. The implication is that privatization is an essential step of economic reform.

Both families of theories clearly bear much empirical relevance, as they are supported by an overwhelming amount of anecdotal evidence. However, it remains a puzzle that the SBC seems to be a persistent problem in many transition economies despite radical reforms of privatization, decentralization, and liberalization.[3] Thus, there seem to be other independent causes of the SBC.

This chapter argues that there is another cause of the SBC, i.e., excessive insider (manager) control of a firm. When insiders obtain critical control of the firm and enjoy substantial control benefit but do not have full claim rights to the liquidation value of the asset, they would obstruct liquidating an existing project, unless they are properly compensated for their loss of control benefit. Thus, the insiders are shielded from the downward risk of an investment. Consequently, insiders would propose many socially inefficient (low profitability) projects. Increasing insiders' profit shares may not help, since ex *post* insiders have limited wealth to sustain large amounts of negative profits so that higher profit shares only stimulate insiders' desire to propose bad projects. In contrast, when outsiders (investors) have full control rights, hard budget constraints arise, since the investors would close profit-losing firms and the insiders have limited wealth to compensate the outsiders for not doing so. *Ex post*, hard budget constraints may well be *socially* inefficient, since they cause frequent losses of control benefit for insiders. However, *ex ante*, hard budget constraints force insiders to refrain from proposing unprofitable projects. In general, we show that hard budget constraints increase firms' average profitability. As for social welfare, the insider control system is better when projects' downward risk is limited – a common scenario of early industrialization in a catching-up economy. The outsider control system is better when R&D projects are important for economic growth as in industrialized economies.[4]

After presenting a formal theory in the spirit illustrated above, the chapter provides supporting evidence from surveys of Chinese state enterprises. The evidence shows that in the reform era, insiders of China's state enterprises have obtained significantly more autonomy than before and often times abuse their autonomy. Excessive bonus expenditure is a major manifestation of this phenomenon and accounts for a large proportion of negative profits in many enterprises.

Finally, the chapter explores its policy implications for state enterprise reform. It is argued that the long-run task of the reform consists of two parts. First, it needs to replace the government as a control right holder of state enterprises by private large stakeholders, such as large creditors or shareholders. Second, at the same time, it needs to establish institutions of corporate governance, i.e., stable rules that enable outside investors to properly monitor and discipline enterprise managers. However, in the short-run, before large private stakeholders emerge and institutions of corporate governance are established, maintaining a proper degree of government control of state enterprises is called for, given that there are few alternatives to curb the abusive behavior of the enterprise insiders. After all, the government is one of the largest stakeholders of a state enterprise, relying on the latter for tax revenues and employment.

A Simple Theory of Insider Control and the Soft Budget Constraint

The model is embedded in the long literature of property rights starting with Grossman and Hart (1986). It is closest to the literature on debt and bankruptcy by Diamond (1991), Aghion and Bolton (1992), and Dewatripont and Tirole (1994). A major difference is that the current model is not concerned with the optimal control rights structure and the corresponding capital structure of the firm. Rather, it focuses on the consequences of given (often poorly designed) control rights arrangements and link these to the concept of budget constraints.

There are two agents in the model: the insider (manager), M, and the outside financier/investor, F. M refers to employees of a firm.[5] F refers to providers of financial capital for the firm. In market economies, they are either bondholders or equity holders. In socialist and post-socialist economies, F often represents the government officials (bureaucrats) who are in charge of approving the firm's investment projects.

A key assumption, which should be highly realistic in many situations, is that F is indispensable for the project because of M's initial wealth constraint and limited liability. M thus cannot be given all the residual income of the project and is not entitled to the liquidation value of project.

We model a typical investment cycle of the firm. At time 1, M discovers a project and proposes it to F, who decides whether to approve the project. Financial investment and labor input are needed in an approved project. If the project is approved, simultaneously a profit sharing rule is determined: s_M for M and s_F for F with $s_M + s_F = 1$. The profit sharing rule will be honored unless re-negotiation arises at time 2. After the initial investment, at time 2, the profitability of the project is revealed. Either M or F decides whether to terminate now or to continue the project for one more period. We shall treat the profit sharing rule s_F and s_M as exogenous, since our focus is in the consequences of control rights arrangements.

Without losing generality, assume that the project needs one unit of physical capital. As an extreme assumption, we shall assume that the physical capital is recoverable or reversible, i.e., if the project is terminated at time 2, the capital can be re-used in another project without loss. The purpose of such an assumption is to highlight the effect of insiders' control rights on budget constraints. When the capital is sunk or partially sunk, the paper's results will be strengthened, since the logic of Dewatripont and Maskin (1995) comes into play. Let the prevailing interest rate be r. Thus, if the project is terminated before period 2, then capital earns r elsewhere.

Similarly, assume that the project needs one unit of labor input by M. Suppose that the wage rate is w so that the per-period labor compensation is w. In addition, controlling a project gives M a control benefit B, which is non-monetary and can take on many forms of non-wage benefits. The benefit of control is a common observation in corporate finance. At time 2, if it is decided that the project is to be terminated, then M can still be employed elsewhere and obtain w but will lose the control benefit B. A simple scenario to support this assumption is that M cannot be trusted for proposing new projects at least for one period of time.

If M chooses not to propose a new project, we assume that he continues getting wage w and a control benefit which is slightly below B, i.e., B$^-$. Conceptually, such a technical assumption is needed to maintain the equilibrium where other things being equal, M prefers to propose new projects. It will not change any of the calculations so that we will not distinguish between B and B$^-$ in the analysis. Alternatively, we can assume that without proposing projects, the control benefit is $B_0 <$ B. All the following results will go through with a only few notational changes.

We assume that the control benefit B is higher than the one-period wage w. This assumption is not essential, but it serves to highlight the potential social cost of the hard budget constraint, which terminates projects at the cost of forfeiting M's control benefit. All of the following results still hold qualitatively without this assumption.

Assumption 1: $B \geq w$

Let θ be an index of the project's profitability so that the net profit of the project is $\theta - r - w$, where θ can be thought of the price of the product that the project produces. θ is a random variable at time 1 and its randomness is not resolved until time 2. Also, we rule out the possibility that M and F can sign a contract which is contingent upon θ. This is the so-called incomplete contract assumption. In former socialist or transition economies, due to poor market institutions, such as formal bankruptcy, this should be a very realistic assumption. There are four possible realizations of θ at time 2: θ_1, θ_2, θ_3, and θ_4 Let π_1, π_2, π_3, and π_4 be the four correspondingly associated net profit levels. At time 1, the corresponding probabilities are: $q_1, q_2, q_3,$ and $q_4.$ We assume:

Assumption 2: $\pi_1 = \theta_1 - r - w > 0$

Assumption 3: $-w \leq \pi_2 = \theta_2 - r - w < 0$

Assumption 4: $-B \leq \pi_3 = \theta_3 - r - w < -w$

Assumption 5: $\pi_4 \le \theta_4 - r - w < -B$

From the social welfare point of view, if $\theta = \theta_1, \theta_2$ or θ_3, the project should continue since the loss of B can be avoided; otherwise, the project should be terminated. The social welfare consideration takes into account M's potential loss of control benefit.

For the following analysis, we will maintain an assumption that the wage cost w is relatively small compared with the worst possible financial loss of the project. For modern industrial enterprises, which are physical capital intensive, this should be a common scenario. Specifically, we assume

Assumption 6: $w \le -\frac{1}{2} \pi_4$

Another assumption, which is already implied above, is that M is liquidity constrained so that its financial payoff cannot be negative. This implies that the most M can give up is his per-period wage w. The information structure is the following. At time 1, M knows (q_1, q_2, q_3, q_4) before proposing it to F. F on the other hand, however, only learns a *prior* distribution of (q_1, q_2, q_3, q_4). As a simplifying assumption, we treat both M and F as expected payoff maximizers with 0 discount rates.

The Case When M Has Complete Control Rights

In order to highlight the consequences of insider control, let us consider an extreme case where the insider M has complete control rights of the firm, i.e., M is fully entrenched and makes decisions on the project at time 2.

Following backward induction, we start with time 2. Suppose that a project is already in place at time 2. If $\theta = \theta_1$, clearly the project will continue. If $\theta = \theta_2$ or θ_3, given assumptions 3 and 4, then it is still in the interest of M to keep the project in order to avoid the loss of B.F, however, F would prefer terminating the project, since F can reuse the capital in another project and earn r. Given that M has complete control rights, the *status quo* of the negotiation between M and F is for the project to continue.

In order to persuade M to agree to terminating the project, F has to pay M at least:[6]

$$s_M \pi_i + B > w, \; i=2 \text{ or } 3$$

which is the difference between F's payoff in the *status quo* and when the project is terminated. Thus, F's net payoff with the project being stopped after compensating M is no more than

$$r - (B + s_M \pi_i), \qquad (1)$$

while with the *status quo*, F obtains a payoff of

$$s_F \pi_i + r \qquad (2)$$

The difference between (2) and (1) is

$$s_M \pi_i + r - (r - s_M \pi_i - B) = \pi_i + B > 0, i = 2 \text{ or } 3$$

according to assumptions 3 and 4. Therefore, the equilibrium must be that with $\theta = \theta_2$, or θ_3, the project will continue and no contract re-negotiation will arise.

In the case of $\theta = \theta_4$, M would still choose to keep the project and this is the *status quo* in the subsequent bargaining. F prefers terminating the project in order to re-use the capital elsewhere. The maximum amount that F is willing to compensate M is the difference between the payoff to F if the project is terminated and that if it continues:

$$r - (s_F \pi_4 + r) = -s_F \pi_4$$

With this maximum compensation, M's payoff is

$$w - s_F \pi_4, \tag{3}$$

and with the *status quo*, M's payoff is

$$s_M \pi_4 + w + B, \tag{4}$$

since M earns wage w and enjoys control benefit B. The difference between (4) and (3) is

$$s_M \pi_4 + w + B - (w - s_F \pi_4) = \pi_4 + B < 0.$$

Therefore, the project will be terminated after F properly compensates M. To summarize:

Proposition 1 (The Soft Budget Constraint) When M has complete control rights, an investment project will continue when $\theta = \theta_1$, θ_2 or θ_3. When $\theta = \theta_4$ the project will be terminated after a proper compensation from F to M. In other words, the project will only be terminated in the worse state of profitability.

The intuition is straightforward and best illustrated by the Coase Theorem. When M has complete right rights, F needs to buy M off. Since F has no wealth constraint and we do not assume any informational or institutional frictions, the outcome of the negotiation has to be Pareto optimal. Thus, Proposition 1 is a direct translation of assumptions 2 to 5.

Now that we have analyzed the outcome of negotiations at time 2, the next issue is what kind of projects M proposes at time 1. For this purpose, we need to calculate the payoff to M at time 2. Without losing generality, let us assume that in the negotiations when $\theta = \theta_4$ is realized, M and F have equal bargaining power, i.e., each has relative bargaining power of ½.[7]

Suppose that M proposes a project (q_1, q_2, q_3, q_4), then M can expect to get the following payoff. With realization of $\theta = \theta_1$, θ_2 or θ_3, the project will continue and no re-negotiation is involved. M expects to obtain

$$q_1(s_M\pi_1 + w + B) + q_2(s_M\pi_2 + w + B) + q_3(s_M\pi_3 + w + B).$$

With θ_4, given our simple Nash-bargaining assumption, M and F split the welfare gain from closing the project. Thus, M expects to get

$$q_4[s_M\pi_4 + w + B + \tfrac{1}{2}[w + r - (\pi_4 + w + r + B)]]$$
$$= q_4[s_M\pi_4 + w + \tfrac{1}{2}(B - \pi_4)].$$

Overall, M can expect to obtain from (q_1, q_2, q_3, q_4) an expected payoff of

$$q_1(s_M\pi_1 + w + B) + q_2(s_M\pi_2 + w + B) + q_3(s_M\pi_3 + w + B) + q_4[s_M\pi_4 + w + \tfrac{1}{2}(B - \pi_4)]. \quad (5)$$

M compares (5) with the payoff from the default option, i.e., obtaining a flat payoff of $w + B$ by proposing no projects. Therefore, if

$$s_M E(\pi) + w + (q_1 + q_2 + q_3)B + \tfrac{1}{2} q_4 (B - \pi_4) \geq w + B$$

or

$$s_M E(\pi) = \tfrac{1}{2} q_4 (B + \pi_4). \quad (6)$$

M will propose a project (q_1, q_2, q_3, q_4).

From the social welfare point of view, a project (q_1, q_2, q_3, q_4) should be invested, if and only if

$$q_1\pi_1 + q_2\pi_2 + q_3\pi_3 + = q_4 B, \quad (7)$$

i.e., when the expected net profit of continuing the project is higher than the expected loss of control benefit.

Comparing (6) and (7), we can show that an M-controlled firm proposes more projects than what is socially desirable. The reason is that M expects to exercise his control rights to extract compensation from F when a project is terminated. Also, in state 2 and 3, M is only exposed to the financial loss up to the amount of w. This is what Kornai (1980) refers to as investment hunger. It was a wide-spread problem in former socialist economies.

Proposition 2 (Investment Hunger) When M obtains full control rights, unless $q_4 \equiv 0$, M proposes more projects than what is socially desirable.

(All proof is in Appendix)

Interestingly, a higher s_M may not alleviate the severity of the investment hunger. To appreciate the intuition, let us focus on the marginal project that M is indifferent between proposing and not proposing. When s_M is very small, such a marginal project has negative expected profit, since essentially M does not care about the firm's financial losses. Thus, an increase in s_M is welfare improving. When w and s_M are relatively large, then M is exposed to relatively large financial losses. The marginal project may actually have positive expected profit (which is smaller that q_4B). A higher s_M now makes M better off due to the positive expected profit. Thus, a higher s_M makes M more aggressive in proposing projects. The following proposition is a precise summary of these intuitions.

Proposition 3 (The Effect of Increasing s_M)
1) When $s_M < -w / \pi_4$, then a higher s_M induces M to propose less socially undesirable projects;
2) when $s_M \geq -w/\pi_4$ and $w \geq -\frac{1}{2}(\pi_4 + B)$ then an increase s_M in makes M propose more socially undesirable projects.

Consider F's decision when facing a proposal by M. Anticipating the bargaining over the termination decision at time 2, F's expected profit from a project (q_1, q_2, q_3, q_4) is

$$E[s_F q_1 \pi_1 + s_F q_2 \pi_2 + s_F q_3 \pi_3 + s_F q_4 \pi_4 + \tfrac{1}{2} q_4 (-B - \pi_4) + r \mid (6)], \tag{8}$$

where the expectation is taken over condition (6). Obviously, F approves the project when

$$E[s_F q_1 \pi_1 + s_F q_2 \pi_2 + s_F q_3 \pi_3 + s_F q_4 \pi_4 + \tfrac{1}{2} q_4 (-B - \pi_4) \mid (6)] > 0. \tag{9}$$

The Case When F Has Complete Control Rights

We now assume the opposite of the previous case, i.e., F has complete control rights of the firm and makes decisions at time 2. When $\theta = \theta_1$, the profit is positive. F has no incentive to terminate the project. Neither does M. The project will continue.

If $\theta = \theta_2$, F wants to terminate the project, since $\pi_2 < 0$ and F can reuse the capital elsewhere and earn r. M, on the other hand, would like the project to continue, since with continuation, F gets[8]

$$s_M \pi_2 + w + B, \tag{10}$$

while with termination, M gets w. By assumption 3, w is smaller than (10). Therefore, F and M will re-negotiate. Given that F has complete control rights, the *status quo* of the re-negotiation is termination. Assume for the moment that M's relative bargaining power is δ. Then, resorting to the Nash bargaining solution, the project continues and F expects to get

$$r + (1-\delta)(\pi_2 + B) > 0,$$

i.e., the *status quo* payoff plus a share of the efficiency gain. This implies that

M must make a monetary transfer to F in the amount of

$$r + (1-\delta)(\pi_2 + B) - (r + s_F\pi_2) = (1-\delta)B + (1-\delta)\pi_2 - s_F\pi_2$$

which is the difference between F's payoff after bargaining and the payoff with project continuation without bargaining.

Let us compare this monetary transfer from M to F with the total monetary income that M can actually obtain with continuation, $s_F\pi_2 + w$,

$$s_M\pi_2 + w - [(1-\delta)B + (1-\delta)\pi_2 - s_F\pi_2] = w - (1-\delta)B + \delta\pi_2. \quad (11)$$

By assumptions 1 to 3, expression (11) is negative when θ is small enough. Notice that due to our limited liability assumption, M's payoff cannot be lower than 0.

Here, we need to make a simplifying modeling assumption, i.e., θ is small enough so that (11) is negative.[9] In plain English, we are assuming that F is so tough in his bargaining stance that M has to give up all of monetary income w (but obtains non-monetary payoff B), in order to persuade F to continue the project. In this case, F's payoff is θ which is bigger than the liquidation value of capital r. In summary, when $\theta = \theta_2$, the project continues but M gives up all his wage and keeps control benefit B.

When $\theta = \theta_3$ or $\theta = \theta_4$, F prefers termination unless M can compensate F enough to keep the project continue. From the above analysis, the most M can compensate F is w. Therefore, the most F can expect by keeping the office open is θ_i (i=3 or 4), which is less than the reuse value of capital r , by assumptions 4 and 5. Thus, the project will be terminated. Notice that in the case of $\theta = \theta_3$, this is not a Pareto efficient outcome, since the loss of control right is larger than the benefit of terminating the project.

Proposition 4 (Hard Budget Constraints) When F has complete control rights, a project continues if either $\theta = \theta_1$ or $\theta = \theta_2$. A project is terminated if either $\theta = \theta_3$ or $\theta = \theta_4$.

An intuitive interpretation of this result is that when F has complete control rights, he would terminate the project whenever the net profit is negative. In the case of θ_2, he would force M to give up all wage income w before allowing the project to continue.

We can calculate M's payoff from a project (q_1, q_2, q_3, q_4). In the case of $\theta = \theta_1$, M expects to obtain a payoff of $s_M\pi_1 + w + B$. With $\theta = \theta_2$, under our assumptions, M expects to have only control benefit B but no wage. Lastly, if $\theta = \theta_3$ or $\theta = \theta_4$, M will get only wage w from switching to another job but not B. Overall, M's expected payoff is

$$q_1(s_M\pi_1 + w + B) + q_2B + (q_3+q_4)w,$$

which has to be bigger than w+B in order for M to propose a project. That is, M proposes a project (q_1, q_2, q_3, q_4) only if

$$q_1 s_M \pi_1 \geq q_2 w + (q_3 + q_4) B. \tag{12}$$

Comparing (12) with (7), it is obvious that less than socially desirable number of projects are proposed by M when F has full control rights. Also, when the M's profit share s_M is increased, then M can benefit more from proposing a project and therefore will propose more.

Proposition 5 When F has complete control rights of the firm, unless $q_2 \equiv q_3 \equiv q_4 \equiv 0$, less than socially desirable amount of projects will be proposed by M. Furthermore, a higher s_M induces M to propose more projects.

Given that a project (q1, q2, q3, q4) is approved, we can calculate F's expected payoff in the following way. In state 1, F's payoff is $s_F \pi_1 + r$. In state 2, the payoff is θ_2, since M gives up all wage income in order to ask F to continue the project. For the rest of the states, F's payoff is simply r, from the re-use value of the capital. Overall, F expects to obtain a payoff of

$$E[q_1(s_F \pi_1 + r) + q2\theta_2 + (q3 + q4) r | (12)],$$

which has to be no smaller than r if F is to approve the project. That is,

$$E[q_1(s_F \pi_1 + r) + q_2 \theta_2 + (q_3 + q_4) r | (12)] - r$$
$$= E[q_1 s_F \pi_1 + q_2 (\theta_2 - r) | (12)] = 0.$$

Therefore, when F has complete control rights of the firm, F would always approve the proposed projects. The intuitive reason is that when F has complete control rights, F is insulated from any financial losses *ex post*. This is a direct outcome of our assumption that capital is completely recoverable.

Comparisons between the Two Bench-mark Cases

We can compare several aspects of investment decisions in the two benchmark cases. In particular, we compare the demand for investment, average profitability, and social welfare.

A direct corollary of Propositions 2 and 4 is that the demand for investment is higher if M has complete control rights than if F has complete control rights. This result is independent of the profit sharing rule (s_M, s_F).

Corollary 1 The demand for investment is higher when M has complete control rights than when F has complete control rights, even though the two systems may have different profit sharing rules s_M.

We can also compare the average profitability under these two alternative systems. From Propositions 1 and 3, it is easy to see that conditional on that a project survives after time 2, the average profitability is higher if F has complete control rights. The intuition is that projects with profit θ_3 cannot survive when F has complete control rights, while such projects survive when M is in control. How about the overall expected profitability of all invested projects at time 1? Again, the F control arrangements yield higher expected profits. The intuition is that F does not have discriminating information on the projects and either approves all proposals or none of them. Thus, the set of all invested projects at time 1 is the same as the set of all proposed projects. From the last proposition, we know that if F has complete control rights, the proposes projects have higher quality.

Corollary 2 1) Among all projects that survive two periods, the average profitability is lower in an M control system than that in an F control system. 2) Among all invested projects, the average profitability is lower in an M control system than that in an F control system.

Finally, we can compare the social welfare level associated with these two alternative systems. The M control system makes better time 2 decisions — it does not incur un-necessary loss of control benefit B by only closing *socially inefficient* projects. However, the M control system does a poor job in project selection at time 1 — many socially inefficient projects are proposed at time 1 due to the lack of punishment on M at time 2. The F control system is just the opposite.

We characterize two representative cases for the purpose of comparison. The first case is when the downward risk of the project is very high, i.e., either q_4 is very high *a priori* or θ_4 is very negative. This is true of R&D projects, which are the driving force of growth for industrialized and developed economies. In such cases, most investment projects involve extensive experiments with new technologies. When a new technology is not successful, continuing running the project is costly. Also, the chance of failure is very high compared with projects of copying existing technologies. In this case, the M control system can be very inefficient, since once π_4 is realized F has to compensate M before M agrees to stopping the project. In equilibrium, F may avoid approving any such projects altogether. On the other hand, π_4 does not affect the decisions in the F control system. There are always some socially efficient projects proposed and approved.

The second case is almost the opposite. When q_4 is very small, the downward risk of the project is very low. The closest situation to this case is the early stage of a developing economies or the early days of socialist economies, when technologies can be easily copied from advanced industrial countries. It is unlikely that the return to investment is very low. In this case, since F expects very small chances to have to persuade M to terminate projects, the over-investment problem with the M control case is greatly mitigated. On the other hand, in the F control system, many projects are terminated prematurely when π_3 arises. To summarize:

Proposition 6 1) There exist $\underline{\theta}_4$ and $\overline{q}_4$, such that when either $\theta_4 \leq \underline{\theta}_4$ or $q_4 \geq \overline{q}_4$, the F control system is better than the M control case in terms of social welfare. In fact, in this case, no projects are approved in the M control system, while some socially efficient projects are proposed and approved in the F control system. 2) When $q_4 \to 0$ and $q_3 > 0$, then the social welfare level associated with the M control system is higher than that associated with F control arrangement.

Empirical Evidence and Policy Implications

After examining theoretically the consequences of excessive insider control of the firm, we now turn to empirical evidence on the extent of insider control and its impact on the budget constraint. The evidence is based on two surveys of Chinese state enterprises in the reform era. The first survey covers 769 enterprises from 1980 to 1989 and the second covers 800 enterprises from 1990 to 1994. There are about 600 enterprises belonging to both surveys. For a description of the data set, please refer to Li and Liang (1998).

The first empirical issue is how to measure the effect of insider control on the SBC. In the context of Chinese state enterprises, the amount of excessive bonus expenditure can be used as an index of the severity of insider control, since bonus is the main variable component of compensation to insiders. Although there are regulations that total bonus should not exceed 25 percent of total basic wage, many managers choose to go beyond the official level at the risk of paying fines.

Table 18.1 describes the situation of extra-bonus expenditure in firms with financial losses. The table is from Li and Liang (1998) and is based on the sample of 680 Chinese state enterprises from 1980 to 1994. It shows that among the profit losing enterprises in the sample period, on average, more than 80% of them issued extra bonuses, i.e, bonuses at least 25% of the basic wage bill. For those enterprises, the extra bonus expenditure could explain over 38% of their financial loss. In other words, over one third of financial losses could be avoided had the insiders of those state enterprises be prevented from distributing extra bonuses for themselves. This shows that insider control is a prominent cause of the SBC in Chinese state enterprises.

A related question on insider control is whether those state enterprises which expensed extra bonus and incurred financial loss in the same year were disciplined some way so that next year their bonus level decreased. Table 18.2 from Li and Liang (1998) shows a regression result which is based on the same sample as in Table 18.1. It shows that there were no such indications at all. That is, those enterprises issuing extra bonuses and incurring losses went unpunished. This paints a worrisome picture that insider control is a persistent cause of the SBC.

The second empirical question is what causes or restrains insider control. Obviously, the answer to this question has important and direct policy implications. Table 3 is from Li (1998) which is based on the first survey of 1980-89. It runs a Probit regression on whether a firm increases workers' average compensation in a year while the performance decreases at the same time. It shows that managers appointed by lower level governments (provincial or municipal) rather than elected by workers or appointed by high level of governments are less likely to show this kind of lack of accountability. When the manager doubles as a senior communist party leader in the firm, he/she is also less likely to lack accountability.

TABLE 18.1 Losses due to Extra-Wage Compensation (For Cases of SBC=1)

Year	% of Cases with Ex-bonus >0	N	Mean	St.Dev
1980	74.7	71	19.6	33.3
1981	70.4	100	26.6	52.3
1982	76.0	79	21.4	43.4
1983	73.6	64	21.1	37.3
1984	86.8	66	56.7	116.2
1985	81.8	54	19.1	25.5
1986	85.1	80	26.9	39.5
1987	81.7	49	42.9	75.8
1988	92.3	60	47.0	66.5
1989	97.0	131	48.9	63.3
1990	77.5	79	62.0	82.4
1991	84.7	111	52.8	80.6
1992	84.1	132	43.7	60.2
1993	79.7	122	43.3	64.3
1994	72.2	184	34.3	65.7
All	80.3	1382	38.6	65.3

This indicates an important cause of insider control in transition economies such as China. During transition to market economy, government control of state enterprises is generally weakened. As a result, enterprise insiders took advantage of the opportunity and consolidated or strengthened their control rights. (see Aoki and Kim 1995) In China, granting managerial autonomy to enterprise employees was the key component of enterprise reform during the 1980's. Subsequently, problems of insider control have become very prominent (Fan and Woo 1996, Qian 1996). By early 1990's, insiders' self-dealing and asset stripping had become a wide-spread problem.[10] In

Russia, employees of formerly state enterprises obtained large amounts of shares of existing capital at very low prices and consequently have consolidated their control of their firms.[11] Meanwhile, these insiders have limited liquidity and have to rely upon outside creditors for capital to restructure. Relative to the final capital requirement of the enterprise, the insiders are not sole or even large shareholders but they do possess disproportionately large control rights.

Even in market economies, corporate insiders sometimes obtain excessive control rights. Such situations arise when corporate governance fails, i.e., when owners (investors) lack effective means to discipline or to replace incompetent managers. As a result, insiders are entrenched and are shielded from outside investors' interference. A large number of literature in corporate finance has documented this.[12] A very common cause of weak governance is that outside shareholders are very small and dispersed so that insiders become very powerful in terms of control rights.[13] Also, excessive institutional shareholding can also lead to the failure of corporate governance, since managers of institutional investors may collude with corporate insiders to advance their own interests.[14]

TABLE 18.2 Changes in Excess Bonus after Financial Losses Occur

Dependent Variable:	Growth Rate of (Bonus - 0.25* Basic Wages) in Year t+1		
	Regression 1	Regression2	Regression3
SBC	-3.1	-3.93	3
	(-0.400)	(-0.446)	
RBLOSS*SBC	-	-1.05	-3.13
		(-0.100)	(-0.330)
RBLOSS* (1-SBC)	-	-9.42	-8.47
		(-0.776)	(-0.709)
R-Squared	0.001	0.0012	0.001
# of Observations	3948	3948	3948

Notes: 1) Also included in the regressions are year dummies (1981 – 1994) and industry dummies (for mining, heavy, and light industries). 2) SBC=1 means that the enterprise is in financial difficulty; SBC=0, otherwise. 3) RBLOSS < 0 if bonus < 0.25*BasicWage. 4) All independent variables are in year t. 5) Heteroskedastic-consistent t-statistics are in parentheses. *, **, and *** indicate statistical significance at 10 percent, 5 percent, and 1 percent level, respectively.

TABLE 18.3 The Benefits of Government Control: Reducing Insider Control

Regression I: Does Compensation/Worker Increase When the Enterprise's Real Value-Added Decreases? (Yes=1)}
Probit Regression: N=1494, Freq(Yes)=0.252.

	Central Gov. Supervised	Provincial Gov. Supervised	Lower Gov. Supervised
Appointment	-.316	-.879	-.268
	(-.803)	(-3.10***)	(-3.24***)
Autonomy	-.00396	-.00139	-.00207
	(-1.36*)	(-.474)	(-2.08**)
Incentive	-.00240	-.00867	-.00227
	(-.6318)	(-1.89**)	(-1.65*)
Party	-.141	-.200	-.497
	(-.473)	(-.807)	(-6.80***)
Selection Dummy	.2555	.801	.141
	(.819)	(2.89***)	(1.86**)

Regression II: Does Compensation/Worker Increase Tax+Profit+Interest Is Lower? (Yes=1)
Probit Regression, N=1501, Freq(Yes)=0.260.

	Central Gov. Supervised	Provincial Gov. Supervised	Lower Gov. Supervised
Appointment	-.0827	-.751	-.260
	(-.199)	(-2.78***)	(-3.19***)
Autonomy	-.00429	-.00106	-.00173
	(-1.33*)	(-.404)	(-1.78*)
Incentive	-.00109	-.00667	-.00190
	(-.271)	(-1.60*)	(-1.38*)
Party	-.226	-.197	-.461
	(-.701)	(-.828)	(-6.43***)
SelectionDummy	.254	.627	.142
	(.786)	(2.43***)	(1.92**)

Notes: 1) Appointment is 1 if the director was appointed by the government and it is 0, otherwise; Autonomy is the percentage of the enterprise's output sold to the market; Incentive is the ex ante contractual percentage of marginal profit retention; Party is 0 if the director is also the first- or second- secretariat of the Communist Party Committee in the enterprise and it is 0, otherwise; SelectionDummy=1 if in one or two years, either Appointment=0 or Party=0 and it is 0, otherwise;
2) Please refer to Equation (4) for model specification;
3) T-statistics are in parentheses. *, **, and *** represent 10 percent, 5 percent, and 1 percent significant levels, respectively.

Three policy implications follow the theoretical analysis and empirical evidence. First, the theory shows that the consequence of the SBC is more damaging to economic efficiency in industries facing high uncertainty and volatility than industries with stable return rates to investment. Therefore, policy makers may find it worthwhile to focus on mitigating the SBC problem in the first group of industries. In the Chinese context, they include export-oriented, high-tech, and highly competitive industries. Second, in the long-run, in order to resolve the problem of the soft budget constraint associated with insider control, it is necessary to replace the government as a major stakeholder of the state enterprises by private large stakeholders. Private large stakeholders (e.g. creditors and shareholders) have both the interest and resources to watch for insiders' abusive behavior. Meanwhile, it is necessary to establish institutions of corporate governance, by which private large stakeholders are able to discipline insiders. Third, in the short-run, before large private stakeholders replace the government and institutions of corporate governance are established, an effective means to fight insider control is maintaining a proper degree of government control of state enterprises. In many cases, this indicates that delaying privatization of state enterprises may be called for. Moreover, according to the Chinese experience, local governments' control of state enterprises is more efficient in curbing the tendency of insider control that control of central government. Therefore, a simple and effective approach to reform the state enterprises is decentralization, i.e., delegating the control rights of the state enterprises from the central government to local governments.

Summary

Existing formal theories point out two independent causes of the SBC phenomenon: creditors' lack of information and commitment and politicians' control of the enterprise. In this chapter, we show that there is another cause for the SBC, i.e., excessive control rights enjoyed by enterprise insiders, or, insider control. In such cases, budget constraints become soft and the so-called investment hunger arises. In the early stage of socialism, when the economy was trying to catch up with industrialized countries, the insider control arrangement may be more socially efficient than the outside investors' control. However, beyond that stage, the insider control system is less desirable than the alternative.

Three policy implications are discussed in the chapter. The first is that in order to control the damage of the soft budget constraint, efforts should be focused on enterprises in industries facing high uncertainty and high volatility. Second, the long-run solution for mitigating the soft budget constraint consists of replacing the government by private large stakeholders and establishing institutions of corporate governance. Finally, in the short-run, maintaining a certain degree of government control of state enterprises is an effective means to curb insider control and the soft budget constraint. Of course, such a short-run solution has its costs. As argued by Li (1998), there is a trade-off in the short-run between the cost and benefit of government control of state enterprises.

Appendix

A.1. Proof of Proposition 2

Notice that when $s_M = 0$, given our assumption that control benefit is slightly higher a new project, M proposes any projects. Proposition 2 holds. The following are the non-trivial cases.

Case 1: $0 < s_M \leq -w / \pi_4$

This is the case shown in the text. (6) can be rewritten as

$$q_1\pi_1 + q_2\pi_2 + q_3\pi_3 \geq q_4 (B + \pi_4) / (2 s_M) - q_4\pi_4.$$

Define

$$B_1 = q_4(B + \pi_4) / (2 s_M) - q_4\pi_4.$$

Define $A = q_4 B$, the right-hand-side of (7). Thus, if we can show that $B_1 = A$, then proposition 2 holds. Notice that from Assumption 6, we know that in Case 1, $s_M < \frac{1}{2}$ Therefore,

$$B_1 \leq q_4 (B + \pi_4) - q_4\pi_4 = q_4 B = A.$$

Case 2: $-w / \pi_4 < s_M \leq -w / \pi_3$

Given our limited liability assumption, if the project were to continue with $\pi = \pi_4$ then M would expect to get only B, the non-monetary payoff from control and this is the *status quo* of the re-negotiation. Therefore, when $\pi = \pi_4$, then the project is terminated and M gets $B - \frac{1}{2} (\pi_4 + B)$. Overall, in this case, M's expected payoff is

$$s_M (q_1\pi_1 + q_2\pi_2 + q_3\pi_3) + (q_1 + q_2 + q_3) w + B - \frac{1}{2} q_4(\pi_4 + B)$$

and M proposes a project $(q_1 + q_2 + q_3 + q_4)$ if the above expression is bigger than $B + w$. In other words,

$$q_1\pi_1 + q_2\pi_2 + q_3\pi_3 \geq q_4 (B + \pi_4) / (2 s_M) + q_4 w / s_M.$$

Define

$$B_2 = q_4 (B + \pi_4) / (2 s_M) + q_4 w / s_M.$$

Notice that if $B + \pi_4 + 2w \leq 0$, then $B_2 < A$. Otherwise,

$$2s_M(B_2 - A)/q_4 = B + \pi_4 + 2w - 2s_M B \leq B + \pi_4 + 2w - 2Bw/(-\pi_4)$$

$$= (B + \pi_4)[1 - 2w/(-\pi_4)] \leq 0,$$

where the last step is aided by Assumption 6.

Case 3: $-w/\pi_3 < s_M \leq -w/\pi_2$

Similar to case 2, M's expected payoff is

$$q_1(s_M\pi_1 + w + B) + q_2(s_M\pi_2 + w + B) + q_3 B + q_4[B - \tfrac{1}{2}q_4(B + \pi_2 4)]$$

and M proposes the project if the above expression is bigger than $B+w$. That is,

$$q_1\pi_1 + q_2 s_M\pi_2 + q_3\pi_3 \geq q_3\pi_3 + \frac{1}{s_M}(q_3 w + q_4 w) + \frac{1}{2s_M}q_4(B + \pi_4),$$

whose right-hand-side is defined as B_3. From the definition of this case,

$$B_3 < q_4 w/s_M + q_4(B + \pi_4)/(2s_M).$$

From the proof of case 2, $B_3 < A$, since the current s_M is higher than that in B_2.

Case 4: $s_M \geq -w/\pi_2$

The proof for this case is very similar to that of case 3 and therefore is omitted.

A.2. Proof of Proposition 3

1) $s_M < -w/\pi_4$

Notice that in case 1 of the proof of Proposition 2,

$$B_1 = q_4(B + \pi_4)/(2s_M) - q_4\pi_4.$$

Now that $B + \pi_4 < 0$ from assumption 5, an increase in s_M makes B_1 higher.

This proves part
1) of Proposition 3.
2) $s_M \geq -w/\pi_4$

Let us focus on cases 2 in the proof of Proposition 2. Other cases can be similarly proved.

$$B_2 = q_4 (B + \pi_4) / (2 s_M) + q_4 w / s_M$$
$$= q_4 (B + \pi_4 + 2w) / (2 s_M),$$

which decreases with s_M given the condition in part 2) of Proposition 3.

A.3. Proof of Proposition 5

Rewrite condition (12):

$$q_1\pi_1 + q_2\pi_2 + q_3\pi_3 \geq q_2\pi_2 + q_3\pi_3 + q_2w/ s_M + (q_3 + q_4) B/ s_M$$

and define

$$C = q_2\pi_2 + q_3\pi_3 + q_2w/ s_M + (q_3 + q_4) B/ s_M.$$

Notice that by Assumptions 3 and 4, we have $q_2\pi_2 + q_2w / s_M > 0$ and $q_3\pi_3 > - q_3B / s_M$, since $s_M \leq 1$. Therefore, $C > A$. Also, apparently, an increase in s_M makes C lower. Thus, Proposition 5 is proved.

A.4. Proof of Proposition 6

Part 1): All we have to show is that when π_4 is negative enough, it is no long worthwhile for F to approve any projects. Meanwhile, our analyses show that the F control system can always pick at least the best projects. Without losing generality, we confine ourselves to the case of $s_M < - w / \pi_4$. Notice that B_1 increases in π_4. Therefore, when π_4 is very small, $q_1\pi_1 + q_2\pi_2 + q_3\pi_3$ can be arbitrarily small and s_M has also to be very small. The expected payoff to F from approving a project is:

$$E [s_F (q_1\pi_1 + q_2\pi_2 + q_3\pi_3 + q_4\pi_4) + \frac{1}{2} (\pi_4 + B) | (6)] + r,$$

where the expectation is taken over the updated belief of F conditional on (6), which is satisfied with increasingly low q_1 projects. Eventually, the first term of the above expression is negative, i.e., no projects will be approved by F. The other condition of q_4 can be similarly shown.

Part 2): When $q_4 = 0$ and $s_M < - w / \pi_4$, from the proof of Proposition 2, we know that $B_1 = B_2 = A$, i.e., M's demand for capital is socially efficient. From the proof in Part 1), we also know that F will approve the proposal according to the first-best criteria. There is no efficiency loss at all with the M control system. On the other hand, the F control system still closes the project when $\pi = \pi_3$. This is efficiency losing.

Notes

1. I am grateful to Janos Kornai, Eric Maskin, Andrei Shleifer, and Martin Weitzman for their advice on an early version of this chapter and to the R.R. Shaw Foundation for financial support.
2. See Kornai (1992) for comprehensive discussions on these related issues. See Qian (1993) for a formal model explaining shortage based on the SBC.
3. Mass privatization of state enterprises was quickly implemented in Russia between 1992—94. At the same time, hundreds of small banks were founded during the reform. However, many privatized firms are still heavily subsidized for their financial losses. See Boycko, Shleifer, and Vishny (1993) and World Bank (1995).
4. Qian and Xu (1998) explain the same pattern of technological innovation in centralized and decentralized economies based on Dewatripont and Maskin (1995) theory of the SBC.
5. We intentionally ignore the difference between the managers and workers, since for the current discussion, they share the same interest.
6. For ease of illustration, in the following we assume that s_M is very small so that $s_M \pi_i + w = 0$. For other cases, please see Appendix A1.
7. In fact, so long as M has non-zero bargaining power, all of the following results will still be valid qualitatively.
8. Again, we assume s_M is very small for the ease of exposition. Appendix A1 covers the general case.
9. One can easily check that by keeping a general θ and letting M's payoff be the larger of (11) and 0, the following analyses will still go through and the same results hold qualitatively.
10. According to Li (1994, page 69), Chinese state enterprises lost a total value of $22 billion due to insiders' asset stripping between 1988-1993.
11. See Boycko, Shleifer and Vishny (1993). A report of the Economist (1996) wrote that: "...privatization, which swept Russian industry in 1992-94, has helped less than expected, because it merely strengthened the position of the existing managers by giving them control of a big slice of their firms' equity."
12. For example, see Jensen (1993) for an analysis of failures of corporate governance.
13. Morck, Shleifer, and Vishny (1985) report that when insiders have significant voting rights, the firm's value suffers.
14. See Jensen and Ruback (1983) for a survey of empirical evidence in this regard.

References

Aoki, M., and H. Kim. 1995. *Corporate Governance in Transitional Economies: Insider Control and the Role of Banks*. Washington, DC: The World Bank.

Aghion, P., and P. Bolton. 1992. "An 'Incomplete Contracts' Approach to Bankruptcy and the Financial Structure of the Firm." *Review of Economic Studies* 59(3):473-94.

Bai, C., and Y. Wang. 1998. "Bureaucratic Control and the Soft Budget Constraint." *Journal of Comparative Economics* 26(1):41-61.

Boycko, M., A. Shleifer, and R. Vishny. 1993. "Privatizing Russia," *Brookings Papers on Economic Activities*. Winter.

Dewatripont, M., and E. Maskin. 1995. "Credit and Efficiency in Centralized and Decentralized Economies." *Review of Economic Studies* 62:541-556.

Dewatripont, M., and J. Tirole. 1994. "A Theory of Debt and Equity: Diversity of Securities and Manager-Shareholder Congruence." *Quarterly Journal of Economics* 109(4):1027-1054.

Diamond, D. 1991. "Debt Maturity Structure and Liquidity Risk." *Quarterly Journal of Economics* 106(3):709-737.

The Economist. 1996. "Please Adjust Your Set." April 13, 57-58.

Fan, G., and W.T. Woo. 1996. "State Enterprise Reform as a Source of Macroeconomic Instability: The Case of China." *Asian Economic Journal*.10(3):207-24.

Grossman, S., and O. Hart. 1986. "The Costs and Benefits of Ownership: A Theory of Vertical and Lateral Integration." *Journal of Political Economy* 94(4):691-719.

Jensen, M. 1993. "The Modern Industrial Revolution, Exit, and the Failure of Internal Control System." *Journal of Finance* 48(3):831-80.

Jensen, M., and R. Ruback. 1983. "The Market for Corporate Control: The Scientific Evidence." *Journal of Financial Economics* 11(1):5-50.

Kornai, J. 1992. *The Socialist System: the Political Economy of Communism*. Princeton, New Jersey: Princeton University Press.

_____. 1980. *Economics of Shortage*. Amsterdam, Holland: North-Holland.

Li, D., and M. Liang. 1998: "Causes of the Soft Budget Constraint: Evidence on three Explanations. *Journal of Comparative Economics* 26(1):104-116.

Li,. 1998. "The Costs and Benefits of Government Control of State Enterprises during Transition: Theory and Evidence from China." mimeo, University of Michigan.

Li, Y. 1994. *Zhongguo Xiandai Qiye Zhidu. (China's Modern Enterprise System.)* Beijing: Zhongguo Shanye Chubang Che (China Commerce Publisher).

Morck, R., A. Shleifer, and R. Vishny. 1988. "Management Ownership and Market Valuation: An Empirical Analysis." *Journal of Financial Economics* 20(2):293-315.

Qian, Y. 1996. "Enterprise Reform in China: Agency Problems and Political Control." *Economics of Transition* 4(2):427-48.

———. 1994. "A Theory of Shortage in Socialist Economies Based on the `Soft Budget Constraint.'" *The American Economic Review* 84(1):145-56.

Qian, Y., and C. Xu. 1998. "Innovation and Bureaucracy under Soft and Hard Budget Constraints." *Review of Economic Studies* 65(1):151-64.

Shleifer, A., and R. Vishny. 1994. "Politicians and Firms." *Quarterly Journal of Economics* 109(4):995-1026.

World Bank. 1995. *Russian Federation Towards Medium-Term Viability*. World Bank: Washington, DC.

19

Transparency and China's Aspirations

Hilton Root[1]

If China is to acquire superpower status in the next decade and beyond, it must develop competitive capital markets to fund the nation's gigantic infrastructure requirements. Inadequate information about the credit worthiness of national financial institutions and unpredictable behavior by government are significant obstacles to capital market development.

It is now often the case that the information required for Chinese financial markets to work is known to intermediaries, allowing them to take advantage of their clients.[2] This problem is amplified because personalized networks of power brokers within the party bureaucracy are the main source of an intermediary's credibility, making the quality of the information proffered difficult to evaluate publicly. It is too early to tell what kinds of institutions specific to the Chinese environment will emerge to cope with these uncertainties. Reducing asymmetric information, however, is essential for financial markets to function effectively. When intermediaries are able to overcome the problem of asymmetric information, they can reduce information costs. So far, the measures taken to provide information to sources outside government have subjected the flow of information to political considerations. As long as politics, rather than rules, control the information needed to price financial assets, markets will be unstable as political risks are added to ordinary business risks.

Relationship-Based Trade-Guanxi

To overcome the absence of formal, rule-bound decision making, relationship-based trade (guanxi), has flourished in the People's Republic of China. When a Chinese company seeks U.S. finance, for example, it will emphasize the existence of a power broker in the party who is on the company's management board.[3] The confusion between the interests of the party and the state has been compounded by officials' inability to distinguish their private interests from those of the party. Official directives acknowledge the practice of public security officials acting on behalf of Chinese entrepreneurs disgruntled with their partners.[4]

The extensive involvement of China's military in the nation's civilian economy exemplifies the confusion between private and public roles. Civilian output from China's military plants accounts for 70% of plant production, and civilian contracts bring profits of more than $5 billion yearly and $7 billion in foreign investment.[5] Thus, the West need not fear a military takeover ushering in a return to socialism. The true threat is deepening corruption, as the army attempts to circumvent a new rule subjecting its business empire to audits.

China's financial intermediaries trade on their presumed privileged access to political decisions, which significantly enhances their credibility as deal makers. These intermediaries are in effect private brokers of public information.[6] Secrecy or ambiguity in the rules is essential to their deal-making role. Intermediaries who possess valuable *guanxi* have information about the state, its assets, and the decisions that will determine the performance of those assets. The emergence of networks based on these officeholders has substituted for financial markets. International business groups wanting to do business in China depend on the expertise of these government officials, thus heightening their ability to pursue opportunistically either their own particular interests or those of the party.

Guanxi also shapes real estate transactions, which are often based on contracts of one or two paragraphs in length and do not anticipate the wide range of contingencies or liabilities that owners may incur. The contractual weakness may be surmounted by a public ceremony in which a ranking party official shakes hands with the would-be owner. A photograph often accompanies the contract, implying that, in the case of contract noncompliance, an important official will risk losing face. The consequences of losing face are credible as long as the hierarchy of command is rigorously maintained, but the emergence of rights based on economic power seriously conflicts with rights founded on party discipline.

Philip Tose the chief of Peregrine, an investment firm that has done particularly well in the China market, explains that his formula for success is "to sit down over a cup of tea with the top guy; there isn't documentation; the deal is done."[7] Although this is possible when a company is wholly owned by a single wealthy tycoon or a family conglomerate, deals without documentation are not tenable when the company is owned by shareholders. Thus, Allied Bank, owned by Lucio Tan, a single wealthy tycoon and a crony of the Marcos family, can maneuver successfully in China (i.e., set up China's first private bank), whereas Merrill Lynch or CitiBank would have difficulty entering such deals because they must be accountable to their shareholders. Corporate rules require documented statements of earnings and assets.

The availability of information about government debts, assets, and policies can moderate information asymmetry and thereby reduce interest rates. By contrast, the present system imposes significant liquidity constraints on China's emerging financial markets. At the least, guanxi reduces the liquidity of financial markets and increases interest rates. But there may be graver dangers. Because of the private information possessed by the intermediaries, and because investors lack accurate information about how much debt the system is carrying, the failure of a handful of firms may be read as a signal of massive failure. Thus, uncertainty about some of the nation's intermediaries or firms could produce a default spiral that could jeopardize the entire financial system (Root 1994, Stiglitz 1993).[8]

Futures Markets with Curious Characteristics

China's attempts to develop futures markets reveal considerable foresight, as in the future such markets will be critical to the development of the Chinese economy. Trade in commodity futures markets mushroomed after Li Peng's call in March 1988 for a reform of China's commercial system in which he advocated wholesale and commodity market development to provide allocative, price discovery, and risk reduction mechanisms (Wall 1993:39). A 1990 report further anticipated a possible role for futures markets in the creation of a socialist market economy. Futures markets would provide a mechanism to replace state control over the allocation of commodities and a price discovery function that would help managers move from a planned to a market economy without the guidance of world market prices. The markets would also help state-owned enterprises manage the risks associated with their entry into the market economy.

Of the exchanges that emerged, the metals exchanges did relatively well, with Shenzhen Metals becoming the third largest futures market in the world (Wall 1993:45). A number of Chinese firms also used the markets effectively, including Shanghai Metal Materials Company, which purchases 80% of its metal needs through the markets. As the prices of nonferrous metals became more stable, volatility intensified in agricultural products and building materials markets where traders faced government risks, not market risks. In those markets, where government policies rather than market forces determine prices, *guanxi* structures the sales of goods. Large state-owned enterprises are not "price takers" but trade on a personalized basis; the terms of trade depend on the transacting agents. Establishing futures contracts does little to reduce the fundamental source of risk-government-in those markets." Thus, a basic criterion whereby futures markets might operate effectively was not met.

Outside China, futures markets arose to cover the risks of price changes and marketability, which are borne by an entity that holds property rights in a commodity. Another reason parties enter into futures contracts is to reduce the costs of maintaining stocks where warehousing is a specialized activity. A firm with a disadvantage in warehousing might purchase a series of futures contracts intending to take delivery rather than to warehouse the stocks. Thus, risk and inventory management are the two principal motivations for futures contracts. Futures markets work effectively when property rights are efficiently traded. A clearinghouse usually registers the deals. An investor must maintain a deposit equal in value to the open contracts with the broker. The brokers maintain margin accounts based on the net position of their clients, which ensures against default by either investors or brokers. It is important that quick, low-cost methods of moving orders, providing information, and establishing the creditworthiness of clients exist.

In addition, markets for derivatives depend on liquidity in the underlying physicals that are to be traded. Those who take positions must be sure that they can deal in cash or in spot markets without being subject to a squeeze. Therefore, the market must be liquid enough and broad enough that buyers will be available should players wish to change or sell. Moreover, all players in the market should be equal, meaning that anyone who meets the market's requirements should be able to sell. Brokers should place clients' interests over the brokers' own interests and therefore must not be allowed to take positions until they have terminated all deals requested by their clients. Finally, participants must be sure that property rights conferred by the contracts are secure and transferable and that a system of guarantees is in place to cope with defaults. A third-party referee must exist to ensure compliance with the rules governing the above conditions. Commercial law must be robust enough to deal with the wide range of contingencies that may give rise to disputes.

The Chinese markets lack all the above-mentioned conditions that account for the success of futures markets elsewhere. Property rights do not exist, and prices for most traded commodities are set by the government, not by the market. The process of exchange lacks transparency because the major trades are initially closed-door negotiations. Owing to inadequate transport and warehousing facilities, Chinese markets require excessive spreads, which prevent optimal inventory management techniques from emerging. The control over warehousing and transport allows officials to provide preferential services to firms they control and to create hardships for firms they seek to remove from the market. Unlucky firms may attempt to circumvent these controls by side deals with military cargo carriers. Uncertainty will prevail, however, as long as the government controls warehousing and trucking licenses.

In China, a few large players dominate the cash market and usually conduct trade through relationships. Most are large, state-owned enterprises with monopoly or monopsony power in the particular markets in which they operate. Thus, market squeezing by big traders is commonplace. David Wall (1993:54) reports that "non-competitive advantages usually determine who wins and who loses in China's futures markets." An informal survey reports that "in several major futures markets in China about three-quarters of the participants are consistently losers and the remaining one-quarter are consistently winners" (Wall 1993:58). The spectacular profits these few winners make draw other hopefuls into the markets.

Because regional markets are not integrated, systemic shortages or gluts characterize the economy. *Guanxi*, not open markets, helps firms negotiate these shortages. *Guanxi* allows for overinvoicing by buyers and underinvoicing by sellers, generating a cash margin that is shared among the participants. Commission agents have sprung up to broker the trades. They, not the futures markets, are the key intermediaries for goods in short supply.

Is it possible that Chinese officials do not understand futures markets? Indeed, the absence of fundamentals means that the social benefits from futures trades are limited. Most traders lose money, but this has had little effect on the markets' popularity. The speculators have little to lose because firms use public funds, and people make promises to deliver property they do not own! State-owned enterprises are the biggest group of both producers and consumers operating on the futures and forward markets, but their losses will eventually be compensated by state fiscal subsidies. Their gains could be transformed into perquisites for company management. Because the biggest player is the Ministry of Finance, the markets can be viewed as a perverse form of taxation. The central government gambles against other administrative organs, such as provincial governments and collectives. Nevertheless, the trade in futures contracts proliferates, allowing management to secure private benefits at no risk. Because party bureaucrats keep the winnings, they use, in effect, both stock and futures markets to parlay public assets into private profits.

A concentration of futures trading is generally needed to ensure adequate liquidity in futures markets. In China, by contrast, because of the large number of protected exchanges that emerged, none could provide adequate liquidity. Numerous markets arose because each exchange was established by a central ministry or bureau, which originally administered the production and distribution of the traded products. At the same time, each block or regional government was eager to set up its own futures exchange. In the best of all possible worlds, however, only one market is needed. For example, Japanese bonds are traded in London around the clock. Dissipating the national market into several markets reduces liquidity and increases uncertainty and volatility. The greater the number of players in an efficient market, the more financial liquidity and depth will result.

The price volatility associated with these risks, however, may bring players into the market strictly to speculate. Where markets are small, any given movement has a large impact. But in China different bureaus and agencies all want their own markets over which they have monopoly powers. An economy of sectors and regions emerged whose primary function was to award officials shares of the local economy and the right to collect rents from those who traded in that economy. The development of a labyrinth of local trade and licensing restrictions serves the same function. By creating futures markets, management was able to appropriate the assets of the firms it managed. The development of stock markets followed the same logic.

China's road to a market economy has been paved by the creation of local privileges as the price of coalitional support. Susan Shirk (1990) points out that fiscal decentralization and the creation of special local tax exemptions were the cornerstones of Deng Xiaoping's strategy to build support for reform. The resulting labyrinth of administrative units and procedures and the sheer volume and complexity of loopholes created by preferential policies make it difficult for the central government to coordinate and exercise effective administrative control. The plethora of regulations opened up extensive opportunities for bureaucratic rent seeking. The regulations and the profits thus produced have converted members of the socialist bureaucracy into champions of reform but at great cost. Of the many dangers China faces, a return to communalism and central planning is not nearly as grave as the threat of systemic corruption.

The regulatory labyrinth that has sprung into existence in China allows administrators to garner the assets of would-be entrepreneurs. In fact, a recent study of corruption notes that bureaucratic corruption is concentrated in the local bureaus and licensing offices (Manion 1994). Elaborate licensing requirements allow officials to share in the profits of entrepreneurial activity. For example, licensing officials, using various commercial codes, can prevent firms from acquiring benefits they are entitled to. Bribes are needed to avoid costly delays in obtaining enterprise licenses. Because the relevant regulations are frequently revised to reflect policy reorientations, firms are never sure which standards apply. The economic departments increase the number of permits required so that the gatekeepers oversee a labyrinth of procedures out of which they alone know the way. Entrepreneurs have no choice but to offer bribes because, as Melanie Manion has calculated, the probability of encountering clean licensing officials is below 0.5%. Because applicants for licenses are aware of that probability, they have no choice but to offer bribes if they want to succeed.[9]

The New Corruption: Caught Between Markets and Hierarchies

Until now, the credit of public financial instruments has been confidence in the credibility of party personalities. Today, credit is eroding as a result of leaders' diminished ability to supervise their expanding networks of intermediaries, many of whom operate as government officials in the morning and private businesspeople in the afternoon. Officials frequently manage economic enterprises without resigning their government positions.[10] Business costs have escalated sharply because the vast complexity of intermediaries is without centralized control and supervision. At one time, an information broker was an officeholder monitored by superiors in a clearly defined administrative hierarchy. That is less the case today; the growing complexity of the system of privileges has fragmented ties among officeholders. This fragmentation is one of the dangers in a gradual transition to a market economy, giving rise to the possibility of developing an administratively managed economy like India's, which is designed to enrich the gatekeepers at the expense of both consumers and producers. In effect, China's corruption is becoming systematized into an intermediary form of bureaucratic capitalism, a system well described by the same Steven Cheung who predicted long before anyone else that China would go capitalist.

> Once rights were defined by how highly an individual placed in the administration, and by how many years in the Party. That system has been under pressure from two sources: the spread of economic markets and the rise of provincial privileges to win support for the market system. Although the hierarchy has lost its centralized structure, it has not yet been replaced by pure property rights in the capitalist sense. Instead, an intermediary system has sprung into existence. Finally, there's a third kind of system in which neither property rights nor hierarchical rankings are well-defined. The rights to corruption, on the other hand, are well-defined. This is what I have called the India system: One official is in charge of iadies' handbag imports, another in charge of exchange control, and a third in charge of men's watches, and so on. It is difficult to corrupt efficiently without regulations. In Panarna, corruption rights are so well-defined that Official A makes it his business on Monday, Tuesday, and Wednesday, and Official B on Thursday and Friday, and Saturday, and it is all part of the system (Cheung 1982).

Manion's account mirrors Steven Cheung's analysis:

> Local licensing offices have territorially based monopolies on issuing licenses for enterprises in their localities. Officials in charge of evaluation of application materials can also enjoy a monopoly: in large licensing offices, individuals often specialize in applications for particular forms of enterprise (organized by territorial scope of operation, ownership sector, or economic activity). In smaller offices, applicants in a single queue usually present themselves to officials on a first come first served basis (Manion 1994).

Unlike East Asia's high-performing Chinese economies-Singapore, Hong Kong, and Taiwan-the mainland has failed to draw the distinction between the private and public roles of officials. Deng Xiaoping's son, Deng Pufang, publicly flaunts his entitlement to 5% of the profits of any transaction he brokers on the grounds that he is acting no differently than a CEO in a Western capitalist firm. He is mistaken; his rights to the 5% are defined by hierarchical ranking. The CEO's rights of private property are obtained from competition in the market. The CEO is equal before the law with other citizens; Deng Pufang is not. His share in the new corruption represents the fundamental confusion between property rights grounded in law and hierarchical rights defined by party discipline.

Steven Cheung draws out some of the implications of the mainland's failure, exemplified in Deng Pufang's remarks, to separate political and economic elites:

> Corruption in transition is one thing, corruption as a well-defined rights system is another. The grave danger of the Chinese reform process is that it may get stuck in the middle and become another India! That's the part which I called the passage to India, and that is why from early on I have firmly held the view that gradualism in reform is a silly thing to do.

Cheung implies that only immediate and total liberalization will prevent this new corruption from spreading. If liberalization is introduced before legally defined property rights and the institutions to enforce them, economic actors in China could become dependent on a private mafia, such as those that proliferate in the former Soviet Union, to sustain deals. It seems that gradualism produces one set of ills, the big bang another. The laws to govern a market economy must be introduced so that powerful private interests that thrive on lawlessness do not emerge to block reform later on.

Let us go back to the futures markets to see another dimension of China's transition problem. To reduce speculation, the China Securities Regulatory Commission (CSRC) has closed many illegal markets and has also banned all indexing and currency futures, demanded the registration of all brokers, and prohibited foreign involvement in futures markets. Futures markets, however, still have no national legal framework governing the operation of futures exchanges. Each exchange developed its own regulatory code, supervised by a council and management committee. The industry grew without control, benefiting a few privileged firms and nonstate, informal, illegal brokers. To restructure the industry and reduce the number of exchanges to those carefully supervised by a government representative, the CSRC has resorted to issuing administrative circulars that have State Council (effectively China's cabinet) approval. Because the circulars are not backed by enforceable laws, however, the CSRC can obtain compliance only through the State Council and, by implication, the Chinese Communist Party. The CSRC acknowledged that a lack of a central authority has resulted in an unenforceable national legislative framework.

After most futures exchanges were closed in the spring of 1994, the Shanghai Metals Exchange obtained permission to reopen by putting Yu Guocong, a party veteran, in charge. As Yu explained, "In risky new areas, it's best for the party to be in control" (Kahn and Brauchli 1994:79). Party backing will, it is hoped, restore confidence, but the lack of constraint on party behavior was often the source of uncertainty in the first place. Thus, a vicious circle is established; because the party refuses to submit its authority to a legal framework, it alone can guarantee contracts and enforce rules. The irony is that the party's above-the-law status produced the problem in the first place. The proposed solution does not get to the source of the problem: Who will monitor the party officials who take advantage of their above-the-law status to prey on the profits of the nascent capitalist economy? The centralized controls will concentrate the profits into the hands of a limited few, meaning that the reforms will be resisted and that many regions will allow illegal exchanges and unregistered brokers to continue in operation. For example, it took a year for central authorities to close Szechuan's stock market in Chengdu because of stiff provincial resistance.[11]

Lacking an elaborate legal system, East Asian high-performing economies depend on credible bureaucracies to enforce contracts. Korea, Taiwan, and Japan all ensured that civil service appointments are based on job-related ability and, by the same token, that bureaucrats are constitutionally protected from political meddling so that the bureaucracy could be a neutral partner in development (Campos and Root 1996). In China, by contrast, efforts at civil service reform have been dominated by the party's desire to control personnel management. Viewing itself as the representative of all legitimate social interests, the party objects to judicial or bureaucratic independence. Because China's civil service system includes the top administrators, no distinction is made between political appointees and career civil servants. The party manages the civil service directly, transferring and dismissing civil servants through the nomenklatura system (Burns 1989). The party also directs policy, drafts the rules and regulations on civil service management, and supervises the implementation of personnel policy. To protect bureaucratic neutrality, governments usually separate these functions into agencies that supervise one another but not in China, where membership in the party is a prerequisite for upward mobility in the civil service and where politics heavily influences decision making.[12] Thus, the Chinese civil service can neither play a neutral role in the policy process nor control corruption once it spreads to the top.

Despite more than 700,000 reports of corruption received, only one vice-ministerial-level official was convicted of corruption during the first half of the decade (Burns 1994). Attacks on corruption reflect a power struggle within the party, for no government agency has the power to impose discipline at the problem's source. Patronage and personnel relations, on which civil service appointments depend, make efforts to cleanse the bureaucracy from inside unlikely. By insisting on hegemonic control over personnel, the party has weakened the government's ability to stem moral decay from within. Because the party will not allow any authority to stand above it, external sanctions on party members that abuse their power do not exist. The other Chinese societies (Hong Kong, Taiwan, and Singapore) created corruption control authorities that stand outside political control as a means of stemming corruption. The Control Yuan that supervises official behavior in

Taiwan is an independent branch of the government. Singapore and Hong Kong have both endowed their corruption control boards with autonomy from the civil service (Campos and Root 1996). In China, however, officials can short-circuit corruption investigations by appealing to their protectors in the party hierarchy.

Formal, Rule-Bound Financial intermediation

Chinese officials show considerable foresight when they consider commercializing financial services to create financial depth. While seeking to increase the market capitalization-to-GDP ratio, China must consider that the financing pattern of corporations depends on the firms' legally defined assets, liabilities, and responsibilities. A firm's optimal capital structure depends on an effective legal system. An effective legal system enforces a separation of the economic and political systems, but when the legal system is weak, political risks and business costs are not clearly separated. In the absence of independent legal, regulatory, and supervisory structures in China, it is the political authorities who supervise and enforce the rules of the game. If the fundamental legal requisites of responsible corporate behavior are absent, it should come as no surprise that Chinese managers act opportunistically.

One variable that predicts the capital structure of firms is the character of the property rights regime. Firm-level differences in capital structures within countries arise from the way that agency conflicts are contracted, which in turn is influenced by the legal system. Township-village enterprises arose as vehicles for investment because an absence of explicit property rights prevented direct investments in private enterprises. An ownership structure emerged in which administrative backing compensated for absent property rights. Attracting investment capital from private sources requires that the government commit political capital. In China, an explicit tie to a government entity substitutes for weak property rights.

The observed capital structure of a firm depends on the potential for opportunistic behavior in that firm. The strength of the legal system is a critical variable of that potential, which depends on the extent to which the agent's actions affect value and the extent to which contracts that regulate actions can be written and enforced. Thus, agency costs depend on the firm's technology, financial institutions, and markets; the investors' incentives to monitor; and the legal system (Dernirguc-Kunt and Maksimovic 1994). The composition of a firm's assets determines its ability to limit its opportunistic behavior. Fixed assets usually have collateral value; thus a firm that freely disposes of its fixed assets can issue secured debt, thereby limiting its ability to expropriate the debt holders. Firms with greater amounts of fixed assets, then, will issue more long-term debt than firms with fewer assets (Dernirguc-Kunt and Maksimovic 1994). Liquidity in the economy thus depends on the protection of property rights. For this reason, in countries like the Philippines, the landed elites dominate the market for credit and dictate access to the market for other goods requiring credit because they possess the major source of collateral. The Philippines will not be able to industrialize without the participation of the landed classes. When collateral is weak, monitoring by creditors must be extensive. In Korea and Japan, highly leveraged firms were subjected to extensive guidance by government ministries that allocated credit at subsidized rates. In general, firms with a high ratio of sales to net fixed assets have cost structures requiring more monitoring and are therefore expected to have more short-term debt and less long-term debt.

If the asset structure or property rights of a firm is clearly defined, it can issue stocks. For example, when a closely held firm has a desirable project that requires a large capital outlay, the owner will require a relatively high return to compensate for the risk of a concentrated portfolio. The high-return requirement implies that some relatively profitable projects will go unexploited because owners cannot effectively diversify risk. An efficient stock market, however, allows the owner to diversify project risks so that the project proceeds. In a more dynamic context, the more developed the stock markets, the easier it is for individuals to price and diversify risks, allowing projects to be undertaken that would not otherwise have been feasible. For this reason, countries with more-developed stock markets have financial systems that issue more credit to the private sector as a share of GDP than do countries with less-developed stock markets.[13] The source of new capital needed to finance these additional projects, however, is not necessarily the stock market. Although the stock market may facilitate risk diversification, the firm finances the project through banks and other financial intermediaries. In this case, a more developed stock market would also increase borrowing, in the form of bonds, commercial paper, bank debt, and so forth.[14] If the essential role of financial markets is to obtain and process information, then China lacks all the preconditions of effective capital markets, the most important of which is information transparency.

Because China's Communist Party prefers to stand above the law, the Chinese state has not developed the needed institutions to appropriately monitor its agents. As investors learn that they cannot rely on those financial markets, they will allocate fewer resources to them To reduce the instability of Chinese stock markets, the government has begun cracking down on sources of inaccurate information. The problem is that those who monitor the agents are often beneficiaries of, or partners in, the crimes they monitor. Information brokers behave opportunistically because they are not subjected to a rulebound criterion that is independent of the party.

Getting Stuck in the Transition

The party is losing control of the transition as corruption causes business costs to skyrocket. The causes of this loss of control are political. They began in 1984, when the personnel management of the party was decentralized.[15] and when the Central Committee and other party committees were given nomenklatura authority over only one level down the hierarchy.[16] The hierarchy was thus weakened because it became difficult for the top to be responsible for the activities of those below.[17] At the same time, economic decontrol gave those below the ability to participate in local economic transactions with limited supervision from the center. As power moved away from the hierarchical pattern of the prereform era, bargaining and competition increased and the center lost the ability to certify the actions of the lower level. Once the split between local and central officials emerged-compounded by the rift between reformers and conservatives-the extralegal routines of the past ceased to be effective. Only binding constitutional boundaries can establish rules among the competing power blocs within the party and among regions.[18]

A constitutional basis for independent third-party enforcement of contracts is necessary for the system of impersonal exchange to work. Today, the Communist Party, not the law or the constitution, stands as the ultimate source of authority in China.[19] Investors need assurances that political bodies will not violate contracts or engage in practices that will radically alter the wealth of parties. Achieving third-party enforcement involves major political changes because it means subjecting the party to independent oversight and distinguishing the interests of the party from those of the state. Constitutional reforms to restrain the absolute exercise of political power by the party must be nurtured into existence. Nevertheless, until there is a credible legal system, there is no substitute for the guarantees of central party officials. How to increase the level of impersonal exchange without effective third-party enforcement may become an intractable problem and choke growth.

The latest developments in China's transition to a market economy suggest a fundamental rethinking of the Asian transitional pattern. The risk of gradualism-getting caught between private and political property rights-may postpone the day of reckoning. Gradualism, however, may make a complete transition less likely, allowing an administered market to emerge that allows the gatekeepers extravagant rents. Those rents will ultimately discredit the party, diminish entrepreneurial profits, and discourage capital investment. Great fortunes are still to be made in China, but the speed with which administrative and legal reforms are undertaken will determine how broadly the fruits of future prosperity will be shared.

Transparency and China's Aspirations

The same disclosure issues that handicap capital market development handicap private large scale-businesses. An arbitrary legal environment, tenuous property rights, unpredictable levels of taxation, provincial officials that apply rules capriciously and complex regulatory codes that invite bribery are all reasons why entrepreneurs must minimize exposure to external scrutiny. With limited means to verify company or public debt investors face uncertainty which will make it difficult for strong professionally managed firms to emerge in China.

By monopolizing the information upon which private investment depends, the state will prevent the development of independent large-scale economic organization that can undertake complex manufacturing or long-range research. State run companies have information and authority to engage other state run entities and government agencies, whereas private firms cannot compete with government entities that have access to cheap credit and are supported by the state's coercive authority. Without the institutional capacity to support strong private firms. China's only alternative to an omniscient state will be dependence on direct investment by foreign multinationals in complex manufacturing or technology intensive production. This approach is fine for Singapore, but China's very size and ambitions dictate the need to find a path toward large professionally managed indigenous corporations.

Real industrial prowess will require the strengthening of monitoring institutions. This in turn will require the erection of boundaries between party and government administration. Separating politics from public administration is an essential step towards creating the conditions for information transparency. More publicly available information will support capital-market development and allow the emergence of professionally managed firms not dependent on owner's political connections. So long as economic information is controlled by the party access will be subjected to political considerations, making guanxi critical to success in China. In turn, the size of the market will be limited to those individuals who possess political proximity not enjoyed by competitors while adding political to ordinary business risks.

Notes

1. This chapter is a revised reprint of "Corruption in China: Has it Become Systematic?" which was originally printed in *Asian Survey* 36(8):741-57

2. As markets expand, China requires intermediaries to bring together buyers and sellers and solve the problem of asymmetric information that bedevils asset markets. When specialized intermediaries do their job well, they reduce adverse selection problems between savers and entrepreneurs by transmitting accurate information about investment opportunities. This transmission, however, requires overcoming the moral hazard that arises between the intermediaries and their clients: when intermediaries play a substantial role, they acquire important information about the participants in asset markets. Typically, such intermediaries will have more information about their clients than intermediaries who, without access to such privileged information, offer their clients service of lower value. As a result, clients may not easily change networks or contacts should the intermediary fail to provide optimal services. Because the client's intermediary will undoubtedly be cognizant of this, he can easily take advantage of his client. At present, the moral hazard is only partly overcome because intermediaries

often possess privileged information by virtue of links to government officials. These officials are not explicitly accountable to the legal system. See Stiglitz and Weiss (1995).

3. When Huaneng Power made its pitch to U.S. investors, the presence of the Chinese prime minister's son, Li Peng, on the management board was emphasized. See *The Economist* (1994).

4. One U.S. businessman was detained without charge when his Chinese partner requested the return of his investment in a joint project. The American was held in a detention center run by his partner's brother-in-law after being arrested by his partner's friends. See Rosario (1995).

5. See *Japan Times*. 1995. "Jiang Hits military Corruption." January 9, p. 3.

6. The Chinese Securities Regulatory Commission estimates that five hundred brokerage firms were operating but that only three hundred were registered. See *Financial Times* (1994).

7. See *The Economist* (1994:26).

8. Although the personalized character of the system limits financial liquidity by limiting contracts to personal networks, the present system is efficient, taking into account the Communist Party's preference for giving up as little control as possible. The party does not want to give equity in the state to intermediary bodies that can then broker the nation's debt independent of party control. An alternative might be the creation of a parliament to create equity, but it cedes control of the firm (i.e., the nation's economy) to shareholders, a solution called for by China's National People's Congress. To avoid giving the reforming Central Bank too much autonomy, the National People's Congress called for tightened government supervision. The Central Bank, it argued, should report on issues such as money supply and credit balance to the legislative body to assure effective supervision. To distance itself from provincial-level political interference, the Central Bank is being requested to no longer engage in commercial or policy lending. See *International Herald Tribune* (1994).

9. An additional problem is that entrepreneurs are no longer sure whether a bribe here reduces the need to provide a bribe there. See Shleifer and Vishny (1993).

10. The practice has become so widespread that, in March 1993, Vice Premier Zhu Rongji criticized vice-ministers and deputy bureau chiefs who became managing directors of companies established by their government agencies without first retiring from their positions. See Bums (1989).

11. Instead of laws, administrative policies supervise the market. Administrators are thus able to add additional expenses and uncertainties to the investment environment. However, contracts and economic rights require administrative backing in the absence of explicit property rights.

12. A single cadre personnel file owned by the party moves with a worker from one position to another. Party core groups are organized in most government or mass organizations. The *nomenklatura* system offers further control to the party over all leadership positions. See Bums (1989). In Singapore, where party and bureaucracy are sharply bifurcated, being a member of parliament or a party member is a handicap to promotion within the civil service.

13. Without a stock market in which company shares are openly traded, the value of a company's assets are difficult to price. Stock markets do not replace banks but take a burden off the banks. Firms still finance projects through banks, but the existence of a stock market helps the firm accurately price and diversify risks. A developed stock market would also increase borrowing in the form of bonds,

commercial paper, and bank debt. See Demirguc-Kunt and Levine (1993). For the opposite point of view, see Stiglitz (1994). Equity markets are an extremely costly way of raising funds, as the transaction costs amount to 25% of all new investment.

14. The ratio of deposit money-bank credit to GDP is an indicator of (1) the size of the banks in the economy, (2) the ratio of deposit-money bank credit to bank credit plus central bank credit as an indicator of the importance of banks relative to the Central Bank, (3) the ratio of nonbank financial intermediary assets to GDP as a measure of the importance of financial intermediaries other than banks in the economy.

15. Large-scale corruption emerged in China about 1984 and 1985. See Steven N. S. Cheung, "Economic Interactions: China vis-à-vis Hong Kong," manuscript, School of Economics and Finance, University of Hong Kong, 1994.

16. The center still directly controlled the appointment of key provincial posts but not the lower levels. See Cheung (1994).

17. When the Chinese firm Unipec lost a fortune on its foreign exchange and swap positions, company officials repudiated responsibility. The firm now claims its trading was unauthorized, although carried out by top executives. Lehman Brothers claims the firm made money from foreign exchange trading in 1992 and 1993, but the suspicion is that the profits were used to play financial markets abroad. When assets are traded overseas, their path back to China is difficult to follow. Domestic assets are often converted into foreign assets rather than returned to deal with the liquidity crunch at home. The Japanese have also registered complaints that loans made to Chinese firms are not being paid back. See *The Economist* (1994).

18. "The Constitution still empowers the central government to intervene in local affairs as long as it sees fit, but it fails to provide a clear and authoritative power map." See Cheung (1994:209).

19. Moreover, the party is nominally entitled to approve every decision in every social unit of more than ten people.

References

Bums, J. 1989. *The Chinese Communist Party's Nomenklatura System*. Armonk, N.Y: M. E. Sharpe.

Campos, E., and H. Root. 1996. *The Key to the Asian Miracle: Making Shared Growth Credible*. Washington, D.C.: Brookings Institution.

Cheung, S. 1994 "The Case of Guangdong in Central-Provincial Relations." In *Changing Central-Local Relations in China (Reform and State Policy)*. Boulder: Westview Press

_____. 1982. *Will China Go Capitalist? An Economic Analysis of Property Rights and Institutional Change*. London: Institute of Economic Affairs.

Demirguc-Kunt, A., and R. Levine. 1993. "Stock Market Development and Financial Intermediary Growth: A Research Agenda." *Policy Research Department Working Paper 1159*. Washington, D.C.: World Bank.

Dernirguc-Kunt, A., and V. Maksimovic. 1994. "Capital Structures in Developing Countries." *Policy Research Working Paper 1320*. Washington, D.C.: World Bank.

Economist, "Asian Finance: Survey," November 12, 1994, p. 26.

Financial Times April 11, 1994.

International Herald Tribune, December 28, 1994, p. 13

Kahn, J., and M. Brauchli. 1994. "China's Communists Seek a New Rule: Fearing Irrelevance Party Tries to Inject Itself into Business World." *Asian Wall Street Journal* 19(December 20):79.

Manion, M. 1994. "Corruption by Design: Bribery in Chinese Enterprise Licensing." Manuscript. Faculty of Social Sciences, Lingnan College, Hong Kong.

Myers, R. 1994. "Me Socialist Market Economy in the People's Republic of China: Fact or Fiction?" Manuscript. Hoover Institution, Stanford University.

Root, H. 1994. *The Fountain of Privilege: Political Foundations of Markets in Old Regime France and England*. Berkeley: University of California Press.

Rosario, L. 1995. "Risky Business: Does China-Style Disorder Lie in Store?" *Far Eastern Economic Review* 26(January):20.

Shirk, S. 1990. "Playing to the Provinces: Deng Xiaoping's Political Strategy of Economic Reform." *Studies in Comparative Communism* 23:230.

Shleifer, A., and R. Vishny. 1993. "Corruption." *Quarterly Journal of Economics* 58:3:599-617.

Stiglitz, J. 1994. "The Role of the State in Financial Markets," *Proceedings of the World Bank Annual Conference on Development Economics, 1993*. Washington, D.C.: World Bank.

Stiglitz, J., and A. Weiss. 1995. "Credit Rationing in Markets with Imperfect Information." *American Economic Review* 73:5:912-27.

Wall, D. 1993. "Special Economic Zones in China: The Administrative and Regulatory Framework." *Journal of East Asian Affairs* 7:1:39.

20

Provincial Distribution of Direct Foreign Investment in China: A Pooled Time-Series Empirical Study

Yi Feng with Hui Zhang

Introduction[1]

During 1993-1995, foreign direct investment made up more than 70% of total capital flows to China. The high composition of direct investment in China is, in part, due to China's financial restrictions on its equity market, which compel foreign investors to convert their investment funds — originally committed to China's equity market — into direct investment in the asset market.

Domestic financial liberalization enhances both savings and the efficiency of the banking system in allocating investment funds. It includes the removal of interest rate ceilings, reduction of reserve requirements and desegmentation of financial markets. The essence of domestic financial liberalization is that domestic financial markets could offer investors, both domestic and foreign, more options to invest their money. International financial liberalization implies the relinquishment of government control over the capital account and free movement of capital. However, China's highly regulated equity market has so far provided limited choices for both domestic and foreign capital. In China, transaction costs are not evenly distributed across asset and equity markets. As the government implements policies to promote foreign direct investment, foreign investors in the asset market receive more favorable conditions in the form of tax and tariff benefits, leading to an increase in foreign direct investment. Therefore, domestic financial restriction on the equity market has an indirect positive effect on foreign direct investment in China, as funds intended for investment in equity are converted into direct investment. With the recent financial crises in East and Southeast Asia, the Chinese government has increased its wariness of the flows of short-term funds and will further regulate the equity market to increase its stability. At the same time, it will continue to entice long-term foreign investment in infrastructure build-up, factory installation and equipment acquisition.

This strategy seems to have been confirmed by recent experience in the city of Tianjin, as reported by the China Press (September 14, 1998, A8). From January to August 1998, the number of newly established foreign firms in Tianjin reached 617, which agreed to spend a total of 2.44 billion U.S. dollars as investment. Several characteristics of foreign direct investment in Tianjin in 1998 were summarized as follows. First, foreign direct investment by Southeast Asian nations decreased in Tianjin, while foreign direct investment by Europe, North America and Latin America increased. Take U.S. investors for example. Compared to the same period the year before, U.S. investors' committed capital in Tianjin increased by 25 percent in 1998 and their utilized capital increased by fourfold. Second, the number of projects that exceeded 5 million U.S. dollars rose; the committed capital in these large projects increased by 40% over 1997. Third, the investment in infrastructure projects increased most when compared to others. Fourth, foreign firms added new capital to their existing enterprises in Tianjin. A total of 154 foreign firms committed new capital to their investment, an increase of 90 percent. The increase in the amount of new capital reached 4.5 hundred million U.S. dollars, an increase of 50.5 percent over 1997. The trend and experience of foreign capital acquisition in Tianjin in the context of ongoing Asian financial crises may indicate the robustness of the Chinese capital market, which has important implications for the recovery and resurgence of economies in Pacific Asia in the aftermath of the financial crisis.

This essay studies the determinants of foreign direct investment across China's twenty-one provinces, six minority autonomous regions and three municipalities under direct supervision by the central government. This constituted all thirty political and economic sub-entities on Mainland China until Chongqing, a populous city in Sichuan Province, became a fourth municipality directly under the central government after 1996. The time span is from 1992 to 1996. This study demonstrates that expenditure on fixed capital, the degree of openness of the provincial economy, transport systems, and communications networks encourage foreign direct investment. We also find that wages, indicating labor costs, are negatively related to foreign direct investment. Measuring the availability of relatively inexpensive labor, unemployment is positively related to foreign direct investment. Additionally, the number of employees in the environmental protection sector has a negative effect on the amount of foreign direct investment, suggesting that foreign direct investment and environmental protection may not be compatible in China.

Literature Review

The issue of direct foreign investment is important for at least two reasons. First, developing and former communist countries attach great importance to foreign direct investment (Pomfret 1994; McMillan 1995; Radice 1995) and private investment (Riker and Weimer 1993) as the very first step toward stimulating their economies. Second, recent research has suggested that the investment share in Gross Domestic Product (GDP) has a positive effect on output growth (Kormendi and Meguire 1985; Barro 1989, 1997; Levine and Renelt 1992; Feng 1997) and that domestic private investment or foreign direct investment in low-income countries is crucial to their economic development (Khan and Reinhart 1990; Firebaugh 1992; Borensztein, Gregorio and Lee 1994). For former Eastern European Communist countries, foreign direct investment is an essential component in their political and economic transformation to democracy and capitalism (Radice 1995).

Foreign direct investment has been identified as a major stimulant for economic growth. For instance, in comparing the effects of domestic and foreign direct investment, Firebaugh (1992) finds that, though homegrown capital outperforms imported capital in generating economic growth, both have a positive impact on the economic growth of the recipient country. By contrast, Borensztein, Gregorio and Lee (1994) suggest that foreign direct investment is an important vehicle for the development and proliferation of technology, contributing relatively more than domestic investment to growth. Amirahmadi and Wu (1994) link the shortage of foreign investment to economic decline. The acquisition and utilization of foreign capital are especially important for capital-scarce countries with accelerating economic growth. To create conditions favorable to the attraction and accommodation of foreign capital, it is essential to first identify these conditions so that relevant polices can be devised accordingly.

Some cross-country analyses establish that bilateral political or security relationships, as a consequence of international conflict, may improve or impede economic relations, including trade and foreign direct investment (e.g. Nigh 1985; Gowa 1994; Feng 1994). Oneal (1994) finds that foreign direct investment by the United States has performed better in developed democracies, though the rates of return may have been higher in autocracies. Among other national characteristics, cross-country studies of foreign direct investment have demonstrated that extra-constitutional government change, strikes and riots have negative impacts on domestic or international private investment (e.g. Schneider and Frey 1985; Lucas 1993; Chen and Feng 1996). The results in Amirahmadi and Wu (1994) indicate that the level of economic development, credit rating, the technological infrastructure, the institutional environment, and political stability are among the factors conducive to foreign indirect investment. By contrast, other studies of foreign direct investment focus on sub-regions within a country, rather than cross-country analysis. For instance, Carlton (1984) and Coughlin, Terza and Arromdee (1991) examine the state characteristics and location of foreign direct investment within the United States. Little (1978, 1983) and hUallacháin (1985) investigate the locational choice of foreign investors in a number of geographical regions of the United States. Using counties as the unit of analysis,

Mason and Howell (1992) study the pattern of Japanese investment in the United States. Williams and Brinker (1994) conduct a survey analysis of decisions by foreign firms located in Tennessee. The advantage of within-country study lies in the exclusion of extraneous effects which may be important only when compared to other nations. In other words, within-country analysis automatically controls for political variables which tend to be unique and have significant variation only at a national level. For instance, under the circumstances of the diplomatic relationship between the United States and China in 1989, investment by the former in the latter decreased among other economic transactions and cultural exchanges between the two countries. However, it is plausible that the relative distribution of American investments in different regions of China remains independent of the foreign relations between the two governments. Once politics is addressed at the national level, factors specific to these sub-national entities — rather than international politics — are likely to determine the relative amount of foreign capital across sub-regions. Isolating and excluding the influence of international politics, this study adopts the within-country approach to investigate the economic determinants of foreign direct investment in China's thirty provinces, autonomous regions and municipalities over the period of 1992 through 1996.

Regional Patterns of FDI in China

Foreign investment in China has taken a quantum leap since economic reform was initiated in 1978. Two views have been offered to predict the prospect of foreign direct investment in China. Kamath (1990) argues that the policy of the Chinese government to attract foreign investors is doomed to fail, as its centralized institutions and hierarchical decision-making processes will negate any positive effect of foreign direct investment in terms of productivity and technology transfer. By contrast, Pomfret (1994) maintains that these undesirable factors can be reduced or modified because China's economic reform is a dynamic and broadly accommodating process that responds to the emerging problems related to foreign direct investment. Pomfret (1994) demonstrates that the Chinese government has made substantial changes in domestic institutions in order to attract and accommodate foreign direct investment. The data presented in Wei (1995) seems to support the latter view on the prospect of foreign direct investment in China. The amount of annually realized foreign direct investment was $3.49 billion in China in 1990; it rose to $4.37 billion in 1991, $11.20 billion in 1992 and $25.76 billion in 1993. Given that the policy of the Chinese government to attract and accommodate foreign direct investment has been generally successful, it would be interesting to uncover particular factors that contribute to the increase of foreign direct investment in China. Such findings will not only help explain China's ability to obtain and absorb foreign capital, but will also indicate policy areas that require improvement so that more foreign capital can be acquired.

China's State Bureau of Statistics reports foreign direct investment in both contractual value and realized value. While the former indicates the size of the investment contemplated by the investor at the time the contract is approved by the Chinese authorities, the latter is the amount of investment that has actually been made in the calendar year. As the investor's future investment is not constrained or bound by the contract (which only shows an intention to invest), the difference between the contractual value and realized value of foreign direct investment may be substantial.

FIGURE 20.1 FDI Inflows across Province in 1996

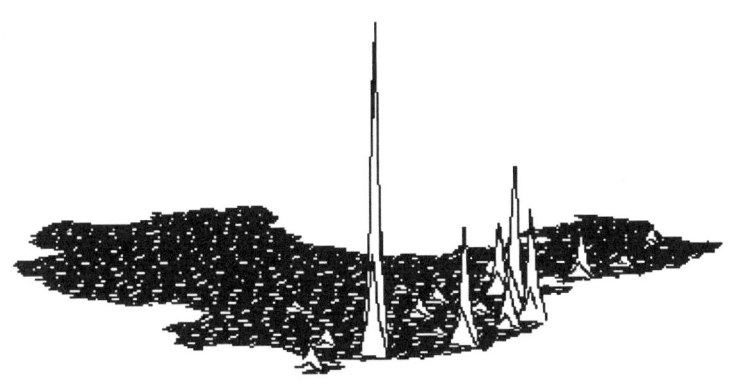

Foreign direct investment usually takes the form of equity joint ventures, contractual joint ventures, wholly-owned foreign firms, and joined explorations. In China, foreign investment also involves loans and "other foreign investment" (the term used by the State Bureau of Statistics). The former includes loans from foreign governments, international financial institutions such as the World Bank and private foreign banks, as well as export credits and purchases of stocks and bonds. The latter comprises leasing and compensation trade in addition to export processing and assembly. Since 1992, the State Bureau of Statistics has combined "other foreign investment" with foreign direct investment in its statistical yearbook. Therefore, foreign direct investment (FDI), as studied in this chapter, includes both foreign direct investment and the category of "other investment" as defined above.

Over the years, coastal areas have received a large proportion of foreign investment in China. As reported in the Appendix and Figure 20.1, the top ten provinces or municipalities (except Beijing, the national capital) all lie on the ocean (Guangdong, Jiangsu, Fujian, Shanghai, Shandong, Tianjin, Liaoning, Zhejiang, Beijing, and Hebei). The only coastal province that does not make the top ten list is Hainan, a province established in the 1980s. The poor performers in attracting foreign capital are those located in the inner area of China or the Eurasian continent, such as Shaanxi, Jiangxi, Yunnan, Gansu, Shanxi, Inner Mongolia, Guizhou, Xinjiang, Ningxia, and Qinghai. There is no FDI data on Tibet. However, it is certain that if the data were available, Tibet would belong to the poor performer group.

In terms of the number of FDI establishments, as reported in Column 2 of the Appendix and Figure 20.2, the coastal provinces still have a dominant advantage in the numbers of firms which absorb and utilize foreign capital. The ten provinces or municipalities with the largest number of firms set up by foreign investors, from most to least are: Guangdong, Jiangsu, Shandong, Fujian, Shanghai, Liaoning, Zhejiang, Beijing, Tianjin, and Hainan. The provinces that have the lowest number of foreign firms are inland: Tibet, Qinghai, Ningxia, Guizhou, Gansu, Inner Mongolia, Yunnan, Shanxi, and Shaanxi.

FIGURE 20.2 Number of FDI Firms across Province in 1994

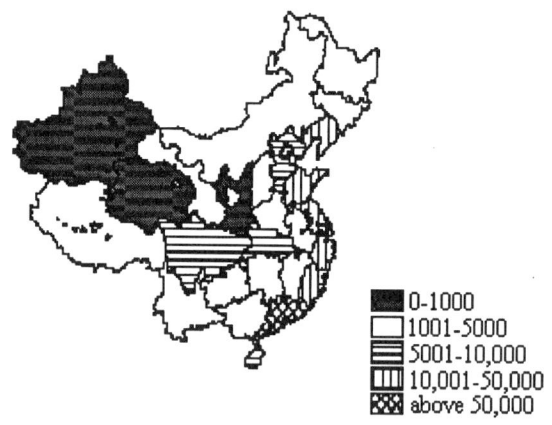

Column 3 of the Appendix is the average annual growth rate of foreign direct investment over the period 1992-1996. The inland provinces have increased their FDI amounts by a large margin. For instance, the average growth rate of FDI during this period was 990 percent for Gansu, 810 percent for Ningxia, 390 percent for Inner Mongolia, 110 percent for Shaanxi and Anhui, and 100 percent for Sichuan. Because their initial levels of FDI were low, these high growth rates have not enabled the hinterland to catch up with the coast. The two coastal units that have maintained an average annual growth rate above one hundred percent are Shanghai (175 percent) and Tianjing (157 percent), followed by Zhejiang (93 percent) and Hebei (85 percent). As these provinces started with a high volume of FDI in the early 1990s, growth rates like these imply a tremendous increase in the amount of

FDI. Column 4 of the Appendix presents the average annual growth rate for FDI firms. Some inland provinces have again shown good progress. Of them, the annual growth rates in Gansu, Yunnan, Xinjiang, Guizhou, and Ningxia have all reached 50 percent. By comparison, Shanghai is the only one of the coastal units that has reached this level. The high growth rates in FDI for some coastal places, however, do not mean that these places are high performers in attracting FDI, given their potential. As the analysis of this study will indicate, despite their levels of FDI, some of these coastal provinces have not lived up to their potential to attract FDI and therefore, are actually low performers. By contrast, despite their low levels of FDI, some inland provinces are high performers, as they have attracted more FDI than expected on the basis of their potential.

Determinants of FDI across China's Provinces

For several reasons this study focuses on the domestic economic determinants of foreign direct investment—excluding other dimensions. Regardless of its impact on the investing country or the recipient country, international conflict (bilateral or multilateral) should not be a very important concern when it comes to sub-national regional distribution of foreign direct investment. Given the level of a country's foreign capital flow, which may be determined by the political and economic relations among the investing and recipient countries, the sub-national regional distribution is mainly conditioned upon domestic economic factors, which vary from region to region, province to province.

Under certain circumstances, the central government may impose restrictions on the regional distribution of foreign investment, based on political considerations. One example of non-economic considerations is the government reducing foreign direct investment or prohibiting it in a certain region for fear that it may significantly increase income disparity (which can prove deleterious to political regime stability) or for reasons of national security. Whether or not the central government adopts such non-economic criteria is determined by country-specific and time-specific variables. For the period of time under study, the Chinese government, while perhaps trying to encourage investment in some provinces for reasons of equity and stability, did not seem to impose region-specific restrictions based on domestic or international political considerations. In addition, political stability is relatively homogenous across provinces and regime type is a constant nationwide. Therefore, the following analysis investigates the domestic economic determinants of foreign direct investment, which vary from province to province in China.

1. *Level of economic development.* The size of the economy is a major determinant of foreign direct investment. As observed in Wei (1995), FDI is largely a phenomenon among developed countries. The developed

countries accounted for 97 percent of all FDI outflows in the 1980s while accounting for 83 percent of inflows in the 1985-1990 period (Wei 1995). Even among developing countries, those with higher income receive more foreign direct investment than others. The newly rich nations of the developing world in Pacific Asia received more than half of all the FDI which flowed into less developed countries in 1989; of the $30 billion or so of FDI that went to all developing countries, $17 billion went to Pacific Asia. The size of the economy is a broad indicator of a nation's level of economic development. For instance, higher GDP per capita indicates a healthier national economy and brighter prospects for profits, thus attracting more foreign investment (Schneider and Frey 1985; Coughlin, Terza and Arromdee 1988; Mason and Howell 1992). By contrast, a depressed economy leads to a decline in foreign direct investment (Amirahmadi and Wu 1995).

2. *Capital expenditure.* Domestic capital investment is positively related to foreign direct investment for a couple of reasons. First, an increase in fixed domestic capital formation may lead to better facilities that help relax production constraints so that productive capabilities can be strengthened. Second, a high level of domestic fixed capital accumulation in the form of equipment acquisition and plant installation may be correlated with both a general improvement of the investment environment and political stability favorable for long-term growth. Foreign direct investment becomes a better investment option when the increase in physical capital improves production potential and signals long-run political or financial stability.

3. *Labor cost.* One of the reasons that foreign direct investment is initiated is that inexpensive labor can be utilized abroad, decreasing the cost of production and increasing the profit margin. Bartik (1985) finds that higher wages were a negative determinant of the probability of locating a new branch plant in a state; Luger and Shetty (1985), Schneider and Frey (1985) and Coughlin, Terza, and Arromdee (1990) all identify a similar effect on foreign direct investment of labor cost. Little (1978) finds that wage differentials across states are more important for foreign than domestic investors. By contrast, Glickman and Woodward (1987) do not find any significant effect of wage differentials on employment growth of foreign owned firms across states, and Mason and Howell (1992) find that Japanese firms tend to select their locations in states where wages are relatively high. In a recent study, Lucas (1993) identifies the cost of labor as a highly negative factor for foreign direct investment in Pacific Asian economies, except Taiwan.

4. *Unemployment.* In connection with wages, the unemployment rate is another variable indicating labor cost. As it reflects a pool of potential workers, the unemployment rate is likely to be positively related to foreign direct investment (Coughlin, Terza and Arromdee 1990; Mason and Howell 1992). In China, unemployment has been kept low for

the sake of political stability (Feng 1997). The cross-province variation of unemployment, however, reflects the degree of relative availability of low-cost labor. If the cost model of multinational corporations is correct, there should exist a positive relationship between unemployment and foreign direct investment in China.

5. *Exports and imports.* Amirahmadi and Wu (1994) point out that liberalization of economic policies is conducive to foreign direct investment. The degree of openness (often measured by the percentage of exports and imports in a nation's Gross Domestic Product) is positively associated with the level of liberalized economic regimes, including trade policies. An open economic environment is consistent with decentralization, deregulation and relaxation of state control, all of which are instrumental in developing both assurance and expedience to foreign investors. Lucas (1993) finds that export income is positively related to foreign direct investment in seven Pacific Asian countries. By contrast, Levine and Renelt (1992) show that all findings using the share of exports in GDP could be almost identically obtained using the total trade or import share. Thus, cross-country studies that use export indicators should not be interpreted as studying exports *per se*, but rather as more broadly defined trade.

6. *Transportation and communications.* The regional transport system and communications network are highly important for international investors, as the start-up and expansion of foreign-owned firms depend upon such facilities. Bartik (1985) presents empirical evidence showing a positive connection between highways and new branch plants. Root and Ahmed (1979) find that commerce and the infrastructure, proxied by the average percentage of a country's gross domestic product attributable to wholesale and retail trade, transport and communication, are critical for nonextractive direct foreign investment. The two studies seem to confirm the view that countries actively building infrastructure facilities are in a better position to acquire foreign investors than others.

7. *Environmental protection.* Economic growth and foreign direct investment are not always consistent with a nation's goals for long-run development. For instance, short-term growth may be achieved at the cost of natural resources, as the investment decisions of foreign business interests may not be subject to the long-term concerns of the recipient country. In addition, environmental protection normally implies constraints on certain economic activities, such as industrial practices that generate toxic emissions. Therefore, a negative relationship between environmental protection and foreign direct investment can be stipulated.

Other factors affecting cross-regional foreign direct investment may include unionization and local taxes. Contrary to the hypothesis that unionization reduces foreign direct investment, Coughlin, Terza and Arromdee (1990) find that higher rates of unionization are related positively to foreign direct investment. They tentatively suggest that this surprising finding results from an improvement, stemming from unionization, in the productive efficiency of manufacturing. The effect of local taxes on foreign direct investment is not statistically significant in the literature (e.g. Carlton 1983; Coughlin Terza and Arromdee 1990; Mason and Howell 1992). While unionization and taxation may be theoretically interesting in a country where political power is shared with local governments and the government does not try to maintain its political control of union activities (such as the United States), these variables may not make much sense in a nation like China, where local taxation has just been emerging and unions are the government's grassroots organs.

Statistical Analysis

The data used in this essay to test the determinants of foreign direct investment are all from the *China Statistical Yearbook* compiled by China's State Bureau of Statistics, except for the data on trade obtained from *China's Provincial Statistics* by Hsueh, Li and Liu (1993). The Yearbook was first published in 1982, but the method of data collection and the standard of variable selection by the Bureau have changed over the years. To maintain a basis of comparability over years, we focus on the time series from 1992 through 1996. The data on foreign direct investment, broken down to the provincial level, is available from 1985 to 1991. Since 1992, foreign direct investment has been combined with "other foreign investment," as defined in Section 1. The data on the number of foreign-owned firms, broken down to the provincial level, begin in 1992. The complete time series for some of the other relevant variables for statistical testing, such as Gross Domestic Product (GDP) and the unemployment rate, only begin in the early 1990s. This study focuses its statistical examination on the period of 1992 through 1996 for the thirty provinces, municipalities and minority autonomous regions.

The dependent variables are the amount of foreign direct investment and the number of foreign-owned establishments. The independent variables are selected in accordance with the discussion of the determinants of foreign direct investment in Section 3. They include real Gross Domestic Product per capita (*GDP*), real expenditure on fixed capital (*INVEST*), the average wages (*WAGES*), the unemployment rate (*JOBLESS*), exports and imports as a percentage of GDP (*TRADE*), kilometers of roads adjusted for the area of the province (*ROAD*), number of telephones adjusted for the population (*PHONE*), and the number of employees working in environmental protection agencies as a ratio to population (*ENVIRON*).

As in Coughlin, Terza and Arromdee (1990) and Wei (1995), a linear specification of natural logarithmic form is adopted:

$$\log(FDI_{it}) = \alpha_i + \beta_1\log(GDP_{i,t-1}) + \beta_2\log(INVEST_{i,t-1}) + \beta_3\log(WAGES_{i,t-1})$$
$$+ \beta_4\log(JOBLESS_{i,t-1}) + \beta_5\log(TRADE_{i,t-7}) + \beta_6\log(ROAD_{i,t-1})$$
$$+ \beta_7\log(PHONE_{i,t-1}) + \beta_8\log(ENVIRON_{i,t-1}) + \varepsilon_{it}$$

where subscript i stands for province, municipality or minority autonomous region, t indicates time, namely year, and ε is the error term. As discussed in the third section, the expected signs of the parameter estimates on the independent variables are presented in Table 20.1.

TABLE 20.1 Expected Signs of Independent Variables in a Parametric Model

Independent Variable	Parametric Sign
Real Gross Domestic Product per capita	+
Real expenditure on fixed capital	+
Average wages (adjusted for inflation)	-
Unemployment rate	+
Exports and imports as a percentage of GDP	+
Road length adjusted by area	+
Number of telephones adjusted by population	+
Number of employees in environmental agencies adjusted by population	-

There are a total of 30×5=150 observations for thirty cross-sections and four years, among which there are ten missing values in the estimation of FDI flow and nine missing values in the estimation of FDI firms: Tibet has neither the data on the amount of foreign direct investment nor the data on trade for all five years; Xinjiang does not have FDI data for 1992; Qinghai does not have trade data for 1989; Hainan does not have trade data for 1985 and 1986. In order to alleviate the reverse causality problem, all the independent variables take a one-year lag t-1, except $TRADE$, which assumes a seven-year lag since the data for trade volume broken down to the provincial level is only available for the 1978-1989 period (Hsueh, Li and Liu 1993).

Ordinary-least-squares (OLS) estimation is used to test the statistical model. Autocorrelation may not be a serious concern, as there are only five time-series points for each cross-section. Heteroscedasticity arising from cross-provinces tends to inflate the true standard error for the parameter estimate, thus rendering the latter statistically less significant than it is in reality. Certain statistical methods, such as Fuller-Battese (1974), Parks (1967) and Da Silva (1975), have been designed to correct for autocorrelation, heteroscedasticity and contemporaneous correlation among cross-sections. The major problem in using these methods lies in the assumption that the covariance matrix is correctly diagnosed, which is not practicable. Beck and Katz (1995) show that using one of the methods (i.e. the Parks method, which assumes first-order autocorrelation with contemporaneous correlations between cross sections) can lead to a serious over-fitting problem, making it more likely to obtain a "statistically significant" parameter estimate. They also demonstrate that the statistical result from Ordinary-Least-Squares (OLS) estimation is robust, and therefore recommend the use of OLS estimation on time-series, cross-sectional data. Given the implications concerning the time-series and cross-section errors, the results we obtain in this study tend to be conservative. The error term structure of the data here implies that the parameter estimates from the OLS method may tend to have a larger standard error than the true one, making it more likely to reject the null hypothesis of no statistical effect. In Table 20.2, ***, **, * indicate that the parameter estimate is statistically significant at the 0.01, 0.05 and 0.10 level, respectively, all in a one-tail test. Regressions, using the model as specified above, are run on two dependent variables: the flow of foreign direct investment and the number of foreign-owned firms.

As shown in Table 20.2, for the estimation of both the amount of FDI and the number of FDI firms, all of the signs for the parameter estimates are as expected given the earlier discussion on determinants of foreign direct investment. Real GDP per capita in Column (1) is not statistically significant, though it has the expected positive sign.

Expenditure on fixed capital is found to be a major determinant of foreign direct investment in China. As noted earlier, investment in physical capital may indicate the friendliness of the investment environment, including political stability and government capacity. When committing capital to a country, foreign investors may study the patterns and trends of domestic investment and follow the activity of domestic investors.

Like GDP per capita and domestic physical capital formation, the openness of the provincial economy is a good indicator of foreign direct investment. The open economy may indicate a high degree of economic liberalization, generally favorable to foreign direct investment as well as international trade. In addition, as noted in Section 1, foreign direct investment as operationalized in the data source also includes leasing and compensation trade, as well as export processing and assembly, which leads to a positive correlation between trade and foreign direct investment as defined here. Because a seven-year lag is adopted for *TRADE*, the reverse effect of foreign direct investment on trade is significantly reduced.

The transport system and communications networks — as indexed by the length of roads adjusted by the provincial area and the number of telephones adjusted by the provincial population — are consistently significant. The better the transport infrastructure and the more telephones, the larger the foreign direct investment.

Concerns about labor cost appear to characterize the decisions of foreign investors. Wages, indicating labor cost, are found to be negatively related to foreign direct investment. Similarly, it is found that unemployment, indicative of the availability of labor, is positively related to foreign direct investment. Additionally, the number of employees in the environmental protection sector is negatively related to the amount of foreign direct investment, suggesting that foreign direct investment and environmental protection may not be compatible in China.

TABLE 20.2 Regression Results, 1992-1996

	(1)	(2)	(3)	(4)
Independent Variable	FDI Flow	FDI Firms	FDI Flow (weighted by pop)	FDI Firms (weighted by pop)
Intercept	10.468***	8.616***	-0.029**	-0.023**
	(1.989)	(1.390)	(0.017)	(0.012)
GDP	0.070	0.034	1.530***	1.289***
	(0.276)	(0.193)	(0.307)	(0.221)
INVEST	1.304***	0.957***	0.491**	0.138
	(0.288)	(0.201)	(0.259)	(0.187)
WAGES	-0.064***	-0.023*	-0.083***	-0.048***
	(0.020)	(0.014)	(0.024)	(0.017)
JOBLESS	0.167	0.175*	0.309**	0.241***
	(0.020)	(0.014)	(0.024)	(0.017)
TRADE	0.816***	0.550***	0.575***	0.241*
	(0.151)	(0.105)	(0.231)	(0.165)
ROAD	0.576***	0.520***	0.494***	0.669***
	(0.118)	(0.079)	(0.125)	(0.087)
PHONE	0.629***	0.276**	1.100***	0.646***
	(0.188)	(0.132)	(0.274)	(0.198)
ENVIRON	-1.131***	-0.501***	-1.868***	-0.739***
	(0.289)	(0.202)	(0.430)	(0.310)
Adj. R^2	0.841	0.857	0.920	0.935
σ	0.810	0.566	0.021	0.015
N	140	141	140	141

As it is likely that heteroskedasticity exists in the data, we use population to weight all variables in the model to conduct a Generalized Least-Squares analysis. The results are reported in Columns (3) and (4). They corroborate the findings in (1) and (2) and improve the precision of the estimates. GDP has become statistically significant. A higher level of GDP per capita leads to a higher level of foreign direct investment. GDP per capita is a broad indicator of social and economic development. It is substantially correlated with "the degree of literacy, the size of the middle class, the school ratio, and the extent of modernization. All of these factors were hypothesized to attract foreign investment" (Root and Ahmad 1979, 762). Therefore, foreign direct investment tends to go to the provinces where the level of social and economic development is relatively high.

Columns (3) and (4) also reveal some nuances between the amount of FDI and the number of FDI firms. Investment in fixed capital and trade are better explanatory variables for the amount of FDI than for the number of FDI firms. Unemployment is a better indicator for the number of FDI firms than the amount of FDI. As the flow of foreign direct investment is biased toward larger investors and the number of foreign-owned firms is biased toward smaller investors, smaller foreign investors may be sensitive to labor cost as indicated by unemployment, and larger investors to the degree of domestic investment and provincial international trade. Overall, the variables previously identified are quite robust across the four regressions.

Table 20.3 reports the standardized coefficients for Column (3) and Column (4), which indicates the change in the standard deviation of the dependent variable, given the change of one standard deviation in the independent variable. As the standard coefficient is based upon the variation of both the dependent and independent variables, as well as the parameter estimate, the standardized coefficient reflects the usefulness of an independent variable in estimating the change in the dependent variable. *GDP* and *PHONE* appear to be the most important variables for both the amount of FDI and the number of FDI firms. A healthy general economy and good facility of telecommunications seem essential for the accumulation of FDI. With respect to labor cost, where wages are important for the amount of FDI, unemployment is for the number of FDI firms. Additionally, compared to the number of FDI firms, the amount of FDI is sensitive to the change in fixed capital investment, international trade and environmental protection, with their standardized coefficients doubling those for the number of FDI firms.

TABLE 20.3   Standardized Coefficients

Variable	FDI Amount	FDI Firms
Intercept	0.000	0.000
GDP	0.818	0.860
INVEST	0.136	0.048
WAGES	-0.337	-0.244
JOBLESS	0.074	0.137
TRADE	0.270	0.141
ROAD	0.216	0.371
PHONE	0.852	0.624
ENVIRON	-0.194	-0.096

Table 20.4 makes use of the statistical analysis of Column 3 in Table 20.2 to study the relative performance of the provinces in FDI acquisition. The average of predicted values of the dependent variable for the five years is calculated against the average of observed values of the dependent variable for the same period of time. The average residual, which is the difference

between the averages of the observed and predicted values, indicates whether a province on the whole has acquired the FDI amount it should have, based upon its potential as indicated by the independent variables. The results are both similar to and different from Broadman and Sun's (1997) cross-province study of FDI in China in 1992. Hainan, Tianjin, Fujian, Shanxi, Jilin, Henan, and Shaanxi are over-performers. The levels of FDI in these provinces have exceeded the levels predicted by the model; they have acquired more FDI than their potentials would suggest. By contrast, Shanghai, Zhejiang, Beijing, Ningxia, Hebei, Yunnan, Anhui, and Inner Mongolia are under-performers. They have acquired less FDI than their potentials would predict. The residuals for the other provinces are within the range of [-0.005, 0.005].

TABLE 20.4 Performance of FDI Acquisition

Under-performing		Over-performing	
Province	Residual	Province	Residual
Shanghai	-0.024	Hubei	0.001
Zhejiang	-0.018	Guangdong	0.001
Beijing	-0.015	Jiangxi	0.001
Ningxia	-0.014	Jiangsu	0.002
Hebei	-0.012	Guizhou	0.002
Yunnan	-0.012	Qinghai	0.005
Anhui	-0.009	Shandong	0.005
Inner Mongolia	-0.008	Hunan	0.005
Heilongjiang	-0.005	Shaanxi	0.007
Liaoning	-0.004	Henan	0.008
Gansu	-0.003	Jilin	0.008
Xinjiang	-0.002	Shanxi	0.009
Sichuan	0.000	Fujian	0.011
		Guangxi	0.012
		Tianjin	0.020
		Hainan	0.074

The only province that is a high performer here, but a low performer in Broadman and Sun's (1997) study is Shanxi. This province is well endowed in coal and iron and has a well-educated labor force. Its FDI annual inflow has increased from $54 million in 1992, the year which Broadman and Sun (1997) studied, to 138 million in 1996. Shanghai, Zhejiang and Beijing are under-performers. There is still room for increasing FDI inflow in these provinces or municipalities. Broadman and Sun (1997) ascribe Shanghai's shortfall in acquiring FDI to the strict FDI screening process. It is plausible, though, that foreign investors desire to diversify their investments in China, spreading their assets to inland provinces that show potential and promise, such as Henan, Jilin and Shanxi, or coastal provinces where labor is cheaper, such as Fujian, Hainan and Guangxi.

Policy Implications and Conclusions

This section presents a descriptive approach toward some events in China's recent development. A number of implications relevant to policy can be derived from the statistical results in Section 4. A major result in the statistical testing demonstrates that domestic investment in fixed capital promotes foreign direct investment. It has been known that domestic investment may "crowd out" or "crowd in" foreign direct investment. In the former case, domestic investment replaces foreign direct investment by utilizing fully domestic labor or financial resources, reducing the need for foreign direct investment. In the case of "crowding in," domestic investment leads to better production conditions made possible by additions and improvements to existing production capacity, thus increasing the marginal product of foreign capital and attracting foreign firms. The statistical results clearly indicate the latter scenario.

In 1994, Hebei province spent a total of 70.9 billion yuan on investment in fixed assets, which was 31.3 percent higher than the previous year; 33.6 billion yuan was invested in state-owned enterprises, 13.8 percent more than the year before. Of this investment in state-owned enterprises, 18.8 billion yuan was spent in capital construction investment (Hebei province witnessed the largest number of such projects in its history) and 11.8 billion in technological innovations. All this seems consistent with a large rise in foreign direct investment in the province: the total actual utilization of foreign capital increased by 52.2 percent, reaching $737 million. Similarly, 1994 saw the total investment in fixed assets increase by 40 percent in Tianjing: state-owned enterprises increased their capital investment by 42 percent, collectively owned enterprises by 31.8 percent and private enterprises by 51.9 percent. Meanwhile, foreign direct investment in Tianjing was 87.5 percent higher than the previous year.

Central and local governments in China should improve the production capacity of their enterprises so as to increase foreign direct investment. The improvement of the domestic industry's capacity and the influx of foreign capital are not a zero-sum game; the relationship between the two is positive. Domestic capital expenditure appears to have a positive spill-over effect on the influx of foreign direct investment. Incidentally, an increase in domestic investment may send a signal of assurance to foreign investors that the macropolitical situation in China is stable.

Furthermore, a trade policy oriented toward openness and liberalization should be continued, promoted and advertised. Since 1978, export promotion has been an important component of China's strategy to increase its economic power. In light of Caves (1971), international trade leads to an increase in foreign direct investment, because consumers (through experiencing diverse imported products) demand more choice in products from domestic manufacturers and foreign firms that produce and sell in differentiated markets. Baldwin (1979) finds that trade and foreign direct investment are likely to be positively associated with the same set of variables, e.g. industries utilizing comparatively large numbers of highly educated employees. The factors that account for trade, such as human capital and physical investment, also have an influence on the formation of foreign direct investment. In order to promote trade and FDI, the Chinese economy should be further liberalized. The recent effort by the Chinese to join the World Trade Organization indicates a long-term strategy to promote growth and development through international trade. Meanwhile, a liberalized trade regime is also conducive to foreign direct investment.

Liberalization of economic policies characterized by deregulation, decentralization and relaxation of state control results in an open economic environment positively associated with the inflow of foreign capital. Economic liberalization has been a major driving force of foreign direct investment in China since the beginning of the "open door" policy. For example, during the transition from a centrally controlled economy to a market economy in Anhui province, market prices became the major signal for resource allocation by the end of 1994, when the market determined about 98 percent of commodity prices. At the same time, raw materials, capital, real property, and other production factors began to be absorbed and released by market mechanisms. By the end of 1994, there were 167 markets for raw materials, 49 markets for other production factors and at least 10 stock brokerages. From 1978 to 1994, international trade grew at an average annual rate of 21.9 percent in Anhui, which saw its foreign investment, by agreement, reach $1.92 billion for 1994.

The policies regarding the reform of state-owned enterprises provide one important aspect of economic liberalization. Jiangxi province succeeded in reorganizing and privatizing state-owned enterprises in 1994 by requiring each of thirty-two large industrial enterprises owned by the state to establish a private corporate structure. Three goals were achieved by legalizing the internal and external relationship of those state-owned enterprises. First, economic and political ties between companies and the government were tremendously reduced. Second, management was forced to be market-minded. Third, the smooth transition induced the government to adopt further reforms in the midst of economic and political stability. Jiangxi also privatized medium-sized or small state-owned industrial enterprises by leasing or selling them to individuals or private corporations. In addition to these instruments of privatization, the provincial government promoted the "state-owned-privately-managed" policy that allowed owners or managers of private enterprises to run the business of state enterprises directly. In 1994, there were about 800 state-owned, privately-managed enterprises in Jiangxi. Combined with other liberalization policies, Jiangxi's openness was enhanced and its exports reached $1.66 billion, 20.6 percent higher than the previous year, while the utilization of foreign capital was $452 million, 31 percent higher than 1993.

Coastal provinces, particularly those with special economic zones, have implemented more liberal economic policies than their inland counterparts, as the degree of openness of the investment environment is much higher in the former than in the latter. For instance, the Zhuhai special economic zone has undergone considerable economic restructuring in recent years. This includes the reform of its local taxation system, which has provided new incentives for private and foreign investors and induced capital inflow from other provinces. To promote international trade, policies to reduce foreign exchange control and trade barriers have been implemented. The administration of the Zhuhai economic special zone was the first local government agency to abolish the quota on foreign currency for investing firms; it has also improved the ease with which companies exchange foreign currency. Although these actions by Zhuhai officials were within the limits set by the central government, these local authorities pushed the boundary as far as possible, trying their best to take the advantage of the "gray areas" within the central government's regulations. The payoff is immediate and clear: in 1994, exports rose by 42.2 percent, and imports by 46.6 percent. In contrast to other coastal areas, Zhuhai is a newly developed industrial city with a stable and economically efficient financial environment due to the financial and banking reforms of the local government. Accordingly, foreign direct investment in Zhuhai increased by 35.6 percent and reached $763 million in 1994.

Improvements in infrastructure and communications are required for sustainable and continued growth. While promoting long-term development by relaxing the constraints on domestic production capacity, they are also instrumental in attracting foreign capital which, in turn, accelerates economic growth. One way of generating capital to improve the highway and communications system is through international loans from such institutions as the World Bank. The virtuous cycle of infrastructure improvement-FDI flow-economic growth can be immensely beneficial to the development of a nation's economy.

Transportation systems and communication networks are critical for foreign investors. The central and regional governments in China have expended considerable capital in building these facilities, especially freeways and telecommunication networks. Finding a telephone in a typical urban household was inconceivable in 1980, but today a telephone is considered a necessity by most urban families. Convenient transportation and communication facilities offer foreign investors better opportunities to expand their manufacturing and marketing interests. In 1994, the railway density of Anhui province ranked first in eastern China, its high quality freeways per square kilometer ranked second and its mileage of river transportation ranked third. This convenient transportation system in Anhui province provided opportunities for 2,656 foreign investment firms.

The newly developing province of Shandong has also been investing heavily in the construction of transportation and telecommunication facilities, with 4,192 kilometers of new freeways, most graded upper-quality. By the end of 1994, there were fifty-nine domestic air routes through Shandong as the number of passengers and tonnage of commodity delivery through airlines increased by 38.5 percent and 35.2 percent, respectively. In the same year, the number of long distance telephone lines in Shandong increased by 71.9 percent, and the rate of telephone possession (number of telephones per one hundred people) rose by 50 percent. Hence, it is no surprise to discover that Shandong's actual utilization of foreign capital has increased by a large margin in recent years.

There has been a noticeable disparity in China's regional development. Provinces in the hinterland have been unable to reap as much benefit from economic reforms as coastal provinces have. Inland provinces are characterized by low levels of GDP per capita, capital expenditure and international trade, as well as a poor transportation and communications infrastructure. The lack of economic growth in these areas could be reversed by foreign direct investment. Local governments should adopt a set of policies to improve investment conditions for a regional increase in foreign capital. Such policies should, in particular, make an efficient use of capital spending to improve the industrial capabilities in the region a priority. This can be made possible through enhancement of the transportation and communications systems and upgrades in the working facility of plants and equipment. Additionally, economic institutions should be liberalized so that the marketplace operates in better accord with price mechanisms, allowing a reasonable rate of return on foreign capital.

Compared with coastal provinces, inland provinces have an obvious advantage in attracting foreign investment: low labor cost. Cheap labor is considered a critical determinant of foreign direct investment in developing countries. In the early stages of economic reform, China used low wages as a major incentive to encourage direct foreign investment. Since the early 1990's, real wages have increased at a substantial rate and therefore, wages, as a factor price, seem to be less attractive to foreign investors than before. However, the wage differentials between coastal and inland areas can still be an important factor for determining foreign direct investment. The inland provinces should exploit this advantage to obtain foreign direct investment, as this and other studies find that wages are negatively related to foreign capital utilization.

In Heilongjiang province, for instance, most industry is state-owned, a majority of which is in the technologically underdeveloped and mismanaged heavy industrial sectors. Their debts far exceed their assets. The only reason that the government has not allowed these firms to go bankrupt is that the central and provincial governments do not want to leave the majority of labor in Heilongjiang unemployed, which could present the prospect of political instability. Although the unemployment rate is as low as 2.4 percent, wages for the employees of most state-owned enterprises are in reality only social welfare on a considerably low scale. The average nominal annual wage for an employee in Heilongjiang Province was 3,200 yuan in 1994, an increase of 20.3 percent over the previous year. However, real wages adjusted for inflation actually decreased 1.4 percent. Concurrently, foreign direct investment increased 63.9 percent and the total utilization of foreign capital reached $490 million.

Inland provinces should make use of low cost labor in acquiring international capital that is particularly profitable in labor-abundant sectors. While coastal areas may have a comparative advantage in locating foreign direct investment which requires the sophistication and complexity of industrialized societies, interior provinces can enhance their capital formation by yoking their inexpensive labor to foreign capital that works better with low-skilled labor, such as light industry. Meanwhile, the spill-over effects of foreign direct investment — in terms of technology transfer and management training, both within the inland provinces and between the inland and coastal provinces — will be conducive to the development of the interior provinces. According to Romer (1995), access to ideas in less developed countries is the key factor in their economic growth, and China is just one of many examples in which the use of foreign ideas on management and technology can rapidly change the economic fate of a country.

Further research on foreign direct investment should focus on the composition of foreign capital across different regions in China. The roles played by various kinds of foreign direct investment (such as manufacturing, agriculture and services) in different regions should be closely examined when such data become available. Studies along this line will differentiate components of foreign direct investment according to distinct endowment features of the individual provinces of China. Additionally, the economic conditions of the investing countries should be closely examined, as there is great need for a study based upon the breakdown of details by industry and region, both at home and abroad.

Appendix: Cross-Provincial Foreign Direct Investment in 1996

Province/ Municipality	Foreign Direct Investment (in $10,000)	# Foreign Direct Investment Firms	Avg Annual Growth Rate of FDI Amount 1992-1996	Avg Annual Growth Rate of FDI firms, 1992-1996
Guangdong	1175407	60597	0.380	0.256
Jiangsu	521009	23891	0.412	0.332
Fujian	408455	17877	0.353	0.262
Shanghai	394094	15927	1.748	0.500
Shandong	263355	18742	0.316	0.414
Tianjing	215273	9235	1.565	0.474
Liaoning	173782	12400	0.453	0.429
Beijing	155290	9797	0.547	0.338
Zhejiang	152050	11388	0.930	0.430
Hebei	83022	5389	0.847	0.335
Hainan	78908	7219	0.190	0.403
Hunan	74530	3249	0.764	0.415
Hubei	68079	5890	0.476	0.434
Guangxi	66313	4338	0.899	0.323
Heilongjiang	56691	4596	0.825	0.430
Henan	52356	4392	1.334	0.487
Anhui	50661	3277	1.126	0.438
Jilin	45155	3123	0.831	0.464
Sichuan	44090	6229	1.028	0.301
Shaanxi	32609	68	1.132	0.163
Jiangxi	30126	2804	0.373	0.309
Shanxi	13808	1316	0.537	0.374
Gansu	9002	1086	9.906	0.676
I-Mongolia	7186	1134	3.888	0.432
Yunnan	6537	1425	0.554	0.687
Xinjiang	6390	600	0.070	0.573
Guizhou	3138	1008	0.275	0.504
Ningxia	555	377	8.143	0.567
Qinghai	100	117	0.700	1.672
Tibet	-	2272	-	11.955*

Notes

1. Part of the result in this chapter was presented at the Chinese Economists Association Annual Meeting at the University of Southern California, Los Angles, August 1-2, 1997, and appeared in *Reforming China's Financial Market: Establishment of Modern Financial Mechanisms and Centers*, edited by Baizhu Chen, Li Yang, and Fang Xinghai (Beijing: Economics and Management Press, 1998). We thank Claremont Graduate University for a Fletcher-Jones Faculty Research Grant.

References

Amirahamadi, H., and W. Wu. 1994. "Foreign Direct Investment in Developing Countries." *The Journal of Developing Areas* 28:167-190.

Baldwin, R. 1979. "Determinants of Trade and Foreign Investment: Further Evidence." *Review of Economics And Statistics* 111:40-48.

Barro, R J. 1991. "Economic Growth in a Cross-section of Countries." *Quarterly Journal of Economics* 106:408-443.

_____. 1997. *Determinants of Economic Growth: A Cross-Country Empirical Study.* Cambridge: The MIT Press.

Bartik, T. 1985. "Business Location Decisions in the United States: Estimates of the Effects of Unionization, Taxes, and Other Characteristics." *Journal of Business and Economic Statistics* 3:14-22.

Beck, N. and J. Katz. 1995. "What To Do (And Not To Do) with Time-Series and Cross-Section Data." *American Political Science Review* 89:634-647.

Borensztein, E., J. De Gregorio and J. Lee. 1994."How Does Foreign Direct Investment Affect Economic Growth?" *International Monetary Fund Working Paper.*

Broadman, H. and X. Sun. 1997. "The Distribution of Foreign Direct Investment in China." *Policy Research Working Paper 1720.* China and Mongolia Department, Country Operations Division, The World Bank.

Carlton, D. 1983. "The Location and Employment Choices of New Firms: An Econometric Model with Discrete and Continuous Endogenous Variables." *The Review of Economics and Statistics* 65:440-449.

Caves, R. 1971. "International Corporation: The Industrial Economics of Foreign Investment." *Economica* 38:1-27.

China Press. 1998. "Four Characteristics in Foreign Direct Investment in Tianjin." September 14:A8.

China State Statistics Bureau. 1992. *China Statistical Yearbook.* Beijing: China Statistics Press.

_____. 1993. *China Statistical Yearbook.* Beijing: China Statistics Press.

_____. 1994. *China Statistical Yearbook.* Beijing: China Statistics Press.

_____. 1995. *China Statistical Yearbook.* Beijing: China Statistics Press.

_____. 1996. *China Statistical Yearbook.* Beijing: China Statistics Press.

_____. 1997. *China Statistical Yearbook.* Beijing: China Statistics Press.

Chen, B. and Y. Feng. 1996. "Some Political Determinants of Economic Growth." *European Journal of Political Economy* 12:609-627.

Coughlin, C., J. Terza, and V. Arromdee. 1991. "State Characteristics and the Location of Foreign Direct Investment within the United States." *The Review of Economics and Statistics* 73:675-683.

Da Silva, J. 1975. "The Analysis of Cross-Sectional Time Series Data." Ph.D. dissertation, Department of Statistics, North Carolina State University.

Feng, Y. 1994. "Trade, Conflict and Alliances: An Empirical Study." *Peace and Defence Economics* 5:301-313.

———. 1994. "China's Economic Reform: Logic and Dynamism." *International Interactions* 23:315-332.

———. 1997. "Democracy, Political Stability and Economic Growth." *British Journal of Political Science* 27:391-418.

Firebaugh, G. 1992. "Growth Effects of Foreign and Domestic Investment." *American Journal of Sociology* 98:105-130.

Fuller, W. and G. Battese. 1974. "Estimation of Linear Models with Crossed-Error Structure." *Journal of Econometrics* 2:67-78.

Gowa, J. 1994. *Allies, Adversaries, and International Trade.* Princeton: Princeton University Press.

Hsueh, T., Q. Li and S. Liu. 1993. *China's Provincial Statistics 1949-1989.* Boulder: Westview Press.

hUallacháin, B. 1985. "Spatial Patterns of Foreign Direct Investment in the United States." *Professional Geographer* 37:155-163.

Kamath, S. 1990. "Foreign Direct Investment in a Centrally Planned Developing Economy: The Chinese Case." *Economic Development and Cultural Change* 39:107-130.

Khan, M. and C. Reinhart. 1990. "Private Investment and Economic Growth in Developing Countries." *World Development* 18:19-27.

Kormendi, R. and P. Meguire. 1985. "Macroeconomic Determinants of Growth: Cross-country Evidence." *Journal of Monetary Economics* 16:141-163.

Levine, R. and D. Renelt. 1992. "A Sensitivity Analysis of Cross-Country Growth Regressions." *American Economic Review* 82:942-63.

Little, J. 1978. "Locational Decisions of Foreign Direct Investors in the United States." *New England Economic Review* July/August:43-64.

Little, J. 1983. "Foreign Investors' Locational Choices: An Update." *New England Economic Review* January/February:28-31.

Lucas, R. 1993."On the Determinants of Direct Foreign Investment: Evidence from East and Southeast Asia." *World Development* 21:391-406.

Luger, M., and S. Shetty. 1985. "Determinants of Foreign Plant Start-ups in the United States: Lessons for Policymakers in the Southeast." *Vanderbilt Journal of Transnational Law* 18:223-245.

Mason, T. and F. Howell. 1992. "Japanese Investment in the United States: A Study of Trends and Site Selection Behavior." Paper presented at the Annual Meeting of the International Studies Association, Atlanta, March 30-April 4.

McMillan, C. 1995. "Foreign Direct Investment in Eastern Europe: Harnessing FDI to the Transition from Plan to Market." In *Foreign Direct Investment in a Changing Global Political Economy*, ed. Steve Chan. New York: St. Martin's Press.

Nigh, D. 1985. "The Effect of Political Events on United States Direct Foreign Investment: A Pooled Time-Series Cross-Sectional Analysis." *Journal of International Business Studies* 16:1-17.

Oneal, J. 1994. "The Affinity of Foreign Investors for Authoritarian Regimes." *Political Research Quarterly* 47:565-588.

Parks, R. 1967. "Efficient Estimation of a System of Regression Equations when Disturbances Are Both Serially and Contemporaneously Correlated." *Journal of the American Statistical Association* 62:500-509.

Pomfret, R. 1994. "Foreign Direct Investment in a Centrally Planned Economy: Lessons from China: Comments on Kamath." *Economic Development and Cultural Change*. 43:413-417.

Radice, H. 1995. "The Role of Foreign Direct Investment in the Transformation of Eastern Europe." In *The Transformation of the Communist Economics*, ed. Ha-joon Chang and Peter Nolan. New York: St. Martin's Press.

Riker, W., and D. Weimer. 1993. "The Economic and Political Liberalization of Socialism: The Fundamental Problem of Property Rights." *Social Philosophy and Policy* 10:79-102.

Romer, P. 1993. "Idea Gaps and Object Gaps in Economic Development." *Journal of Monetary Economics* 32:543-573.

Root, F., and A. Ahmed. 1979. "Empirical Determinants of Manufacturing Direct Foreign Investment in Developing Countries." *Economic Development and Cultural Change* 28:751-767.

Schneider, F. and B. Frey. 1985. "Economic and Political Determinants of Foreign Direct Investment." *World Development* 13:161-175.

Wei, S. 1995. "Attracting Foreign Direct Investment: Has China Reached Its Potential?" *China Economic Review* 6:187-199.

Yuan, B., et al. Eds. 1994. *Almanac of Chinese Economy*. Beijing: China's Economy Almanac Publishers.

_____. 1995. *Almanac of Chinese Economy*. Beijing: China's Economy Almanac Publishers.